God's First Love

God's First Love

Christians and Jews over two thousand years

Friedrich Heer

Translated from the German by Geoffrey Skelton

WEIDENFELD AND NICOLSON
5 Winsley Street London W1

TRANSLATOR'S NOTE: Very substantial assistance in the preparation of this translation has been given by Heather Nicholas, Peter Heller and Derek Masters, to whom I express my thanks.

Original German version 'Gottes erste Liebe' published 1967 by Bechtle Verlag, München und Esslingen. English translation © 1970 Weidenfeld and Nicolson Ltd.

SBN 297 17865 2

Printed in Great Britain
by Ebenezer Baylis and Son, Ltd
The Trinity Press, Worcester, and London

This book, by an Austrian Catholic, is dedicated to the Jewish, Christian and non-Christian victims of the Austrian Catholic, Adolf Hitler.

We realize now that many, many centuries of blindness have dimmed our eyes, so that we no longer see the beauty of Thy Chosen People and no longer recognize in their faces the features of our firstborn brother. We realize that our brows are branded with the mark of Cain. Centuries long has Abel lain in blood and tears, because we had forgotten Thy love. Forgive us the curse which we unjustly laid on the name of the Jews. Forgive us that, with our curse, we crucified Thee a second time.

POPE JOHN XXIII
Prayer composed shortly before his death

———————————————————

To restore itself to health, Christianity must make good the most grievous sin committed by it against the world and itself.

NIKOLAUS KOCH, a German Catholic,
writing in *Evangelisch-Katholisches Forum,*
October–December 1964

Contents

A*

Marranos – Racialism and brainwashing – Jewish Messianic faith and the discovery of America – The Society of Jesus and the 'Aryan' Christ – 'Come, Holy Ghost!' – Marrano pride – Return of the prodigal son

CONTENTS

Second Vatican Council – Christendom faced with
suicide: the 'final solution' of the Christian problem –
Loving God at the expense of men – Outraged
Christians – Freud's three great outrages – The
church as a permanent place of execution – Pathological traits in the church – Paul Schütz – A self-
defensive church – Crisis in Catholic education – Post-
Fascist society in Germany – The church's exodus
from history – The Liturgy – Congar and *Le Mystère
du Temple* – Dogma and compulsion – Monophysitism,
Manichaeism and the cult of the Virgin Mary – The
false deification of Christ – Uprooted and replanted
Christianity – 'The church needs the Jews' – Protestant and Catholic invitations to a Christian self-analysis
– Manès Sperber – 'The Jew Jesus is to blame' – Back
to the sources: rooting Christianity in Judaism – The
Jews today – Simon Dubnow – Hermann Cohen –
Martin Buber – Leo Baeck – William Schlamm –
Jewish voices in the years of destruction: emergence
of a new psalter – Katzenelson – Nelly Sachs – Paul
Celan – The Christians' last word: hell for the others?

Foreword

Mankind is on the point of an explosion. In the wake of technological progress, nowhere humanly controlled, each of us, whether we realize it or not, is involved in a future which has already begun and which is rife with danger.

Will mankind be able to adapt itself? After thousands of years spent in sailing first the Mediterranean and then the oceans, colonizing the world, will it have the mental, spiritual, physical and social capacity to colonize in space? To what goals are the explosions in the armaments industry, in advertising, in luxury articles, in the sex industry leading us?

The best minds, not only in the birth-places of the technological revolution, but in the developing countries as well, are busy with the problem of how the future of humanity can be humanly mastered – in such a way that explosions, and not least the population explosion, can be steered away from new mass murders and outbreaks of mass suicide.

In our day suicide, like murder, assumes many new forms. There is now such a thing as *white murder*, office-desk murder, planned and carried out coolly with 'clean' weapons by greater or lesser Eichmanns. So too in our large industrial societies many people prefer a gradual form of suicide spread over several acts to one single dramatic act, a suicide based on suppression of the personality, overwork, sex, alcohol and drugs.

In past eras delicate problems of growth and stabilization within larger or smaller social groups were mastered often enough by religious forces. When this did not happen, such social groups usually came to a quick end. We cannot know what form religious forces, arising out of the deep resources of humanity, may take in the future of a new mankind. But this we do know – and there is a remarkable concensus of opinion between Christians and atheists, between open-minded representatives of the churches, members of the great old world religions and people who have long turned their backs on all traditional gods on the point – in no present-day industrial community are churches or other religious bodies, upholders of the idea of Faith in the Christian sense, playing an effective or creative part in the gigantic process.

Christian churches, synagogues, nonconformist chapels – all of them are sewn almost invisibly into the prevailing pattern, whether that is the American way of life or the forms of government, democratic, semi-democratic, authoritarian or totalitarian, which vary from country to country, but in the past few years have begun to appear remarkably like one another.

Millions of Christians work peacefully side by side with millions of atheists on the production of atomic weapons. The church in Germany had nothing to say about Hitler's war. The American bishops were silent in 1945 on the subject of Hiroshima. There is no sign of any effort on the part of any of the great religious communities to bring about a new world order, a Great Peace organization in which the inevitable squabbles of mankind, great or small, can be dealt with and either solved or led into new channels which do not end in genocide and suicide.

The Austrian Catholic Adolf Hitler once defined conscience as a Jewish invention. And he was right.

Today Adolf Hitler is the model of not a few dictators, politicians and generals, though, unlike some of the dictator-generals in Vietnam, they usually do not acknowledge him as their model.

Adolf Hitler was able to become a world power, a murderous power, because the conscience of several millions of Christians either was not stirred or assented to his deeds. This conscience was a private conscience, only concerned with internal matters. It had nothing to do with those outside – the Jews, the Poles, the gypsies, the Italians.

Theologians of both great Christian churches, Roman Catholic and Protestant, could point with a good conscience to venerable religious traditions, which led straight to Hitler. Once, in a conversation with Cardinal Faulhaber, Hitler pointed out – apparently without being contradicted – that he was doing only what the church itself had been preaching for centuries and also practising against the Jews.

Auschwitz, Hiroshima and its successors rest on fifteen centuries of illustrious church tradition.

People who do not dare to look this fact in the eye understand neither themselves nor the very precarious condition of society, particularly our late Christian, Westernized industrial society. It can be seen daily how many Christian people, who no longer subscribe to any church creed, are still deeply influenced by the conceptions of Heaven and Hell, the anxieties manufactured by Christians and Christian theologians. When vast organizations, such as world religions, fall into decay, the cancerous growths of their decomposition processes continue to infect succeeding generations, often for hundreds of years. That happened in the late eras of the ancient world, when non-Christian and pre-Christian religions and attitudes affected a Christian millennium. And it has happened and is happening in the nineteenth and twentieth centuries, in which millions of late Christians, with no old gods to believe in and no new gods in sight, live in the diseased atmophere spread by the *ecclesiological neuroses* of the post-Christian era.

Christianity today is rather like a tree, or a forest if you will, on a mountaintop: uprooted by a storm, one suddenly sees how little soil it had to hold it up. At the Second Vatican Council in Rome several of the participants discovered to their surprise that they had nothing of their own to say to the world about nuclear warfare and the other great problems of modern life, because the church has never had and still does not have a theology based on earthly realities.

The reason for this alarming fact is that Christianity is not rooted in the soil from which it stems – from Jewish piety, the Jewish fear of God, love of humanity, love of earthly pleasures, joy in the present and hope for the future.

Looking back now on the funeral pyres which the Austrian Catholic Adolf Hitler set ablaze with the help of his Catholic and Protestant henchman (Heinrich Himmler's godfather was a bishop of Bamberg), we can see that Christianity today has a chance to become influential and creative if it bases itself on the ideals and attitudes of ancient Israel – that Israel which St Paul, the terrible destroyer, the greatest revolutionary in the history of man, nevertheless recognized as *God's first love*.

Adolf Hitler and his henchmen – he had, and still has, allies in all churches and in all countries of the Western world – clashed with a Jewry which was mentally and spiritually wholly unprepared for the events with which it had to deal. The few lonely warning voices among this Jewry were as little heeded – though heeded in time by those who came to silence them – as the lonely warning voices in the Catholic church and among non-Catholic Christians.

This is a point worth noting. Since the Jewish catastrophe is so closely connected with the internal catastrophe of Christianity, there is a possibility which ought not to be overlooked: namely, that a true revival, a rebirth of Jewish piety could possibly depend on whether the synagogue would assume the role of mother in the Mother Church and elder sister of the younger daughter churches. The return of Jesus the Jew to the community of His brothers who have borne His cross as crusaders from the fourth century to the twentieth century – this could be an event of extraordinary and vital importance.

Christianity got itself into a dangerous position through its identification with the religio-political state of Constantine. Since Pope John XXIII some real opportunities have arisen to break free of the Constantine influence. But Jewry too has got itself into a dangerous position with the founding of the state of Israel. To avoid any misunderstanding, let me say at once that I consider the creation of the state of Israel to be not only perhaps the boldest sociological and political experiment of this century, but also an act of historical necessity. Jewry needs a place in the world in which it can call the soil its own. But the founding of Israel and the struggle to preserve it raises an important question. Jews who are not Israelis nevertheless recognize their calling as witnesses of the living God (Whom no man can visualize and Whose name cannot be spoken) in all countries and among all the peoples of the earth. In what spiritual realm shall these Jews find their roots, if no outward persecution forces them to proclaim their God through an independent existence which is highly exclusive yet at the same time sympathetic to all other human beings?

It could be possible that the Jews of tomorrow might find new ideas for the development and growth of their own religious life in the experiences of Christendom over the centuries. But these experiences will become viable – for Christians and Jews alike – only when Christianity succeeds through a process of self-analysis in rooting itself anew in the spiritual soil of ancient Israel.

However, this is a matter for the future. The immediate task is to look at the position today – a position of bankruptcy, with centuries of venerable Christian church tradition lying in the dust.

Mankind gains the power to shape its future in a creative way only if it pays heed to its whole collective past. The Bible, beginning with the Old Testament, has given men strength over many long centuries with its account of the past history of the people which was God's first love. There is only one mankind, ranging from Cain and Abel to Adolf Hitler and Pope John XXIII, from the first moulder of clay to Picasso, from Stone Age men to Einstein.

The world religions can exercise their influence on this life process only if they dedicate themselves to it utterly. He that findeth his life shall lose it. Every nation, every church, every religion that cares only for itself seals its own doom. The deaths of the three Catholics Adolf Hitler, Benito Mussolini and Pope Pius XII – the subject of my next book *Der Glaube des Adolf Hitler* (The Faith of Adolf Hitler) – provide a clear warning.

Vienna, Second Sunday in Lent, 1967. FRIEDRICH HEER

Today the whole world has its eyes on Israel. Day after day, night after night, for more than ten years now, the Arab radio has been proclaiming the extermination of Israel, holding out to its conquerors the promise of rape and murder of all Jews, including the children.

Genocide – the extermination of nations and peoples: nowadays as little heed is paid to it as to suicide, the deliberate extermination of the self, with nuclear and other weapons, produced in order to be used.

Can this vicious circle of death be interrupted? The answer is yes, but only on one inexorable condition: that the power of those centuries-old traditions which today rule the lives of hundreds of millions of human beings is deliberately broken and rendered ineffective. Should this not happen, the chain of violence, in which Adolf Hitler was a link, will continue to lead to new acts of murder.

Vienna, 6 June 1967. FRIEDRICH HEER

I

God's First Love

'How was it possible for such a thing to happen?' 'I fear it will not be possible in this present trial to lay the roots of this evil fully bare. That is a task for historians and sociologists, for writers and psychologists.'

THE PUBLIC PROSECUTOR AT THE EICHMANN TRIAL, 17 April 1961

'I was an idealist.'

ADOLF EICHMANN, 12 July 1961

'The following book was composed by a group of idealists, all of them fervent Catholics, who believe as Catholics that the Catholic Church is at this very moment going through one of the most dangerous times in its whole history.'

From the introduction to the Italian edition of the book CONSPIRACY AGAINST THE CHURCH by MAURICE PINAY, Madrid, 1962. Copies of this book were given to all participants at the opening of the Second Vatican Council in Rome. Its themes are:

'Nearly two thousand years ago the synagogue was not a temple of God, but rather the headquarters of the most powerful and dangerous band of criminals in history.' 'The centuries-long struggle of the Holy Church against the Jewish religion and its rites was due not – as is falsely claimed – to the religious intolerance of the Catholics, but to the utter infamy of the Jewish religion, which constitutes a deadly threat to Christianity.'

'In response to numerous requests reaching us from religious circles in both Germany and Austria, we have decided to print the book.'

1963: Extract from the Austrian edition of this book

'Filled with dismay by your article about the Jews – and with satisfaction at the indignation it has everywhere aroused – I am writing to you to

protest most vehemently against the purpose of your arguments, which is to force the peoples of the earth even more under Jewish domination, and even to press the church into its service.' 'Who are you, sir, that you cannot acknowledge what is acknowledged by millions of right-thinking people everywhere? And this you call, in defiance of all the facts, "the cancer of Christianity"! Sir, what are you? Perhaps you are yourself a Jew or part-Jewish, so that with typical Jewish blindness to your own failings you profess not to recognize this "infamy"? Or have you been bribed with Jewish money to work, against all ideas of right and justice, for the subjugation of all peoples under the Jewish yoke?' 'We have no wish to wipe out the distinctions which God in His wisdom made between the various peoples, not to tolerate amongst us parasitic agitators such as the Jews have in fact always been. God has not only asked us, He has commanded us to fight against wrong. And that is why we ask Christ, our beloved immortal king, to deliver us from our and His enemies and to destroy all efforts to betray us for ever to our murderers.'

1964: ERNST RICHTER in a letter to FRIEDRICH HEER

1970: ?

2000 AD: ?

Prayer

I cannot hate.
They strike me. They kick me with their feet.
I cannot hate. I can but pray
for you and me.

I cannot hate.
They throttle me. They pelt me with stones.
I cannot hate. I can but weep
bitterly.

ILSE BLUMENTHAL-WEISS, 1945

Ilse Weiss corresponded regularly with Rainer Maria Rilke in the years 1921–5. From April 1943 onwards she was in the concentration camps of Westerborg and Tereczin. Her husband, Dr Herbert Blumenthal, died in the gas chambers of Auschwitz. Her son was murdered in the concentration camp at Mauthausen.

'I am the best and severest judge of myself here . . . I should like to ask God to give me a nature which does not set everyone against me . . . All humans are born the same, they were all helpless and unblemished. All humans breathe the same air, and many believe in the same God . . . All

2

*humans are born the same, they all have to die and have nothing left of
their fame on earth . . . Why must we have so little from the few years
we spend here on earth? People who have something to give should not
just throw it in one's face : everyone has a right to friendliness . . . Human
worth does not lie in riches or power, but in character and in goodness. We
are all just human beings, with all our faults and weaknesses, but
everyone is born with a lot of good in him. If people would only begin to
develop this goodness, instead of stifling it, and give the poor some human
sympathy, one would need no money or possessions, for not everyone has that
to give away . . . How wonderful it is that nobody needs wait a single
moment before starting gradually to improve the world!'*

ANNE FRANK, 1944 (*Geschichten und Ereignisse aus dem Hinterhaus*)

Let us consider the realitics. The fires of Auschwitz have not succeeded in
purging the violent hatred against the Jews. A quarter of a century after
Adolf Hitler caught the Jews in his murderous trap, the world looks on while
Nasser prepares the extermination of Israel. Well-known European firms –
Swiss, German and others – and European scientists are helping Nasser to
arm for the declared purpose of destroying the Jews in Israel. If it does not
happen every day – as happened to the protocol chief in Berne in 1964 – that
the mask slips from the faces of diplomats and politicians, revealing un-
disguised hatred, nevertheless the facts speak for themselves. Anti-Semitic
meetings, demonstrations, proclamations have come to light since 1945 in
almost all countries whose way of life has been formed by Christian principles,
from Russia and Poland to Great Britain and America.

Is this bloody anti-Semitism remediable? It can be cured like any of the
other great sicknesses of whole communities: plague, starvation, disease,
war. But there is no magic formula, no one single medicine which could cure
it like a sort of improved penicillin. Murderous anti-Semitism — and every
form of anti-Semitism carries the seed of murder within itself – fulfils certain
functions at periods of crisis in the growth process of nations, societies,
religions and also individuals. A cure is therefore possible only if the process
of humanizing human beings, collectively as well as individually, is energetically followed. Social relationships must be changed – every form of society
possesses an infinite potentiality for harm – and at the same time people must
be taught to examine themselves critically. Those are the tasks, and, if they
are not mastered, our society will slip down into slavery. We shall all become
murderers and suicides.

'How wonderful it is that nobody needs wait a single moment before
starting gradually to improve the world!' That is a Credo, an acknowledgement of faith in human dignity. A fourteen-year-old girl wrote it, just before
being dragged off to her death.

3

Anti-Semitism is a many-sided problem, and both Jews and Christians, the two main groups concerned, often tend to obscure it. The Jews, because they do not dare confront the Christians openly with it. The Christians, because they do not dare admit to themselves that only a revision of Christian theology and tradition, a return across more than fifteen centuries to the theological roots of Christianity, can prevent ever-recurring outbreaks of anti-Semitism. The hidebound Christian, following harsh subconscious psychological impulses, has to overcome in his own heart doubts about the divinity of the Jew Jesus by liquidating the blood brothers of Jesus of Nazareth. The liquidation can be brought about by destruction or by conversion (or both together). In this connection the first centuries of Christianity give us a remarkable demonstration. Often then it seemed that, through the active support of some emperors in Constantinople, Christianity would become Arian. Arian Christianity puts the emphasis on the humanity of Jesus of Nazareth, and could therefore be more humanitarian, more tolerant towards other men. The inhumanity of 'orthodox' Christians towards others with different views and beliefs (Christians, heretics, Jews, and so on) throughout the centuries may very well arise from the frequently unacknowledged fact that belief in the divinity of Christ is too difficult for very many Christians, when many of them are only superficially believers. Since these Christians do not wish to, in fact cannot, reveal their non-belief in the divine being Jesus Christ, and mostly lack all means of self-analysis (confession provides no substitute for most, since it seldom reaches to the depths of the individual), they are forced to shift their repressed sense of guilt on to another. The Jew is the chief scapegoat for all those Christians who wish to eliminate all the embarrassing family relations of the Jew Jesus in order to clear the way for the divine Christ, who – long before he was proclaimed Arian – was already seen as a being of a different order: a splendid celestial being, an omnipotent being – in fact a 'Christ King', as represented to me in the letter from a Catholic correspondent quoted earlier.

For both Jews and Christians the opening of a discussion aimed at self-criticism on both sides can effect a return to the roots. Like all religions today (atheistic as well as theistic), both the Christian and the Jewish religions are in danger of withering at the roots, of becoming petrified, however outwardly active they may appear in societies and associations of various kinds. Christianity is not capable of taking over the responsibility for mankind in an extended universe unless it tends its roots in a centuries-old Jewish culture. A Jewish religion for which Moses and the prophets are nothing more than a legend is heading towards its own downfall.

The problems of anti-Semitism are thus for Christians and Jews, as the most closely affected, much greater than either wish or dare to admit. But they also concern other non-Jewish, non-Christian, non-religious people. For they raise basic questions of importance to us as individuals as well as members of a society which we so lightly call a free democracy.

2

Exodus into History

Although the fig tree shall not blossom,
Neither shall fruit be in the vines:
The labour of the olive shall fail,
And the fields shall yield no meat:
The flock shall be cut off from the fold,
And there shall be no herd in the stalls:
Yet I will rejoice in the Lord,
I will joy in the God of my salvation.
The Lord God is my strength,
And he will make my feet like hinds' feet,
And he will make me to walk upon mine high places.

HABUKKUK 3, 17–19, written in the period 605–598 BC, between Nebuchadnezzar's decisive victory over the Egyptians at Carchemish and his invasion of Israel, which ended with the destruction of the temple.

'And the remnant of Jacob shall be in the midst of many people as a dew from the Lord, as the showers upon the grass, that tarrieth not for man, nor waiteth for the sons of men.'

MICAH 5, 7

We Go
Do not ask: where?
We go.
We have been told to go
From the days of our fathers' fathers.
Abram went, Jacob went,
They all had to go,
Go to a land, go from a land,
All of them bent
Over the path of the farer,
Of those who never spared themselves,

5

All of them went, staff in the road-hard hand,
Promise in their hearts, eyes filled with Him,
Our God who bade us go on and on,
Turned to the one and only goal.
A hounded rest when he called a halt,
Strange farings from Nile to Rhine,
Long farings in dread
Until wells brim,
Meagre wells
For wavering, restless rest –
My roots reached down before those rooted
Who hunt me now, but I was a guest
In the land of others – always a guest.
Unthinkably long I rested there,
But never knew a rest that gives repose.
Our rest was drowned in tears and sweat and blood,
A sudden lightning and it cracked
In a cry :
Gone by, gone by!
In the full flare of sun –
We go.
Again He drives us,
Again He dooms us
To His eternal law :
To go on,
To go on!

KARL WOLFSKEHL, 1933. He and his friend, the poet Stefan George, edited the famous anthology of German poetry *Deutsche Dichtung*, published 1901–3. He died in 1948 in Auckland in New Zealand – thus far had his flight taken him. Wolfskehl was a member of the well-known Kalonymos family, settled in Mainz since the early Middle Ages.

Israel : the name means 'God's fighter', 'God fighteth', 'Fight of God', 'God rules'. It is a proper name. Jacob was known by it. So too after thousands of years were all of his male descendants living in the land of Adolf Hitler, and through the name Israel were held liable for the death of Christ. Since the bond of union at Sinai the name has also been applied to the people of the sons of Jacob arising out of that covenant.

The first historically authenticated mention of Israel concerns its destruction : the victory inscription of the Pharaoh Merenptah in 1223 BC.

Canaan is taken   *With all its evil*
Askalon captured   *Seized Gezer Jenoam conquered*
Israel   *Its people are few its seed destroyed*

Israel, its people are few, its seed destroyed: a small country, constantly threatened – by enemies without, by betrayers within. Threatened too by its God: 'Shall there be evil in a city, and the Lord hath not done it?' (Amos 3, 6). This terrible God destroys, almost destroys His beloved people. 'As the shepherd taketh out of the mouth of the lion two legs, or a piece of an ear; so shall the children of Israel be taken out that dwell in Samaria in the corner of a bed, and in Damascus in a couch' (Amos 3, 12). This destroyed, partly destroyed people yet believes in the word of its God. 'The grass withereth, the flower fadeth: but the word of our God shall stand for ever' (Isaiah 40, 8).

In the last quarter of the second millennium BC the Israelite tribes began to move into Canaan. Nomads became peasants. The Jews received their decisive historical identity at the time of the Babylonian captivity, 596–38 BC. 'The downfall of Judaea marked the rise of the Jewish people' (Erich von Kahler). Jews: 'Y'hudi' from 'Y'hudah' meaning 'Praise the Lord' (Genesis 29, 35). The people appointed to praise the Lord is the outcome of disaster – of Nebuchadnezzar's destruction of the temple in Jerusalem, of the overthrow of the kingdom of Judaea and the sending of its inhabitants into Babylonian exile. Up to the founding of the state of Israel in AD 1948, the Jews were to live in a perpetual state of dispossession.

In the fifty years of Babylonian exile, priests and prophets rallied all the despairing, uprooted and banished, and turned them into the Jewish people, moulding them by explaining the disaster and evolving the Law. Their reason for the disaster: Israel, God's chosen people, was always turning away from its God, with Whom on Mount Sinai it had sworn an eternal bond. The priests and prophets (often regarded as in opposition to one another, yet they were not) would lead the people back to God. So they built a wall around the people in the form of a Law. This Law should not be looked on through the eyes of the later St Paul. Both written and unwritten (the Torah), the Law was felt by the people as a protective wall and greeted with joy. It was a wall within which Paradise should be created anew and outside which the evil jackals of the wilderness, the traitors and the idol worshippers, would howl in vain.

The priests evolved the Law, seeking to lead everything that had happened in the long centuries back to Moses. And the prophets were the watchdogs, guarding the herds of Israel and driving back the straying sheep. Yet not infrequently the whole people seemed to stray from the path, to lose its way and

7

seek absorption into the life of the heathens, the *gentes*. The prophets sought to bring it back on the right path: to the living God. Yet this people, described in Deuteronomy (7, 7) as 'the fewest of all people', in Exodus (34, 9) as 'a stiffnecked people', in Amos (3, 2), in Isaiah (62, 12) and elsewhere as a people of more importance to God than any other, this people lived in the constant temptation 'that we also may be like all the nations' (1 Samuel 8, 20).

It is a great and burning temptation, and not only for the privy councillors and professors of Prussia who felt themselves different from the 'Asian hordes' of East European Jews. The fleshpots of Egypt; the golden gods of Mesopotamia and of the Ancient World; Greece, offering pleasure of body and soul; Spain later; and then Germany – for this 'little troop', this 'little lantern of God' (as Martin Luther was later to call the true hidden church, the true Christianity) the temptation of losing itself, like a river in the sea, a drop of blood in the blood-stream of mankind, was ever present.

Certainly it is one solution of the Jewish problem, and Jews, even before Arthur Koestler and other ex-Jews surviving the catastrophes of our days, had felt the temptation. It was to happen at later periods, above all in non-Christian countries such as China and India. In Christian countries the hatred of others kept them from it.

The Law was felt as bulwark of a prosperous life, even of life itself, flowing from God. The Law was fervently adored, not only by the priests, but by the prophets as well. It was the prophets above all who wanted to see the Law fulfilled down to its smallest detail. Thus it was up to the time of Jesus of Nazareth – and beyond.

The Law formed a wall around Israel, now spread out among all the other peoples of the earth, with no home of its own, no temple, no holy city, no Jerusalem on earth. Refugees, scattered after the downfall of their own land throughout Asia Minor, Syria, Egypt, felt the wall around them as an invisible protection. But, if invisible to them, it was visible to others. Look at the Jews, it was said, they keep themselves apart and do not join in our festivals and celebrations. Society in the classical world and in Europe right through to the First World War was based on the idea of festal community, expressed through religious services, food and drink, celebration of gods in heaven and on earth (the kings and presidents of this world). All who stood apart shut themselves out of the community, became outcasts. And outcasts are suspect. What do they do at their own festivals? Maybe they even butcher human beings and eat them!

So, long before anti-Semitism in the modern sense was evolved, the hatred of Jews was born, based on fear of a people who dared to stand apart from the life-giving celebrations of the *great community*. Loathing became a part of the non-Jewish experience of this Law, which preserved Jewry by creating the Jew as a being apart, whose prayers, eating habits, celebrations and family life had nothing in common with the rest of mankind. The Law created and preserved the Jew and began very early to *turn him in on himself*. The Law is the first Jewish ghetto – a voluntary ghetto. The very first mark of the Jew was assumed voluntarily in the form of outward signs and customs dictated to him by the Law.

The Law that preserved the identity of the Jew, the law of life, was in time to become for him a law of death. The invisible wall would come to arouse hatred, fear and loathing in others. But not yet.

In the days of the kings of Judah a Jewish culture had developed, enriched by many non-Jewish influences. Israelite art at the time of the kings showed a feeling for elegance, for drama, for distinctive accuracy. A love of simple, graceful form is noticeable, particularly in Jerusalem, where again and again strong ties with pre-classical Greece can be discerned. In the disaster of 586 BC this spirit disappeared. The new leaders – the priests and the prophets – led the people in other directions.

The word synagogue comes from the Greek 'synagein', meaning 'to bring together'. The synagogue, a revolutionary idea for its time, probably arose during the Babylonian exile. The heathen temples were empty, both of men and of God. The synagogue was a house of prayer for all, not only for a few priests. It was an assembly point for the renewal of religious life, for the meeting of the people of Israel in the Diaspora. The synagogue pointed to Jerusalem, the heavenly Jerusalem and the earthly Jerusalem.

The first archaeological proof of the existence of synagogues was discovered outside Palestine: an inscription dating from the third century BC in Shedia, a part of Alexandria. Alexandria was the largest Diaspora community. The synagogue served the Jews scattered among the Gentiles as prayer-house, school, meeting-place and sometimes as a hostel for penniless wanderers. Christ was to preach in them, St Paul to visit them. The synagogue is the spiritual mother of the Christian church and the mosque.

A very beautiful fresco in the synagogue of Dura-Europos depicts Moses and the burning bush.

Brought together by priests and prophets, the Jews were, from the time of the Babylonian exile, the people of Moses, the people of the convenant which God made with Moses on Sinai. They are the people of the Bible, of a book. Never before, nor since, has this tremendous experiment been made – to lead a whole people through history and to mould it, day for day and hour by hour, by means of a book: the Bible. When in the nineteenth and early twentieth centuries the ghetto disintegrated, first in Central and Western Europe and then in Eastern Europe, the intellectual energy of the Jews, built up in thousands of years of Bible reading and Bible study, burst out into the world outside. Jews became intellectuals, professors, doctors, politicians, scientists, explorers, Nobel prizewinners – all this through the spiritual energy accumulated over centuries of conscientious application with one single aim in view: to discover from the Bible and later from its interpretation in the Talmud what the Lord wanted from His servant, from

9

each individual Jew as well as from the Jews as a whole, the people of Israel. The individual Jew exists only in the community of God's chosen people.

As a member of this community each Jew carries a share of *collective guilt*, acknowledging his responsibility for everything each other Jew does. A single line leads up to 'Jewish self-administration' in the later ghettoes and in Hitler's concentration camps: the Jew is a Jew within the community of Israel. He is a 'servant of God', of whom the heathens say (Isaiah 53, 3-6):

'He is despised and rejected of men; a man of sorrows, and acquainted with grief; and we hid as it were our faces from him . . . Surely he hath borne our griefs, and carried our sorrows: yet we did esteem him stricken, smitten of God, and afflicted. But he was wounded for our transgressions . . . The chastisement of our peace was upon him; and with his stripes we are healed.'

Israel speaks about itself: 'I gave my back to the smiters, and my cheeks to them that plucked off the hair: I hid not my face from shame and spitting' (Isaiah 50, 6) . . . 'The only Christians in Europe, turning the other cheek.' In a poem 'Israel' by Israel Zangwill and in poems and songs written by Jews in the nineteenth and twentieth centuries this consciousness remains alive after thousands of years: Israel, the Jew, the people of God, is born to suffering, to a Messianic suffering.

The Jewish sense of a Messianic mission is bound up inseparably with the consciousness and experience of pain. Jewish sensibility, mentality, spirituality, all are formed by this experience and consciousness, which Moses put in words to remain valid for thousands of years: 'The Lord shall scatter thee among all people, from the one end of the earth even unto the other . . . And among these nations shalt thou find no ease, neither shall the sole of thy foot have rest; but the Lord shall give thee there a trembling heart, and failing of eyes, and sorrow of mind . . . And thou shalt not prosper in thy ways: and thou shalt be only oppressed and spoiled evermore, and no man shall save thee . . . So that thou shalt be mad for the sight of thine eyes which thou shalt see' (Deuteronomy 28).

The Bible overflows with accounts of pain. Modern man tends to evade pain through sickness, neuroses, aggression against himself and others. At the very least he takes refuge in nervous conditions, in hatred, envy, in antipathies against others, in numerous forms of self-pity and self-deception. The Bible became the consolation and guide to mankind because it understood how to mould and educate men, to build their personalities, through the consciousness of suffering. The Psalms provide a striking proof of this.

Greek monks, Irish nuns in the Middle Ages, Catholic priests and dignitaries through fifteen centuries, members of the Eastern church – all these have based their lives, their thoughts, their piety, their devotion on the Psalms. Roman Catholic liturgy lives on the Psalms and other books of the Old Testament. The Huguenots sang the Psalms as they were burnt in their cities and flung to their death or sent to prisons and galleys. Calvinism, Puritanism, Lutheran Protestantism, the later religious movements of the sixteenth and seventeenth centuries, they all partake of the glow, the fire, the verbal strength of the Psalms.

Without the Psalms there would be no Europe, no Christian past, no Christian future.

The great editors of the Bible, priests and Jewish clerics, who selected, edited and shaped the colossal amount of material from previous centuries into the book which was to become the Bible, were teachers of the very first rank – possibly the greatest teachers in the history of the world. Their work gives constant new life to the people of Israel by holding continually before its eyes its own unconquered past.

Today many peoples and civilizations are still groaning under the burden of their own near or more distant unconquered past. In the United States the civil war is not yet put behind. As in the sixteenth century, 'two Frances' confront one another. In Spain, Germany, Poland and in Russia blockages caused by actual historical defeats and disasters at various times still bar the way to the future.

The Bible daily turns the hearts and heads of Jews to a contemplation of their unconquered past. How many sins has God's chosen people committed against its God and against itself, all set down in this history of God and men! Perjury, betrayal, incest, adultery, murder, treachery: anti-Semitic literature thrives to this day on the self-portrayals and self-criticisms of the Jews in the Bible.

A great German Jew, Franz Rosenzweig, analysing a poem 'Aus dem Elend' by Jehuda Halevi, wrote, 'The uniqueness of this people, which, when one attempts to show it out through the front door of reason, insists on re-entering through the back door of emotion as expressed in the paroxysms of Jew-hatred (which was never more rabid than in the 120 years when the attempt was made to present the Jew as a normal person) – this uniqueness arises from the fact that the Jewish people sees itself exactly as it is seen from outside. The whole world calls the Jewish race infamous and predestined. And the Jewish race, instead of replacing the words of others with words of its own, simply confirms them.' Rosenzweig also remarks that the cups of grace and disgrace are so closely related that the one cannot overflow unless the other is also full to the brim.

The Psalms have become the greatest source of consolation and enlightenment for millions of Jews and non-Jews alike, have led them to confession, self-analysis and self-understanding because they have dared to present the human being in all humility as a creature bleeding from a thousand wounds; as a being crying to God from a broken heart; as a being that, all but at the end of his resources, stands upright before his God and asks: Why sleepest thou, O Lord?

Jewish self-criticism, self-communion, in the midst of all piety, puts Man and indeed God in question. Jewish condemnation of other religions, Jewish atheism springs straight from the Bible. Is God perhaps the Devil? Can Jehovah, the Inexpressible, 'I am that I am', this tremendous potential of all things possible, good and bad – can the Devil be part of Him? In the oldest parts of the Bible which did not entirely fall victim to the editors, God's shadow, the Devil, belongs inseparably, with all its destructive implications, to the idea of godhead.

This raises the essential problem for religions of a later generation: whether the separation of the Devil from the idea of godhead does not deprive the religion of its whole inner strength. Is not the tension of *amor dei*, God-loving, and *timor dei*, God-fearing, an essential part of individual piety?

The people of the Bible wrestles with its God. In every hour of its history it demands from Him proof of His godhead and wrings from itself the proof of its humanity. Leon Werth, a French Jewish philosopher, went back to the beginnings of Jewish knowledge when he said in 1940, describing the human condition in our modern days, 'It is not so important to seek proofs for the existence of God as for the existence of humanity.' The Bible reminds us again and again that Man is nothing without God, and God nothing without Man. Man's wrestling with the problems of self, of pain, of God reaches its biblical culmination in the Book of Job.

What still remains to us of Job's book, after passing through several editings and clerical tidyings, still resembles a rock that has not succumbed entirely to the onslaught of the waves in the sea of co-ordinations, excisions and 'improvements'. In the Book of Job we can still discern how close cursing lies to praying in its earliest forms. A pious man hurls his pain and despair in the face of a terrible, murderous God. What sort of God is He, to allow the faithful, *His* people to suffer so, to let His loyal servants end miserably in the slaughter-houses of history? What sort of God is He – to apply Job's questions to the events of our own age – that lets small children and naked women stand outside in the rain and snow waiting for admittance to the gas chambers?

Whoever wishes to feel the force of this seething element of Jewish piety, revealed in Job's questioning of God, and work his way (a rewarding task) through the vast pile of glosses which Christians and others have put over Job and his book, should first of all turn his attention to a modern Job.

Professor Jizchak Katzenelson, head of a secondary school in Lodz, living in the Warsaw ghetto until sent in January 1943 to the concentration camp of Vittel in France, buried there three bottles, in which he concealed his 'Song of the Last Jew'. On 29 April 1944 he was taken to Auschwitz and murdered. This is what he wrote in his 'Message to the Seven Heavens':

Not a single one was spared. Was that
just, ye heavens? And, were it just, for whom?
For whom? For us? Then tell us why.
We are full of shame for you. And for the guilty world.

Away, away with you!
Ye heavens, do you think a crushed worm can love you still?

I believed in you, ye heavens, and
pledged to you the loveliest songs I knew.
You I have loved as I
have loved no other but my wife. She is dead. Smoke, froth . . .

Away. Away. You have deceived
my ancient people, stemming from the start of time.

You deceive us still,
as you deceived our fathers. Before you prophets trembled,
since you deceived them. And
they looked up to you. Inspired, enflamed. By you.
How true they were to you
on earth, ye heavens! And living how? Poor. Starved. Pursued.
It was you they sought. To you the herald
of the Commandments cried: Hear, ye heavens!
Heavens, have you still thoughts
for Moses? Or for Joshua, who cried aloud to you?
Jeremiah too cried out:
Hear, ye heavens! And who should hear but you? Is no one there?
The heavens drained of love? You open
light-drenched skies, are you asleep? Heavens, slumbering deep?
Do you not know us now? Why? Are we
changed? Or is the change in you?
We are the people whom God charged
to spread His word. We are God's witness
and our fathers were holy men.
And we are better still. Not I!
I am no prophet. Yet on the Cross my people,
that expiates earth's guilt, was blessed.

Jizchak Katzenelson, a modern Job, sings in this poem of the children of
his people ascending to Heaven, the children small and big, burnt, gassed,
journeying in the smoke up to the empty heavens. It is prayer and curse at
the same time, invocation and imprecation.

The earth consumed by fire.
May earth's flame now rise up that shall consume you too.

Scorched men. Scorched earth. Scorched heaven.

'All is but a puff of air.' 'Puff of wind' is the keyword for that book of the Bible called in the Authorized Version (following the Greek translation) Ecclesiastes, or The Preacher: the book Quohelet. *Vanitas vanitatum*, 'vanity of vanities': Life is *vanitas*. The theme of this book is known and quoted by many authors and other people who know almost nothing of the Bible and the God of the Bible.

The book of Quohelet, whose thoughts many different peoples have made their own, was written probably in the third or fourth century BC – at any rate not earlier than the fifth and not later than the first century. Many see in it an amalgam of Greek and Egyptian influences. Oswald Loretz has demonstrated that it owes much to the Babylonian Gilgamesh Epic, which was written twelve centuries earlier.

This tells us something: The Jews, from the beginning of known history almost to the present day, are a remarkable mixture of age-old and, at the same time, contemporary elements.

All is but a puff of air. 'He that increaseth knowledge increaseth sorrow' (Ecclesiastes 1, 18). This sentence could be affixed to all the knowledge of outstanding Jews up to Sigmund Freud. Wisdom is better than strength, than weapons of war. To everything there is a season: a time to be born, a time to die. A living dog is better than a dead lion. A man hath no better thing under the sun, than to eat, and to drink, and to be merry.

Life and joy are both constantly endangered: by men. And by God. The place of evil is in Man. But where does evil come from, if not from God? God is the greatest troublemaker in the life of His creatures. God distorts the rights of a human being. *He* brings disorder.

And what of divine justice? That is the great question in Babylonian literature, the question that goes all through the Bible – unanswered.

In the book of Quohelet occurs, among other Persian words, the word *pari-daida, paridais* – in Greek *paradeisos* and in Hebrew *pardēs*. In Persian it means first and foremost a game preserve, an artificial park such as princes create out of a wilderness for the delight of their mistresses. Paradise is something to be won on earth, to be fought for by deeds of bravery.

The second paradise, after the first was lost in the Garden of Eden, must be fought for on earth – through a striving for justice. The Jew's sense of responsibility towards his fellow beings, his mission as a member of God's chosen race to lead the way to the kingdom of God, his belief in *progress*, brings the Messianic element into the history of mankind. This universal consciousness of a Messianic mission, spreading tidings of joy, combined with Jewish 'exclusivity', brought about the first great clashes with other races and other cultures: with the Greeks and then with the Romans. But the first accurately recorded historical clash occurred in that land where, in the days of Moses, the conflict first broke out and where it has broken out again today – in Egypt.

3

Jews, Greeks and Romans

Xenophobia is inherent in the Egyptian nation. At the end of the third century BC, and then again in the second, it was directed against the Greek population of Egypt. In the second century BC Hellenism clashed with Jewry in Alexandria, the great centre of trade and home of a floating intelligentsia. Later we shall see how in the mid-nineteenth century the French intelligentsia in Paris, terrified by the proletarianization threatening it, developed at the instigation of Drumont a similar anti-Semitism. Alexandria had its Greek Drumonts, who whipped up the feelings of the common people against the affluent Jews. In Alexandria, moreover, there existed a very active and well-to-do intellectual Jewish set, and this was as proud of its superiority over the 'heathens' in the sphere of religion, as it was sensitive about its inferiority in the fields of literature, philosophy and education.

This Jewish intelligentsia became aggressive. In speeches and writings it stressed the superiority of monotheism and the Bible over Greek philosophy; for the Bible was older than any monument of Greek thought. This was the constant theme, which we find again in a more recent poem, 'Jewish Sibyl':

> But you, poor Greece,
> Should give up your proud designs
> And pray to the bountiful immortal.
> Take heed!
> No longer set against this city your imprudent people
> Who are strangers in the land of the great God.

The following anti-Greek comparison occurs in the poem 'We Jews' by Paul Mayer (born 1889), which was often called to mind in the years 1934–44.

> In all places and at all times
> We changeable people are unchangeable.
> Others come, conquer and fade away,
> Even the god of the Greeks, with a wreath in his hair.

It was no easy matter to wrench the wreath from the Greek gods – the wreath of Apollo, Plato and Aristotle, the dazzling crown of supreme wisdom. In cosmopolitan Alexandria bold Jewish writers falsified texts of Homer, Hesiod, Aeschylus and Sophocles, to increase the glory of the single God. In the great religious and political struggle *pia fraus*, pious falsification, was for centuries the order of the day. From the Donation of Constantine onwards, the Christian Middle Ages drew considerable support from celebrated frauds, perpetrated to enhance the reputation either of Papal Rome or of national saints and ecclesiastical princes, or, as was especially the case in the twelfth century, of the monasteries.

The Graeco-Egyptian intelligentsia, no less proud than its Jewish counterpart, was angered by this arrogant and provocative behaviour. The first tangible display of anti-Semitism, at first Greek, then Graeco-Roman, was, as Jules Isaac has pointed out, a reaction to Jewish expansion. The affluent Jewish intelligentsia in Alexandria has been aptly compared with the Jewish upper class of Wilhelmine Germany in the nineteenth and early twentieth centuries. These Jews, once assimilated into the German nation, looked down equally on uneducated Gentiles and on the unassimilated Jews of the East. In Alexandria, Hellenized upper class Jews provoked the anger of upper class Egyptians and Greeks, and the two Hellenized castes – the Egyptians and the Jews – inevitably clashed. The Jewish literary offensive, which prepared the way for a powerful religious offensive, had a particularly striking effect. A large-scale plan of Jewish propaganda was set in motion to win proselytes, first among the Hellenized Egyptians themselves, and then in Rome.

Today we can hardly imagine that there was a real possibility of the message of Judaism, rather than that of Christianity, gaining supremacy in the Roman Empire – just as, later, it was for a long time uncertain whether Arianism or Catholicism would prevail.

Before the clash – on Egyptian soil – the intellectual relations between Greeks and Jews were very cordial. A Jew took part in Aristotle's colloquia in Assos, not far from Homer's Troy. Aristotle lived here from 347 to 345 BC. According to Clearchus, this Jew was Greek 'not only in his speech but in his soul', and in his familiar intercourse with the Greeks 'he gave more than he received'.

What did these Greeks think of the Jews? Aristotle called them the 'descendants of the Indian philosophers'. Hecataeus of Abdera, at the court of the Ptolemies in Alexandria, repeated Aristotle's definition in 300 BC, but he went further. He devoted a whole book to the Jews in his *Aegyptiaca*, which has come down to us through Diodorus, who incorporated this account in his own work in the time of Augustus. In it a verse from the Bible is literally transcribed for the first time, and Hecataeus defines the essence of the Jewish religion as follows: 'He (Moses) did not create an image of God, because God is not like Man, but he believed that the heavens surrounding the earth were God, the Lord of All' – a cosmological misunderstanding of the supra-cosmic nature of God. The Jews were later described as a philosophical race by Theophrastus in his work *On Piety*.

The Greeks, then, both esteemed and misunderstood the Jews.

To summarize the position in Egypt and Greece up to the time that Apion went to Rome: The first Egyptian manifestation of anti-Semitism developed in the third century BC as a result of an intensive Jewish campaign of conversion. In pamphlets written to counter this campaign, an Egyptian religious writer described the Jews as lepers and descendants of the Hyksos, the archetypal plague-bearers. It took the Egyptians more than a thousand years to rid themselves of their fear of the Hyksos.

The decisive event was the Jewish resistance to Hellenization in the religious sphere in the second century BC. The Jews were violently persecuted by the Seleucid Antiochus IV. The victorious uprising of the Maccabeans led to the establishment of a Jewish state in Palestine. This uprising was carried out by uneducated Jews, and was directed against their own Hellenized upper classes. The Jews, now conscious of their calling and their strength, unleashed a vast proselytizing movement and created a Jewish-Greek propaganda literature, especially in the large towns where Greeks and Jews, both numerous, were in competition with each other. The first wave of anti-Semitism arose in the first century BC in the urban centres of the Hellenized East – in Antioch, Alexandria, Cyrene. Its instigators were mostly Alexandrians, though three of them – Lysimachus, Chaeromon and Apion – were possibly Greek Egyptians. The first two troublemakers, Poseidonios and Molon, were Greeks from Syria and Caria, living on Rhodes; for the same wind was blowing in Rhodes as in Alexandria.

The Alexandrian Apion, a very vain and ambitious writer whom the Emperor Tiberius described as *cymbalum mundi*, was a product of both the Egyptian and the Greek brands of anti-Semitism – both of which were against Jewish separatism and the isolation of Jewish religious practices from the ordinary social and ritual life of other races. Apion, like Drumont in nineteenth-century Paris, repeated the well-worn charges against the Jews: they were a race of shameful origins, lepers who had been cast out of Egypt in the days of Moses; Jewish separatism had its roots in hatred of mankind and hatred of the gods; the Jews were a godless people who undermined all other religions; they were superstitious and worshipped a golden ass's head; they practised ritual murder against the Greeks; Jewish civilization was sterile and had produced nothing great or useful. All the weapons used by Christians and Nazis in the twentieth century are already to be found in the writings of Apion and his like.

Apion went from Alexandria to Rome, taking with him this Graeco-Egyptian anti-Semitism, which appealed to the element in Rome hostile to the great Caesar's pro-Jewish policies. Caesar's statute in favour of the Jews, which really did give the Jews privileges, unlike Pétain's in 1942, remained in force, apart from a few interruptions, until the new legislation of the

Christian Empire. Jews held influential positions with some of the imperial families, and there had even been cases of members of the emperor's family being converted to Judaism. Was Rome becoming Jewish?

In Ethelbert Stauffer's words, Rome and Jerusalem were not two cities, but two different worlds. The golden eagle of Imperial Rome gripped its prey – the subjugated peoples – in brazen claws. Rome's domination was harsh and ruthless: Hegel said that 'the Roman Empire broke the hearts of the people it conquered'. This was a prerequisite for the triumphal march of Christianity through the Empire, along the roads built and trodden by Roman legionaries.

The *Pax Romana* reached its zenith under Augustus in the year 9, when a peace altar was erected on the Field of Mars, the shrine of the god of war and the centre for military gatherings. This *Pax Romana* held the same meaning as the Spanish peace later: *paz entre cristianos, y guerra contra los infieles*. Peace – the peace of a closed as opposed to an open society – meant war against enemies threatening any of its boundaries. And it meant satisfying the faithful, whose politico-religious belief pledged them to the support of their state. The Roman raised his right hand in a salute which was to be imitated by the *Sieg Heil* salute of the Nazis. It was the duty of every citizen, subject, ally, friend – every person bound in any way to the religious and political community of the Roman Empire – to believe in the prosperity and supremacy of Rome.

The small population of Jews refused to share this faith. The bloody suppressions of the risings in Judaea were not, from the Roman point of view, anti-Jewish persecutions, but quellings of national rebellions similar to those in other parts of the Roman Empire, which were dealt with just as harshly in the first century AD. Up until almost the middle of the century there were very few signs of anti-Semitism in Rome. Then Apion, the Drumont of Alexandria, came to Rome and found his best pupils there: Seneca, Juvenal and Tacitus.

The Roman battle for Jerusalem, which was waged alongside Jerusalem's proselytizing campaign in Rome, naturally had religious undertones. It is a popular notion that the Romans showed great tolerance towards the various gods of the peoples they conquered. But it must not be forgotten that most of these multifarious gods appeared to the Romans as no more than local variations of their own gods. A similar situation exists today in the United States, where Jews, Catholics and Protestants of various denominations all appear to have common characteristics, because they all share a politico-reilgious belief in America, in the *American way of life*. We must imagine a similar norm prevailing in the Roman Empire, where, amid the manifold temples and cults, a single belief was held: that *victoria*, *nike*, victory, would always be Roman.

The Jews did not share this belief. Even before the Romans, the Seleucid Antiochus Epiphanes (175–64 BC) had tried in vain to 'co-ordinate' the

Jews. 'One empire, one culture, one religion, this is what he hoped to achieve during his reign' (cf. 1 Maccabees 1, 43). In 167 Antiochus set up an altar to the imperial god Zeus in the temple in Jerusalem. During his reign of terror the Jews suffered the proscription of their Law. They were forbidden, under penalty of death, to worship in their temples and forced to participate in Greek religious practices, including the eating of pork and the Dionysian orgies. The servants of God were tortured and murdered.

Antiochus' power, like that of the Romans in Jerusalem, was upheld by collaborators – a wealthy upper class with a taste for power and good living which came to terms with the Seleucid and then with the Romans. These collaborators, like those of many centuries later, must have presented a widely differing spectrum of views. Around the hard core of a clique which had direct relations with the occupying power were grouped individuals who participated in Greek and later Graeco-Roman culture, but were not completely assimilated into it in the religious and political sense.

From what background does St Paul come, the Roman citizen with a Graeco-Roman education?

The simple uneducated people of Judaea rebelled against the Seleucid under the leadership of Judas Maccabeus, son of a village priest in the house of the Hasmonaeans. In December 164 BC the traditional cult of Jehovah on Mount Zion was restored. In 153 BC the Hasmonaeans secured for themselves the office of high priest. From 142 BC onwards they were more or less princes of Jerusalem, and from 105 BC they bore the royal title.

The Romans then destroyed the Seleucid's empire and in 63 BC the great Pompey entered Jerusalem, which was to remain for exactly seven hundred years under Roman domination, up to the Arab conquest of AD 637. In Jerusalem and Judaea the collaborators and the opponents of Rome now stood face to face. The collaborators were after 37 BC grouped around Herod, an Arab who became king of the Jews with Roman help, and later around Pontius Pilate and Caiaphas, who was high priest for eighteen years under the Romans. The opponents of Rome were not united. There were zealots who were always willing to risk their lives against the Romans. There were also the devout who were awaiting the Messiah. From AD 38–135 the country was in a continuous state of Messianic upheaval. Other opponents of Rome went out into the desert, or settled in Jerusalem or little inland towns – praying and fasting for the fall of Rome, for the liberation of the temple and Jerusalem from the golden eagle. Jewish prophecies of religious and political import circulated widely. The same atmosphere of fervent expectation was to be found later in Christian Europe, at the time of Luther, then in the English civil war period among the Puritans and to an even greater extent among the radical sects, and yet again in Paris on the eve of the French Revolution. The most eloquent testimony to the great hatred felt towards the religious and political domination of Rome is to be found in a Christian document which was received into the canon of the Bible only after much hesitation – the Revelation of St John, the number, six hundred threescore and six, representing the devilish enemy, actually referred to Rome.

After Herod's death on 1 April 4 BC, riots broke out, and Augustus divided up the Jewish kingdom among Herod's sons. On the death of Augustus in AD 14, Tiberius became emperor. During his reign the effective ruler was his prefect of the guard, Sejanus. Eusebius said of him that 'he aimed at the extermination of the whole Jewish race'. What could have provoked such violent anti-Semitism in a Roman living in Rome? The leaders, both military and political – it came to the same thing in Rome – were scandalized that the puny little Jewish race should dare to rebel against Rome in all its greatness. Their feelings were the same as those of Tacitus who, on the occasion of Hadrian's execution in Rome, characterized the Jews as a permanently rebellious people.

But now let us look at the facts. Perhaps seven or eight per cent of the population of the old Roman Empire consisted of Jews. The Jews were everywhere – in Rome and in all the big cities of the Empire. At this critical time the Jewish religion appeared as a proselytizing religion – commending itself through its Bible, its proclamation of a single God, the purity of its morals, its history of achievement, suffering and martyrdom as God's chosen people.

'The practices of this criminal race are spreading so fast that they have followers in every country and have thus imposed their laws on their conquerors.' *Victi victoribus leges dederunt.* This is a great law of world history. It is neither a Roman nor a written law, but it is certainly a law of life. Conquered races remould their conquerors to their own pattern. In the Roman Empire it was the Greeks who, though vanquished by Rome, were the true conquerors.

Seneca and the Roman upper classes feared these Jews, at any rate since Caesar's policy of friendliness towards them. For there were Jews at the imperial court, and Jews within the old patrician families. Patricians received Jews like St Peter and St Paul in their own houses, just as later Jews were admitted to the court of Charlemagne, and particularly of his son, Louis the Pious and the Empress Judith.

But let us return to Sejanus, the man behind Tiberius. Sejanus banished the Jews from Rome in the year AD 19, and in AD 26, after Tiberius' retirement from Rome, he despatched a new procurator to Palestine – Pontius Pilate. He was manifestly Sejanus' creature. Pontius Pilate was a terrorist and a provocateur, under whom a continuous stream of executions occurred. He was guilty of a viciously provocative gesture towards the Jews, when he had a copper coin struck bearing a design of the sacrificial instruments of the Roman religion. His predecessors had chosen emblems less likely to cause religious and political friction. In the year 30 Sejanus made preparations for a campaign against the Jews throughout the Roman Empire. In the same year the supreme Jewish court of justice, the Sanhedrin, lost its jurisdiction over its own people. In Jerusalem, the Rabbi Zadok started a forty-year fast to save the city from the catastrophe threatening it. In the following year Pilate ordered a massacre of pilgrims coming to Jerusalem for the Feast of the Passover. And Pilate was awarded the title of *Amicus Caesaris* (Friend of the Emperor).

The catastrophe was once again averted at the last moment, or rather, in the context of history, postponed. On 31 October Tiberius had Sejanus, whose powers were now almost absolute, arrested and executed. Provincial governors were ordered to put an immediate stop to anti-Jewish measures. Pilate had reason to fear for his position, but he did not fall.

'The Roman eagle went on hovering over Jerusalem, ready at any moment to swoop down on the defenceless city.' In the year 40 Caligula planned to erect a statue of himself in the temple of Jerusalem, but he was murdered before it could be done. The Jews felt more and more harassed, and feared either annihilation by the Romans or absorption into Rome as a result of the Graeco-Roman leanings of their own educated upper classes. The lower classes and their prophets took up the cause and fought to the bitter end. In August of the year 70 Jerusalem and its temple were destroyed and 73 saw the fall of the last stronghold of the zealots – the fortress of Masada in the wilderness near the Dead Sea. The last battle took place in the years 132–6. The 'Son of the Stars', Bar-Cochba, proclaimed a holy war for the freedom of God's chosen people. The greatest of all interpreters of the Torah – Rabbi Akiba ben Joseph – supported him. But the uprising collapsed in 136; Bar-Cochba fell in battle and Rabbi Akiba died a martyr's death. The Romans erected a temple to Jupiter on Mount Zion, and shouted their 'Salus et victoria' in Jerusalem. Jews were forbidden to enter the city on punishment of death.

Thus began a new epoch for the Jews: that of the Diaspora – an epoch of total vulnerability, during which they were protected only by their own Law and the Talmud. Throughout these battles in and for Jerusalem, one man distinguished himself by forty years of fasting and prayer, earning himself the title of Oblias, bulwark of the people: this was Jacob ben Joseph, the brother of Jesus.

4

Jesus and the Jews

Thee, Brother Jesus
I saw Thee as I wandered through the town,
My brother, whom the rabble hunted down
Because Thy world did not resemble theirs.

These words from GEORG MANNHEIMER's *Gang durch die Via dolorosa* (Passing through the *via dolorosa*) were written in 1933. Georg Mannheimer, a Viennese Jew, died in Dachau in 1942.

'In the fourth Gospel, and only in this, did the Jews deny Christ. The Evangelist John was simply a Jewish prophet who used the Qumran mode of expression to fulminate against the leaders of the synagogue, who so tragically misled his own beloved people.'

(GREGORY BAUM, Augustinian lecturer in theology, at the Second Vatican Council.)

The Jew Jesus of Nazareth grew up, lived and died among Jewish surroundings. In the ninth hour on the Cross (between 2 and 3 p.m.) He spoke the 22nd Psalm. After that He spoke the Sabbath, night and dying prayers of His forefathers. The dying Jew Jesus spoke the same prayers that His Jewish brothers and sisters were to speak during persecutions over fifteen centuries: at the stake, before taking their own lives in the face of their Christian oppressors, in Auschwitz. The Jew Jesus was laid to rest in a grave of honour.

The Gospel of Jesus Christ, the 'Good News' of the Redeemer, became for millions of Jews the messenger of death. Millions of Christians have based their hatred of the Jews on it, have taken it as a call to destroy or at the least enslave the Jews, 'the people who killed Christ'. Are the Gospels the indestructible cell from which new life stems for Christians – and death for Jews? Do they preach an anti-Semitism on which Christians and anti-Christians can legitimately draw to this day?

With the three synoptists – St Matthew, St Mark, St Luke – the answer to this problem seems relatively simple. The Gospel according to St Matthew can be rightly regarded as 'the Jewish Gospel'. According to St Mark the Jewish people was sympathetic to Jesus: only the leaders were against him. St Luke was writing for a Christian community in which Jewish and Gentile Christians lived peaceably together. But St John is still being quoted as a crown witness by Christian and anti-Christian anti-Semites alike.

It is a significant fact that those notorious sentences in the Bible, which later theologians and practitioners of anti-Semitism, particularly in the millennium of Western civilization, like to quote against the Jews, held no particular significance in the first centuries of Christendom. The people's cry in St Matthew 27, 25 – 'His blood be on us, and on our children' – has been interpreted in the thousand years since Constantine as a divine command to persecute the Jews. But Christian authors in the first centuries saw no significance in the cry of an enraged mob.

Jewish Christians in the early days of Christianity read the Gospels as accounts of an internal Jewish dispute. But after their separation from the other Jews, things began to look very different . . .

The Gospels reflect – in their very different ways – the gradual estrangement of Jewish Christians from their orthodox Jewish brothers. The experiences of the evangelists and other Christians among Jews in the first generations after Christ are projected back on Jesus' own relations with His people, the Jews. There was one particularly important political aspect: the early Christians – all of them Jews – were treated by the Romans as Jews, as a Jewish sect. They knew of the Roman hatred for Jews, and wanted to dissociate themselves from it. In their accounts of the trial of Jesus – and these accounts supply the basis for the traditional definition of the Jews as 'the people who killed Christ' – the evangelists were concerned to convince the Romans that adherence to the Christian faith did not imply hostility to the imperial authorities. All four evangelists go out of their way to leave the question open as to whether the death sentence was imposed by the Roman governor. The historic Pontius Pilate, a cruel persecutor of the Jews, is transformed into a hesitant, vacillating man, becoming gentler and more amiable with each successive Gospel. The 'Christian' career of Pontius Pilate ended with Constantine, for then the church had no more need of Roman witnesses to testify to its political innocuousness.

The fourth Gospel, the Gospel according to St John, is the most pro-Roman and anti-Jewish of them all. It is also furthest away in time from the historical Jesus. The Gospel according to St John takes the theological argument that the Jews have been the enemies of Jesus right from the beginning of time, coming straight from the Devil. St John's thinking owes something to

Gnosticism (a fact that is very often denied): all men belong either to the realm of the Devil or the realm of Light. St John was certainly basing himself on Qumran writings. These Jewish sectarians, escaping to the desert, described themselves as 'children of the Light'. Their Jewish enemies, triumphant in Jerusalem, were in their eyes 'children of Darkness'. Puritans and Manichaeans have tended at all times to divide mankind up into two sorts. They themselves (as for instance in New England in America) are 'children of the Light'; Catholics, heathens and Communists are 'children of the Darkness'.

St John brands the Pharisees as enemies of Jesus. This is simply not true. During Jesus' lifetime the Sadducees were his enemies – and St John does not so much as mention them. Jesus moved a great deal in Pharisee circles, and certainly up to AD 62 the Pharisees enjoyed good relations with the leaders of the original church. The disputes between Jesus and the Jews, reported in St Mark, reflect, without exception, disputes between the later church of the apostles and its social surroundings. They have no place in the historical life of Jesus.

It would, of course, be very useful to know when St John wrote his Gospel, which maintains that the Jews rejected Jesus, and which, with its attack on the 'devilish' synagogue, exercised and still exercises so devastating an influence on anti-Semitism. Bible researchers in the nineteenth and early twentieth centuries ascribed it to the second century, but today it is put earlier, at the turn of the century. In either case St John's portrait of Jesus was separated by more than a century from Jesus of Nazareth, the son of Mary. His Christ is no longer a Jew, hardly even a human being, but rather a prince of Light, 'the true light', a cosmic world leader who triumphed over the powers of Darkness. This majestic Christ did not concern Himself with sinners, like the Jesus of the three synoptists. The words repentance and conversion appear nowhere in St John. In this Gospel He is already the unapproachable mystery, looking down from the apse of Constantinian, Byzantine and Roman basilicas on men and dividing them at a glance into the chosen and the damned.

The Jews belong to the damned. The synagogue is as ynagogue of Satan. In St John Christ is the new Moses. He has completely taken over Moses' power. It was His anyway, before the world was made.

'At the time of St Paul's death Christianity was still a Jewish sect' (James Parkes). The diminutive Jew Saul, who as Paul became the founder of an anti-Jewish Christianity, was – like all great creative men – full of contradictions. St Paul was the only apostle who never set eyes on the young Jew Jesus who died on the Cross in Jerusalem. (Who can visualize Jesus as middle-aged or old?) St Paul's Christ – a Christ who ousted the Christ of Jewish and other Christians only after centuries of hard fighting – first seen in a vision on the road to Damascus is, in many ways, the product of St Paul's creative imagination. He is the Christ of Pauline theology. Into this theology went

24

everything that the Jew Saul had experienced in his Jewish and Hellenistic surroundings and in constant internal and external confrontations with Jewish contemporaries of many different religious persuasions. St Paul's Christ is – if not entirely, nevertheless essentially – a child of suffering, the painful sufferings of St Paul among the Jews of his own time. St Augustine, like St Paul a fervent, volcanic theologian and one who did much, both good and bad, to shape Western civilization, described himself as 'a child of his mother's tears'. St Paul might have described himself, or rather his theology, as a child of the tears he wept over his 'stiff-necked' Jewish people. St Paul, the revolutionary, tore infant Christianity out of the womb of Israel and Jewry, and from that time forward Christianity has been bleeding from many wounds, has become for many a religion of the uprooted, the *déracinés*.

A religion of converts, torn from another, older soil and still clinging in hate and love-hatred to their 'old Adam'. St Paul achieved rebirth in Christ, the 'other Christ', only by the terrible agony of tearing the umbilical cord that bound Him to His people.

This man, who was 'against the Jews' to his dying day and who accused them at the bar of world history of betraying Christ the Lord and crucifying their Messiah, became – without knowing it or wishing it – the revered progenitor of a Christian anti-Semitism. Both Catholic and Protestant churches – logically enough from their own particular standpoint – referred to him around 1933 as non-Semitic, as a deadly enemy of the Jews. Yet this same man remained all his life true to his Jewish people. *His is the theology of 'God's first love', which was given to Israel.*

'What advantage then hath the Jew? . . . Much every way: chiefly, because that unto them were committed the oracles of God. For what if some did not believe? Shall their unbelief make the faith of God without effect? God forbid: yea, let God be true, but every man a liar' (Romans 3, 1–4).

Gregory Baum, an Augustine monk and a converted German Jew, interprets St Paul in the following way: 'Israel is always to remain God's first love, even when overshadowed by the cloud of unbelief. Certainly with the coming of Christ the Jewish people lost its distinctive position as the chosen people, but if it joins the community of the believers, the blessed people of God, then it will not lose, but rather gain by its loss. Yet nevertheless the boundless love which God extends through Christ to all mankind detracts nothing from God's first love, which He gave to the people of Israel.' St Paul declares the equality of Jews and Gentiles in the church of Jesus Christ. 'God sent the grace of Christ to the Jews to confirm the promises made to their fathers. He sent it to the Gentiles to reveal His pure and voluntary mercy' (cf. Romans 15, 8).

St Paul is the apostle of God's grace and God's wrath. The word 'grace' (*chen* in the Old Testament) is found only in the writings of St Paul. St Matthew, St Mark and St Luke do not use it at all, and St John does not put the word into Jesus' mouth. The word 'wrath' is never used by Jesus.

The conceptions of grace and wrath lie close together in St Paul's mind. He sees them in fact as one. God comes on him in thunder and lightning and tears him wide open, releasing the streams which flow to the surface of his being, enabling him to sing a new song: the song of grace and of mankind's new freedom, the song of victory over death and disaster, the song of resurrection, experienced as a re-awakening and a reformation of the individual personality. St Paul's Epistles are a single paeon of praise about this experience of a great inner liberation, of the unleasing of the deepest forces of personality. God's revolutionary omnipotence is revealed through His wrath: that is St Paul's belief.

In this spirit St Paul approached the Jews: grimly determined to convert them. The Jews, he declared, were the people that Jehovah, their God, had chosen as His sons. The gift of divine glory had been presented to the people of Israel. The Jews took part in the covenants. The Jews possessed the Law. The Jews had received the promises. With this word St Paul summarizes all divine assurances regarding the coming Messianic age (cf. Romans 15, 8). The Pauline church of Christ is the new and genuine Israel. 'St Matthew is the only one among the evangelists to use the word "church", meaning an organization and an authoritative body.' St Paul was the founder and first organizer of the church. His proclamation, naming it as the new and genuine Israel, is one of the most revolutionary and portentous in world history. It tore Christianity from the womb of old Israel and laid the foundations, historically and theologically, of what the Jews regard as the greatest act of robbery in history, compared to which the destruction of the temple in Jerusalem by the Romans, the plundering of the Alexandrian Library and all the other terrible onslaughts on the treasures of the Ancient World by barbarians, Romans, Arabs and Mongols seem almost petty.

This greatest act of robbery in history (and the sincere Christian should try to see it from the Jewish point of view) brought the Old Testament into the service of the Christian church. All that Jewish prophets, priests and sons of the Jewish people had produced in the way of prayers, liturgy, poetry and speeches in more than a thousand of years of untold suffering before and after the Babylonian captivity – all this now became the inviolable property of the 'new Israel', the Christian church.

Christians think, meditate, pray, sacrifice – in their liturgy, their hymns – in terms of this property, without which no event in the church calendar would be thinkable. And they use it against the Jews, the 'perfidious Jewish people'. *De perfidis judaeis*, the axis of Christian anti-Semitism, a formula whose power was to be broken only in the days of Pope John XXIII, may not have entered the liturgy until the early Middle Ages, but it is Pauline in its theological conception. The Jews are the treacherous, perfidious people, even if Jewish-Christian theologians have recently tried to give the word *perfidia* as innocuous a meaning as possible.

Like his great follower Martin Luther, St Paul was deeply hurt by Jewish

26

reluctance to be converted. If Christians are still to this day unable to appreciate the true meaning of Israel (just as most Jews today are ignorant of the spiritual nature of Israel), they can blame their lack of grace on St Paul, who – amid many real acts of grace – shared the inability of all great revolutionaries to see his adversaries other than through a distorting mirror: for him there was no Jew but a converted Jew. He turned the Law, which was for the old Jews a source of life and joy, into a monument of misery and enslavement. As a Jew St Paul knew very well that the Torah contains not only the *halachah*, the legalistic interpretation of the Law, but also the *haggadah*, which interprets the Law mystically and humanly. St Paul chose to ignore this latter part and thus to establish the superiority of the Gospel over the Law. There are learned Christians even today who do not know that the commandments to love one's neighbours and one's enemies are contained both in the Old Testament and in the Law. They also do not know that one of the main principles of rabbinical ethics is, 'You shall not put anyone to shame.' This is equivalent to the *neminem laedere*, the 'you shall not hurt anyone' of the Roman Stoics, the basic principle of a later humanistic Catholicism based on the teachings of Erasmus. But St Paul, with his belief in the liberating efficacy of God's wrath, felt it his duty to shame his Jewish people by means of theological shock tactics. (At the time of the Second World War some Catholic theologians in France evolved a *théologie du choc*, which was designed to shake the comfortable, thick-skinned bourgeoisie out of its spiritual complacency.)

The Law appeared to St Paul as the wall which cut off the Jewish people from God, whereas priests, prophets and Bible editors had erected it expressly as a protective wall to keep the blossoming vineyard of Israel safe from the jackals outside. The church was later to adopt this protective function of dogma and church discipline and to call its own jackals, the heretics, to account in its name.

The distorted image of the Law as defined for the church by St Paul brought disaster primarily to the Jews. '*Cette omission frauduleuse a produit au cours des siècles les fruits les plus empoisonnés, persécutions et massacres.*' ('This treacherous omission brought forth over centuries bitter fruits in the shape of persecution and blood-baths.') Thus wrote a prominent Jew of our time, Josué Jéhouda, who spent over forty years wrestling with Christian anti-Semites and trying to arouse the conscience of the world, in order to save the Jews after 1933. His statement should be regarded by all Christians with respect. But this too should not be forgotten: the rejection of the Law opened the doors to young Pauline Christianity and enabled it to become a universal religion. But this very universality, the ability to speak for all men and all peoples and to bring them freedom, was already contained in Jewish theology and Jewish faith. However, in the centuries before and after Christ this great universal message – openly proclaimed in the Old Testament – could not be sufficiently conveyed to the other peoples, simply because the ambitious

27

proselyte movement foundered on the Law itself. To quote another prominent Jew, Erich von Kahler: 'What prevented the Jewish religion, then and in later times, from becoming the universal religion that its offshoot, Christianity, subsequently became, was its spiritual rigidity, its insistence on the absolute authority of the Law and its refusal to form alliances with the outer manifestations of pagan beliefs.' (To which we might add: the history of Catholicism from late Antiquity up to the present day is a process of osmotic relationships with local customs, with non-Christian and pre-Christian gods and powers of very varied origins, as for instance in Poland, Spain and South America.) 'It was this very inviolability of the Law that prevented a distinction being made between its universal ethical concepts and ancient tribal rituals. Circumcision was one ritual which proved an insuperable obstacle for the majority of Gentiles who sympathized with the Jewish idea of God. And thus there arose around the Diaspora communities groups of half-believers, of "God worshippers" (*sebomenoi*) who adopted only the purely spiritual and generally applicable parts of the Jewish religion as their own. These became the fertilizing cells of the first Christian communities.'

For many people, and not only Christians, St Paul appeared in the role of a liberator from the Jewish religion and its ritual, from the Law and from the first church, the synagogue; later too from the second church, which he himself helped to found, the Roman Catholic church. Jesus had lived all His life within the Law, which He altered by filling it with His life blood and the power of His love. But it was the Jew Paul who destroyed the Law.

From the time of St Paul Jews and Christians went different ways. It was at first an internal separation; the actual separation began in about AD 70. And, with the Law, Pauline Christianity gave up a priceless heritage: the Messianic idea. Clericalism, de-Messianization and self-sufficiency replaced the Jewish beliefs in the direct fulfilment of God's commandments in any given historical situation. And these three concepts are bound up closely with Pauline distinctions between the spirit and the flesh. We know that *sarx*, St Paul's word for flesh, is not identical with the word as understood and condemned by Puritans and Manichaeans. St Paul's man of flesh is not the old Adam, not simply the libidinous man at the mercy of his carnal lusts. St Paul knew that the lusts and cravings of the spirit are just as dangerous, if not even more so. For him flesh includes the undisciplined, licentious spirit.

After all the deviations and failures of various forms of Christianity during the past fifteen centuries, there is one fact we should acknowledge: St Paul began, and St Augustine completed, the process of turning the 'true church' into a religion of celibates. At the Second Vatican Council in Rome in 1964 the Patriarch Maximos referred openly to the 'bachelor psychosis' in Christian theology. And the Jew Alexandre Weill defines Christianity rather unkindly as the religion of celibates, pointing to Jesus, St Paul, and Pascal, Kant and Schopenhauer. Clericalism is bound up with priests and the training of a body of men to hold themselves aloof from the sinful world, the sinful flesh, the sinful woman, sinful lust. St Paul condemns women to silence in the church. And if later researches suggest that this edict was not St Paul's own, it has nevertheless earned the weight of authority by having been regarded for a thousand years as his. Original sin has come increasingly to be identified with concupiscence, with the libido, the sexual urge itself. The Jewish religion has on the other hand become a religion of the family, the Jewish rabbi being a family man and, like all family men, living and working in intimate daily contact with historical events. He is part of the family of men, whose wars and civil wars daily affect and threaten his family. The celibate theologian is not personally affected by war: he can quite calmly refer to atomic warfare as a Christian enterprise. A Christianity of celibate priests and laymen instructed in their image is not concerned with actual history – that is the work partly of the Devil and partly of God – but primarily with the salvation of its own soul. But this sort of salvation is connected primarily with the sins of the flesh, the temptations of a man living in celibacy. The greatest part of his energy is spent in battling with the sin of carnal lust. This clericalized and self-sufficing Christianity, striving to turn all men into monks, has no strength left to cultivate the Messianic idea. Israel and the Jews believe in and accept their duty to build the kingdom of God here on earth. Every single Jew is pledged to prepare for the Messiah and for the sake of his fellow-men to work actively, whatever the suffering and sacrifice, for His coming.

History is progress towards the kingdom of God, and each single Jew bears with his own personal progress the responsibility for it. The kingdom of God is not to be found in some vague – preferably self-sufficient – Beyond, in the distant heavens, but here on this earth. Jews like Marx, Freud and Einstein stand with many non-professing Jews in the service of this idea of progress, and share the same belief of personal responsibility for the founding of God's kingdom on earth that inspired Israel. A very mundane German Jew, Walther Rathenau, Germany's economic director during the First World War, author of a social plan for the twenty-first century and foreign minister in the Weimar Republic up to his assassination in 1922, wrote at the end of the First World War to a German officer friend, 'You love the Old Testament and hate, or rather disapprove of, us Jews. And you are right, for we have not yet fulfilled our mission. Do you know what we have been sent into the world to do? To summon all men to Sinai. You don't want to go there? If I don't summon you, Marx will. If Marx doesn't summon you, Spinoza will. And if Spinoza doesn't, then Christ will.'

In this letter Rathenau goes on to say, 'It is not the noble people who are responsible for the ignoble ones. No, it is Kol Jisroel, the whole of Israel, that is responsible for each single one of us – yes, each single one. But the whole of Israel is every man created in the image of God. That is to say, it is you and your commanding officer and your batman and myself and all the rest of us.'

If Spinoza doesn't summon you, then Christ will ... Israel is all of us. But St Paul came (not consciously, not deliberately, but factually) between Jesus and the Jews, Israel's Messianic deeds and hopes and the Christians. St Paul invalidated Messianic hopes with his clericalism and so in practice put an end to them. St Augustine, the killer of hope and recognized by the Jesuits as such, followed closely in St Paul's footsteps. The salvation of the 'new Adam', earned in communion with a remote, unearthly Christ, conveyed through the sacraments and above all in a communion which by its very exclusivity implies an excommunication of all men holding different views – this form of salvation swallows up all Messianic hope, deprives both Jews and Christian Jews of their Messianic mission. 'Our Jerusalem is in heaven.' The heavenly Jerusalem which the church extols and presents exclusively to its believers inside its church walls and stately palaces has, it seems, nothing more to do with the tears and miseries of 'poor sinners' here on earth.

The Messianic idea was banished in and from the church in bitter disputes during the first centuries after Christ. *Docta spes*, the 'principle of hope', as the atheistic Jewish believer Bloch calls it today, was denounced and left to the visionaries, the heretics, the nonconformists and the Communists.

So, through St Paul, Jews and Christians were set on completely different paths. The church, the new Israel, became the persecutor of the old Israel, from which hope was filched as the first and last heritage and channelled in a completely different direction. The hope of the Jew, rejoicing in life, his family, his sexual power and desire for a numerous progeny, is centred on the coming kingdom of God on earth. The Messiah will create the great festive community of God's people. A Jewish song in folk style, emanating from Poland, gives lively expression to this hope that has not been extinguished in two thousand years:

'Rabbi, dear Rabbi, what will there be when the Messiah comes? A great feast there will be. Rabbi, dear Rabbi, what will happen at the feast? The *Schor habor* will be slaughtered at the feast to come. Rabbi, dear Rabbi, what will happen at the feast? The leviathan will be slaughtered; there will be meat and fish to eat at the feast to come. Rabbi, dear Rabbi, what will be drunk at the feast to come? There will be holy wine to drink and meat and fish to eat at the feast to come!'

The last verse runs, 'We shall dance and leap, we shall cheer and sing and bring holy sacrifices. Our father Jacob will lead us, our father Isaac will hold the cup. Ezra the Scribe will write our wishes. Our father Abraham will bless us. Our teacher Moses will teach us the Law, the Levites will sing to us. Aaron the priest will dance for us, David the king will play for us. There will be holy wine to drink and meat and fish to eat at the feast to come.'

Jewish festivities retain to this day this note of joy. Early Christian love-feasts basked in a similar joy. Christianity after St Paul denounced the fleshly, earthbound hope of the Jews and branded the Jews as lascivious, fleshly and sexually obsessed – right up to the trials of the Third Reich. The hope of the sexually terrified Christian man was fixed on his private salvation and a kingdom of God on the far side of history and time. The cosmocrat Christ will descend from His throne in the skies above to judge the world and gather His sheep from the ranks of the damned, the sinners of the flesh. He is a Christ who moves further and further away from the Jew Jesus, the Jewish man on earth.

5

Christianity on the Way to the Imperial Church. Imperial Church versus the Jews

During the Jewish war against the Romans from AD 66 to 70, the Sanhedrin, the supreme religious and civil authority, fled from Jerusalem to Jabne, a small town east of the Jordan. The leaders of the Jewish-Christian church had left Jerusalem possibly even earlier, and taken refuge in Pella, another small Transjordanian town. So now – at a time of national Jewish emergency – there were two churches in exile, with separate identities. The Jewish community, the older of the two, began first of all to close its ranks against the Jewish-Christians, who were living among them and attending the synagogue and Jewish services.

The acrimonious disputes in sixteenth- and seventeenth-century England, among Protestant refugees from the Continent, give some idea of the sort of struggle for ascendancy that was now beginning to take place between the two Jewish communities. The synagogue began to shut itself off from Jewish-Christians and tried to stop them making converts. From this bitter life in exile grew the fanaticism of Jewish orthodoxy, which contorted the life of the Diaspora Jews, making them turn in on themselves and cast anxious and angry eyes on the Jewish-Christians. It was a form of fanaticism that had nothing to do with the alleged exclusiveness of the Pharisaic scribes towards Jesus during his lifetime.

In the second half of the first century Samuel 'the Small' composed a prayer against heretics, to which Jewish-Christians could not ascribe; but it was inserted in the Eighteen Benedictions as part of the Jewish service. All synagogues throughout the Diaspora presumably knew of this condemnation before the end of the first century, and from that moment onwards Christians could no longer participate in Jewish life. Since the Jewish-Christian church used the Septuagint translation of the scriptures and the Bible interpretations of the Egyptian Jews, the Sanhedrin revised the canonic writings and rejected the Septuagint with its universalist-Greek flavour.

'If any member of the church of Jerusalem had been asked "Are you a Jew?" or "Are you a Christian?" he would, even after the flight from

Jerusalem, have unhesitatingly answered "yes" to both questions. But those days were gone. In the eyes of the Sanhedrin one was either Jew or Christian. The synagogue had said "No" to Christ, once and for all.'

The author of the Fourth Gospel lived through those agonizing times. 'The Gospel according to St John reflects the feelings of Jewish-Christians who had been cast out from their national community.'

The tragic history of the Jewish-Christians after this separation has yet to be written. The sources lie buried. Perhaps some will one day be unearthed. These Jewish-Christians should have formed a bridge, but they were rebuffed, first by the church, then by the Jews, for they believed both in Jesus the Messiah and in the Law. Some of them were presumably accepted by one or the other of the numerous Christian sects which sprang up in the first centuries after Christ.

In the second century AD the church was completely under non-Jewish leadership, and most of its members were non-Jews. By the middle of that century the Christian and Jewish religions were entirely separate, and Christian apologists laboured to demonstrate to the Romans and Greeks the indigenous origin, dignity and political loyalty of Christianity.

The Jews were now beginning to set up their voluntary spiritual ghetto. Feeling themselves threatened and encircled by the Romans, Greeks, Egyptians and Jewish-Christians, they portrayed Jesus as a deceiver and fraud to their frightened co-religionists. Christianity, they asserted, was a denial of God; it was wicked atheism and a rejection of the Law.

Out of this attitude Talmudic Jewry of the first centuries after Christ evolved a story in which Jesus was described as the illegitimate child of a Roman soldier of the name of Panthera. His miracles were worked by magic which He had learnt in Egypt. After His death, His disciples had stolen the body and invented the story of His resurrection. Jesus, the Talmudic story claimed, had deceived Israel. And the Talmud described the Jewish-Christians as *minim*: frauds, traitors and heretics.

The distinguished Anglican theologian and historian, the Rev. James Parkes, has suggested that in those days Jewish attacks on Christians were probably less vehement than those by Christians on Jews. Despite this animosity and hostility, the first few centuries saw long, lively and good-neighbourly relations between Jew and Gentile. It was only centuries later that separate dates were laid down for the Christian Easter and the Jewish Passover. The powerful impact of sermon and worship in the synagogue on Jewish-born Christians roused St John Chrysostom to lash out against the Jews. The church never ceased to fear the rival influence of Jewry. It feared infection, conversion to the Jewish faith, and therefore sought to limit, if not entirely prohibit, all contact and personal relations between Jews and Christians. This fear and anxiety of the church was openly admitted in Visigothic Spain in the sixth and seventh centuries, in Poland in the thirteenth century and in nearly all European countries in the late Middle Ages and modern times. And it was clearly manifested in 1928, before Hitler's access to power, in the proscription by the Roman Curia of the Society of the Friends of Israel.

The first law which the church imposed on the Roman Empire, when it became Christian, was to forbid the Jews to make proselytes.

Between the second and fourth centuries a violent anti-Judaism and anti-Semitism were born which to this day supply the enemies of the Jews with ammunition. The great Jew-baiters and Jew-killers of the twentieth century may have committed worse deeds, but their utterances scarcely surpass the violence of the anti-Jewish attacks and denunciations of those days. The origin of that early anti-Semitism can be understood only in the closest context with the difficulties besetting the early Christian communities before they were absorbed into, brought into line with, or destroyed by the victorious imperial church. Those inflammatory days produced explosive personalities, full of tension and inner conflict. Their fight for Christianity and the church was eloquently mirrored in their aggressiveness against the Jews. St John Chrysostom, St Jerome and St Augustine created an image of the Jew which, for one and a half thousand years, hypnotized the world, above all in times of crisis and upheaval, and had a special effect on neurotic people

The Swiss Protestant theologian, Martin Werner, has summed up the situation in these words: 'After the early days of the apostles, as Christianity continued to spread, it immediately split up into numerous separate sects and groups, and conspicuous rifts appeared. Round about 375, Epiphanius had to contend with no less than sixty such Christian "heresies". A little later, about 390, Philaster of Brescia listed well over a hundred heresies. Disputes among the many groups and sects sharpened, and much of contemporary Christian literature was devoted to combatting adversaries of some sort.'

What was more convenient than to suspect the evil seducer, the Jew, the 'synagogue of Satan' as the power behind all kinds of opposition and heresy?

'Only thanks to its recognition by Emperor Constantine was the Catholic Church, in alliance with the might of the Roman state, able to crush its old and new rivals. It destroyed their churches, confiscated their Bibles and other religious works, used compulsory conversion and resorted to other means of force.'

Catholic church historians are naturally more cautious in their accounts of the struggles and upheavals in those centuries, but, whenever they manage to be objective, their descriptions resemble those of this Protestant theologian.

'Until the middle of the second century, traditional church circles, in accordance with St Paul's views, accepted only the Old Testament as the strict canon of the revelation.' The Old Testament belonged to the Christians, the orthodox Christians.

Their duty was to defend the Old Testament and its God against both the Jews and the rigidly disciplined Marcionite church, which from the middle of the second century began to expand throughout the Roman Empire in dangerous rivalry to incipient Catholicism.

Marcion was the brilliant son of a bishop who had rejected him. He saw in St Paul the only true apostle, and spurned the Old Testament as a contrivance of the Jewish God. Marcion 'purged' the New Testament of all reference to the Old Testament and declared everything that contradicted his own teaching to be a forgery by Jewish apostles and their followers. Basing himself mainly on St Luke and St Paul's Epistles, Marcion produced a 'pure' gospel of his own.

'At the beginning of the third century, Tertullian, in his disputes over dogma, concluded that it was senseless and unprofitable to argue with heretics over the interpretation of the Holy Bible. The right procedure was to deny them, *a priori*, the right to invoke the Scriptures.'

'During the fierce contests of the fourth century, Bishop Hilary of Poitiers once complained that ever since the Council of Nicaea (325) there had been endless dogmatic arguments over new formulations of the Creed. No one knew what the Creed would be in the coming year, and in the end a stage would be reached when nothing that the church held sacred would remain untouched.'

At times it seemed as if any means were permissible in this all-in fight: forgery, slander, manslaughter, murder and rebellion. Harnack speaks of the increasing mendacity of theologians which, he says, began in the fourth century. That was the climate in which the ecclesiastical dogmas of the Trinity, of God Incarnate and of the Two-Substances Christ were created. 'Just as it was considered unnecessary to be truthful to an adversary, thus forgetting the evangelical command, so theologians now began to insinuate that Christ and the apostles had been less than truthful; and even God Himself was charged with having deceived His opponent, the Devil. But if God Himself cunningly deceived His enemy, Man also should be allowed to do so. In the circumstances it was not surprising to find forgeries a common occurrence. Of course, even in the second century, there had been many reports of forgeries and misrepresentations . . . but these falsifications were minor affairs compared with the mendacity which began to pervade official writings in the fourth century . . . In those days no one any longer trusted a written document, file or deposition. Contemporary episcopal letters abound in charges of forgery. The letters of earlier church fathers were falsified and alien views were imputed to them. Conversely, the simplest way of defending an early church father who might have been cited as a supporter of the opposition or whose orthodoxy had come under suspicion, was to claim that heretics had arbitrarily altered his writings. The official literature on the dispute between Nestorians and Monophysites is a morass of lies and villainy with but a few rocks emerging to offer a firm foothold.'

Patriarchs, bishops, religious communities, indeed whole nations, were fighting each other, covering their rabid nationalism in 'Christian' garb – especially in Egypt, North Africa and Asia Minor. 'The clerics of Carthage, who in Cyprian's day were fighting for power, charged one another with fraud, adultery and murder.' In the middle of the fourth century Rome was the scene of a bloody clash between the two contenders for the papal office, Ursinus and Damasus, and their followers. The fight took place in the church and one hundred and thirty-seven lay there dead after the battle.

The still valid doctrine of the Trinity and of the dual substance of Christ were established during the perpetual hot and cold wars and civil strife of the fourth century. That terrible century, engulfed in hatred, murder, expulsion, banishment and endless denunciation was the great watershed: Judaism and Christianity are still in many ways the religions of the fourth century. The Councils of Nicaea and Constantinople and the schools of Pumbeditha and Sura left their stamp on both religions. St Ambrose, St Augustine, St Jerome and St John Chrysostom were alive then. At the same time great Talmudic teachers were at work; Rabbah bar Nahmani, Joseph bar Hama, Abbaye and others. The Babylonian Talmud was centred on Sura. There was no theological discussion between Christians and Jews, although most of their works were based on the same books of the Bible. St Jerome was the only Christian father with a knowledge of Hebrew and of Talmudic and rabbinical thought. He lived in Palestine, in close touch with Jews, but to him they were merely objects of mockery and derision. St Jerome despised the Christian Jews of Palestine just as much as the Jews did.

This was the century of destiny for the Jews and the synagogue. The fourth century was the era in which the fires of Christian hate and murder were lit: they are still burning.

Christian orthodoxy was evolving slowly and in trying circumstances amidst many battles against heresy – and each day brought new suspicion and fresh charges. Everywhere the old foe, the Jew, was encountered. Nearly all Judaizing heresies originated in places with strong Jewish communities. The church fathers went much further in denouncing the Jews as demons than the great heathen anti-Semite Apion, whose slogans they borrowed. Nearly all the church fathers brought along their pieces of rock for the stoning – so far only metaphoric – of the Jews: St Hilary of Poitiers (rightly described as the sole Western theologian who had an intellectual grasp of the deep theological arguments in the East), St Jerome, St Ephraim, St Gregory of Nyssa, St Ambrose, St Epiphanius (a Jew by birth) and St Cyril of Jerusalem. But two stood out among them: St John Chrysostom and St Augustine.

To the church fathers and other ecclesiastical authors of the fourth century the Jew was not a human being but a monster, a theological abstraction, a being of superhuman cunning and malice, yet at the same time struck with superhuman blindness. The attack was always directed against the Jews in general, never concretely against a particular Jew.

Psychologists may readily agree that a tremendous mental effort of repression must have been needed to substitute for the man and Jew Jesus a God who no longer had anything in common with the evil Jews, the kinsfolk of Miriam and Mary. Hence Mary had to be elevated, to become the Mother of God, a being more divine than human.

St Hilary of Poitiers did not acknowledge a Jew's greeting in the street. He believed that before the Jews received the Law they were possessed by an unclean devil, who immediately returned after their rejection of Christ. Eusebius of Caesarea made a sharp distinction between Hebrews, who were good men in the Old Testament, and Jews, who were evil.

The eight sermons which St John Chrysostom (*c.* 350–*c.* 407) delivered in 387 against the Jews in Antioch are of epoch-making significance: they provided all the weapons used against Jewry ever since. The Jew was denounced as carnal, lascivious, demonic, avaricious and accursed. The Jews had murdered the prophets and they had murdered Christ. They were deicides. The Jews worshipped the Devil. They were drunkards, whore-mongers and criminals. St Jerome hurled a much-quoted insult at the synagogue: 'If you call it a brothel, a den of vice, the Devil's refuge, Satan's fortress, a place to deprave the soul, an abyss of every conceivable disaster or whatever else you will, you are still saying less than it deserves!'

St Jerome was embittered by the sight of Jews in Antioch, where they formed a large part of the town's population, living with Christians and successfully engaged in missionary work among them. In this context the Catholic author Karl Thieme remarks: 'It goes without saying that there was but a short step from this kind of calumny by ecclesiastical authority to setting synagogues on fire. The same rowdy mob that as heathens stormed the Jewish quarter of Alexandria, and as Christians murdered the heathen neo-Platonic philosopher Hypatia in the same city, was perfectly willing to set fire to Satan's fortress. When in one such instance (in 338 at Callinicum on the Euphrates) the Emperor Theodosius ordered the arsonists to be punished and the damage to the synagogue to be made good at the expense of the local bishop who had instigated it, no less a man than St Ambrose protested. "I hereby declare," he said, "that it was I who set fire to the synagogue; indeed, I gave orders for it to be done so that there should no longer be any place where Christ is denied." And, interrupting a public church service, he morally compelled the emperor to rescind his order and ultimately to let all the culprits go unpunished.'

St Ambrose was St Augustine's great mentor. But, before turning to the latter, let us say a word about St Jerome, the man who for many centuries formed the last link between Eastern and Western Christianity. St Jerome's personality was extremely complex and his attitude to St Ambrose was full of hostility. There is one particular reason why St Jerome merits attention: to this very day monks and ascetic Christians are the most inveterate enemies of the 'carnal' Jew. Monks led the Jew-killing mob in Spain and in the

Rhineland during the Crusades, and in England and France in the twelfth and thirteenth centuries. Monks led the attack on the Jews in Spain from the fourteenth to the sixteenth centuries and in Germany in the days of Pfefferkorn and Reuchlin.

Monasticism has attracted many mature men and women who are rightly credited with great spiritual and humanitarian achievements, both in Europe and the East. But many Christians, living monastic lives in this wicked world, have failed to achieve such physical and spiritual maturity. Sexuality runs wild and distorts them. Fearful and jealous of sex, they persecute the filthy woman, the lazy mob, all sinful mankind. To them the 'worldly-wanton' Jew embodies and magnifies every sexual impulse, in the same way that the Devil was depicted in the Middle Ages as a Jew, and as the father of all Jews with oversized genitals. If Christians of the male sex happen to be intellectuals as well as monks, their sharp intelligence tends to combine with their undeveloped, repressed and brutalized sexuality to produce a harsh and bitter enemy to those devilish adversaries – women and Jews.

St Jerome appears to us the archetype of such a neurotic, monastic intellectual. Modern monks who realize the potential dangers know that immature, undisciplined sexuality can lead to murder and suicide. For this reason a study of St Jerome's sexual problems by a doctor, Charles-Henri Nodet, was incorporated by French Carmelites in their *Études Carmélitaines* (1952).

A brief summary of St Jerome's life reveals that the young Dalmatian received a wide classical education in Rome from the age of twelve. When he was twenty he was baptized by Pope Liberius. Disgusted by the lascivious life of luxury in Rome, he went to Antioch after travelling through Gaul, Trier and the Syrian desert. Here ordained, he learned Hebrew from a Jewish convert and studied with St Gregory of Nazianzus. Commissioned by Pope Damasus, he completed his famous revision of the Bible. For thirty-five years he lived in ascetic retirement in Bethlehem, near the birthplace of the Jew Jesus, surrounded by Jews, without ever understanding Jesus the man or seeing the Jews as fellow humans.

There is a close link between St Jerome's savage condemnation of the female sex and his denigration of the Jew. St Jerome knew from experience what the wealthy, licentious women of the Roman aristocracy were like, and he may well have based his portrayal of sexy women on them. Like many other neurotics, he made a distinction between love and sexual lust. Love was divine, virginal, manly, asexual. Sexual lust was obscene, fit for pigs and dogs rather than human beings. In marriage a woman should become as a man, practise continence and serve Christ – but only after the children were born. Why have children, in any case? Childbirth was a dirty, strenuous affair and brought nothing but worries. Even before the advent of Christianity, a wave of hatred of sex swept the last days of the Ancient World. St Jerome took it up and intensified it. The Ancient World foundered on a low birth-rate.

To St Jerome marriage was the Old Testament, the Law. It was 'carnal' and thus stood condemned. Virginity, however, was the Gospel. To be Christian meant to be or to become virgin – as a widow or a man to renounce sinful life. Adam and Eve had a sexual relationship only after the Fall. Marriage and sex were dominant from the Fall till Salvation through Christ. Christ was man living without sex.

Rebirth in Christ conferred 'virginity'. Time and again St Jerome invokes St Paul in his attacks on sex, sensuality and women.

St Jerome displays the colossal egotism of the bachelor who refuses to have anything to do with the 'filth' that is woman. His invective betrays the fear of the neurotic who had never been able to follow his own sexual nature to maturity. Often he compares marriage with Sodom. A husband could love his wife only if he abstained from all sexual intercourse with her. Fear of sex induced St Jerome to speak out even against bathing.

St Jerome gave vent to his pent-up aggressiveness, the evil fruit of his warped sensuality – and also supplied a model for the next fifteen hundred years – in furious attacks on all and everything he considered his enemies: camels, dogs, pigs, forgers, madmen, scorpions, hydras, wild boars, sows – such was the vocabulary Jerome applied to his dear neighbours.

In such surroundings there was no place for Jews. He was now and for ever more the 'carnal', 'lewd' and 'materialistic' Jew. This is well worth noting. Long before the Jew was condemned for his business acumen and denounced as a devilish capitalist, he had been unmasked theologically as a materialist, a child of the wicked carnal world, and the product of filthy sexual lust.

In this context the reinterpretation of the Song of Songs is significant for the light it throws on the reassessment of the Jew. Shir-ha-Shirim, the Song of Songs, the Song of Solomon . . . world literature knows few other love poems in which the love of two young people is sung with such fervour and splendid eloquence – love for the maiden whose breasts are like two young roes that are twins. Countless generations of young Jews, confined within the narrow walls of the ghetto, have sung this song of youthful love, sighing and dreaming the visions of the Song of Songs. To this day Arab wedding songs in Syria recall the Song. But in the second century the famous Rabbi Akiba was angered when he encountered a group of young men happily singing verses from the Song of Songs. Rabbi Akiba thought this was frivolous.

On the Sabbath of the Passover, the Jewish Easter, devout Jews sing the Song of Songs. This ritual was presumably established in Babylon in the sixth century. For Easter was originally a festival of Spring, of the renewal of life. Only later was it linked with the national life of the Jews and the memory of the exodus from Egypt.

For the later Cabalists the Sabbath was the bride and Israel her lover and protector. In a somewhat contrived medieval interpretation by rabbinical theologians the beloved Shulamite of the Song of Songs appears as Israel. During those centuries we are now reviewing Talmudic rabbis were already working on an allegorical interpretation of the Song of Songs which was eagerly adopted by the fathers of the church. 'Thy two breasts are like two young roes that are twins . . .' The breasts of Israel, so these Talmudists declared, were the brothers Moses and Aaron. Here was a transformation of the faith into something masculine, a repression of the female and erotic and the emergence of neurotic traits – and that among Talmudic Jews of the fourth to the sixth centuries. At the same time a parallel development began among Christians and persisted all through the Middle Ages: the Song of Songs lauds the marriage between the church and Christ. The bride was the virginal soul and Christ her spiritual bridegroom.

This use and misuse of the Song of Songs deprived the Jews also of Eros, all-embracing love. The love expressed in the Song of Songs was turned into something masculine, monastic, spiritual, asexual. And the Jew was damned as a sex-ridden libertine.

In the West this process of depriving love of sex, a move of such lasting significance for Christendom and of such disastrous consequences for the Jews, was pushed vigorously forward by St Augustine.

Next to St Paul, St Augustine is the Western world's greatest Christian authority. Popes and anti-popes, orthodox and heterodox reformists of the Church alike quote him. So do Luther and Jansenius and the dualistic religious movements and sects which so harshly stamped modern European history in wars and civil wars between the sixteenth and twentieth centuries. The well-worn image of the Jew which still replaces broad historical truth in the minds of anti-Semites and philo-Semites owes quite a lot to St Augustine's theology.

In the great St Augustine, African passion was wedded to a borderland Roman nationalism. (The most rabid Roman nationalists came from Africa and Spain, just as the most nationalistic French come from Algeria and Alsace, and extreme German nationalists from Slavonic Central Europe). St Augustine never managed to escape from his Manichaeian past and, especially in his last years, relapsed back into it.

Mani's predecessors were Marcion and Bardesanes. Mani was the son of Maryam (Mary), of the Parthian dynasty of Kamsarakan, and Prince Hamadan, and was born in the Babylonian village of Mardinu – in a part of the world where the Persian empire and the influence of the Romans and Greeks clashed – presumably on 14 April AD 216. Mani said of himself: 'I am a grateful scholar, who has sprung from the land of Babel.'

Mani, a God-seeker, a man of genius with great artistic and intellectual gifts, probably spent his childhood among a Baptist sect. At the age of twelve Mani – like the twelve-year-old Jesus in the temple – had his first revelation.

Later he had a decisive vision: 'In this same year, when King Ardashir was about to be crowned, the living Paraclete descended and addressed me. He revealed to me the mystery that had been hidden from aeons and generations: the mystery of light and darkness, the mystery of struggle and war and of the great war.' Mani claimed to be the Paraclete, the Holy Ghost whose coming was promised by Jesus in the Gospel according to St John.

His hands manacled by three chains, three shackles fettering his feet and with a chain around his neck, the sixty-year-old Mani spent his last days from 19 January till 14 February 276 (other accounts put the time from 31 January to 26 February 277) in the gaol of the Parthian king. In accordance with ancient oriental custom he was permitted – as was John the Baptist in Herod's prison – to receive his disciples and give them religious instruction. But, emaciated through fasting and penance, he died of exhaustion.

'At eleven o'clock in the morning he ascended from his body to the high abode of his greatness.' The Great King ordered Mani's body to be pierced with a burning torch to ascertain whether the hated leader of this sect was really dead. The body was cut into pieces and the severed head nailed above the gates of Bet-Lapat.

Out of the confluence of Gnostic, Christian, Jewish, Mesopotamian and Persian streams of thought, Mani created the Manichaean church which temporarily out-rivalled Christianity in the Near East and along the silk route to China. Manichaeans travelled to every part of Europe and deeply penetrated Christendom with their doctrines, especially with their concept of history. Even now a type of Manichaeism, associated with certain Monophysite traits, is the cancer of Christendom. If anti-Semitism in the nineteenth and twentieth centuries is to be regarded as a cancerous growth in the womb of Christianity, its origin lies, like all other similar growths, in Manichaeism.

How deep-rooted the Manichaean image of the world became in the West, thanks to St Augustine and his disciple Orosius, can be demonstrated by referring briefly to two of its offspring in the nineteenth and twentieth centuries: the interpretation of history as found in the Communist Manifesto and among leading anti-Semites in the circle of supporters of the Protocols of the Elders of Zion.

In the Communist Manifesto, Marx and Engels interpret history as a struggle in which the children of Light (the proletariat) defeat the children of Darkness (the capitalists). Their victory is historically pre-determined and necessary for the salvation of mankind. The class struggle – like the Aryan 'racial struggle' – is a contest in which a wicked world power, born of the Devil (capitalism, 'international Jewry') is and must ultimately be defeated. It was a particularly dangerous phenomenon that a vulgarized, plebeian party-church Communism of the Stalinist stamp succeeded in uniting these two Manichaean components. There was the 'orthodox' Communist Party line, admirably suited to the mentality of the old

41

exseminarist Stalin, who enjoyed using liturgical phrases when handing out praise or thundering condemnation. And there was that popular form of anti-Semitism which flourished among the peoples of East Europe and which also fed on ancient Manichaean sources. Stalin's last indictment of Jewish doctors directly parallels the sixteenth-century execution of Jewish physicians in Spain, who were accused of poisoning and killing the pure children of Light.

Manichaeans, in the form of orthodox Augustinian theologians, Communists and anti-Semites are convinced that they hold the key to world history in their hands. Like Mani, they believe that the Holy Ghost has revealed Himself to them alone. History is a struggle between the children of Light and the children of Darkness; and he who knows that and holds the secret of it is infinitely superior to all other men. The orthodox Communist and the convinced German-Aryan anti-Semite alike feel contempt and pity for the ignoramuses who simply cannot grasp what history is all about and what men of good-will have to do.

But let us return to St Augustine. His philosophy, based on St Paul, was deeply pessimistic. To him Man was the child and the prisoner of original sin. This, in essence, was concupiscence, the wicked sexual appetite, and it was rooted in *superbia*, the revolt of Satan and the fallen angels. Like St Thomas Aquinas, his great adversary and critic of later days, St Augustine was entirely moulded by the political and social order of his time. There was an exact parallel between his concept of original sin and the compulsory hereditary service decreed by the Roman Empire. In late Antiquity, the Roman Empire imposed draconic laws of taxation. Whip and torture became common instruments of the tax gatherer, and tax debts could lead to execution. Anyone who was given an office had to retain it so as to remain liable for tax. Originally, immunity meant exemption from the *munus*, the office bestowed on the clergy. In AD 325 Emperor Constantine made the service of municipal *decuriones* hereditary and compulsory; in 331 the same rule was applied to soldiers and lower officials; in 332 to the *coloni*, the small tenants of the landowners, who were able to meet their taxes only if assured of the requisite number of agricultural labourers. St Augustine taught that Adam's disobedience was an inherited burden, a *res obnoxia*. As the descendants of Adam, all human beings were *hereditarii debiti*, hereditarily burdened bearers of original sin. Man cannot free himself of this terrible inheritance, and St Augustine's principle of 'grace' amounts in fact to a denial of individual initiative. In St Augustine, the great political reactionary, there lies hidden a narcotic, quietistic element which is alien to the glad tidings of the Gospel.

St Augustine became and remained a monk all his life: only the monastery could offer ultimate refuge. Ascetic life was real, full Christianity. But since all people could not enter monasteries, they needed a corrective on this sin-ridden earth to keep them in check. They must have some overall protection against carnal and spiritual excesses. The Roman Empire and the church were St Augustine's chosen instruments for the protection of the slaves of sin: it was the duty of these bodies to work together to provide for the wretched human being a maximum of security – security against himself and his freedom, which, for the descendant of Adam, could only be an abuse of freedom.

'There is no salvation outside the church.' On this point St Augustine fully agreed with St Cyprian. St Augustine, the intellectual who for many years had lived a life of profound spiritual insecurity, confessed that he could believe only in a collective salvation. He would not take the word of an angel or indeed of the Gospels unless the church – the authority – confirmed it. The church *must* impose salvation upon sinful man, and the church appealed for help to the state – the Roman Empire. For more than a thousand years St Augustine has been the great ecclesiastical authority always invoked where inquisition, torture, the stake or secular aid for the church are involved. St Augustine invoked the *anti-rebel* laws of the Roman Empire in his campaign against the heretic Donatists in North Africa. Admittedly, he wrote to the Roman pro-consul Donatus in 408, 'We beg you not to have them killed.' But this can easily have been a mere formula, a pious wish not to be involved oneself in the shedding of blood. The situation was later portrayed in Spanish pictures, showing the ecclesiastical authorities enthroned high above the popular masses, the laymen who were 'instruments' of the clergy. 'Instrument' was an ancient designation for slaves. Even in the nineteenth and twentieth centuries laymen are referred to as instruments in this sense. And in the thirteenth and fourteenth centuries, canonists spoke of them as *servi adscripticii*, serfs tied to the soil. This is pure St Augustine: bishops and theologians seated on their exalted thrones while at their feet heretics and Jews burn at the stake.

St Augustine's pessimistic theology was the foundation for many extreme, reactionary theories and practices of church and state. The first rebel against God was the Devil. The majority of human beings were adherents of the Devil, they were damned and predestined for the torment of Hell. Even unbaptized babies were included. All acts of inhumanity in Europe's Christian countries are rooted in the theological concepts of St Augustine. According to him the whole human race since Adam's day had been in rebellion against God. Rebellion was the sin for which the church inflicted punishment on heretics. And the church appealed for help to the state, the Roman Empire.

Only in this context can St Augustine's condemnation of the Jews be understood. He used the magic power and demagogy of his great oratorical talent to impress upon the young catechumens (converts under instruction seeking acceptance into the realm of Light) that the Jews had maltreated, sadistically tortured, violated and killed Jesus. The Romans disappeared completely from St Augustine's version of Christ's Passion – an approach which was historically logical from his point of view, since he sought the Roman Empire's protection for the church. In his account of the Passion, St Augustine totally ignored the facts of history and the Holy Scriptures.

Although he tried for years to shake off the fetters of his Manichaean past (he had been a member of the Manichaean community for sixteen years), St Augustine was quite unable to free himself from its fatal dualism. He saw the whole world, history and mankind strictly divided into two opposing camps: pagans and Christians, Catholics and heretics, Romans and non-Romans, Christians and Jews. Although men of very different intellectual and religious origins were living at Hippo, where he held office, he declared, 'Here we have two kinds of people, Christians and Jews.'

What was to be done with these two types of people? The Christians could of course be compelled to join the church, if necessary by force. The Jews were bound, until the end of time, to serve as witnesses to the truth of the church's teaching – as slaves. St Augustine's dualistic teaching was to dominate the middle period of Christianity (which for many people is still not ended). On the one hand, the Jews must not be wiped out. They must be preserved to the end of time, when they will turn to Christ at the Last Judgment. But in times of crisis for Christianity this leads to a special temptation: since people believe Doomsday to be at hand, they endeavour quickly to convert the Jews so as to fulfil the prophecy. Yet the Jews, as the people who murdered Christ, must not be allowed to live in freedom and comfort on this earth, for that would offend the faithful. 'A Roman Emperor, who had already embraced Christianity, issued a decree prohibiting the Jews from setting foot in Jerusalem. And so – scattered across the globe – they have become as it were the custodians of our books, like the slaves who carry their masters' law books to court – and then wait outside.'

Thus St Augustine. His reference to the Roman Emperor draws attention to his own devotion to Rome. St Augustine, a citizen of Rome from latinized North Africa, knew no Hebrew, nor did he understand enough Greek to be familiar with such great Greek humanists as Basil the Great of Cappadocia. That (due to St Augustine) Greek optimism, the progressive teachings and faith of Greek and other Eastern church fathers did not penetrate Roman Christianity is a deficiency that has caused lasting damage to Western Christianity to this day. St Augustine simply did not want to know about such things as Origen's theology of reconciliation, which interpreted the world as a *varietas animarum*, a place of great diversity and multiplicity. The Cosmos was a *kosmos poikilotatos*, a variegated, wonderfully beautiful universe. God was the Lord of the free and the loving, opposed to all despots. St Augustine was ignorant of St Gregory of Nyssa and his faith in spiritual progress, which anticipated Teilhard de Chardin; his life of Moses (*Vita Moysis*) was based on the Song of Songs. Goethe referred to it in *Faust* and derived his vision of the superman, which he passed on to Nietzsche, from these Greek models.

St Augustine was both master and slave of the Latin language and the dualistic, authoritarian legal approach of the Romans which allowed no bridge between right and left. This legalistic mentality was something utterly alien to the Greek experience and thought which plays so great a part in the Gospel – *Zoé, phos*, Light, Love and Life; all flowing, moving concepts.

Christianity was being undermined by hundreds of different sects, a number of brilliant heretics, such as Arius and Pelagius, and all the dubious oriental theologians. St Augustine, looking around for help, turned to Rome and the Roman state. To him the fall of Rome in 409 was a terrible disaster. The Empire was mankind's last realm, ordained by God to protect Man to the end of time by its laws, armies and judiciary. With the fall of Rome St Augustine's outlook darkened. To him this political catastrophe was also a religious disaster. And it contributed to the resurgence of Manichaean traits in the ageing man's mind.

Nonetheless, it took one hundred and fifty years – from 430 to 580 – before St Augustine was posthumously recognized as orthodox. During that period the Roman Empire and its heirs actively assisted the church, which was perpetually threatened by disintegration.

The Roman Empire meant the emperors and their courts, their ladies, minions, generals and governors. They all came decisively to the aid of Christianity in the fourth century.

Christianity became the official religion of the Roman Empire. So it has been written, and Christians and non-Christians alike speak of Christianity's victory over paganism, achieved by the great Emperor Constantine in the battle of the Milvian Bridge. Constantine, whose monumental statue stands on the Capitol looking at us with big, heavy eyes, was a worshipper of Helios, the invincible God of the Sun, whom he identified with Christ. To the Christians, Constantine became the thirteenth apostle, to the heathens the thirteenth god. In his era the ancient pagan belief in the salvation of the world through the emperor's power, the faith in Victoria, sacred Rome's goddess of victory, merged – and was deliberately blended by orators and theologians – with the faith in salvation through Christ. Bishop Eusebius, Constantine's great preacher of salvation, dismissed the Jewish people from the story of redemption. And so God's realm became reality among man, embodied in the emperor in Heaven and the emperor on earth. The two became one in the hall of kings, the basilica, in worship. In the congregation's sacrifice in the gold-laden basilica, the heavenly household of the heavenly Emperor Christ (who to this day bears the imperial title 'Kyrios' and whose blessing is invoked at Catholic mass in Greek, 'Kyrie eleison') was liturgically combined with the secular emperor's household, in which bishops and theologians began to play an ever increasing role.

Bishop Eusebius' act in dismissing the Jewish people from the story of redemption caused the history of the Jews henceforward to be a story of disaster. The people, who up to the time of Christ had borne witness to

45

salvation, was now a people damned by God, obliged until the end of all time to bear witness of misfortune for the edification of all believers. In the sight of all Christians, God's displeasure was to rest upon the Jews and so to testify to the grace of Christ and to the truth that the prophecies of the Old Testament applied to Him alone.

To help Christianity prevail was not the problem of the Christian emperors after Constantine or that of their theologians and jurists. What concerned them was which form of Christianity was to become the religion of the empire. Arianism stood the best chance. According to the Arian doctrine Christ was more man than God, and in any case He was subordinate to the God-Father. Pressed by the emperor, most bishops at the Councils of Sardica in 343 and of Rimini in 353 voted for the oriental Arianist doctrine. Angrily St Jerome wrote, 'Overnight the world has turned Arian.'

St Ambrose of Milan, Augustine's mentor (mentioned earlier in connection with his defence of the synagogue raiders of Callinicum), persuaded the Emperor Theodosius that church unity could not be founded on a compromise with the Arians. (Theodosius was a Spaniard, and the Spanish have been deeply worried about their orthodoxy for more than a thousand years.) At the Ecumenical Council of Constantinople in 382 Arianism was overcome, that is to say it was condemned by secular and canonic law.

The most violent and furious resistance to Arianism came from Egypt. Here the ancient worship of the dead, documented with great artistry in stone, paintings, mummies and offerings to the deceased in the pyramids, the sphinx and the tombs of the Pharaohs, began to be transformed in the Christian period into a passionate belief in the resurrection of the flesh. Only a Christ who is all God could achieve anything as miraculous as that. Athanasius, patriarch of Alexandria, supported by armies of monks, was the great adversary of Arianism. Five times the Emperor Constantius sent him into exile, but Athanasius proved stronger, for the religious and political nationalism of the Egyptians could not be broken. Egypt defied Arian Syria, westernized Constantinople and oriental Asia Minor – comparable in every way to Egyptian nationalism in Nasser's struggle against the Western Powers.

'Athanasius' formula of God become Man incarnate, so that mankind shall be deified, aims at the resurrection and glorification of the flesh. And Cyril's formula that we *syssemoi* must be incorporated in the *corpus mysticum* emphasizes the mystic effect of the Eucharist as an aid towards immortality and thus the church of the Sacrament.'

One flesh with the risen Christ, in a church, in a communion of the faithful from which all dogs, pigs, scorpions, fornicators, Jews, Arians and heretics were excluded. But who was a heretic? He whose side was defeated, whether at the imperial court, in the councils of the church, in filling episcopal seats or in theological controversy. Ultimately, the battle was between two conflicting viewpoints: Is Christ God or only God-like? It was a matter of a single letter in the alphabet: *homoousios* or *homoiousios?* Into this contest the awakening peoples of the declining Roman Empire put all their nationalistic feeling; in Egypt, Syria, Cappadocia, in the Balkans, Lower Italy, North Africa and Spain.

We have already seen one side of the Janus head of the Roman Empire in its struggle with Jerusalem and the Jews of Palestine. This is the iron mask of power which destroyed all who rose in rebellion against it. Virgil, court theologian of the Augustan Empire and poet of the Pax Romana, which he lauded as the Great Peace of Emperor Augustus, had proclaimed the ancient sacred maxim of Rome: *parcere subiectis et debellare superbos.* The *superbi* (remember the fiendish *superbia* of the Devil and fallen Man in St Augustine's writings) were all who openly resisted Rome and whose rebellion had to be crushed. The *subiecti* were those who submitted to mercy and justice – that is to say, to Rome's jurisdiction. They must be spared, protected and guarded, body and soul. Since Constantine, the Christians in particular were among these *subiecti*, subjects of the Empire. Statesmen and jurists of the Empire thereupon undertook the herculean labour of attempting a reconciliation among the bitterly feuding Christians.

These imperial jurists and politicians can be compared with their counterparts in the era of Charles v and Ferdinand i who, as disciples of the Dutch humanist Erasmus, tried with unending patience to bring the religious parties of the Holy Roman Empire to the conference table to negotiate a compromise. Naturally, the imperial jurists, theologians and politicians were attacked on all sides. A similar fate befell the party of politicians around Henry iv of France, the party of the *Third Force*, who strove to save their country from permanent civil war between the 'two Frances' – the Huguenots and the monarchical Catholics.

The imperial jurists performed a Sisyphean task. In the Eastern part of the Empire their success was remarkable. There, in the sixth century, many jurists and laymen took part in the evolution of a balanced theological system. Justinian's Code, that outstanding codification, selection, compilation and annotation of Roman laws – comparable to the completion of the Babylonian Talmud around AD 500 – was based on the groundwork undertaken at the law faculties of Beirut and Constantinople.

Besides the Christians, the imperial jurists also tried for a long time to protect the other *subiecti* of the Roman Empire, the pagans and the Jews. But in this pursuit they were frustrated by the pressure and brutality of the masses, stirred up by theologians, church leaders and monks. Once again we must emphasize the fact – since even reputable theologians in our day continue to maintain the opposite – that in Christian Europe anti-Semitism came from above, not from ordinary and lowly people. It originated in theology and in theological concepts of world history. It was at the top that the popular image of the Jew was created, and below that it was turned into such horrifying reality.

47

In the early days of the Christian Roman Empire, at the beginning of the fourth century, the state was fully prepared to behave legally in relation to its Jewish subjects. After all, the great Caesar had encouraged them, and the nephew of Emperor Domitian, Flavius Clemens, even became a Jew. Emperor Caracalla had granted all Jews in the Empire the right to hold offices of state.

Now, in 418, the Jews in the Western part of the Roman Empire were excluded from all public posts and positions of honour. The gallant imperial officials and jurists, who sought to defend the honour of the Empire by upholding the law, succumbed more and more to the increasing terrorism of ecclesiastics. More and more synagogues were destroyed with impunity, more and more murders of Jews failed to reach the courts. Confiscations of Jewish property multiplied; and in the big trading cities there was no short-age of well-to-do Jews.

We are already familiar with St John Chrysostom's attacks on the Jews of Antioch. Cyril of Alexandria raged in similar fashion. 'The legend of ideas grew naturally in the Middle Ages, but their origin lay in the image created by such men as Chrysostom and Cyril' (James Parkes). One of St Jerome's friends, the bishop of Salamis in Cyprus, St Epiphanius – a kind of fourth-century Makarios – showed himself in his spiteful polemics to be a true scourge of Jews and heretics. By birth a Palestinian Jew, St Epiphanius was converted to Christianity at the age of sixteen. Converted Jews were later to play a terrible role among the Jew-haters.

The councils of the fourth century attempted to separate the Jews from the Christians both in Asia Minor and Spain. Jews were forbidden to keep Christian slaves. Imperial legislation sought to meet the wishes of the church. Constantius decreed that Jews who married Gentile women employed in imperial factories (*gynaecea*) were to be executed, and the women brought back to their places of work. Julian the Apostate tried to ease the lot of the Jews, but that was only an episode. Theodosius the Great issued a law under which marriage between Jew and Gentile amounted to adultery. From this time onwards the words chosen to designate the Jewish communities in Roman law reveal the desire to humiliate and punish: *fecalis secta*, dirty sect; *turpitudo*, Jewish infamy, *sua flagitia: sacrilegi coetus* – damned, dirty, sacrile-gious, lecherous community – such were the Jews.

The nationalistic Patriarch Athanasius of Egypt exemplifies the tradition of the Egyptian party in Alexandria, which was violently opposed to both Jews and Greeks.

The fourth century brought raids on synagogues in Italy, Africa and Asia Minor. St Ambrose warned his flock against staining their honour by talking to Jews.

The Code issued by Emperor Theodosius made use of malicious language in relation to the Jews. Its phraseology was something new in Roman law. The process was completed by Justinian, whose legislation stripped the Jews of all rights. They were now completely at the mercy of the ruler, and were outlaws, like heretics and heathens. At an early date Justinian confiscated all synagogues in Africa and handed them over to the Catholic church. He was the first to legalize the destruction of synagogues. He was the first directly to invite the 'ecclesiastical arm' to formulate laws against the civic rights of the Jews. They were completely excluded from normal life and confined to a few permitted occupations. This is when the Jewish type was created and the foundation laid for the centuries-long middle period of Christianity. The Jew was stamped, deformed and recast as a warped, sickly, abnormal and alien being, barred from all normal occupations and activities.

In the West, Arian régimes sprang up among the Ostrogoths in Italy and among the Visigoths in Spain. They were tolerant towards the Jews. Theodoric even ordered that reparations be paid to the Jews when synagogues in Rome and Ravenna were burnt down. The Jews loyally supported the Ostrogoths until their downfall. In Naples, Jews fought to the end on their side against troops from Byzantine under Belisarius.

What was the Jewish reaction to Christian persecution in this era of the later Roman Empire?

In the sixth century under Emperor Justin II, Jews and Samaritans rebelled, for example in Caesarea, and destroyed Christian churches. Open resistance of this kind was rare, but it already signified the end.

How was it in the beginning? Earlier historians accepted as common ground the allegation that the Jews were responsible for the persecution of the Christians in the first few centuries. But not a single concrete case of persecution, of Christian martyrdom, or of Jewish connivance in such persecution is recorded by any historical authority. In view of the growing animosity of the church against the Jews and more frequent anti-Jewish sermons and legislation, the 'in-group' of the Jews naturally felt increasingly bitter towards the 'out-group' of Christians, the *Minim*, who had been excluded from the synagogue since the end of the first century. Considering that the Jews had been exposed to hatred for 1,500 years, it is astonishing that the whole of Jewry did not become neurotic and filled with pathological hate against the Gentiles. Not even a saint could have withstood so much hatred with impunity. Yet how many saints are to be found among the leading assailants of the Jews!

After the armed opposition in Palestine had been crushed by the Romans in the first and second centuries, Jewish resistance to Christian attack turned inward. Aggression was deflected against themselves. From then on Jewry, especially in Babylonia, produced an orthodoxy which over-anxiously, at times even neurotically, turned the Torah into a powerful fortress. That is how it seemed to St Paul in his time of heart-searching.

Talmudic Judaism is based on the Palestinian and Babylonian Talmud. The Palestinian version rests chiefly on the Mishnah of Rabbi Judah the Prince (with a commentary). This rabbi (AD 135–217) can be regarded as the greatest rabbi of all time. His work embodies the entire legal system governing and directing Jewish life, as it was taught in Palestinian schools in the early third century. The codification of this Talmud of Jerusalem was completed in about AD 350. The Babylonian Talmud emerged from discussions in Babylonian schools concerning the Rabbi's Mishnah. This Babylonian version was finished round about AD 500. The powerful hold of the Talmud on the Jews, scattered as they were all over the world in the Diaspora, dates from this time.

It is interesting to note the parallel: Christianity (church) and Judaism (synagogue) came into being at the dawn of the Middle Ages, both as closed societies. Codification of the Babylonian Talmud was completed in 500. In 511 the Exilarch Mar Sutra II organized an almost independent Jewish state in Babylonia under the sovereignty of Kobad, king of the Parthians. Integrated Jewry now had its national home. In 537 Justinian deprived the Jews of civic equality and religious freedom. All was set for the start of the Middle Ages.

6

The Christian and Jewish Middle Ages

In Europe the Christian and Jewish Middle Ages existed side by side until the French Revolution, and indeed until the beginning of the nineteenth century. The Rabbinical Epoch of 797–1789 (Edmond Fleg) corresponds roughly with that of the Holy Roman Empire, in the various parts of which Jews found a certain protection as servants of emperor and princes – a protection not enjoyed in England and France after the height of the Middle Ages.

Medieval Christian practices, such as the burning of witches, still occurred in Goethe's lifetime; and even in the nineteenth century the Spanish Inquisition burned to death a Jew and a Quaker. Medieval punishments and medieval conditions of hygiene survived, together with the belief in witches, until well into the nineteenth century. In the sixteenth century belief in witches partly supplanted belief in the Jewish Devil, which regained supremacy, however, in the nineteenth century. The Witches' Sabbath ousted the Synagogue of Satan, and from the time of Goethe's *Faust, Part II* to Hitler's 'final solution' of the Jewish problem, the celebration of Walpurgis Night in Germany took on the additional character of a witch-hunt against the Jews.

In nineteenth- and twentieth-century Germany, large areas of the bourgeoisie and petty bourgeoisie were as deeply rooted in medieval superstition and imagery as they were in their own small towns and villages. One of the signs of this was a militant anti-Semitism which revived all the anti-Jewish slogans that the Augustinian Luther had hurled among the excited masses. In Spain, France, Italy and the countries of Eastern Europe at this time the majority of people (apart from little islands of enlightenment among the bourgeoisie and nobility) lived in a state of mind highly susceptible to devilish inventions. Politicians and high priests of sects and churches, of revivalist and political movements, have often tended to paint their enemies as an embodiment of the Devil – orthodox Calvinists referred to Roman Catholics and Protestants of other persuasions as Papists, Lutheran dogs, satellites of Satan; and at times of great religious crisis in Europe the Jews were always the scapegoats, represented as incarnations of the Devil.

51

This stigmatization of the Jews was particularly popular with both Christian demagogues (many of them in monk's robes) and politicians, since throughout the thousand years of the Middle Ages the Jews had formed a separate group in Europe and there was something uncanny about this. Jewish art in Europe, up to the time of the emancipation in the nineteenth century, has a strange, early oriental quality. This is the more striking since in their architecture the Christian influence is predominant – one has only to think of the synagogues of Worms and Regensburg, designed in 1519 by the great Ferdinand Altdorfer, who was later to participate actively in their destruction. Many of the synagogues of Spain show Islamic influence, and medieval Jewish illuminated manuscripts were strongly influenced by the Christian miniaturist art of the time. But in spite of these and other contemporary non-Jewish influences, Jewish art – especially in their ornaments and sacramental implements and the interior design of their synagogues – testifies to the fact that here, among the Germans, Celts and Slavs of Christian Europe, a race was living which clung to customs and religious rites imported with it: a traditional culture retaining its oriental stamp even in the ghettoes of Prague, Leghorn, Vilna and Rome.

This distinctive Jewish world was itself split into two hemispheres. In the Middle Ages the Ashkenazim differed in customs, liturgy and religious ways of life from the Sephardim. The Ashkenazim preserved many of the ancient traditions of Palestine, notably the movable screen in the synagogue. The Sephardim apparently continued the tradition of the Babylonian exiles, for whom the ark was an essential feature of the inner area of the synagogue.

The synagogue and the family life of the Jews together provided protection for the traditional Jewish culture, with its regular times of prayer, its celebrations, fasts, feasts, hymns, thanksgivings and its Bible. The Jew is the great conservative of history, and by the same token the true revolutionary. This is the message of the synagogue and Jewish art in the Middle Ages.

The European synagogue is familiar to us from the ninth century onwards as the school for Jews – *schola Judaeorum, Schule, escuela, scuola*. These schools produced a race of people, disciplined by God's law and obedient to His word, which was worlds apart from its Christian contemporaries. A page of a fifteenth-century German Haggadah manuscript, illustrating the Jewish maxim 'Go forth and learn', shows a youth setting out with a Bible, a lance and a sword. They are the lance and sword of his faith, and he is striding into the land of the Bible. The path of the devout Jew leads inwards, into his own heart. His aggressions, his hopes, his fears (of losing his God), all these look back thousands of years to Sinai and Jerusalem – and at the same time look forward to the coming of the Messiah.

Today the single family of mankind suffers great difficulties of communication, because races and continents, though geographically neighbours, belong to quite different ages and have quite different forms of consciousness.

The Arab Semite in Egypt today may be a student, an officer or a politician, but, in spite of technological progress in his own country, he is not a contemporary of the neighbouring Semites in Israel, who belong to a modern American and European civilization. The mentality of the Arab Semite is largely as it was during the thousand years of the Islamic Middle Ages. The outlook of political and religious preachers of Islam, who nowadays call for the destruction of Israel, is no different from that of the fanatical anti-Greek and anti-Jewish monks of the fourth century. In the same way, Jews and Christians in Europe were not contemporaries in the Middle Ages – apart from certain exceptions with which we shall deal later. Church and synagogue provided completely different spiritual worlds for their worshippers. The Christian bestowed crowns on emperors, kings, princes, bishops, abbots, popes – then made images of them in stone, wood and bronze. The Jew gave a crown only to the Torah. And he did not make images of men – that would be blasphemy. The first Jewish portraits, apart from some very few earlier attempts, appeared in the eighteenth century, the time of Lessing and Moses Mendelssohn. The Christian placed a crown on Christ the King, hanging on the Cross. In the Romanesque period from the eleventh to the thirteenth century the crucified Christ was always depicted triumphantly wearing a crown. But the Jew crowned only the Torah.

The custom of placing silver crowns upon the scroll became established during the period of the Babylonian Gaonate, certainly not later than the tenth century. Through the centuries the Sephardic Torah-crowns became smaller and smaller, until they acquired the shape of a king's crown. Here the element of rivalry with the Christian coronation became apparent – but only as far as the Western Jews were concerned. The Ashkenazim – particularly those in Eastern Europe – avoided the characteristics of the royal crown as far as possible. They made particularly large and heavy Torah-crowns. The difference between a Torah-crown – for instance an eighteenth-century crown made in Vienna of gilded silver – and a Christian crown was as great as that between Jehovah, the ineffable, imageless God of Sinai, and the Christian Trinity, which was represented and crowned in statuary.

Jews and Christians inhabited, throughout their respective Middle Ages, completely different worlds of imagination, thought and emotion. In our day the special world of the Jews has been brilliantly and magnificently conveyed to us by great Jewish artists. Samuel Joseph Agnon, who was born in Galicia in 1888 and emigrated to Jerusalem in 1909, recreates in his novel *A Guest for the Night* (written after a visit to his old homeland, Poland) this special world in describing life in a small Jewish town in Poland. Marc Chagall's illustrations of the Bible (published in Paris in 1956) provide unique documentation of the way in which this separate world of the Jews was aware of its roots in the wanderings, prayers, struggles and celebrations of the little race which made its way across the desert into the Promised Land. This great Jewish art stands apart from Christian civilization, despite certain formal similarities.

It is almost as if Christianity, the West, and technological, industrial Europe had never existed.

The reverse side of this splendid affirmation of separateness by the Jews – a separateness which went to the point of shutting themselves off physically from other races – is shown by the dreadful dangers which accompanied, and still accompany it.

'During the first centuries of the Middle Ages [and these continued to exert their influence up to the nineteenth century] the Jewish world was influenced by two parallel processes, which permitted cultural developments to take place only within the narrowest confines. Christian prejudice had, to an ever-increasing extent, banished the Jews from the shared environment and the authority of the Talmud had pushed the Jewish community more and more into a position of cultural autarchy and isolation, in which the study of the Torah was held to be the only legitimate spiritual occupation' (B. Cecil Roth). Two great adversaries contributed – sometimes consciously, sometimes unconsciously – to the development of this thousand years of Jewish isolation in Europe. There were the rabbis – the orthodox rabbis – who wanted to protect the Jews from the evils of the wicked world by voluntary confinement to Talmudic ghettoes. And there were the orthodox Christian clerics, who wanted to protect their flock from dangerous contact with the fascinating Jews. A similar isolationism occurred within Christianity itself. At the height of the Middle Ages the Hanseatic League was able to take over from the Russians the whole trading area of the Baltic and the North Sea, from Novgorod to the British Isles, because the Orthodox clergy of the Eastern church forbade their devout Russian flock to go abroad and expose their souls to the baneful influences of the corrupt and heretical West. They were also forbidden to learn foreign languages. In similar fashion Lutherans, Calvinists and Roman Catholics constructed their own separate worlds, which existed side by side, but desired no mutual contact.

The Christian insistence on ghettoes for the Jews in the Middle Ages held other special dangers for both sides. Each effort to confine the Jews to ghettoes implied a mortal insult to human nature, demoralizing both to the victims and the oppressors. 'To the Christian the ghetto was a cage where certain dangerous and repulsive animals were confined. To the Jew it was the prison in which he was shut up from the free world outside. In that prison there were no jailers, and the prisoners kept order amongst themselves' (R. Travers Herford).

The gift for self-government which the Jews demonstrated in the medieval ghettoes all over Europe was exploited in a masterly fashion by the bureaucrats of the Third Reich, when they made the Jews contribute to their own destruction by allowing them self-government in the new ghettoes in Poland and in Hitler's concentration, labour and extermination camps.

The eleventh to thirteenth centuries saw a movement towards an ever-increasing isolationism, with the closed community of the Jews cut off completely from a closed Roman Catholic civilization. Previously there had been an open period, in which Jews and Christians in France, and Christians, Jews and Moslems in Spain had lived together quite freely. Jews were popular guests – and indeed benefactors – at the court of Charlemagne, and even more so under his son Louis the Pious and his wife, Empress Judith. In twelfth-century England Jews were living in Oxford and London, conducting scientific and religious discussions with English clerics, eager to further their knowledge. A flourishing German Jewry enjoyed the protection of the king, the emperor and the bishops in the Rhenish towns, where some of them had settled as early as the time of the Roman occupation. The great luminaries of Christian intellectual life – Albertus Magnus, his pupil St Thomas Aquinas, and Meister Eckhart – owe as much to Jewish as to Arab thinkers. The greatest poet of the Christian Middle Ages – Dante – had Jewish friends, and his death was lamented by a Jewish poet of the *dolce stil nuovo*.

This open period of the Middle Ages, when Jewish thinkers, scientists and travellers had the freedom of the courts of Emperor Frederick II in Palermo and Christian kings in Spain and Portugal, and when even popes were prepared to have Jewish physicians, had a very remarkable precedent in Visigothic Spain, where the later European pattern – great splendour followed by annihilating catastrophe – was foreshadowed.

It seems possible that the Jews came to Spain with the Phoenicians. The oldest Jewish settlements of Europe are in Spain. Spain earned on two occasions the reputation of a 'new Judaea' or a 'new Jerusalem' – first at the time of the early Arian rule of Visigothic Spain, and later in Arab and Christian Spain. This was still remembered at the beginning of the twentieth century by descendants of the Jews who were driven out of Spain in 1492, in the towns in the Balkans where they had now settled.

Spanish ecclesiastical councils had also begun as early as the fourth century, to fight against the corrupting influence of the Jews, against all contact between Jews and Christians, and against Christian girls turning to the Jewish faith. The year 418 saw the destruction of the synagogue and the compulsory baptism of 540 Jews in the town of Magona on Minorca. The conquest of the Spanish peninsula by Arian Visigoths brought peace to the Jews, who in return gave considerable financial support to the Arian kings. Their tragedy began with the kings' conversion to Roman Catholicism. The Catholic clergy now had two enemies to fight – the Arians and the Jews, who both denied the divinity of Jesus of Nazareth, though for different reasons.

King Reccared I (586–601) was converted to Catholicism and undertook the task of converting his Gothic subjects and fighting the Jews. At the third Council of Toledo twenty-three bulls of excommunication were directed against the Arians, and war was declared against the Jews. It was the beginning of that fateful struggle for the 'preservation of the purity of the Catholic faith' which has cost Spain so much blood and self-mutilation right up to the present time. The Spanish orthodox believer was to become one who was continually trying to cleanse himself of the stain of the Jewish, Moorish, Marrano and heretical blood in his own race.

The Jewish faith was branded as a pseudo-faith, as a Hebrew perfidy worthy of damnation (*Ebreorum execranda perfidia*). It is largely due to Spanish influence that in the ninth century the significant formula *De perfidis judaeis* was included in the liturgy of the Roman Catholic church.

In 613 King Sisebut decreed that all Jews who refused compulsory baptism must leave Spain. The great Bishop Isidor of Seville, famous throughout the Middle Ages as a luminary of learning, acclaimed this as a heroic deed.

The Councils of the Spanish Visigothic church have, to this day, been admired by fanatical anti-Semitic Catholics for their anti-Jewish measures and laws. Their particular target was the group of compulsorily baptized Jews who were, rightly or wrongly, suspected of secretly adhering to the Jewish faith. The fourth Council of Toledo in 633 declared these Jews to be in the bondage of the church. King Swintila (636–40) was the first Christian prince to receive the title 'Most Christian Prince' – *christianissimus princeps* – a title which the French kings later sought to justify by 'orthodox' great deeds. Swintila won it by his vow to persecute the suspect converted Jews. All future kings were to vow, on their accession to the throne, to carry out zealously all decrees of the Council which were directed against the Jews. Failure to do so would mean excommunication and eternal damnation.

Extirpation of the false doctrines of Judaism now became the chief aim of these weak Visigothic kings, who, under continuous threat of insurrection from their family and the nobility, sought protection from an arrogant and presumptuous clergy. Morally weak and lacking popular support, these kings desperately sought to strengthen their position, in a country permanently threatened by civil war and anarchy, by the ostentatious profession of an extreme orthodoxy, and by an aggressive anti-Jewish policy which would win them the support of the powerful clerical party.

During the reign of terror of King Recceswinth (649–72) – 'a Visigothic Justinian' – a confession of repentance, containing the most dreadful self-accusations, was drawn up, and a group of compulsorily baptized Jews was made to voice it. These ex-Jews had solemnly to renounce their 'obdurate unbelief' and 'the deep-rooted aberrations of our forefathers'. 'We will avoid all association with the despicable community of unbaptized Jews, and we will contract no lewd marriages with relations up to the sixth degree, as was hitherto our custom; marriages will only take place between practising Christians.' These ex-Jews swore to renounce all Jewish customs and ceremonies. They swore that in the case of any infringement of these vows they would either impose a penalty of death 'by fire or stoning' themselves, or hand over the guilty person to the state authorities for punishment.

It is worth noting that the word *Judaeus* in the laws of Recceswinth's reign designated both practising Jews and Jews who had received Christian baptism. Baptism did not wash the Jews clean, it was no ticket of admission into free society, as it was later in Heine's time. On the contrary, the baptized Jew had even more hardships to bear, as he was continually watched and threatened by the church authorities, who justifiably doubted the actual authenticity of these compulsory baptisms.

In the last years of Visigothic rule – before the conquest of the Spanish peninsula by the Moors – persecution of the Jews, both orthodox and compulsorily baptized, reached its climax. The driving force behind these actions was the archbishop of Toledo, Julian, who possibly himself came from a compulsorily baptized family. The compulsorily baptized were now threatened with banishment, confiscation of their property, flogging, tearing out of hair and other forms of mutilation. Julian's main efforts were directed against Jewish Messianism. We shall see later how this played a particularly important role in Spain and among Spanish Jews. It is at the root of the revivalist movements of the fifteenth and sixteenth centuries, it animated the reform movement within the church, and was perhaps the mainspring of Columbus' expedition.

These Jews, oppressed in Spain and banished from Spain, now found allies and protectors in the Arabs who were preparing to conquer the peninsula. King Egica and his prelates decreed at the sixteenth Council of Toledo – these councils simultaneously embraced the functions of state parliaments and courts of justice – that all Spanish Jews were henceforth and for all time vassals of the state. The king had the right to make presents of these Jews to his subjects. Their children were to be taken away when they were six years old and brought up by Christians.

In July 711 the Berbers sailed to Spain and the conquest of the Iberian peninsula began. Spain, with its Moorish, Jewish and Christian population – and hence three-fold culture – was to become the most highly cultivated and flourishing region of Europe.

Theodoric the Great and his Ostrogoths protected the Jews, who in turn gave their loyal support to the Ostrogoths against the Byzantine armies. In the areas of the Roman Empire occupied by the Germanic races and tribes, the Jews lived as foreigners under their own Mosaic law (as among the Franks), but were mildly, even benevolently treated. The church, admittedly, still treated the Jews as a body apart, and through its regional councils kept close watch on them and imposed restrictions on their association with Christians. But the Germanic people themselves did not fear or hate the Jews. Good businessmen themselves, they welcomed Jewish and Syrian traders, and allowed Jews to acquire and cultivate land. This is a fact that can never be too much emphasized: for a long period of time – seven centuries in fact, from the sixth to the end of the twelfth century – the Germanic (Celtic) Christians maintained a harmonious co-existence with the Jews. It is a fact that has proved particularly annoying to Catholic anti-Semites in the nineteenth and twentieth centuries, who abhor the pro-Jewish policies of Charlemagne, Louis the Pious and the German bishops and dignitaries of the Roman church.

This seven-hundred-year epoch of co-existence, even conviviality, between Christians and Jews cannot be explained away by the assertion that there were so few Jews in Central Europe that it was not worth the trouble of exterminating or banishing them. For in the nineteenth century – in France, for instance – anti-Semitism flourished particularly vigorously in areas where there were no Jews, or only very few. On the eve of the Dreyfus affair, which plunged France into something like a civil war, it was in the very *départements* and dioceses which were free of Jews that anti-Semitism, propagated by country priests and newspapers, was most active. No, the true reason for this remarkable absence of anti-Semitism was the absence of a vigorous, anti-Semitic propaganda putting the blame on the Jews for all the disasters of the age – plague, war, famine and religious crises.

In Frankish Gaul, especially in the southern districts adjoining Spain, the Jews held long-established and highly respected positions in society. Jews settled in the Roman and post-Roman towns and travelled as merchants through the land. In the Carolingian epoch they spread along the old Roman roads and trade routes, down the valleys of the Rhône and the Saône to Lyon, and along the Rhine to Mainz, Cologne and Aix-la-Chapelle. They had been established in Trier since the days of the Romans. Their favoured position was due not to any particular patronage on the part of Charlemagne – there is little evidence for that, though he used them as envoys to the Caliph Harun al Raschid, and as agents of East-West trade in the Mediterranean. The reason was rather that the intellectual and religious climate of Charlemagne's court and of other cultural centres in his Empire was sympathetic to the Jews.

Thirst for knowledge and receptivity to interesting influences from outside were the chief characteristics of Charlemagne's court. Clerics from the British Isles, from Lombardy and from Spain came, bringing with them an atmosphere of restlessness and intellectual curiosity. The British clerics in particular introduced an element of Greek and Celtic 'curiosity' into the sluggish, rural Catholicism of the Continent, which, with its large heathen inheritance, was tough and not exactly nimble in its intellectual processes.

This new intellectual curiosity was manifest, for instance, in the interest shown by the Irishman Vergil, the first archbishop of Salzburg, in the

Antipodes – the part of the world in which the other half of humanity lived. This involved him in a trial for heresy. Intellectual clerics helped, or perhaps even forced Charlemagne to conduct his politico-religious and dogmatic dispute with Byzantium in terms of literary polemics. And they brought with them the whole armoury of dogmatic argument which was in regular use in Spain, and was now to be put to use in Charlemagne's councils. But they also brought with them Spanish anti-Semitism.

This intellectual receptivity to Greek and oriental influences developed into friendly relations with the Jews at the court of Louis the Pious (814–40) and his second wife, the beautiful Bavarian Judith. Louis gave the Jews his special protection. They were allowed to buy and sell foreign, Islamic and heathen slaves, and these slaves could not be baptized without the permission of their masters. Jewish testimony was to have the same validity as Christian in the courts of law. An imperial official was appointed 'Master of the Jews' with the task of ensuring that this pro-Jewish legislation was observed.

In their thirst for knowledge, intelligent young clerics and ladies at court were fascinated by the Jewish intellect and erudition. As was to happen later in Spain, this upper class preferred to listen to Jewish sermons rather than boring Christian sermons, clumsily constructed out of a string of ill-digested or misinterpreted quotations. The educated Jew held the same fascination for the intellectual ladies of Empress Judith's court as did the clerics of the twelfth and thirteenth centuries, who outstripped the illiterate knights in a bid for feminine favour. The steadily improving position of Jews at court was bound to cause offence to the envious clergy, and this turned to alarm when they saw that the Jews were also receiving a sympathetic hearing among the ordinary people. The peasants and country people of the Carolingian period were as susceptible to Jewish preaching as they were to be later in Poland, and as they were in the ninth-century empire of the Khazars, when the whole nation followed the example of the royal family and adopted the Jewish faith, remaining true to it until they were conquered by the Greeks and Russians in 1016. The mighty empire of the Turkish Khazars extended in the eighth century along the coast of the Caspian Sea to Crimea.

The Kaghans – the princes of the Khazars – and their heathen subjects were wooed simultaneously by Islamic, Byzantine-Christian and Jewish missionaries, just as the Russians of the tenth century were wooed by Western Catholics and Byzantines. They chose Judaism. After the fall of the Khazar empire some of these Jewish Kaghans went to Spain, where they were still to be encountered in Toledo in the twelfth century.

The anti-Semitic tradition of the Spanish church can be seen in the actions of Agobard, archbishop of Lyon, who was possibly of Spanish descent. He fought vigorously against the 'Jewish' court of Louis the Pious and against the Jewish mission in Lyon and the surrounding countryside.

Despite the fact that many great classical histories of the Middle Ages – particularly ecclesiastical and theological accounts – hardly mention the

Jews, there was a genuine possibility, though it seems scarcely credible today, that the Carolingian Empire might have become Jewish. This danger must have haunted Archbishop Agobard and his successor. Christianity had not yet taken a firm hold on the population as a whole, and the country people were easily swayed by Jewish preaching based directly on the Bible. A similar thing happened in 1944–5, when a whole village in Italy was converted to Judaism by a peasant who had got hold of an Old Testament. The example of the highly-respected deacon Bodo, father-confessor of Emperor Louis, could well have had a contagious effect on the educated clergy of the court. Under the pretext of making a pilgrimage to Rome Bodo fled to Spain, was converted to Judaism, adopted the name Eleazer and married a Jewess.

Agobard's successor, Archbishop Amulo of Lyon, cited the case of Bodo as an example of the Jewish danger in his polemical epistle against the Jews. He accused the highly educated and well respected Bodo of becoming entangled in the devilish nets of the Jews, betraying Christ, his country and the church. 'And now he lives in Spain, amidst the Saracens and allied with the Jews ... Completely Jewish in his pseudo-faith and way of life, his bearded figure squats in the synagogues of Satan and joins with other Jews in blaspheming against Christ and His church.'

Bodo gave the reasons for his conversion to Judaism in letters to friends. He had been disillusioned chiefly by the degenerate way of life of the Carolingian clergy. But he also had doubts about the dogma. The final persuasion had been his impression of the barbaric and corrupt way of life in Rome, where a protracted process of degeneration reached its nadir in the eighth to tenth centuries, with noble families murdering each other to gain the papal throne.

Was there really a danger of the Carolingian Empire becoming Jewish? Agobard of Lyon openly admits that in straight debate contemporary Christianity was no match for Judaism. The Greek, Arabic and ancient Jewish heritage of the Jews gave them the advantage over Carolingian Christianity in three ways – their level of education, both religious and secular, their knowledge of the Bible, and their devout and total absorption in the word of God. But it was a different story in the sphere of power-politics, for the Christian clergy was indispensable to the Empire, compensating for the Empire's lack of a bureaucracy, an urban middle class, and a secular educated élite. This clergy was by no means a uniform body; its members came from all levels of society and possessed widely differing degrees of education. The correspondence of the Carolingian humanists, such as Lupus or Ferrières, shows that they were as gifted in the art of rhetoric as were the humanists of the early Renaissance. But country priests, whose scanty knowledge of Latin hardly sufficed for reading the mass, passed their parish on to one of their sons and remained rooted in the heathen customs and way of life of the village community. Rich and powerful Carolingian bishops and abbots of the wealthy, landed monastic foundations formed the kernel of an intellectual aristocracy which remained intact up to the collapse of the Holy Roman Empire and its church in the years 1792–1803. Differing as the members of this clergy did in their social and economic status and levels of education, they nevertheless formed a vested interest of insuperable strength. Their secular contemporaries were bound to them by the fear of hell and the hope of heaven. So sociological reasons alone would have prevented the conversion of the Carolingian Empire to Judaism. The Franks' reverence for the great saints, with St Peter in golden Rome at their head, the popular Merovingian saints with their miracle-working relics, and the great founding saints of the Frankish Empire, like Martin of Tours, the awakener of the dead and St Denis – stood in the way of their conversion to Judaism with its imageless God.

This people, or rather the peoples and tribes of the Carolingian Empire, were deeply rooted in heathen pre-Christian beliefs and superstitions. Archbishop Agobard in particular was painfully aware of this. This 'first great anti-Semite of the Christian West' – and still celebrated as such by racialist, Nazi and Catholic anti-Semites – was by no means an ignorant obscurantist. On the contrary, he was a highly educated man. He was a great ecclesiastical reformer who fought against the belief in relics and other Catholic superstitions with a degree of courage which many theologians of the twentieth century might envy. Agobard was weighed down with anxiety and fears for his missionary and reform work within the church when he took up the fight against the Jews – and against Emperor Louis, who became his deadly enemy.

Agobard saw that Jewish missionary efforts were far more successful than those of his church. And he saw with horror the imperial officers entering his town of Lyon to protect the Jews from the clergy. Agobard declared that this imperial protection had made the Jews insolent, so that they dared to abuse Christ quite openly. His letter to Emperor Louis *De insolentia Judaeorum* was the first of his anti-Jewish writings, which were to be brought up again and again in the next thousand years.

Agobard, together with two other bishops, then composed a pastoral letter concerning Jewish superstition (*De judaicis superstitionibus*), in which he listed the invectives of the fathers of the church and all ecclesiastical laws pertaining to the Jews. Agobard demanded that Christians should no longer eat together with Jews, and that no further synagogues should be built. He painted a vivid picture of the Jewish menace. Drawing support from St Paul and the early church fathers, he declared that peaceful co-existence of synagogue and church was impossible. In the true spirit of Augustinian doctrine, which the Carolingians regarded primarily as a doctrine of religious political tactics (Charlemagne was a keen student of St Augustine's *De civitate dei*) Agobard declared, 'It is unworthy of our faith that a shadow should fall on the children of Light through their intercourse with the sons of Darkness. It is also unseemly that the church of Christ, who should be conducted immaculate and unblemished to her heavenly bridegroom, be defiled by contact with the unclean, senile and corrupt synagogue. It is strange to see the immaculate virgin, the promised bride of Christ, seated at table with a whore.'

Agobard was particularly afraid that Christian women might be enticed into service or employment by Jews, 'sons of the Devil'. Christians should remember that 'the Jewish prophets themselves branded their race for all time as a sinful, useless race, as children of profligacy . . . they are the descendants of the princes of Sodom and the people of Gomorrha.' John the Baptist had called them 'a generation of vipers', and the Lord Himself described them as an evil and adulterous generation of serpents. 'The common people, the simple country folk, listen to them and succumb to the mad idea that the Jews alone are the chosen people of God, and then they persuade others that the Jews possess a purer and truer faith than our own. Thus does this evil gnaw at the people entrusted to our care, and like a plague claims more victims daily.'

The eminent French ecclesiastical historian, Monsignor Bressolles, honorary vice-rector of the Catholic Institute in Paris, is in complete agreement with Agobard. In his work *Saint Agobard, évêque de Lyon (760–840)*, written in 1933 and published in 1949, he claims that Agobard's polemic against the Jews displays good sense, wisdom and Christian charity. Agobard had declared the Jews to be the true enemies of God, the synagogue to be the synagogue of Satan. The Jews are 'a race cursed to their very bowels', and contact with them should be avoided as a foul contamination.

Monsignor Bressolles goes on to declare that there was no anti-Semitism among the people in the reign of Charlemagne.

Oremus et pro perfidis judaeis – this petition in the Good Friday prayer is the core of the church's doctrine of contempt for the Jews.

It was precisely here in the ninth century that the Good Friday liturgy was altered to exclude the prayer for the Jews. *Pro Judaeis non flectant*: genuflection for the Jews was eliminated from the great prayer for all sections of humanity. Prayers for Jews seem to have played an important part in the pre-ninth-century liturgies; this can be seen from the *Liber mozarabicus sacramentorum*, in which the liturgies of Arabic and Christian Spain are preserved. Pro-Jewish prayers became progressively scarcer and changed their character, manifesting an increasingly hostile attitude towards the Jews. The suppression of the genuflection for the Jews in the Good Friday prayer was intended expressly to remind the congregation of the people who murdered Christ. The liturgy of Holy Week, closely bound up with the folk customs of Eastertide, became the focal point each year for anti-Jewish feelings in the Christian West. Even in more modern times the magistrates of Frankfurt ordered the Jews to remain in their ghetto during Holy Week, so as to protect them from the people and its priests.

Did this disastrous change in the Good Friday liturgy come from Gaul, where so many Spanish emigrants had settled? Or did it come from Rome, which had authorized it? A laudable attempt to establish less abusive connotations for the ominous words *perfidia, perfidus*, was made by the Protestant convert Peterson in 1930 and by the Jewish convert Osterreicher, who devoted himself to pastoral work among converted Jews (in Vienna and later in America) and to the improvement of relations between Catholics and Jews. But medieval words and the Good Friday liturgy still, a thousand years later, speak their own terrible, unmistakable language.

In the Middle Ages the common people were taught, in church prayers and sermons, that the Jews were the people of Judas, born of the Devil. The Jews were to blame for war, plague and famine. What was the beginning of the popular belief that the Jews were responsible for war – a belief which Goebbels was still able to exploit in the twentieth century? In AD 848 Norman pirates invaded and plundered the rich city of Bordeaux. The bishop of Troyes, Prudentius, alleged that the Jews were responsible for this looting, ignoring the fact that the Jews suffered just as much as the Christians from it. In 876 Ansegis, archbishop of Sens, banished the Jews from the town; the Normans were approaching. When Charles the Bald died in 877 his Jewish physician, Sedekias, was accused of poisoning him, though Charles was renowned for his protection of the Jews. A hundred years later the same accusations were made against the Jewish physician of Hugh Capet.

A strange custom still survives today in Catalonia, where, on both sides of the Pyrenees, special clappers and mallets are made for the Easter celebrations. At the end of the service on Maundy Thursday the priest gives a sign, and the congregation beats around with these instruments. The blows signify 'We are killing the Jews' – an ancient formula probably going back to the time of Charlemagne. When Jules Isaac taxed Bishop Bernard of Perpignan about the survival of this practice, the bishop replied that nowadays the implication of Jew-killing no longer applied. If this were not the case, he wrote in a letter dated 16 September 1949, he would ban the custom. The terrible *Pro perfidis judaeis*-prayer remained in the Good Friday liturgy until Pope John XXIII took a personal decision to suppress it. That was after the Second World War, after the death of Pope Pius XII.

Around about AD 1000 rumours spread through the Christian West that the 'Prince of Babylon' had, at the instigation of the Jews, desecrated the tomb of Christ in Jerusalem. The connection with the Good Friday liturgy is obvious – at this time of year people were in a state of emotional excitement. These rumours sparked off massacres of Jews and forced conversions in Rouen, Orleans, Limoges and Mainz (1012) and also in Rome. These were the first symptoms of the spirit of the Crusades. But in the same period there were also constant conversions to Judaism. Ecclesiastical sources naturally mention only the most striking cases, such as the conversion of Duke Renant of Sens in 1015, and Duke Conrad's chaplain, Vezelin, in 1005.

We can start our account of the post-Carolingian imperial policy of protection for the Jews (which lasted until the dissolution of the Holy Roman Empire) with an incident in which an emperor was protected by a Jew.

In the summer of 981 Emperor Otto II decided to conquer Lower Italy and make war against the Saracens. On 13 July 982 the Germans lost a battle at Cape Colonne which was already in their grasp (and in which the leader of the Saracens, Emir Abulkasem, fell), because the advance troops lacked support. Almost the whole of the German army was lost, among them Bishop Henry of Augsburg, Duke Udo II of Rhenish Franconia, and other noblemen. Emperor Otto II was in danger of being taken prisoner. He fled to the coast and saw two large Greek ships. How could he get to them? Then he noticed a Jew, Kalonymus ben Meschullam of Lucca, who had a horse and was willing to place it at the Emperor's disposal. The Emperor mounted the horse and swam out to the first ship, but was refused permission to go on board. So he returned to land, where the Jew awaited him, anxious for the safety of his beloved master. Just as the Saracen riders were approaching, the second ship drew near, and the Emperor once more sprung on to the Jew's horse and swam out to the ship. (Anticipating Shakespeare's Richard III, he might well have cried 'My empire for a horse', or indeed 'My kingdom for a Jew'!) Fortunately for Otto, a Slav who owed him allegiance was on board this ship and saw to it that he was taken on.

The Emperor later showed his gratitude to the Jew Kalonymus. He invited him to Mainz, where he earned a great reputation as a learned rabbi. (The German-Jewish poet Wolfskehl was a descendant of this Kalonymus.) In the reign of Otto the great German cathedrals on the Rhine were built. These cathedrals, rebuilt in the twelfth and thirteenth centuries on their Ottonian foundations, stood intact (with the exception of Speyer Cathedral) until the air-raids of 1943-4 – the very years in which German Jews, who had for centuries been able to rely completely on the protection of the Holy Roman Empire and the German Reich, and hence had not wished to emigrate, were being deported to Auschwitz and Maidanek.

Speyer Cathedral – which is perhaps the greatest manifestation of the imperial glory of Otto's reign, and of the great faith in the true God and His servants on earth, the bishops – was rebuilt by Henry IV, who allowed the Jews, forcibly baptized during the terrible Crusade years, to return to their former faith.

The reign of terror began in 1096 with the First Crusade. In the rich towns along the Rhine Jews were massacred by gangs of Crusaders passing through on their way to the Holy Land, their emotions whipped up and distorted by fanatical priests and monks. *The first epoch of popular mass anti-Semitism was the product of propaganda associated with the Crusades.* It was the emperors, kings, bishops, popes, people in high positions, who opposed this anti-Semitism of the common people, just as Emperor Franz Josef did in Lueger's time in Austria, the classical land of popular anti-Semitism. These leaders sensed – to a certain extent at least – the anarchical element in this popular anti-Semitism; they knew that this popular feeling might well turn against themselves if, for instance, demagogic preachers were to accuse them of heresy and bring them to the stake. Such a thing had indeed happened in Germany in 1230. Crusading zeal could also be directed at targets nearer home. In the thirteenth century papal canonists formulated the doctrine that a crusade in Europe against heretics and heathens – such as the Albigenses and their protectors, the pro-Jewish Counts of Toulouse, and against heathens in Prussia – was just as meritorious as, if not more so than, a crusade in foreign lands. Even in the twelfth century the Rhenish bishops had had experience of a popular outcry against their own possessions. The high clergy themselves, together with rich noblemen, were the victims of the remarkable crusade of the 'Pastoureaux' in thirteenth-century France in the reign of St Louis. There is a direct connection between the fanatical folk-preachers and leaders of plebeian movements in the Middle Ages and the emotional religious movements of the nineteenth century. 'The German cathedral protects our home from Jews and Hapsburgs and from Rome' sang the followers of Georg von Schönerer, the new St George, the latter-day German crusader against the unholy power of the emperor in Vienna, the pope in Rome and Jews out for world domination. Adolf Hitler was the pupil not only of Lueger, the propagator of popular anti-Semitism in Vienna, but also of Schönerer and of the renegade Cistercian monk, Jörg Lanz Liebenfels, who revived the old Manichaean-Augustinian doctrine of the struggle between the children of Light and the children of Darkness. It was Liebenfels who, some years before the First World War, hoisted a swastika flag over a castle on the Danube. Adolf Hitler was depicted as the new crusader and the new knight of St George on picture post-cards, a popular method of mass propaganda ever since the invention of post-cards during the Franco-Prussian War of 1870–1.

Hitler thus takes his place beside Santiago Matamoros (St James), the slaughterer of the Moors and potential slaughterer of Jews, who emerged, in his call for an internal crusade in Spain, as a forerunner of the Crusades. Pilgrims travelling across Europe along the great pilgrim routes, accompanied by all the rumours, fears and hopes of the ordinary people (there are echoes of them in Chaucer's Canterbury Tales) wore a badge bearing the shell of St James.

This connection between crusades, folk movements, war against heresy and revolt against bishops (there were many assassinations of bishops and other prelates of the church in the twelfth century) draws our attention to a fact which is almost totally overlooked in accounts of the history of anti-Semitism. According to these accounts disaster burst unexpectedly, like a storm from a clear sky, upon a flourishing European Jewry, who lived peacefully in rich Jewish communities in the south of France, Italy and along the Rhine, spreading in the course of the twelfth century eastwards to Vienna. Only in fringe areas, like Spain, had the five or six centuries of peace been occasionally disturbed by grumbles of thunder. Prussian Jews in 1933 – among them privy counsellors, professors and bankers – were bewildered when they found that the wave of anti-Semitism that broke over them was no superficial affair, but that it drew on vast reserves of fanatical hatred which enabled it to keep renewing its murderous onslaughts right up to 1945. In the nineteenth and early twentieth centuries Jews assimilated into the German and West European nations had done their utmost to conceal the approaching catastrophe from themselves.

'Baptism or death' was the war-cry of the mass gangs who fell upon the Jews under the leadership of adventurers, ex-priests and inferior monks – first in Rouen in August 1096, then in Metz and then in the Rhineland. The first leader of the First Crusade, Godfrey Bouillon, swore to 'avenge the blood of Christ on Israel, and to leave no single member of the Jewish race alive'. Godfrey withdrew this oath at the command of Emperor Henry IV. Nevertheless, after the conquest of Jerusalem the synagogue there was burnt to the ground, with all the Jews still inside.

So it is wrong to consider these fanatical gangs as a sudden inexplicable phenomenon. In the Christian West the sky had become heavily overcast in the eleventh century, and saw only occasional outbreaks of sunshine until the early thirteenth century, when at the height of a crisis in European Christianity, Pope Innocent III set the points in a direction which orthodox Catholics, heretics and Jews were to follow for centuries. In the middle of the eleventh century Europe entered into a period of commotion. The great battle between Pope Gregory VII and Emperor Henry IV concerning the use and abuse of investiture, shook the foundations not only of the Holy Roman Empire and its churches but also of the papacy itself. This battle was temporarily ended with the extinction of the Hohenstaufen line of emperors, whose last representative, the young Conradin, was beheaded in the market-place of Naples, but it did not really end until the dissolution of the Austrian empire in 1918. Franz Josef's veto of the choice of Cardinal Rampolla as pope was in line with a tradition which went back to Ottonian and even Carolingian times.

In that eleventh-century quarrel the revolutionary papal party used all the weapons of propaganda and preaching to gain the upper hand. In its attack on the worldly, simoniacal bishops and prelates, the popular movement of the *pataria* – which enjoyed the support of Gregory VII – employed fanatical demagogic slogans of a sort previously used only by heretical anti-clerical movements. The monks and clerics who supported the great revolu-

66

tionary Gregory vii called the emperor and his loyal bishops precursors and harbingers of the anti-Christ, and made public throughout Europe the most intimate details of Henry's private life. The reciprocal viciousness of this battle aroused the horror of the more moderate elements of each side. One of Gregory vii's own party, horrified at the demonic strength of this low-born monk, called him a sort of 'holy devil'.

In the turbulent state of Europe which resulted from this conflict the lower classes became active for the first time in religious and political spheres. The conflict reverberated in England throughout the twelfth and thirteenth centuries, where it led to the murder of Thomas à Becket, and in France from the twelfth to the fourteenth centuries, where it led to the fatal outrage of Anagni against Pope Boniface viii and to the 'Babylonian captivity' of the church in Avignon. In the eleventh and twelfth centuries heretical movements of very different kinds broke out in Italy, the South of France, Flanders, the Netherlands and the Rhineland. 'Heretics are everywhere' – in all the towns of Italy. This cry of alarm can be seen in relation to the cry, 'Jews are everywhere'.

Agobard of Lyon openly admitted that the church was not equipped to compete against the Jews. Church leaders in the twelfth century saw that the old church, with its old methods, was powerless against the intensive propaganda of the heretics. The great Pope Innocent iii's counteraction was a counsel of despair: a crusade which in twenty years led to the extermination of the Albigenses and the devastation of the South of France. St Bernard of Clairvaux had to concede that he was no match for the heretics of Cologne. St Bernard was the greatest and most passionate Christian preacher of the first half of the twelfth century, and was the instigator of the Second Crusade. He preached against the 'bestial' Jews, saying that they were lower than animals (Lavisse in 1901 thought the same), that they were descendant of the Devil and had been murderers from the beginning of time. But at the request of the archbishop of Mainz St Bernard spoke against the extermination of the Jews, which was being advocated particularly by Ranulf, a monk who had escaped from the archbishop of Mainz.

In the archdiocese of Mainz lived the great St Hildegard, of Bingen, whose fame reached as far as England and Iceland in the twelfth century. For more than ten years she stood with her abbey of St Rupert under the interdiction of the church, because she had, against the will of the archbishop, permitted the burial of an excommunicated knight in the grounds of her cloister. The rich feudal prelates of the Rhineland, however, were quite incapable of preaching effectively against the heretics, or of conducting a countermission with the weapons of their own church. This was pointed out to them by Ekbert of Deutz, who was a fellow-student of Archbishop Rainald of Dassel, Frederick i's chancellor. So, at the request of the hierarchy of the Rhineland, St Hildegard undertook missionary journeys along the Rhine and the Nahe, preaching against the heretics. This episode illustrates the total powerlessness and inarticulateness of the higher clergy, who simply could not find any way of swaying the excited people, as could the Jewish preachers and the heretics.

Petrus Venerabilis, Peter the Venerable, abbot of Cluny, who took a great interest in the Jews and the Koran, expressed the opinion that the Jews should pay the costs of the Crusades. The same sort of view was expressed by Lieutenant-General Sir Evelyn Parker, G.O.C. in Palestine, in a circular to his troops on 26 July 1946, in which he said that the Jews should bear the costs of the war there. Highly respected Catholic historians of the eighteenth to the twentieth centuries, right up to Georges Goyau, G. K. Chesterton and even later writers, have sought to approve, excuse or play down the slaughter of Jews during the Crusades of the twelfth century. A famous dissenter from this view was the father of Scholasticism, Peter Abelard, friend and lover of Heloise during his early period of fame as a teacher at the university of Paris, before he was ruined by the persecutions of St Bernard of Clairvaux. A nascent European intelligentsia gathered round him in Paris, which through him became for the first time an intellectual centre of Europe.

In one of his late writings, *Dialogue between a Jewish and a Christian philosopher*, he makes the Jew say:

One would be accusing God of cruelty if one thought that the Jews' steadfast bearing of suffering could remain unrewarded. No other people has borne so much for God's sake. Dispersed among strangers, without king or prince, the Jews are oppressed with the heaviest taxes, as if each day they had to buy anew the right to live. The maltreatment of the Jews is thought to please God. For the servitude of the Jews can only be interpreted by Christians as a sign that Jews are hated by God. The lives of the Jews lie in the hands of their deadliest enemies. If they want to travel, they have to pay large sums to gain the protection of Christian princes, who in actual fact desire their death so that they can seize their possessions. Jews cannot own fields or vineyards, because they have no one to guarantee their ownership. So the only profession open to them is that of usury, which only increases the Christians' hatred of them.

Abelard died in 1142. His words read like a vision of Jewish life in a closed Europe from the thirteenth century onwards. Abelard was the first spokesman of a new European intellect, which was to be decisively influenced scholastically by Jewish and Arabic philosophers. But in the same epoch – from the mid-twelfth to the fourteenth century – in which a European intelligentsia of young, widely educated clerks, in Paris and at all the schools and new universities, was studying the great Jewish thinkers, a new monasticism was propagating anti-Semitism among the people, and a restored papacy banishing the Jews into ghettoes.

What was this new monasticism? Benedictine Europe of the sixth to twelfth centuries had not taken over any of the Eastern forms of monasticism, such as the stark asceticism of the Stylites or of church fathers like St Antony who wrestled with their temptations in the desert; it had nothing of the harsh military discipline which reigned in the vast Egyptian monasteries, where the monks knelt to pray on command, flagellated themselves on command, appeared in troops of three to five thousand at the daily distribution of rations, wore sword belts at the annual distribution of clothing, and in fights for the possession of the patriarch's throne, and against 'troublesome foreigners' like Greeks and Jews, called up storm troops reminiscent of the SS and the SA: the *Totenkopf-Standarte* of Coptic Egypt.

Benedictine Europe, which flourished between the sixth and twelfth centuries – the same six centuries of (relative) peace for the Jews in Europe – made an important contribution to European culture, through its *ora et labora* (prayer and work), practised in the thousands of Benedictine monasteries. Benedictinism advocated moderation (*Discretio est mater omnium virtutum*), stability of abode (*stabilitas loci*) – a monk usually spent his whole life in his monastery – and the paternal authority of the abbot (*abbas*) over his monks, whom he strove to mould in accordance with patrician values, both ancient Roman and Christian. Benedict of Nursia, who founded the first Benedictine monastery at Monte Cassino, was himself descended from a Roman patrician family.

These Benedictine monasteries acquired riches and land through the liberality of the old European nobility. Often in need of reform, they gave birth to a long series of reform movements and councils. In the course of generations the spiritual life in the monasteries might very well have declined, but the Benedictines were completely free of that aggressiveness which was a feature of the new monastic movements of the mid-eleventh and twelfth centuries. Stormy young reform movements started among the Cistercians and Premonstratensians in the twelfth century, but they were outstripped by the new mendicant orders of the Franciscans and Dominicans. These monks went out among the people, militant politico-religious preachers in the service of the restored papacy, preaching at first against Emperor Frederick II and then against heretics, heathens and Turks.

The Dominicans became officials of the Inquisition (*domini canes* – watchdogs of the Lord). Franciscans, in the course of their movement's long and strife-ridden history, became first and foremost preachers to the common people and whippers-up of popular emotion. In the thirteenth century the practice of flagellation reached pathological proportions. These, with other new orders and monastic movements, introduced into Europe a new mobility and spirit of aggression, which was as foreign to the Benedictine spirit and the comfortable town and country clergy as it was to the aristocratic bishops and cathedral chapters. The mendicants overcame the resistance of bishops, chapters, town clergy and university professors to win the right to settle and preach in towns and to take over professorships at the university of Paris. These youthful orders produced vigorous preachers and heretic-hunters, and their popular sermons were not seldom directed against the Jews.

These orders grew in strength under the protection of the restored papacy, which found in them militant champions. The papacy, which having humbled the Empire in the thirteenth century, was now out to realize its dream of papal world domination, owed its strength in the time of Innocent III and Innocent IV to Gregory VII, who enforced the rule of celibacy. This pledge to live unmarried and without sexual relations with women was designed to free the clergy from the bonds of flesh and family which tied other men.

Even by the time of the Counter-Reformation, in the seventeenth century, total enforcement of the rule of celibacy had not been achieved; but one thing emerged from these measures: a new type of priest who, though secular, submitted himself to hardships and penances previously undergone only by the enclosed orders. This increased the clergy's energy, and developed in them a feeling of aggression which added to the vigour of their sense of mission. However, the tensions resulting from this mortification of the flesh rarely produced a psychologically mature personality. The frustrated mental and emotional energies turned inwards, or, in the case of aggressive natures, outwards, and joined battle with the various manifestations of the Devil on earth: women, heretics – and, of course, Jews. *Suppression of the inner self leads to death for others.*

With this new celibate clergy and these new monks, the popes after Gregory VII entered upon the great Crusade, first to the Holy Land and then in Europe against the heathens of Prussia, the rebellious peasants (the Stedinger) of North Germany, the Albigenses in Provence and Italian, French and German heretics. In the early part of the thirteenth century, side by side with Crusades to the Holy Land, European crusades became increasingly frequent.

This turbulent Europe of the twelfth century saw a wave of accusations of ritual murder against the Jews – and this plague of prejudice survives to the present day. Bishops like Dr Paul Rusch of Innsbruck and others still give credence to stories of the ritual murder of Christian children by Jews. It is still difficult, and sometimes impossible, to remove illustrations on the ritual murder theme from country churches and places of pilgrimage. From the twelfth century onwards the whole of Catholic Europe was poisoned by this infection.

Allegations of ritual murder have always occurred somewhere at some time. In China such accusations were made against Christian missionaries in the nineteenth century, and in the twentieth the theme was exploited by the Communists. In Indo-China and Madagascar, the island considered by Himmler and Eichmann as a possible site for a Jewish settlement, similar legends were directed against French government officials. In the Ancient World Greeks made this accusation against Jews, and Romans against early Christians; subsequently orthodox Christians made it against heretics, Gnostics and Montanists. Between 1141 and 1150, for the first time in Christian Europe, there were three separate allegations of a Christian child having been killed so that its blood could be mixed in the unleavened bread of the Jewish sacramental meal.

This meal was seen as the 'murderous' Jewish people's equivalent of the Christian communion. The devout Christian consumes the body of Christ at Holy Communion, and the priest drinks the blood as wine. (A violent controversy raged from the eleventh century onwards over transubstantiation. Heretics in the Rhineland, and later the Albigenses, openly disavowed this doctrine.) The rise of the legend of ritual murder in the twelfth century must have been connected, if only subconsciously, with deep and widespread doubts about the reality and efficacy of the Holy Communion. The Albigenses and Waldenses developed a highly effective propaganda against what to them was the 'synagogue of Satan' – the Roman Catholic Church. Its sacraments were denounced as works of the Devil, as black magic. Roman Catholic counter-propaganda was for a long time totally ineffective against the heretical aristocracy and rural population of Italy and the South of France.

It was in this atmosphere of controversy over the validity and significance of transubstantiation, and of the Catholic mass in general, that the legend of ritual murder arose.

The first allegation occurred in 1144 in Norwich, the second in Würzburg in 1147, in connection with preaching efforts to win support for the Second Crusade. The vicious Norwich lie was probably brewed by the monk Theobald – a converted Jew – and committed to paper by Thomas of Monmouth shortly before the Second Crusade. The third allegation was in 1171, in Blois (France). The cult of worshipping the child victims as saints, with all the paraphernalia of pictures, statues, miraculous happenings and pilgrimages, spread throughout Europe in the late Middle Ages. The Scottish Catholic Malcolm Hay remarks, 'Every pilgrim was an apostle of hate.'

Emperor Frederick II – the heretic so often attacked by the popes – defended the Jews against allegations of ritual murder in his Golden Bull of 1236. And one pope – Innocent IV – also issued a bull (1247) denouncing the legends, which, he said, were merely a pretext for robbing the Jews. In Lyon in 1245 (fleeing from Frederick II), Innocent had moved from hostility to a more favourable opinion of the Jews.

The ritual murder movement, with its canonization of child-victims, gained new impetus on the eve of the Reformation and subsequently during the Counter-Reformation. Anderl of Rinn, who died in 1482, was decreed a saint by the bull *Beatus Andreas* of 22 February 1755.

A series of articles on ritual murder was published in 1881 in the Jesuit periodical *La Civiltà Cattolica*, which had long been virulently anti-Semitic. In English Catholic circles around 1901 it was accepted as historical fact.

In 1758, the Holy State condemned the cult of canonized children and denounced the legend of ritual murder. So in particular did Cardinal Ganganelli, who later became Pope Clement xiv. But two exceptions were acknowledged: Anderl of Rinn and Simon of Trent. These two exceptions sufficed to keep the belief alive in the minds of many Catholics. They believed that the race which murdered Christ was continuing in the same tradition; that this people poisoned springs and wells and that Jewish physicians poisoned their Christian masters; and that the Jews were in league with all the enemies of Christ – with the Saracens in Spain and the Moslems in the Holy Land, and with heretics everywhere.

Heretics had to be exterminated, for their disease was contagious. And the Jews, no less deadly, had to be separated from the Christians. The edicts against heretics and Jews passed by the Fourth Lateran Council in 1215, when the reputation of the papacy was at its height under Innocent iii, are manifestations of the same feeling. This council created the Papal Inquisition and ordered the Jews to wear special emblems. Innocent iii declared that the Jews were destined by God to eternal slavery, as a punishment for the death of Christ. St Thomas Aquinas accepted the idea of Jewish slavery in his teaching; he laid down that churches, kings and princes had the right to dispose of the possessions of Jews as if they were their own.

The Lateran Council, which permanently changed the position of the Jews in Europe, branding them with a special sign like lepers and whores and confining them to ghettoes, was the result of an extremely critical situation in Christianity. It was also the personal creation of Innocent iii, a man of extraordinary legal and political skill.

Count Lotario of Segni – Pope Innocent iii – considered Roman Catholic Christianity and the papacy to be threatened with destruction. In Italy he feared political and military isolation through Emperor Frederick ii, his ward, and a Hohenstaufen dynasty which in all parts of Italy and Sicily, held the Holy State and the legacy of St Peter in a vice-like grip. Italy, the South of France and the Rhineland were full of heretics; the Waldenses and Albigenses were able to carry out among the nobility and the common people, in town and country, a large-scale programme of anti-Catholic propaganda, reminiscent of that of the young Luther. The high secular clergy of the various countries concerned were unequal to the task of countering this propaganda, and were moreover politically unreliable, often supporting their kings in disputes between king and pope. This was the case in England and France. Germany was split between a papal party and two secular parties – the Hohenstaufen and the Guelfs. The Fourth Lateran Council of 1215 aimed at the reorganization of the church and its internal and external consolidation through dogmatic reform. Ten years earlier, in 1205, Innocent iii had dispatched to France two important letters which reveal clearly his attitude towards the Jews. A letter to the king of France (16 January 1205) stated that Christ was of royal blood, whereas the Jews maintained that He was the son of peasants. Innocent was here attempting to bring about an alliance of kings, princes and nobles against heretics, Jews and rebellious common people. The pope declared further that the Jews exploited every opportunity secretly to murder their Christian hosts. In a letter to the archbishop of Sens and the bishop of Paris (15 July 1205) he wrote, 'The Jews are condemned to eternal slavery as a punishment for crucifying our Lord.' He had already advocated this Augustinian doctrine in his *Constitutio pro Judaeis*.

In the early years of his pontificate Innocent III had hoped for the conversion of the Jews. As an educated Italian he recognized the intellectual and scientific qualities of the Jewish doctors, scholars and travellers who lived in or visited the rich Jewish communities of the Italian towns. As was the case with the Augustinian monk Martin Luther, disappointed hopes may have increased, perhaps even first kindled, his feelings of bitterness against them. The firmest foundation for his anti-Jewish policies, and indeed for his whole authoritarian political philosophy, was provided by his Augustinian theology. His work *De Contemptu Mundi* was read and quoted long after the end of the Middle Ages. It expresses an extreme pessimism concerning the wretched and sinful nature of Man and the wickedness of the world. Man is given over to sin, the flesh and the world and can be redeemed only with great difficulty. Authoritarian and totalitarian ideologies and régimes always have their roots in an anthropological and theological pessimism, which believes that the sinful beast which is Man, the accursed masses – the *massa damnata* – must be ruled with a rod of iron, wielded by emperor-popes and their servants the secular kings.

And who is more a prey to the evil, carnal world than the 'lecherous' Jew? Innocent III did not contemplate the extermination of the Jews. He subscribed to the view of St Augustine, who explained the Jews' strange survival throughout history, in his *Adversus Judaeos* and elsewhere, with the argument that God had branded them with the mark of Cain, so that no one who met them should slay them. And now the Lateran Council compelled the Jews to wear a special sign – a yellow patch or stripe on their garments, and later a pointed hat. In 850 the Caliph of Baghdad had decreed that all unbelievers, Christians and Jews must wear a yellow cap and a badge; but this was rarely enforced. It was quite different in Christian Europe. From the beginning of the fourteenth century onwards artists painted even the Old Testament patriarchs with the Jewish sign. Jewish manuscript makers themselves took up the practice, and Abraham, Jacob and Joseph all wear the Jewish sign in fourteenth- and fifteenth-century miniatures. An odd capitulation of the Jews to their enemies. Later, in the concentration camps, both Jewish and non-Jewish prisoners were often remarkably similar in clothing and behaviour to the SS, their murderous enemies.

St Augustine also said that, though Jews should not be killed, they should always remain servants of the Christian people. *Ecce judaeus servus est christiani.*

73

Such degradation would be a testimony to their wrongness and to the truth of Christianity. Pope Innocent III followed these Augustinian maxims in the decrees of the Fourth Lateran Council. The Jews should not be too heavily oppressed, because their existence served to prove the truth of the Christian faith. So the Jews were to be preserved – in a state of wretchedness. In a letter to the archbishop and bishops of Germany (5 March 1233) Pope Gregory IX, a relative of Innocent III and himself a Count Segni, complained that the Jews in Germany were not living in the state of utter wretchedness to which God had condemned them. He deplored the over-friendly relations between Jews and Christians in Germany; Christians were being converted to Judaism, he complained. And he forbade all conversation between Christians and Jews.

Over-friendly relations between Christians and Jews – one thinks of Spain, and of the young intelligentsia at the university in Paris, and later in Padua and Naples. It was one of the glories of the period of Scholasticism that men like Albertus Magnus and St Thomas Aquinas created in the universities an arena for free discussion between questioning Catholics and heathen, Greek, Arab, Jewish and atheistic thinkers, at a time when debate between Christians and Jews was forbidden in a Europe increasingly divided into ecclesiastical, national and Jewish ghettoes.

'Israel is to the other peoples of the earth what the heart is to all the other parts of the body: it suffers for the whole body and feels the pain more sharply than any other part. It was not for nothing that God said to Israel: "I have chosen you from among all others, and therefore I will persecute you more than all the others." '

Judah ben Samuel Halevi wrote (c. 1130–40) in his *Sefer Kuzari* (Book of the Khazars):

God speaks

> May hope stay young,
> And thy heart hold firm to it.
> What is won by misery
> And spirit faint?
> Rise up, speak, and sing thy song anew.
> Thy slandered name bids thee
> Trust thyself and heed not
> Those who scorn, though loud their voice.
> Drive thy flocks gently:
> Thou shalt find shelter at the end.

The Jew

> It is for Thee I bear the spite
> Of those that worship idols in the night.

74

I answer them: to serve my God is right.
What stands that finds not favour in His sight?
When He frowns, I am the meanest wight;
Yet when He smiles, boundless is my might.

The songs and prayers of the poet and thinker, Judah Halevi, who lived
in Spain in the twelfth century – the century of Crusades and of cross-paths
for European Jews – have become part of the Jewish liturgy, providing it, to
the present day, with an irreplaceable core. Halevi is a child of the period of
religious tolerance in Spain, when since the eighth century Christians, Jews
and Mohammedans had developed a community of co-existence.

'The perfect man should be of East Persian descent, of Arab faith, Iraqi
(Babylonian) upbringing, Hebrew cunning, Christian conduct; he should be
as pious as a Syrian monk, a Greek in his knowledge, Indian in his appreciation of the mysteries, and lastly, and most essentially, a Sufi in his spiritual
life' (Iswan).

An enlightened Islamic intelligentsia, inheritors of the educational ideals
of the Hellenistic world, sought to realize this ideal in Spain with its triple
culture. (Educated Byzantine Christians in fifteenth-century Constantinople
still felt they belonged to this Hellenistic world, and their forbears in the
twelfth century had felt nearer to Baghdad than to the barbaric Franks and
Latin Christians.)

From the tenth to the thirteenth centuries Jews in the Mediterranean area
acted as ambassadors between East and West. Jewish sects had kept company
with Islam from its birth, and had followed in the wake of the conquering
Islamic armies, as physicians, translators, astrologers, merchants and diplomats: thus we find them in the tenth century negotiating between Otto I –
the founder of the Holy Roman Empire – and the Arab princes in Spain.
Jewish culture included Hellenistic and Islamic elements, and their religious
and philosophical thinking was deeply influenced by Aristotle and his Arab
interpreters, by Arab neo-Platonism and their own Cabbala.

'In a cultural sense the Jews were the first Europeans' (Charles and Dorothy
Singer) – by virtue of their activity as travellers, as communicators of Greek,
Near East and Arab thought, and as translators. Ibn-ezra, who was born in
Toledo in 1090, was in Rome in 1140, in Salerno in 1141, in Verona in 1145,
in Lucca in 1148, in Béziers in 1156 and in Narbonne in 1160. He died
in 1167, probably in Calahorra. This Spanish Jew, who was a translator
from Arabic into Hebrew, and one of the greatest commentators of the Bible
in the Middle Ages, was admired by Spinoza as a pioneer of modern
biblical criticism. On his propaganda missions among the Jews of Western
Europe, Ibn-ezra disseminated the new scientific methods of the Arabs and
Jews in Spain. His compatriot Pedro Alfonso (died 1110) became physician
to King Alfonso VI of Castile and later, for a time, court physician to Henry I
of England. His thirty-three tales were translated into many languages and

were a source for Chaucer, Shakespeare and many other Christian writers. Pedro Alfonso was converted to Christianity, and wrote a tract against the Jews, thereby founding, together with other Jewish converts, the anti-Jewish movements and literature which were to play so great a part in the history of Spain, and in which the leading figures were often ex-Jews and descendants of Jewish families.

The great Jewish philosophical activity of the eleventh century culminated in Spain in the neo-Platonism of Ibn Gabirol (also called Avicebron and Avencebrel by Christian scholastics) and in Ibn Pakuda's *Guide to the duties of the heart*. Ibn Pakuda was the preacher of an inner ethic which went far beyond all external convention and morality. He anticipated the great pioneer of an inner personal ethic, an ethic of heart and mind rather than of subservience to social pressures: Peter Abelard – himself a lone defender of the Jews.

Contemporary with Ibn Pakuda were Ibn-ezra and Halevi. There were three centres of Jewish education and learning – Salerno, the South of France and Spain. Salerno, whose famous medical school was probably of Jewish origin, served the whole of Lower Italy, including Naples and Sicily. In Toulouse, the centre in the South of France, the Counts of Toulouse were both friendly towards the Jews and at the same time protectors of the Albigenses. In Spain, Toledo was the centre. Toledo produced – in the field of biblical scholarship – the first Jewish works of philological criticism. It was here, in 1168, that Abraham ben David Halevi ventured to connect the Revelation to Aristotle. The great physician, theologian and philosopher, Maimonides lived here; he died in 1204 in Old Cairo, while fleeing from Spain across Egypt to Palestine. Maimonides, who came of a family which had been physicians for seven generations, was a philosopher of unique power, the bulwark of an enlightened Judaism in the following five centuries. His *Moreh Nebuchim* (Teacher of the Perplexed) became a sort of bible for intellectual believers, and his *Dogmas* still form an essential part of the religious instruction of Jewish children today. This second Moses (Rabbi Moses ben Maimon was his full name) had a powerful influence on scholastic philosophers such as Albertus Magnus and St Thomas Aquinas, as well as on Meister Eckhart, the master of German intellectual mysticism, Nicholas of Cusa, Leon Hebreo, Spinoza and Kant.

Ubique sunt Hebraei, the Jews are everywhere, wrote a chronicler in the early thirteenth century. As early as the twelfth century there was a wealth of polemical Christian literature disputing Jewish propaganda – by such writers as Rupert of Deutz, Petrus Venerabilis and Peter of Blois. Gilbert Crispin, abbot of Westminster (who died in 1117, and whose grave can still be seen today in Westminster Abbey) recounts, in a light courtly tone, conversations with an educated Jew from Mainz, who had come to England on business. The twelfth century produced a large number of accounts of such conversations in England, France and Spain. Public discussions between

Jews and Christian theologians were forbidden in Paris in 1208, in Trier in 1223 and (by Pope Gregory IX) in the whole of Germany in 1231. However, they were still taking place in Paris in 1240 before Louis IX, and in Barcelona in 1263 before James I of Aragon – under royal protection.

In a Europe which was being separated into isolated compartments, discussions grew increasingly hostile towards the Jews. The Jews were abused as a *gens prava atque perversa*, as a devilish, accursed race. The culmination of these later discussions was banishment or compulsory baptism. In the 'open' twelfth century, disputations were a feature of places, such as Palermo and Spain, in which Byzantine and Arabic manners were habitual at court. In Toledo, where Arabic was still spoken in the twelfth century, Archbishop Raimundo I (1126–51) founded with the help of his archdeacon Gundissalvi (a converted Jew) a school for translators which became a magnetic centre for the élite of Western Europe. It attracted Adelard of Bath – 'the first natural scientist of Western Europe' – Walter of Malvern, Robert of Chester, Michael Scotus from England. From Flanders came Heinrich Bate and Rudolf of Bruges; from Dalmatia Hermann of Dalmatia; from the South of France and Italy came many Jewish and non-Jewish 'seekers after truth'.

In the entrances of Gothic cathedrals the synagogue is represented as a female figure side by side with the church. Beautiful and graceful, it hints of the great possibility of a Christian self-awareness without hatred of the Jews at the time the cathedrals were built. The Third Lateran Council had in 1179 advocated a tolerance of the Jews on grounds of pure humanity (*pro sola humanitate*). Christian chivalry in the twelfth and thirteenth centuries recognized in its equally well-born and chivalrous Islamic antagonists 'the noble heathen'. Thomist Scholasticism preserved religious disputation within the universities when it was forbidden to an ever-increasing extent in the outside world. Today the fact cannot be too much emphasized how much this learned university scholasticism contributed to the shaping of Europe's intellects (including the rationalists), from the twelfth century right up to the nineteenth century.

European intellectual discipline and integrity – the foundations for scientific discoveries yet to come – were first developed at the university of Paris and later at other universities in the great running debate between theologians and secular teachers of philosophy on the one hand and atheist, Arab and Jewish thinkers on the other. The great Christian literature of the time reflects this fact. Boccaccio does not allow himself to use the plague (the great instigator of Jewish persecution in the Europe of 1350) as an excuse for anti-Jewish outbursts in his *Decameron*. Dante consigns popes and emperors to hell, but it is a very remarkable fact that in the *Inferno* there are no Jews.

Immanuel di Roma (1265–1330) was a friend of Dante. This Jewish court poet of young Italy was one of the first poets in Europe to compose sonnets in Hebrew and Italian. His *Ha-Tafet weha Eden* (Hell and Paradise) has the same theme as Dante's *Divine Comedy*: the ageing Jewish poet, in a state of remorse for his past life and fear of the Last Judgment, is led by the spirit of a dead friend through hell-fire and Paradise.

A medieval miniature depicts the German Jewish Minnesinger Süsskind von Trimberg singing before a bishop. In the miniatures of the *Sachsenspiegel* – the great codification of German law – Jews are shown as free men carrying arms. In 1225 they shared with the Christian citizens the duty of defending their towns.

Fifty years later the powerful influence of the church can be seen in the *Schwabenspiegel* with its theory of the eternal slavery of the Jewish race. Despite serious portents for the future, Jews and Christians were living in close contact with each other in the thirteenth century, even in Germany. Jews bore arms and had, like all free men, to submit themselves to the judgment of God. Jewish mysticism in the Rhineland in the thirteenth century testifies to two things: to the shock caused by the pogroms which burst upon the Jews in the Rhenish towns during the Crusades; and to the fruitful relationship between this Jewish mysticism and the German mysticism which flourished at the time in the area between Strasbourg and Cologne. Whereas the forefathers of these Jews had stimulated Christian Scholasticism, it was now the turn of Jewish orthodox Scholasticism to be influenced by Christian ways of thinking.

Jews and Christians still formed a true cultural community in the twelfth and thirteenth centuries. This close relationship occasionally found tragical or tragi-comical expression – for instance, when Jewish orthodox rabbis appealed to the Dominican Inquisition, as they did in Montpelier in 1233, for support against 'heretics' within their ranks, that is to say, against followers of Maimonides. Here we find the first signs of alliance between different totalitarian orthodoxies, which in the twentieth century led, among other things, to the remarkable team-work of Stalinist and Nazi bureaucrats.

Let us return to the figure representing the synagogue on the doors of Gothic cathedrals – the cathedrals of Bamberg, Strasbourg, Freiburg, Trier and Magdeburg. The sculptured frieze on the 'gateway to the heavenly city' represents the history of man's salvation, from the fall of Adam to the Last Judgment. 'Here the witnesses of the old and new covenants stand united, this is the place for church and synagogue' (Wolfgang Seiferth).

Today the beauty and charm of the allegorical figure representing the synagogue in Strasbourg Cathedral captivates tourists from all parts of the world who are not conscious that this graceful figure took her place there in an atmosphere of hate and contempt. Only a few decades previously bands of Crusaders had persecuted the Jews in French and German towns along the Rhine, and a new exodus of Jews was already under way from England and France to Italy, Germany and Spain, and thence to Eastern Europe, in particular to Poland.

'Synagogue', 'Jerusalem', and 'Judaea': these took on flesh and blood form in the Middle Ages. Synagogue is a creation of prophetic poetry, conceived by Jeremiah, evoked by Christ in St Matthew 23, and woven by St Paul into his typological interpretation of the scriptures. The same can be said of Ecclesia, the church. St Paul paints a picture of her in his Epistle to the Ephesians 5. But the image of the synagogue as a blind outcast, which dominated the thousand years of the Christian middle period we owe to St Augustine – in his interpretation of the Song of Songs! Again and again we find Christian hostility to sex, monastic spirituality and stark asceticism joined with feelings of aggression towards Jews. St Augustine paints the mystical marriage in glowing colours and insists on the necessity of separation from the synagogue: 'Ecclesia is the bride, Christ the bridegroom . . . Let the bride, the beloved of the Lord rejoice . . . The people who formerly believed the Jews now turn against the synagogue . . . as the bride herself turns against the mother of the bridegroom . . . He will leave father and mother . . . And who is the mother he is leaving? She is the race of the Jews, the synagogue. What an epithalamion! Behold, between the joyful songs the bride herself steps forward. For the bridegroom has come . . . he steps steps forward with her. The queen stands at his right hand (Psalm 44) but she who stands on his left is no queen. To the one who stands on his left he will say: "Get thee hence, into everlasting fire." But to the one who stands on his right he will say: "Come, you who have my Father's blessing, inherit the kingdom that has been prepared for you since the beginning of the world".'

The synagogue is consigned to the flames, the church – Ecclesia – takes her place. Sedulius, a younger contemporary of St Augustine, wrote: 'Let the synagogue depart, blackened with disgrace, for Christ has taken the church as his beloved bride . . .' And in a poem written in the ninth century by the monk Notker of St Gall occurs the line:

'The synagogue will be driven out into the darkness of blackest night.'

Through Europe's black night – a night lasting centuries – Jews were driven, from West to East. The most glorious hour of Christian poetry and intellectual life, when St Thomas Aquinas talked with Maimonides and Dante with his friend Immanuel di Roma, also marks the apogee of an art which in the sculpture of the Gothic cathedrals returns for the first time to a true classicism.

Concordia – the concordance of the Old and New Testaments – becomes reality here: flesh, spirit and life enshrined in blossoming stone. One of the greatest sculptors in the history of European art, the Bamberg Master, represents church and synagogue in the cathedral of Bamberg as two related noble women. Synagogue is blindfold (an artistic convention which began to appear in the second half of the twelfth century). Her lance is broken, the tablets of the Law slipping out of her left hand. Ecclesia has the dignity and ceremonial bearing of an enthroned goddess, but the synagogue figure is younger, softer, more attractive. 'Thus the sympathy of the sculptor, as of the beholder, is with her. The greater emphasis on her physical qualities makes her seem a doomed victim, a figure of tragic stature' (Seiferth).

In the mid-twelfth century the *Ludus de antichristo* (Play of Anti-Christ) – a religio-political play probably written, and certainly performed in the Benedictine monastery of Tegernsee – gives the synagogue an important role: it is she and not the Roman church, who breaks the spell of anti-Christ in calling him by name. The original function of the synagogue is very hazily visible here – the function of unmasking all false gods and destroying their images.

The history of the Bamberg synagogue figure is interesting. The door for which it and Ecclesia were destined was never built, and, for centuries the two figures were standing beside the prince's door, the synagogue figure on a pillar depicting a Jew whose eye is being gouged out by the Devil. This is the work of a later period. Since 1938 (!) both figures have stood inside the cathedral, in the southern transept beside the pillars flanking the choir-screens, with their magnificent thirteenth-century reliefs of disputing prophets and apostles. The dignity and passion of these disputing figures can be seen in relation to the great religious debates in the period of Scholasticism.

At Strasbourg Cathedral the figures of church and synagogue still stand today in their original places on either side of the double doors. Here Ecclesia, the victorious queen, is looking at her vanquished opponent, who is blind – but very beautiful.

The glorious hour of Concordia, of true humanity, was of short duration. The representations of the synagogue and of the Jew in the art of the later Middle Ages reflect the propaganda of hatred and denunciation which the new monks and a plebeian parish clergy preached to the masses. Anti-Semitic propaganda was also disseminated by means of the passion plays, which were becoming increasingly hostile to Jews, and have continued to be so right up to the Oberammergau plays of today.

Synagogue became a personification of the Jewish community, of the Jewish people, particularly in popular art. At the main doors of Notre Dame in Paris – built under Philip Augustus, who banished the Jews from France – the dragon of Hell is seen winding itself round the head of the synagogue figure, covering her eyes. France was, from the height of the Middle Ages to the time of Dreyfus and beyond, a classical land of anti-Semitism. On the southern door of Chartres Cathedral, St Jerome (we may recall the important role he played in intensifying the neurotic Christian fear of women and Jews) is depicted taking a scroll from the synagogue figure. This can be interpreted literally, as symbolizing the translation of the Bible into Latin, but it can also be interpreted in a more sinister way, as an act of expropriation. In Freiburg Cathedral the synagogue figure is shown preparing for an unequal contest with Ecclesia: blindfold, in a yellow robe on a lame donkey, her lance broken. 'Her most significant distinguishing mark is the head of a goat, which around 1300 no longer stood for the Old Testament sacrificial beast, but for unchastity, since it is also used as the emblem of lust (*luxuria*) in the entrance to the cathedral.'

From 1400 onwards the 'Jewish sow' began to appear in churches (Erfurt and Magdeburg, for example): a sow – symbolizing the synagogue of Satan – is shown suckling little Jewish monsters. In wood-carvings, which played a vital role in Luther's propaganda campaign, in religious folk-songs and hymns and in broadsheets passed from hand to hand, popular hatred of the Jews was portrayed in countless unpleasant images. In the debates with the synagogue which formed part of the passion plays of the late Middle Ages, the synagogue no longer has any say. She is just the defenceless object of derision. As early as 1150, a Salzburg antiphonary – a masterpiece of illumination – replaces the Roman soldiers leading Christ to the Crucifixion by Jews.

The Concordia seems here to have been forgotten. But after a long period of self-laceration in the cold and hot sectarian wars which culminated in the Thirty Years War, a pietistic German Protestantism turned determinedly inwards: the true Christ was not to be found in 'protective' churches built of stone, He was not to be reached through the humiliation of others. The text of a hymn written on the eve of the Reformation attributes the Crucifixion to the sins of humanity. 'So we must not abuse you, poor Jews, since the blame is ours.' In the mellower years of a victorious Protestantism, in the eighteenth century, Johann Sebastian Bach composed his great works, which were then totally neglected until rediscovered by a Jew – Mendelssohn. We already know something of the part played by liturgy and art in the creation of an image of the Jew which had the power to trigger off dangerous (and not only emotional) reactions in broad sections of the people. Bach kept strictly – but with inner freedom – to the liturgy of his Evangelical church, which takes as its text for the Twenty-seventh Sunday after Trinity the parable of the wise and foolish virgins.

In medieval sculpture, as we have seen, the synagogue as leader of the foolish virgins had sunk down to a wretched woman ensnared by the Devil. Theological interpretations of the Song of Songs had taken the beautiful Shulamite, the splendid Jewish woman (Synagogue) and turned her into a proud church, awaiting not the young Jew of the Song of Solomon, but Christ the King, who as judge over the synagogue of Satan was shaping His Last Judgment in the daily judgment of history. Now Bach, in his Cantata No. 140 (based on the chorale by Philipp Nicolai: *Wachet auf, ruft uns die Stimme*) interweaves the mystical experience of Christ's marriage to the church with the characters of the Song: Zion, the wise virgin of the first theme, is also the loved one, for when the Song of Songs is sung. 'Bach's virgins are all pure expectation, preparedness and faith'. There is only one love: the love of God for Man, for Man of the new, as of the old, covenant. God's first love – for Israel – merges with the love of Christ to form a love embracing the whole of mankind, in the true spirit of ancient Jewish Messianism. This all-embracing love finds expression in the music of Bach, as later also in the Ode to Joy of Beethoven's Choral Symphony.

A song born of joy: but Jewish song in the Middle Ages was born of sorrow. David ben Meschullam wrote the following poem about the suicide of the Jews in Mainz who were oppressed by forerunners of the First Crusade:

> O God, do not forget the blood that was spilt:
> Leave not unscathed those who rose up against me:
> Avenge all this blood upon my destroyers . . .
> Women and children laid down their lives for the sake of Thy name.
> Do not spare us, the little ones said to their pitying mothers,
> Heaven herself demands from us this sacrifice . . .
> So women like men wielded the knife of the priests . . .

> *The Jewish liturgy for days of mourning and fasting*
> *includes an elegy by Kalonymos ben Judah:*

> My tears fall fast over the dead of Aschpira (Speyer),
> Over the graceful youth and the venerable old man . . .
> Bitterly will I lament
> The community of Warmaisa (Worms),
> The community of holy ones who twice in their death pangs
> Sanctified before the world the Unity of God the Almighty . . .
> And my elegy shall remember too the victims of Magenza (Mainz),
> Those spiritual heroes who, with the wings of an eagle
> And the courage of a lion, raised themselves to die for God.
> On the third day of the third month grief was unending:
> On this day was the Torah given us, the fount of our felicity;
> Now on this same day it returned to Heaven, its home,
> Borne by the spirits of those who had lived by and within its word.

The burning of Jews in Blois on 26 May 1171 – thirty-eight Jews died singing their hymn *Alenu* in a wooden tower surrounded by a pyre – is echoed in magnificent songs of lamentation. An unshakeable sense of victory is expressed in the song of the martyrs of Troyes (1288):

> Elle est mise à grand mal, la malheureuse gent;
> Et ce n'est pas si faute, si la rage la prend,
> Car d'entre eux sont brûlés maints preux braves et gens,
> Qui n'ont pu pour leur vie donner rachat d'argent.

No wonder this brave company is enraged: proud and honest men were among those burnt because they could not pay the ransom which would have saved their lives. A pregnant woman dies after her husband. Two brothers are burnt. The little one is frightened of the fire, but the older one comforts him: You are going to Paradise, I swear it!

> Deux frères sont brûlés, un petit et un grand;
> Le plus jeune s'effraie du feu qui lors s'éprend:
> 'Haro! Je brûle entiers,' et l'aîné lui apprend:
> 'Au paradis tu vas aller; j'en suis garant.'

The Passion of Christ is repeated in the suffering of these French Jews in 1288. The older brother comforts the younger with the assurance Christ gave on the Cross to the thief on His right. These Jews knew the Gospel. Did they also know that the Jew Jesus spoke on the Cross the old dying prayers of His (and their) race?

> D'une voix tous ensemble, ils chantaient haut et clair
> Comme des gens de fête qui dussent caracoler.
> Leurs mains étaient liés, ils ne pouvaient baller,
> Jamais on ne vit gcnssi vivement marcher.–
>
> Les prêcheurs sont vcnus, Isaac Cohen quérir:
> Qu'il abjure, ou sinon il lui faudra périr:
> Que me demandez-vous? Pour Dieu je veux mourir.
> Prêtre, je veux l'offrande de mon corps lui offrir.

They sang loud and clear, like people going to a festive dance. Catholic witnesses in the twelfth and thirteenth centuries tell of heretics facing death with joy and singing: in Cologne and Strasbourg, for instance, the joyful demeanour of men, women and children at the moment of death deeply impressed the ecclesiastical chroniclers. The passage in the song of the martyrs of Troyes, plcading that the undeserved death of these martyrs might be avenged, is particularly significant, for it presents a counter-liturgy to the liturgy of the Catholic mass. The preachers (Dominican monks) came to persuade Isaac Cohen (who bears the priest's sacred name) to conversion to Christianity. He refused, preferring to die for God and offer his body as a sacrificial gift. *The true sacrificial lamb (agnus dei) is the people of Israel, the Jew butchered by the Christians.*

The thirteenth century, in particular, furnishes us with many clear instances of such Jewish-Christian confrontations, in which faith clashes against faith. In 1263 a debate concerning the Messiah took place between Rabbi Moise ben Nachman and Paul of Santa Clara – a Jewish apostate turned monk. The rabbi recounts: 'And I answered him: "The prophet says that, when the Messiah comes, the people will beat their swords into ploughshares and their spears into pruning hooks ... Yet ever since the

83

coming of Jesus the world has been full of war and plundering, and the Christians spill more blood than any other nations. Your Jesus is not the true Messiah. The true Messiah will come and gather together the twelve branches of Israel and rebuild the temple. Jesus only destroys. The Messiah will have to rule over all the peoples of the earth: but Jesus was not even master of himself." '

This Jewish reproach reappears today in the Buddhist argument that Christians are not bearers of good tidings, but bearers of violence and discontent wherever they go.

In the thirteenth century, too, we find in a Jewish letter to an apostate – *La missive de Prophiat Duran* – a sharp distinction between the Jewish belief in one God, and the Christian belief in the Trinity and in God's incarnation in Christ. The Jewish author declares that the Christian belief is not compatible with physics, mathematics, logic or with anything the sciences teach us. Nor is the belief in transubstantiation. This Jewish argument is similar to that used by Bertrand Russell in explaining why he is not a Christian.

Modern English anti-Semites who consider the Jews more dangerous to mankind than the atom-bomb (and who amassed a fair proportion of guilt in Palestine in the years 1918–45) like to point out that, until Edward I's 'meritorious' expulsion of the Jews in 1290, England was sucked dry by Jewish money-lenders.

The twelfth-century Jews' House in Lincoln is probably the oldest surviving stone house in England. The first Jewish communities to appear in England were those in Oxford and Cambridge in the eleventh century. The pogroms which resulted from the First Crusade sent the first wave of Jewish refugees from France to England, where, under the protection of the king, they grew rich through usury. The notorious and much maligned 'Jewish money-lender' owes his existence to an ecclesiastical prohibition. The Old Testament and the rabbis forbade the Jewish people to lend at interest, and it was on this Jewish prohibition that St Jerome based the similar Christian prohibition. The Third Lateran Council of 1179 insisted on its observance – and that in a century in which the up and coming Western states, England and France, the fashionable young nobility, the Crusaders, and not least the high clerics all desperately needed money. It could only be acquired through borrowing. And the Jew became the chosen instrument.

The Jews were the property of the king, of the Christian princes. Their position of slavery provided the basis both for their wealth and for their subsequent downfall. As agents of kings and as creditors of feudal lords, bishops and prominent citizens they amassed great capital. Fortresses, castles and churches were built with money borrowed from them. The Jewish quarters in London and in other English towns were adorned with new stone buildings. The English kings possessed great financial skill – inherited from their acquisitive Norman forbears – and they were adept at squeezing their Jews dry. As early as the reign of Henry II it became the established custom to divert to the crown all debts owed to a deceased Jew. But no amount of royal protection could prevent occasional pogroms in this century of Crusades and pathological mass-movements. The ritual-murder scare – first felt in Norwich in 1146 – together with the demagogic preaching of the monks, stirred up aggressive feelings among the common people. The Third Crusade unleashed massacres of Jews in London, York, Norwich, Stamford and King's Lynn. They started outside Westminster Abbey at the coronation of Richard Coeur-de-lion on 3 September 1189, before he set out on Crusade, and reached a climax in York in 1190, after the king had left the country.

Benedict, the first leader of the rich Jewish community in York, lost his life in London, where he had gone to take rich gifts for the coronation of King Richard. The second leader of the York community, Josce, found refuge for his family and other members of the community in Clifford's Tower when his house was stormed. Under the leadership of a Premonstratensian monk the townspeople besieged the Tower. Before the final assault some of the Jews followed the advice of Rabbi Jomtob of Joigny, and the example of German Jews in the Rhineland, and committed suicide. Josce killed his wife Anna and his two sons with his own hand, and then let the rabbi put him to death. This happened in the night of the Great Sabbath, on 17 March 1190. The survivors gave themselves up the next morning, ready to submit to baptism. But the Christians rushed in and killed them all, and then charged into the church and burnt all the promissory notes recording Christians' debts to Jewish money-lenders. To the burning of Jewish houses and the murder of Jews, we can now add the burning of promissory notes as the third form of medieval Jewish persecution.

These are some of the landmarks in the Jews' history of suffering in England, before their final banishment in 1290. On his return from the Crusade, King Richard I instituted a royal Exchequer of the Jews, which was to supervise all money transactions, keeping them under the control of the Crown. English kings turned out to be masters in the art of extorting money from their Jews. King John, nicknamed Lackland, the unhappy signatory of the Magna Carta, that great document of freedom wrung from him by rebellious barons, asked a stiff price from the Jews for their safety. For instance, he demanded 10,000 silver marks from the rich Abraham of Bristol, who had a tooth pulled out every day till he managed to produce the sum. It cost Abraham seven teeth. To escape this arbitrary domination some English Jews emigrated, together with a group of French Jews, to Palestine. It was to some extent the Jews who bore the brunt of the struggle for possession of England between Henry III (1216–72) and his nobles. Oppressed Jews were – on very rare occasions – provoked into demonstrations against the church, as were the Huguenots later in France. In 1268, for instance, a Jew in Oxford seized the crucifix from a priest and stamped on it. Jews in England began to seek permission to leave a land that was becoming increasingly hostile to them. But as the property of the king they were refused this permission: their money was too valuable. The struggle between the king and the rebellious nobles was swallowing up a lot of money, and both sides depended for it on the Jews.

Under Edward I the position of the Jews became even more perilous. In 1275 a ban on all lending at interest crippled the Jewish money-lending business. The famous archbishop of Canterbury, John Peckham, ordered all Jewish places of prayer in London to be closed. Henry III had already appropriated the great London synagogue. One of the most able thinkers in the whole of the Middle Ages, the Franciscan Duns Scotus proposed that Jewish children should be removed from their parents and given a Christian baptism and a Christian upbringing. In the middle of the nineteenth century (1858–60) the abduction and baptism of a Jewish child – the Edgar Mortara affair – led to the foundation of the Alliance Israélite Universelle, an international Jewish aid organisation.

In a letter to the archbishops of Canterbury and York (1286) Pope Honorius IV supported the English royal and church policy towards the Jews. Four years later, on 18 July 1290, Edward I signed a decree ordering all Jews to leave England by I November. He had already banished the Jews from the province of Gascoigne in the South of France. The English Jews went mostly to France, and were driven from there, together with French Jews, in 1306. Smaller groups went to Flanders, Germany and Spain.

And now to the position in France. The burning of the martyrs of Troyes in 1288, ordered by the Inquisition which had found them guilty of ritual murder, was recorded in four contemporary elegies – three in Hebrew, one (from which we have already quoted) in Old French. The martyr now became an institution: he gave his life to glorify the name of the Lord, and he was given the title *Kadosch* – a sort of canonization. In the thirteenth century the constant threat of persecution engendered a specifically Jewish mentality which countered Christian hatred with Jewish hatred. Against the closed Christian church they set up a closed Jewish church, which disastrously imitated the orthodoxy, the exclusivity and intolerance of the Roman Catholic church, which had become increasingly hard of heart under Pope Innocent III and his successors. A narrow and narrow-minded Talmudism, at first centred in Germany, spread to France and Spain. 'It is our duty to destroy, burn and root out the pernicious ideas spread by heretical books, even when their authors wear the mask of piety.' So preached Abba Mari Jarchi, under his French name Don Astruc de Lunel, in Montpelier.

'To destroy, burn, root out' harmful books – Jewish converts to Christianity agitated for the burning of the Talmud in France in the thirteenth century (and again in Germany in the sixteenth century). This book-burning movement, the fatal danger of which was pointed out by Heinrich Heine ('people who burn books will also turn to burning people'), was instigated by the Dominican Nicholas Donin, a baptized Jew from La Rochelle, who denounced the Talmud to Pope Gregory IX in 1239 as a book particularly dangerous to Christians. In 1242 twenty-four cart-loads of Talmud manuscripts were publicly burnt in a Paris square. The German Rabbi Meir von Rothenburg composed an elegy on this burning – a synagogical *Kinnah* which is still sung in synagogues throughout Europe on the *Tish ba' Ab* – the day of mourning dedicated to the Roman destruction of the temple in Jerusalem.

From the time of Philip Augustus – the great architect of the French monarchy, in its struggle with the nobility and the English kings who owned a large part of France in the twelfth and thirteenth centuries – the French kings were mostly oppressors and exploiters of the Jews. King Louis IX (St Louis) hated the Jews for religious reasons. But most of them were more concerned with extorting money from their Jews. This extortion reached a climax under Philip IV. In 1299 Philip, called Le Bel, bought from his brother, Count Charles of Valois, two thousand Jewish land workers for 20,000 livres. He treated them as his serfs, as did Russian landowners their 'souls' (as they called their peasants) in the nineteenth century – and it was not uncommon for them to lose several thousand souls in a night's card-playing.

Philip IV decided in 1306 to take a radical step. He banished all Jews from France, so that he could seize all their property for himself. Royal officials auctioned land belonging to Jews. These 'commissioners of Jewish affairs' received constant exhortations from Paris to carry out their work 'more quickly and thoroughly'. Their 'work', and above all the cold-blooded, large-scale, organized plunder of the Jews by their 'protector', Philip IV, foreshadows in a macabre way what the Jews were to suffer at the hands of their later 'supreme protectors' the German government under Adolf Hitler.

This brutal French king is also famous for his similarly large-scale campaign of destruction against the rich order of the Templars, and for his frequent persecution of Italian financiers, the Lombards. The latter regained the right to return after some years, as did the Jews after nine years. But, until Charles VI finally banished them from France in the year 1394, they constituted only a small group, which never recovered from the heavy blow of 1306. A French Christian folk-song of the time maintained that 'the Jews had acted more honestly than the Christians' and that the land was made poorer by their banishment.

In 1321 a rumour spread through Aquitania that Jews and lepers had sworn to kill all Christians by poisoning wells and springs; and that they had concocted a special poison out of human blood, urine and the juice of three plants. *This is an early form of the conspiracy theory – the theory that Jewry was determined to exterminate the whole of Christianity.* This theory was propounded on the eve of an actual massacre of the Jews themselves. France is *the* place for conspiracy theories. The most successful of them was disseminated throughout Europe by emigrés at the time of the French Revolution, and large areas of Catholicism are still poisoned by it today. This theory maintains that evil forces – freemasons, Jews, Germans, and such like – have been undermining 'pure' France and Christianity, ever since the Middle Ages and are responsible for all revolutions, regicides and subversive actions.

France, which was relatively free of Jews – what few there were lived in seclusion or near the frontiers – up until the French Revolution, nevertheless became the classical land of a classical anti-Semitism. Sermons, passion plays and religious folk literature constantly presented the image of the devilish Jew in a country where most of the population had never actually seen a Jew. The greatest thinkers of France are anti-Semites, or at least have anti-Jewish tendencies, from the Scholastics to the great preachers of the seventeenth and eighteenth centuries, including Bossuet, and from Pascal and Voltaire to Marcel Proust. Even among non-Christians the latent Christian foundation of French anti-Semitism is clearly perceptible.

Giovanni Papini called France the classical land of the Devil. In no other country in Europe, with the possible exception of Spain, has imagination been so concerned with Satan. Poliakov calls the fourteenth century 'the century of the Devil'. In the late Middle Ages saints ardently believing in the existence of the Devil took particular pleasure in persecuting the Jews. One such was St Vincent Ferrier, whose passionate sermons enflamed the masses in France and Spain. At his instigation the first Spanish ghettoes, the *juderías*, were created in 1412, and they were followed by anti-Jewish legislation. The powerful and persuasive Giovanni di Capestrano preached, mainly in Italy, that hell was an indivisible trinity: Antichrist, the Last Judgment, the Jew. His preaching burned with hatred of the Jews. The same was true of Bernadin of Feltre.

Clerics of this sort, even today, are frequently completely apolitical in their outlook and unaware of the complicated social processes involved. They are masters of the simple formula (right up to the militant preachers of the civil war period in Europe, from 1918–45, to Father Lombardi and Father Leppich). The scarifying, demagogical style of their politico-religious preaching set the example for the war-preaching of the eighteenth and nineteenth centuries. Adolf Hitler inherited their methods.

This preaching tirelessly hammered a few frightening images into the minds of the neurotic masses, whose belief in the Devil from the late Middle Ages onwards was commonly stronger than their belief in a benevolent God. An age-old popular Manichaeism was now on the increase, together with despair over a church which, as an *ecclesia judicatrix* – a juridical church of officials and judges – had shown itself incapable of communicating joy, salvation, spiritual health and freedom: a church in which anti-popes were always fighting one another, and in which all favours were exorbitantly priced.

The masses despaired – this is proved a hundred times over by contemporary sources – of the possibility of a Christian life on earth. The worldly clergy seemed as much a prey to the Devil and uncontrolled carnality as the people themselves. Salvation could only be found within monastery walls, if then. The young Luther grew up in this atmosphere. The monasteries produced those passionate ascetics with their imperfectly suppressed instincts and obsessive sexual neuroses, which showed themselves in attacks on the sinful flesh and the lewd and wealthy Jew, the servant of the Devil.

Sexual neurosis, fear of the world, of sin, of their own immature and unemancipated instincts – all these helped to promote the ever-increasing belief in the Devil in the late Middle Ages. This belief demanded sacrifices, visible sacrifices. Witches and Jews were chosen to fulfil this function. Later, Protestants, freemasons, Communists, Socialists and others were alleged to be agents of the Devil and punished as such. *An insatiable appetite for hatred, enormous fears were aroused, channelled and mobilized by preachings against Jews and the Devil.*

In 1298, in a Germany constantly threatened by anarchy after the popef had brought about the downfall of the Hohenstaufen, a man by the name os Rindfleisch began in the little town of Röttingen, in Franconia, to form gangs of murderers, who went from place to place killing Jews and burning down their houses. It was perhaps the first case of genocide in modern Christian Europe. One thing certainly was new: an accusation of sacrilege made against a single Jew was enough to put the whole Jewish population of a particular place in danger of arrest and punishment. The fourteenth century was a century of catastrophes, crises, peasants' revolts and civil wars in the whole of Western Europe, in the Netherlands, in England and in France. Many place-names – such as Judenloch, Judenbühl, Trou-aux-Juifs – commemorate the murder of Jews at this time. The same climate produced the many place-names associated with the Devil: from Spain to Germany there are bridges, mountains, forests and villages named after him. Present-day believers in the Devil in Spain have even gone to the trouble of collecting them all.

The great plague in Europe (1347–9) mobilized the fears which since the twelfth century had oppressed the despairing masses, who no longer found salvation or spiritual reassurance in the 'protective' church. Who was to blame for the plague? The answer was simple; it was the Devil, and the Devil's agents on earth were the Jews. In vain did Pope Clement vi point out in his Bull of September 1348 that Jews died of the plague just as often as Christians, and that the plague raged in areas where there were no Jews. The authority of the popes had reached its lowest ebb in Europe in the fourteenth and fifteenth centuries.

In 1348 Jews were butchered in every town in the German-speaking countries, with the exception of Vienna and Regensburg. German Jews had already lost their civil rights in 1343 – before the plague. Emperor Louis the

Bavarian, who was in continuous conflict with the pope and with his political and ecclesiastical enemies in the Holy Roman Empire and in Italy, put a poll-tax on the Jews and readily accepted the doctrine of their eternal slavery. An international group of Franciscans had gathered at his court, radical Franciscans who were in conflict both with the pope and other groups within their order, on the question of poverty. These Franciscan radicals, fighting for the restoration of the 'poor Christ', the 'poor Franciscan', and renunciation of possessions within the order, saw – at least to some extent – the rich Jew, the usurer, as an incarnation of Satanic corruption.

In this epoch of permanent civil war, peasants' revolts and rebellions, animosity towards the Jews grew out of the massacres themselves. The killing was inspired by fear of the Devil (real or imagined) and followed by loathing. Where there were no Jews they had to be invented – in religious plays and pictures and lampoons. The growth of Christian anti-Semitism in Europe in the late Middle Ages was closely associated with the development of folk art and folk literature. Popular fables, farces, ballads, wood-cuts, broadsheets, pictures in pilgrimage churches, all betray the longing for a legitimate outlet for enormous waves of fear, hate, envy, mockery, greed and aggression, which was found in the Jew.

Even in Italy, a country in which anti-Semitism was rare and, when it occurred, took a moderate form (the Jews were to benefit from this in the Fascist period), the short story *Il Pecorone* (1378) by the Florentine Ser Giovanni Fiorentino presents the Jew as an incarnation of the Devil. In the late fourteenth century Italian artists began to depict Jews as scorpions. We remember the admirable moderation and open-mindedness with which the Scholastic masters – St Thomas Aquinas, for example, his teacher Albertus Magnus and Meister Eckhart – conducted their disputes with their Arab and Jewish teachers, with Averroes and Maimonides. Later illustrations of these disputes give a very different impression. The altar-piece by Francesco Traini in Santa Caterina in Pisa (1345) depicts St Thomas Aquinas' victory over Averroes, and in this Averroes is a tiny figure, lying at the feet of a gigantic St Thomas Aquinas. He is wearing a Jewish emblem on both shoulders, although Averroes was not a Jew. A little Christ sits enthroned above the saint, rays of light leading from His lips to Moses, John and the Evangelists.

The Jew and the Devil – no less a figure than St Thomas Aquinas provided weighty theological arguments for the popular belief in human incarnations of the Devil. He himself believed in the 'child of the Devil': *succubus* (if born of a man and of the Devil in the shape of a woman), or *incubus* (if born of a woman and of the Devil in the shape of a man). He considered the Huns to be descendants of demons (Summa Theol. I, Quaest. LI, art. III, 6). From here it is only a short step to those religio-political ideologies, still alive today, which see in the 'devilish' Eastern nations (associated with the Gog and Magog of Revelation) the triumph of anti-Christ and the threatened domination of the world by the Devil: the Russians, the Bolsheviks, the 'Jewish-Bolsheviks'. This Devil's ideology, brutally exploited by Hitler and by ecclesiastical reactionaries in the twentieth century, goes back basically to the medieval belief in incarnations of the Devil in whole nations as well as in the Jew.

In the fifteenth century, when the spiritual degradation of the people corresponded with the disintegration of almost all ecclesiastical authority (between the Council of Constance 1414–15 and the reign of the Borgia Pope Alexander vi, 1492–1503), the first large epidemics of witch-hunting broke out. The belief in witches was alive in many ancient nations (and is still alive in France today). The Jews of the Old Testament had the witch of Endor and many wicked magicians. Romans, Greeks, Celts and ancient Germans had magicians and witches both good and bad. Long after the end of the Middle Ages they continued to flourish in Italy, where every town and village had its professional sorcerers and witches practising their wicked trade along with panders and prostitutes. But witch mania, witch psychosis, is something quite different. It first appeared in Christian Europe in the late Middle Ages and spread during the time of the Reformation and the religious wars, gaining a particularly firm hold in Protestant countries. Whole social groups, particularly unmarried women, both rich and poor, both outstandingly beautiful and outstandingly ugly women, were its victims: a sinister foreshadowing of the mass-persecution of the Jews.

Nobles, bishops, educated laymen and clerics tried in vain to stem this witch-mania which had seized hold of the ignorant, tormented masses, but Pope Innocent viii gave it the sanction of the church in the Bull *Summis Desiderantes* (1484). Of Innocent viii (Giovanni Battista Cibo) who became pope through simony, a Catholic author (Hans Kühner-Wolfskehl) has written: 'How deeply corrupted and blunted all notions of dignity and principle had become Innocent showed when he married his disreputable bastard son, Franceschetto, to Maddalena de' Medici, the daughter of Lorenzo the Magnificent, celebrating this marriage in the Vatican with as much pomp as in the same year the marriage of his granddaughter Battistina (the daughter of Teodorina) to Luigi d'Aragona of Naples.' Franceschetto took up residence in the Vatican as the official son of the pope; while his father-in-law Lorenzo had his fourteen-year-old son Giovanni de' Medici (later Pope Leo x) appointed cardinal, after he had already been made a protonotary by Sixtus iv at the age of seven.

'Though Innocent summoned a Crusade Council in 1490, he found it more profitable to keep the royal pretender, Dschem (the brother of Sultan Bajasid ii), as a hostage in the Vatican, and to extort money from his family. He incurred an even heavier burden of guilt with his notorious bull on witches, which sanctioned the bloody deeds of two fanatical German Dominican Inquisitors. The primitive mentality which led him to accept the far-fetched stories of these two sinister figures, giving them the opportunity to compose one of the most dreadful works in the whole of literature – the *Hexenhammer* (Witches' Hammer) of 1487, and furthermore his threat of the heaviest ecclesiastical penalties against anyone who interfered in the work of the two villains – these had a more damaging effect than anything else on his reputation and on the respect in which the institution of the papacy was held.'

Innocent VIII complained that all German countries were full of agents of the Devil, sorcerers and witches. The *Hexenhammer* of the two Germans Sprenger and Institoris had his full backing. We can see here a dangerous and calamitous partnership between Rome and German psychopaths, a macabre foretaste of the partnership, in the time of Pope Pius XII, between papal purists and German Catholics, who found themselves fighting in a common cause with Hitler – against the 'Jewish-Bolshevik danger'.

To return to the Devil and his connection with the Jews: the Devil had by this time been given the masculine attributes of horns, claws, tail, goat's beard and lewd, oversized genitals. In fifteenth-century legends the Jews received these new attributes of the Devil and those of sorcerers: horns, tail, goat's beard, and a fiendish smell. German professors of the twentieth century did some research on the *foetor judaicus*, the 'fiendish smell of the Jews' (thus Hans Günther in his *Rassenkunde des judischen Volkes*, Munich, 1930). These German professors can be seen as the descendants of Lutheran theologians, whose Jew-hatred and sexual neuroses derived directly from Luther's own personality, and also of the Roman Catholic intellectuals of late Scholasticism who speculated about the incarnation of the Devil in human form and sexual intercourse between devils and humans. The whole pandemonium of devils and devil-men was given new life at the height of the nineteenth century by one of the most brilliant Catholics in Germany, Joseph von Görres, in his four-volume work *Mystik* (Mysticism).

The German *Walpurgisnacht*, that Witches' Sabbath of the gloom-ridden German soul, found approval and support – on the eve of the Reformation – in Rome. It was an alliance between a helpless Papacy (well aware of the low regard in which it stood in Europe, with troubadour songs in England, France, Italy, Spain and Germany expressing open derision) and an equally helpless German people. The German people felt itself doomed, caught in a death-trap set by the old enemy – the Devil, the Jew, Rome, the pope. (A few decades later the pope himself was depicted in Lutheran propaganda as a devil-Jew, grasping greedily at German souls with his claws, like Rothschild in French anti-Semitic caricatures after 1871.) Since the witch-epidemics of the mid-fifteenth century, since the raging of the supporters of Sprenger's and Institoris's *Hexenhammer*, since Innocent VIII's Bull on witches, Germany was spiritually ripe for the Reformation, for Luther's belief in devils, and

Luther's violently anti-Jewish writings, on which the Nazi Julius Streicher, publisher of *Der Stürmer*, not surprisingly based his defence at the Nuremberg trials.

Pope Innocent VIII died on 25 July 1492. On 2 January of that year Granada, the last outpost of the Moors in Spain, fell to the 'Catholic kings'. The tomb of Innocent VIII in St Peter's is a masterpiece by Pollaiuolo. The inscription – added later – relates that nine days after the pope's death, Columbus set out on his first voyage to 'God's India' – America. Columbus, who was possibly, even probably, of Jewish descent, set out immediately after the banishment of the Jews from Spain.

In both Spain and Germany – the two 'promised lands' of European Jewry – there was a period of the most harmonious and fruitful coexistence between Jews and the native inhabitants: in Spain in the Middle Ages, in Germany in the nineteenth and early twentieth centuries. The catastrophes which befell the Jews in Spain and then in Germany are the greatest Jewish catastrophes since the destruction of the temple in Jerusalem by the Romans.

7

Spain: Heaven and Hell of the Jews

What happened in the past is happening still, and the issues are burning as fiercely as they did four hundred years ago: in the tragic events of the twentieth century Spain is re-living her tragedy of the fifteenth and sixteenth centuries; the Jew is no less a subject of controversy in our age than when the Ecclesiastical Councils of Toledo met in the seventh century or when the stakes were burning at the autos-da-fé in the fifteenth century.

In 1935 President Alcala Zamora of Spain declared: 'This outrage stains our national history to this day.' He was referring to the expulsion of the Jews in 1492. Spanish orthodox Catholics replied that the expulsion was inevitable and necessary for national self-preservation. In 1941 the Arias Montano Institute was opened in Madrid. Among other things it was to look at this cardinal issue scientifically, and determine the past and present significance of the expulsion. In 1959 a history book for primary schools entitled *I am a Spaniard* entered its nineteenth edition. The book, approved by the bishop of Jaén and officially authorized for use in education, tends to instil in the Spanish child a deep hatred of the Jews. As an edifying incident it described the murder of a little boy, St Domingo de Val. 'He was pious, and with his comrades he walked through the town singing songs in praise of the Virgin Mary. That annoyed the Jews more than anything else. And that was why they wanted to kill him.' The Jews (so the book said) crucified the seven-year-old boy, as they had crucified Jesus. Instructions for the use of the book laid down that children should be reminded of all examples of Jewish treachery against the Spanish, starting with the 'betrayal' on the River Guadalete in 711, the scene of Arab victory over the Visigoths, allegedly because they had been betrayed by the Jews.

In 1960 an aristocratic Spanish lady, Isabella Monios, made a journey to Jerusalem. She was the daughter of a pro-Franco general who had been highly decorated during the Spanish Civil War. A Marrano, she had decided to revert to the Jewish faith her ancestors had abandoned in 1492. Openly appealing to her own kinsfolk to return to Judaism, she called on other Spanish Marrano families to do the same.

In 1962 the book *Conspiracy against the Church* appeared in Madrid under the pseudonym of Maurice Pinay, first in Italian for the ecclesiastics of the Vatican Council, and then in 1963 in Spanish and German.

The book purports to show that 'throughout nineteen centuries the church energetically fought against the Jews, which will be proved by means of authentic documents.' It would 'demonstrate that Christ Himself, the Gospels and the Catholic church were among the sources of anti-Semitism...' By condemning anti-Semitism at the Second Vatican Council, the church would damn itself, since it would put numerous ecclesiastical councils, popes and saints in the dock. The book devotes seventy-four pages to the Visigothic Councils of Toledo and their struggle against the Jews alone. Christians are exhorted to fight fanatically against Jews, described as the 'chief enemies of Christendom and the human race'. At the end of the fifteenth century Christianity 'thanks to the Inquisition, was on the point of final victory' over all adversaries of Christendom. But with devilish cunning the Jews managed to extricate themselves with an appeal to Christian charity.

In this book the Vatican Council was urged to resume the old, hallowed methods of the Inquisition – investigation of intermarriage of Christians and Jews so as to purge the church of Jews and their descendants. 'We are convinced that, if today we had a court with methods of investigation as efficient as the tribunal of the Inquisition, we should soon find out how many of these cardinals, archbishops, abbots, canons, priests and monks who so zealously (if hypocritically) promote the advance and triumph of freemasonry and Communism and defend the Jews so much more frantically and effectively than they defend the Holy Church, are themselves Jews.'

The pogroms and massacres of the Jews by the Nazis are described as the fulfilment of God's just laws. The Franciscan Giovanni da Capistrano, who in fifteenth-century Spain and France had preached and acted so successfully against 'the Jewish beast', deserved 'to be regarded as a patron saint by patriotic organizations now fighting against the Jews'.

The description of Spain as the 'second Judaea', the Promised Land of the Jews, was first applied to Moorish Spain. The second time it was used for Christian-Muslim-Jewish Spain – which came under the rule of Christian monarchs in the centuries of the Reconquest. With the Reconquest a golden age began for the Jews. During this 'holy war' Jewish financiers and administrators – as indispensable court bureaucrats and high-ranking officials – rendered incalculable services to the Christian monarchs. In the Christian monarchies of the Spanish peninsula Jews assumed the civic and administrative duties which were slowly evolving in towns and courts of other European countries.

For at least seven hundred years the Christian nobility in Spain (as in Hungary and Poland) considered it undignified to engage in such 'dirty' activities. To them only *iglesia, mar, o casa real* – service in the high ranks of the clergy, at the royal court or overseas – were appropriate to their rank. And so the Jews, playing a vital part in helping the Spanish Christian monarchs to develop their realms, were bound ultimately to become the targets of hate.

Don Alonso de Cartagena, Castile's representative at the Council of Basle in 1434, seems to have been the first to describe the Reconquest officially as a holy war. He probably wanted to demonstrate Castile's precedence over England. This first ideologist of militant Christian Spain was the son of Rabbi Salomon Ha Levi of Burgos.

For their Christian rulers Jewish officials carried out a re-organization in the lands reconquered from the Arabs. In this capacity they can be compared with present-day European experts on development aid working in Tunisia, Morocco and other parts of Africa and Asia. After the Reconquest, the Spanish kings called themselves 'Kings of the Three Religions', and the first to do so was probably Ferdinand III of Castile. Since under these kings Jews occupied the leading positions in administration, finance and the diplomatic service, it might be said that the first proverbial 'proud Spaniard' was a Spanish Jew. Jewish grandees took pride in their wealth, knowledge and consciousness that they were 'the oldest aristocracy of the world'. Spanish Jews preserved this pride throughout centuries of exile from Spain and carried it with them to all parts of the world.

In these exalted positions Jews could get from their kings mosques, which were first converted into synagogues and later into churches. To Spanish children a synagogue even now is a 'mosque dedicated to Christian worship'. During the golden age of the Spain of the three religions, the 'three nations' gave a ceremonial welcome to King Alfonso III, each people greeting him in its own language. In this period of Spanish history intermixture developed on a broad scale. Jews acted as godparents at Christian baptisms. Gentiles took part in Jewish rites. Jewish women were hired as attendants at Christian weddings. Spanish Christians liked listening to the sermons of learned rabbis – right up to the eve of the expulsions of 1492. Jews attended Christian services, heard Christian sermons, and Jews and Gentiles joined in prayer. But a decision by the Ecclesiastical Council in 1322 criticized this practice. As late as 1449 Christians and Jews marched in solemn procession through Seville, with Jews carrying their Torah. The procession – to ward off the plague – was organized with the archbishop's permission. Pope Nicholas V afterwards protested against it.

Before the unhappy fourteenth century, conversions of Jews to Christianity were very rare. Jews played an important role as tutors. From the early days they cultivated Spanish, which thus became the leading language in European literature. Spanish Jews of those days had a profound distaste for Latin. Friendly relations between rabbis and Christian theologians formed the foundation for the works of Ramón Lull, the great Spanish mystic and poet.

'Great is the Jewish nation of Spain' : the leading Jewish families of Toledo and Barcelona took pride in their descent from King David and in the purity of their families – even after conversion to Christianity. This was attested by the rabbi of Burgos, Salomon Ha Levi, after his conversion in 1391, in a polemic on the origin and nobility of his family. To this day Spanish Jews detest Salomon Ha Levi, while Christian Spaniards honour his memory.

Like many of his co-religionists and fellow rabbis, the learned Salomon Ha Levi was familiar with Christian teachings (just as in the nineteenth century German Jews knew Schiller, Goethe, Kant and German idealistic philosophy). Highly educated Spanish Jews who had spent all their lives among Christians had few scruples about becoming converts if necessary. It did not mean that in their hearts they had abandoned their Jewish origin. The Aristotelian Rabbi Salomon Ha Levi became a bishop. He took his new name from the Jew St Paul and called himself Pablo de Santa Maria, being convinced that, like the mother of Jesus, he was a descendant of the family of Levi.

This bi-polarity of the voluntarily converted Spanish Jew was variously affected when compulsory conversions began. In Christian monks and theologians of Jewish origin the Messianic feeling greatly enriched their Christian belief: such was the experience of the great theologian and poet Luis de León, who recalled his Jewish ancestry as he lay in the prison to which the Inquisition had consigned him. The same consciousness of being Jewish strengthened the resolve of other forced converts surreptitiously to remain Jewish in their private and family life. The masses of the Christian population saw something sinister in this Jewish-Christian bi-polarity and the elliptical life of Jewish *conversos*, for whom the Catholic psalter was a repository of a more ancient wisdom and an expression of Israel's yearnings.

In the thirteenth century the kingdom of Aragon, with its Jews, occupied a leading position in Spain: in the fourteenth century this role was taken over by Castile, the land of castles and mountains, whose centre was Burgos. Jewish *almojarifes*, the king's tax gatherers and financiers, were inevitably involved in the struggles among the various cliques of the nobility and their followers. (Spain remains to this day a land of civil wars.) The career of the *almojarife* Joseph Benveniste, confidant of the young King Alfonso XI (1325–1350), reminds one of Feuchtwanger's *Jew Suess:* a proud and haughty Jew, who in his time played host to the leading nobles of the country, ends up in prison after a series of intrigues.

The high living and often arrogant attitude of Jewish *privados*, the king's confidants, their rise to power and sometimes sensational fall, caused anxiety not least to the Jewish communities themselves. In 1415 Salomo Alami declared in his *Writ of Indictment* – an early example of Jewish self-criticism which, incidentally, has been going on especially in Spain since the end of the fourteenth century to the present day: 'The life which many representatives of our society were leading was by no means honest. These nobles posed as leaders (of Jewry) at the royal courts. The kings raised them to high office and entrusted them with the keys to their treasury; but the wealth these Jews acquired made them arrogant; and they no longer wanted to be reminded of their former poverty and degradation. They had palaces built, harnessed the most magnificent mules to their carriages, and their wives and daughters began to dress up like noble ladies and flaunt their jewellery. These people were contemptuous of learning [i.e., rabbinical study of the Bible], work and handicrafts, and they preferred idleness, arrogance and ostentatious pomp . . . . At the same time they were jealous of one another and slandered each other before the kings and high nobility, not realizing that they were thereby causing their own ruin . . . But they exploited and robbed the little man. Their sole aim was to shake off the burdensome taxes and get the poor to pay them. Their entire conduct degraded them in the eyes of their enemies, who were only waiting for an opportunity to get rid of them and chase them with scorn and contempt from the palaces of the kings and nobles.'

This illustrates the abyss between the ordinary and humble Jewish people and a thin layer of parvenus. It is the tragedy of the Jew whose assimilation appears suspect. Sephardic Spanish Jews managed to uphold their special position even until the days of the Nazi concentration camps at Terezin. Haughty Spanish and West European Jews in England, France, Holland and Germany held aloof from the poor Jewish immigrants from Eastern Europe. A small, wealthy and influential upper layer of Jews succeeded in buying their freedom from the murderers in Germany, Hungary and other European countries occupied by the armies and bureaucrats of the Nazi apparatus of annihilation. In effect they bought their liberty at the expense of the millions who were sent to the gas chambers.

In the increasingly explosive fourteenth century it was in Spain in particular that some very outspoken debates took place between Christians and Jews; and the Christian side was often represented by newly-converted Jews. Moses de Tordesillas, a distinguished Jewish scholar of Christian theology, warned the Jews against excessive candour. In a guide to discussion which he sent to the Jewish community of Toledo he wrote: 'The Christians have power, and they can silence truth by a single blow.'

The first blow fell in 1391, which became a year of massive persecution and suppression of the Jews in Spain. Clerics preached against the Jewish menace: Christian Spain, they said, would perish unless it purged itself of Jews and Moors. Their property must go over to the Christians. This slogan proved of great appeal to the masses and the impoverished lower nobility. Ferrand Martinez, archdeacon of Seville Cathedral, raised the spectre of a Jewish plot: the Jews would enslave all Spain and before long they would make all

Christians, from the king down to the last Spanish citizen, their docile tools. Ferrand Martinez was apparently quite unaware of the fact that his argument was a complete reversal of the learned scholars' prevailing theory about the 'eternal serfdom' of the Jews, whom God had presented to the church and Christian princes as slaves and tools. Kings and archbishops defended the Jews against these fanatics. But when in 1390 the king and the archbishop of Seville died, Martinez gained the upper hand in the bishopric and, as former father confessor to the new regent, Queen Mother Leonora, he acquired great political power. (Bigoted queens, female regents and princesses have always played an important role in anti-Jewish legislation.) Against the will of the royal authorities, which stood for peace and order, Martinez succeeded in stirring up the populace in Seville by his perpetual agitation and inflammatory sermons. On 6 June 1391 they stormed the *Juderia*, the Jewish quarter. Some four thousand Jews were beaten to death, many others were sold into Arab slavery and some accepted baptism.

The conflagration quickly spread from Seville to Cordoba, where the streets were littered with the corpses of two thousand men, women and children. In Toledo the rabbis were the first to meet their death in the name of their God. About seventy Jewish communities in Old and New Castile were devastated. From Castile the fire spread to Aragon and then to Majorca. In Palma de Majorca not only were the Jews murdered, but the houses of Christians who had sheltered them from persecution were stormed. It was here, 540 years later, that Georges Bernanos, a pupil of the French Jew-baiter Drumont, witnessed the bestial killing by Spanish Fascists of Christians who opposed Franco – and the ecclesiastical authorities did nothing to intervene. Bernanos, a Frenchman with a militant right-wing background, at last had his eyes opened to the 'huge cemeteries in the moonlight' and the silence of church leaders in the face of blatant mass murder.

But the most momentous sequel to the bloodshed of 1391 was this: overwhelmed by the sudden explosion of terror, tens of thousands of Jews submitted to baptism. They were Spanish Jews who for centuries had been accustomed to living in peace with their Christian brothers. Christianity was not unknown to them; they were familiar with its teachings, usages, festivals and rituals, in many of which they had quite often taken a part. This intimate acquaintance with Christianity worked together with the sudden shock to produce a chain reaction of compulsory conversions. The enforced baptisms – which were only an emergency solution – contributed to the creation of a terrible problem: from then on and for generations, even centuries to come, Spanish Jews were simultaneously Christians and Jews – Christians in public worship, Jews in carefully preserved family traditions, hidden from the outside world.

Spanish Jewry was now faced with a dual danger: on the one hand, it might be submerged in Christianity through friendly relations; on the other, its 'little flock' had to be shielded against apostacy and baptism. In this situation the Jews protected themselves by an orthodoxy which became increasingly rigorous throughout the fourteenth and fifteenth centuries. This Spanish orthodoxy solemnly renounced all later Jewish 'interpretations' and the teachings of Maimonides. It disowned the epoch of Jewish co-existence and the dialogue with Moors and Christians. In its struggle against Jewish heretics – nonconformist and worldly elements – the Spanish rabbis received strong support from Germany. From the late Middle Ages onwards Germany was the bulwark of a hard, narrow-minded and intolerant Talmudism whose ghetto outlook (turning a bitter need into a doubtful virtue) grew in fanaticism with Christian exclusivity. Such are the dreadful concepts which persecutors breed in their victims. The Jews were facing the dawn of a gloomy, anguished middle age, which was to last nearly up to the French Revolution of 1789.

The year 1413–14 – the 'Year of Apostasy' as devout Jews came to call it later – marked a sinister start to the fifteenth century. Rabbis were tortured, subjected to the terror of brain-washing and forced into baptism. The Spanish anti-pope, Benedict XIII, who had been excommunicated by the Council of Pisa in 1409, sought his rehabilitation by attempting something that hardly anyone had achieved so far: a mass conversion of Spanish Jews. Under the influence and with the collaboration of his personal physician, the distinguished Talmudist Josua of Lorca, who as a Christian had assumed the evocative name of Jerome of the Sacred Faith – Geronimo de Santa Fe – he decided to challenge the rabbis to a public debate. With the consent of the king, the Jewish communities of Aragon were ordered to send their chief rabbis and scholars to Tortosa. The debate began in February 1413 under the leadership of Benedict XIII and continued in sixty-nine sessions till November 1414. Since it failed to induce the assembled Jews to become converts, scores of compulsorily baptized Jews were brought from various towns to Tortosa and compelled to recite in chorus before the Jewish leaders the formula of abandonment of the Jewish faith. For Benedict this Jewish Christian Council proved a total débâcle. In the following year he was condemned by the Council of Constance as being chiefly responsible for the schism of the church. It was solemnly decided that he, 'a withered branch of the tree of the Catholic Church, must be cut off'. The offensive against the Jews was called off. They were granted a respite in Spain which lasted until the middle of the century.

What was Spain like in the fifteenth century? From that time to this day Spain has subscribed to the maxim: one state, one faith, one Spanish race. This meant that Spain's purity must be preserved by repeated acts of self-purification. All Jews, and descendants of Jews all Moors and their descendants, all heretics, all who denied the 'pure doctrines' of the church (the church of Spain, which often was at odds with Rome) had to be exterminated or at least banished.

Man himself became the battlefield: from now on every true Spaniard, every nobleman, had the duty as a hidalgo (i.e. *hijo de algo*, son of a 'somebody') to cleanse himself every day of his life of all impurities of blood and thought. The orthodox Spaniard is one who is perpetually suppressing the Jew, the Marrano and the heretic in his own heart, often at terrible cost.

At the start of the fifteenth century, Spain (excluding the small kingdoms of Granada and Navarra) had a population of about eight and a half million. Of these, seven million lived on the land, in various degrees of dependence on their ecclesiastical and secular landlords. One and a half million of the peasants were Muslim Moriscos, descendants of Moors. It must be remembered that most of the Moors in Spain were themselves of Spanish-Christian origin and had been converted to Islam by the small band of true Moors who conquered the country. The town population was estimated at about one and a half million, of which ten per cent were members of the aristocracy and the upper class. Seventy per cent belonged to the *pueblo menudo*, the lower classes who as *menu peuple* in France or *piccola gente* in Italy have taken part in many urban uprisings since the Middle Ages. They correspond to the German *Kleinbürger* and dispossessed middle class which were the first sections of the nation to be affected by Hitler's mobilization.

The vast vacuum between aristocracy and lower class was filled by the clergy and the Jews. Jews formed the middle class, the bourgeoisie. It was a property-owning section whose wealth, or even only modest comfort, was a constant temptation to the thousands of have-nots and mendicant friars. The driving force against them was the lower clergy, a poor, ignorant unsettled band of men who played much the same part in the struggle against the Jews as restless, semi-educated Christian *literati*, teachers and frustrated petty officials in Alexandria in the fourth century, Paris in 1880, and in Berlin, Munich and Vienna in 1930.

In the late fifteenth century the Jewish chronicler Ibn Verga wrote in a critical analysis of anti-Semitism in Spain that the lower classes hated the rich Jews for their exclusivity and arrogance. These Jews had entered the country as paupers; but now the once wealthy Christians were poor and the Jews were rich. The Verga lists six causes for anti-Semitism, as defined by a Christian king. They include the following questions: Why do Jews teach their children to sing when they ought to be weeping and mourning all their lives? Why do they have their sons instructed in fencing, when they do not go to war? Why do they wear princely gowns and so arouse envy and hatred? In 1432 Jewish local councillors decided to launch an austerity programme (similar in intention to the British austerity measures in 1945). All Spanish Jews were urged to wage war on luxury and all forms of ostentation offensive to the Christians.

But the problem of the Marranos was much more serious. The name may be derived from the old Castilian *marrano* (swine) or perhaps from the Arabic *mahran* (forbidden). The Marranos, the accursed, the swine, the damned, were (it may be recalled) those compulsorily converted Jews and their descendants who outwardly had become Christians but in their hearts and within the bosom of their families remained Jews. Coerced in the fourteenth and early fifteenth centuries by acts of terror, they considered themselves slaves of the church, *Anussim*, and did not have their children baptized. When forced to do so, they washed off the holy water after the ceremony. They met secretly in the synagogue, celebrated Jewish feast days, observed the Sabbath (God's Rest, the holy axis of cosmic order, 'Israel's greatest gift to the world') and Jewish diet laws. As early as 1429 the Council of Tortosa turned against these 'Judaizers'. Just as in Cologne in the twelfth century the 'heretics' met in underground vaults, so the Marranos held their religious services more and more often in barns, remote houses and subterranean halls. And driven into ever greater secrecy, they passed on their legacy: 'Honour Christ with your lips, but serve God with your heart; pretend to be a Christian but secretly remain a Jew.'

The schizophrenic, split-personality European first became reality in the Marrano. He was born between semblance and truth, external conformity and inner rebellion. A split personality can take various forms. It can, for instance, explode into hatred. Spanish Marranos rejoiced in the fall of Constantinople in 1453 because, they thought, it heralded the coming of the Messiah. He would destroy the Christian churches and honour the synagogues. In Marrano prayers, discovered in the archives of the Inquisition, two Gods, two religions and two forms of worship, old Jewish and Christian liturgy, prayer and dogma, intermingle and clash. Sensitive Marranos took refuge in the peace of the monastery and became preferably Jeronomites. This, the wealthiest order in Spain became, with its devotion to learning and religious thought – at least temporarily – the sanctuary of the Marranos. Others went to Rome. (Later Ignatius Loyola deliberately brought Spanish Jews to Rome, where he enlisted them in the Society of Jesus.) This of course heightened Rome's age-old animosity to Spain. Rome regarded all Spaniards as either Jews or heretics, or both.

Yet other Marranos, especially those of high theological and philosophical education, became aggressive atheists. (European atheism is a direct offspring of European Christian theology, as Leibniz pointed out.) They wrote in Hebrew about the 'three deceivers': Abraham, Jesus and Mohammed. Among a people so profoundly divided, both within and without, the two religions, Judaism and Christianity, dissolved into festering, cankerous growths. Jewish self-hatred encountered and mingled with Christian self-hatred; Jewish doubts about faith reinforced Christian questioning of faith. Marranos became radical exponents of Reason. The Marrano Job accused God and Man, and endeavoured to see through both: the false heaven above and the false, murderous hierarchical structure below.

In this tormented Spain confessional hatred turned into pure race hatred: Christians hated Jews, Marranos, Moors and Moriscos, the converted descendants of Moors. And against this race hatred Pope Nicholas v and Bishop Alonso de Cartagena, the son of the former rabbi, and Bishop Pablo de Santa Maria appealed in vain.

This was the hour of the Inquisition. King Ferdinand the Catholic had Jewish blood. By virtue of their Portuguese connections the *reyes catolicos*, King Ferdinand and Queen Isabella, and their descendants (the Hapsburgs) were closely related to Jews. In both Spain and Portugal descendants of Jews played an important role in the Inquisition. To this day the shadow of the Castilian Inquisition lies over the land. De Maistre and his political disciples are still convinced that the Inquisition saved Spain for ever. In 1814 Ferdinand vii revived the Inquisition. And in 1948 twelve Spanish Catholics sent a letter to a Protestant pastor, informing him that they had decided personally to eradicate heresy in their town: 'Do not compel us to soil our hands with your blood. For even if the Holy Inquisition has officially been terminated, it continues in the mind of the nation . . .'

The Spanish Inquisition developed the technique of brainwashing to perfection. It was, after all, able to work on eminently suitable human 'material' – Marranos, New Christians, Judaizers, Moors, Moriscos and heretics on both sides. The technique of brainwashing: make your victim suffer, humiliate him, lower his power of resistance and reduce him to a near-infantile state of mind. (Later, ex-Jesuits pointed out that similar practices aimed at the transformation of a man's personality could be found in St Ignatius Loyola's spiritual exercises). It is terror and persuasion – the *and* is most important – the combination of constant threatening with sweet and gentle persuasion: *fortiter in re, suaviter in modo*. When the will is broken, the tortured victim can be 'made' into a new man. This difficult and laborious operation can sometimes be made to succeed, sometimes not.

The Inquisition in Castile was instituted by a papal bull of 1478. It was conceived as an instrument of the kings of Spain with a view to unifying their country and purging it of 'impure elements' and 'subversive' subjects. But the kings, cardinals, bishops and aristocrats (both secular and ecclesiastical) often lost control of it, for it created a vast bureaucracy and could be used to whip up jealousy and greed among the masses and all who were interested in confiscating the property of Jews and heretics.

To begin with, the Spanish Inquisition operated only in Castile. First it decreed a strict distinction between *conversos* (Jewish New Christians) and professed Jews. Heretics were invited to denounce themselves. They were given a thirty-day 'term of grace'. 'Good Catholics' (meaning to the papal purists of Rome in the nineteenth and even in the twentieth century Catholics who in their own country – that is to say Rome – denounce as dangerous as many theologians and laymen as possible) were ordered to report all 'suspect subjects', even their own fathers and mothers. In the service of the terrorist Hitler, the Gestapo used the very same methods of inciting children against their actual parents for the benefit of an abstract parentage: in the one case 'spiritual father' and 'mother church'; in the other 'fatherland' and 'mother party'.

The church handed the guilty over to the secular power to be burnt at the stake. Justification for this procedure was found in the Gospel according to St John (15, 5–6): 'I am the vine . . . If a man abide not in me, he is cast forth as a branch, and is withered; and men gather them, and cast them into the fire, and they are burned.' Justification for the all-important confiscation of property was found in the story of Adam and Eve, the first heretics, cast from the Garden of Eden. Greed for the possessions of Jews, Marranos and heretics time and again rekindled the dying flames of inquisitorial proceedings.

The theoreticians of the Inquisition, who were under the spell of St Augustine's teachings, regarded original sin and heresy almost as one and the same thing: a dreadful stain on the human race, a plague to be rooted out by fire. The Spanish Inquisition had many facets: one of them was that of a huge and highly accurate machine, carefully and bureaucratically controlled, which after long years of processing either ejected or absorbed its victims. Kafka, in his novels *The Castle* and *The Trial*, describing Jewish-Christian Prague, offered an inspired insight into the essence of Spanish Inquisition bureaucracy.

Another aspect of the Spanish Inquisition was the insatiable greed of individual inquisitors. A huge fortune was gathered from confiscated wealth. Occasionally the very rich were able to buy their freedom. There existed a kind of 'honorary Aryan', as in the days of Hitler and Goering. (Even Hitler, the arch-torturer and murderer, 'aryanized' nearly 340 Jews.) But, as happened earlier in the thirteenth century in neighbouring Provence, the excessive zeal of the Inquisition could turn against the inquisitors themselves: the mob stormed the prisons of the Inquisition and burned its archives. Many Spanish Catholics, angered by the Inquisition, had themselves circumcized and became Jews.

On 2 January 1492 the Catholic King Ferdinand and Queen Isabella made their entry into Granada. The last Moorish principality in Spain had fallen. On 31 March they issued an edict expelling the Jews from Spain. The reason given was that the Jews were seducing the New Christians to embrace Judaism. On the day the expelled Jews left Spain, Christopher Columbus –

who is presumed to be of Jewish descent – set sail. Many years later, in a letter to the Catholic monarchs, he linked his first voyage with the expulsion of the Jews. His son Fernando was meanwhile engaged on a hunt for prohibited writings of religious nonconformists, seeking in Brussels, Venice and other places additions to his library. Jewish friends and colleagues enabled Columbus to undertake his historic voyage: Diego de Deza helped him prepare his great plan, and the king's financiers, Abraham Senior, Abarbanel and Gabriel Sanchez, gave him money. The Marrano Luis de Santangel, a high state official, won over Queen Isabella for Columbus' project by personally raising five million marevedis. Columbus compared himself with David and Moses, and likened his first trip to America to the exodus from Egypt. (Some of his Franciscan enemies called him King Pharaoh.) 'I am a servant of the same Lord who raised David to this rank,' wrote Columbus in a letter to the tutor of Don Juan. His son Fernando, writing about the 'secret' of Columbus' descent, also compared his father with King David.

The tremendous mental strain, the constant fear of being unmasked as a Jew, an improperly converted Jew, steeled Columbus' will to succeed and kept him in a perpetual state of anxiety. Even in Hispaniola, the place of destiny for Las Casas, rebellious Spaniards in 1498 cast his Jewish descent in his teeth. Columbus had to change his tack with great circumspection to avoid the stake and the gallows. In 1489, when he was already sailing in the service of the Catholic monarchs, the Inquisition in Tarragona sentenced three baptized people of the name of Colon (Colombus' Spanish name was Cristobal Colon) for engaging in Jewish ritual practices. Colon-Colombus' scientific knowledge was based on the Jewish-Catalan tradition of cosmography and on the knowledge of making instruments which he had gained in Portugal, where many learned Jews, astronomers and cartographers, were employed by Prince Henry in Sagres. There the spirit of religious tolerance was still alive. Columbus wrote to his monarchs: 'I maintain that the Holy Ghost can manifest itself in Christians, Jews, Moors and all kinds of people, and not only in the wise but also in the simple-hearted.'

As a young man Columbus was struck by a passage in the Spanish-born Seneca's *Medea*, which he interpreted as follows: 'When the world gets old, it will be time for the Ocean to loosen its grip. A new land will appear and a new seafarer will come. He will discover a new world . . .' This prophecy of the ancient Sybil (as one may put it) merged in his mind with the ancient Messianic element in the Jewish prophets, which, as we shall shortly see, was to set in train two other world-wide 'youth movements': the Jewish-Spanish illuminists and the early Jesuits.

Esdras and Isaiah guided Columbus across the seas into the Promised Land. He dreamed of discovering the Western passage to India for his king; there he would visit the priest-king Prester John, and conclude a holy alliance with him which would apply a pincer movement against the number one enemy of the world, Islam, from India on the one side and Spain on the other. After the defeat of this world enemy he, Columbus, would establish the Messiah's realm of peace in Jerusalem.

The discovery of America sprang from the spirit of Jewish Utopia and was inspired by all the fervour of Jewish Messianic faith. In 1502 Columbus wrote to the Catholic monarchs: 'In carrying out my Indian venture I was helped neither by my intelligence nor mathematics, nor even by the map of the world. All that happened was simply that Isaiah's prophecy found its splendid fulfilment.' In 1501 Columbus calculated that the end of the world could come in a hundred and fifty-five years. This meant that by that time the many prophecies of the Old and New Testaments would have to come true. Deposed as viceroy, Columbus collected prophecies to prove that Spain should and must liberate Jerusalem. 'The Abbot Joachim said it would be someone coming from Spain.' Abbot Joachim of Fiore had predicted a 'third age' of the Holy Ghost, characterized by love, which would supersede the 'ages' of the Father (fear of the law) and of the Son (grace and faith). From the thirteenth to the nineteenth century, this Abbot Joachim exercised a mysterious power whose radiating force could only be compared with that of Origen. He lived under the Hohenstaufen in southern Italy, the battlefield of the popes and Emperor Henry v and a melting pot of Greek, Arabic and Jewish spirit and culture. Abbot Joachim's haughty Messianic attitude, and later especially that of his left-wing Franciscan disciples, led to several crises in the Franciscan order and disaster among his spiritual heirs. The abbot, who had quickly become suspect to the church, was accused of being of Jewish origin.

Columbus soon found help and shelter among the Franciscans, an order that is still fanatically anti-Semitic. (It was a Franciscan who paved the way to South America for Adolf Eichmann, knowing full well who he was.) But Franciscans following the Catalan tradition of Joachim of Fiore and his spiritual disciples, such as Antonio de Marchena and Juan Perez, helped Columbus to launch the expedition which was to lead to the discovery of America.

Columbus first set foot on Castilian soil wearing the robes of a Franciscan monk. It was Columbus who started the exodus to America of Franciscan spiritualists and believers in Utopia, of Erasmists like Diego Mendez de Segura, Marranos and the sons of Spanish itinerant shepherds – a very varied conglomeration of religious feeling and thought.

The discovery of America by Columbus is unthinkable without the groundwork and help of Jews and Jewish-Christians in every field – economic, scientific and political. It was a parallel phenomenon to the Jewish exodus from Spain. For this expedition a Messianic faith was mobilized which in the same epoch and during the next two generations inspired two other great developments: a revival movement which was first confined to Spain alone; and then what Eugen Rosenstock called the exuberance, the *synblysma*, of the early Jesuits.

Rabbi Leo Baeck, leader of the elders of the Jewish community in Berlin, who was later taken to Terezin concentration camp, once described Christianity as the romantic youth movement of Judaism. What is the relationship between romanticism and Judaism? The great early romanticists of Germany – associated with Novalis, the two Schlegel brothers and their periodical *Athenaeum* – aimed at 'world revolution' (a term later coined by Heine and modelled on English and French examples). Such a revolution would totally change the human character and all aspects of the living world. This romanticism had nothing or very little to do with the petty bourgeois pseudo-Gothic romanticism of later years, or with the romanticism of aristocratic refugees from the French Revolution, fleeing from the dawn of modern times. It was a youthful romanticism, which was at home in Berlin in the salons of Jewish and Jewish-Christian ladies. The Spanish revival movement in the time between 1480 and 1550 was also to some extent the work of men and women of Jewish descent.

Besides the Jewish New Christians and Marranos of whom we have already spoken, there were other Jewish-Christians in Spain who brought all the fervour of their Jewish faith, especially the Messianic element, into their young Christian religion. These people sometimes became fanatics – fanatical anti-Semites, tools of the Inquisition, preachers who misled the people into persecution of the Jews. But some of them became devout men of prayer, monks, Christian mystics, humanists and church reformers. It was a conciliatory form of Catholicism based on the teachings of Erasmus of Rotterdam and aimed at reviving the withered religious branches of a barren Spain with the spring waters of a Christian humanism that did justice both to God and Man. Long before Europe split into two hostile camps, Roman Catholic and Lutheran, long before the mighty river of the Reformation divided and was deflected into a variety of channels, there did exist this one inwardly pure and variegated European reform movement in Spain. It aimed at a return to the sources of the Bible in both Testaments. (How attractive must this slogan have been to Jewish New Christians – the *conversos*!) Back to the purity of the simple evangelical faith : this was what should be preached to the simple man, to the peasant, by missionaries (including laymen) inspired with the message of the Gospels. Back to the sources – this meant new and purified editions of the Bible; it meant combining all the wisdom of antiquity, of the devout pagans of Greece and Rome, with the gentle wisdom of God and Man contained in the Gospels. A threefold reformation was involved : reformation of the soul and reformation of the individual personality which was to be achieved by daily instruction and Bible readings. And this called for a reform of studies (early Franciscan reformers around Ramon Lull had already in the thirteenth century called for trilingual education for Christians, Jews and Muslims). The reformation of the individual personality served both church and nation : Spain was to be wrenched from her ghetto-like existence and made accessible to the whole intellectual world.

Jewish New Christians in Spain above all flung themselves into this revivalist movement with a Messianic zeal comparable to the fervour with which German Jews in the nineteenth and early twentieth centuries set about social and political reforms. To some of them it brought death. The confused, bewildered men of the Inquisition and a rigid church order fished among the religious enthusiasts for presumed heretics. It is in the nature of great reform movements that very often what is to become orthodox or unorthodox, which people are right and which wrong, is far from clear at the beginning. Tomorrow's victor is the one who decides what must be rejected as heretic and what may be accepted as orthodox. This is what happened in the second to the fourth centuries to Origen: stigmatized eventually as a heretic, his influence lived on underground and made him the secret spiritual father of European development.

There was quite a possibility, indeed at times a definite danger, that the revivalist movement might be submerged in the welter of nonconformist movements and share the fate of the Waldenses, if not the Albigenses. But by his intellect, toughness, patience and circumspection Ignatius Loyola, a Basque of ancient lineage, was able to free himself and his young Society of Jesus from the clutches and fires of the Inquisition and the mortal enmity of the pope. Ignatius categorically forbade all members of the Society of Jesus to work with the Inquisition. He was the only great ecclesiastic during the incipient Counter-Reformation in Spain who thought nothing of *limpieza de sangre*, the purity of blood on which the Inquisition insisted.

The task of the Inquisition in Spain was made easier in various ways. In their exuberance some individuals or small groups of religious enthusiasts went much too far for their attitude to be acceptable to orthodox clerics of the time. Their zeal, their missionary devotion and Messianic faith were unmistakably Jewish in origin. And mendicant friars, inquisitors and the mob recognized and attacked them as Jews.

'*Dadnos, hermanos, de vuestras obras, y tomad de nuestra fe.*' 'Brethren, give us of your good works and receive in return our faith.' Thus spoke Hernando de Talavera at the fall of Granada in 1492, addressing himself to the Moors, those 'good pagans' whose lives (as he freely admitted) were so much more Christian than those of many Christians. Hernando de Talavera, Queen Isabella's counsellor and confessor and first archbishop of Granada, was of Jewish descent. He was a friend of Ximenes, the first patron of the great reform movement in Spain.

The Franciscan Francisco Ximenez de Cisneros, the Queen's confessor from 1492, primate of Spain from 1495, Grand Inquisitor from 1507, struggled for twenty years for an inner renewal of the Spanish church. His opponents were the indolent, wealthy ecclesiastic nobles who did not regard such a rebirth as necessary. In 1498 Ximenes founded the university of Alcala de Henares, where there were to be chairs in Greek, Hebrew, Arabic and Syriac. In his palace Ximenes set up a small academy for Bible studies, and from 1502 onwards engaged humanists to work with him. On 10 July 1517 (Luther's year) the entire Polyglot Bible was ready in print – in Latin, Greek and Hebrew. This work of baptized Jews and humanists trained in Paris and Venice was designed to convert Spain to the 'pure Gospel'. But then Ximenes died. His protégés were defamed as Lutherans and denounced and persecuted as *alumbrados* (or Illuminists).

In his old age Hernando de Talavera, Ximenes's friend, learned Arabic, used revolutionary methods of popular liturgy and ordered his clergy to preach to the Moors in Arabic. Many of the Jewish New Christians in his entourage were full of prophet-like zeal to convert the whole world as quickly and thoroughly as possible. They also brought to their new office the knowledge and education of an enlightened Arab-Jewish intelligentsia. Some of them inclined towards illuminism. In a sense the Illuminists stood half-way between a Catholic piety and a spirit of enlightenment. They combined traits of Islamic mysticism, 'evangelical' fervour and belief in grace with a critical attitude, derived from Erasmist humanism, towards corruption in the church and the martial lust of Christian princes. One of the friends of the Illuminist Fray Melchor (Melchior) was Ximenes's chaplain, the Jew Juan de Cazalla, later bishop of Verissa and one of the most illustrious Franciscans of his day. Fray Melchor himself came from a Jewish family of business aristocrats in Burgos, who were in constant touch with Bruges and London. Melchor spent his youth at the English court. Then he had a 'call' – such Pauline 'awakenings' were not rare among this type of convert – and, after going through all the Spanish orders, became a Franciscan. Filled with Messianic ecstasy he proclaimed his prophecies, invoking St Francis and the Fraticelli of the fourteenth century. In five years, he prophesied, the great rebirth of Christianity would come; the Roman Empire and the kingdoms of Europe would tumble. The pope and the ecclesiastics would be killed. Only those Christian princes and clerics who took part in the great work of renovation would be saved. The church would make its home in Jerusalem. And then the human race would live in virtue and happiness on this earth. The man chosen by God to perform this great task of liquidation and reformation was Melchor himself. Heavenly Jerusalem would be God's empire on earth.

And now to more modern times: the Messianic faith of the Jews and the Old Testament-based Messianic belief of the Christians were an essential ingredient of European revolutions between the sixteenth and twentieth centuries. Revolutionary Puritanism in England and Scotland fed on this belief in a Messianic mission. On the eve of the French Revolution in 1789, Paris overflowed with Messianic enthusiasts who had much in common with Fray Melchor's type of Illuminists. In modern times numerous Communist magazines unwittingly remind us that in the nineteenth and twentieth centuries it was the Jewish intelligentsia, inspired by Messianic faith, who became involved in all types of Socialism and Communism. The exodus of this intelligentsia from Communism – when it became a closed church with its own inquisition under Stalin – was marked by the same critical enthusiasm and the same Messianic zeal as its entry. There were analogous developments in sixteenth-century Spain: when Jewish-Christian Illuminists and other enthusiasts saw that the established church was resisting new reforms and the advent of the Holy Ghost, the rejected reformers became the bitterest opponents of the fortress church of the 'old guard'.

Fray Melchor felt confirmed in his calling by 'many God-fearing men and women in monastic orders' in England, Spain and Naples. Cazalla wrote admiringly about him to Ximenes. But Melchor's case was significant also in another respect: in 1512 he went to France, which, like Spain and Germany at that time, was filled with Illuminists. It was in that year, too, that the term *alumbrados* (Illuminists) made its first appearance, denoting ecstatic Franciscans. Particularly women, among them many Jewish-Christians, had this sense of inspiration. Ximenes became their protector.

These enthusiasts, who were forming communities and study circles in Spanish towns between Sevilla and Burgos, took up the mighty intellectual impulse of Erasmism after 1516. Ximenes urgently invited Erasmus to Spain in 1517 (the year of Ximenes's death and of Luther's Wittenberg Manifesto). But Erasmus did not go. In a letter to his friend Sir Thomas More, Erasmus said he was repelled by Spain, a country which seemed to him strange, sinister and Jew-ridden. (Erasmus was in fact no more anti-Semitic than Goethe, who also made some sarcastic comments on the Jews.) The Erasmists in Spain and their enthusiastic supporters were thus thrown back on their own resources. They were dragged into the whirlpool of persecution. The Inquisition made the job easy for itself: it simply threw all these Spanish humanists, Illuminists, *alumbrados* and 'Lutheran heretics' together into one pot, and was delighted to find among the victims so many Jews, *conversos*, New Christians and people of Jewish descent.

At the inquisitorial trials it was particularly these people of Jewish descent who bravely and openly confessed their beliefs. One of them, Dr Vergara, freely admitted that, like everyone else, he had sympathized with Luther at the beginning. The general attitude of the Spanish public towards the *Communeros*, the great reformist rebel movement in the towns, was similar: to start with, everyone was for the *Communeros* because they seemed to aim at only a few specific reforms. The most sympathetic turned their backs on Luther and the *Communeros* only when both plunged into excess.

Dr Vergara's line of argument and his political position can be compared with that of American left-wing intellectuals who, in the McCarthy era, tried to explain to their harsh inquisitors why years ago they had sympathized with Socialism or Communism.

At his trial Dr Vergara proudly proclaimed his adherence to the church of scholars, critics and intellectuals. He attacked ignorant fanatical monks and church officials who smelt heresy wherever their superstitious mentality prevented them from keeping up intellectually with what was going on. One of the chief prosecution witnesses was Dr Pedro Ortiz, a one-time sympathizer with Briconnet's early evangelical reformists in Paris. Later, however, he denounced Ignatius Loyola to the Dominican Inquisition. In political terms, Dr Ortiz switched from being a left-wing church reformer to a right-wing reactionary. We are familiar with such characters – they were the accusers and denunciators in the trials of the McCarthy era.

The entire Cazalla family, which played an outstanding part in the ecclesiastical reform movement, was put on trial. The inquisitorial procedure set great store on proving the Jewish origin of the accused. Maria Cazalla, Bishop Cazalla's sister, gallantly defended her ideal of pure love and unselfish good-neighbourly service, with no thought of reward from God or men. Maria Cazalla, a Jewish-Christian, spoke up for the much-stigmatized *alumbrados* (whose name was as much abhorred as that of the Communists in modern times). She admitted her early sympathy with the teachings of the 'arch-heretic' Luther, based on her feeling that the church had become deeply corrupt. Maria Cazalla endured all tortures without renouncing her beliefs.

It was against this background of terror that Ignatius Loyola reached his spiritual maturity. It was a terror that threatened not only religious enthusiasts, but also the whole of Spain's great religious literature – the Valdes Index of 1559 proscribed all religious writings in the vernacular and threatened death to the possessor of forbidden books. Even the most illustrious and enlightened leaders of spiritual reform and Spanish mysticism, St Teresa of Avila, Luis de León and St John of the Cross stood in danger of being swept under. Nine times Ignatius Loyola fell into the clutches of the Inquisition. Pope Paul IV, the protagonist of Rome's most rigorous Inquisition, which raged against heretics, Lutherans and people of Jewish descent, was his bitterest enemy.

The Society of Jesus achieved world-wide success: it had sprung from an association between Ignatius and six of his friends in Paris, and at the time of his death in 1556 it was already established in twelve provinces with 101 houses and one thousand members. In 1542 the Society set up branches in India (the land of which Columbus dreamed), in 1549 in Japan and Brazil and in 1563 in China. In the seventeenth and eighteenth centuries the Society of Jesus, with its six hundred colleges and academies, became the greatest scholastic Order and the most influential educational institution in Europe. The Jesuit state of Paraguay was the embodiment of Joachim of Fiore's vision of a state of monks, Sir Thomas More's Utopia and the dreams of the Jewish-Christian religious enthusiasts around Columbus. The Jesuits' global success was basically the work of the religious genius of the founder of their Society, Ignatius Loyola. With his spiritual exercises he shaped 'new men';

through brilliant organization, which involved enlisting, above all, the aid of ladies of Europe's high nobility, he created the new and unique system of Jesuit colleges. Ignatius Loyola, as *il padre*, the father, gathered around him the angry, depressed and deserted sons of the European nobility (and later of the bourgeoisie) – rootless young men who found no inspiration from their natural fathers in either secular or ecclesiastical affairs. The Jesuit order was a movement of the young (although, like Ignatius himself, its members might already have been quite advanced in years), who cut themselves off from their old, corrupt and indolent fathers and chose Ignatius as their new parent.

Let us briefly return to Maria Cazalla. The Christian and Christian-Jewish women of Spain, full of religious fervour, would also have liked to adopt Ignatius as their father. Some of them urged him to establish a women's branch of his Society. But he resisted, and allowed only one woman, a member of the Spanish Hapsburg family, to join under a man's name. Ignatius did, however, accept Jews and people of Jewish descent into his Society. The exuberance, the missionary élan, the critical honesty of the Society of Jesus, especially in the decisive first decades of its existence, would have been unthinkable without the 'young' Jews and the descendants of Spanish Jews, whom Ignatius brought to Rome to save them from the fires of the Spanish persecution.

No history has yet been written of the contribution Jewish-Christians and men of Jewish origin have made to the rise of the Society of Jesus. This is understandable when one remembers that the Jesuits later became violent anti-Semites and have remained so to this day. The anti-Semitic movements of the nineteenth and twentieth centuries in Germany, Italy and France have all in their time pointed legitimately to the 'Aryan clause' of the Society of Jesus which excluded Jewish-born men from membership from the end of the sixteenth century until 1946. Under the shadow of Hitler and the 'final solution' of the Jewish question, distinguished Jesuits wrote theological treatises bristling with resentment, even hatred against the Jews. In such an atmosphere (which still persists) it is of course difficult to realize just how much the initial advance of Europe's young intelligentsia and its mobilization through the Society of Jesus owed to Jews and Spaniards of Jewish origin. Men see only what they want to see.

While the great battle to cleanse Spain of impure blood was still in full cry, Ignatius Loyola chose a *converso* from Spain, Juan Alonso de Polanco, to be his secretary and confidant, and selected another *converso*, Diego de Laynez, as his successor. It was the enthusiasm, devotion and Messianic faith of Jesuit theologians and leading members of Jewish descent, such as Laynez and Salmeron, that gave the young Society its particular youth-inspiring character.

After the death of Ignatius in 1556 – the same year in which Emperor Charles v, the great protector of the Jews in the Holy Roman Empire, died – the Society's pro-Jewish attitude endangered its position in Rome and in

Spain. Italians rose to greater prominence in the affairs of the Society in Rome. To them Spaniards and Jews were almost identical. It was hoped (and achieved) that by excluding Jews, Spanish predominance in the Order could be broken. The capitulation of the Society of Jesus began in 1592, when its statutes forbade the admission of men of Jewish origin. This move ensured the take-over of the Order by Italians. The Jewish-born Laynez was falsely said to be of 'pure Christian' descent, and in the case of other less prominent members of the Society Jewish ties were simply not mentioned. In Spain the great struggle to cleanse the Christian church of all people of Jewish origin was by now well under way. The archbishop of Toledo, Juan Martinez Siliceo, was the first theologian of an 'Aryan Christ'. He ignored the fact that the mother of Christ was the Jewish Mary.

The Castilian Inquisition was established by a papal bull in 1478. Exiled Jews later said that in ten years the terror of the Inquisition did more to revitalize Jewish faith than centuries of admonitions by rabbis. A remarkable urge to emigrate, for an exodus, sprang up among the persecuted Jews (long before 1492). 'Let us go joyfully from Egypt' (which Spain had now become to them).

We do not know how many people were burnt at the stake in Spain between 1480 and 1834. Llorente, the renegade inquisitor and historian of the Inquisition who was in charge of its undamaged archives, put the number at 341,021. But this figure is too exact to be convincing. Protestant researchers, such as Schäfer, believe that at the most one-third of this number was actually burned – possibly one hundred thousand. The majority of the victims of the Inquisition were *conversos*, baptized Jews and people of Jewish descent.

The first Grand Inquisitor, Torquemada, who died in 1498, is said to have sent some ten thousand 'heretics' to the stake and to have imposed other sentences on a hundred thousand 'penitents' (*reconciliados*) during his fifteen years of office. The special interest of the Inquisition was focused throughout on the wealthy Marranos. Writers and commentators of our time maintain that the cold-blooded bureaucratic exploitation and plunder of the Jews was a specifically Nazi innovation – something unique in world history. They were wrong. The Spanish Inquisition, with its extensive bureaucratic apparatus (above all at the permanent tribunals in Toledo, Seville, Cordoba, Valladolid, Saragossa, Barcelona and Valencia) systematically organized the search for Marranos, apostates and suspects and then, with equal business-like thoroughness, arranged for the confiscation and sale of their possessions and property.

The proceeds went partly to the king (i.e. firstly to Ferdinand the Catholic of Castile), partly to the host of inquisitorial officials, and partly to the denunciators. All this required an elaborate system of bureaucracy. *Spain provided the first prototype of an over-developed bureaucracy*, if we leave aside the Curia. King Philip II has gone down in history as the 'bureaucratic king'.

E 113

He reigned from his writing desk with the aid of thousands of files and documents. The total bureaucratization of the Spanish Inquisition held both advantages and disadvantages for the people detained for investigation – especially in later days, after the first orgy of killing had passed. These people often had to wait for years, indeed decades, for their trials to be convened and this allowed time for intervention on their behalf. And not a few bureaucrats found – as did later 'enlightened' leaders of the SS-bureaucracy – that more could be extracted from living prisoners than dead ones.

One significant sociological aspect of the Spanish Inquisition is unmistakable. Protected by the anonymity of this *société anonyme*, this corporation without liability, a host of 'small men' found employment as clerks, inquisitors and assistants – men from the lower classes, from the small towns and from the country, full of hatred for rich Jews, Marranos, aristocrats and the high church dignitaries. If, in the end, cardinals, archbishops, church prelates and kings trembled before the Inquisition, one of the reasons was that here, far beneath the surface, the permanent war of the underdogs against their overlords was being waged.

This can be seen from the monster trial which the Inquisitor Lucero staged in Cordoba in 1505. Lucero ordered the arrest of about one hundred members of the Spanish aristocracy, which had long been heavily 'Jew-ridden'. A 'prophetess' was made to confess under torture that a meeting had been held at the house of the archbishop of Granada, Talavera, at which the early coming of the Prophet Elijah and the Jewish Messiah had been foretold. (What a distortion of the true relationship between Jewish-Christian Messianic ideas and the religious revivalism of the time!) Lucero's intention was to induce the pope to have Archbishop Talavera himself thrown into prison. The very same tactic is being used in our time by Lucero's spiritual heirs, as seen in Maurice Pinay's request to the Second Vatican Council to have the Jewish origin of all princes of the church, monks and priests of the last few centuries investigated so that they might be held to account.

But Lucero went too far. A nobleman stormed the Inquisition's residence in Cordoba with his troops, and Lucero fled. But the rumour he had started persisted: the story of an alleged plot by Jews, people of Jewish blood and their friends to Judaize Spain and hand it over to the anti-Christ, who would appear as the Jewish Messiah.

Under the youthful King Charles I (Emperor Charles V) the Marranos tried to get to the roots of the matter. They offered to pay four hundred thousand ducats to the king, who was always short of money, as compensation for the sums he would otherwise receive from the Inquisition. Charles, who later maintained good relations with Josel von Rosheim, appointed by him as protector of the Jews in Germany, may not have been averse to this financial solution, and Pope Leo x showed himself also to be on the side of the Jews and Marranos. But both eventually yielded to Spanish resistance against any practical protective measures. Resistance to the pope's wish for a reform of the Inquisition came too from the head of the Inquisition, Cardinal Adrian (later Pope Adrian vi), who was a compatriot of Erasmus of Rotterdam.

Preachers and propagandists for the Inquisition, and many other people who had an interest in its activities, systematically aroused and kept awake a panic fear of the 'Jewish menace' among the Spanish lower classes. It is rather like certain press and publishing organizations today, for instance in the United States, which are dependent on and allied with the armament industry, and therefore try to frighten the nation with the dangers of Communism. There was of course some truth behind the propaganda, just as there does really exist a Communist threat today (though most people have not the courage to look for its true causes). Jewish-Christians and Marranos were in fact allied and intermarried with the nobility, high clergy and holders of high public offices, although their number was insignificant. From the eighth to the fifteenth centuries, indeed, Spain owed its cultural and economic wealth to these bonds. But now the Spanish began to organize their systematic destruction. Under pressure of public opinion, as always 'created' by a relatively small clique, the Hieronymites at the end of the fifteenth century decided to exclude men of Jewish descent. In 1525 this example was followed by the Franciscans, who, particularly through their Joachimite cross-links with Provence, Italy and the Netherlands, had attracted Messianic Jewish-Christian enthusiasts. The attitude of the Dominicans varied from monastery to monastery. As an order of preachers and intellectuals they had a number of important Jewish-Christians in their ranks.

The main battle against the Jewish-Christians, *conversos*, Marranos and people of Jewish origin was begun by Archbishop Juan Martinez Siliceo of Toledo. He came from a simple peasant family, like many anti-Semitic clerics in France and Austria in the nineteenth and twentieth centuries. He hated the aristocracy and threw his chief adversaries, the 'Jew-ridden nobles' of Toledo, into prison.

This first prominent theological protagonist of an 'Aryan Christ' naturally deserves particular attention today. In 1547 Siliceo, at one time tutor to the crown prince who was later to become King Philip ii, wrote a momentous tract on the purity of Spanish blood, the *limpieza de sangre*. Siliceo claimed that only clerics who could prove from genealogical records that they were of pure-blooded descent ought to be allowed to hold office. Their lineage must be untainted by Jews, Marranos or New Christians. Although the chapter of Toledo approved Siliceo's suggestions (we are reminded of the Councils of Toledo of Visigothic times), he failed to secure support from the pope or from Emperor Charles v for this revolutionary change.

Like the Tsarist propagandists of the *Protocols of the Elders of Zion*, Siliceo then resorted to forgery. The archbishop claimed that in the archives of Toledo he had discovered an ancient correspondence between Jews in Spain and Constantinople which proved the Jews were plotting to usurp power in Spain. In these letters (the archbishop alleged) the Spanish Jews complained of persecution in Spain and the cruelty of the Spanish king. The reply from Constantinople read: 'You say that the Spanish king forces you to accept baptism. Accept it then, for you have no other choice. You say that he deprives you of your possessions; then let your sons become merchants so that they in turn can deprive the Christians of their wealth. They take your lives; well then, have your children trained to become doctors and chemists so that they can shorten the lives of your enemies. They destroy your synagogues; then let your sons become priests and theologians, whereby you will destroy their churches. You say you are being put upon in many other ways; see then that your children become lawyers, prosecutors, notaries and officials, whereby they will acquire influence on public affairs and you, by dominating and subjugating the country, will take revenge on your enemies.'

This forgery, which meant exactly what Siliceo meant it to mean, strikingly illustrates all the guilt Christian consciences repress when they know what they themselves have done to Jews and blamed on Jews. All the lust for power, all the avarice and envy and immature instincts fermenting in their own hearts are projected on to the Jews.

Siliceo's tract and his allegation of a Jewish plot produced the desired effect: the process of poisoning the minds of the Spaniards continued relentlessly. And once again the indications of a hidden class war are unmistakable. A widely-read pamphlet, attributed to Cardinal Mendoza de Bobadilla, alleged that the entire aristocracy of Spain was riddled with Jews. And this obsession with the purity of the blood now began to take on the form of a concealed civil war. The roads were choked with people on their way to other towns to search their archives for proof of the purity of their own blood and the impurity of their adversaries. The closed society of Spain was hardening into a *communauté d'angoisse et de haine* – a community of hate, fear and jealousy, as the new Catholicism was called in France. Scoring a kill became a national sport, a Spanish disease.

The doyen of Spanish historians, Menéndez y Pelayo, declared four hundred years later: 'This internal racial dispute and permanent civil war, this struggle for the purity of blood, caused the downfall of the Pyrenaean peninsula.'

The whole of Spain fell into the grip of a neurosis, a psychotic obsession. Everybody depended on his neighbour's good or bad testimony. Such is the background to the Spanish struggle to preserve 'honour'. Every day honour was in mortal peril: this or that nobleman would allege that this or that other nobleman was of 'impure blood'. A duel would decide the issue. What had begun as a national act of suicide, when Spain decided to purify itself of the Jewish and Moorish elements which had helped since the seventh century to form it, became now – from the seventeenth to the twentieth centuries – an act of personal suicide.

And now to the fate of the Marranos. After 1492 many of them had fled to Portugal, where they were compulsorily baptized and then, in 1497, given an assurance by King Manuel that they would not be persecuted by the Inquisition during the next twenty years. In 1506 the first popular rising took place there against the Marranos, who were quite openly carrying on a Christian-Jewish double life in Lisbon. Monks led the masses with the cry, 'If you are for the Christian faith and the Holy Cross, do not stand aloof when the Jews are rooted out!' King Manuel had two of the guilty monks burnt at the stake and ordered the other ring-leaders to be punished.

But under his successor John III and his Spanish Queen Catherine the situation became explosive. In February 1539 posters appeared on church gates in Lisbon: 'The Messiah has not come. Jesus was not the true Messiah.' The Marrano Manuel da Costa was convicted of having put up the posters and burnt at the stake. The leaders of a too lenient Inquisition were replaced. The Inquisitor John de Mello set up subterranean torture chambers and turned Lisbon into a veritable hell for the Marranos. They were whipped, their heels singed and skin torn from their bodies.

In an enthusiastic letter to the king, John de Mello described one of the autos-da-fé he had organized in Lisbon: 'About one hundred of the condemned marched in solemn procession, led by a lay judge and escorted by the clergy of two dioceses. When the procession reached the place of execution the hymn *Veni creator spiritus* was intoned. One of the monks mounted the pulpit, but his sermon was brief, as there was still a great deal to be done that day. The sentences were read out, first the punishments of exile and temporary imprisonment, then of life imprisonment and finally the death sentences. There were twenty of these. Seven women and twelve men were tied to the stakes and burnt alive. Only one woman was pardoned, because she had repented at confession.' In Coimbra the Dominican Inquisitor, Bernardo de Santa Cruz, caught a couple of his fish, the wealthy Simon Alvares and his wife, for his frying-pan by inducing their six-year-old daughter to give false evidence. 'He placed the child in front of a bowl filled with burning coals and threatened to burn her hands on them unless she confessed that her father and mother had done something to insult a crucifix.' The child confessed, and her parents were burnt to death.

Insulting the crucifix could mean insulting the honour of God, Spain or European Catholicism. This concept of wounded honour has played a large part in Christian thinking right up to the present century. Austria's criminal laws at the time of Empress Maria Theresa were particularly severe on such insults. What Christians themselves had perpetrated against Jews, heretics and nonconformists they found impossible to forgive when they discovered themselves on the receiving end.

In Portugal the Marranos went deep underground and established a syncretic religion of their own. While conforming strictly to Catholicism outwardly, they took to reading Messianic, apocryphal books on the Bible. Their crypto-Jewish faith was maintained largely thanks to their womenfolk, who became veritable priestesses, *sacerdotisas*, within the family. Marranos from Portugal and Spain journeyed to the Netherlands, Turkey and India. For two hundred years their travels and international relations were closely watched by the Inquisition. Its archives contain the dossiers of forty thousand cases brought to trial. Under the Portuguese there were fewer burnings than under the Spanish Inquisition. After several generations the Marranos who had stayed in Portugal began to lose their old faith, and their attitude gradually changed into a silent but stubborn anti-clericalism. The active, strong and enterprising elements of the Portuguese Marrano population emigrated to Protestant countries. No intellectual history of Europe should ignore the part played by those Marranos who became critics of both Judaism and Christianity and were often persecuted by the closed ranks of the synagogue just as much as by the closed ranks of the church.

In 1772 Pombal forbade in Portugal any legal discrimination between Old and New Christians. In 1821 the Inquisition was abolished in Portugal. After the First World War several thousand Marranos were discovered living, under the leadership of their womenfolk, their *sacerdotisas*, as humble craftsmen and peasants in the Portuguese hinterland. They went on living a hand to mouth existence there, like the Jews in China, until quite recently. Their descendants say of themselves: They call us Judeus, Jews, because we help one another, *ajudarnos*.

From Spain and Portugal Marranos went to the Levant, especially to Constantinople and Salonica. These towns became centres of Eastern Jewry. Nazi hirelings closed down the Spanish-Jewish community of Salonica and transported its members to the death camps in Poland.

In the sixteenth century Marrano settlements also sprang up in Antwerp, Bordeaux, Venice and Ancona, which as papal territory formed an important gateway to the East. In the seventeenth century Amsterdam, Hamburg and London were added to the list of Marrano centres. It was no accident that these towns became the focal points of Christian and European enlightenment which developed through study and criticism of the Bible.

The West European Marranos clung to their Hispanic ties and their Jewish aristocratic rank. They emphasized their descent from King David and despised other Jews, like those from Germany or Poland. When Holland was occupied by the Germans, their pride and exclusiveness became their downfall. The Spanish Jews of Holland simply could not conceive that they could be lumped together with the 'rabble' from Germany and East Europe, and could be sent with them to a single gas chamber.

The proverbial pride of Dutch and Western Hispanic Jews is evident in a remark which Isaac de Pinto once made to Voltaire. Portuguese and Spanish Jews (he said) would never mix or intermarry with other Jews, such as those of Germany. For this reason they had preserved the purity of their customs and won great respect among the Christian peoples. Voltaire agreed with Pinto. Perhaps neither was aware that the Hispanic Jews (just like those modern Jews who take on the habits of their persecutors) had assumed the concept of *limpieza de sangre* – that doctrine of pure-bloodedness which had claimed and was still claiming so many victims among their relatives in Spain and Portugal.

If a Portuguese Jew had married a *Tudesque*, a German Jewess, he would have become a social outcast, and probably even been excommunicated by his synagogue. In the large synagogues of Amsterdam and London German Jews had to occupy pews separated from the rest by barriers. In Venice, German and Levantine Jews were ejected from the *ghetto vecchio*, the time-honoured Portuguese ghetto. The tragic and suicidal refusal of wealthy Western Jews in Holland, France and England after 1933 to take heed from the fate of their co-religionists in Poland and Hitler's Germany has its historical foundation in the exclusive outlook of these Hispanic Jews and Marranos.

The Marranos were torn within themselves. They were Spaniards; banished from Spain, they yet belonged with every fibre of their being to their Promised Land of Spain. They were top show Christians, attracted by the power, prestige, wealth and glamour in *their* Christian churches. They yearned for and believed in success – just as German Jews believed in Hitler and wanted to form his 'most loyal Jewish opposition'. Many Marranos wished to remain Jews at heart, yet were unwilling to bow to the Law, the Torah, and they looked down on their orthodox brethren as backward and archaic. Here and there Marranos became nihilists. Others preserved a glowing Messianic faith and so became progressives in various Christian denominations, and later in liberal or Socialist reform groups and parties.

The history of the expansion of the Marranos in the sixteenth century is dominated by the Mendés family. They built up a vast commercial enterprise which rested primarily on two brothers resident in Lisbon and Antwerp. Charles v elevated the family to noble rank. From this clan, with its Egyptian and French affiliations, there has come one of the shrewdest politicians of modern France: Mendés-France.

Amsterdam, another Marrano centre in Western Europe, had a Jewish newspaper, the *Gazeta de Amsterdam*, as early as 1675. It dealt with all kinds of topics, in addition to Jewish matters. In Amsterdam Baruch Spinoza, ex-pupil of the 'Etz Haim' rabbinical school, was excommunicated by the synagogue on 27 July 1656. Shortly before his death in 1677 at the age of forty-four, Spinoza burnt a translation of the Old Testament on which he had been working.

Spinoza held the Jews responsible for the Christian hatred of them: Jewish patriotism, he said, meant permanent hatred of all non-Jews. Spinoza fought against the Old Testament and was deeply wounded by the exclusive-ness of the Hispanic Jews in his synagogue at Amsterdam. But subconsciously, deep down, Spinoza spoke a different esoteric language, in which the dialogue with his Jewish God and his Jewish community never ceased. He turned his unrequited love against the synagogue which had rejected him. The anti-Jewish passages in his famous *Tractatus* were taken from his defence of his Jewishness, re-written after his excommunication.

A similar inner conflict to Spinoza's is also detectable in many famous modern Jewish thinkers who have spoken out against the Jews while des-perately nurturing a secret, repressed love for Judaism. Nietzsche recognized this when he compared Spinoza with Jesus of Nazareth; perhaps a better comparison would have been with St Paul.

Spinoza was the pioneer of a belief in mankind. He personifies the 'party of peace and justice' which, as the great French philosopher Alain points out, is the party of all Jews in modern society. Spinoza's anti-Jewish polemics paved the road for the rationalist, intellectual anti-Semitism of modern times, which struck particularly deep roots in nineteenth-century France among intellectuals of Christian origin. Here, in one swoop, they could work off their resentment against their Jewish rivals, the Law, the church, the Jewish God and established Christianity.

Spinoza's 'demonic irony' (Hermann Cohen) sprang from a deeply wounded heart. Carl Gebhardt, publisher and biographer of Spinoza and of the writings of Uriel da Costa, has spoken of the *duplication of the Marrano consciousness*. This provides the clue to a certain form of modern consciousness which, at different levels, thinks and reacts in very different ways. There is an unending conflict between doubt and counter-doubt, belief (which deep down contains an inability to believe) and non-belief (in which there are still buried links with old, even archaic reasons for faith). A leading Catholic philosopher, Reinhold Schneider, has expressed this modern consciousness in these terms: faith nourishes doubt, and doubt nourishes faith.

Let us take one more look at Spain. In seventeenth-century Spain, the land of Don Quixote, whom Cervantes portrayed as an exponent of Erasmist tolerance, the racialist crusade reached a paroxysm of obsession with the fiction of *limpieza de sangre*. It was not enough to be of non-Jewish origin; one had to be able to prove it. The start of the century was marked by the 'final solution' of the problem of the Moors still left in Spain: it saw the 'radical and barbaric expulsion' (Richelieu) of the last Moors between 1609 and 1614 under King Philip III. Europe stood on the threshold of the Thirty Years War.

This final solution, by expulsion, was based on a conception of total and totalitarian racism. No exceptions, such as for mixed marriages, were made. It was in vain that a priest pleaded for his two nephews, both of them pure Christians and one of them hoping to become a priest. It was in vain that Bishop Sobrino extolled the virtue of Sister Maria Vincente. Moorish nuns were dragged from their convents and banished. The Jewish Carmelite nun, Edith Stein, one of the most brilliant intellectuals of German Catholicism, could not be saved by the Catholics of all Europe from being fetched from her convent cell and sent to her death. This undefeated Spanish racism, as strong today as it was in the seventeenth century, provides one of the historical explanations for the inability of the clergy to save mankind.

Just as gallant little peoples such as the Danes and Bulgarians and a few brave Christian individuals stood their ground against the terror of the bureaucrats and hirelings of the National Socialist régime, so did a few people in seventeenth-century Spain – with similar results. The only group of Moriscos (descendants of the Moors) who were able to save themselves – possibly altogether four hundred families – owed their escape to the protection of the bishop of Tortosa.

In 1681 the Grand Inquisitor Valladares objected to the employment of New Christian wet-nurses by the aristocracy: he argued that children were ruined by their milk. Analogous files were found in the archives of the National Socialist ministry of justice which recorded measures taken against the Jewish wet-nurses of Christian children.

In 1778 works by Spinoza, Hobbes, Montesquieu and Voltaire were found in the house of a town councillor, Pablo Olavide. He was stripped of all his offices and honours, sentenced to eight years' imprisonment in a monastery and confiscation of all his possessions. Five generations of his descendants were declared unfit for office. This was Spain, ten years before the French Revolution – Spain, the country that had made so inestimable a contribution to the spirit and culture of Europe during the seven hundred years of Spanish co-existence and symbiosis between Jews, Christians and Mohammedans.

In 1865 a law forbade the publication of information concerning Jewish or Moorish antecedents – documentary evidence until then necessary for marriage, entry into public service and so on. But in practice the law proved ineffectual, and 'good old custom' prevailed.

The depth of the Christian-Jewish tragedy of Spain is illustrated in a long poem by the Jewish poet Zalman Schneour, born in 1887, entitled 'The Last Words of Don Henriquez'. These were the words Don Henriquez spoke before being sent to his death at the stake:

Jesus of Nazareth,
Son of man, and my brother,
Your robe, stained with suffering,
Has darkened the light of the sun . . .
On the spires of the temples
You have fixed your cross.
It is hung in the bedchambers,
And from the necks of women and children . . .
Do not trust these strangers, Jesus!
Wandering through the centuries
I have learned their ways and language,
I have learned to know them now.
Like straw in the mouth of a tiger
Is to them the taste of your compassion.
Moloch still reigns in their houses of worship,
And the beast of prey is in their blood.
Since the wild beasts have gone from the forests,
And the forests are thinned and cleared,
They now hunt men in the cities,
With prayers and with organ chant . . .
Do not believe these strangers, Jesus.
The day will come, it is not far off,
When they will hunt you too from their churches,
From their steeples and their domes,
From the throats of their wives and children . . .
It is the fate of us both,
Henriquez today, and Jesus next . . .
You will be deserted, Jesus,
Forsaken on your breaking cross,
With your outstretched arms –
And on your bleeding feet you will limp,
As we do, along strange roads,
And the hem of your garment
Will sweep up the filth of the nations and lands
That you will pass on your flight.
And out of each town and land,
Out of cathedrals and museums
They will hurl with execration
Your image and your name . . .
And mothers and daughters and sisters,
All the pure daughters of Israel,
Dressed in white and in black
Will stand on both sides of the roadways,
A guard of honour for the hunted,

And they will recognize in you and your effigies,
And in the thousands of ikons,
Each mother her son who was tortured with glowing pincers,
And each wife her husband whose tongue was torn out in the market-
    place,
Each sister will find her brother who was massacred,
Each orphan her murdered father . . .
And each Jewish woman will press to her heart
A picture, a statue, the image of her lost one,
Tormented and crucified,
And each will be a Madonna weeping for her dead.
Oh, what a vast number of Pietàs,
All the way from Europe to the hills of Zion!
And you, noble martyr, who will head the procession,
A new Sanhedrin will welcome you.
    (*Jesus returns as prodigal son to Israel.*)
They come, to lead you to the banks of the Jordan,
To bathe in the holy water,
To heal your wounds . . .
And being clean as Naaman when he was healed of his leprosy
They will receive you with new psalms,
With open arms and with hearts full of love.
As today we receive a Marrano
Who returns to his faith.
No Pilate will be able to judge you by Roman law,
Nor any zealot or Pharisee to denounce you,
For ours will be the land,
And the courts of law will be ours.
No stranger will interfere in a dispute between brothers.
Jesus of Nazareth,
My breath fails me,
My word is being carried to heaven by horses of fire,
The stake has become like the throne of Solomon,
I am clad in purple,
And my burning hair is my crown.
I shall not cry out as you did, Jesus,
'My God, why hast Thou forsaken me?'
I have been favoured by the God of Jacob
Far beyond the lot of other mortals,
And therefore I will glorify God's Name,
That He has found me worthy to be a torch for the erring,
Burning with my blood and flesh,
And pointing in the dark and the mist
The way to eternity to my brothers.

The fire is near my heart,
The wet clothes steam and my tongue roasts between my teeth,
Strengthen me, God of Jacob, for one more moment,
That I may cry even as I die,
'Hear me all peoples!
Hear oh Israel,
And you too, Jesus, cry with me –
"The Lord our God is One God!" '

8

Eastwards

Westward Ho! Towards the Golden West, Eldorado! The greatest German historian of the late Middle Ages, Bishop Otto von Freising, son of an Austrian duke and uncle of Emperor Frederick Barbarossa, took the old traditional view that the trend of history was from East to West. The first great empires were in the East; but the last were in the West: the Roman Empire and its successor, the Holy Roman Empire. Eastwards was the watchword of the Crusaders – to Constantinople and the Holy Land. The great victors of the wars of the Crusades, the Genoese and Venetians, built up an empire on the shores of the Eastern Mediterranean and the Black Sea. But after that the interest of the major powers seemed to turn entirely westwards. The Mediterranean lost its significance, the region fell under Turkish rule, and in 1529 the Turks were, for the first time, at the gates of Vienna. The rise of the West had begun: France, the Netherlands, England and then the American continent.

Europe became the West: Calvinism, the Protestant sea-powers, the Netherlands and England, brought about the downfall of Spain. *And the Jews moved eastwards.* This great eastward migration, spreading over several stages, seems like an involuntary counter-movement against European civilization centred in the West and steadily pushing westward. This Jewish migration could be said to have begun with the eastward flight of Spanish Jews from the Islamic 'crusaders', the Almohades. These African fanatics stormed Seville in 1147, Cordoba in 1148 and destroyed the synagogues in these two towns, as they did in Lucena, Malaga and other places in Andalusia. Before the invasion by the Almohades, who had overrun Almoravides, which by then had become more peaceful, Spanish Jews fled to the northern and eastern regions of the country.

The Christian Crusades drove the Jews eastwards. From 1096 onwards they began to move from Germany via Bohemia to Poland. In the second half of the twelfth century Polish princes were protecting the Jews from molestation. By about 1200 the Jews had a village of their own near Breslau (Wroclav). Jews settled in Russia during the Kiev period. They were presumably in direct contact, via the Crimea and the Caucasus, with the Jewish centre in Babylonia, which once again flourished briefly.

Jews migrated eastwards, Germans and Russians migrated eastwards.

The Germans reached Riga, Reval and Dorpat in the twelfth and early thirteenth centuries. Communities acknowledging German law were established in East Prussia, Poland, Hungary and Transylvania. Cathedrals, churches and houses of the Hanseatic League provide testimony in stone of this far-flung German expansion, which had a parallel in the Russian move to the East: from the twelfth century onwards Russian peasants pushed eastwards with indefatigable, stubborn resolve. The Russian colonization of Siberia – an attempt by a few bold reformers in the late nineteenth century to create a Russian America from which old Russia might be reformed – can justifiably be compared with the settlement of North America.

Germans and Russians moved to the East: in the nineteenth and twentieth centuries these two nations were destined to determine the fate of the Jews who had been emigrating eastwards ever since the twelfth century. In the last century and the present century masses of Eastern Jews fled from Russia and Russian-occupied Poland to America, to the countries of the Austro-Hungarian monarchy, to the German empire and later to the Weimar Republic. This desperate, turbulent rush to the West was intercepted by the henchmen of the Third Reich: endlessly the trains from France, Holland, Germany, Hungary and Rumania rolled back eastwards: to Upper Silesia and Poland – towards the 'final solution'.

In the thirteenth century Jews were moving along with the Germans into sparsely populated Poland, which became a 'colony of German Jewry'. German-Jewish towns flourished in Poland's western territories, especially in Greater Poland (Posen, Kalisch and Gnesen). In 1264 Prince Boleslaw the Chaste granted the Jews a charter similar to the one granted a little earlier in Austria and Bohemia. The Austrian-Jewish statute of 1244 guaranteed the Jews inviolability of life and possessions. Murder of a Jew was punishable by death and confiscation of the murderer's entire property; and heavy fines were imposed for physical assault. Attacks on Jewish cemeteries, synagogues or schools, and the abduction of Jewish children for the purpose of compulsory baptism were strictly prohibited. In Austria the Jews were given unlimited freedom of movement, the right to settle and to carry on trade.

The pro-Jewish policy of the author of this statute, Frederick the Quarrelsome, last duke of the Babenbergs, was based on an ancient Babenberg tradition. Austria and the lands of the Hapsburgs became Jewish sanctuaries. The Edict of Tolerance issued by Emperor Joseph II was ahead of the French Revolution both in time and content. Jews from Poland and Russia fled to the Danubian countries of the Hapsburg monarchy, right up to the time of its dissolution – and then into the Austrian Republic. Spanish Jews settled in Galicia, Ruthenia and in the eastern borderlands of the Hapsburg monarchy. Their descendants include the poets Joseph Roth and Paul Celan, author of *Todesfuge* which, except for poems by the Berlin Jewess Nelly Sachs, is the most important poetic work on the Jewish agony of the concentration camp era. But also from Austria came Odilo Globocnik, who set up the first gas chambers in Poland and Upper Silesia, Adolf Eichmann and the Nazi Governor of the Netherlands, Seyss-Inquart, who was responsible for the Dutch Jews' death journey to the East. From the twelfth to the twentieth centuries Austria was a country where the Jews enjoyed a certain amount of freedom. But in the nineteenth and twentieth centuries Austria became the very centre of popular anti-Semitism.

The Babenberg Statute of 1244 provided the model for the charters given to the Jews by King Premysl Otakar of Bohemia and Austria, by King Béla of Hungary and the Polish Prince Boleslaw of Kalisch. This pro-Jewish policy angered Pope Clement IV, who sent his legate Guido to Austria and Poland to take counter-action. The Synod of Breslau, over which he presided, resolved on a number of anti-Jewish measures in 1267 and insisted, in particular, on a strict separation of Jews and Christians. It laid down that the Jews were to live in separate quarters and to sell their houses in Christian parts of the towns. In public the Jew had to be clearly distinguishable by wearing a pointed hat and a red badge.

The reasons given for forcing the Polish Jews to live within the walls of the ghetto are interesting. The Synod of Breslau openly declared: 'Since the Poles represent a new plantation on the soil of Christendom, it is to be feared that the Christian population, among whom the Christian religion has not yet taken deep root, may succumb to the influence of the counterfeit faith and evil habits of the Jews living in their midst.' As in Carolingian France at the time of St Agobard of Lyon, the danger of the Jews exerting some kind of fascination on the 'young Christians' and of converting them to Judaism was very real.

Understandably, ecclesiastical sources of the Middle Ages only rarely reported cases of conversion to Judaism (just as Roman Catholic statistics in England today show only conversions to Catholicism, but not conversions to the Church of England, or other moves away). All the more noteworthy, therefore, are such infrequent reports, showing that it was not only sects that threatened this middle period of Christendom, but also the 'Jewish danger', the conversion of Christians to Judaism.

In 1233 Pope Gregory IX warned the German clergy that relations between Christians and Jews were becoming too close. Quite a few Christians were inclined towards Judaism. And six years earlier the episcopal Council of Trier had issued a warning against too close an association with Jews. In the Alsatian town of Weissenburg a ritual murder trial in 1270 ended with seven Jews being sentenced to death and broken on the wheel for the alleged killing of a Christian child. Among the seven were two Christians converted to Judaism, one of them a former Franciscan prior. (In modern times European converts to Buddhism quite often include former Franciscan monks.) The contemporaneous anti-Jewish sermons of the German preacher, Berthold of Regensburg (who described Jews, heretics and pagans as children of Satan), needs to be assessed in the light of this Christian-Jewish competition. The old lament, first heard in Spain and France, was still quite common in Poland in later centuries: Christians listen to the sermons of learned rabbis rather than to boring Christian priests.

While the Synod of Breslau was meeting in 1267 to consider the situation in Poland and Silesia, a parallel council, for Austria and Bohemia, was held in Vienna. Here the clergy were especially reminded of the need to observe the anti-Jewish decisions of the Lateran Council of 1215. 'In view of the fact that owing to the boundless impudence of the Jews the purity and sanctity of the Catholic faith of so many Christians has been harmed, we decree that the Jews, already obliged to wear distinctive clothing, shall again wear the pointed hat . . .' Here, too, we see a reflection of the fear that Christians might be infected by the Jewish faith. It was the monks, the 'new' wandering monks of the two mendicant Orders, Franciscan and Dominican, and later missionary Orders dedicated to work among the masses, who rekindled anti-Jewish feeling or – where it did not already exist – created it.

In Germany, along the route from West to East stood, in the region between Erfurt and Wittenberg, the figure of Martin Luther – the great monk whose anti-Jewish writings and pithy sayings provided an inexhaustible armoury for German anti-Semites in the nineteenth and twentieth centuries.

Luther was not the first in Germany, as events in Nuremburg between 1494 and 1499 showed. An anti-Jewish pamphlet *Defence of the Faith* by a Spanish monk, Alfonso de Espina, printed in Nuremburg, set processes in motion. On 10 March 1499 the last Jews left the town. Their entire fixed assets – houses, synagogues and cemetery – were confiscated by the city. The cemetery was ploughed up and a road built across it, Jewish tombstones being used to pave it. That was in Nuremburg – the city of the Nazi rallies.

In Cologne, on the eve of the Reformation, monks and baptized Jews – such as Johann Pfefferkorn, an ex-butcher, and Rabbi Viktor von Karben, who became a Catholic priest – began to agitate for the burning of the Talmud and all writings in Hebrew. They were opposed by the humanist Johannes Reuchlin. The 'Obscurantists' of Cologne, who were discredited for all time by humanists in Erfurt and by Ulrich von Hutten in his *Epistolae Obscurorum Virorum* (1515–17), received support from university theologians in Cologne, Mainz and Erfurt. The Cologne monks around Pfefferkorn alleged that Reuchlin had been bribed by the Jews and demanded that he should be tried by the church. Pfefferkorn himself suggested in his *Brandspiegel* that all adult Jews should be made into slaves, as had been done in ancient Egypt, and their children baptized.

For centuries tension had been building up in Germany, and the atmosphere was approaching flash point. To many Germans Martin Luther was the 'cleansing storm' or 'theological atom bomb', as he was called four hundred years later by the Catholic prelate and historian Karl Eder. Luther was the great deliverer. In this capacity, in relation to the German nation, he can be compared only with the much inferior twentieth-century 'deliverer' –

Adolf Hitler. Luther released all the fears, despair, hate, passion, wrath, sorrow, resilience, energy, passivity, melancholy and joy in the German people, and – last but not least, a colossal thirst for vengeance. Revenge at last against the noble lords, the aristocratic scoundrels, the high clergy, against the monks, Rome and all Germany's internal and external enemies. *Revenge ultimately against its God* – that terrible, incomprehensible, murderous God of vengeance – the God of the Jews.

Luther said that the Jews had changed God into the Devil. The Jews themselves were devils. His last sermon at Eisleben, his native town, delivered on 18 February 1546, four days before his death, was entirely given over to the Jewish problem. Luther demanded that they be expelled from all German lands. He called for practical measures: burn their synagogues, confiscate all books in Hebrew; prohibit Jewish prayers; force them to do manual labour; but, best of all, drive them out of Germany. 'I have done my part! I am excused.'

Luther was rent by deep fear: is God Himself the Devil? Or am I, Dr Martinus Luther, making a devil out of God? Deeply troubled by apparitions of the Devil, he once confessed that at certain times of temptation he no longer knew who was God and who the Devil.

One is tempted to dismiss Luther as a specifically German explosion and catastrophe. But the conclusions reached by Theodor Adorno and his team of researchers in the United States during the Second World War – investigating the correlation between authoritarian personality and upbringing by oppressive parents, hatred and aggressiveness against Jews and other outsiders – suggest that this problem personified by Luther was not confined to the German situation of the sixteenth and twentieth centuries. The American psychoanalyst Erik H. Erikson's searching study of the young Luther was directly prompted by his therapeutical work with American youths.

Luther's 'problem of the generations' is still a burning issue. This is so especially in any closed society or group, caste or section of the community which seeks exclusiveness and in which ambitious fathers are anxious that their sons should one day be their successful heirs. Luther never dared admit to hating his own father, a successful miner who had risen in life through diligence and energy and wanted his son to get on in the world. Luther transferred his hatred of his father to God. His fear of the Devil and disaster mirrored his persistently bad conscience. 'All his life Luther felt himself to be some sort of criminal' (Erikson). The young Luther's troubled conscience exploded in his deadly fear of Christ the Judge. The torments of Hell which Luther suffered were the product of conscience, dogma and terror combined. The Jewish religion, race and money – this devilish tryptich of Luther's was a reflection of his personal experience of a three-fold Hell. This is of great significance, for Luther's barbaric, desperate hatred of the 'devilish Jews' can only be understood in closest relation to his own personal development and the profound crisis of Germany and Christendom in his day.

We shall see later that Hitler in his conversations with Dietrich Eckart in 1923 (before his attempted Munich putsch) constantly invoked Luther. The despairing masses of Germany, and particularly Christians who no longer saw any hope for their country in a Western, Roman God, looked for salvation to the charismatic *Führer*, Adolf Hitler. Luther, too, called for a German *Führer* and held up to his people such German heroes as Arminius, prince of the Cherusci. But Luther himself was hailed as this German leader by the country's youth, by scores of monks and nuns who had deserted their monasteries, by spiritually and physically enslaved, proletarianized priests, and by a bourgeois intelligentsia that was yearning for inner freedom.

As a young man Luther had had such a liberating experience; he broke through the terrible images of father and father-god, devil, fear and hell to the archaic womb, in which lay embedded sublime trust, joy, deep peace and the certain knowledge that neither Heaven nor Hell, God nor Devil, and none of the powers of this or any other world could harm him there.

To this day the young Luther's experience of liberation provides something for Lutherans to feed on. His music, his eloquence, his songs, his translation of the Bible; the thawed waters of his soul pour forth free and untrammelled. Liberation and release from fear became something positive. To a man who experiences the awakening of God in himself everything, anything is possible! Luther was gripped by the power of German mysticism. A man thus laid open to the sources of his strength and the springs of his own personality is a 'man of potential' in the best sense of the term. Liberated, the young Luther felt strong enough to challenge the emperor, the pope and the whole world and to present to his beloved, desperate Germans Christ the Redeemer (and himself in his Christ) – not the false Christ of a negative conscience, whom he knew only too well – ('Christ, a more terrible tyrant and judge . . . than Moses').

Salvation was in this Redeemer. Salvation was in the Bible. The Bible became Luther's mother image. Salvation flowed from this God who sprang from the depth of the heart.

Here, in and with the young man Luther, the German revolution begins – to this day the only German revolution. Trusting in the great leader and deliverer Martin Luther, monks, nuns, priests and ministers left their churches, Germany's Christian nobles drew their swords and German peasants rushed to arms.

Barely twenty years after this great awakening came the great débâcle: the peasants were beaten, their leaders tortured and strung up on the gallows. The clergy wanted nothing more than to return to their old mother church. Many Protestant parsons committed suicide. Doctrine and religious teaching was thrown into chaos. Now Luther lashed out against the most genuine and spirited friends and disciples of his younger days. The Lutheran left-wing found it impossible to maintain itself against the persecution of the new 'exclusive' Lutheran church and its inquisitors, and fled, pursued, from country to country.

Luther himself sank into an abyss of despair. He sought help in strong beer, militant speeches and a new, harsh church discipline. 'Damned be love to the bottom of hell if it be pursued to the detriment and harm of doctrine.' The world was an 'arsehole' and Luther again felt he was 'dung'. They must wash their hands 'in the blood of cardinals and popes'. Shortly before his death he once more cast his curse on the 'whore Reason' and the 'swinish pope' in 'Against the papacy in Rome, founded by the Devil' (1545). Luther demanded that the pope and his Curia should have their tongues torn out and nailed to the gallows like seals of the papal bulls, according to their rank. Then they could meet in council on the gallows or in Hell amidst all the devils. In his later years Luther refused to talk to devilish papists and devilish Jews.

He openly confessed that he could not pray without cursing. He had wood-cuts made, depicting the church as a whore. Early in life he himself had experienced that God devoured Man; 'He is a searing, consuming flame'. In the ex-Augustinian monk Martin Luther, who was never able to shake himself free of St Augustine's teachings or of his monkdom, the sad old conviction once again struck root: Man was a miserable sinner. The nation was an accursed flock of miserable sinners fit only to be trampled upon, tortured and hanged by miserable princes. 'His words could adorn the gates of the police headquarters and concentration camps of our time' (Erikson).

The Lutheran Spring in Germany was of short duration, from approximately 1516/7 to 1524/5. From 1527 onwards fear, melancholy and self-hatred began to mount within Luther. *Sancte Sathana, ora pro me*: Holy Satan, pray for me. 'My heart quivers'. Luther, growing heavier and ever more obese, had heart trouble; he often broke out into severe sweats – his old 'devil's bath' – and into severe fits of crying; he suffered from buzzing in his ears and kidney stones. Luther, 'probably the most provincial of all universal leaders' (as Erikson put it); Luther the 'barbarian'; Luther, a 'man of such terrifying naïveté and unpredictable impetuousness' (Jaromir) – this tormented giant Luther, so it sometimes seemed to him, now only had one firm friend left, the Devil.

'At the end, Luther lived with the Devil on terms of mutual obstinacy, an inability to let go of each other, as tenacious as his old fixation on his father and his later fixation on the pope.'

Luther's attitude towards the Jews can only be understood within the context of his own life: as a young man he was pro-Jewish. Between 1523 and 1543 his views changed completely. His new hatred of the Jews was a reflection of his personal decline. At a time of great distress, when the Diet of Worms was meeting, the young Luther received a visit from two Jews at his hostel in Worms. But in his old age Luther refused even to talk to Jews.

His essay *Jesus Christ was born a Jew* (1523) was directed against the Jew-haters: 'Fools, popes, bishops, sophists and monks – the coarse dolts – have treated the Jews in such manner that a good Christian would rather be a Jew

. . . [Let us add that this was one of the reasons why quite a few Christians went over to the Jewish faith.] The Jews were treated like dogs, scolded and robbed of their possessions . . . And yet they are friends, cousins and brothers of our Saviour; no other people has been treated with such distinction by God; it was to them that he entrusted the Holy Scriptures.'

Luther pleaded that the Jews be treated more humanely, in a more Christian spirit: 'But if we treat them only with violence, accuse them of needing Christian blood so that they do not stink, and other such foolish things . . . how can that help to make them good? Deny them the right to work among us, to go about their jobs and associate with other human beings, and thereby force them to usury: how shall that make them better? If we want to help them we must use toward the Jews not the pope's but Christ's law of love, must accept them with friendship, allow them to earn their living and to work, so that from their own experience they get to know the teachings and life of the Christians.'

That was still the young Luther – the great hope in Germany and of a youthful, spiritually and emotionally stirring Europe. They all looked to Luther – English humanists and theologians in Cambridge; and French and Spanish as far as Seville. So did devout Spanish humanists and Italians in Naples, Rome, Florence and Venice. The Slav intelligentsia of the Balkans and Poland; Hungary's and Rumania's youth were inspired by Luther. *Of all the shining hopes which were ultimately buried in the vast cemeteries of Europe, Luther was one of the very greatest.* Luther knew that himself. His anger, hatred and rage against the 'whoring' church, the pope, the Devil, the Jews, religious fanatics and the left wing of his own movement – basically these outbursts sprang from sadness and despair at his momentous failure.

First of all he was disappointed in the Jews. Luther had hoped to become a new St Paul and convert them. Was the Day of Judgment not at hand? How long still before God would gather in the final harvest? And the Jews were part of that harvest. Early Lutherans in Germany had been hoping to convert the Jews; later they looked towards a grand alliance with the Eastern church, the Greeks and the Russians against Rome. Both hopes were dashed.

Luther, the ex-monk reared on St Paul's and St Augustine's doctrines, was driven like many Roman theologians and popes, from disappointment to hatred of the 'stiff-necked' Jews – a turn entirely in line with his general disillusionment and deepening gloom. As early as 1537 he refused to receive Josel von Rosheim, whom the emperor had appointed spokesman for the German Jews. Josel intended to ask Luther to put in a plea with the elector of Saxony, Prince Johann-Friedrich, on behalf of the Jews who had been expelled from his lands. Luther informed Josel that he was working on a thesis against the Jews: this was published the following year under the title *Epistle against the Sabbatarians*. It was of particular significance, as it eloquently expressed Luther's fear of the Jews infiltrating his Reformation. In fact, Jewish people and Jewish ideas were at that time penetrating into Christian revivalist movements in Russia, Poland, Italy, France and Spain. (In Scotland and England the Puritans openly accepted them.) Luther was afraid of the fascination the Bible, the *Jewish* Bible, might exert on them. He was also afraid of the Jewish intelligentsia. Were not Reuchlin and other German humanists, who were pro-Lutheran, under the spell of the Talmud and the Cabbala, of Jewish mysticism which was in many ways so close to German mysticism, and of Jewish Bible study and interpretation?

To whom did the Bible belong? To the Christians or the Jews? Monk, Augustinian disciple and Pauline theologian, Dr Martin Luther fought heart and soul against this Jewish peril: had he wrested the Bible from the pope only to let it fall into the hands of the Jews? A thousand-year-old tradition of Christian theology, whose prisoner both Luther and his opponents had become, clouded his view of reality.

The diabolical Jew, filled with hatred of Christ and the Christians and now threatening to 'seduce' the awakening youth of the Reformation, was causing Luther as much anxiety as the Devil. More and more often in his sermons and table talks, Luther called for the expulsion, even the extermination, of the Jews. In 1543 he published the two tracts which Christian anti-Semites to this day cite as King's evidence: *On the Jews and their Lies* and *On Shem ha-Mephorash.*

Luther's wrath, feared by friends and foes alike, descended on the accursed Jewish people who for fifteen hundred years had rejected the Redeemer. Luther, a man of old primeval fears, shared the popular belief in witches, sorcerers and black magic. The Jews, he believed, did commit ritual murders, poison wells and springs, violate and kill Christians wherever they could. The Jews were a nation of traitors. He believed all the wicked things of them that Protestant preachers and theologians of the nineteenth and twentieth centuries believed of the 'Reds'. Luther accused the German Jews of being in league with the Turks, the arch-enemy of Christendom.

The Jews (he said) deserved the most rigorous punishment. Their synagogues should be burned, their homes destroyed and they themselves be forced to live in tents, like gypsies. (It will be recalled that the Nazis included gypsies in their plans for a 'final solution' in 1941-4.) The Jews should have their religious writings taken from them. Their rabbis must no longer teach the Law. Jews must be barred from all professions. They should be permitted none but the heaviest and roughest labour (this was how the German armament industry 'used' the Jews whom the SS had sold or hired out to the factories). Rich Jews must be deprived of their wealth, which should be used for the maintenance of those of their co-religionists who were willing to accept baptism.

If all these measures were ineffective, it was the duty of Christian rulers to drive the Jews from their countries like rabid dogs. Luther praised King Ferdinand the Catholic and his Queen Isabella for expelling the Jews from Spain.

In a letter to Butzer, the great reformer of Strasbourg, the Swiss theologian Bullinger comments that Luther's anti-Semitic utterances gave the impression of having been written 'by a swineherd and not by a renowned shepherd of the soul'. If Reuchlin's famous hero Kapnion were to rise from the dead, he would say that Tunger, Hochstraten and Pfefferkorn had come to life again in this Luther.

Unwittingly Bullinger had touched upon Luther's deep wound : for in his heart Luther had never overcome the monk in himself, nor his desperately aggressive, unresolved sexuality. The monstrous aggressiveness which, shortly after his death, Lutheran churchmen displayed in ordering the persecution, torture and execution of Calvinist theologians and crypto-Calvinists, for instance, show how little these inner conflicts had been resolved. The fanaticism of the new married monks, who exercised a neurotic power over their wives and children, was no less brutal than that of the 'old' monks.

In Germany, a fanatic Protestant anti-Semitism was centred particularly on Giessen. From the sixteenth to the twentieth centuries numerous anti-Semitic tracts and pamphlets appeared there as sequels to Luther's anti-Jewish writings. Examples were the *Judenfeind* (The Jewish Enemy), published in Giessen in 1570, the *Judengeissel* (The Jewish Scourge) and a *Short Extract from the Dreadful Blasphemies of the Jews* (both 1604). In 1817, when the three-hundredth anniversary of the Reformation and Germany's liberation from the French were simultaneously celebrated on the Wartburg, German students, mostly from Protestant homes, made great bonfires of books. It was the first occasion, and Heinrich Heine commented : 'This was only a curtain-raiser. For where books are burnt, they finally burn human beings.' In 1829 Heine recalled his meetings with the fanatics of Giessen. These radical, nationalist student gangs now seem like forerunners of the SS : 'At the very time when nearly all nationalities were vanishing, there arose a black sect which indulged in the most foolish dreams of nationhood, and even more foolish plans for realizing them . . . They were able to determine the precise genealogical grade at which a person became eligible, under the new order, for removal from this world. But they could not agree on the method of execution. Some considered the sword would be the most truly German way, while others thought the guillotine would do, since it was, after all, a German invention.'

'While the Jews were leaving Spain and Portugal for exile in the Turkish East, countless groups of emigrants were streaming from the narrow ghettoes of Germany and Austria to the Slavonic East, Poland and Lithuania. This significant sixteenth-century shift of European Jewry's centre of gravity from Western to Eastern Europe, led to the simultaneous establishment of the Sephardim in Turkey and the Ashkenazim in Poland' (Simon Dubnow).

Ten years before the catastrophe of the Polish state and its Jews in 1648, the Venetian rabbi, Simone Luzzato, published a book *On the condition of the Jews*. At that time, he pointed out, the Jews were most numerous in Poland and in Turkey, and in both countries they were enjoying much greater freedom than in Western Europe. Towards the end of the sixteenth century there were thought to have been more than one hundred and fifty thousand Jews in Poland and Lithuania. Half a century later their number exceeded half a million, which reflected a remarkable population growth, considering that health and living conditions all over Europe were still largely medieval. It is believed that hundreds of thousands of Jews were murdered in 1648, the year of terror.

In Poland, a 'Jewish nation' arose. King and aristocracy protected their Jews, to whom they had entrusted their financial affairs and the administration of their estates. Poland became the Jews' Promised Land. (The name Poland was read as Po-lan-ia, meaning 'God resides here'.) Polish clerics (many of whom are still bitterly anti-Semitic today), the bourgeoisie and members of the lower aristocracy declared that there were Jews everywhere in Poland. The misery of the impoverished Polish peasantry could be explained thus: 'We have to feed the master, the priest and the Jew.' 'What the peasant earns, the master spends; and the Jew takes his profit.' 'The Jew, the German and the Devil are sons of the same mother.'

These same uneducated, primitive, distressed Polish peasants, receiving no enlightenment from their own anti-Semitic clergy, later looked on as the Germans set up their death camps in Poland. They approved of this German 'final solution', some of them quite openly, even after 1945!

King Sigismund (1506–48) was the great protector of the Jews, who found an excellent refuge in his residential city of Cracow. The high nobility stood their ground against the lower aristocracy, the clergy and the citizens who were pressing for emergency laws against the Jews. On their huge estates these aristocrats were what the kings of France had claimed to be in their royal dominions since the twelfth century: pope, emperor and king all in one.

The Reformation, the spread of nonconformist movements, such as that of the anti-Trinitarians, and the need to protect Protestant emigrants from Italy induced the proud leaders of the aristocracy in Poland's golden age, the sixteenth century, to create preserves of freedom in their towns and villages for their Jews and these refugees from Western Europe. Often there were links between the two groups: the followers of Sozzini and the anti-Trinitarians were, in their non-dogmatic Christianity, close to the early Arians and were attacked as such by orthodox Calvinists and Lutherans. Men and women who were more interested in Jesus the man and in his humanity than in the deification of Christ were frequently denounced as Judaizers. (These people, expelled from Europe after the fall of Poland, were later to be of exceptional importance in the spiritual development of the United States.)

The lives and possessions of the 'Crown Jews' and those who enjoyed the protection of their aristocratic overlords in Poland were the object of incessant attack. Robberies, murders and other acts of violence were the orders of the day. Only by energetic intervention was a strong king able to prevent an epidemic of Jew-killing. Once a menacing situation arose when a Jewish convert from Turkey reported to King Sigismund that he had met on the way whole columns of Poles who had embraced Judaism and were emigrating to Turkey. He also told the king that the Turks were planning to invade Poland. The first reaction to this report was a panic-stricken wave of arrests, which was only brought to and end in 1540 when the report was discovered to have been untrue.

But it was in these years that Poland became, and remained for several centuries, a publishing centre for anti-Semitic pamphlets which had the backing of the clergy and quite often followed Western, especially German, models. One of them *Saints who were killed by Jews* appeared in 1543, the same year as Luther's two libellous attacks on the Jews.

King Sigismund's successor, Sigismund II Augustus (1548–72), greatly extended Jewish communal self-rule in Poland. The Jews were allowed to govern themselves in accordance with their own *kahal* system of jurisdiction. The *kahal* or local organization tied the Jews to the royal system of taxation. The Polish kings merged the offices of collector-general of taxes and head of all Jewish communities with the spiritual office of chief rabbi. Even before the fifteenth century, Spanish monarchs had adopted the same solution in their realms. And in the later sixteenth century the *kahal* was further developed along these lines. Originally *kahal* meant two different things: the community *kehila* and its executive. Later it came to denote the councils of the various Jewish communes and their assembly or 'parliament'. Attached to the *kahal* were a number of societies engaged in economic, cultural and charitable activities. The *kahal* system became increasingly centralized: the king was trying to simplify the collection of taxes and apportion fixed sums of revenue and the *kahal* relieved the governmental authorities of the task of seeking out individual taxpayers (just as under the Hitler régime Jewish self-governing communities made it easy for the Nazi henchmen to trace and seize Jewish citizens and their property). The *kahal* associations were responsible for raising very large sums of money. They then formed their own diets (the *Vaadim*), and by about 1580 a provincial diet had been set up as the central administrative institution of Polish Jews. In this council delegates met from the five provinces of Great and Little Poland, Podolia, Volhynia and Lithuania. Lithuania left the diet in 1623 and formed its own association, after which date the body was called 'Vaad of the Four Provinces'. It was a powerful organization, which looked after all the interests of the Polish Jews.

The special position of the Polish Jews had meanwhile begun to worry the supporters of the Counter-Reformation in Rome, where under Pope Paul IV (Giampetro Carafa) the Roman Inquisition had been revived. The fight against heretics and nonconformists was combined with sharp attacks on the

Jews. To the men around Pope Paul IV, Poland appeared as the promised land of both heretics and Jews. When Bishop Lippomano, whom the pope sent as papal Inquisitor to Poland in 1555, failed to make any headway against the various Protestant sects, he turned the wrath of the Catholics against the Jews.

A miracle of the sacred host was staged, and a Jewish girl and three Jewish men were executed on charges of having maltreated a stolen wafer until it had begun to bleed. Before they went to their deaths, these Jewish victims of Plock declared: 'It never occurred to us to pierce the host, for we could never believe that it was the body of God. God is incorporeal, just as a wafer is bloodless.'

This testimony is most important. To torture a sacred host could not make any sense to a Jew. *In charging Jews with such offences, their Christian accusers are pretending, as they have repeatedly done on other occasions, and at other times, that Jews believe things which Christians want to make themselves believe.* Violation of the Eucharist only makes sense in a Christian context. Such acts have, of course, taken place: for example among French Protestants, even earlier among the Albigenses and to this day among the sinister practitioners of 'Black Mass'. But the culprits everywhere have been Catholics and former Christians hoping to work off their spiritual bonds with the church, in part by a perverse ritual that is nothing but a malicious counterfeit of church liturgy. It never struck the Christian killers of those four Polish Jews that they were imputing to them a Christian, indeed a specifically Catholic, belief. And so they regarded the Jews' statement before their execution as blasphemy. The ecclesiastical judges ordered the executioner to ram burning torches into the victims' mouths.

King Sigismund II was shocked by this action of the bishop of Cholm and his adviser Lippomano, and in 1557 decreed that in future Jews charged with ritual murder or desecration of the host were to be arraigned only before the Sejm (the Polish Parliament) in the presence of the king and the highest dignitaries of the state.

Ten years after Lippomano's visit to Poland, Cardinal Commendoni reported on the situation of the Jews there, which he found astonishing: 'In these parts one finds large numbers of Jews who are not yet met with the contempt they arouse elsewhere. [He obviously regarded Poland as 'backward', because various religions still co-existed there in early medieval fashion.] Their situation is by no means wretched and not all their occupations are humiliating. [That is to say, as Pope Innocent III and St Thomas Aquinas considered they should be.] Indeed, there are landowners, merchants and students of medicine and astronomy among them. They own great wealth and are not only counted respectable members of the populace, but in some cases even hold superior positions. Far from wearing any marks distinguishing them from the Christians, they are even permitted to carry arms, and altogether enjoy the full rights of citizenship.'

This Polish golden age, in which art, science, humanistic education and poetry flourished in an atmosphere of Christian-Jewish co-existence, recalls the situation in Spain between the eighth and fourteenth centuries and in the Carolingian Empire under Charlemagne, Louis the Pious and Charles the Bald.

After the extinction of the dynasty of Jagello in 1572, Poland became a country of elected kings and deteriorated into a more characteristic disunity. Civil strife tore the country apart: contestants for the throne and their noble supporters intrigued and bargained with ever-changing allies. Under Sigismund III (1588–1632), a Swede from the house of Vasa, Poland became a land of latent civil war. And within this struggle clergy and townspeople waged a war of their own against the Jews. Inevitably Cracow became a battle centre. A local citizen, Sebastian Miczynski, acting on directives from the Cracow municipal authority, published a pamphlet *Mirror of Poland*, subtitled 'An Account of the Grave Iniquities Inflicted on Poland by the Jews, Drawn up for the Sons of the Realm Assembled in the Sejm'. The chief targets were the Jewish merchants and 'capitalists'. The author recommended the expulsion of the Jews from Poland and called for a pogrom. The date of the publication was 1618 – the year in which the Thirty Years War began.

Between 1621 and 1623 a doctor in Kalisz named Sleszkowski wrote three books attacking Jewish physicians as sorcerers, murderers, poisoners of Christians and carriers of the plague. During those years numerous trials for ritual murder were held in Poland, providing a medical chart of the fever that had seized the land. A book by Father Mojecki published in 1598 under the title *Cruelty, Murderous Acts and Superstition of the Jews* collated German anti-Semitic writings and showed particular interest in acts of desecration of the host and ritual murders. With the country disintegrating about them, Polish priests and Catholics, peasants and the lower classes saw the devilish Jew at work everywhere, violating Christ and Christian children. Their attitude had a great deal to do with economic rivalry. In 1648, Poland's fateful year, Jan Kmita, an employee at the rich salt mines of Bochnia run by Jewish leaseholders, published a lampoon entitled *The Raven in the Golden Cage, or The Jews in the Free Kingdom of Poland*, in which he said: 'No one in Poland is more prosperous than the Jew: there is always a fatted goose or chicken on his table, but the needy Catholic must eat his bread with tears for gravy.'

This is the anti-Semitism of the little man, such as could be encountered in Vienna around 1910 and again in 1930. But that same year 1648 saw the Polish Jews overwhelmed by a true and catastrophic deluge.

Wladislaw IV (1632–48), the 'wisest of the Polish Vasas', the son of Sigismund III, highly gifted and popular with the masses, found it increasingly hard to resist the Cossacks: they were Orthodox and allied to the Orthodox Russians, the Tartars and the Turks. On his death he was succeeded by his brother John Casimir, who had been living in France as a priest and had attained the rank of cardinal. Under his reign (1648–68) Poland fell apart. The Cossack rebellion and invasion led to a war with Russia which lasted thirteen years and in cruelty even surpassed the Thirty Years War. Ukrainian Cossacks, Russians and even the Poles themselves, fell upon the Polish Jews. (During the Second World War Ukrainians served as auxiliaries with the SS in the mass slaughter of the Jews.) Hundreds of thousands of Jews are said to have been beaten to death. Survivors were sold as slaves to Constantinople. The deluge of 1648 was one of the worst disasters in the whole of Jewry's disaster-ridden history. From thenceforward, the tradition of brutality took hold: new massacres in the civil war, and then, on the eve of Poland's first partition, more slaughter at the hands of Russian insurgents, to be followed by killings and pogroms in the eighteenth and nineteenth centuries; the blood bath of 1918–20, following close upon the heels of the First World War and continuing through the Russo-Polish war – all leading in the direction of Polish co-operation with Hitler in the 'final solution' of the Jewish question.

The Russians had long feared Poland as a superior power. Now, encouraged by the Cossack and Turkish thrust and by the internal disintegration of Poland, they went over to the offensive. Ever since the twelfth century Orthodox clergy had been doing its best to nurture in the Russian people, who in any case disliked foreigners, fear and horror of the 'corrupt West', of the warlike Franks. Had not these people under their bishops' leadership (during the Fourth Crusade in 1204) fallen upon and plundered Constantinople, the Holy City, the Jerusalem for which the Russians were yearning? Then the Russian clergy stirred up popular fear of the Germans and their merchants, who were obliged to live and house their wares in a German ghetto at Novgorod, entirely separated from the Russian population. In Russia's critical years under Ivan III a handful of Jews – Judaizers who had come to Moscow from Novgorod – threw the Orthodox clergy into a state of panic.

In about 1470 a man named Zacharias (also called Skarguina, Shkaria – possibly a symbolic name) is said to have come to Novgorod, where he allegedly convinced a number of clerics of the superiority of the Jewish faith. The Judaizing sect denied the Holy Trinity and Christ's divinity. They smashed the sacred ikons. (This type of iconoclasm, of gnostic and oriental origin, persisted in Russia till the early days of Bolshevism.) Jesus and Moses were considered to be equals. Similar ideas had been put 'about in early Byzantium by the followers of Photius and Marcellus in the fourth century, and they frequently crop up among newly baptized peoples – in the Carolingian Empire in the ninth century, in Russian territories in the fifteenth and sixteenth centuries and among Africans in the twentieth century.

In Moscow the Judaizers won over Ivan III's favourite, Fedor Kuritzin, as well as several of the monarch's relatives, and even the metropolitan of Moscow, Zossima. The counter-blow came in 1504. The leaders of the

Judaizers were burnt in Moscow. Princess Helen, Ivan's daughter-in-law, who had sponsored the movement, was sent to prison, where she died in the same year. The terrible fear of the Jews, however, persisted.

In the eyes of the Russian people the Jew was a wandering anti-Christ, a sorcerer, seducer, a sort of German Faust figure, and their fear made them keep out of his way. In 1526 the ambassador of Grand Prince Vassily III of Muscovy told Paulus Jovius, the Roman humanist and historian: 'We Russians fear most of all the Jewish people, to whom we have barred entry; after all, it was the Jews who not long ago taught the Turks how to use firearms.'

This old Russian belief that the Jew served hostile foreign powers has persisted through the centuries; first it was the Germans, then the Austrians, then, under Communism, the capitalist West, and yet later the state of Israel, the Americans and Zionism who were accused of making use of the Jew to undermine the Russian state.

When in 1550 King Sigismund II Augustus of Poland intervened with Ivan the Terrible on behalf of his Lithuanian Jewish merchants, the tsar declared: 'We have told you repeatedly of the evil deeds of the Jews – they have alienated our people from Christendom and have imported poisons into our dominions. [This idea that Jewish doctors were poisoning the Russian people and its leaders survived right up to the days of Stalin's indictment of Jewish physicians.] In all the countries to which Jews have been admitted, they have caused great harm, and have in consequence been expelled or condemned to death. How can we permit Jews to enter our dominions? We do not wish for any evil in our land, but are much more concerned that God may bestow on our peoples a peaceful and carefree life. We must ask you, our brother, to refrain from ever mentioning the Jews in your letters to us again.'

A peaceful, carefree life – in a closed society under an authoritarian régime, an existence without spiritual and intellectual excitement, peaceable, obedient, unquestioning, with not too many schools, and no Jews! For Jews are seen as elements of unrest, heresy, rebellion and, like bacteria and viruses, carriers of pestilence, destroyers of a nation's soul. And since their positive function as dissector, driving force and critic are not acknowledged, authoritarian leaders of state and church, from Ivan the Terrible up to the present day, do their best to keep the Jews out – or at least confined inside ghettoes. American anti-Semites of the twentieth century will have no difficulty in relating the policies of the autocratic rulers of All the Russias to their own ideal of a purely American society, in which all 'un-American activities' are prosecuted by the courts.

Ivan III, obsessed with hatred of all foreigners and Jews and fear of the Last Judgment, had all Jews drowned in the River Dvina when the Polish town of Polozk was captured. He also had the Catholic clergy of Poland put to death – killing two birds with one stone.

The Jews survived only in the borderlands of the tsarist empire – in the Baltic region, the Ukraine and in the Crimea. Catherine I expelled them from the Ukraine. In the western part of European Russia the Jews were confined to special areas right up to 1917. In the late nineteenth century all tsarist governments lived in perpetual fear of revolution: the government and its upper class political allies, such as the Black Hundreds (who had many affinities with the SS) systematically fomented fanatic nationalism and anti-Semitism in order to divert the discontented masses. This was quite freely admitted. These Russian anti-Semites, organized from above by the tsarist government, carried out officially approved pogroms – one of which has become famous through Lord Melchett's description. The beginning of the twentieth century saw the Easter pogrom at Kishinev in 1903 and another one in Bialystok in 1906. In October 1905 no less than 690 pogroms were organized to provide an outlet for the bitter disappointment occasioned by Russia's defeat in the war against Japan and the 'Bloody Sunday' of St Petersburg.

Between 1881 and 1914 a total of two million Russian and Polish Jews fled from the tsarist empire.

In 1889, the year Adolf Hitler was born, the English anti-Semite, Germanomaniac and pioneer of an arrogant nationalistic German ideology, Houston Stewart Chamberlain, moved to Vienna, where he stayed for twenty years. It was in the Austrian capital that the young Hitler was later to experience his first paroxysms of hate. Also in 1889 a Russian, Viktor Petrovich Klyushnikov, published his novel *Egyptian Darkness*, a story of barbaric anti-Semitism. The imperial tsarist printers at Tsarskoye Selo were the first to print the *Protocols of the Elders of Zion* in 1905. The historical impact of this forgery continues unabated today.

The great role played by forgeries of sacred books, testimonies, letters and documents in the history of Christendom has already been dealt with in a previous chapter. And to this day *pia fraus* (pious fraud) is regarded as a legitimate instrument to be used by integralists who consider themselves responsible for the preservation of the 'right order' on earth. Forgery continued unashamedly in the context of the Second Vatican Council, and regrettably nothing has been done under Pope Paul VI to identify the exalted authors of various forgeries in the reproduction of the encyclical *Pacem in terris* and of Council documents. Such people are convinced that their opponents are satellites of Satan. (This ominous term of denunciation, first employed in the political struggle of the church and later as a general politico-religious phrase of denigration, was coined by Calvin, who himself made masterly use of it.) They look on their adversaries as agents of anti-Christ, tools of the 'Jewish-Bolshevik conspiracy', set on destroying the church and the righteous. They therefore regard any method of combat as justified. The forgers themselves (though not always the hacks who work for them) believe in the legitimacy of their fraud, convinced that their work is false only in form and represents the real truth. By this logic, a forgery which upholds the pope's 'sacred claim' to Rome and the pontifical state, the rights of a monastery or a saint's power of salvation, can be held – in the opinion of the forgers – to be true.

According to this interpretation, 'believing' forgers are satisfied that they are doing the right thing (as those French men and women are satisfied who believe that the forged dossier in the Dreyfus trial served the salvation of the church, the army and the nation). This attitude is still openly professed by Catholic defenders of the *Protocols of the Elders of Zion*. Both they and National Socialist 'believers' in the *Protocols* declare that their outward literary form is of no significance. What alone matters is their 'inner truthfulness'. Since this is beyond doubt, they conclude that it is important to disseminate the *Protocols* throughout Christendom and the free world.

In the early twenties of this century millions of copies of the *Protocols* were distributed in the United States. An explanation had to be found for the deep malaise that followed the victory of the First World War and for the economic depression: it was all the fault of the Jews . . . In order to secure the widest circulation of the *Protocols* Henry Ford founded a journal *Dearborn Independent*, which had three hundred thousand subscribers.

The dissemination of the *Protocols* in Germany, France, Palestine and the Arab world after 1918 brings us to contemporary issues. But some attention should first be paid to the Russian background of the whole affair. It was not only by chance that the *Protocols* were concocted in Russia, in the service of Imperial Russian propaganda. A minor Stalinist parallel can be found in the richly documented story during the Korean War, when Russian and Chinese Communists and Communist governments spread the news that the Americans were trying to infect Korea and China with bubonic plague.

There were two large anti-Semitic organizations in tsarist Russia, both enjoying official government support: the *Sojus Russkogo Naroda* (Union of the Russian People) and the *Douglavij Orel* (Two-headed Eagle). Both served an extremist policy of Russification, which established itself under the last tsars: its aim was to 'Russify' all the peoples of the empire, convert them to Russian Orthodoxy and instil in them faith in the tsar and Holy Russia. Among those who put up a most obstinate resistance to this total co-ordination were the Jews. They would have to be exterminated. In any case, they were plotting to overthrow the tsar and preparing the dominion of anti-Christ.

Plots: French emigrés who had swarmed to Germany, Switzerland and Russia during the French Revolution made use of pamphlets, sermons and society salons to spread the story that, long before the revolution, Holy France had been undermined by a conspiracy of Jews, freemasons and Jacobins. This French plot theory found willing audiences in Berlin, Vienna, Munich, Madrid, Rome and, above all, among the reactionary circles of St Petersburg. (Most of the present-day plots, theories and ideologies derive from that source.) Metternich finally succeeded in separating Tsar Alexander I from his German adorers around Madame de Krüdener by convincing the tsar that there was a real foundation to the plot theory: all lawful rulers were threatened by revolution. The revolution was being prepared from a centre in Paris.

The French emigré plot theory preyed on old Russian fears. The Russian Orthodox clergy had felt itself encircled by Rome ever since the Middle Ages. Tsarist politicians were aware of the anti-Russian mood in Western Europe, where a widespread fear of the 'Russian peril' existed in the late eighteenth and throughout the nineteenth centuries. Russian reactionaries, feeling isolated, afraid of being denounced as backward, as well as worried by their political, technological and military inferiority to the West, began to think of the Jews: were the Jews not born traitors, agents of the West and world revolution?

The author of the *Protocols of the Elders of Zion*, Sergei Nilus, was a minor official in the office of the Holy Synod, the tsarist church ministry in Moscow. The *Protocols* first appeared in 1905 as a chapter of a pamphlet by Nilus entitled *The Great and the Small – the Advent of Anti-Christ*. From 1905 onwards Sergei Nilus asserted that the *Protocols* had been read out at a secret session of the Zionist Congress in Basle in August 1897 to acquaint the Jews, assembled there by Theodor Herzl, with the grand design of the Jewish world conquest. According to Nilus, a secret agent sent to the congress by the tsarist government had made a copy of the *Protocols* which, after many adventures, had fallen into the publisher's hands.

In 1921 the London *Times* revealed the history of the *Protocols*. *The Times* correspondent in Constantinople discovered a thin volume, originally owned by a former tsarist officer and member of the Ochrana (the political police), with the title *Dialogue aux Enfers entre Machiavel et Montesquieu, ou La politique de Machiavel au XIX siècle* (first edition, Brussels, 1864). These conversations in hell between Machiavelli and Montesquieu were a political satire against Napoleon III. Apart from this, Sergei Nilus also made use of a pamphlet written in 1905 against the Russian minister Witte.

In this the 'Elders of Zion' declare: 'We will establish a central world government of great splendour and complete despotism. The wheels of the machines of every state move on fuel which is in our hands – gold. We will set up a supra-government and subjugate all resisting countries by war, if necessary by a world war. Everywhere in Europe and, through our relations with Europe, in other continents too, we must sow discord, hostility and unrest. After our final victory we will root out all other religions; only the Jewish faith shall be allowed to exist. Should the *goyim* dare to rise against us, we will answer them with the guns of America and China or Japan.'

The *Protocols of the Elders of Zion* include a detailed plan of Jewish world economy which shows a most striking ignorance on every question of economy, industry and technology. A specifically Russian charge is made against the Jews: wherever they come to power they advocate technical and scientific education of the young.

The immediate aim of the *Protocols* in 1905 was to prevent the manifesto of 30 October from becoming a political reality. The manifesto, wrested from the tsar in the Russian uprising following the defeat in the war against Japan, promised 'true inviolability of the person, freedom of conscience, of speech, of assembly and the right of forming associations'. A few days after its proclamation a wave of 'spontaneous' right-wing demonstrations, organized by the police, swept the country. The demonstrators objected to any renunciation of the sacred, time-honoured rights of the tsar – and a wave of pogroms began.

Sergei Nilus himself published new editions of the *Protocols* in 1911, 1912 and 1917. In the autumn of 1919 a German captain, Mueller von Hausen, using the pseudonym Gottfried zur Beck, translated the *Protocols* (not the entire work of Nilus but only this appendix) under the title *Die Geheimnisse der Weisen von Zion*, and dedicated it to 'The princes of Europe'. (It may be recalled that Metternich had repeatedly warned Pope Gregory xvi, the tsar and all those whom he regarded as 'Christian princes' against a world-wide plot of revolutionaries and sectarians. Let the princes heed the warning and understand it aright – here was a threat of a great Jewish conspiracy against throne and altar!)

Members of the German Protestant aristocracy sponsored the dissemination of the *Protocols*; among them Prince Otto of Salm, Prince Joachim Albert of Prussia and ex-Emperor Wilhelm ii, who recommended the book to his visitors at Doorn. (We shall see in a later chapter how it was the French nobility who gathered round Drumont in the Dreyfus affair.)

Count Reventlow's *Deutsche Volkszeitung* and the Prussian Protestant conservative *Kreuzzeitung* publicized the *Protocols*. Throughout the nineteenth century in France, and especially after 1918, in Germany, aristocrats and conservatives (who were really reactionaries) had widely indulged in the wishful thought that it might be possible to use anti-Semitism to turn the masses against 'Jewish' Socialism and 'Jewish' democracy, bring them back to the monarchy and the church and build up an authoritarian and national mass movement or party. This was why so many of them later slithered into National Socialism and similar political creeds.

Round about 1920 a Polish edition of the *Protocols* appeared, and three French versions followed in quick succession. In the early twenties editions appeared in England, America (three), Scandinavia and Italy. The first Arabic version, which spread like wildfire in the Near East, appeared in 1925.

Adolf Hitler refers to the *Protocols* in his book *Mein Kampf* to justify his call for special measures in the struggle against the 'Jewish world menace'.

Sergey Witte, who as prime minister in 1905–06 made some liberal concessions to the reform movement in Russia and who was the target of criticism in the *Protocols*, is reported to have discussed the Jews with the tsar. Witte is said to have remarked ironically that if it were technically possible to drown all Russian Jews simultaneously in the Black Sea he would be in favour of such a solution. But, since it could not be done technically, one would have to put up with the continued existence of the Jews. Witte, who died in 1915, did not realize how soon technology – always a child of war and the armament industry – would make it possible.

In the nineteenth and early twentieth centuries anti-Semitism persisted or grew in East Europe, carefully nurtured by authority in the tsarist empire. Among the Estonians, Lithuanians, Latvians, Rumanians and Hungarians it turned into a murderous anti-Jewish drive. In Poland anti-Semitism had a strong Catholic tinge. It pointed, via Austro-Hungary and Germany, in the direction of the country which in the nineteenth century became the motherland of revolution and counter-revolution and the cradle of all pre-Fascist and National Socialist movements and parties in Europe: to France.

Shattered by the experience of the Dreyfus trial, Theodor Herzl, feature editor of the *Freie Presse* in Vienna and Jewish member of an Austrian students' association, became interested in Zionism.

The Dreyfus affair grew out of the permanent civil war which has convulsed France ever since her defeat in the 1870–1 war with Prussia.

9

The French Versus Jewry

'*By'ei Zhidov!*' Kill the Jews! That was the official Russian battle-cry. It was taken up with enthusiasm in France by Edouard Drumont and the many Catholics who with him welcomed the pogroms in Russia. Drumont declared that the Jews had infected Russia with syphilis. Drumont considered himself a pioneer, the precursor of some later great man who would produce a final solution. Jean Drault, one of the last survivors of Drumont's short-lived party, said in 1935 that Hitler had achieved what Drumont proclaimed. Drumont wanted to burn Zola, the defender of Captain Dreyfus, and drown the Jews in the Seine. They should not be burnt alive, since a young roasted Jew would give off a dreadful smell (*Libre Parole*, 12 February 1898).

Georges Bernanos, right up to his death one of the greatest defenders of freedom, was as late as 1931 praising Drumont's *La France Juive* as a masterpiece of learning, analysis and observation. These facts reveal to what extent France, a country which had hardly any Jews since the expulsion of the Jews in the Middle Ages and then (after the conquest of Alsace-Lorraine) only in territories of the former Holy Roman Empire, was a cradle of anti-Semitism in Europe.

The *Protocols of the Elders of Zion* had predicted the coming of anti-Christ, the Jewish Messiah bent on establishing on earth the kingdom of the Devil. Orthodox Russia was the last bulwark against him. Darwinism, Marxism and Nietzscheanism all owed their success to the Jews.

Something has already been said of the French literary sources of the *Protocols*. Charles Péguy, that lone defender of the true honour of France and French Catholicism against the rabid anti-Semitism of Catholic aristocrats, priests, bishops, country parsons and laymen, has acknowledged the existence of a long anti-Jewish and anti-Semitic tradition in France, comprising not only the masses, their anti-Jewish feelings nourished and kept alive in sermons and passion plays from the Middle Ages onward, but also the most enlightened French minds: Pascal, and above all Bossuet, the great preacher, from whose fulminating, scintillating rhetoric Paul Claudel could still draw strength.

Bossuet took a truly sadistic delight in the misfortunes of the Jews in world history. Rousseau, Voltaire, Catholic France in the age of Enlightenment, all were anti-Jewish, even anti-Semitic in the strict sense of the word.

Lamennais, 'the druid who sang of freedom', as Lacordaire called him, put the Jews on a lower level than slaves.

In Paris, on 14 October 1789, Isaac Berr made a great speech in the National Assembly. In the name of God and of humanity he begged for justice for the Jews, those people who were persecuted in all countries. Men should accept us, the Jews, as brothers. In 1791 the National Assembly passed, and Louis XVI ratified, a law emancipating the Jews in France. In Austria Emperor Joseph II, a true friend and a brotherly adviser to Louis in the problems of his marriage with his sister Marie Antoinette, had already shown the way with his charter of religious tolerance. This charter (1782) ordered among other things the abolition of the Jewish stigma and of the poll-tax.

For the Jews in Europe the French Revolution meant the beginning of a new age. It opened up for them new homelands, *nouvelles patries*. Edmond Fleg, notable French-Jewish poet and philosopher, stressed the fact that for the Jews the French Revolution had as great a meaning as the destruction of the second temple in Jerusalem. Forces and energies which had for centuries lain in bondage were now made free. France was followed in the emancipation of Jews by Holland in 1796, and by Prussia in 1812. The French Revolution, in the view of Catholics in France, Spain, Italy, Latin America, bears the greatest share of blame for the spread of the Jewish peril.

In 1792, amidst the jubilation of the populace, a venerable old Jew of ninety was elected president of the town council of Fort-Louis in Alsace. His name was Abraham Dreyfus. The family of the future Captain Dreyfus left their native home when Alsace became part of the German empire, and went to France. They would have been able to live there unmolested at least until 1933, were it not for the tragedy that brought them into the history books. This name of Dreyfus, encountered here in 1792, draws attention to an aspect of the French Revolution that is often overlooked: its leading men were not interested in preserving or rescuing Jewry as such. Their aim was to emancipate the individual Jew and make him into a full man. With the help of the Revolution he would be liberated from his Jewishness, his 'superstitious' Jewish manners and customs, from his exclusiveness.

It was – in its own way – a 'final solution'. The emancipated Jews were to seek complete assimilation in the nation, both physically and spiritually, and sacrifice themselves to it on all battlefields.

Jewish anti-Semites of the nineteenth and twentieth centuries, from Karl Marx to Arthur Koestler and beyond, could find in the French Revolution a legitimate precedent for their call to the Jews to abandon their suicidal separateness and to assimilate themselves in a single humanity.

Devout French Jews early recognized the great threat of the French Revolution. In 1807 the Sanhedrin convened in Paris by Napoleon drafted a statute for Jews in modern society.

The Dreyfus affair, as Robert F.Byrnes has said, 'was the most serious crisis of modern democratic society faced between the Civil War in the United States and the rise of Communism and Fascism throughout Europe after the First World War'. Fascism and all the rest of our modern totalitarian ideologies and movements are deeply rooted in our social conditions. And the internal dissensions in France, which were let loose (or rather brought into the open) by the Dreyfus affair, and which in the Fourth Republic almost led to a new catastrophe for France and Europe, were essentially a reflection of tensions within the whole European situation.

In about 1880 the European system of alliance, which, in its essentials had held together from the Vienna Congress of 1815 until between 1866 and 1870, collapsed. The collapse of the European 'balance of power', for which England had struggled for centuries, and which Metternich, Talleyrand and Castlereagh had revitalized as a defence against Russian and Prussian aggression, was basically responsible for the Jewish tragedy culminating in the events of 1945.

In 1886 – the year of catastrophe for Austria-Hungary, which, weakened beyond redemption by Prussian victory at Königgrätz, was split into two unequal halves – Rumania declared all Jews in its territory to be foreigners. This was later to be the pattern for the extermination of Jews in Nazi Europe. First the Jews are made stateless, declared to be troublesome foreigners, and then left to the mercies of native or foreign persecutors and murderers.

In 1878, at the Berlin Congress, Rumania had been coerced into granting equal citizenship to its Jews. Between 1887 and 1902 Rumanian laws excluded Jews successively from all public offices, limited their civil rights, granted Jewish workers only a restricted opportunity to work, and prepared by statutory means that 'final solution' which, much to Hitler's astonishment, made the Rumanians his pacemakers. He found it necessary to apply the brakes to them – for technical reasons.

In 1895 the first Dreyfus trial took place.

The Third Republic in France was the child of defeat in the Franco-Prussian War of 1870–1 (just as after 1919 the Weimar Republic was seen as the offspring of German surrender in the First World War). The rise of the Paris Commune was not a Socialist or even Communist revolution (as militant Catholics right-wingers in France and Europe like to denounce it to this day), but a desperate rising of patriotic Parisian workers who were convinced that they were being betrayed to Bismarck. The bloody week from 21–8 May 1871, in which about twenty thousand workers lost their lives, and fifty thousand were arrested, was one of the cruellest episodes of recent history. Appalled, Victor Hugo watched French Catholicism locked in murderous hate, its only hope the army, the dictatorship of the sword.

The fear of the workers' vengeance poisoned French Catholicism and its allies, the atheistic, politically liberal upper-middle-class intelligentsia, at least up to 1914.

Militant French nationalism and chauvinism, building up to 1914 and then after 1918 blossoming even more poisonously to destroy Briand's efforts for peace, was the offspring of an unholy alliance between a neurotic French Catholicism and an anticlerical, non-Christian middle class which saw in the church a means to keep the masses in check.

This new nationalism became a sort of religion, which bound Catholics and non-Catholics together in the 'holy cause' of France. The most radical and anticlerical governments in France gave warm support to Catholic missions such as those in the Lebanon, in Africa and in China. The White Fathers, France's leading Catholic Order of missionaries, were fervent nationalists and French chauvinists.

The alliance, however, existed only on the surface and did not last long. The old discord between the 'two Frances' – royalist France, which wished to return to the Ancien Régime and stamp out the French Revolution, and post-revolutionary secular France – broke out again. The majority of France's Catholics – peasants, middle and lower middle classes, aristocrats and military officers – joined the camp of the enemies of the Republic. In 1882 Bishop Freppel preached that the Fourteenth of July, the national day of rejoicing for the detested Republic, was the remembrance day of the most odious massacre in history, the French Revolution. In 1884 he declared in the Chamber of Deputies that the whole anticlerical campaign was a Semitic movement.

From 1879 to 1884 the political defeats of the monarchists and the church nourished the anti-Semitic campaigns. The Jews, it was said, were responsible for the hostility towards the church, for the defeat of 1871, for the general corruption, for the Republic itself. Surplus intellectuals gathered in Paris, which was also the centre of French Jewry. These men of letters – poor, ambitious journalists fallen on hard times – began to criticize the rich, corrupt Republic, leading lights in society and Jews. Most French men of letters, as well as many politicians, started out on the left wing, but ended up on the right.

An interesting light on this period is thrown by Hippolyte Taine in his seven-volume *Origines de la France contemporaine* (1871–93). This romantic writer explained the catastrophe of 1871 in terms of the French Revolution. All that was evil came from that.

Taine's work became the classic of French reaction: France should return to the monarchy and to the aristocracy. Both Barrès and Maurras have their origin in Taine, who maintained that Man is shaped by his race, environment and the spirit of the age. Fatalistic determinist that he was, Taine saw Man as 'a rudderless rabbit', incompetent to control the vast powers. His great disciple Charles Maurras acknowledges himself to be both an atheist and a Catholic. To this day he delights church leaders in Rome and France with his call for order and a strong power to enforce it. His *Action Française* was proscribed in Rome after the First World War and then, in 1939, on the eve of the Second World War, was rehabilitated by Pope Pius XII. Maurras, an anti-Semite, like almost all the Catholic right wing in France, declared (*Chemin de Paradis*): 'I should not wish to sacrifice the learned procession of church councils, popes and the modern élite of great men with their anti-Semitic proclamations, in order to place my trust in the gospels of four obscure Jews.'

Almost every blasphemy against God and Man from such illustrious spirits of the right is overlooked or even benevolently tolerated by churchmen, while every left-wing critic of church and society is angrily repulsed. The poor, pacific Marc Sangnier with his mild criticism of society in *Le Sillon* is condemned by the church.

French Catholic anti-Semites were attentively watching the rise of anti-Semitism throughout Europe. There was the court chaplain Adolf Stöcker in Berlin with his 'Christian Social Movement'. Anti-Semitic votes in the Reichstag elections rose from 47,500 in the year 1890 to 285,000 in 1898 and to 461,000 in 1910. In Austria-Hungary popular anti-Semitism centred around Georg von Schönerer and the 'German Club' in Vienna (1882). Schönerer agitated in beerhalls, as did later his admirer Adolf Hitler. Hitler also admired Karl Lueger, master of the Catholic 'anti-Semitism of the little man'. In oppressed and divided Poland the hate of the uneducated masses, particularly of the rural population, was turned against the Jews. The assassination of Tsar Alexander II was the signal for officially sanctioned anti-Semitism to become violent in Russia. In 1881 more than three hundred pogroms took place, and the May Laws of 1882 confined the Jews to enclosed ghetto areas. Between 1905 and 1916 the tsar gave approximately twelve million roubles to support anti-Semitic propaganda. More than twelve million copies of anti-Semitic books and brochures were distributed in this period.

Russia seemed to French anti-Semites to be the Promised Land of the 'Jewish solution'. Leading foreign anti-Semites were invited to write for the French Catholic press. Kalixt de Wolski published a book on *Jewish Russia* in Paris in 1887. Catholic, anti-Semitic France showed particular interest in anti-Semitism in Germany and Austria-Hungary. One of the first documents on anti-Semitism in the Third Republic was an article in the influential *Revue du Monde Catholique* (1881) about anti-Semitism in Germany, written by Hermann Kuhn, German correspondent of the Catholic newspaper *Le Monde*. At the climax of the Dreyfus affair two books appeared in Paris on anti-Semitism in Austria. The effusion by Canon (later Professor) August Rohling entitled *Der Talmudjude* (1873) underwent in 1889 (the year of Hitler's birth), three translations into French. One of them was made by Father Maximilian de Lamarque. Father Henri Desportes took over Rohling's role in France: he even fabricated a ritual murder affair (*Tué par les Juifs. Histoire d'un meurtre rituel*, Paris 1890).

In 1872 there were 49,439 Jews in France, which is 0.13 per cent of the total population. Proportionally Russia had forty-two times as many Jews, Austria sixteen times more, Holland eight, Germany five, Turkey two and a half. Even Switzerland had proportionally more Jews than France. Yet Drumont claimed in *La France Juive* in 1886 that there were more than five hundred thousand Jews in France. His disciple Jacques de Biez raised this figure to six hundred thousand. The anti-Semitic Jewish journalist Arthur Meyer (Paris and Vienna were also centres of anti-Semitic and anti-Jewish Jews) falsely declared that there were six to seven Jewish prefects in France. Peter Isidore Bertrand, a Jewish convert, raised this figure to forty-two!

For patriotic reasons – because they preferred to be French rather than German – Jews emigrated after 1871 from Alsace-Lorraine to France, among them the family of Léon Blum, the family of Dreyfus. Like France's intellectuals and politicians, the Jews made Paris their target. They were for the most part insignificant, even needy people. Sixty per cent of them died poor. In Paris, however, Rothschild was the archetype of the 'Jewish capitalist', and as such ardently envied. In the press, in the theatre, in the worlds of criticism and the law, in medicine, in political management, Jews worked their way upwards. Marcel Proust (himself half Jewish, yet a child of the anti-Semitic reactionary social circle into which he was born) portrayed in his masterpiece *À la Recherche du Temps perdu* the flight into childhood, back to the womb (the equivalent for French reactionaries of a return to pre-revolutionary France) in the figure of a theatre manager who changed his name to Samuel in order to win more success.

How did rich and poor Jews act when faced with the rising wave of anti-Semitism? The attitude of French Jews in the Paris of the 1880s was already prophetic of the attitude of German Jews in the Berlin of the 1930s. The poor Jews, the small people were not consulted: they sought simply to keep out of the way. Rich and distinguished Jews were anxious to avoid a clash: their best policy was to pretend that anti-Semitism did not exist. At the same time the emancipation drive was intensified: the goal was – cost what it might (and the cost grew from country to country) – to become, to be, to appear to be a good Frenchman, a good German. Most French Jews at first accepted the verdict on Dreyfus as just. A characteristic conservatism joined hands with fear to dominate a French Jewry which with growing sophistication had lost its faith. Devout Jews like the great Jewish poet Alexandre Weill, who spoke out against Drumont, and like the atheistic, yet in his own way deeply devout Jew Bernard-Lazare, were extremely rare. The chief rabbi of France, Zadoc Kahn, a native of Alsace-Lorraine, stood up for the Jews, but as a French nationalist.

In 1890 the National Anti-Semitic League was founded. In 1892 it was replaced in Paris by the anti-Semitic newspaper *Libre Parole*.

There is no anti-Semitism in literature to rival in brilliance that of France. For more than two hundred years the French theatre presented Jews as evil and despicable (thus unwittingly proving its descent from medieval church drama). Countess Sybille Martel de Janville, a member of an old royalist family, wrote best-selling anti-Semitic novels under the pseudonym of Gyp: her father was a papal officer. But more significant than Gyp and the many other literary 'females of both sexes' was the fact that some of the greatest men of letters in the nation professed the anti-Semitism of a Drumont. Edmond de Goncourt reveals it in his nine-volume Journal. Alphonse Daudet, the great French novelist, introduced Drumont and his work to the publishing house of Marpon and Flammarion and gave him much support.

A conservative and racial anti-Semitism was propagated in his life's work by Count Gobineau and by the 'Soldier of Christ' (as Henri Gougenot des Mousseaux called himself). Gobineau was the son of an army officer under Louis XVIII, was educated in Switzerland and in 1844 became de Tocqueville's secretary. As a professional diplomat he never attained his ambition, which was to become ambassador in Constantinople. He was a frail, sensitive, lonely, remote and deeply pessimistic man, who felt himself forsaken by his age, which he hated. He hated 'weak' men and also hated himself for being a weak man. Towards the end of his life he fell under the spell of Wotan. A friend of Richard Wagner since 1876, his influence was greater in Germany than in France. In Freiburg a Gobineau Society was set up in 1894. His *Essai sur l'inégalité des races humaines* (1853–5), says in four learned, speculative and digressive volumes (likely of course for that very reason to impress German readers) what every young royalist nobleman and officer in the Third Republic was saying in one word to his fellows, confident of its truth: namely, that he, as a French nobleman, came of better stock than the 'canaille', the reds, the Republicans and the Jews.

In 1870 Plon published *Le Juif, le Judaisme et la Judaization des peuples chrétiens* by Henry Gougenot des Mousseaux. It was a warning to the Christian peoples to protect themselves from increasing Jewish influence. Issued on the eve of the First Vatican Council, it can be compared with Pinay's book published on the eve of the Second Vatican Council. The preface was written by Father Voisin – head of the Paris Seminar for Foreign Missions.

Pope Pius IX blessed the author for his courage. The motto of this book was that everywhere perverse Jews were leading the campaign against the church. The Jews were using the liberal ideas of the eighteenth century and also freemasonry to gain domination over the world and to destroy the church. Gougenot explained the defeat of Catholic Austria in 1866 at Königgrätz (felt in France equally as a French defeat) by the Protestant Prussians as the result of Jewish manipulations.

French anti-Semitism belonged from the 1880s onwards to the right wing. Before 1880–5, however, the most virulent political anti-Semitism in France came from the left, which could look back to a great tradition: Voltaire, Diderot and the great period of Enlightenment had all been anti-Jewish.

Whereas the French Revolution aimed to assimilate the Jew in the 'free citizens' of the nation, early French Socialism and utopian Socialism were anti-Semitically inclined. The invective of Charles Fourier anticipates the early Nazis tracts of the 1920s. It was from early French Socialism that the Nazis took over the picture of Rothschild as the embodiment of 'Jewish capitalism'. These small early Socialists saw Rothschild as the frightening 'super-father' eating up the children of France. Fourier's disciple, Alphonse Toussenel, presented the Jews to the workers and people of France as the kings of the epoch (*Les juifs rois de l'époque*, 1845). In the Paris of 1941 L. Thomas portrayed Toussenel as a National Socialist anti-Semite, to be regarded as a model for the present day (*Alphonse Toussenel – Socialiste national antisémite*, 1803–85; Paris 1941).

Pierre Joseph Proudhon, the great French master of forward-looking *political* fantasy, was also an anti-Semite. He pointed his finger at capitalists, bankers, Jews. Early French Socialism – more liberal and more individualistic than the Socialism of the anti-Jewish Karl Marx – suffered to some extent from a Rothschild complex. It saw the whole world ensnared and sucked dry by the Rothschilds in Paris. National Socialists and Vichy French honoured Proudhon as the great pioneer of their ideas.

Conservatives and Catholics were the main upholders of anti-Semitism on the right. The French Revolution appeared to them as a plot hatched by occult powers: Jews and freemasons. Pope Leo XIII's encyclical against free-masonry (20 April 1884) was directed in particular against French masons. The pope, following St Augustine's fatal theology, divided mankind into two classes: one belonging to the kingdom of Christ, the other to the empire of Satan. A decree issued by the Holy Office (heir to the Inquisition) on 20 August 1884 declared the Oddfellows, the Sons of Temperance, and the Knights of Pytheas to belong to the 'Synagogue of Satan'. And who was at the bottom of the synagogue of Satan? The Jews, of course. French clerics and literary laymen regarded freemasons, Jews and Germans (the Jew is an agent of the Germans!) as much the same thing. Between 1880 and 1885 there appeared twenty-four anti-masonic books and twenty-three pamphlets. Fourteen of these were written by Catholic priests, five by bishops.

All the misfortunes of France can be traced back to masonic and Jewish influences. Thus did French Catholicism give the finishing touch to the plot theory which French emigrants had spread throughout the world after 1789. France, long considered the 'land of Satan' through its various preoccupations with the Devil, began to develop a political form of satanism to put beside literary, libidinous satanism, the satanism of black masses and the black literature of the *poètes maudits*. The anti-masonic, anti-satanic French Catholic newspapers were the first to declare war on the Devil by publishing anti-Semitic articles. Father Chabauty was a leading pamphleteering journalist in this vein.

The storm broke. Boulanger, whom French Catholics wanted to make their leader in the fight against Germany and the effort to 'purge' France of all 'traitors' and Republicans, became minister of war. Three months after his appointment and three months before his great triumph at the parade of the Fourteenth of July, *La France Juive* appeared – on 14 April 1866. Its *leitmotiv*: throughout French history the Jews had been the main cause of all national crises and misfortunes: and especially after 1870. The Jews were by their very nature spies, traitors and criminals. Every Protestant was half-Jewish, and the Germans were both Protestants and Jews. The Third Republic was denounced (as was later the Weimar Republic) as being 'infested with Jews'.

In 1887 the first illustrated edition of *La France Juive* appeared. The picture on the jacket shows Drumont bearing a cross and advancing on an old man bearing the tablets of the Ten Commandments from Mount Sinai. (We are reminded of that picture in Siena, with the triumphant St Thomas Aquinas towering above the 'little' Jew at his feet.) Illustrations inside depict, among other things, a ritual murder and Huguenot as well as Jewish – masonic anticlerical atrocities.

The publisher was the leading Catholic house of Gautier. Edouard Drumont, the author, now became a hero of French Catholics anti-Semitism and a leading figure in the Dreyfus affair. Drumont, the son of a small provincial official, was born in 1844 and lived all his life in fear of poverty. He concealed his money all over his house in hiding places within easy reach. Drumont had begun work with a Jewish publishing firm, and for several years all his social contacts had been with Jews. In 1886 he was a hard-working and ambitious journalist who had hitherto got nowhere. An only child and early widowed, he remained throughout his life a solitary, basically shy man without children or any real personal friends.

Drumont carried a mandrake around with him, believed in fortune-tellers and was in touch with spiritualists. In the 1890s one of his disciples, Gaston Méry, wanted to start a holy war of the Celtic against the Latin races. With other journalists in Drumont's circle, Méry founded the magazine *L'Echo du Merveilleux*, which was entirely devoted to witchcraft and the occult sciences. This 'magical' Paris was intrinsically related to 'magical' Munich, and was in many ways associated with it in the nineteenth century. The four-volume *Christian Mysticism* of Joseph von Görres, a farrago of satanic practices, magic arts and demons, circulated in two translations in this royalist and anti-Republican France, kicking against the technological advances of the nineteenth century, which seemed to it to be totally under Jewish domination. Hitler also believed in mandrakes and nature cures, and in the early years of Munich was immersed with Dietrich Eckart, Hess and Himmler in a similar atmosphere.

Drumont, in his younger days more a Catholic on paper than in conviction, all of a sudden became a militant political Catholic and at the same time an anti-Semite. In the summer of 1884 he made a pilgrimage to Canterbury to his rich Jesuit friend Father du Lac (the Jesuits having been driven out of the French Republic), in order to check that the manuscript of *La France Juive* contained no theological errors.

Before the end of the year 1886 more than one hundred thousand copies of *La France Juive* had been sold in France. Translations appeared in Germany, Spain, Italy, Portugal and the United States of America.

Drumont found followers on the left, right and in the centre of the political spectrum. The 'revolutionary working man', as presented by the *Revue Socialiste*, was a fighter inside a National Socialist movement. The main targets were Rothschild and capitalism. Until the Dreyfus affair Drumont's move was disguised as a kind of Socialism. Cheap editions of *La France Juive* preached a socio-political gospel of salvation to the working classes: deliverance of the people from Jewish capitalist slavery.

Jacques de Bièz, Drumont's first disciple and vice-president of the Anti-Semitic League, declared in 1889: 'We are Socialists, we are National Socialists, because we are attacking international finance. We want France for the French.' This movement foundered, because, as Léon Daudet later explained, it became a meeting place for people of all shades of opinion. Hitler rose to power when he succeeded in promising everything to almost everybody: to the workers the smashing of capitalist slavery, to small shopkeepers the destruction of Jewish department stores, to Catholics the liquidation of Jewish-Liberal influence in the Weimar Republic.

Though putting himself forward as a Socialist, Drumont was in fact a romantic and melancholic reactionary. He dreamed, like Major Esterhazy, the sorry hero of the Dreyfus affair, of a 'march on Rome', of *la dernière bataille*. Five hundred determined anti-Semites could conquer Paris and become masters of France within a year. But France no longer had men of that sort, and so the future of the world would needs rest in American hands. Drumont did not feel himself called to be a political leader.

His Nazi type of anti-Semitism did, however, infect Socialists, such as those around Auguste Dirac and Edmond Picard. It was not until the battle of the Dreyfus affair that Socialism woke from this dream.

Real, heartfelt and enthusiastic acceptance Drumont found only among the French Catholics. Country parsons – poor, uneducated, despised by the Republic and its intellectuals, ignored by the higher clergy – these were Drumont's most enthusiastic readers. But the royalist, anti-Republican higher clergy was not far behind. One solitary French bishop raised objections to the denunciation and condemnation of the Jews in *La France Juive*, which anticipates in so many respects the Vichy *Statut des Juifs*, Pétain's special legislation which delivered up the Jews in France to Hitler's henchmen.

In *La Croix*, the influential Assumptionist newspaper, *La France Juive* met with an enthusiastic reception from Father Georges de Pascal on the day of its first publication. Eugène Veuillot's *Univers* reprinted the last page of *La France Juive* on Easter Saturday 1886 as a reminder that, just as Christ rose from the dead after his crucifixion at the hands of the Jews, so would Christian France free itself from Jewish dominion. For centuries during Easter Week Jews had had to be protected by the civic authorities from massacre. Now there were new calls to new massacres. But where were the civic authorities?

Extreme anti-Semitic, Catholic, conservative writers like Father Georges de Pascal and Father Joseph Lémann (a converted Jew), displayed considerable journalistic activity. Father Isidore Bertrand declared that Jews, masons, Protestants and Germans were responsible for the downfall of the papacy! A particularly sinister figure in this devil's kitchen was Father Henri Desportes, who was active in Rouen, Amiens and Lille. In 1889 – once again we encounter this fatal year! – and in 1890 he brought out a fat book and two pamphlets about Jewish human sacrifices and ritual murders. Through the close links existing between the conservative and reactionary circles of French Catholicism and the Curia in Rome (*La Civiltà Cattolica* supported the French anti-Semites in the Dreyfus trial), these atrocity stories had a great effect on Roman Catholicism. Father Desportes's periodical *La Terre de France* called for the destruction of Jewish and masonic might. In *Le Mystère du Sang* (1899) he combined all the themes of his blood-and-soil mysticism together to produce a work horrifyingly prophetic of the later blood cult of Nazi fanatics.

Monsignor Justin Fèvre, an extremely prolific writer, summed up his hatred against democracy in the single statement that rationalism, socialism, and liberalism were the causes of France's misery. During the Dreyfus trial he wrote: 'We Catholics and Frenchmen *must* all of us – even at the risk of being punished for high treason – be anti-Semitic.'

Within the Catholic publishing industry, which was anti-democratic and anti-Semitic, Victor Palme was particularly active. His great combine published, among other things, August Rohling's *Der Talmudjude* in French.

The popular Catholic press, in which the Assumptionist Father Vincent de Paul Bailly played the leading role, fed the Catholic masses with demagogic journalism. *La Croix du Dimanche*, the Sunday edition of *La Croix*, had in 1899 a circulation of 525,000 copies. In 1897 the Vatican refused a request from the French government to persuade *La Croix* to cease its immoderate campaign against the Republic. In January 1900 the French government banned the Assumptionists.

Just how deeply French Catholicism was influenced by this ceaseless propaganda is shown by the socio-political Christian Democratic youth movement. Its members – mostly young priests interested in a reconciliation with the Republic – were strongly influenced by Drumont. Father Hippolyte Gayraud was one of the leaders of this Christian Democratic anti-Semitism: 'A convinced Christian is by his very nature a practising anti-Semite!' Jews are the enemy of Christ and the enemy of Christian France, declared Father Hippolyte at the first congress of the Christian Democrats in Lyon. Lyon is the town of Archbishop Agobard, recognized to this day as a patron saint of ecclesiastical anti-Semitism.

Six thousand representatives of anti-Semitic clubs were gathered at this first congress of the Christian Democrats of France in Lyon in the last week of November 1896. The congress proved to be the climax of organized Catholic anti-Semitism in France, and at the same time the climax of the Christian Democratic movement. Both very soon collapsed. People argued amongst themselves and could not agree on a programme. Nevertheless, among the resolutions passed was a demand for the exclusion of Jews from all public offices and all positions in education, the civil service and the army.

Father Garnier, a great spokesman for political Christian democracy, who reminds one in many ways of those worker-priests in the docks of Marseilles, often visited Socialist and anarchist meetings in order to challenge his political opponents in open debate. On 28 May 1890, among the dockers of Saint Nazaire, he encountered Aristide Briand. Briand, later the great champion of Franco-German understanding in the Briand-Stresemann era, was at that time not a Socialist, but a revolutionary syndicalist. In front of the workers Father Garnier attacked the Jews. Briand answered that the Catholic church had always attacked the Jews in order to have a scapegoat for its own lapses.

Christian Democrats, Christian Socialists, conservatives and reactionaries were all at this period trying to win the people's support through vigorous anti-Semitism.

It was in this climate that Morès rose to prominence – the 'first National Socialist', as he was called. Maurice Barrès devoted a study to him in 1902. Morès appealed to the upper classes, particularly to the aristocracy. In order to retain their position in business, society and politics, he declared, they should take on the leadership of a national and National Socialist revolution. The discontented lower classes could be won over by the expropriation of Jewish and foreign possessions in France, by cheap housing, credits for workers and gifts of food.

R.F.Byrnes called Morès the 'first SA man'. Political 'storm-troops', cohorts of roughs formed by early Fascists and Nazis can be seen as the invention of this man, whose ancestors had fought in the service of the kings of

Aragon and the dukes of Savoy against France. (A history of aristocratic German SS leaders and of the few aristocratic SA leaders has yet to be written). Morès's father bore the Italian title of duke of Vallombrosa, but both parents were of Spanish origin. Morès was thus an adopted Frenchman. As has already been pointed out, radical, conservative, reactionary and supra-national Frenchmen are either borderland Frenchmen (like de Maistre) or adopted Frenchmen (with Algerians moving more and more into the foreground since the Dreyfus affair).

The young Morès became a soldier: in 1877 – only a few years after the catastrophe of 1870–1 – he was a fellow student of Pétain at the military academy of Saint Cyr. Marshal Pétain was never to conceal his contempt for the Republic, long even before the founding of the Germano-French Vichy state.

Morès left the army and in 1882 married Medora Hoffmann, the daughter of a rich New York banker. This imaginative and enterprising young man, in whom there was something of Saint Simon's 'French Faust' (who took part in the American War of Independence), became involved in many unsuccessful business ventures in the United States, in industry, agriculture and cattle-breeding. Returning to France, he later made the discovery that Jews were to blame for all his unsuccessful transactions. (In 1936 his eldest son, the duke of Vallombrosa, handed over his father's mansion and estate in Dakota to the North Dakota Historical Society.)

Always inclined to flamboyance and deeds of daring, he invented his own uniform, which united elements of the gangster, the cowboy and the Wild West film star. He wore a sombrero and a purple cowboy shirt, and later on in France he made this the uniform of his storm-troopers. He flitted between mass meetings in New York and tiger hunts in Nepal and Burma before returning to France in 1888. He toyed with the idea of building a railway along the Red River from Hanoi to Yunnan. After an unsuccessful attempt to enter politics, he lived the life of a rootless aristocrat. And then, in 1889, he read Drumont's *La France Juive*. His eyes were opened. He had found the key to world history and the key to the secret of his many failures: the Jews.

In late September 1889, as a Boulangist, he made his first national and anti-Semitic speech to workers in Paris. 'Comrades, the hour has come! Let us fight together, nobility and common people, let us unite our blood on the battlefield.' For *la patrie*, the holy fatherland, the Ancien Régime – against the Jews.

Romantic National Socialists of this kind could, even at that early stage, have become a real danger to the Third Republic, had they been able to unite with the middle classes and the bourgeoisie. Morès did not know how to do that. His militant anti-Semitic alliance between the highest and lowest ranks of society was politically a failure. Moreover, he had run out of money. His opponents established that he was in debt to rich Jews. He went to prison for three months.

In 1891 he founded the organization 'Morès and his Friends', with his cowboy dress as uniform. The uniform created group consciousness and a brutal inclination towards street fighting. The 'Friends' broke up the meetings of their opponents, terrorized Jewish festivities and learned the art of carrying out raids.

Morès declared at meetings of his supporters that anti-Semitism and syndicalism could alone save France. The influence on him of Louis Blanc and Proudhon, of early anti-Semitic utopian Socialism became apparent. In the period 1893–4 he began to preach Socialism, but at the same time attacked organized Socialists as 'internationalists' in the pay of Germans, Jews and British. In Algeria – that powder magazine of French politics until it became independent – Morès gave blazing addresses to anti-Semitic organizations.

An imperialist form of anti-Semitism now began to inspire his political vision. (Something similar happened in the SS later, when plans were mooted to fight England and Judaism with the help of Arabs and Islam.) Morès tried to build up in Africa a great anti-Semitic front, starting in Constantine, Bone and Algiers. He worked to form a Franco-Islamic alliance to drive the English out of Africa. He made a pact with the Mahdi of the Senussi in the Kufra Oasis in the Lybian Desert against the English on the Nile. (The later alliance of Himmler, Hitler and the Great Mufti of Jerusalem is here called to mind.)

In Africa Morès realized that all his plans had come to nought. France had not adopted him as leader, deliverer and saviour. His death fighting against the Tuareg on 9 June 1896 – similar to the death of the son of Napoleon III – was a kind of suicide. His body was given a ceremonious reception in Marseilles. The cardinal archbishop of Paris and the foreign minister of the Republic, together with many highly placed people, took part in the funeral service in Nôtre Dame on 15 July 1896 (the 'other France' gathering round the altar of the French God Almighty on the day following the Fourteenth of July ceremony of the accursed Republic!) A statue of Morès was unveiled during the period in which the Dreyfus affair was dragging on.

France on the eve of the Dreyfus affair: Paris was naturally the centre of Catholic anti-Semitism, but it also flourished in the provinces – around Rennes, which had less than a dozen Jewish families, in Normandy, Maine, Anjou and Poitou. In the area around Lille two Catholic legitimist papers, *Lillois* and *Vraie France* held the banner high. In Bordeaux and Toulouse the anti-Semites actually had some Jews to work on. In the East, in Dijon, Besançon, Nancy and Bar-le-Duc, there were Jews from the province of Alsace-Lorraine.

As far as class was concerned, anti-Semitism found passionate believers among the poor, uneducated provincial clergy, as well as among the nobility and the officer class. Saint Cyr took young men particularly from Jesuit schools and from the nobility. The general staff had the nickname 'la Jésuitière'. Officers on a low income, looked upon with mistrust by Republican politicians, formed an officer proletariat. The petty bourgeoisie showed itself to be particularly susceptible. Drumont himself is a classic example of the sort of individual sociologically predestined to be anti-Semitic. His paternal grandfather was an artisan, his maternal grandfather a small trades-man, his father a minor official in the Paris market. This petty bourgeoisie had its mouthpiece in a white-collar proletariat of lawyers, journalists and artists in Paris.

This intellectual Parisian proletariat of the 1890s can be compared with the German petty bourgeois intellectual proletariat after 1918 which produced a Dr Goebbels. Many frustrated intellectuals rushed to join the anti-Semitic movement, like Jacques de Bièz, who tried to prove that Christ was a Celt and who developed a racial theory which came close to that of National Socialism. In Paris anti-Semitism flourished among the lower stratum of unemployed or poorly-paid journalists, writers and hack play-wrights. In 1903 three or four journalists were out of work for every one who was employed. They became election agents and threw themselves into the campaign against the Jews.

The three most famous caricaturists were anti-Semites: Willette, Emmanuel Poiré and Jean Forain. Among lesser talents Blass, Steinlen, Léandre, Gerbault and Huard can be mentioned. In postcards, books and hand-bills a stereotype of the Jew was presented, attracting by means of its repulsive hideousness. German anti-Semites of the late nineteenth and twentieth centuries up to the *Stürmer* itself liked to imitate these French caricatures, which were not just distortions but in fact deadly daggers, inviting to murder.

The social and political situation does not fully explain why the French intelligentsia, including as it did some authors of high rank, was so passionately anti-Semitic. There was nothing comparable to it, neither in Germany nor in any other country in the literature of the period from 1870 to the present day. We might venture a speculation: possibly a specifically French form of intellectuality and sensibility – easily offended, nationally sensitive and vulnerable, proud, arrogant and vain – felt jealous of Jewish competition. The Jews possessed those very qualities of sensitivity, stylistic elegance and skill in formal expression which the French intellectuals themselves were struggling to achieve. And so they appeared to be aping French Gallic *esprit*. In the Middle Ages the Devil was referred to as *simia dei* (the ape of God). In the same way, the Jewish author and intellectual was the ape of the French spirit. Envy is the secret god of the literary intelligentsia, particularly among artists, journalists and playwrights, but also among professors and theologians. The fanatical anti-Semitism of French men of letters always contained in the background the question: Who made these Jews, these

Germans, into Frenchmen? Who permitted them to use the holy language of France and to compete with us in its use?

The Jews are either Germans or agents of the Germans. Long before and long after the Dreyfus trial the French clergy and right-wing Catholic laymen held this view. In 1919 a French newspaper declared that Germany was being rebuilt by international Jewry. Another French writer screamed that international Jewish capital was aiding Germany. The papal prelate Monsignor E. Jouin declared in Paris that the Jew was the enemy of the human race. The Jesuit Joseph Bonsirven stated in 1935 that Drumont still had many disciples in France, and that a latent anti-Semitism dominated Catholics everywhere. In 1940 the Catholic disciples of Drumont in France united openly with their anti-Christian fellow-believers in Germany.

France in the epoch of the Dreyfus trial: A third of all anti-Semitic books published in the period 1870–94 were written by priests, by authors like Chabauty, Lémann, Pascal, Charles, Gayraud, Fesch, Naudet, Garnier, Desportes, Bailly. Ninety per cent of the French clergy came from rural families. In their seminaries these youths, who believed as deeply in the Devil as any medieval monk in his cell, were taught that the Jews were to blame for all evils in history. This clergy was lacking in all self-criticism, all critical faculty. These young priests around Loisy, busy with their analytical Bible study, were reproached by the higher clergy with subservience to German Protestant scholarship.

This chauvinist clergy was, moreover, very anti-American. De Gaulle's anti-Americanism stems in fact from an old Catholic source. America, like Germany, was accused in Rome of modernism, of a diabolic Americanism that was undermining the church. Monsignor Ireland puts his finger on the political basis of this French anti-Americanism in his statement: 'Their hatred of America was only an expression of their hatred of democracy.' America signified the victory of this hateful democracy, and now Rome was being untrue to itself, seeking through Pope Leo XIII to reconcile the Catholics of France with the diabolic Jewish, masonic Republic. Father Henri Delassus, one of the greatest enemies of Leo XIII's programme of reconciliation and publisher of the influential *Semaine réligieuse de Cambrai* (which was much read by the clergy), accused Cardinal Gibbons and Monsignor Ireland of conspiring with the Jews and freemasons to overthrow the Catholic church and to prepare for the Anti-Christ.

French Catholicism, cutting itself off out of fear from all hints of scientific, technological and industrial progress, easily fell victim to crazy political and politico-religious ideas. The career of Gabriel Jogand-Pagès, who, as Leo Taxil, won a massive following for himself among French Catholics, began in a climate in which clairvoyance and occultism united with anti-Semitism. Many French anti-Semites, as we have seen, occupied themselves with occult practices, and one of the leading American Fascists and anti-Semites, William Dudley Pelley, chief of the 'Silver Shirts', believed in his own powers of magic.

Leo Taxil, product of a Jesuit school, first won success as a writer of anti-clerical pamphlets. His pamphlet against Pius ix *À bas la calotte* achieved an edition of 130,000 copies. However, Taxil soon saw that his best chance lay among the bigotted French Catholics with their susceptibility to every crazy notion. He became converted three or four years after Drumont, was received in 1885 by the nuncio and in 1887 by the pope. One of his new books contained as preface letters of recommendation from seventeen bishops.

Taxil's conversion was a business venture: he decided to exploit French Catholic belief in the Devil in order to line his own pockets. In *Le diable au dix-neuvième siècle*, written in conjunction with Dr Charles Hacks (pseudonym Dr Bataille) and published by the much respected Catholic firm of Delhome and Briquet, he provided a panorama of the nineteenth century. In their voluntary self-isolation French Catholics needed the assurance that they were beseiged by devils. Lutherans were representatives of the Devil, sitting in Germany, America and England. England was a state ruled by the Devil through scoundrels.

Taxil invented a Miss Diana Vaughan. A descendant of the famous Rosicrucian Thomas Vaughan and the goddess Astarte, she was born on 29 February 1874. (There was of course no such date, but that did not disturb Taxil's episcopal admirers.) The beautiful diabolic Miss Diana was brought up as a follower of Lucifer and became engaged to the god Asmodeus who took her with him on trips to Purgatory and the planet Mars. Initiated into the highest grades of masonry, Miss Diana declined to take part in ceremonies at which terrible things were done to the Holy Eucharist. (The Eucharist had a special role to play at that time of Eucharistic Congresses – an invention of French Catholics who wanted to present the evil world of the Republic with solid proof that the Eucharist must be defended constantly against the insults and profilations of Protestants, freemasons and Jews.)

At this point Miss Diana went on strike. She was replaced by another beautiful young lady, Sophia Walden, who rose to the highest ranks of masonic leadership. Her father was the devil Betru. Her official father, however, was a Protestant pastor, her mother a Rosicrucian Jewess. Sophia became the grandmother of the Anti-Christ, who was to be born in 1962.

Taxil now revealed to the masses, waiting greedily for every new revelation from the diabolic realm of the masons, Jews, Protestants and English, that through Miss Diana's refusal to become the high priestess of masonry, a schism had arisen (in this synagogue of Satan, this anti-church). To strengthen

Miss Diana's position, an extreme anti-Catholic monthly appeared in Paris in 1895. It revealed that the mother of God had broken with Lucifer. The Anti-Christ and a Jewish pope would achieve mastery and control over the Catholic Church in the year 1995.

With these publications Leo Taxil reached the height of his business success. Many priests, prelates, even bishops (like Bishop Fava, whose anti-Semitic remarks are once again, in 1965, being quoted), wrote enthusiastic letters to Miss Diana. Here we see to what pathological condition a deeply confused, neurotic French Catholicism had been reduced.

Taxil received letters of recommendation from many French bishops for a prayer book which was published by Miss Diana – now converted to Catholicism – in 1896. She was converted through Joan of Arc. (After the First World War Joan of Arc was canonized: a politico-religious act of reconciliation between the Republic and the Curia). For this prayer book Taxil received the blessing of Leo XIII.

Leo Taxil appeared again at the international congress against free-masonry which was held in Trient in September 1896 (Leo XIII gave his blessing to the congress as a new crusade against the hell of Satan). At this congress a six-member commission was set up to study the Miss Diana problem. Passionately French clergymen begged to be allowed to see and speak to the girl who had been freed from bondage in hell to serve in heaven. Was this heavenly maid of satanic origin not a portent sent by God to show that the desecrated Mother Church and desecrated France would be liberated from the devilish embrace, from domination by Jews, masons, Germans and Englishmen?

Miss Diana had no intention of resisting for ever the pleas of her many spiritual and temporal admirers. Leo Taxil had achieved all he wanted: a hysterical mass movement had been let loose which broke all bounds of reason, taste and sense. Miss Diana called a conference in Paris on Easter Monday, 19 April 1897, at which she would appear.

This was Leo Taxil's last diabolic irony, indeed blasphemy. On Easter Monday the church reads the Gospel according to St Luke, 24, 13-35: Mourning, the disciples go to Emmaus. The Lord comes to them, but they do not recognize Him. Not until He goes are their eyes opened. 'Did not our heart burn within us, while He talked with us by the way, and while He opened to us the scriptures?' Then they realize: 'The Lord is risen indeed . . .'

The many priests who, together with countless journalists, flocked to this conference had all just been reading this passage. Their hearts were burning with longing at last to see with their own eyes the heavenly maid who had flown to Purgatory and to distant planets and resolutely withstood on earth the terrible temptations of the sinful flesh.

The place in which the conference was to be held might have aroused their suspicions. It was the auditorium of the Geographical Society – a place devoted to the dreaded subject of natural science. Here Taxil told his story, revealing all his accounts of the Devil and freemasonry as inventions of his pen. Miss Diana Vaughan was his typewriter. Taxil reviled his believers as ignoramuses, fools, superstitious lunatics.

Indignation, dismay, laughter. But Taxil's revelations could not destroy the faith of many of Miss Diana's admirers. Men like Father Mustrel and Bishop Fava continued to believe in her. And Leo Taxil's satanic books continued to be read at the beginning of the twentieth century as truthful accounts by Catholics both in France and outside.

It was in this intellectual atmosphere that the Dreyfus storm broke out. The Catholic anti-Semitic right wing proclaimed its destructive mood in a speech made by the famous Father Didon at a prize-giving ceremony at his educational institute:

'When I speak of the necessity of power for a nation, I must emphasize that I am referring to naked force, which does not prevaricate, but simply acts. Its finest embodiment is the army, of which one can say what has been asserted of the cannon: that it is the final argument of both state and people ... The enemy is intellectualism, which affects to despise force; the enemy is the civilian mentality, which wishes to subordinate the army to itself. When persuasion fails and love grows weary, then there is nothing for it but to draw the sword, spread terror, cut off heads, swoop down and punish. Woe to all governments that seek to hide their criminal weakness under a threadbare cloak of legality. Woe to all who permit the sword to become blunt!'

Father Didon demanded on 19 July 1898 that heads should roll: Jews and all enemies of France must be wiped out.

For the Catholic right wing, out for a new St Bartholomew's Eve massacre, the obscure little Captain Dreyfus was of no interest in himself. They had no wish to dirty their hands with him. When a review of the trial was demanded, the church refused to intervene. Mathieu Dreyfus turned in vain to the archbishop of Paris, Cardinal Richard.

The time for a final reckoning with the satanic Republic was at hand. For that reason this Jew had to fall. This time the success of the necessary coup d'état must be assured. A strong man was needed, as *La Croix* and other Catholic papers pointed out. This strong man had to be a man of the sword, an army man (Morès? Or Pétain, his contemporary at Saint Cyr? In 1899 *his* time had not yet come.) And so the army had to be defended against every insult. *The army cannot lie, just as the church cannot lie.* And if the army did lie, then it was in the service of the nation, holy France and the church.

But how were the masses to be whipped up? Obviously through anti-Semitism. Once one had succeeded in selling the Jew to the masses as the prototype of a traitor, then the final battle for power could begin. 'The Jew was created by God to serve as a spy wherever treason is being prepared.' This sentence can be read in *La Civiltà Cattolica* of 5 February 1898. This periodical, published in Rome, had been founded – against the will of the Jesuit leadership – to defend the absolutism and centralism of the Curia. It fought against modernists, Catholic reformers and against the Jewish-German-Republican-masonic conspiracy in France, personified in Dreyfus.

Count Albert de Mun, one of the great figures of political Catholicism (and in himself a man of integrity) said in the Chamber that it was an insult to suggest that the army was capable of even one single mistake – the army in which 'the imperishable hopes of all French people are united'.

The Dreyfus affair began as a purely army matter. Alfred Dreyfus (born 1859) died as a retired lieutenant-colonel on 11 July 1935, having lived to see the dragon's teeth sown by Drumont in his *Libre Parole*, by *Le Pélerin* (which on 10 November 1894 congratulated the tsar on the expulsion of the Jews) by *La Croix* and by *La Vérité Française* spring up in Hitler's Reich. (Following pogroms in Algiers, in which Jewish women were stripped naked and 158 Jewish department stores were looted, *La Croix* observed on 2 February 1898: 'This day Algiers has declared itself for Christ.')

Alfred Dreyfus, an inoffensive, honourable, unimaginative bourgeois, was the youngest son of a rich Jewish family in Mulhouse, his father Raphael Dreyfus having emigrated to France after the annexation of Alsace-Lorraine. Alfred became an army officer, passing in 1892 an examination that qualified him for the general staff. This was to be his misfortune: *La Jésuitière* was a nest of radical anti-Semitism.

Esterhazy, the tool of Colonel Henry in the forgery of the documents which Dreyfus was alleged to have betrayed to the Germans, died in England in 1923. The spy and counter-spy, forger of documents, liar and slanderer, Major Marie-Charles-Ferdinand Walsin-Esterhazy was a descendant of various great historical European families. After spending some years in Austria and Germany and 1869 as an officer in the service of the pope, he entered the service of France in 1870.

Esterhazy, instrument of the strongly anti-Semitic general staff, hero of the French Catholics and idol of their chauvinism, indulged in letters to his cousin and friend Madame de Boulancy, in intoxicated dreams of a German bloodbath among the French and pogroms among the Jews and their friends. This is what he thought of the general staff: 'Our great commanders, the cowards and idiots, will once again people the German prison-camps . . .' – 'I could not bear to hurt a little dog, but I would willingly kill a hundred thousand Frenchmen, those detestable, garrulous men who peddle their gossip from salon to salon under the cover of an anonymous, cowardly *on dit* – what sorry figures they would present under the red sun of battle, with Paris taken by storm and looted by a hundred thousand drunken soldiers. That is the festival I dream about. Amen.'

During the Dreyfus affair Esterhazy's hatred grew, on the one hand against the general staff which was beginning to drop him as their tool, and on the other hand against Jews. In February 1898 he told the English journalist David Christie Murray that the affair would almost certainly end in violence. As far as he was concerned, he asked for nothing better than to lead his regiment against the Jews of Paris, where he would kill them like rabbits, without hate or anger, in the general interest.

To a reporter of the *Pall Mall Gazette* he confided that he lived now only to revenge himself. If Zola were acquitted, all Paris would rise up in revolt, and he (Esterhazy) would be at the head. If Dreyfus were to put foot again on French soil, five thousand Jewish corpses would lie in the streets of Paris.

Esterhazy is here speaking for the majority of French Catholics. He was closely connected with Edouard Drumont, who opened the columns of *La Libre Parole* to him and paid him a monthly allowance. *La Libre Parole*, in touch with the general staff through Esterhazy, fired the first round: on 1 November 1894 it called Dreyfus a traitor.

When Esterhazy himself later described the evil game in which he had become involved through the general staff, he mentioned his friend Drumont and others who for a long time had prevented him from breaking his silence: 'It was very painful for me as a *soldier, Catholic and reactionary* who detested the form of government to which France was subjected, to play the game of those whom I had always hated.'

When Lieutenant-Colonel Hubert-Joseph Henry, fabricator of the forged documents which had been laid at Dreyfus's door, died, *La Libre Parole* wanted to put up a monument to this 'martyr of Catholic France', bearing the inscription 'murdered by the Jews'. The list of subscribers towards the cost of the monument contained the most famous names of the ancient French aristocracy (the Bonapartist new aristocracy did not sign). Thirty-two generals and several hundred priests signed the subscription list, which was hailed by *La Croix* on 17 December 1898 as a 'great and consoling spectacle'.

Henry was murdered not by the Jews, but by the general staff. A suicide was simulated while he was under arrest, when it became clear that the mouth of this most dangerous fellow conspirator could no longer be stopped. (How strange it is that extreme right wingers and authoritarian Catholics, who are always thinking and dreaming of Jewish plots, are themselves always plotting). Henry genuinely believed that he was serving his fatherland by his forgeries, lies and perjuries (like so many pious forgers in the fifteen centuries before him). Fundamentally, he was a typical non-commissioned officer of the sort that would go through thick and thin for his staff commanders. After his death his wife continued to do battle on his behalf, supported by Drumont.

Drumont had an inscription set up at the offices of *La Libre Parole*: 'For the widow and orphan of Colonel Henry, against the Jew Reinach!' (Reinach: supporter of Dreyfus and author of *Histoire de l'affaire Dreyfus*). In four weeks 130,000 gold francs were raised from about 15,000 donors. Many thousands of officers and three hundred and fifty clerics gave their contributions, identifying themselves gladly in accompanying letters.

'One wanted to grind Reinach's nose under his heel, another (a priest) wished he were as adept with a dagger as with a water sprinkler, yet another wished for a bedside mat of Jews' skin (here we come near to the reality of 1943: lampshades of human skin). There was, however, no high church dignitary among them, a fact which frankly "disgusted" one obscure abbé. The aristocrats were represented in masses distinguishing themselves with the brutality of their language. Their wish was to thrash, put out eyes, tan hides, roast, throw to the dogs, drown and boil in oil.' (S. Thalheimer).

Reinach comments in his book on these lists: 'Many Republicans, and even the oldest revisionists, were dismayed. They could scarcely trust their eyes when they saw the eighteen lists following one after another. This exoneration of a forger, this flood of jesuitical, besmirching, base hatred appeared to them as a disgrace and as the beginning of the end of civilization in France.'

Charles Péguy gave the attitude of the vast majority of French Catholics its right name: a pact between the Catholics and the Devil.

'Had it come to a coup d'état – and there was an immediate danger of that happening – then France would, in all probability, have received a dictator and the first Fascist constitution of the era.' – 'In this affair the church was in the vanguard of the Republic's attackers. The clerics fought ruthlessly and without restraint as demagogues.' (S. Thalheimer).

J'accuse: I accuse. The open letter of Emile Zola to the president of the Republic appeared on 13 January 1898 on the front page of *L'Aurore*, Clémenceau's paper. Zola entered the lists as a solitary champion against the strongest forces in France. Zola, condemned in all the many court cases which were now brought against him, finally fled to England to escape imprisonment.

In the long fight for a retrial and then for the acquittal of Captain Alfred Dreyfus, atheists, Socialists and freethinkers displayed a pure, unshakeable belief in the idea justice. The 'defenders of the holy rights of religion' relied cynically and without any regard to spiritual decrees solely on themselves, their power, their cunning and the superiority of their weapons. They laughed at the belief of Emile Zola, who wrote to the president of the Republic: 'If one buries truth, it develops underground such an explosive force, that on the day it finds release, it destroys everything.'

France's rich Jews were cautious and for a long time hesitated to reveal their hand in this tricky matter in which the church and army were so deeply involved. The honour of clearing the way for the fight for truth belongs to an obscure, needy Jew who had fought his way laboriously through the mountains of lies, forgeries and concealments and begun at his own cost to fight for Dreyfus. Bernard-Lazare (a pseudonym for Lazare Bernard) started by writing pamphlets which for years went unnoticed. (The way in which rich French Jews and their friends among journalists and men of letters shut their eyes to the Dreyfus affair, this ostrich-like attitude in the face of their own murderers, was to repeat itself: around 1933 and after 1945 when 'representative' spokesmen for Jewry thanked the silent men who shared the responsibility for the massacres.)

Bernard-Lazare collapsed from overwork and died exhausted. Daniel Halévy described his funeral: 'There was no pomp whatsoever. Nothing but the conveying of the body to the cemetery, followed by only a small number of people. A handful of friends, a handful of poor East European Jews who remained loyal to the man who had defended them. In addition Péguy and Bourgeois walked with them.'

Charles Péguy saw in the atheist Bernard-Lazare a man filled with the spirit of God, a man with the unmistakable characteristics of true holiness. 'I can still feel his short-sighted gaze resting on me, I can still see his intelligent, kind, imperturbably clear, radiant expression, which reflected an inexhaustible, comprehending, much-tried goodness.' This man had 'a heart which bled in all the ghettoes of the world, and perhaps even more in the open ghettoes, as in Paris, than in the closed ones ... ' – 'His heart was consumed by a fire, by the fire of his people; he himself was a soul aflame.'

This characterization of Bernard-Lazare may be applied to its author, to Charles Péguy himself. Péguy (1873–1914), son of a master joiner in Orleans, who died shortly after Charles's birth (his mother and grandmother learned basketmaking in order to be able to support the family) was awakened by the Dreyfus affair to the knowledge of his mission. He saw it very clearly in all its perspectives: 'The Dreyfus affair was a God-given affair. It was the highly significant crisis of three historical entities, which in themselves are highly significant. It was a significant crisis in the history of Israel. It was patently a significant crisis in the history of France. It was above all a significant crisis – and the extent of its importance will become more and more apparent – in the history of Christendom, and perhaps also of various other historical entities. It was, perhaps by some unique stroke of providence, a threefold crisis. It had a threefold importance, it was truly a climax.'

'Catholics do not love the truth.' André Gide's well-known saying was brought home to Charles Péguy as a fearful and painfully real experience. Péguy was 'the witness of truth'. He recognized from the Dreyfus affair that the concealment of only one single truth can bring 'a whole nation into a state of mortal sin'. *He recognized that Catholicism was dying of a self-administered poison, of its inability to acknowledge truth, because truth is always bitter.* There is no such thing as sweet truth.

The Dreyfus affair revealed disquieting aspects for the twentieth century: for France, for Europe, for Jews and for Christians.

For France: The country would, if the general staff had achieved its goal, probably have fallen into the hands of a dictator and become the model of a fascist state. The defenders of democracy were for a long time uncertain, weak and evasive towards their insolent attackers.

For Europe: An aggressive reactionary right wing was watching this spectacle from Russia to Spain.

For the Jews: The great majority of French Jews tried to ignore this unpleasant affair, to have nothing to do with it. Protesting voices like that of the poet Alexandre Weill were rare exceptions. How would the Jews act if faced by a new attack? A Viennese Jew, Theodor Herzl, reporting for his newspaper in Vienna, saw the extraordinary danger that lay in the Dreyfus trial. Herzl began to seek a way out of the European murder-trap. He became, for Christendom and especially for Catholics, a pioneer of Zionism.

Leading circles in the Curia were on the side of Dreyfus's enemies. Italian Jesuits backed up their French fellow Jesuits in the great fight. As early as 1881–2 *La Civiltà Cattolica* revived, in unsigned articles written by Father Guiseppe Oreglia de San Stefano, the old accusations of ritual murder. Every practising Jew, according to the issue of 4 March 1882, was bound by his conscience to consume the flesh or dried blood of a Christian child in his food and drink. (Here we see the expression of a monstrous and unconscious fear of a Jewish anti-Communion – after one thousand five hundred years of a Christian 'communion' against the Jew Jesus, consummated in the murder of the Jews, his blood relations.)

There was no papal protest against this series of articles. Only Cardinal Manning lodged a complaint with the Holy Father on a visit to Rome in 1883 – privately, according to Purcell's *Life of Cardinal Manning*. The articles were based on German and Austrian sources. Sebastian Brunner (1814–93), the influential spokesman of a rejuvenated Catholic press, had been in Rome in the previous years. As publisher of the *Kirchenzeitung* this anti-Semitic priest played a large part in anti-Semitism in Austria-Hungary. Abbé A. Kannengiesser wrote appreciatively of him in a series of articles in *Le Correspondant* in 1895 on the theme: 'Abbé Brunner, the father of Austrian anti-Semitism'.

La Civiltà Cattolica referred in a leading article on the Dreyfus affair (5 February 1898) to the *Protocols of the Elders of Zion*. 'Dreyfus is both a Jew and a freemason.' Against poor Christian France the Protestants had made common cause with the Jews. The money came principally from Germany. *Pecuniae obediunt omnia*, that was the motto of the Jews. In all the countries of Europe they had bought up people and newspapers susceptible to bribery. 'The Jew was created by God to serve as a spy wherever treason is being prepared . . . '

'As a people accursed by God, the Jews attested, by their appearance everywhere in the world, to the truth of Christianity.' That was written by the editor of *La Civilta Cattolicà*, Father Raffaele Ballerini, in his (also unsigned) articles on the Dreyfus affair.

(In an interview with the Catholic writer Boyer d'Agen in March 1899, Pope Leo XIII tried to moderate the unrestrained passions of the French Catholics: 'Where is French magnanimity in all this wild outburst of partisan strife?' The pope earned for himself furious hatred in Catholic France, which he wished to reconcile with the Republic. Drumont called for a French knight, who, as Nogaret stood up to Pope Boniface VIII in Anagni, would now throw his iron glove into the face of Pope Leo XIII. Masses were read in many churches praying for the conversion of the pope to (French) orthodoxy.

Since the declaration of infallibility, which formed the stormy close to the First Vatican Council on the eve of the Franco-Prussian War, the papacy has been a prisoner of reaction within the church. The pope is thus immured in his Roman ghetto, shielded from the evil world outside (at least until the Lateran Treaty of 1929 – but the inner wall did not begin to crumble until the time of John XXIII).

Cardinal Rampolla expressed his joy at Dreyfus's conviction at a diplomatic reception at the Vatican. Even after the rehabilitation of Dreyfus in 1906 many clerics continued to regard people who believed in his innocence as heretics and enemies of France. The nuncio in Paris, Monsignor Montagnini, warned the Holy See in July 1906 of the *mauvais esprit* which was spreading among French seminarists: these young men were inclining towards 'Loisy, Dreyfus and disarmament'!

Loisy, the great Bible scholar, was an excommunicated priest. In 1915–6, as a professor at the Sorbonne, he was later to give his lectures on the war of the Christian Gods in the First World War. The Christian God of Germany was fighting against the Christian God of France, the God of Italy against the God of Austria. Nobody recognized the bankruptcy of Christianity in Europe more clearly than Loisy – or spoke more openly about it.

The bishop of Nancy declared in 1916 that belief in Dreyfus's innocence was tantamount to apostasy. Even today many French Catholics are hurt when they hear someone say that Dreyfus was innocent.

At the time of the Dreyfus affair there arose that militant French Catholic right wing which found in the *Action Française* around Charles Maurras an extremely effective dynamic centre. The Catholic atheist Maurras, bitter enemy of the Jews and of democracy, had influential supporters (cardinals and bishops) in Rome, and in France powerful patrons in the high episcopate. From the Dreyfus affair a road leads direct to the Pétain-Laval régime in Vichy; a Christian *Führerstaat* which abandoned the Jews to the mercies of Hitler's henchmen. In 1929 the Catholic organization of the 'Friends of Israel', was abolished by the church in Rome – on the eve of Hitler's rise to power. In 1939 – on the eve of the Second World War and of the 'final solution' of the Jewish problem – Pius XII lifted the church ban on the *Action Française*. Rome did not move a finger to save Dreyfus. And later it would prove incapable of snatching even the Jews of Rome from the murderers' grip – *incapable, in the final analysis, both intellectually and spiritually.* Authority – ecclesiastical, religious and political – held fast to its politico-religious dogma: the Jews are the people that murdered Christ. 'Every Jew is a Judas', a traitor to Christianity and the church.

10

The Great Dream

European Jews – with the exception of roughly a hundred families – lived up till the nineteenth century in a world of their own making which had no contact with European history. *The Christians had pushed the Jews out of history*, in the sense that all the great movements, like the Reformation and the Renaissance, passed them by. It was only lonely and often tragic existences on the edges of Jewish life who were caught up in the great epochs of European history, and then spat out by their Jewish communities.

In the nineteenth century the ghetto broke open – in fact was broken open. The explosion released enormous forces of energy: intellectual and spiritual forces, which for hundreds and thousands of years had been schooled, steeled, sharpened, tamed and bound in a study of the Scriptures.

St Augustine's great command to Christians to seek God and their own salvation – this and nothing else – had held sway unchallenged for fifteen centuries. The Jewish faith had been kept alive in splendid isolation by concentrating all its efforts on obedient service to the word of God and the interpretation of the word of God by the sages, scholars and martyrs of God's people. A threefold awareness of suffering – experienced, remembered (Jewish liturgy pays as much heed in its sacred calendar to the sufferings of the sixth century BC as to the massacres on the Rhine in the third century AD) and acknowledged – had created in them a sensitivity and an intellectual energy against which the Christian peoples of Europe, still caught up in the slumber of centuries, could offer nothing comparable.

But now in the eighteenth, then in the nineteenth century, the peoples of Europe began to awake. England, the mother country of European Romanticism, was the first to be stirred by great evangelical revivalist movements. Then Germany, France, Italy, Poland, Hungary, Greece, Russia – and Germany once more, around 1930.

Right in the middle of the religious, political and intellectual revivalist movements in the nineteenth and early twentieth centuries, with its revolutions and counter-revolutions, the exodus from the ghettoes began which put great stores of energy at the disposal of the awakening European peoples. German and German educated European Jews contributed alike to the rise of German science in the nineteenth and early twentieth centuries.

Marx, Einstein, Freud and the German-Jewish scientists and doctors who have been awarded the Nobel Prize in this century bear witness to this fruitful union. In France there is not only the special case of the house of Rothschild; in literature, economics and politics Jews played a significant role in the second, third and fourth Republics. A Jew became Britain's master-builder: Disraeli, Lord Beaconsfield, who brought Queen Victoria the imperial crown of India and inaugurated the epoch of British imperialism. In the Austro-Hungarian monarchy, with its three centres of Vienna, Budapest and Prague, Jews helped to transform old feudal structures into a modern industrial society. A new Jewish nobility came into being and married into families of the Christian aristocracy, in the Austrian empire as also in the early German Reich, where Bismarck looked favourably upon the union of Christian 'stallions' with Jewish 'mares' as a means of breeding a dynamic class of society leaders.

Only in one large European country were the Jews forbidden entry into Christian society: in the empire of the tsar. And thereby the tsarist régime signed its own death warrant. In Russia too, Jews would have helped in the transition from medievalism to a twentieth-century industrial society. Russia's Jews would have put themselves at the service of any tsarist policy of reform as zealously as they served the German economy at the time of Wilhelm II and the Weimar Republic after 1918.

The fact that in Russia the Jews were socially rejected, deprived of their rights and officially persecuted until the middle of the First World War, was to have momentous consequences for world history. Jewish youth and the Jewish intelligentsia in Russia saw a Europe stirring beyond its boundaries, and put all their longing and their faith into revolutionary movements: Socialism, then Communism, then Bolshevism. The phenomenon of 'Jewish Bolshevism', which is linked inseparably with Trotsky, with the early Jewish Bolsheviks and the Jewish Communist critics and opponents of the Stalinist faction, is too often misinterpreted. It can be understood in terms of world history only if it is seen in the living context out of which it arose: in Jewish emotional participation in the national movements of all Europe. Germany around 1800 provides a striking example. Bettina Brentano-von Arnim had read the signs of awakening and it was in her salon that Russian and Polish revolutionary refugees were to meet in a later reactionary time. Heinrich Heine, the strongest intellect of the *Junges Deutschland* (Young Germany) of 1830, was the first to write in German of a 'world revolution', and he foresaw not only the coming world war and world revolution, but also the National Socialist counter-revolution.

The commitment of Jews, and particularly intellectual Jews, to left-wing movements in both the Europe and America of our own century is a direct result of these commitments in Europe during the nineteenth century.

The emergence from the ghettoes offered European Jews opportunities for fulfilment and expansion such as they had never before experienced, but at the same time brought them into deadly danger. Not till 1840 did the total of living Jews regain its level of AD 70: four and a half million people. 'During the 105 years between 1825 and 1930 the population of the world doubled. In lands where the Jewish population was relatively strong, it increased three and a half times. But the number of Jews increased five- or nine-fold from 1650 onwards.' (H.L.Goldschmidt).

The crumbling of the Jewish ghetto (at irregular intervals in the years between 1790 and 1920) precipitated Jews into a Christian world which had been very badly prepared for this intrusion. For centuries there had been few or no Jews in many areas of Europe, and during this time theology and religious instruction had fabricated a dangerous image: the image of the devilish Jew (with all the physical characteristics of Satan) of the 'Jewish pig'; the image of Judas, of the people who killed Christ.

And now here they were, coming from all the ghettoes of Germany, then from Poland, Russia, Lithuania, the Ukraine, the Levant. They streamed into towns which were growing rapidly and already bursting out of their walls. Berlin, once so small, became a large city in only a few generations. Frankfurt, Breslau, Vienna, Prague, Budapest and hundreds of smaller towns in Germany and Central Europe experienced a rapid growth in their native Jewish communities, and an even more rapid influx of Jews from outside.

The Jewish explosion – a tropical growth comparable in heat and power to the Industrial Revolution – produced violent reactions. Piece by piece after 1815 a reactionary Europe took back the promises made to its peoples during the wars of liberation against Napoleon, and the Jews too were to lose the rights and the freedom which the French Revolution and the age of Napoleon had brought them. Reactionary régimes seized their opportunity to channel the anger of the disappointed middle classes against the Jews. The year 1848 saw the Jews fighting as European revolutionaries, for the first time together with non-Jews, on the barricades. The 1848 revolution failed. Jewish and non-Jewish freedom fighters alike fled: many emigrated to America. But in spite of this political defeat, the middle years of the nineteenth century brought a middle class liberalism in the economic and social spheres, which offered the Jews many opportunities. It was not until 1871 that that wild and aggressive anti-Semitism began in Germany, France and Russia whose descendants were the butchers of 1943.

World history has three times seen how Jews and non-Jews can live together in an atmosphere of fruitful harmony. The first time was in Greek Alexandria, where Jews educated in the Greek tradition translated the books of the Old Testament into Greek, and Philo's philosophy envisaged a comprehensive synthesis between Athens and Jerusalem. The second was the Arab-Jewish-Spanish era in the Middle Ages. The third took place in German lands and might, if it had not been destroyed, have led to the emergence of that 'third great power' which could have brought its powerful descendants in Russia and America together. The life and work of the German Jew Walther

Rathenau is a clue to what might have been achieved in our present century. The man who created the German war economy in the First World War was already in his essays talking about the world economy of a single human society. The assassination of Rathenau, Foreign Minister of the Weimar Republic, in 1922 provided a terrifying omen of the impending assassination of German democracy.

In 1743 a shy boy applied for admittance at the Rosenthal Gate in Berlin – the only gate through which Jews were allowed to pass. The boy came from Dessau, and his name was Moses, the son of Mendel. In 1933, 190 years later, the story of the new German Jewry, which began with this Moses, came to an end. Moses Mendelssohn led his people of Israel into the Promised Land of European culture and Enlightenment.

The split in the Jewish ranks into a Western and an Eastern camp began with Moses Mendelssohn, the first Western Jew. At the time of Mendelssohn and his school Jewish public opinion was divided into a West European and an East European section; 'each of which was centred around a single vital question: the Western group on the question of equal rights for Jews and the degree of Jewishness which would have to be sacrificed to gain them, the Eastern group purely on the question of how rightly to serve God.' (Ernst Simon).

'Moses Mendelssohn was a ragged, misshapen lad, capable of no other language than the debased Middle High German of his fathers which sounded terrible in German ears' (Hilde Spiel). He died as an intellectual prince of the Enlightenment; as creator of an educated German Jewry and friend of Lessing (who gave him a lasting memorial in his drama *Nathan der Weise*); as one of Kant's correspondents; and as father and grandfather of a family which was almost without exception to become Christian.

The Berlin of Frederick the Great and his heirs, who were by no means comparable, was, at least up to 1815, a young city in which newcomers could do well for themselves: Huguenots, French adherents of the Enlightenment from Paris and a restless young German intelligentsia, the founder of early Romanticism. All of them were rootless, *deracinés*, starting with Frederick the Great himself, who with characteristic independence created a highly artificial state and cultivated for his officials and subjects a form of princely enlightment which was highly repugnant to all in Germany who felt the pressure of authority as a burden rather than a blessing. The rapid rise of Mendelssohn and his Jewish pupils occurred in that young and restless small-town Berlin: a place with no intellectual traditions of its own, but one in which the disintegration processes of Lutheranism and Calvinism formed a good breeding-ground for enlightened and romantic movements.

Israel Samosz, a Polish-Jewish schoolmaster, was Mendelssohn's first teacher in Berlin. The way to get on in Berlin was by study and by participation in the Prussian form of Enlightenment that was patronized from above: to become a citizen in the kingdom of the mind. The boy Moses set to with a good will and became an excellent scholar. In 1763, twenty years after his arrival, he won the prize of the Prussian Academy by affirming unconditionally that metaphysics were capable of proof as mathematics. (At a later date assenting to assertions by the state and the church, and to modern ideas would prove the greatest strength and weakness of the German Jews.) In doing so, Mendelssohn beat his rival Kant.

But this was a hollow victory, typical of so many hollow victories which German Jews were to win in the following 150 years. Mendelssohn wanted to give everything to everyone (that is, everyone who meant well). For Christians and Jews, non-Christians and non-Jews alike he evolved a 'natural religion', one which all decent, educated citizens could embrace; its dominant features were tolerance, reason and a common code of good behaviour. Enlightened Prussian officials and patriots were tolerant towards him: they wanted – like the Prussian minister of war, Christian Wilhelm Dohm, whose essay on the civic rights of Jews was criticized right up to Hitler's time – to make good citizens of the despised Jews.

Dohm thought that the Jews were 'morally lepers' as a result of their oppression for hundreds of years, and that they ought to be liberated socially. The Prussian minister suggested moreover – with the purest of motives – the setting up of independent Jewish communities, whose leaders should have powers of jurisdiction and discipline within the community. This was a foreshadowing, though with a completely different purpose, of those self-administered Jewish centres which were set up by Hitler's murderous henchmen as collecting bases in 1939 after the victory over Poland.

Mendelssohn did not want to abandon his Jews any more than he wanted to abandon his Jewish faith, and he steadfastly rejected all attempts to convert him to the faith of the Son.

Yet orthodox rabbis banned his works and persecuted him, just as their fellow rabbis had persecuted Maimonides and Spinoza before him. For Mendelssohn did not want to protect his Jews only from the outside world, but also from within. Nothing should take away the Jew's freedom of thought and freedom of service to God and Man – neither state nor church, not even a strictly orthodox synagogue with its dogmas and disciplines. He developed this theme in his essay *Jerusalem*, subtitled 'Religious Power and the Jews'.

In 1783 – the same year in which the American War of Independence came to an end – Moses Mendelssohn, the 'Jewish Luther' (W. Kaufmann) and free-thinking 'heretic', published his German translation of the Pentateuch and the Psalms. Mendelssohn's German Bible seemed like an act of sacrilege to orthodox rabbis; the sacred writings stripped of their protection of the original Hebrew and delivered over to the mercies of a profane language. Bonfires, Jewish bonfires, were lit to burn his German Bible in

Posnan, Lissa and Vilna. In 1779 rabbis in Fürth, Frankfurt and Hamburg had also threatened to ban the project.

But the 'profane language of the heathens' thus rejected by orthodox rabbis (who by this act confined their adherence to a ghetto mentality and condemned Mendelssohn's Berlin as well as Joseph II's Vienna) became, as a result of Moses Mendelssohn's work, the sacred language of German Jews. As poets, philosophers and scientists in London, New York and even Jerusalem, they refused to give up the mother-tongue which Mendelssohn had given them.

Mendelssohn was no more willing to abandon his Christian friends than he was to abandon his Jews. In 1783 he founded the 'Society of Friends of the Hebrew Language' with Jewish friends in Berlin, and began to publish the *Collector*, the first Hebrew magazine devoted to modern themes.

The chief rabbi of Berlin, Leo Baeck, who was there to comfort his people in the concentration camp of Theresienstadt, was convinced that Jewry both in the present day and in the future, would be unthinkable without Moses Mendelssohn. It is a Jewry of world wide culture, in which the Jewish religion is a matter of conscience and morality. All Jewish world-citizens, whether German, French, English or American, are in this sense descendants of Mendelssohn. Through Moses Mendelssohn 'the God of Israel has become a denominational God' (Arthur A. Cohen). This denominational God does not concern Himself with affairs in the nation to which the Jews now belong.

Without wanting or realizing it, Moses Mendelssohn became the great leader for more and more individuals who were longing to escape from the oppression of mind and soul (so their religion now seemed to them suddenly, whereas to the Torah scholar of the old faith it was a sweet burden) into the great freedom of the world of knowledge. Mendelssohn became the great seducer, starting with his own children who, with one exception, all became Christians.

From the beginning of the nineteenth century onwards many Jews fled from their faith. 'It was widely thought that the end of Judaism had come. In Berlin Schleiermacher declared that it was dead, and around 1800 the Prussian minister Friedrich L. von Schrötter gave it only another twenty years to live' (R. Weltsch). In Berlin Jewish women who had renounced their faith became the midwives of the early 'German Movement', a movement made up of a mixture of free-thinking and bigotry, of high intellect and a passionate Prussian patriotism. These women remind one of those Jewish women in the tragic epoch of Spain's history around 1500, 1520 and 1530: they too were passionate, converted Christians, inspired by the humanism of Erasmus, reform movements within the church and Messianic movements stretching from Spain to England. With their clerical and lay friends and blood relations they formed circles and small communities which may justifiably be compared with the Berlin salons.

The first salon of this kind in Berlin was established by Henriette Herz, who came of a Sephardic, Spanish-Portuguese family. She was a beautiful, highly educated woman who lived from 1764 till the eve of the revolution in 1848, and was married at the age of fifteen to the physician Marcus Herz, follower of Mendelssohn and Kant. Her salon was visited by Count Mirabeau (who in London in 1787 demanded the liberation of the Jews in his essay on Mendelssohn), by Friedrich von Gentz, the great reactionary and anti-Semite, by the brothers Humboldt and by men and women of the early Romantic movement and the *Junges Deutschland* of Börne and Heine.

Henriette clung by only one single sentimental thread to her Jewishness. In 1815 she refused to be baptized, even though that meant giving up the prospect of becoming governess to the Prussian princess Charlotte, who later became empress of Russia. Two years later, after the death of her mother, whom she had not wished to hurt, she was converted.

Spanish Jewesses – both in Spain and in their new adopted countries – developed a Spanish nationalism which was an amalgam of Jewish faith in a new Jerusalem and Spanish awareness of being among the chosen. Henriette Herz's salon was a cell in the *Tugendbund* (League of Virtue) in which the revolt against Napoleon was being prepared. Women were Napoleon's bitterest enemies. His greatest opponent was a non-Jewess – Madame de Stael – but even she was excelled in hatred by Dorothea Schlegel, who turned angry eyes on the still restless France of the 1830s from her home in Vienna. Dorothea Schlegel, who was to become even more bigoted, impatient and Catholic as the years went on, was Moses Mendelssohn's eldest daughter, and she met her future husband, Friedrich Schlegel, in Henriette Herz's salon. At that time she was still the wife of a Jewish businessman, David Veit, and her affair with Friedrich Schlegel became the biggest scandal in Berlin society, particularly since Schlegel portrayed their free love very frankly in his novel *Lucinda*. Schlegel was a hot-headed young man at that time, a Romantic who with his brother August edited the periodical *Athenäum*, which championed a world revolution in morals, education, art and all ways of thought.

In contemporary Christian pamphlets directed against this 'Jewish sow' (Dorothea) ominous notes could be heard which were to be sounded more and more frequently after 1820.

In 1804 Dorothea Mendelssohn-Veit was finally able to marry her Friedrich – in a Protestant ceremony. Friedrich Schlegel was a highly gifted, deeply unhappy soul who toyed intellectually with his Christianity and his Catholicism till his life's end. He entered the service of Metternich and became an Austrian civil servant. Until her death in 1839 Dorothea Schlegel enjoyed her role as a quick-witted, malicious critic of Protestantism, Judaism, France, Germany, Poland and revolutionary Europe, in which she could see only chaos. Moses Mendelssohn's eldest daughter ended up the advocate of counter-reformatory Catholicism during the Restoration period in Vienna.

In Berlin Protestant Jews became the advocates of a Prussian neo-conservatism preaching loyalty to throne and altar, an established Protestant church and an exclusive elite of civil servants. The time was between 1848 and 1860.

All that was best and free and most typical in Berlin was to be found in Rahel Varnhagen's salon. She was the charming hostess of the most brilliant and attractive of Berlin salons, admired by Jean Paul, Kleist and the Romantics, to say nothing of Prince Louis Ferdinand of Prussia and the Prince de Ligne. But in her personal life Rahel was anything but free. She could not come to terms with her own Jewishness, which she bore like a burden, unable for many years to understand it. Her first fiancé, Count Finkenstein, gave up his suit at the instance of his family, who were against his marriage to 'that Jewess', Rahel Levin. Eventually she married Karl August Varnhagen von Ense, who was in the Prussian diplomatic service. On account of his talkativeness it was usual – and still is – to poke fun at him, yet as a Prussian nobleman Varnhagen was one of the politically most enlightened thinkers in the whole of the nineteenth century. He loved and honoured Rahel, to whom he set up a memorial in his memoirs. Together with Bettina Brentano (whose love for the Jews was genuine, in contrast to her poet-husband von Arnim and her poet-brother Clemens Brentano), Prince von Pückler-Muskau and the Prince de Ligne, Varnhagen can be ranked among the most upright Christians of that time in relation to their Jewish friends.

Rahel, the intellectual godmother of so many romantic and truly German souls, with their Prussian patriotism and gentle brand of humanism, turned to the Christian evangelical faith on her wedding day in 1814. A Christian study of the Bible brought her closer to the God of her forefathers and her blood-brother Jesus. The anti-Jewish disturbance in 1819 distressed her deeply. Like Bettina Brentano, she saw with her feminine intuition the true cause more clearly than many men; it lay in the silence, the hostile silence of the Christian clergy, who praised the Old Testament in their sermons, but had nothing to say about the burning of synagogues and Torah scrolls.

Refreshing herself at the spring of Christian mysticism, with the words of Angelus Silesius, ('And were Christ born a thousand times in Bethlehem, And never in thy soul, still wert thou lost . . . ') an older, wiser Rahel knew how firmly she was still tied to her Jewish forebears. Five days before her death in 1833 she referred to herself as a refugee from Egypt and Palestine who had found help and affection in Germany.

But while Rahel and some other of her blood relations were being courted in their salons in Berlin and Vienna by an enthusiastic group of aristocrats and young German poets, evil omens were appearing in the bright skies of the 'new age'. Violent anti-Semitism raged in speeches and publications during the Wars of Liberation, in the writings of Arndt and Jahn, in the right wing of the *Junges Deutschland* movement. Students burned Jewish books in 1817. A reactionary legislature in the different states of the German Confederation, created at the Vienna Congress of 1815, sought to deprive the Jews of rights which had only just been promised them, or even to some extent granted.

During the Vienna Congress the death occurred of a loved and respected representative of the true ancient aristocracy of Europe. Prince de Ligne considered himself, in his own words, 'a Frenchman in Germany, a citizen of the German Reich in France and a Westerner in Russia'. This man – the happiest man in Europe, according to Goethe – early recognized the complexity of the Jewish problem in Europe. Already in 1797 he was outlining in a letter to a friend a plan for a Jewish state: 'The Christians obviously possess neither the skill nor the goodness of heart to liberate the Jews from their present condition and do something sensible with them. I only wish one of the Jews living in Turkey would be clever enough to gain such influence over his ruler there as to win back for them the kingdom of Judaea.' ' – When I speak of a return to Palestine, I am thinking only of the paupers and the class between the rich and the poor.'

Prince de Ligne, mercifully free of self-hatred and an inferiority complex, and therefore able to look on the Jews as fellow men, recognize that a gap was beginning to grow between wealthy European Jews in the process of assimilation and the others, the masses of poor, insignificant Jews.

Fichte, the philosopher of the first German national movement, came out strongly against student anti-Semitic excesses when he was rector of Berlin University. Earlier, in September 1799, he had written to his beloved wife about Dorothea Mendelssohn: 'It may seem strange to hear me praising a Jewess, but this woman has altered my belief that nothing good could come out of this people ... ' In his youth Fichte had been strongly anti-Jewish, convinced that the Jews were allowed to exploit Christian citizens and get away with it unpunished: 'I cannot see any means of giving them full civil rights, except by cutting off all their heads and putting on new ones with no Jewish ideas in them. Moreover, I can see no other means of protecting ourselves from them, except by conquering their Promised Land and sending them all there.' Were these the models for the Kristallnacht of 1938, when Nazis burned Jewish synagogues and shops, or for Eichmann's and Himmler's plans to ship the Jews off to Madagascar or Palestine, or were they for something much worse?

A young man whom Kant selected to correct the proofs of his book *On Everlasting Peace* and who later made a career for himself in Vienna as Metternich's assistant and secretary of the 1815 Vienna Congress, was often to be seen at the salons of Henriette Herz and Rahel Varnhagen. This was Friedrich von Gentz, who also frequented Fanny Arnstein's salon in Vienna for a time and kept a Jewish mistress. Nevertheless he became during his life maliciously anti-Semitic. Friedrich von Gentz can be called symptomatic of his time in many respects, and not least in his anti-Semitism. Up to and beyond the Nuremberg trials many leading anti-Semites were to maintain that they personally had or used to have a whole host of Jewish friends. Even Adolf Hitler is known to have had three hundred Jews made into 'honorary Aryans'. To this day the standard self-justification of Jew-haters is the statement: 'I've got nothing against individual Jews.'

Friedrich von Gentz, who was both gifted and ambitious, was filled with envy of Jewish intelligence at an early age. In 1801 he was already talking of 'the cursed Jews'. The great Humboldt was on friendly terms with him, yet Gentz declared: 'It is indeed a disgrace that one can no longer see Humboldt's name except linked with a Frenchman or a Jew.'

Gentz laughed, as he confessed he had not laughed for years, over an anonymous pamphlet, written in fact by his Berlin lawyer Grattenauer, *Against the Jews: a Word of Warning to our Christian Fellow Citizens.* It poured scorn on 'the Jewish stench' and 'Jewish quackery' as well as on the intelligent Jewish salon hostesses in Berlin. Gentz wanted to send this document by courier to Rome, where Humboldt was Prussian ambassador.

We have already mentioned how Metternich (who was not an anti-Semite) frightened Tsar Alexander with news of a plot which was supposedly being spread through Europe by French emigrés. Paris was the centre of a masonic conspiracy, whose sects were aiming at the overthrow of the church and all crowned heads in Europe. In Friedrich von Gentz hatred of the French (of which Metternich was also completely free) was fused with hatred of the Jews in a pitiful conspiracy theory. The Jews appeared to him as 'born representatives of atheism, Jacobinism and so-called Enlightenment'.

It is sad to see a man as highly gifted as Gentz reduced here to a *terrible simplificateur*, a malicious demagogue. 'No Jew has ever seriously believed in God. No Jewish woman has ever known true love – and I make absolutely no exceptions. Everything bad in the modern world, if you go back far enough, stems from the Jews; it was they alone who made Bonaparte emperor; they alone struck with such despicable blindness at the north of Germany . . . But enough of these cannibals!' Here, from one of the foremost voices in a Europe dedicated to the preservation of an old sacred order, we hear the bitter note that characterized, then and later, the anti-Semitism of the unsuccessful, the plebs in the form of teachers, country parsons, hack writers, soapbox politicians and beer-hall demagogues in Vienna, Munich and elsewhere. But here it was being sounded by a man who was a leader of opinion, a guest in the leading salons of his time. Friedrich von Gentz got up from the luxurious tables of his Jewish hosts in Berlin and Vienna – and betrayed them: 'The Devil take the Jews!' he wrote, not spelling out the word 'devil', but leaving it at the initial letter: the completion he could safely leave to his contemporaries and successors. This early advocate of a counter-revolutionary Christian *Abendland* declares all Jews to be godless, atheistic, completely lacking in love – the Jews, the authors of the Psalms and the Old Testament, from which spring the liturgies and prayers of every Christian nation!

Friedrich von Gentz, the great reactionary, did not believe in the promise of the future. His condemnation of the Greek and Polish uprisings demonstrated his certainty that the forces of reaction would not and could not win. Behind all his hatred of Jews and French, behind the mockery of Greeks and Poles, lay the fears of a basically very lonely man who found it impossible to believe in the future or in the power of love and freedom.

Love and revolution, woman and freedom, emancipation of peoples, races and women : all these things were inextricably bound together in the mind of Heinrich Heine.

Heine's all too often quoted definition of baptism as a ticket of admittance to Western culture did not obscure or solve – either for himself or for other Jewish Christians – the real problem of the emancipation of the Jews. Heine stands out as one of the exceptional minds between Goethe and Nietzsche, and not even a Karl Kraus (the victim of a Jewish self-hatred) can minimize his greatness. The magnitude of Heine's wrestling with his own German, Jewish and Christian identity can be measured against the doubtful attempts of some other converted German Jews to solve the problems involved.

All the personal recognition accorded a man like Moses Mendelssohn, and other Jewish bankers and scholars, could not conceal from the Jews emerging from their ghettoes in German lands what was expected of them : a complete loss of identity – either by baptism or disappearance.

'Show some respect, Jew !' Every Jew in the free imperial city of Frankfurt was forced to respond to this cry by a servile demonstration of respect towards the caller. A Frankfurt Jew related this as a childhood memory to the German chancellor Prince Bülow at the beginning of the twentieth century. The Jew was Baron Mayer Anselm Rothschild.

Loeb Baruch, a child of the Frankfurt ghetto, longed for the freedom which emerging German intellectualism would give him. In 1818 he was baptized and took the name Ludwig Börne. The following year he published *Für die Juden* (On Behalf of the Jews), appealing to the reason and goodwill of the Germans towards freedom and self-enlightenment. In his book Börne drew attention to the centuries-old persecution of Jews and heretics. It was a bloody river flowing through eighteen centuries, and on its banks stood Christianity. Time and again religion had become a murderous weapon in plundering hands. Börne knew from experience all about the sufferings of the Jews at the hands of their Christian neighbours. He begged his German friends to give full civil rights to the Jews, declaring that the emancipation of Germans could not really be complete as long as the Jews had lesser rights.

The young Börne was full of confidence. The Jews would dissolve in the great sea of freedom just like other nations who had emerged from a constricting past. Hatred of the Jews was a relic of the Middle Ages, an artificial plant with no real roots in the new age. But an ageing, disillusioned Börne saw the rise of a new and massive hatred of the Jews, systematically encouraged even by his fellow-fighters in the *Junges Deutschland* movement, men like Wolfgang Menzel, who had gone over to the side of reaction.

Menzel, 'that devourer of the French' as Börne called him in one of his pamphlets, is a disturbing symptom of the future. In his old age Börne gave much thought to the great qualities and traditions of the Jews. He knew that he was still considered Jewish, even though he was a Christian. But he had chosen for ever: he had set forth as 'a German and a Jew' to fight for the freedom of both in his writings. What would become of Germany and German freedom? Börne was sceptical now. He looked across the sea and thought things might be better in America. There all the nations of old Europe would go into the melting-pot and a new freedom would emerge. America would complete the assimilation of the Jews.

Vienna, seat of Christian-Socialist, anti-Semitic Catholics and German nationalists, danced to the music of Strauss's *Blue Danube* waltz. The words set to music by Strauss were written by Karl Beck. He belonged to the group of German Jews who, with Börne, were prominent in the *Junges Deutschland* movement and who for a time believed in the spring awakening in Germany with the same fervour as the Jews of 'Young Spain' in 1510. Beck's German friends compared him with Byron. With shame and growing scorn he looked down on his Jewish people and in 1843 became a Protestant – in that secularized, worldly Protestant church of German culture which celebrated its Sunday services in the concert hall and the theatre and in lecture meetings.

Here and there among the young German nationalist Jews and Jewish Christians of Börne's generation a hatred of the Jews was slowly growing. It grew, for instance, in the man who came of a long line of rabbis, was baptized Heinrich Marx and passed his aversion to the Jews on to his son, Karl. Years later, in his London exile, Karl Marx recalled how his father had sung in Trier the praises of the Prussian king in a fervent patriotic speech.

These early German nationalist Jews were not yet the equivalent of those Nazi Jews in Prague, Vienna and Berlin who ardently admired Adolf Hitler (one has to have known these tragic figures personally to be able to appreciate the extent of their tragedy), but they throw a disquieting light on a future which was to reveal the hitherto unsuspected possibilities of a Jewish betrayal from within.

Joel Jacoby and David Friedrich Koreff may be taken as representative of these unfortunates. Jacoby came from Königsberg, a centre of Enlightenment where Jewish emancipation was actively supported by high Prussian officials intent on making worthy Prussian citizens out of the Jews. In his *Jew's Lament*, published anonymously in 1837, Jacoby sang of the sombre fate of the Jews in the past. He wanted to throw off the burden of Jewishness, and called upon himself and all Jews to become German in thought and feeling. With fatal facility he sang the praises of the old heathen Germany, his true, second fatherland. He bitterly condemned a decree by King Frederick William III forbidding Prussian Jews to take names of Christian origin. In 1840 Joel Jacoby became the Prussian Catholic Franz Carl Jacoby, who openly cast aside the burden of his Jewishness – and with it some years later his belief in democracy and neo-paganism. Jacoby died in 1863 as an official of the Prussian propaganda machine, in whose service he had foresworn both his Jewish identity and his *Junges Deutschland*.

In 1851 David Friedrich Koreff was buried in the dismal cemetery of Père-la-Chaise, which bears witness to the lives and deaths of so many lonely souls who came to grief in Paris. There Börne too found lasting peace. Koreff was a native of Breslau – the town which also gave birth to Ferdinand Lassalle, an arrogant Prussian Jew who, in a conversation with Bismarck, declared his longing for a *Führerstaat* under the leadership of the Kaiser in which highly disciplined worker armies would storm Constantinople and set up a German world empire, after destroying the smaller nations that had no part to play in history.

Koreff practised as a doctor in Berlin, Paris and Vienna; as a faith-healer he was the darling of the ladies. He became the personal physician of Napoleon's family, and after that the leading doctor in the Prussian army headquarters and Hardenberg's physician. King Friedrich Wilhelm of Prussia decorated him with the Iron Cross and got him a professorship at Berlin University. Koreff extolled Prussia as the fatherland of science and learning. He never mentioned Jews in his writing, but at table, amidst the pleasures of dining, his jokes and invectives against the Jews could often be heard.

Koreff, the favourite of the Prussian king and patronized by the Prussian nobility, rose high in the Prussian academic world. When Bonn University was founded he was called in as adviser to the faculty of medicine. His pupils and protegés showed him no gratitude, however; for them this emphatic ex-Jew was still a Jew who had to go. Koreff could not hold his position in Berlin. He went back to Paris where, acclaimed at the beginning of the century, he was now after 1822 denounced as a Prussian. Humiliated and abandoned, he became one of a circle of Jews including the composer Meyerbeer and his brother, the playwright Michael Beer; and he became physician to another lonely spirit in Paris – the great Heinrich Heine.

Chaim Bückeburg: that was Heine's real name, according to Adolf Bartels, one of the many Nazi historians of literature who did their bit to see that Heine's works were publicly burned in 1933 (one hundred years after they had been banned by the German Bundestag in 1835). Thomas Carlyle attacked him as a 'dirty blasphemous Jew', and the Comte de Soissons declared in 1920 in the *Quarterly Review* that he, together with Spinoza, Herzen, Marx and Lassalle, prepared the way for Bolshevism and the Jewish world revolution. (The reactionary Comte de Soissons did at least do Heine justice in one respect: he treated him as a figure of world importance.)

Heinrich Heine (1797–1856) was stunned as a young Jewish student in Berlin to learn from Hegel that this celebrated man, the saviour of Christianity in philosophy, personally did not believe in an after-life, nor in any heavenly reward for good or punishment for evil. Heine joined the short-lived 'Society for Jewish Culture and Science', and then on 25 June 1825 was converted to the Protestant faith. Shortly afterwards he was shattered by a sermon preached by a rabbi in Hamburg against apostates, and as a result he saw himself as a man hated by both Christians and Jews.

Heine was the most clear-sighted poet of the nineteenth century in Germany. He saw himself as a Jew, a German, a Christian, an Ancient Greek, a heathen, an Asiatic and wrote of 'civil war in my heart'. He was aware of the death of Jehovah and the death of Christ, and equally aware of the resurrection of the gods, the resurrection of mankind and the cosmic Christ, and he wrote: 'God is in movement.' Heine was aware of the two peoples in every nation, and aware of the connection between revolution and reaction. He foresaw the German plebian movement, National Socialism, the World War and the world revolution. No other man in nineteenth-century Germany expressed so much of the suffering of a split Jewish soul.

German, French and Polish visitors professed to see Christ-like features in the dying Heine.

Heine saw Christianity falling into decay behind the façade of a Christian state, dying in millions of hearts. 'Our hearts are full of an unbearable pity – it is the old Jehovah himself who is preparing for his death. We knew him well from the cradle onwards, in Egypt, where he was raised among sacred calves and crocodiles, holy onions, sacred ibises and cats. We saw how he said farewell to these playmates of his youth and to the obelisks and sphinxes of his native Nile valley, and became a small god-king in Palestine among a poor little tribe of shepherds, living in his own temple-palace . . .' 'We saw him come into contact with Assyrian–Babylonian civilization, and then emigrate to Rome . . .' 'We saw how he turned ever more and more to the realm of the spirit, how he softly pleaded, became a loving father, a friend of all mankind, a philanthropist. But nothing could save him. Do you hear the bell ringing? Kneel down – they are bringing the sacraments to a dying god.'

Jewish atheism, arising as it does from the Jewish tendency to analyse, is frequently misunderstood, but recognizable for what it basically is: treating all images of God as graven images, which stand in the way of man's growth and his deeper experience of the deity.

Heine saw Christianity as being sick unto death and no longer capable of taming, healing and redeeming mankind, since in Germany the power of

Christianity had been broken ('the Cross, that taming talisman, snaps'), the 'old stone gods' before which the world would tremble. Its destructive power would make the 'French Revolution look like a harmless idyll.'

Heine loved Germany, especially the dark, unfathomable Germany of fairy-tale and legend, of Paracelsus and Faust; yet he saw the ancient forces piercing the thin covering of civilization all over the world – in Germany, in North and South America, in Asia, India and Africa.

The thought of the Jews on their tragic wanderings through world history moved Heine to the depths of his being. He saw them persecuted and reviled in all the lands of the earth, including his German homeland. His unfinished work *The Rabbi of Bacharach* is one of his greatest creations, combining German and Jewish history with the story of his own soul.

As a psychologist Heine anticipated much of Nietzsche and Freud, and he himself gained in creativity from his three-fold burden as Jew, German and Christian. His rabbi says to the young Jew who wants to fight for his faith: 'Noble lord, if you wish to be my knight, you must fight against whole peoples, and in this fight there is little reward and still less honour to be gained. And, if you want to wear my colours, you must sew yellow rings on your cloak or bind a blue striped sash around you, for these are the colours of my house, which is called Israel and which is exceeding cast-down and mocked in the streets by the children of fortune.'

The German Jew Heinrich Heine wrote one of the greatest poems about Christ in a century singularly lacking in Christian works: 'Peace' (The North Sea I, 1825):

> He strode gigantically tall
> Over land and sea.
> His head touched heaven.
> He spread his hands in benediction
> Over land and sea;
> And for a heart in his bosom
> He bore the sun,
> The red fiery sun,
> And the red, fiery sun-heart
> Showered its beams of grace
> And its pure love-bestowing light,
> That illumines and warms
> Over land and sea . . .

Heine believed in love and in a world revolution. In 1842 (in *Lutetia*) he foresaw the coming world war: Germany and France would start it, then England and Russia would join in. However, England, the great sea serpent, could withdraw into the sea, and the Russian bear hide in the steppes and tundra of Siberia. Germany and France would emerge fatally wounded from the war, which would lead to world revolution – the great struggle between capitalism and workers' movements. National boundaries would disappear, and differences of faith would gradually lose their importance. There would remain only one mother country, the earth itself, and one faith: joy in existence, in this life on earth.

Heine was no guileless optimist. He foresaw great inner struggles after the wars and the political revolution. Europe might well see a new absolutism in the twentieth century with new slogans: tyranny in new garb. Heine foresaw Fascism and National Socialism. New and brutal times would come, bringing new monsters compared with which the old symbolic beasts of the Apocalypse would seem like doves and cherubim. The future smelt of blood, murder and crime.

Some free spirits would save themselves as Europe collapsed, by escaping to America: they would flee from the prison of Europe to the last stronghold of freedom-loving men. Heine recalled that America was discovered in the same year as the Jews were driven out of Spain. America would become Europe's last hope. In America the conflict between East and West, between Jew and German, would be resolved.

Heine considered himself a prophet. In the Bible a prophet is a man who can understand the reality of his own day. Since God has opened his eyes, he can reveal what others hide from themselves.

'I lightened your darkness, and, when the battle began, I fought in the front line. Around me lie the bodies of my friends. Joyful songs of triumph mix with the funeral hymns. But we have time neither for joy nor for mourning. Once again the trumpets sound, calling to new battles – I am the sword, I am the flame.'

Heinrich Heine, the 'good European' (Nietzsche, who coined the phrase, considered Heine as the greatest German poet beside Goethe), was one of the most valiant fighters for Man's liberation from spiritual terror and intellectual and mental self-imprisonment. Heine proclaimed a new message of joy, beauty and freedom from fear.

On a day in May, during his last visit to the Louvre, Heine collapsed before the Venus de Milo. The year was 1848 – that fateful year in European history, whose abortive revolution directly led to the Franco-Prussian War of 1870–1, to violent nationalism and to the First World War. In his 'mattress-tomb' his life gradually ebbed away.

It was in Heine's beloved Paris, the hope of political refugees from many European countries, that Karl Marx, that 'shameless Jew' (as his early companion in battle Arnold Ruge called him), wrote poetry together with Heine. Marx, the object of police attention in his humble rooms in Dean Street, Soho, declared in 1858 that he was plagued like Job. Three of his children died in misery. Sometimes the whole family's clothes had to be pawned, and then they would lie in bed in the dark with neither light nor food. When his favourite son Edgar died in 1856 at the age of six, he collapsed. His wife loyally shared the misery of his hell, through seven births and the deaths of their children. One of her brothers became the Prussian minister of the interior under King Friedrich Wilhelm IV. She was born Jenny von Westphalen, daughter of the Prussian privy councillor Ludwig von Westphalen, and on her mother's side she was descended from Scottish nobility. Her ancestor was the rebellious Archibald Campbell, earl of Argyll, who tried to seize power in Scotland and, after his defeat by the English king, was beheaded in the market-place in Edinburgh.

Karl Marx, who died in poverty in his armchair on 14 March 1883 and who was followed to his grave in Highgate cemetery by only a small group of friends and representatives of workers' movements, was a descendant of Europe's oldest intellectual nobility. His forebears included such great rabbis as Joseph ben Gerson Cohen, rabbi of Cracow at the end of the sixteenth century, and Meir Katzenellenbogen, who died in 1565 as rabbi of Padua, much respected by the university of Padua, which honoured his memory with a portrait in its great hall. Karl Marx's father, Herschel Marx – who became Heinrich Marx after baptism – belonged to a family that had provided the rabbis for 150 years to Trier, a town to which Jews had come with Caesar and Augustus.

Karl Marx, the 'Red Prussian' (as the Jew Leopold Schwarzschild called him in a malicious portrait), who would sing German folksongs as he walked with his family from Hampstead to Soho on feast days, was 'the last great manifestation of the Jewish prophet, coming unbidden from the wilderness to pour forth his curses on the lost and erring of a vain world' (René König).

It was in his London wilderness, during the period of intense inner loneliness between 1849 and 1883, that the fires which accompanied the people of Moses on their journey flared up in Karl Marx, the wanderer between two worlds, between the ancient past and the distant future of mankind. Marx penetrated right through the Jewry of his time, through the orthodox ghetto and through Europeanized, assimilated Jewry back to the great early prophets, to Isaiah and Amos.

He was the most passionate and radical prophet in a century which was swarming with small and lesser prophets, preaching disaster and salvation of many kinds. The anger of Moses against his faithless people was heard again on Marx's lips and seen in Marx's eyes. Woe betide all on whom this prophet's judgment fell! Hardest hit were friends, colleagues and disciples who betrayed what he thought weakness or deviance: Ruge, Bauer, Kriege, Grün, Hess, Kinkel, Willich, Weitling, Schweitzer, Lassalle. Of Mikhail Bakunin, who handed over the torch of total revolution to Lenin and whom Alexander Herzen called 'a Columbus with no ship and no America' Marx wrote to Engels: 'This Russian obviously wants to be dictator of the European workers' movement. He had better be careful. Otherwise he will be officially excommunicated.'

From his London den the Amos of the nineteenth century (as H.D. Sanders called him), head of a new synagogue of the future, launched his lightning shafts into the world. These flashes – his critical analyses of society – announced the time, place and form of the coming storm, which would cleanse the air of the whole world and – to use the words of his friend Engels – make possible 'mankind's leap from the realm of necessity into the realm of freedom'.

The German romantic poet and idealist philosopher Dr Karl Marx became, during his Paris years (1843–5), the historical figure Karl Marx. Here he discovered his identity as prophet of the world revolution, of the liberation of Man from the alienation inflicted on him by himself and others. The gnostics, St Augustine and Hegel all speak of Man's estrangement from himself. Marx is a descendant of Hegel; and his thinking on the problem of alienation is that of a Jew struggling consciously and subconsciously with the problem of Jewry.

Marx's explicit dealings with the Jewish problem are inadequate and not entirely free from an element of Jewish self-hatred. Bruno Bauer, at one time a friend of Marx and one of the most intelligent members of the Hegelian Left, had, in two of his essays, *The Jewish Question* and *The Capacity of Modern Jews and Christians to Become Free*, denied the Jews the right of assimilation and of equal civil rights with Christians. For him the Christian was far above the Jew. The Jew was an interloper, a feeble and malevolent creature who stood outside the true development of world history. Bauer put his view even more emphatically in *Jewry Abroad* (1863): in this Jew became a manifestation of evil on earth.

The theologian's hatred of the evil God Jehovah was intensified to hatred of the whole Jewish people, whom Bauer called the arch-enemies of future human prosperity. Bauer became the spiritual leader of an overt German anti-Semitism, which sought to build up an international movement. It was represented before 1848 by Wilhelm Marr, and in Wilhelmine Germany by Rudolf Todt, the court preacher Stöcker and his Christian-Social party and by the *International Monthly* (Chemnitz, from 1882), a cultural and literary magazine. After Bauer's death this was renamed the *Antisemitische Blätter* (Anti-Semitic Journal). Bauer himself did not wish to be called an anti-Semite.

Was Karl Marx, who in 1844 reviewed Bauer's two anti-Jewish essays, himself an anti-Semite? This allegation is often made, but it cannot be sub-stantiated. Marx defended the Jews, but not as an independent racial and religious unit; rather he wished to free them in order to assimilate them into the single race of humanity (as had the French Revolution before him). Marx treats the Jewish problem as a part of the human problem, and above all of the proletarian problem. His description of the social position of the proletariat is immediately applicable to the Jews. 'Marx in fact secularizes into a general revolutionary philosophy the ancient Jewish promise of a release in this world from unbearable misery and endless suffering. This spirit remains basically alive in him up to Chapter 24 of *Das Kapital*, in which he speaks of the "so-called primitive capital accumulation" as "original sin" in political economy and concludes: "The hour is striking" – that is, the final act of liberation, of redemption has begun. Capital, the demon which holds the world in its claws ("dripping from head to foot with blood and filth", to use Marx's biblical language), the "abomination of desolation" has now reached its end, and the prophet calls for the leap from the realm of necessity into the realm of freedom (as Engels was later to call it in similarly theological language)' (René König).

Marx conceives of Man as the worker, realizing himself through his own labour. In this connection there are four sorts of possible alienation, defined by H. Popitz thus:

'Alienation of the worker from the products of his labour;

Alienation of the worker from his work;

Self-alienation of the hired labourer;

Alienation between men, the effect of which is that men cannot see their relation to the human species in its true light, but merely treat one another as instruments.'

Marx's thought, revolving around the complex problem of alienation and self-alienation, is one of the very greatest intellectual achievements of the modern era. This theory of alienation was further developed by Sigmund Freud; but already in Marx it has its deep subconscious roots in his struggle with the tragic problem of the place of the Jew in the world. The Jew is a stranger in the world of Christian and post-Christian peoples. The German Jew who had left, or been chased out of, the ghetto in the nineteenth century was alienated from his past, his history, his God. And this non-believing baptized Jew (Marx was baptized himself, and he wrote his school-leaving dissertation on the question of the nature, causes and consequences of the union of the faithful with Christ – St John 15, 1–14) still found himself in the same position as Ludwig Börne in 1832: 'Some reproach me for being a Jew, some forgive me and others even praise me for it; but they are all conscious of it. They are all transfixed in this magic Jewish circle, and none can escape from it.'

Can no one escape? Yes, mankind could escape from alienation, the proletariat could burst its chains, and would do so in the workers' revolution heralded by the new gospel of the Communist Manifesto. The Manifesto, composed by Marx in London, was published in February 1848. It promised the victors of the future – the Communists – that they would bring together the vanquished of the present, indeed the whole of mankind, into the single nation of humanity. Only then would the true history of the world begin, the history of emancipated men who had become their true selves.

After 1844 Marx never again concerned himself directly with the Jewish question. This was not in fact just an evasion, but rather characteristic of that specifically Jewish (and hence prophetic) tendency to regard the problem of personal existence and the problems of the Jewish people as problems of all humanity. *All men* are involved in the message of Marx's deep Messianic faith. He explains the task, the means and the end of world history to the suffering, the oppressed and the under-privileged, to the self-alienated proletariat but also to the self-alienated capitalist (Marx's work contains the most generous nineteenth-century valuation of capitalism).

The great, prolific and eloquent prophet is silent, throughout the whole of his vast work, about the actual nature of this shining future, this kingdom of God on earth, the Communist society of men freed for their own true purposes. In thousands of pages there is only one concrete reference to it. This is in *German Ideology*: 'In capitalist society every man has a job which is forced on him and from which he cannot escape; but in Communist society, in which no man is confined to a single sphere of activity but can branch out as he wishes, society itself regulates overall production, and by that very fact makes it possible for a man to do different things from day to day, to hunt in the morning, fish in the afternoon, tend cattle in the evening and criticize after dinner, without being labelled a hunter, a fisherman, a herdsman or a critic.

Marx in these lines is harking back to a primitive society in which hunting, fishing and guarding cattle were part of a free communal life lived close to nature – the mythical time of the original races of the Old Testament and of the people of Israel. At the same time he is looking forward to a future society, some of whose features have now been realized by experts in the art of living in the United States of America, who – thanks to their wealth and to private aeroplanes and modern communications – are able to go hunting in New York State in the morning, to do business in New York City at midday, to go fishing in the afternoon and, after a brief visit to their own farm in the evening, to play the critic among their circle of friends and (with the help of the *New Yorker*) to discuss the theatre, the arts and international affairs.

The way for this society has been prepared during the nineteenth and twentieth centuries by Jews. Applying the dammed-up energies of centuries in all the professions open to them after their liberation from the ghetto, they became active in the new sciences and fields of activity which they themselves in some cases helped to discover – certain areas of psychology, depth psychology, sociology, all the sciences and techniques concerned with the integration of the individual in society; and not least in the techniques of cultural enterprise, the entertainments industry and the mass-media: film, radio, television and show business.

To return now to the world of Karl Marx. It is no coincidence that a Jew with true prophetic spirit was the first to recognize the genius of the young, unknown Marx.

'He is a very young man, but one who will strike the final blow at medieval religions and political ideas.' Such, in 1841, was the judgment of Moses Hess (1812–75) on the twenty-four-year-old Marx, whom he saw as a combination of Rousseau, Voltaire, Holbach, Lessing, Heine and Hegel. Hess, member of a Bonn industrial family and a descendant on his mother's side of Eastern Jewish rabbis, combined within himself the energies and hopes of both Western and Eastern European Jewry. *Die Heilige Geschichte der Menschheit* (The Holy Story of Humanity, 1837) presents Adam, Jesus and Spinoza as representatives of the three ages of the world. Man is the redeemer and the redeemed. Hess longed to identify himself completely with the new young nation of Germany. He married a Christian woman, and took part actively in the 'Poets' War' in which German and French journalists, writers and poets disputed in 1840 whether the Rhine was a German or a French river. Nikolaus Becker's war-song *The German Rhine* enflamed the nationalistic youth of Germany. Hess, more Prussian than many Prussians themselves, set Becker's song to music. Becker returned the composition to him, rejecting it with the words: 'You are a Jew.'

You are a Jew. Moses Hess was to become conscious of this fact in the weary course of his life – at first with pain and bitterness and then with pride and emotion; it was this experience which revealed to him his vocation. In *Die europäische Triarchie* (1841) he pleads for 'a United States of Europe', for a social and political reorganization of Europe under the patronage of Prussia, France and England. The Jew is to play an important role in this united Europe. The law of Moses, founded on justice, freedom and equality, contains the seed of the coming world order – a law from the remotest past providing a model for the social structure of a distant future.

Hess acquired the nick-name of 'the Communist rabbi' – in a way an apt choice, as he was, in his religious fervour and passionate desire to serve the cause of suffering humanity, one of the first German Communists. In his *Kommunistisches Bekenntnis* (Communist Declaration) of 1844–5 he declares the aim of Christianity to be 'the happiness of all human beings through love, freedom and justice.' These are ancient Jewish ideals. The evil in the world is Mammon – money. 'Hell is nothing other than the world under the domination of money.' Christians give an accurate representation of reality, but disguised in symbols. God is love – 'humanity united in love'. In the coming Communist society people will achieve this love, and the kingdom of God will be established on earth.

Hess won over Marx and Engels to Communism and made the young Dr Marx co-editor of his socialistic newspaper *Rheinische Zeitung*. Marx had been greatly impressed by Hess's contributions in Herwegh's *21 Bogen* (21 Sheets, 1843), in which he denounced the terrorization of the state and the tyranny of religion, as the old prophets in Israel and Judaea had once denounced the tyranny of priests and kings.

'The distinction between pleasure and work disappears' in Communism. The transformation of work into 'pleasurable activity' (reminiscent of Marx's reference to the society of the future, already quoted) is to make man free. The goal of all Communism and atheism is 'to convert external restraints into self-restraint, the external God into an inner one, material possessions into spiritual ones.'

The prophets had declared exactly this to be the goal of the Messianic kingdom. It is significant for the whole inner history of 'Jewish atheism', 'Jewish Socialism' and 'Jewish Bolshevism' that what Hess designated as 'atheism' was what he himself, both previously and subsequently, experienced as religion, as Man's religious struggle for liberation of the self.

In 1845 Moses Hess brought out, together with Engels, the *Gesellschafts-spiegel* (Mirror of Society) – the first German periodical to deal with the social conditions of the working classes.

In Paris, Cologne and Belgium Hess lived the typical underground life of the religious refugee. In 1848 there was a rupture between Marx and Engels and himself. Marx was trying to put the Messianic Jewish element in himself on a philosophic footing and to submit it to scientific discipline. But there is no doubt that Hess had a decisive influence on him.

In Moses Hess we have the first break-through to a revolutionary German Socialism, arising from the spirit of Messianic Jews and German revivalists, the socialistic anabaptists who had been living in hiding in the Rhineland and in the Netherlands since the sixteenth century. Hess thought that work which was free, moral, not distorted or alienated through private ownership, must become pleasurable and must finally, when practised by fraternities, overthrow the state. He here anticipated the ideas of Bakunin and of revolutionary anarchists and syndicalists in France, Spain and later Russia.

In the following years Hess immersed himself in the history of Israel and Judaism. In his work *Rom und Jerusalem* (1862) he laid down the basis for modern Zionism. Full of enthusiasm for the cause of Jewish nationalism, he was the first Western European to recognize the significance of Hasidism, and revealed his close affinity with the fanatical underground movement of both Eastern and Western Europe by predicting the fall of the old sacred dynasties of Europe – the Hapsburgs, Romanovs and Hohenzollerns, the dissolution of the Austro-Hungarian monarchy and the political rebirth of the Slav nations. The old struggle of the prophets versus kings and priests was revived in him.

Rom und Jerusalem is an extraordinary work. Moses Hess, the great fighter against the self-alienation of Man, confesses that he had estranged himself from his Jewish race for twenty years. Now returned to his people, he sees that Jews can not and should not try to assimilate. They form a foreign element in their host nations. In Eastern Europe millions of Jews are praying day and night for the restoration of the Jewish nation and its return to Palestine, the Holy Land of the Jews. If Jewry were to remember its own peculiar character, both racially and spiritually, it could be of service to the whole of humanity in the battle for the doctrine of the divine unity of all living beings. The Christian battle for a private and exclusive salvation is beside the point: the individual is inseparably bound to the family, the family to the nation, the nation to the whole of mankind, and humanity, together with all creation, forms a whole in God. The function of Man is to be the guardian of this cosmic life. The kingdom of the Messiah for which Jewry yearns is the kingdom of life on earth, not a remote, timeless kingdom in heaven. In the course of world history all people will be led to this kingdom.

Hess preached that a new start in this direction could only be made if the present egoistic and individualistic social system were transformed into the socialistic and Messianic system forecast by the Jewish prophets. The Jews should return to Palestine. There, on the soil of their fathers, they would lose their inferiority complex, they would put down roots again and become a creative force influencing the whole of mankind. Jewish intellectuals should shake off their vague cosmopolitanism and devote their energies to this cause, the immediate aim being the return to Palestine. At least this remaining few – the famous holy remnant of God's chosen race which did not break faith with the God of Sinai – should not allow itself to be tempted into joining the Mammoth-worshippers in their dance around the Golden Calf.

It was in his descriptions of Mammon, of Mammon-worship, of the devilish, enslaving power of money, and of the 'curse' which such idol-worship brings, that Karl Marx showed himself to be, throughout his life, an ardent disciple of Moses Hess and the prophets.

Moses Hess proclaimed the glad tidings that capitalism, the service of Mammon, the exploitation of Man by Man and class by class was approaching its downfall. Imperialism, with its exploitation of weaker nations by stronger ones (how much had the small Jewish people had to suffer under foreign rule in the ancient world!) could not survive indefinitely.

In the dawning liberation of the oppressed classes, races and peoples Jewry had an active part to play which it could not fulfil as long as it remained dispersed, but only by concentrating all its efforts on building up Palestine – by developing agriculture and crafts, and educating a new youth and a new intelligence. Once the nucleus of a Jewish state was created in Palestine, under the protection of the great powers, this Jewish state would be a growing point of creative life strategically placed on the path of communication between East and West, on the route to India and China.

Hess, the fervent dedicated prophet, possessed great patience and clear-sightedness. He was also aware that perhaps the great majority of Jews would not return to Palestine after their two-thousand year long second exile. Probably fewer Jews would leave the flesh-pots of Western Europe than other parts of the world. But, whether this was so or not, the moral and political disposition of those Jews who did not return to their homeland would be greatly strengthened by the consciousness that there, in Israel, Jews were constructing a Jewish state.

Moses Hess, the German Jew, is the most important Central European

precursor of the Viennese Jew, Theodor Herzl, the founder of political
Zionism.

In 1862, the year he published *Rom und Jerusalem*, Moses Hess collaborated
with Lassalle in preparing the foundation of the Association of German
Workers, which was officially inaugurated on 23 May 1863 in Leipzig. This
was the hour of birth of German social democracy. Its tragedy, its failure
up to the present day, was pre-ordained by the personality of its first leader,
Ferdinand Lassalle (1825–64). Lassalle was the conformist assimilated Jew,
who ingratiated himself with the possessors of power and with high society.
There would be little cause for objection if he had been deciding the fate of
bankers, industrialists or 'Jewish capitalists'. But Lassalle was responsible for
the capitulation of the working-class movement, the squandering of its
revolutionary Messianic inheritance. Through him the hoped-for progress of
the German Socialist working class movement turned out to be no more than
acceptance of the uniforms, weapons, wars, governmental structures, thought
patterns and attitudes of successive régimes right up to the present Federal
Republic.

Alexander von Humboldt called him a prodigy and recommended him
to learned men in Paris, where he associated with Heine. Lassalle, son of a
Jewish silk-merchant in Breslau, was an ardent disciple of Fichte and Hegel,
and wrote a dissertation in 1857 on *The Philosophy of the Dark Heraclitus of
Ephesus*. Marx, Engels and Lenin all poured scorn on this German-Jewish
idealistic Heraclitus with his unmistakable Lassallean stamp. Two years
later he wrote his drama *Franz von Sickingen*, in which he pleaded the cause
of a united Germany ruled by an evangelical emperor. The Austro-Hungarian
empire should be destroyed and the German parts of it should be incorporated
in the new empire. Right up to 1945 German Socialists clung to this pious
wish of Lassalle. The Association of German Workers elected Lassalle as its
president – a five-year office – with the full dictatorial powers he had insisted
upon. This dictatorial leadership of a party of the masses, which suppressed
all opposition, is a small foretaste of the *Führerstaat* of the future.

Lassalle was a belated knight of late Romanticism. He died in Geneva in
a duel arising out of a love affair with Helene von Dönniges, the daughter of
the Bavarian ambassador. Lassalle remained attached to the very circles and
cliques which, according to German Socialist workers, it was his duty as
leader of the workers to overthrow.

In Lassalle's demagogic speeches we can hear the thunder of the 'marching
feet of the workers' battalions'. Bombastically he cried to the workers: 'You
are the rock upon which the church of the present is to be built.' 'The rule of
the Fourth Estate' would bring forth an unprecedented 'blossoming of
morality, culture and learning'.

Lassalle in effect advocated an authoritarian, imperialist state. Smaller, 'culturally inferior' nations should be dominated and absorbed by great nations with great cultural traditions. Lassalle's correspondence with Bismarck in the years 1863–4 was discovered by chance in the 1920s, when a worm-eaten cupboard in the Prussian state ministry fell to pieces. In a letter to Bismarck (8 June 1863) Lassalle says that 'the working classes are instinctively well-disposed towards dictatorship, as long as they are convinced that it will promote their interests. How happy would they be, for all their republican attitudes (or rather because of them), to see the monarchy as the instrument of social dictatorship, rather than the egoism of bourgeois society; if only the crown – and this is admittedly very unlikely – could bring itself to take the truly revolutionary and nationalistic step of changing from an institution representing the privileged classes into a socialistic popular monarchy.'

This is bad, romantic politics. Lassalle was building up a kingdom for himself in the workers' party. He took pains to cure his workers of 'the disease of having an opinion, thinking that they know better'. He looked confidently towards the future, a future which belonged to a national Germany: 'I hope I shall live to see the Turkish possessions in Europe fall to Germany, and German soldiers – or workers' regiments – penetrating to the Bosphorus.'

Lassalle was not an agent in the pay of Bismarck, as many German workers thought during his lifetime. The tragedy of his betrayal lay at a deeper level. This highly gifted writer, speaker, organizer, 'Führer' of the German working class, was an example of Jewish self-betrayal: a self-betrayal which occurred deep in the subconscious. It was here that the coin of his Messianic inheritance was minted – but at the same time squandered in the small change of everyday life.

Lassalle can be invoked by all Jewish leaders and spokesmen of a revisionist Marxism who, from Bernstein on, retain the name and phraseology of the Socialist and Marxist workers' movement, but in reality are furthering the integration of the working classes into a late-bourgeois society. Under the leadership of Jewish 'national' revisionist leaders, the workers' armies marched into the First World War. The first member of the German *Reichstag* to fall was a Jewish volunteer. In Kaiser Wilhelm's empire Jews were active as reformers in almost every party, and particularly in the conservative and bourgeois parties, since Jews were often the only citizens traluistic enough to devote themselves and their time to the demands of party work. The aristocracy and the Christian bourgeoisie stood lethargically aside.

This Jewish political reformism was accompanied in the German states by a parallel phenomenon – Jewish religious reformism. Its first public manifestation was the 'Temple Dispute' in Hamburg in 1818. An organ was installed in the Hamburg temple (the organ is to this day rejected as a heathen instrument by the Eastern church, and in Hellenistic antiquity it occupied the position that jazz holds today). At the same time the forms of the religious service were modernized. This reform split Jewry into two parties – orthodox and liberal. Liberal Jews and reformist rabbinical theologians advocated an ever-increasing conformity of the Jews to the ways of contemporary educated society. The Jewish reformist theology became – as it still is today – a combination of essences and aromas drawn from the tastier pages of the Old Testament with elements of German idealistic philosophy and the liberal Protestant theology associated with it. This Jewish religious reform unintentionally weakened the resistance of European Jewry, undermined its self-assertiveness, and nourished the great dream of total assimilation of the Jews into the German nation. By 1930 this bourgeois, property-orientated Jewish reform movement had been drained of all inner vitality and meaning, and thus it could offer no resistance when faced with the gathering storm which drove it, between the Cross and the swastika, to its death.

Leaders of the Catholic church and theologians, both Catholic and Protestant, painted the Jewish danger in lurid colours for the benefit of the masses inside its own narrow churches and its political parties. Beginning before the First World War, the pressure increased after the Bolshevist victory in Russia in 1918.

Jewish Bolshevism: Russian and Polish Jews became Socialists, revolutionaries, Bolsheviks, from motives similar to those of the Spanish-Jewish revivalist movement of 1500 and the German-Jewish movements of 1795 and 1810. A young generation wanted to take up the fight for freedom and enlightenment by way of reform within the Catholic church, society and the state. On the bleak soil of the tsarist state unruly elements were faced with Siberia or the stake, prison or death; Jews were faced with confinement within certain areas, limited educational facilities and exclusion from certain occupations. All this led inevitably to the creation of underground movements. Here the Messianic fires blazed up, burning in the hearts and minds of young Jews who no longer shared the faith of their forefathers but nevertheless lived off the substance of this faith.

While in prison the great Russian revolutionary, Vera Sassulich, read the life of the arch-priest Avvakum, the great martyr of the Old Believers – the nonconformist movement in the Russian church which resisted the alliance of church and crown. Avvakum took up the cause of the oppressed peasants in the seventeenth century against the tsar, the Patriarch Nikon and a corrupt church hierarchy. Avvakum was burnt at the stake in Moscow, but he had managed to write his autobiography while in banishment in Siberia. The theme of *The Archpriest Avvakum's Life, Written by Himself* is suffering unto death. Trotsky was greatly moved by this book: he read it several times and later recognized it to be an account of his own fate.

Isaac Deutscher, the Polish-Jewish Communist, was an opponent of Stalinism and was excommunicated from the Communist party. He divided his monumental biography of Trotsky into three parts: *The Prophet Armed* (1879–1921), *The Prophet Unarmed* (1921–9), and *The Prophet Outcast* (1929–1940). A comparison of the life and work of Trotsky with that of Walther Rathenau is helpful in providing an insight into the essential nature of Jewish Bolshevism. Both were exceptional men, both burned with a similar prophetic zeal. Both had it in them to make world history. Both were first highly esteemed and then despised in their own countries. Both were assassinated.

Like Lenin (who tended, in moments of excitement at the climax of the revolution, to lapse into his second – or first – mother-tongue, German), Trotsky throughout his life fixed his hopes on Germany. Germany was to be the agent of the world revolution. Trotsky, the Red Origen (as I have called him elsewhere), was excommunicated by Stalin. Stalin, the child of the Orthodox church, often laced his pompous speeches with its liturgical language (not excluding its invective); and, as many people remarked, he became increasingly tsarist in figure, features, speech and behaviour as he grew older. Trotsky was deeply convinced that Stalin, who was responsible for his excommunication, banishment and finally assassination, was the betrayer of the world revolution, the arch-Cain, the murderer of hope, of liberty, of humanity. Moreover, Trotsky believed that he could establish that Stalin's disastrous theory of 'Socialism in one country' was derived from the German writer Georg von Vollmar.

The young Trotsky was an ardent reader of John Stuart Mill, Bentham and Tchernyshevsky; he wanted to become the Russian Lassalle. Like Heine – whom he resembled in many ways – Trotsky was in sympathy with French intellectual life. His love of the great French novels helped to support him through his imprisonment and the period of civil war. He was also profoundly influenced by German intellectual and political activity. As a member of the Austrian Social Democrats he recognized the Austrians' petty-bourgeois and chauvinistic character and contrasted it with the intellectual nobility of Marx and Engels, as revealed in their correspondence.

'The correspondence between Marx and Engels was for me not a theoretical, but a psychological revelation. *Toutes proportions gardées*, I found proof on every page that I was bound to these two by a direct psychological affinity ... They had not the slightest trace of sectarianism or asceticism. Both of them, and especially Engels, could at any time say of themselves that nothing human was strange to them.' 'Vulgarity could not stick even to the soles of their boots. Their appreciations, sympathies, jests, even when most commonplace – are always touched by the rarefied air of spiritual nobility.'

The same could be said of Trotsky at the height of his career, and he was likewise suspect on account of it. Suspicion turned to hate among the Stalinist plebeians and bureaucrats, whom he perceived to his horror to be hard, narrow-minded, nationalistic petty-bourgeois.

Leon Trotsky, the creator of the Red Army, the saviour of the Bolshevik revolution, the man who led the Bolsheviks to victory, often against more than a dozen enemy armies, inspired his army with a politico-religious fervour and fanaticism comparable only to the spirit which pervaded Cromwell's armies and their nucleus, the Ironsides. The model for these Puritan soldiers was Israel, and their thinking was moulded by the Psalms and daily readings from the Old Testament. They believed themselves to be chosen by the Lord of Hosts to establish the new Israel on earth, the supremacy of God over men and the purification of humanity from all uncleanness and depravity.

Red, the colour of Trotsky's army, is in Russian synonymous with beautiful: it was the symbolic colour of salvation in the Eastern church. Trotsky, the Jewish Bolshevik, believed in the world revolution, and viewed world history as a vast progression towards the true humanity of men. He experienced his first great disappointment in 1914: Western European Socialism rushed into the blood-bath of the World War. Trotsky was far-sighted enough to realize that this meant political and moral catastrophe for official Socialism. He never recovered from this inner breakdown. He would never be able to create a new people, a new society. Henceforth he was only the henchman and stooge of others.

But who were the leaders of Socialism? Who possessed the biggest, best-organized Socialist party in the world, with the most tradition behind it? The Germans, the 'nation of poets and thinkers'. Trotsky did not employ such grandiloquent phrases. But he accorded the role of leaders of world revolution to the nation which had brought forth Hegel, Marx, Engels and possessed a great scientific and intellectual tradition. The world revolution must be brought about by the Germans, or it would be drowned in the blood and swamps of Russia, where the revolution was corrupted by the Stalinist terror and the wilful unleashing of the petty-bourgeois spirit within Bolshevism.

Exiled in Mexico, the aged Trotsky voluntarily submitted to a commission of inquiry into the monstrous accusations which Stalin and the orthodox Communist party of the whole world had brought against him, making him, the Jew, the scapegoat for all the failures, crises and defeats of World Communism. Trotsky declared to the commission that in thirteen years Stalin had, with the help of the capitulating leaders of the opposition, erected a 'tower of Babel' because he knew that a single blow would bring it crashing down – and this blow would certainly be struck.

The Jews were the first and by far the most important activists of the Communist movement, and consequently became its greatest critics. They were reformers who wanted to prevent the revolutionary spirit from succumbing to the institutional pressures and inquisitional authority of a 'red church' which claimed to be the only way to salvation. The function of the true revolutionary was to be a prophet on the watch. But before the same commission Trotsky maintained in his very next breath his allegiance to the October Revolution and to Communism. It was not the revolution which was to blame for the tragic deterioration of Bolshevism, but the failure of the revolution to spread beyond the frontiers of Russia. Soviet workers were at that time faced with a choice between Hitler and Stalin. They chose Stalin, and they were right to do so: 'Stalin is better than Hitler.' But this would not do for the future. 'That is why I do not despair. I have patience. Three revolutions have taught me to be patient. A life-time rich in experiences, in successes and failures, has not only failed to shake my belief in the bright future of humanity; on the contrary it has made my faith indestructible, I have preserved in its entirety this faith in reason, truth, human solidarity, which led me, as a youth of eighteen, into the working class areas of the provincial town of Nikolaev. It has grown more mature, but its flame burns as brightly as ever.'

Thus declared Trotsky, in the final speech of his cross-examination in Mexico on 17 April 1937. On 20 August 1940 an assassin split open his skull with an ice-pick.

'His cry will ring in my ears as long as I live,' said the assassin later. With his skull shattered, Trotsky wrestled with his killer, still possessed of a demonic strength. 'I love you, Natasha,' he said to his wife. After an unsuccessful operation he struggled for twenty-two hours against death. 'Please tell our friends that I believe . . . in the victory . . . of the Fourth International . . . Fight on!'

Natasha described the end: 'They raised him, his head fell back, his arms hung down just like the arms in Titian's *Christ Crowned with Thorns*. Instead of a crown of thorns the dying man wore a bandage. His features still preserved their look of purity and pride. He looked as if he might at any moment rise up and regain his faculties.'

'You have borne the heavy cross of the revolutionary Marxist for a long time.' These are Trotsky's own words in his autobiography *My Life*.

Banished by Stalin, he was in 1927 in Alma-Ata, the town on the Chinese border which had been the scene of earthquakes and floods. Here he received a letter from a loyal follower in Moscow, condoling with him on the loss of his beloved daughter, Nina. Rakovsky wrote: 'Dear friend, I am greatly pained about Ninotschka, for you and yours. You have long been bearing the heavy cross of a revolutionary Marxist, but now for the first time you are experiencing the boundless sorrow of a father. I am with you, with all my heart. I grieve that I am so far from you.'

Trotsky wrote: 'On 9 June my daughter Nina, my ardent supporter, died in Moscow. She was twenty-six. Her husband had been arrested shortly before my exile. She continued the oppositionist work until she was laid low by illness – a quick consumption that carried her off in a few weeks. The letter she wrote to me from the hospital was seventy-three days reaching me, and came after she died.' On 16 February 1938 Trotsky's son Ljova died in Paris. After a 'life of hell', he was, at the age of thirty-two, worn-out with over-work and anxiety about his exiled father. He had been literally hunted to death and perhaps even poisoned by the GPU.

In the great lament which the despairing Trotsky dedicated to the memory of his favourite son, he wrote: 'The old generation with whom we . . . once marched along the road of revolution . . . has been swept off the stage. Those who managed to survive tsarist deportation, prisons and penal colonies, the deprivations of life in exile, civil war and illness, have in these last few years been liquidated by Stalin, the worst scourge of the revolution . . . The majority of the middle generation, those . . . who were awakened by the year 1917 and who received their education in twenty-four armies on the revolutionary front have also been exterminated. And most of the younger generation, Ljova's contemporaries . . . have been trampled underfoot . . . '

Trotsky's greatest drama was his struggle to save the revolution from drowning in blood. A few weeks after Ljova's death he prophesied that Stalin and his accomplices would one day be put on trial by the working-class. 'Human language will not be able to be twisted to defend *this most wicked of all Cain-figures in the whole of history*. [Here we see that for Trotsky the history of the world was a history of progress towards salvation, and he thought in Messianic dimensions and categories which – subconsciously – drew on the Bible.] The monuments which Stalin erected will be pulled down and exhibited in museums as relics of the totalitarian terror. And the victorious working-class will review all trials – both public and secret – and erect monuments to the unfortunate victims of Stalinist villainy in the squares of the liberated Soviet Union.'

These views were proclaimed in 1938 by the rejected prophet, Leon Trotsky. But his heart was filled with sorrow on account of the 'abomination of desolation' wrought by the wicked king of Judah, Stalin, upon the chosen race – the proletariat of the whole world. Much earlier, when, living for two and a half years in a train, he travelled around the country raising troops for the Red Army and wooing tsarist officers for support, his unshakeable faith encountered demoralization, treachery, corruption and cowardice on all sides. It was at that time he learned that revolution is a great destroyer of people and character, exhausting the brave and annihilating the weak.

Later, shortly before Lenin's death on 21 January 1924, Trotsky perceived that the bureaucrats of the early Stalinist Communist party were hostile towards him as a Jew. They accused him of unsociability (on account of his individualism, aristocratic leanings, and so on.) This aristocrat of the spirit, this Jewish intellectual who was constantly advocating self-criticism, was a source of great discomfort to them. Stalin succeeded in presenting Trotskyism as the scapegoat for all the mistakes, crimes and disasters of his own brand of Communism: 'Under this banner, the liberation of the philistine in the Bolshevik was proceeding. It was because of this that I lost power, and it was this that determined the form which this loss took.' (Trotsky, *My Life*).

Was Stalin alone responsible for the revolution drowning in blood and becoming bogged down in the marshes of petty-bourgeois party-clericalism? The broken health of Lenin, who warned against Stalin in vain, cleared the path for Stalin's ascent to power. But what about Lenin himself? Throughout his life Trotsky conducted a great spiritual and mental dialogue with Lenin, and eventually acquired a very high regard for this colossal and awe-inspiring figure. The aged, rejected prophet saw Lenin as a monumental figure on the stage of world history. The young, spiritually armed prophet regarded Lenin in 1904 as a Jacobin, another Robespierre, a murderer of the coming revolution. In April 1904 Trotsky left Lenin's periodical *Iskra* and in August he published in Geneva his brochure *Our Political Tasks*. He dedicated it to his 'faithful teacher Paul B. Axelrod', the important Jewish revolutionary thinker and opponent of Lenin.

In this brochure Trotsky declared that Lenin distrusted the masses and looked down on them. Lenin advocated an 'orthodox theocracy'; his aim was to put the party in the place of the masses, the central committee in the place of the party organization, and finally to install himself as dictator of the central committee. In fact, Trotsky saw in the Lenin of 1904 what he was to see in Stalin in 1935. Trotsky accused Lenin of preparing a new Jacobinism, a new reign of terror dominated by the guillotine. A Jacobin tribunal would accuse the whole international workers' movement of the crime of moderation, and Marx's head would be the first to fall under the guillotine. Robespierre used to say, 'I know only two parties, the good citizens and the bad citizens.' In Trotsky's view, this aphorism was also engraved in the heart of Maximilien Lenin.

In 1904 Trotsky delivered a warning against the erection of a totalitarian Communist party 'church'. He pointed out that 'The tasks of the new régime would be so manifold that they could be accomplished only through competition between various economic and political methods. There would have to be lengthy discussions and a systematic struggle not only between the socialist and the capitalist world, but between various tendencies within socialism itself. Such tendencies would inevitably appear the moment the dictatorship of the proletariat established itself, throwing up countless new problems. No strong dominating body would be able to suppress these tendencies and conflicts, since a proletariat able to umpire its own dictatorship over society would not take kindly to dictatorship over itself.'

Trotsky was pleading here, in 1904, for the free competition of ideas and tendencies – and twenty years later he repeated this plea in almost the same words, before the Bolshevik tribunals.

In 1929, banished by Stalin and excommunicated by the new world-church of orthodox Communism, Trotsky was in Constantinople, trying to acquire a visa to a country which would offer him asylum. He described his vain applications to European and other governments in the last chapter of his autobiography, *The Planet without a Visa*. One of his applications was to the German government. In the whole of the Reichstag there was not a single member who showed any interest in the right of asylum. This was the Weimar Republic of 1929. (Otto Wels, the leader and spokesman of the Social Democrats in the Reichstag, announced in one of his last speeches before the dissolution of the Reichstag that his party was willing to support Hitler's foreign policies.)

Trotsky makes this comment about his vain applications: 'I must admit that the roll-call of the Western European democracies on the question of the right of asylum has given me ... more than a few merry minutes. At times it seemed as if I were attending pan-European performances of a one-act comedy on the theme of principles of democracy. Its text might have been written by Bernard Shaw, if the Fabian fluid that runs in his veins had been strengthened by even so much as five per cent of Jonathan Swift's blood. But whoever may have written the text, the play remains very instructive: *Europe without a Visa*. There is no need to mention America. The United States is not only the strongest, but also the most terrified country ... There the right of asylum has been absent for a long time. *Europe and America without a Visa*. But these two continents own the other three. This means – *The Planet without a Visa*.'

The planet without a visa; for this one exceptional Jew Leon Trotsky the idea might have seemed for a moment in 1929 like the theme for a comedy, even though it caused him great sorrow. But in 1939 it was to form the first act of a tragedy for millions of Jews.

Trotsky went on fighting till his dying day, spurred on by his faith and a militant optimism. On 27 February 1940 (the year of his death) he made his will, in which, like Heine, he professed his love for women – in the form of his wife Natasha: 'Fate gave me not only the good fortune of being a fighter for socialism, but also the good fortune to be her husband. Through almost forty years of married life she has been an inexhaustible source of love, generosity and tenderness. She has suffered much. But I feel some relief at the thought that she has also known days of happiness.'

Looking back on his life, Trotsky declared that, though – if he could live it again – he would try to avoid various mistakes, he would not want to change its main course. He would die as a proletarian revolutionary, as a Marxist, as a dialectical materialist and hence as an unswerving atheist. 'My faith in the Communist future is even stronger today than in my youth ... ' 'Life is beautiful. May the next generation purge it of all evil, oppression and unjust force, and enjoy it to the full.'

Jewish Bolshevism is in Trotsky a passionate struggle for justice and freedom, for love of life, of woman and of all that is beautiful: a faith nourished by his Messianic heritage, though it is accompanied by a denial of all the religions of the present day.

In an addition to his will Trotsky reserved the right to commit suicide, rather than to waste away in a prolonged old age (how often have deeply committed Jews taken their own lives under persecution!) 'But, whatever the circumstances of my death may be, I shall die with an unshakeable belief in the future of Communism. This belief in men and their future gives me even at this point a strength which no religion could give!'

No religion? Trotsky was religious through and through; though as a professed atheist his faith lay hidden deep inside his heart. It must remain flexible, must never harden or become constricted by any dogma or church – not even the 'red church' of Communism. It was a faith that obeyed the commandment: 'Thou shalt not make any graven image.'

In his old age Trotsky looked forward to the future. The West, he declared, would one day be forced to see in a refined and purified Marxism its own creation and its own vision of Man's destiny. Thus might Man's history come full circle, when the spirit had created out of glimmers of hope what was promised in the beginning.

Trotsky often compared human progress with the barefoot march of pilgrims who approach their holy shrine by advancing a few steps and then retreating or stepping aside. He saw his own role as that of encouraging the pilgrims onward. But mankind, after a brief moment of progress breaking up in confusion, permits those who urge it forward to be denigrated, sullied and trampled to death. Only later, when they are again advancing, do men pay remorseful tribute to the sacrificial victims and collect their relics. Then they are grateful for every drop of their spilt blood – for they know that it is with this blood that the seed of the future is watered.

Trotsky's image applies equally to the history of the Jews interpreted as the core of the story of Man's salvation. Abraham, the 'father of our faith' (Kierkegaard) gives the order to advance as he himself journeys out of the land of the heathen. The Jewish people is Man on the move, *homo viator*, *populous viator*. New cues for advance are given over the ages by other Jews: Jesus, Maimonides, Spinoza, Marx, Trotsky, Freud, Einstein and innumerable nameless martyrs.

Ernst Bloch, a German Jew, Marxist, atheist and religious thinker, whom the Communist German Democratic Republic first condemned and then expelled as a red heretic, has erected in his powerful work *Das Prinzip Hoffnung* (The Principle of Hope), a memorial to the 'red martyr', which could well be applied to Trotsky. Bloch sees in Messianism the 'salt of heaven and earth'. He sees the God of Moses as the God who says: 'I shall become what I become.' 'God becomes the kingdom of God, and the kingdom of God no longer contains a god.' There is nothing beyond this world, but this world itself has unlimited possibilities. The true *deus abscondi-*

tus, the hidden god of the mystics, is *homo absconditus,* the hidden man, as yet undeveloped and immature, still in the process of discovering himself and his own vast potentialities.

The way for this man of the future is prepared by the red martyr. 'All men take flowers from the past with them into the grave, sometimes dried and unrecognizable. Only one sort of man goes to his death without any traditional consolations: the red hero. Acknowledging up to the moment of his murder the belief for which he has lived, he goes cold and clear-headed into the nothingness in which he, as a free spirit, has been taught to "believe". His martyr's death is thus different from those of previous martyrs; for they died almost without exception with a prayer on their lips and believed that they had earned a place in Heaven. But the Communist – under the tsars and Hitler and later still – sacrifices himself without hope of resurrection. His Good Friday is not mitigated or cancelled out by an Easter Sunday on which he rises in his own person to a new life. Heaven, towards which the martyrs stretched their arms through the fire and smoke, does not exist for the red materialist. Yet he too dies a believer, as triumphant as any early Christian or missionary. Büchner's completely non-religious saying about men is appropriate to such a hero: "We are like the autumn crocus, which only bears its seeds after the winter".'

The Christian will easily see the connection between these words of the German poet, physician and revolutionary Georg Büchner (Bertolt Brecht's spiritual father) and the words of the Gospel: 'Except a corn of wheat fall into the ground and die, it abideth alone; but if it die, it bringeth forth much fruit.' In his red requiem, which could easily be applied to Trotsky, Bloch declares: 'A belief in the mechanical laws of the universe allowed the red hero, when he himself as a corpse became an inert machine, to vanish into dust, without fuss and equally without any pantheistic belief. And yet this materialist dies as though the whole of eternity were his.'

On 8 December 1917, shortly before peace negotiations began in Brest-Litovsk, Trotsky spoke at St Petersburg in a joint session of the government, the central executive of the Soviets, the Soviet and town council of St Petersburg and the union leaders. 'This war has indeed shown the strength and stamina of men, their ability to put up with the most dreadful suffering. It has also shown how much savagery still lurks in modern Man . . . He, the king of nature, has been going down into trenches to spy through little openings at his fellow-men, to stalk them as a hunter stalks his prey . . . So low has humanity sunk. One is overcome with shame when one considers that men who have gone through so many stages of civilization – Christianity, absolutism, parliamentary democracy – men who have absorbed socialist ideas, are killing one another like miserable slaves under the whip of the ruling classes . . .

'The Russian people, which has risen up in the land of the former police-men of Europe, declares that it wishes to speak to its armed brothers . . . not in the language of guns but in the language of the international solidarity of the workers . . . This fact of solidarity cannot be erased from the minds of the people . . . anywhere. Sooner or later they will hear our voice, they will come to us and hold out their hands to help us.'

Trotsky appealed to the Germany of Karl Liebknecht, Klara Zetkin and Rosa Luxemberg (Liebknecht and Rosa Luxemberg were Jewish Communists). But he knew that he had to negotiate with General Hoffman and Count Czernin (for Austria-Hungary).

'Unless the voice of the German workers exerts a decisive influence . . . there can be no peace . . .

'We would fight to the last drop of blood for our life and for our revolutionary honour.'

The voice of the German workers did not come to the aid of the Russian negotiators at Brest-Litovsk. And the peace that was made involved a parcelling out of the Russian state. Valuable and extensive industrial and agricultural resources fell into the hands of the Germans and their satellites. The German armies advanced further, and the Bolsheviks resolved to make peace, in spite of strong opposition within their own Soviets.

In an exhausted Russia, devastated by the armies of its own civil war as well as by enemy armies, Trotsky miraculously raised his Red Army.

Why was Trotsky – for a time the most powerful man in Russia and master of its army – not able to maintain his position? We know that anti-Semitism existed in the various parts of the Russian state after 1918 and again from 1945 to the present day, and in this lies the most important factor in Trotsky's downfall: as a Jew he was unacceptable as a leader to the predominantly anti-Jewish population. Stalin, who was trying to subdue the peasants in a brutal civil war, had to present them and the other oppressed peoples of the Soviet Union with the old scapegoat: the Jew, traditionally suspected of treachery. Stalin painted a picture of the red Judas, and in fact called Trotsky Judas. As a child of the Orthodox church he presented the Trotskyite Jew as the betrayer of Russia, and Trotsky himself, 'this arch-intellectual and aristocrat', as the archetypal Jew with his 'typical Jewish physiognomy'.

Trotsky and the Jewish Communist intellectuals looked to Germany in the hope that the workers would rise up and take over the leadership of the world revolution. Germany had highly gifted Jewish Communists who were considered as potential leaders – especially Karl Liebknecht and Rosa Luxemberg. Both were murdered. The diminutive Polish Jewess Rosa Luxemberg, while in prison, wrote letters which are among the most important documents of political humanism in this period. The 'little Jewess' was in 1917 the first to take a stand against Lenin, and her criticism of the beginnings and early forms of Leninist Bolshevism already foreshadows the whole coming drama, the foundering of the revolution in terror and murder, and the extinction of Red hope. What happened to Bolshevism in Germany? In Bavaria a revolutionary republic was set up under Max Eisner, whose government included Gustav Landauer. Landauer loved Germany and loved the Jews. In an essay written in 1913 he takes up a critical attitude to Zionism. He would not like to become a Hebrew or to learn Hebrew: 'My language and my children's language is German . . . I accept my lot as I have received it. My German and Jewish allegiances do not harm one another; they are in fact mutually beneficial. Like two brothers, a first-born and a Benjamin, they are both loved by one mother.'

In his *Ostjuden und Deutsches Reich* (Eastern Jews and the German Empire, 1916) Landauer defended the Eastern Jews who were streaming to the West and who were being received by established German Jews with anxiety, dismay and hostility. As an internationalist, he foresaw a rejuvenated Germany and a Jewry reinvigorated by the encounter of Eastern and Western Jews – in fact, a whole new humanity.

'Filthy Bolshevik! Finish him off.' He was fired at by soldiers, to whom he called as he sank to the ground covered with blood: 'It is not I who have betrayed you. You yourselves do not know how dreadfully you have been betrayed.' An aristocrat, Freiherr von Gagern, struck the blow that finally silenced him.

Gustav Landauer, the apostle of a new humanity, had thought about the Jewish problem more deeply than many of his predecessors. He strongly influenced the friend who was to collect his writings together – Martin Buber. Martin Buber bears witness to the pure humanity of this martyr and 'Jewish Bolshevik'.

Closely connected with the defeat of the revolutionary republic was the rise of Munich as the chief centre of reaction in Germany. Here Hitler was protected by conservative authorities and politicians; and it was here that a highly gifted young cleric had a very unpleasant experience during the Communist uprising. He was insulted and threatened by Communists, and was in danger of being captured and shot. Many years later he still groaned aloud in his sleep at the memory of this experience, and this lonely, anguished man became deeply imbued with the conviction that Bolshevism was the embodiment of evil on earth. It must be fought by all available means. What could seem more brave and reassuring to him than German armies, German discipline? The young man was a fervent admirer of German scholarship, discipline and powers of organization. He had made vain attempts, in the service of his master, the pope, to persuade the Kaiser to make peace with the Western powers.

The papal nuncio Eugenio Pacelli never recovered from this shock in Munich. As Pope Pius XII he became the 'representative', who saw in Hitler the lesser of two evils.

In Pacelli's beloved Berlin a German Jew was attentively watching developments in Russia. Walther Rathenau was born in 1867 in Berlin and took his doctorate in 1889 (the year of Hitler's birth), after studying philosophy, physics and chemistry. As a director of the great electrical combine AEG, founded by his father, and as a member of the board in over a hundred other companies, he acquired a unique view of international economic developments. In 1914 he was entrusted by the Kaiser's government with the organization of the supply of raw materials to the war industries. It was due to the Jew Rathenau that the German army was able to fight for more than the few months which some staff officers had estimated.

In 1915 he left the war ministry to become chairman of AEG; in 1921 he became minister of reconstruction in Wirth's cabinet, and then in February 1922 foreign minister. In this capacity he negotiated on Germany's behalf at the Genoa Conference. His term of office saw the settlement with the Soviet Union in the Treaty of Rapallo, April 1922.

On 24 June of the same year he was assassinated by young right-wing extremists in Berlin. There are still West German politicians today who praise this act as a contribution to the liberation of Germany from Jewish Bolshevism.

Walther Rathenau was neither Socialist, Marxist nor Communist. At the stock exchange he was referred to mockingly as 'Jesus in a tail-coat'. The Messianic element in this outstanding figure is unmistakable! his life and death can be seen as a fruitless attempt to bring hope to Germany.

Trotsky appealed to the German proletariat, Rathenau appealed to the German middle classes, to educated Germans, to join vigorously in the building of a future in which there should be one single society of mankind. Before 1914 he had given warning of the coming war. In 1915-16 he wrote his prophetic essay *Von kommenden Dingen* (In Days to Come), which was published in 1917 and received with derision, amazement and embarrassed silence. In it he declared that the essential problem was in what way this planet could fulfil its responsibilities towards God and Man. Man must become aware of a 'new responsibility to God'. After capitalism and the machine age, Man had need of an epoch of spiritual growth, which was already being born in great suffering in the minds of perhaps only a thousand men in Europe. 'The fulfilment of the soul is love.' Intellect is old and sterile but the soul is young. The present leaders of the world, 'anxious and greedy men of intellect' had turned the earth into a heap of rubble.

This 'Jesus in a tail coat', the Prussian Jew Walther Rathenau, became a favourite of the National Socialists, by whom he was murdered. Anti-Semitic writings, speeches, popular sermons and picture books (real *biblia pauperum;* illustrated bibles for the people) – not only of Nazi but also of Christian origin – bring him in as witness for the prosecution in their case against the Jews. What had happened?

In 1897 there appeared in Maximilian Harden's journal *Zukunft* (Harden

was the much-feared publicist and ally of the aged Bismarck) an anonymous article *Hear, O Israel!* Five years later Rathenau included it in his
first volume of collected essays, thus openly acknowledging his author-
ship.

In the same year in which Theodor Herzl summoned the Jews to gather
together as a people, to profess their faith and to go to settle in Palestine, the
German Jew Walther Rathenau called on them to give up all the marks of
ethnic distinction which aroused the hostility of their German fellow-citizens
and to become completely assimilated. Rathenau was called up into the
guards on account of his physical stature, but as a Jew he could not become an
officer. Yet he felt himself a German, and wanted all German Jews to become
true Germans.

What then had the Jews in Germany been up till this time? Rathenau's
answer was: a foreign enclave in the heart of Germany (excepting those old
Prussian Jews who had been established for a hundred years or more). And he
went on to paint a picture of these rootless Jews such as the Nazis and other
anti-Semites were glad to take over; the Jew was restless, arrogant, a
parvenu; living in an unseen ghetto; having a repellent effect on others.

That Jews were repellent to the Germans, Rathenau could prove from his
own painful experience. In schools and universities, in offices and factories,
in trains and in public houses – everywhere this German distaste for the Jews
could be seen. And now the Germans faced problems enough in absorbing
their Danes and Poles. To expect them to absorb the Jews as well was asking
too much; the assimilation process must therefore be carried out by the
Jews themselves.

The German Jews should set the example for the Eastern Jews, who
would like nothing better than to disappear as Jews and be reborn as
Germans; the Jews should leave their stifling ghettoes and go out into the
fresh air of the German woods and mountains.

For Rathenau the question of conversion was only subsidiary. As a
product of the Prussian Enlightenment he could see no particular difference
between the faith of a liberal Protestant pastor and of an enlightened rabbi
of reformed Judaism. Old and wealthy German Jewish families had treated
conversion not as a defection but as something completely natural. Their
moral life had long been a fusion of German, Christian and Jewish elements,
a harmony of the Old and New Testaments and of modern culture.

Rathenau asked the German state to further with all possible vigour the
complete assimilation of the Jews. Prominent Jewish personalities should be
given commissions in the army and posts in the higher civil service.

Rathenau assured Herzl in a letter that he himself was not anti-Semitic.
He saw his essay as a plea to both sides: to the Jews to deal with anti-Semitism
from the inside, and to non-Jewish Germans to accept the Jews as citizens
with full rights. Later he denounced his essay as a youthful indiscretion and
withdrew it from sale. From 1933 the Nazis encouraged the dissemination of

Hear, O Israel! in German schools, where it could be discussed by young Germans as a work in which Jewish parasitism and degeneracy stood self-condemned.

The young Rathenau thought the Jewish people had degenerated as a result of centuries of humiliation, and that it needed to be recharged by an infusion of the noble blood of the Northern races. He thought of himself as of German blood: 'If I am driven off my German soil I shall remain a German: nothing can alter that. I share with the Jews only what every German shares: the Bible, memory and the figures of the Old and New Testaments. My ancestors and I were nourished body and soul on German soil and have given all that lay in our power to the German people. My father and I have never had a thought which was not German or which was not in Germany's interest . . .' [The great Emil Rathenau, founder of the AEG, for a long time could not believe that his dilettante, artistically inclined son would be of any use in a leading position in industry.]

'For me the Jews are a branch of the German people like the Saxons, the Bavarians or the Wends . . . From this point of view I would put them somewhere between the Saxons and the Swabians; they are more remote from me than the Brandenburgers and the Holsteiners, perhaps a little closer than the Silesians or the people of Lorraine. Here I am naturally speaking only of German Jews. I consider Eastern Jews as Russians, Poles or Galicians, just as any other German does. Western Jews I see as Spaniards or Frenchmen. For me anti-Semitism is no different from nationalism. Examining my reactions closely, I find that I am more hurt when a Bavarian insults the Prussians than when he insults the Jews.'

Walther Rathenau was convinced that the only nationality to which a respectable and educated Central European Jew could aspire was the German nationality. His answer to Herzl and Zionism was that he would like to make one visit to the Holy Land to explore its economic possibilities; but that he and German Jews like him wanted only to live and die for the empire as their fathers had done before them. The valiant Moritz Itzig – who had boxed Achim von Arnim on the ears for refusing to fight a duel with him – had fallen as a volunteer in the wars of liberation against Napoleon. Albert Ballin, adviser to the Kaiser and founder of the Hamburg-American shipping line, committed suicide because he did not want to survive the defeat of the German empire. In Nazi Berlin members of old Prussian Jewish families silently prepared themselves for the day when they would be dispatched to death: they kept their bags ready day and night and refused the chance to emigrate to America.

Walther Rathenau's answer to the question which Lavater had put to Moses Mendelssohn, 'What stops you from becoming a liberal Protestant Christian?' is to be found in *Eine Streitschrift vom Glauben* (A Polemic about Faith), written when he was fifty. He says that Judaism, like all religions, has developed in the course of centuries, but that throughout these changes certain elements have remained constant. The Jews have developed no church, no dogmas, no hierarchy and no clerical class; any compulsion to a universally binding norm of belief is rejected. Even the Old Testament has no absolute authority. The biblical texts communicate comfort, happiness and hope, care, anxiety and despair; they are purely human creations. When a Jew accepts Christianity, he must leave a free community of believers for an organized church, a mechanized form of belief with priests, dogmas, sacraments and liturgies. He must submit to spiritual compulsion and supervision. This is undesirable. The Jews should certainly accept Jesus among their spiritual guides, just as they should accept Spinoza. They should respect the New Testament as well as the Old. But they should not give allegiance to any church. The German people should aim at greater freedom and diversity in religion, rather than at uniformity.

Invited in 1920 to take part in the fight against anti-Semitism, Walther Rathenau declined, saying that so deeply immoral a movement must inevitably be destroyed by its own viciousness, without any external intervention. In a letter to a racialist friend he opposed the racial theories of the new nationalism. To Aryan fanatics who maintained that the Jews were uncreative one must point out that no other comparably small section of humanity had exerted so much influence on history: Moses, Isaiah, Jesus, St Paul, Spinoza and Marx were beacons in the spiritual history of mankind. Without saying so, Rathenau knew that he himself, with his deeply wounded psyche and all his divisions of allegiance, belonged among the creative spirits of mankind.

In the spring of 1906 Rathenau was in Delphi. Leaning on a rock in the valley, he recorded in his notebook ten aphorisms. Here, in compressed and distilled form, he set down his view of life. The soul is the essence of freedom, the young seed of life and freedom (he wrote). The soul is young, the intellect is old and sterile. The soul is not simply inborn, it must be acquired by effort. The powers of the soul are threefold: imagination, love and awe. It embraces the world through imagination, fellow creatures through imagination and love, and God through all three powers.

Ten years after that visit to Delphi, in 1916, Rathenau wrote his essay *In Days to Come*. Here his ideas often recall those of Pierre Teilhard de Chardin, who, over in the French trenches, was having his first vision of the evolutionary progress of Man. The fate of the planet Earth, the 'planetary process', is entrusted to humanity. We are still living in the machine age, the era created by capitalism and world trade. But now, after developing all the instincts of 'fear, greed, selfishness and hatred' in men to their highest pitch, it is coming to an end in a gigantic final conflict. Rathenau does not deny the greatness of this dying age: its great achievement has been Man's conquest of the forces of nature.

But now there is to be something new: 'Independently of conscious intention or reflection, a sense of the meaning of our being has been awakened;

this meaning lies in the life and growth of the soul . . . But just as we know that the awakening soul is the divinity for which we live, that love is the power which releases our inner goodness and fuses us into a higher union, so also we recognize, in the incontrovertible world conflict of the machine, this one essential truth: the will to oneness. By holding up to the machine the sign before which it pales – devotion to the soul, belief in the absolute; by revealing its true nature and at the same time penetrating to the essence of our own aspiration to union, we dethrone the machine and make it a servant instead of a master. *Our eyes have been opened,* and we shall not sign away our human dignity and spiritual life for the sake of a starvation wage, or for corrupt pleasures and trivialities, or in the cause of idleness, selfishness and irresponsibility. We strive for the unity and solidarity of mankind, for the union of spiritual responsibility and divine confidence. *Woe unto this race and its successors* if it stifles the voice of conscience and persists in materialistic obtuseness, in frivolous pleasure, at the mercy of egoism and hate. We are not here for the sake of property or power or even of happiness; we are here to draw out the divine from the human spirit.'

'Our eyes have been opened', 'woe unto this race and its successors': Rathenau is a prophet in the true Old Testament sense. The prophet sees what is really happening in the present, how things really are; while the eyes of most of his fellows are blinded by their own impenetrable egoism.

What did Walther Rathenau see before – and also after – 1914? First and foremost a spurious conservatism among the upper middle and ruling classes. 'Conservatism has the appearance of being an affirmation of existing values, but in fact it is a negation of life and its development.' It was the treachery of the upper middle class that destroyed Germany. Rathenau's formulations of 1914 and 1918 can be applied to the period around 1933 – and to the present day.

In his large-scale study, *The Kaiser,* which contains both the fairest appreciation of Wilhelm II as a person and the most scathing criticism of his policies by a German writer, Rathenau condemns the upper middle class, who, after 1848, constantly betrayed Germany and German freedom with its national liberalism. 'Here as everywhere the attitude of the upper middle class was a shameful one: they were bribed into a creeping subservience to the ruling class and sought their own advantage in extolling existing institutions. The treachery of this class, its denial of its hereditary responsibilities, dammed up and poisoned the springs of German democracy for the sake of a few petty offices and privileges . . . One of the Kaiser's tragic features was that he loved the upper middle class – as he seemed fated to love all those who were destructive to him and to persecute all those who could have saved him.'

Rathenau saw that the upper middle class, an institutionalized church and the 'pathetic, transient celebrities of majority socialism' together were unable to overcome the post-1918 rulers of the world: the 'anxious and greedy men of intellect', whose mad, unbridled economics were changing the world into a rubbish-heap of superfluous articles, weapons of war and instruments of self-destruction.

Rathenau saw the whole naked wretchedness of a German 'majority Socialism' which was unable to project a real vision of a peaceful future and hence itself became the stooge of the reactionaries. Rathenau saw a 'mechanized church' in which God disappeared behind the priests and piety gave way to politics. The churches had adapted themselves to the machine age of which capitalism, imperialism and nationalism were only certain aspects.

Rathenau the Jew identified the ultimate cause of this petrifaction of Christianity as the absence of the prophetic element, which it had banished. 'The churches have never made a serious attempt to form and influence morality.' They had always fallen in with the social organization dictated by the ruling classes, and had thus betrayed the Gospel, the glad tidings of the Jew Jesus. They had become word-spinners – while for Rathenau word and deed, thought and action were inseparable. 'What I have recognized to be right, that I must do.' 'Thinking involves the highest sense of responsibility.'

What did Rathenau see after the end of the war and the collapse of the German empire? 'Our economy is like a shanty-town built on water, whose supports are rotting away.' 'We are standing at the death-bed of the great capitalist era' (28 June 1920). 'Our whole system of production is artificially kept on a primitive basis.' 'What we need is no longer rulers, but administrations, supervisors, communities.'

Long before 1914 Rathenau had pleaded for a 'reformation', for the 'awakening of an economic conscience'. The childish world of the European dynasties, which created private paradises in their nurseries and within their tightly-knit families and shut themselves off from the people in fear and anxiety – these people were incapable of appreciating the situation. Wilhelm II was 'the embodiment of the self-alienation of the German people' and the perfect incarnation of German infantilism.

Rathenau looked at the Germans through the eyes of a German Jew with deep personal experience of self-alienation and the divided self. The English Jew Disraeli had seen in England 'two nations' divided by an abyss from one another – the rich and the poor. The Prussian Jew Rathenau saw the 'two nations' of Germany – a nation of underlings allowing itself to be used as human raw material on the battle-grounds of the machine age, both in peace and war; and a nation of bosses. Rathenau realized in 1914 and 1920 what Western observers did not grasp until 1940: that the German people of the twentieth century is a completely different one from the German people of 1800. In nineteenth-century Germany a vast social upheaval had begun. It brought strata of the population which had hitherto taken no part in centuries-old European civilization to the top.

Such was Rathenau's conclusion after 1918: 'These are the only ways of thinking we understand: the police are to blame, the war economy is to blame, the Prussians are to blame, the Jews or the English or the priests or the capitalists are to blame. If two hundred years of decency and love of order did not hold us back, we should be like Slavs: the natural expression of our primitive political aspirations would be the pogrom – in the form of peasant wars, religious wars, witch-hunts and Jew-hunts. Our flag-waving patriotism showed clear signs of this, with its mixture of nationalism and aggression towards some bogeyman or other, but never a proud calm, an amiable patience or an idealistic striving.'

Rathenau goes on: 'We have got a republic: no one seriously wanted it. We got parliamentary democracy at the last minute: no one wanted it. We have a sort of socialism: no one believes in it . . .

'Yet are we not the classic land of social democracy and radicalism? Certainly we were and are – with our willing submission to authority and discipline – the classic land of organized objection; but likewise the classic land of anti-Semitism, which took away from us the powers we most need: a fruitful scepticism and a concrete imagination. Organized objection is not creative political action. There has never been a socialism or radicalism more barren of ideas than the post-Marxist German brand, which divided its efforts between mere paperwork and cheap utopian agitation.'

In *Die Neue Gesellschaft* (The New Society, 1920) Rathenau already depicts the German post-war situation of 1945 – and of 1965. He describes the cause of the decline and suicide of the Weimar Republic – a suicide begun at its very birth and continued, by instalments, till its completion in 1933.

As minister of reconstruction (1921) and foreign minister (1922) Rathenau offered his services to the republic whose self-destructive quality he recognized. The sole reason for this decision – which his mother and friends saw as his own suicide and warned him against – lay in his faith. The Prussian Jew Walther Rathenau believed in Germany, as he believed in the efficacy of the new movement of peoples and in the reclassification of the German people and of all mankind.

This is the basis of Rathenau's reflections – so offensive to Jews and so provocative to German anti-Semites – on the constructive dissolution of the Jewish people. (In his old age Bismarck often thought about a 'constructive dissolution' of the German empire.) Rathenau saw that a gigantic process of reclassification had begun, in which the old ruling classes would melt away. This process, in which master races and castes become fused with the formerly faceless, unrecorded masses is both painful and attenuated. It falls together with the world revolution.

In September 1919 Rathenau declared that the war had not simply been a disorderly interruption, but was part of a world revolution which would continue in the future. This vast reclassification of peoples into a new society and eventually a stateless society would tread a path through inferno.

Rathenau presented his timid bourgeois contemporaries with the model of a 'fully socialized' Germany at the end of the twentieth century. This model contains frightening features, and in many respects anticipated the regimentation of men in the East German Democratic Republic.

Rathenau, however, did not want to frighten the German people, but to arm them with patience and to educate them to political manhood. The German people must at last become politically adult. After the lost war the immediate future would bring such heavy burdens that only extreme sobriety, patience, self-criticism and discipline could triumph over chaos. 'The new Germany is the most unknown of all nations.' It presented great opportunities but also great dangers.

Rathenau declared categorically: 'We have never been a people of poets and thinkers.' At the beginning of the war Rathenau told a friend (and he repeated his words in *The Kaiser*): 'The moment will never come when the Kaiser rides through the Brandenburg Gate . . . as conqueror of the world. On such a day world history would have lost its meaning. Not one of the great men who are marching into this war will survive it.'

Rathenau added: 'Moltke fell and died, Falkenhayn, Bethmann, Jagow and Tirpitz all fell; in the last year only the Kaiser remained, and finally he too met his downfall.'

These are the words of a prophet. In the same way the Old Testament prophets predicted the downfall of the Jewish kingdom and its kings – and were struck down for their words. To the many who demanded Rathenau's death the words just quoted provided the final impulse to his murder.

The great dream of German Jewry was to find a spiritual home in Germany. And none sang of his dream more melodiously than Felix Mendelssohn, that boy to whom Goethe was so devoted. (Houston Stewart Chamberlain, Richard Wagner's son-in-law and the spiritual guide of Wilhelm II, who deeply influenced Hitler, Rosenberg and the Nazi mind, was later to reproach his hero Goethe for the kisses he bestowed on this 'Jewish boy'.)

Felix Mendelssohn was a grandson of that crippled Jew Moses Mendelssohn who knew no German when he sought entry to Berlin at the Jews' Gate in 1743. (The log-book of the guard records that 'today there passed through the Rosenthal Gate six oxen, seven pigs and one Jew'.)

In the house of Moses Mendelssohn's banker son, Abraham, Goethe was a religion. Abraham had his children Fanny and Felix baptized in 1816, shortly after the wars of liberation, when Fanny was eleven and Felix seven years old. Just before Fanny's confirmation in 1820 her father Abraham, who had left the land of his fathers to settle in the German fatherland (the Berlin Mendelssohns had a strong sense of their Prussian allegiance), wrote her a long letter on the subject of God.

'Does God exist, and what is He? Is a part of ourselves immortal and destined to live on when the other parts have died? And, if so, where, and how? I do not know, and have therefore never taught you anything about it. I know only that in me and in you and in all men there is an eternal attraction towards what is good, true and just, that there is a conscience which admonishes and guides us whenever we stray away from its dictates. I know and believe in this. I live in this faith and this is my religion.'

Conscience: the faith of emancipated, secularized Jews in the nineteenth and twentieth centuries reduces itself to the credo: God is conscience. Conscience demands exceptional and untiring efforts in every duty which the Jew incurs as citizen, member of a class or profession, as father of a family and as a German. Adolf Hitler called conscience a Jewish invention.

Abraham Mendelssohn commended to his daughter the example of her mother, 'this noblest and worthiest of mothers, this embodiment of religion in human form! . . . When you look at your mother you feel God and are pious. That is all that I can tell you about religion, all that I know about it. The particular form in which your religious teacher has put it to you is historical and, like all human precepts, is open to change. A few thousand years ago the Jewish form was dominant, then the heathen, and now the Christian. Your mother and I were born and educated as Jews and have been able to obey God and our conscience without changing the form of our religion. We have brought our children up as Christians because this is the form of religion of most moral people and because it contains nothing that will lead you away from the good, but rather many things which will direct you towards love, obedience, tolerance and resignation – if only the example of its founder, recognized by so few and followed by even fewer . . .'

Even in the last years of the Third Reich, a high officer of the SS and one of Hitler's governors in the East dared to declare his love for the music of the Jew Felix Mendelssohn and to criticize its suppression. Felix Mendelssohn chose Germany as his home and fatherland 'in the free choice of love', as Heinrich Eduard Jacob puts it. Until 1933 his German folksongs belonged to the repertory of every choir.

On 11 March 1829 – a hundred years after Moses Mendelssohn's birth – his grandson put on a performance of Bach's *St Matthew Passion* in Berlin. Felix Mendelssohn re-discovered and re-awakened interest in Bach in Germany and Europe as a whole. He himself had deep roots in the German Protestant faith. His evangelical hymns, his oratorio *St Paul* and his *Reformation Symphony* (1830 – in commemoration of Luther and the Augsburg Confession of 1530) are not simply mechanical commissioned works, such as appeared in vast numbers in the nineteenth century.

At the same time Felix Mendelssohn composed a truly Catholic Mass as well as *Elijah* (1845), in which the spirit of the Old Testament finds expression in words and music.

This was not simply eclecticism. Felix Mendelssohn lived in an atmosphere of all-embracing piety, which had a frequently overlooked counterpart in Vienna. Here Franz Schubert, the composer of that *German Mass* which is sung by German-speaking Catholics all over the world, also wrote a work for a close Jewish friend who was choirmaster of the Seitenstetten Temple in Vienna; this was a setting of the Hebrew text of the ninety-second Psalm, and it is still sung in Jewish services today.

To the end of his life Goethe remained faithful to the Jewish boy who had been brought to play to him by his teacher Zelter. When he was nearly eighty he told Felix's mother: 'He is my David – and I am Saul.' In spring 1830 he said to Felix, who was passing through Weimar on his journey to that Italy which had once liberated Goethe from his provincial anxieties: 'You are my David. Play to me when I am sad. And I will not cast a javelin at you.'

'I will not cast a javelin at you' – Goethe, the supreme representative of the German spirit, is saturated with the language of the Old Testament. On this visit Goethe's daughter-in-law Ottilie enrolled Mendelssohn as a collaborator in a journal to be called *Chaos*. Could the chaos of the German soul be chained within the confines of a journal? Certainly, at a later period, newspapers and journals managed to *un*leash this chaos.

'To my dear young friend Felix Mendelssohn-Bartholdy, powerful and tender master of the piano, in affectionate memory of the happy days of May 1830. J.W. Goethe.' Goethe wrote these words on a page of his *Faust* manuscript which he presented to Felix. And Mendelssohn later spoke of this, in a conversation with Sir Julius Benedict, as the 'sun of royal favour in my life'.

In Berlin and Potsdam Mendelssohn literally enjoyed royal favour. The whole royal family attended the first performance of *Antigone* in the New Palace in Potsdam on November 1841. In the following year he appeared before Queen Victoria and Prince Albert at Buckingham Palace, and later the queen and her beloved German consort each sang him one of his own songs. The great German Jewish dream of Germany as the home of humanity in which they had found acceptance seemed to become true in the life and work of Felix Mendelssohn and the august people grouped around him.

In the last year of his life (1847) Mendelssohn was particularly taken up with fairy-stories (like Heine in Paris). In German fairy-stories all good and evil spirits are at home, find expression in words and pictures and hence achieve redemption. It was all part of the great dream. In early life Felix Mendelssohn composed incidental music for *A Midsummer Night's Dream*, and between 1904 and 1934 Max Reinhardt staged thirteen different productions of the play with Mendelssohn's music. Was Mendelssohn oblivious of the sinister underground voices of a growing German anti-Semitism, intriguing and plotting against him in Leipzig and Berlin?

There was a young German composer who used to write letters couched in the most respectful and friendly terms to Mendelssohn and to Meyerbeer. This young musician had many Jewish friends during his years of poverty in Paris around 1840, and he embraced the cause of Heinrich Heine, to whom he owed important themes in his own creative work. In late years Jewish friends surrounded him as singers, stage-managers, publicists and conductors (for example Angelo Neumann and Hermann Levi, son of a German rabbi and 'the greatest operatic conductor of his time'). His death caused an inconsolable German Jew to commit suicide.

This German composer, whose name was Richard Wagner, published in 1850, under the pseudonym Karl Freidank, an essay entitled *Das Judentum in der Musik* (Judaism in Music). Felix Mendelssohn had died on 4 November 1847, and now was the time to insult his name and expunge his work from musical history. Karl Freidank asserts that the Jews are uncreative in music as in all other arts. Only 'in a very superficial sense' can the Jews achieve anything comparable to German art. All Jewish music must appear to a German as 'strange, cold, bizarre, mediocre, unnatural and perverse'. The impression Jewish music makes on us is as if a Goethe poem were recited in Jewish jargon.

'Where is this more clearly illustrated . . . than in the work of a composer of Jewish origin who was naturally gifted as few had been before him? All the unsympathetic features of the Jewish nature which our enquiry revealed to us, all its internal contradictions and external conflicts . . . reach fully tragic proportions in the life and work of the short-lived Felix Mendelssohn-Bartholdy. His example has shown us that the Jew may have the richest natural talents, the highest and tenderest sensibility and sense of honour, and yet be unable even once to make that profound emotional effect on us . . . which we have often experienced when one of our own artistic heroes . . . simply opens his mouth to speak.'

Karl Freidank particularly reviles Heinrich Heine, the 'inexorable demon of negation' who drove himself on 'through every illusion that modern self-deception can offer, to the point where he lied himself back to the status of a poet and got his poetic lies set to music by our composers . . .' In these words the author was insulting not only Schubert and Schumann but also himself, since he had set Heine's *Die Beiden Grenadiere* to music in Paris and, from *Der Fliegende Holländer* to *Götterdämmerung* drew heavily on Heine's ideas. Meyerbeer, Wagner's Jewish sponsor, died in 1864. In 1868, eighteen years after its first appearance, Wagner published a new and extended version of *Judaism in Music* under his own name.

Wagner was a hater: at the deepest level a hater of himself. But first of all the others must go. He said of Mendelssohn to his second wife Cosima: 'Such a shadow cannot grow – it can only disappear.'

Even Wagner-lovers, like the French-Canadian André Hémois and the German Thomas Mann, have admitted that Wagner's politico-cultural writings lead straight to Chamberlain and Hitler.

Hitler could fairly invoke Wagner as an ally. Wagner's attack on un-creative, un-German, sterile, lying Jews could be fully exploited in *Der Stürmer* and *Das Schwarze Corps* and all the other Nazi publications.

Richard Wagner's remark about the impossibility of reciting a Goethe poem in Jewish jargon disregards Goethe's love for Mendelssohn and points to future events. In his old age Goethe liked to walk in a beech-wood near Weimar. And one tree from Goethe's time was piously conserved when that beech-wood became the Buchenwald concentration camp.

The important – sometimes exceptional or indeed unique – achievements in German intellectual and scientific life are the product of that tension summed up in 1832 by Ludwig Börne in his remark that no one could ever forget that he was a Jew. Basically insecure, treated as 'foreign bodies', the Jews tried through their achievements to acquire the respect and the established position in Germany which were never fully accorded them. For the Jew in the process of secularization the German universities acted as a secularized Talmudic school; and here Jews deployed intellectual qualities which had been trained over hundreds, indeed thousands of years of study and interpretation of the Bible.

In 1931 Felix A. Theilhaber published his *Schicksal und Leistung* (Destiny and Achievement) with the sub-title 'The Jews in German Scientific Research and Technology'. In 1934 a thousand-page volume edited by Siegfried Kaznelson, with the collaboration of scholars of all faculties, was ready for the press. The Nazi government forbade its publication 'in the interests of public security and order'. It eventually appeared in 1959 as a memorial to German Jewry and a final statement of accounts.

In 1836 an essay was published in Stuttgart entitled *Das Judentum und die neueste Literatur* (The Jews and Modern Literature). It was a defence of the Jews in Germany against the accusations of Wolfgang Menzel and others of like mind, who alleged that the Jews were radicals and revolutionaries, and that they were seeking to overturn every national and divine ordinance. The twenty-four-year-old author, Berthold Auerbach, pointed out that of the six literary leaders of the *Junges Deutschland* movement, four (Gutzkow, Laube, Wienbarg and Mundt) had no personal connections with Judaism; and only two (Börne and Heine) were of Jewish descent – 'and they have long since dissociated themselves from the faith of their fathers'. Auerbach appealed to the Germans: 'Give us the fatherland to which we belong by birth, custom and love; and we will faithfully offer up our blood and our possessions on its altars. Forget, and teach us Jews to forget, the sinister wall which has separated us in the past.'

Auerbach saw himself as a German of the Jewish confession and considered himself to be a German writer. He had originally wanted to be a rabbi and then had attempted a synthesis of Moses and Hegel. In the middle decades of the nineteenth century he acquired a considerable reputation as the author of rustic tales which gave a somewhat romantic view of country life. Towards 1870 and then after the foundation of the German empire in 1871 he had to watch the sorry spectacle of a growing anti-Semitism among the very intelligentsia and middle class whose favour he had courted with his writings.

In 1872 Auerbach was invited to join a committee founded by the New York Jewish lawyer Benjamin Franklin Peixotto to assist Jews emigrating from Rumania to the USA. Auerbach agreed to serve, but wanted the work to be extended to all the persecuted refugees of Europe, without distinction of faith. This was a laudable aim, but its fatal consequences continued right up to the Bermuda conference during the Second World War, which carefully avoided making a special case of the Jews. The examples of Rumania in 1872, and Russia soon after, demonstrate that there are refugees – in this case the Jews – who are in immediate danger of death, and others who are in distress but no danger. Those who do not wish (or do not dare) to refer directly to the former expose them to annihilation.

Like Treitschke and Richard Wagner, Auerbach in his old age saw an abyss opening between Germans and Jews. In 1875 in Vienna – the Mecca of medicine, as Virchow in Berlin called it – the famous professor of surgery, Theodor Billroth, opposed the admission of Jewish students to the medical school and openly stated that he himself felt conscious of a great gulf between Jews and pure Germans. The Jews, he maintained, were incapable of martyrdom. Similar aberrations, ultimately traceable to a suppression of Jesus the Jew in their own consciousness, can still be found today among prominent Christian theologians.

Auerbach's answer to Billroth was that Jewish history had been one continuous martyrdom for eighteen hundred years – and that the end of this martydom was not yet in sight. And he tried to point out to Billroth that Jews had been imbued with German culture before other inhabitants of the country, such as the Wends and the Slavs, had been assimilated into it.

Auerbach saw his life's work in ruins. He could no longer write: what was the point, when Germans were expelling Jews, or at least trying to drive them back into ghettoes (as was requested in a petition to the Reichstag in November 1880 containing four million signatures)? Auerbach turned his hopes to America, knowing that there too anti-Semitism was at work, but hoping that the tradition of freedom would prevail. In his story *Waldfried* (1874) he suggested that, on the occasion of the centenary of the American Declaration of Independence, a German university should be founded in America as an international academy dedicated to the freedom of the spirit. German students would spend a year there and become familiar with American traditions of freedom. After the Second World War the Americans, with the active participation of American Jews, founded the Free University of Berlin and enabled the foundation of the College of Design at Ulm, two centres devoted to the ideal of free and humane education.

Billroth's accusation – which he later withdrew – that the Jews were incapable of martyrdom, has been refuted by the achievements of German

Jews, especially in the field of learning and science. The natural sciences have played the greater part, right back to the Islamic and Christian Middle Ages with their centres in Baghdad, Palermo, Toledo and Padua. In the philosophical sciences any conflict with the dogmas and taboos of Christianity for centuries spelled mortal danger.

An outstanding Jew in the field of the natural sciences was Heinrich Hertz (commemorated in the Hertz unit of frequency), who died at the age of thirty-seven in 1894. Hertz re-created for himself the cultural world of those Islamic-Christian Middle Ages. He learned Arabic, read Homer, Plato and Dante, was a talented artist and sculptor and studied philosophy, physiology, chemistry, physics and mathematics. The world of learning heaped honours on the young Hamburg Jew as the storm clouds were gathering on the political scene. Manchester, Vienna, Geneva, Paris, St Petersburg, Moscow, Naples and London all honoured the young prodigy who was to meet his early death with such courage and resignation.

The line of Jewish scientists in Germany runs unbroken from men like Eugen Goldstein and Robert von Lieben to Lise Meitner, Frisch, Niels Bohr (a Dane, but trained in Germany) and Albert Einstein. Modern scientific history would be unthinkable without physicists like Abraham Michelson, chemists like Adolf von Baeyer, Richard Willstätter and Fritz Haber, mathematicians like Jacobi, Eisenstein, Kronecker, Georg Cantor and David Hilbert.

Jewish medical research in Germany was concentrated especially in the fields of bacteriology, serology, physiology and physiological chemistry, internal medicine, neurology and psychiatry. The founder of bacteriology, Ferdinand Julius Cohn, was the first Jew to be appointed to a full university chair (1870). His work laid the foundations for that of Robert Koch and Emil Behring. Julius Cohnheim, Berthold Auerbach (who was both writer and doctor), Carl Weigert, Neisser, Weil, August von Wassermann (after whom the syphilis blood-test was named), Carl Landsteiner (discoverer of the human blood-groups), Paul Ehrlich (who discovered in salvarsan the first anti-syphilis drug), Moritz Schiff, Gustav Embden, Otto Meyerhof, Richard Willstätter, Otto H.Warburg, Edinger, Hitzig, Mendel and Offenheim: a brilliant line of distinguished researchers leads up to the 'greatest Jewish doctor of modern times' – to Sigmund Freud.

Till well on into the period of the Third Reich the Jewish family doctor played a unique role as confidential friend in many German households – even Hitler's. Imaginative sympathy for the patient, a sober dedication to his welfare: these qualities, born of thousands of years of Jewish experience of suffering, were responsible for the special character of the Jewish doctor, who was a true father to his own family and a fatherly friend to the families of his German fellows.

Viktor von Weizsäcker, a 'grandson and great-grandson of Protestant pastors and Swabian theologians', acknowledges in his book of memoirs

Natur und Geist (Nature and Spirit) what an invaluable lesson he learned from the contrast between a German and a German Jewish doctor. His teacher Ludolf von Krehl always projected his own personality on to his patient, treated him in accordance with his own sympathies and antipathies. In 1918 in Heidelberg Weizsäcker got to know Albert Fraenkel's way of dealing with patients, the way in which he would feel himself into a young soldier's very being and make it part of himself. 'True inner sympathy, which is love itself, can be achieved only by experiencing another person's being, not by projecting one's own.'

As well as their work in medicine, the Jews were pioneers in psychology and sociology (sympathetic understanding of a sick society as an extension of imaginative sympathy for a sick individual). 'Upright' Germans and young people in Germany today still show fear and distaste for these 'Jewish' sciences.

When Otto Walter Haseloff conducted an inquiry into the attitude towards psychology of West German students, 41.7 per cent of those questioned agreed with the statement: 'Most psychologists are and always were Jews.' Fifty-five per cent were convinced of the impossibility of studying human character by scientific means. The product of an authoritarian upbringing cannot believe that a man has a scientific history; the Jewish doctor or psychologist makes scientific use of a patient's medical history, knowing that this can also become, and ought to become, the history of his liberation.

Psychology requires vigilant observation of oneself and others: self-analysis (here used in the pre-Freudian sense); the breaking down of everything that has been taken for granted and passed unnoticed or that has been silenced by taboos; the struggle to uncover the lies in the life of every man. Himself continually subject to hostile observation, continually painted in false colours, the Jewish psychologist feels an existential need to come to grips with the nature of Man, this unknown creature who is so dangerous to himself and to others. The great work of the Jews in psychology is part of a larger effort to clarify the problem of alienation and self-alienation, both in individuals and in oppressed minority groups. Medicine, social medicine, anthropology, ethnology, history – including even pre-history – and sociology are all closely connected with psychology.

The number of depth psychologists in the time of Freud and after Freud is legion. The Jewish contribution to American depth psychology need not concern us here. We shall meet again in Freud's circle some of his fellow-pioneers, such as Rank, Reich and Ferenczi. Here we need only mention a few German-Jewish psychologists before and after Freud: William Stern, Dessoir, Gelb, Goldstein, Katz, Koffka, Lewin, Münsterberg, Wertheimer – and the great deserter from Freud, the 'prodigal son' who would not return to the paternal home of psycho-analysis, Alfred Adler.

After thousands of years, during which their own existence had been called into question, the Jews are now interrogating Man themselves; not in order to kill him (as had been the case with many forms of inquisition), but in order to help him to a better and richer life. There is no 'sweet' truth. Truth in Man's experience is bitter and can be acquired only through suffering. And Jewish psychology is branded as 'disruptive' by non-Jews who have no desire, either in times of peace or war, to be subjected to struggles within their own hearts.

Jews have also played a prominent part in the development of sociology. The Jewish scholar of German literature, Friedrich Gundolf (whose pupil Joseph Goebbels was) once remarked after a sociological congress in Heidelberg: 'Now I know at any rate what sociology is: it is a Jewish sect.' René König, the German-Jewish sociologist, has interpreted Gundolf's remark as follows: 'The word sect here indicates the passionate nature of the discussions, the doubtless incomprehensible jargon which the sociologists used, the fervour with which they emphasized the difference of their science from any other, and their sometimes severe criticism of traditional scientific systems and logic.'

This traditional logic was the logic of masters, of 'men's men', who looked down from the embattled heights of their masculine spirit on the weak and indolent common clay, the unstable, changeable world of women and the masses. The beginnings of sociology between 1871 and 1914 were only made possible by the collapse of a five-thousand-year-old set-up of gods, men, churches, animals – the *urbs diis hominibusque communis*, in which each element strove to protect its own fixed, eternal and unalterable rights. Immediately after the foundation of the empire in 1871, perceptive observers like Bismarck, Crown Prince Friedrich, Fontane, Lagarde and others, sensed the coming collapse of this strange revival of a divinely sanctioned political and social system in which no one really believed any longer: a system in which the state, the church, society, the army, nobles, citizens, peasants and beggars were bound to one another in unalterable master-servant relationships.

Jewish sociology called society into question at a time when it had already shown itself to be highly questionable. The big city was questionable, and its nature was first analysed in Germany by the Berlin-born Jew Georg Simmel. Questionable, too, was the social structure of peoples – those peoples among whom the Jews as a 'pariah-people' (Max Weber's term) had long had the opportunity of studying all forms of social behaviour and attitudes, often through the most unpleasant personal experience. The emancipation of the Jews, which coincided with the rise of the bourgeoisie in the nineteenth century, often brought the individual Jew into a dangerous state of loneliness when he left the centuries-old protection of his own family and people. In a strange, cold, hostile world the Jew looked around and faced the problem of adjusting himself to this 'new society'.

The founder of sociology, Emile Durkheim, was sometimes considered by his audiences to be the visionary prophet of a new religion, which he dressed up as an exact science. For Durkheim, society was the essential element of a man's life. The Jew must study this society, since it always discriminates against and rejects him. The intense activity of Jewish scholars in the development of sociology was thus the produce 'of a unique set of circumstances, which could hardly be simulated by a non-Jew' (René König). 'The Jew alone can find the necessary detachment to study it, since society itself forces detachment on him.'

The Jew is the 'outsider' in society. Simmel is the first to deal with this concept in sociology, and he calls the Jew the prototype of the outsider. The outsider is more able to understand the pathological structures of society than the insider whom society protects and to whom it still seems sound. A large proportion of the work done by Jews in American sociology has been concerned with the problems of constructing a plural society out of different racial, religious, social and ethnic groups with the ways in which integration and mutual toleration can be brought about. A problem that could be regarded as specifically Jewish has become the leading problem both in industrial psychology and in a certain brand of academic depth-psychology. It is this: how can the unattractive individual be integrated into the factory or workshop, so that he can do his job to the best advantage and with the least discomfort to himself and others? How can hatred be overcome, and especially racial hatred? How can the 'authoritarian personality', who is particularly prone to the temptations of Fascism, anti-Semitism and McCarthyism, be educated to enjoy the more difficult but more rewarding challenge of freedom and democracy?

Pascal worked his way to a Christian experience of life through his recognition that the God of Abraham, Isaac and of Jacob was totally different from the 'God of the philosophers'. Jewish philosophy and the philosophy of Jews (which are not always the same thing) attempt to present this God as the God of reason, accessible to the rational insight of all men. Philo, Maimonides, Moses Mendelssohn, Gans (the pupil of Hegel), the German-Jewish neo-Kantians who centred round Hermann Cohen – all these proclaim that *the God of the Jewish people is the God of universal reason*. This reason now calls in question the intellectual conventions, the subtleties, sophistries and rationalizations of Man and tries to show up the metaphysics of the divine-political system of old Europe as mere 'empty formulas' (Wittgenstein). The thought of Jewish philosophers often contains deeply conservative and archaic elements at the same time as revolutionary ones. All the products of human thought and language, all philosophical models, can be subjected to radical questioning and exposure. But the questioner eventually comes face to face with the pre-history of Man and of his soul, comes back to the burning bush of Moses. This thought was expressed in that letter of Walther Rathenau which was quoted in an earlier chapter and which we could extend as follows: if Christ does not speak to you, then Moses will. And if not Moses, then the thorn-bush itself will speak, the eternal fire of Godhead, in whose dialectic the ultimate questions posed by Man blaze up and burn away.

During the nineteenth and early twentieth centuries, which saw the most fruitful intermingling of German and Jewish culture, Jewish thinkers posed and discussed fundamental intellectual, spiritual and religious problems on a scale which is without parallel anywhere else in the world. Hermann Levin Goldschmidt drew up a formidable list of German-Jewish thinkers up to 1900: Mendelssohn, Maimon, Steinheim, Gans, Stahl, Jacobi, Formstecher, Hess, Hirsch, Marx, Steinthal, Kronecker, Lazarus, Lassalle, Geiger, Lasson, Popper-Lynkeus, Liebmann, Cohen, Cantor, Mauthner, Rée, Freud, Marcus, Simmel, Fliess, Husserl, L. Stein, Brunner, Joel, Oppenheimer, Minkowski, Neumark, Dessoir, Rathenau, Lasker, Cohn, Landauer, Adler, Richter, Lessing, Baeck, Cassirer, Scheler, Lask, Gurewitsch, Buber, Liebert, Einstein, Koigen, Reinach, Utitz, Kroner, Weltsch, Bloch, Goldberg, Guttmann, Weininger, Wertheimer, Kelsen, Nelson, Klatzkin, Rosenzweig, Picard, Rosenstock, Heinemann, E. Stein, Benjamin, Horkheimer.

Thought is bound up with language – and language is what thought becomes, unless it is ever replaced by a system of logical and mathematical symbols. Jewry has long had relationships with the German language. Up to the period before the Second World War two-thirds of the world Jewry spoke Yiddish; this is, in essence, a late medieval form of German which had become the Jew's language alongside Hebrew, the language of worship. At the same time the Jews carried correct modern German far into the eastern territories of Europe. Prague, the town which prided itself on speaking the purest German, is also the native town of Kafka, Werfel, Brod and many less important Jewish writers in German.

An unbroken line leads from the Berlin of Mendelssohn, Henriette Herz and Rahel Varnhagen in the period 1800 to 1810 to the Berlin of 1900 and even of 1930, in which Samuel Fischer, the Jewish publisher from Vienna, gathered around him German and Jewish poets and writers. For non-Germans in the nineteenth century it was above all Heinrich Heine who raised German poetry and literature to the status of world literature. No other German poet, not even Goethe himself, has had a comparable influence. Right up to the beginnings of the Third Reich the German authors most read outside Germany were Jews. A considerable number of them lived in Austria, where, during that long Indian summer of the old empire, it was they in particular who sensed the crisis of European civilization and the coming catastrophe.

A few names may be mentioned here to represent a whole epoch of German and German-Jewish literature. In the novel, Kafka, Döblin, Werfel, Broch, Roth, Wassermann and Brod; in lyric poetry, Mombert, Wolfskehl, Werfel and Else Lasker-Schüler; in drama, Toller and Sternheim. Hermann

Broch's *Tod des Vergil* (Death of Virgil), truly the swansong of a thousand-year epoch of poetic dealing with the problematic human word, was begun in a German prison and completed in America; the poet died on the eve of his return to Vienna. Joseph Roth recalls the Austro-Hungarian monarchy in his *Radetzky March* and the suffering of the old people of God in his *Job*. Karl Wolfskehl, poet of a German renaissance, knew that his forefathers came to the Rhine at the time of Charlemagne. His tombstone in Auckland, New Zealand, commemorates in both Hebrew and Latin the German-Jewish poet: Karl Wolfskehl, *exul poeta*. Else Lasker-Schüler remained until her death in Jerusalem a German and a German-Jewish poetess. And yet another exile, Jacob Picard, in *Frühling in Massachusetts* (Spring in Massachusetts) spoke nostalgically of springtime in his lost German home.

The lost home of the Jew and of Man. Happiness belongs only to childhood. We find Sigmund Freud writing: 'Happiness is the subsequent fulfilment of a prehistoric wish. Hence riches seldom make for happiness: money plays no part in a child's desires' (Vienna, 16 January 1898). 'Imagination and work for me go together. I take pleasure in nothing else' (Vienna, 6 March 1910). 'My heart is German provincial' (Paris, 3 December 1885). Writing from Paris on 2 February 1886, he revealed himself to his fiancée in the following words: 'Do you really find my appearance so attractive? Well, this I very much doubt. I believe people see something alien in me, and the real reason for this is that in my youth I was never young, and now that I am entering the age of maturity, I cannot mature properly.

'You know what Breuer told me one evening? I was so moved by what he said that in return I disclosed the secret of our engagement. He told me he had discovered that, hidden under that surface of timidity, there lay in me an extremely daring and fearless human being. I had always thought so, but never dared tell anyone. I have often felt as though I had inherited all the defiance and all the passions with which our ancestors defended their temple, and could gladly sacrifice my life for one great moment in history. And at the same time I always felt so helpless and incapable of expressing these ardent passions even by a word or a poem. So I have always restrained myself, and it is this, I think, which people must see in me.'

To this letter from Paris addressed to his 'beloved sweet darling', he added a few lines concerning a reception at Charcot's: 'Only towards the end I embarked on a political conversation with Giles de La Tourette during which he, of course, predicted the most ferocious war with Germany. I promptly explained that I am a Jew, adhering neither to Germany nor Austria. But such conversations are always very embarrassing to me, for I feel stirring within me something German which I long ago decided to suppress.'

'I have a quite personal hatred of Vienna,' he wrote on 11 March 1900 to his Berlin Jewish friend, Wilhelm Fliess, his one intellectual companion over many lonely years. Thirty-eight years later to the day, Austria collapsed and fell to Hitler.

Sigmund Freud, who was born in a small Moravian town in 1856, fled from Vienna in 1938 and died in the following year in London. He was doctor, poet, depth psychologist and prophet. In 1930 he received the city of Frankfurt's Goethe Prize. His thinking combined motifs from the bold, heroic early German Romantic period of 1795 and 1800 and motifs from Goethe, Bettina Brentano and Nietzsche, with the conclusions that he himself had arrived at in Vienna: the discovery of the conflicts in the human breast. At Easter 1898 he visited the caves of St Canzian in Friuli. He wrote: 'Sheer Tartarus. If Dante had seen anything like this, he wouldn't have had to strain his imagination for his description of the Inferno. The ruler of Vienna, Dr Carl Lueger, was with us in the cave'.

Lueger, referred to by Adolf Hitler as the greatest of all German burgo-masters, had achieved power for his Christian Socialist party in Vienna by exploiting the 'anti-Semitism of the small man'. However, he reserved to himself the right to decide who was a Jew. Sigmund Freud lived in this Vienna for more than a decade. He himself said it was like being in a 'wilderness'. On his eightieth birthday in 1936 – he had of course in the meantime become world-famous – the Austrian authorities managed to bring themselves to send a private message of congratulations, but the Austrian press was not allowed to publish it.

The Austrian poet, Hugo von Hofmannsthal, wrote in a letter to Hermann Bahr ten years before the First World War about the 'profound depths of the hidden kingdom of the ego'. This hidden kingdom of the ego was experienced, explored, and studied by the Moravian Jew, Sigmund Freud, in the Vienna which he both hated and loved. His life was outwardly very similar to that of the Viennese lower middle class – with his weekly card games and excursions into the country. Later it had much in common with that of the patricians, with journeys to Rome and Italy; and not least with that of the Jews at fortnightly gatherings of his 'Jewish brethren', to whom he gave lectures. His happy home life with six children continued a noble Jewish tradition, and his way of working was similar to that of the old Emperor Franz Joseph (with his camp bed in Schönbrunn Palace) and to the puritan style of thousands of officials in the Danube monarchy who had been brought up on Jansenist and enlightened Josephine principles. Such people continued to do their work and carry out their administrative duties conscientiously, although after the decisive defeat by Prussia at Königgratz in 1866 many of them could no longer believe in a resurgence of the Austrian state.

In 1898 Sigmund Freud and 'the ruler of Vienna, Dr Karl Lueger' were together in the caves of St Canzian. In 1938 Gauleiter Bürckel, appointed by Hitler to be the new ruler of Vienna, was to establish himself immediately opposite Freud's home in Grinzing – as Freud pointed out in a letter from

London on 6 June 1938. Between these two dates, 1898 and 1938, Freud's gigantic life work unfolded. It was also the incubation period of two world wars, and it saw the rise to power of Adolf Hitler.

Sigmund Freud explored the depths and infernos of the individual personality and of humanity at large. He was profoundly convinced that, even if it were no solution, the fact of illuminating the conflicts within the individual could make an external war unnecessary. In 1898 Tsar Nicholas invited the nations to a peace conference with a manifesto warning against the dangers of an armaments race, every sentence of which still has burning relevance today. Commenting on this in a letter, Freud observed: 'The tsar's manifesto has touched me personally . . . Two people could be helped if we were brought together. I go for a year to Russia, take from him so much (neurosis) that he no longer suffers, but leave just enough so that he does not start any war. After that we can hold three congresses a year exclusively in Italy, and from then on I shall treat all my patients gratis . . . Incidentally, what is of lasting value in the manifesto is the revolutionary language. Any leader writer of a democratic paper making such observations about militarism would find his paper confiscated if he lived in Austria, or sent to Siberia if he lived in Russia.'

In 1902 Freud received his appointment as professor from Emperor Franz Joseph (he only received the title, not a chair). He remarked: 'Congratulations and bouquets are already pouring in as though the role of sexuality had suddenly been officially recognized by His Majesty, the importance of dreams confirmed by the Council of Ministers, and the necessity of treating hysteria by psycho-analytic therapy accepted in Parliament by a two-thirds majority.'

Here, under a cloak of irony, Freud expressed his conviction that psycho-analysis could become a world movement to give peace to humanity: first, inner peace and then, by restraining the massive material of conflict in the hidden kingdom of the ego, external peace. Peace, Shalom: world peace, peace for all men. Militarists, nationalists, and National Socialists accused the Jews in the nineteenth and twentieth centuries of preparing the way for pacifism. Jewish thought, Jewish belief in progress, Jewish Messianism, sought the goal of world peace.

In 1932, one year before Hitler was brought to power by men and groups who imagined they could make use of him, two 'old Jews' talked about war in a public exchange of letters: they were Albert Einstein and Sigmund Freud. On 30 July 1932 Einstein had asked Freud whether there was any way of delivering mankind from the menace of war. Einstein thought that 'the external or organizational aspect of the problem' was simple. International authorities and arbitration courts could settle conflicts. But he thought the world was then far from possessing any supra-national organization capable of enforcing obedience in the execution of its verdicts. 'How is it possible for this small ruling clique to bend the will of the majority, who stand to lose and suffer by a state of war, to the service of their ambitions?' Einstein also asked

Freud: 'How is it possible that the majority allow themselves to be inflamed to frenzy and self-sacrifice by the methods we have mentioned (the minority of the ruling class at present has the schools and the press and usually the church as well under its thumb)?' Einstein put the cardinal question when he asked: 'Is it possible to control Man's mental evolution so as to make him proof against the psychosis of hate and destructiveness?'

It was a large question put in a modest form: Man was to be made 'proof against' the psychosis of hate and destructiveness.

Freud's reply, headed Vienna, September 1932, was written from the standpoint of a man who had experienced the First World War and the crushing of the twelve-nation state of the Danube monarchy, a very remarkable construction which offered the nations in its domains, and not least the Jews, more security and rights than its individual successor states – a fact which Winston Churchill clearly recognized. In the First World War Freud had been concerned for the sons of his own race who were serving in the armies of the emperor as well as for the many other children of the family of Man. And in 1932 Freud was witnessing the rise of Hitler and seeing Austria slide down into a bloody civil war after enduring decades of latent civil strife.

With his habitual earnestness and honesty (that honesty which caused some friends and pupils to abandon him because they could not bear its tremendous effect on them) Freud faced Einstein's questions. He ended his letter with the words: 'With kindest regards and, should this *exposé* prove a disappointment to you, my sincere regrets.'

Freud states in his letter to Einstein that conflict of interests among men are generally decided by recourse to violence. 'It is the same in the animal kingdom from which Man cannot claim exclusion . . . The slaughter of a foe gratifies an instinctive craving.' Later, violence is content to hold the foe in subjection, instead of killing him. 'Hence springs the practice of giving quarter; but the victor, having from now on to reckon with the craving for revenge that rankles in his victim, forfeits to some extent his personal security.'

Thus, under primitive conditions, it is superior force – brute violence or violence backed by intellect – that prevails. 'We know that in the course of evolution this state of things was modified: a path was traced that led away from violence to law. But what was this path? Surely it issued from a single verity: that the superiority of one strong man can be overborne by an alliance of many weaklings, that *l'union fait la force*. Brute force is overcome by union: the allied might of several units now constitutes the law in contrast to the brute force of the individual.' Within a community there are also continual conflicts of interest which are very often 'settled' by force. 'There is but one sure way of ending war, and that is the establishment, by common consent, of a central control which shall have the last word in every conflict of interests.'

The League of Nations had been thought of as such an authority; but it was not able to fulfil these tasks. Its members refused to transfer power to it. 'We have seen that there are two factors of cohesion in a community: violent compulsion and ties of sentiment ("identifications" in technical parlance) between the members of the group.' Neither the pan-Hellenic ideal nor the Christian sense of community had been able to prevent wars. 'And in our times we look in vain for some such unifying ideal whose authority would be unquestioned.'

How then could war be banished? Freud's answer was that we could get nearer this great goal if we clearly recognized the conflict in the soul of Man. In Man there were instincts of two kinds: the erotic and the death instincts. Freud admitted to Einstein that it had only been in recent years, 'after many gropings in the dark', that he had come in his teaching to accept the existence of a death instinct. 'We assume that human instincts are of two kinds: those that conserve and unify, which we call "erotic" (in the meaning which Plato gives to Eros in his *Symposium*) or else "sexual" (explicitly extending the popular connotation of "sex"); and secondly, the instincts to destroy and kill, which we assimilate as the aggressive or destructive instincts. These are, as you perceive, the well-known opposites, love and hate, transformed into theoretical entities. They are, perhaps, another aspect of those eternal polarities, attraction and repulsion, which fall within your province. But we must be chary of passing overhastily to the notions of good and evil. Each of these instincts is every whit as indispensable as its opposite, and all the phenomena of life derive from their activity, whether they work in concert or in opposition. It seems that an instinct of either category can operate, but rarely in isolation; it is always blended (alloyed, as we say) with a certain dosage of its opposite, which modifies its aim or even, in certain circumstances, is a prime condition of its attainment . . .

'It is the difficulty of isolating the two kinds of instincts in their manifestations that has so long prevented us from recognizing them . . .

'Only exceptionally does an action follow on the stimulus of a single instinct, which is *per se* a blend of Eros and destructiveness.'

Freud refers Einstein to his scientific colleague, the Göttingen physicist, Lichtenberg, who taught physics in Göttingen 'in the age of our classical writers'. He had evolved the idea of a 'compass card of motives' and wrote: 'The efficient motives compelling Man to act can be classified like the thirty-two winds and described in the same manner e.g. Food-Food-Fame or Fame-Fame-Food.' Freud comments: 'Thus, when a nation is summoned to engage in a war, a whole gamut of human motives may respond to this appeal – high and low motives, some openly avowed, others slurred over.'

'Slurred over,' or passed over in silence. Freud devoted his whole life to the task of revealing the great importance of instincts which are passed over in silence in the formation of the volcanic landscape of man's physical and spiritual nature.

Within every living being the destructive instinct is at work, striving 'to work its ruin and reduce life to its primal state of inert matter. Indeed it might well be called the "death instinct"; whereas the erotic instincts vouch for the struggle to live on.' A particle of the death instinct remains operative within the living being, 'and we have attempted to trace back a number of normal and pathological phenomena to this *introversion* of the destructive instinct. We have even committed the heresy of explaining the origin of human conscience by some such "turning inward" of the aggressive impulse.'

It should be remarked here that Adolf Hitler was convinced that conscience was a Jewish invention. If it were only possible to free Germans from their conscience, Hitler thought, they would be capable of the extraordinary efforts needed to rule Europe as a master race.

Freud continues: 'All this may give you the impression that our theories amount to a species of mythology, and a gloomy one at that! But does not every natural science lead ultimately to this – a sort of mythology? Is it otherwise today with your physical sciences?'

Freud has been regarded as a mythologist, a finder and inventor of myths. He himself readily admitted that he preferred reading books on prehistoric times to books on psychology. Here, in this letter to Einstein, it is clear how Freud himself understood his 'mythologies': as models and as aids to make very complex matters intelligible in terms of images and symbols and thus to aid further research.

'The upshot of these observations, as bearing on the subject in hand, is that there is no likelihood of our being able to suppress humanity's aggressive tendencies.'

Equally vain was the Bolshevist hope that human aggression could be ended by the satisfaction of material needs and the equality of all members of society. 'To me, this hope seems vain. Meanwhile they busily perfect their armaments, and their hatred of outsiders is not the least of the factors of cohesion among themselves. In any case, as you too have observed, complete suppression of Man's aggressive tendencies is not an issue: what we may try is to divert it into a channel other than that of warfare.

'From our "mythology" of the instincts we may easily deduce a formula for an indirect method of eliminating war. If the propensity for war be due to the destructive instinct, we have always its counter-agent, Eros, to hand. All that produces ties of sentiment between man and man must serve as war's antidote. These ties are of two kinds. First, such relations as those toward a beloved object, void though they be of sexual intent. The psychoanalysts need feel no compunction in mentioning "love" in this connection: religion uses the same language: love thy neighbour as thyself. A pious injunction, easy to announce but hard to carry out! The other bond of sentiment is by way of identification. All that brings out the significant resemblance between men calls into play this feeling of community, identification, whereon is founded, in large measure, the whole edifice of human society.

'In your strictures on the abuse of authority, I find another suggestion for an indirect attack on the war impulse. That men are divided into the leaders and the led is but another manifestation of their inborn and irremediable inequality. The second class constitutes the vast majority; they need a high command to make decisions for them, to which decisions they usually bow without demur. In this context we would point out that men should be at greater pains than heretofore to form a superior class of independent thinkers, unamenable to intimidation and fervent in the quest of truth, whose function it would be to guide the masses dependent on their lead. There is no need to point out how little the rule of politicians and the church's ban on liberty of thought encourage such a new creation.'

Here Sigmund Freud touches on the crucial question for modern democracies. It was one which, in his own way, John F. Kennedy recognized: a superior class of independent thinkers, unamenable to intimidation, and fervent in the quest of truth is necessary to lead the state. Unfortunately, in our modern German and European states, there are only very few of them available. Freud saw that psychoanalysis had clearly come too late, since there were hardly any of these personalities in responsible positions who could free themselves, or wanted to free themselves, from their inhibitions, fears, self-alienation, alien bondage, and above all, from intimidation. They were also afraid of losing contact with the frenzied masses, even when they could succeed in freeing themselves from the masses' wishful thinking and illusions.

After the Second World War Erwin Stransky, the Nestor of Austrian psychiatry, called for a periodic 'psychological and patho-psychological examination of prominent and leading personalities in the state and international life.'

In 1932 Freud was unable to offer Einstein a proven and, above all, a quickly effective means of curbing war. Men would, therefore, continue to arm and fight wars. Nevertheless we must be pacifist ['we' meaning the old Jews Einstein and Freud] 'because we must be so for organic reasons'.

What were these 'organic reasons' which compelled Freud and Einstein to be pacifists? Let us say at once: they were, in secular terms, the age-old Jewish experience of war and the age-old Jewish Messianic hope of peace. In Freud's case the Messianism appears in its most sober, hardened and pessimistic form, like a piece of refined metal.

'Here is the way in which I see it. The cultural development of mankind had been in progress since immemorial antiquity. To this *processus* we owe all that is best in our composition, but also much that makes for human suffering. Its origins and causes are obscure; its issue is uncertain; but some of its characteristics are easy to perceive. It may well lead to the extinction of mankind, for it impairs the sexual function in more than one respect, and even today the uncivilized races and backward classes of all nations are multiplying more rapidly than the cultured elements.' This organic process of cultural development brings psychic changes with it. 'They consist in the progressive rejection of instinctive ends and a scaling down of instinctive reactions. Sensations which delighted our forefathers have become neutral or unbearable to us; and, if our ethical and aesthetic ideals have undergone a change, the causes of this are ultimately organic. On the psychological side two of the most important phenomena of culture are, firstly, a strengthening of the intellect, which tends to master our instinctive life and, secondly, an introversion of the aggressive impulse with all its consequent benefits and perils. Now war runs most emphatically counter to the psychic disposition imposed on us by the growth of culture; we are therefore bound to resent war, to find it utterly intolerable. With pacifists like us it is not merely an intellectual and affective repulsion, but a constitutional intolerance, an idiosyncracy in its most drastic form. And it would seem that the aesthetic ignominies of warfare play almost as large a part in this repugnance as war's atrocities.'

Freud closes his letter to Albert Einstein with the words: 'How long have we to wait before the rest of men turn pacifist? Impossible to say, and yet perhaps our hope that these two factors – Man's cultural disposition and a well-founded dread of the form that future wars will take – may serve to put an end to war in the near future, is not chimerical. By what ways or byways this will come about, we cannot guess. Meanwhile we may rest on the assurance that whatever makes for cultural development is working also against war.'

'Whatever makes for cultural development . . .'. The doctor, man and depth psychologist Sigmund Freud saw, in the course of his researches extending over more than fifty years, that many factors in the human personality militate against its own maturity and the development of its own culture. There is a tendency to dismiss the increasing emphasis that Freud came towards the end of his life to put on the death instinct, the destructive instinct in Man, as an old man's caprice. This is particularly so in America, where psychoanalysis has degenerated in the hands of assimilation – hungry Jews into a scholastic discipline aimed at fitting both Jews and non-Jews into the *American way of life*.

But in this way they sin against the ethos and whole work of Sigmund Freud, the great lonely figure from Vienna.

Antiquity regarded all philosophy and all thought as a meditation on death. Sigmund Freud saw his research and his analytical work as a constant struggle with death – in the first place with the 'lesser death' of failure. He was honest enough always to make the reservation that an analyst never knows whether an analysis is successful, whether it brings about a genuine and lasting solution and a release for the patient. Freud was always going back on his tracks and correcting himself.

The discovery of psychoanalysis in the years 1898 to 1900 was closely connected with Freud's analysis of his own self.

Freud knew all about the ultimate failures, long before he himself fell ill with cancer and closely observed the destruction of his own body. How few individuals did he manage to cure himself, in spite of all his strenuous work, working to begin with eight to ten hours a day on his analysis in modest surroundings, even carrying his scientific work through into the night, knowing full well that his was a voice in the wilderness! How little did sick society care to listen to him! The huge spectre of death was everywhere at hand. Anyone who wanted to could see it in Vienna in 1900 and in 1930 and in Europe in 1910, 1933 and 1938. He often had the impression, as he noted in Vienna on 7 January 1913, that 'all the evil spirits have been let loose against me'. In 1900 he saw himself soberly yet prophetically as Jacob struggling with the angel and in the process of being defeated. 'No critic . . . can see more clearly than I what misunderstanding arises between problems and their solutions, and it will be a just punishment for me that none of the unexplored regions of the psychic life which I was the first of all mortals to enter will ever bear my name or obey my laws. When, during the struggle, I was in danger of expiring, I asked the angel to desist, and that he has since done. I was not the stronger, and since then I have a perceptible limp. Indeed, I am truly forty-four years of age – an old and somewhat broken-down Israelite . . .'

On 18 February 1926 he wrote from Vienna to his Italian colleague, Enrico Morselli, who had just written a book on psychoanalysis: 'I am not sure that your opinion, which looks upon psychoanalysis as a direct product of the Jewish mind, is correct, but if it is, I would not be ashamed. Although I have been alienated from the religion of my forebears for a long time, I have never lost the feeling of solidarity with my people, and realize with satisfaction that you call yourself a pupil of a man of my race – the great Lombroso.'

In May of the same year Sigmund Freud wrote to his brethren of the Jewish lodge B'nai B'rith in Vienna. He thanked them for receiving him when, in the years after 1895, his 'first insight into the depths of human instinct' and the publication of his 'unpopular discoveries' had brought him to a state of personal isolation. 'I felt as though outlawed, shunned by all.' In this lonely state the Jewish brethren had taken him in. 'That you are Jews could only be welcome to me, for I was myself a Jew, and it has always appeared to me not only undignified but outright foolish to deny it. What tied me to Jewry was – I have to admit it – not the faith, not even the national pride, for I was always an unbeliever and have been brought up without religion (but not without respect for the so-called "ethical demands" of human civilization). When I have experienced feelings of national ex-altation, I have tried to suppress them as disastrous and unfair, frightened by the warning example of those nations amongst which we Jews live. But there remained enough to make the attraction of Judaism and the Jews irresistible, many dark emotional powers all the stronger the less they could be expressed in words, as well as the clear consciousness of an inner identity, the familiarity of the same psychological structure. And before long there followed the realization that it was only to my Jewish nature that I owed the two qualities that have become indispensable to me throughout my difficult life. Because I was a Jew I found myself free of many prejudices which restrict others in the use of the intellect: as a Jew I was prepared to be in the opposition and dispense with the approval of the "compact majority".'

If the idea and reality of opposition (which is often only a corrupt appendage of the other group or party) and of non-conformism was not today so devalued and so restricted, one could say that Sigmund Freud was the born non-conformist. Not from a desire to contradict, but from a love of truth and an awareness of suffering. His obstinate championship of truth (which he acknowledged in a letter to Lou Andreas-Salomé on 28 July 1929) did not originate in herostratic or exhibitionist motives or in the vanity of an assertive ego. It was based on the experience of a manly heart which regarded the path of humanity, of Jewry and of every individual person as a matter of vital importance. His specifically Jewish experience, acquired over the ages, and preserved in the subconscious, made him see the history of gods and Man and the history of the world as something related to the history of the individual. For the Jew, to remember is a pious duty for the male: to forget is feminine, evil and godless.

World history, the history of humanity, and the psychological history of the individual: in all of these it was a question of dethroning idols and of the need to destroy false images. Freud had no fear of the 'enthroned idol, Meynert' who possessed overwhelming authority at the university (2 May 1891). In a letter of 19 July 1915 to the American James J.Putnam, in which he strongly attacked the puritan American attitude to sexual morality, Freud wrote: 'I should add that I stand in no awe whatever of the Almighty. If we were ever to meet I should have more reproaches to make to Him than He could to me. I would ask Him why He had not endowed me with a better intellectual equipment, and He could not complain that I have failed to make the best use of my so-called freedom.'

In this letter Freud acknowledged a 'social morality' – morality as a sense of responsibility towards society, as opposed to a predominantly egotistic sexual morality. He then admitted: 'When I ask myself why I have always aspired to behave honourably, to spare others and to be kind wherever possible, and why I did not cease doing so when I realized that in this way one gets harmed and becomes an anvil because other people are brutal and unreliable, then indeed I have no answer.'

Having no answer to ultimate questions: Freud's immanent atheist piety – his father came from a Chassidim background – proclaimed itself elliptically: Man could know nothing about the 'nothingness' of death. 'Of one thing I am absolutely positive: there are certain things we cannot know now' (letter to Romain Rolland, 19 January 1930). Here he was basically in agreement with the philosopher Wittgenstein with whom he shared an attitude of resolute silence and agnosticism towards 'ultimate things'. About many things – all too many – Man knows nothing and can know nothing with the mental equipment available to him. But about many things – very many things – Man can know much and can learn a frightening amount. Freud illuminated the landscape of the psyche and of the inner man and plumbed down into the secret history of humanity, ages back. He took the path the Jewish people had taken, but in an opposite direction – back to Moses and even beyond.

The history of the psyche with all its sufferings and conflicts and the history of the individual in the modern world become intelligible and discernible only when we recognize that the human psyche has undergone a genuine development from primitive times and still carries within it today the material of conflict derived from those primitive times.

Life is hard for humanity as a whole and for the individual. Who should know this better than the Jew? Here the gods had three functions to fulfil: to exercise the terrors of nature, to reconcile men to the cruelty of fate, particularly as manifested in death, and to compensate for the sufferings and privations that communal cultural life imposes on men.

The God-Father is feared and worshipped by Man (the theology of the church speaks of *timor et amor dei*, the fear and love of God). The majority of people are still in many respects infantile and by no means prepared for the difficult task of facing up, honestly and soberly, to the very serious matter of becoming a human being. Freud gave a warning in 1928 to the Englishman, Richard Dyer-Bennett, who in his *Gospel of Living* expressed the view that the time had come for men to become gods.

'To turn human beings into gods and the earth into heaven would not be an aim of mine. This is too reminiscent of *vieux jeu* nor is it quite feasible. We human beings are rooted in our animal nature and could never become god-like. The earth is a small planet not suited to be a "heaven". We cannot promise those willing to follow us full compensation for what they give up. A painful piece of renunciation is inevitable.'

'A very thin layer may come up to your expectations, otherwise all the old cultural levels – those of the Middle Ages, of the Stone Age, even of animistic prehistory – are still alive in the great masses.'

The reversion to barbarism after 1933, which was deplored by many humanists, had only to remove a very thin skin in order to reveal and release the immature, uncontrollable instincts beneath. Freud was to experience from 1900 onwards something which many people still refused to recognize in 1940: that the luminaries of university science could behave like cannibals and often like the inquisitors of the late Middle Ages. These famous German scientists campaigned against him with an aggressiveness devoid of all principles of decency.

Freud was not unaware of the strength of religious illusions, but he said: 'An illusion is not the same as an error, it is indeed not necessarily an error'. Religious ideas, 'which profess to be dogmas, are not the residue of experience or the final result of reflection; they are illusions, fulfilments of the oldest, strongest and most insistent wishes of mankind: the secret of their strength is the strength of these wishes. We know already that the terrifying effect of infantile helplessness aroused the need for protection – protection through love – which the father relieved, and that the discovery that this helplessness would continue through the whole of life made it necessary to cling to the existence of a father – but this time a more powerful one. Thus the benevolent rule of divine providence allays our anxiety in face of dangers; the establishment of a moral world order ensures the fulfilment of the demands of justice, which within human culture have so often remained unfulfilled; and the prolongation of earthly existence by a future life provides in addition the local and temporal setting for these wish fulfilments . . . It betokens a tremendous relief for the individual psyche if it is released from those conflicts of childhood arising out of the father complex which are never wholly overcome, and if these conflicts are afforded a universally accepted solution.'

Freud did not wish to deprive men of the child's belief rooted in them. But he saw that for the masses in the contemporary world religion no longer had a fruitful and positive meaning. 'Religion has clearly performed great services for human culture. It has contributed towards restraining the asocial instincts; but still not enough. For many thousands of years it has ruled human society; it has had time to show what it can do. If it had succeeded in making happy the greater part of mankind, in consoling them, in reconciling them to life and in making them into supporters of civilization, then no one would dream of striving to alter existing conditions. But, instead of this, what do we see? We see that an appallingly large number of men are dissatisfied with civilization and are unhappy in it, and feel it as a yoke that must be shaken off; that these men either do everything in their power to alter this civilization or else go so far in their hostility to it that they will have nothing whatever to do either with civilization or with restraining their instincts.'

In 1927 these statements appeared in his book *The Future of an Illusion*. Freud saw that, at least in Europe, religion had failed. Religion, he said, was responsible for stunting the radiant intelligence of the child, and it reinfantilized adults. The same problem engaged the mind of Father Delp, who, before his execution in Berlin-Plötzensee in 1945, meditated about the churches' responsibility for the infantile attitude of the masses. Freud saw another transgression of religion: many intellects had suffered untold harm from the compromises they had been forced to make to find a way between the demands of their scientific conscience and the commandments and dogmas of their church. Freud did not know of the untold sufferings of many Catholic and Protestant theologians, scientists and educated laymen and clergy, who between 1870 and 1914, and indeed after, had been physically and spiritually broken in the church's struggle against modernism. But he thought, entirely in the spirit of modern biblical criticism, that all our religious writings were 'contradictory, amended, and forged'.

In what God did Freud believe as he set out through the wilderness of the modern age, through the hells and heavens of the human personality and of world history? He wrote: 'Immortality, retribution and the whole concept of the other life are such representations of our psychic personality . . . Psycho-mythology' (12 December 1897).

'Our god Logos will realize these wishes which external nature permits, but he will do this very gradually, only in the incalculable future and for other children of men. Compensation for us, who suffer grievously from life, he does not promise.'

Freud, the latter-day Moses, would not himself enter the promised land of free humanity: the land of inwardly liberated humanity which lives intensely with and in its conflicts.

This god Logos is the god of Philo, of Maimonides, of Spinoza and of Hermann Cohen: the god of all the great Jewish thinkers who agree with the phrase of St Thomas Aquinas, that Catholic child of Jewish thought: *totius libertatis radix est in ratione constituta*. The origin of all freedom is rooted in reason. Freud put it this way: 'There is no appeal beyond reason.'

But the way he handled this reason in his psychoanalysis was specifically Jewish, the product of a specifically Jewish medical ethos and a specifically Viennese form of *humanitas austriaca*, Austrian humanity. In Vienna, that hive of poison which Freud hated (though in a different way from Hitler), the antidote was also to be found.

Nestroy, the great Viennese master of popular comedy, whom Freud knew well and liked to quote, observed: '*Homo sum*, as the Romans say, which means in German "I'm an ass".' And the doctor and poet, Arthur Schnitzler (to whom Freud confessed: 'I have avoided you from a kind of reluctance to meet my double') noted: 'Most men have no idea of all the things they know – know in the depth of their soul without admitting it.' Nestroy wrote a comedy called *Zu ebener Erde und erster Stock*, showing the lower orders on the ground floor with their joys and sorrows, and the bourgeoisie with its lies and follies on the floor above. Freud saw the psychic drama of every personality as a drama in which the Id, the Ego and the Super-Ego worked together.

In the psychic drama the powerful Id constitutes the deepest layer of the psychological household, the foundation. In it are to be found the death instinct and the Eros. It contains the sources of the libido, the passions associated with life, love and suffering, beyond good and evil. Here exist, in their separate states, both the conscious and the unconscious.

In the old Hapsburg world the Id corresponded to the volcanic depths of the peoples of the Danube monarchy, to the Unconscious of the Christians and not least of the Jews.

Could and should Man rely on this Unconscious – on the volcano within himself? Freud's answer to this, as to all large questions was a conditional yes and no. The Id is the foundation supporting both life and personality. But, as it is also the embodiment of the unrestrained pleasure principle, it needs to be regulated by a restraining force, a reality principle. That is the Ego.

The Ego is in fact that part of the Id which is modified by contact with the external world and its influences. The Ego provides the elements of perception and the conscious activity of human thought. It thus forms the buffer between blind instinct and external reality.

This Ego consequently has no easy task. And it is made even more difficult by the fact that it has to mediate between a still rebellious ground floor, and a very awkward tenant on the floor above: the Super-Ego. On this upper floor, in the Super-Ego, dwell the laws, statutes, ordinances, religions and arts – in fact, all the cultural achievements of humanity. The Super-Ego, therefore, has a truly imperial function, similar to that provided by the God-Father and (for the Austrian people) by the super-father figure in Schönbrunn, Emperor Franz Joseph. In the late nineteenth and early twentieth centuries hundreds of thousands of Jews fled from the East to the protection of His Majesty in Vienna. The most perceptive amongst them, in the years 1889–1900 in which psychoanalysis was born, wondered uneasily what the fate of the Jews and the people of Central Europe would be if this imperial father became feeble and sick and collapsed.

Sigmund Freud discovered this Super-Ego in his self-analysis as a direct result of his psychological relationship with his own father, Jacob Freud, the man of Chassidim background.

The death of his father in 1896 profoundly affected Freud. In July 1897 he began his self-analysis: the uncovering of the heavens and hells in his own personality which originated in childhood and in the corresponding early period of humanity. In the preface to the second edition of the *Interpretation of Dreams* (the first edition appeared in 1900), he intimated that this work could be regarded as part of his own self-analysis and his reaction to his father's death.

Joseph Nuttin has written: 'The analysis of his dreams of incest helped him, among other things, to understand the meaning of those scenes of seduction described by his parents which he had hitherto regarded as memories of real events. At the same time, this self-analysis led him to formulate his theories about the Oedipus complex and infantile sexuality generally.'

Jewish children, boys and girls of Polish, Czech, German and Dutch origin had plenty of opportunity in the concentration camps to study at first hand the hellish backgrounds of their 'sunny' childhood, in the presence of their murderers as well as their mothers and fathers. They did this with sobriety, acuteness and self-questioning – all in the imaginative and picturesque language of a child and elaborated in drawings, paintings, poems and songs. All this was movingly foreshadowed in Freud's attempts to penetrate into the 'profound depths of the hidden kingdom of the ego' as Hugo von Hofmannsthal wrote to Hermann Bahr in 1904, ten years before the First World War.

When Freud looked into the depths he saw how a child wrestles with its parents. A boy wants to be his own father, to win his mother and to possess her entirely. A girl tries to win her father for herself from her mother. This is the Oedipus complex: incest, the incestuous union of mother and son. Greek tragedians wrote of it, as did Homer in the eleventh book of the Odyssey. In his *Republic* Plato describes the stirring of the instincts during sleep, when 'one part of the soul', reason, sleeps and the 'animal and wild part of the soul' rises up: 'You know that in this condition the latter allows itself everything conceivable, because it is now alone and free of all shame and reason. Then it has no qualms about cohabiting with its mother, if it so fancies, or any other object of its desire, be it god, man or animal ... *In all men* there is a wild, powerful and unrestrained species of desires, even if some seem to be very respectable people, and of this ... we have clear proof in dreams.'

As for happiness, Freud never tired of saying that it is to be found only when the individual succeeds in rooting himself in his childhood, in the prehistoric experience of the human being who wishes to have everything and be everything.

The child cannot just become the young King Oedipus. He represses the wish to kill his father and to possess his mother by imagining that he is the father. By this sort of 'introjection' the child transfers the father to his Ego, as his 'Ego Ideal'. The Super-Ego is the image of the parents within the child. The father's strictness, authority and complete power and the mother's goodness and wisdom gather in the Super-Ego. The protective yet threatening power of the father and mother, of the God-Father and possibly the divine Mother, form within the Super-Ego that element which, in the shape of conscience, makes demands on the individual man. The Super-Ego intervenes, as a sort of father and God-Father present in the child-man, when something 'impermissible' is thought or done.

'It's a work of art to serve three masters', as Peter Hofstätter has said. And so it is with the Ego between the Id and the Super-Ego. Its life is as difficult as was that of any citizen in the twelve-nation state of the Danube monarchy. He had to serve the emperor, (the Super-Ego) in the army or as an official; he had (if he were a Czech, for instance) to serve his own awakening Czech people; and he had to serve his deeply hidden loves and passions, in and outside his family.

Metternich's régime had shown great skill in developing the censorship into a fine instrument to which press, theatre and literature were all subject. In post-Metternich high society a generally accepted form of language was evolved which by a kind of voluntary censorship went far towards eliminating whatever might cause offence to authority. In addition, there arose the neo-puritan voluntary censorship of bourgeois society. Beginning with the 'unmentionables' in underwear, it censored and suppressed everything sexual and banished it to the underground of the psyche.

Censorship by the state, by the church, by society, and by the puritanically educated or miseducated individual: Freud's 'dream censorship' fed itself on all these daily realities. In his analyses Freud noticed how in dreams the Id, the Ego, and the Super-Ego, can work together to an extraordinary degree. The Id bursts out, agog to reveal its impulsive desires. The Super-Ego attempts brutally to suppress and repress these impulses. Then, like journalists trying to assuage the censor by presenting their burning themes in acceptable disguises, the Ego intervenes, clothing the ugly passions of the underground in seemingly harmless words and images.

Freud's neurotic patient (and also Man as member of a sick society) has a great deal within himself to repress or to conceal. His inner condition is rather like that of an authoritarian state, having to deploy all its armed forces to hold down the masses adjudged rebellious.

Freud was convinced that the neurotic, the mentally and physically sick person can only be cured by illuminating his inner hells and making him aware of them, by bringing to light the whole history of his sufferings in its often distorted and devious development. This history of individual suffering had its counterpart in the suffering of mankind as it has occurred and recurred in many periods and epochs.

As a doctor, Sigmund Freud learned when treating a patient how the latter would always develop and use, unconsciously, the same techniques of repression and resistance to the analyst. In uncovering these techniques, Freud succeeded in making one of his greatest discoveries, that of 'transference'. The patient transfers his instinctual impulses, first experienced in his relations with his parents and other persons, to substitute persons, and in the case of analysis, to the doctor providing the treatment.

Hate and love, trust and hostility, aggression and despair, are all transferred to the doctor. He becomes the healer and saviour, leader and god, father and lover – as well as the victim, the final sacrifice.

In analysis there can be both 'negative' and 'positive' transference. Both can endanger the process of healing, indeed make it impossible, if they are not resolved. Some patients, (usually women) when their inner hells are revealed, suddenly see the doctor, whom they have already secretly desired, as a devil and seducer. They run away and do not return. No less serious and dangerous can be the effects of an undissolved 'positive transference', when the patient cannot free himself from his doctor but continues to regard him as leader, healer, saviour, lover, father, son, etc.

The great risk in all this is only perceptible by implication. It arises from one human being offering himself to another as a sort of father confessor, redeemer and guide through the victim's inner hells. What Freud, the Viennese Jewish doctor, was venturing to do was nothing less than this: for fifteen hundred years Christians had made the Jew their scapegoat and had attributed to him all their physical and mental illnesses, hunger, plague, spiritual fear, fear of the Devil, of sex, of witches, of death and of the enemy (as we have seen, the Jew was always regarded as being in alliance with death, the Devil and sex). And now Freud was introducing to the sick individual and the sick society of his time the analyst, the doctor working with analysis in the capacity of what I should like to call the 'voluntary Jew'.

The Jewish depth psychologist must take on himself the patient's guilt and seek to dissolve it in a sympathetic partnership with the sufferer.

But Freud knew that it would require much Eros, much love – a sober and discreet love – to dissolve the transference altogether. After establishing the bond the doctor must thrust the patient away back into his own life. Freud treated his patients through a screen, in order to ensure conditions of the greatest possible discretion. In an obituary tribute to one of his greatest pupils, Ferenczi, in 1933, he gave a kind of self-portrait: 'The need to heal and help was predominant in him. Perhaps he had set himself aims which cannot be achieved with our present therapeutic methods. He had the invincible conviction that one could do much more for the sick if one gave them enough of the love they had longed for as children . . .'

Human beings, like children, need unlimited help, care and healing treatment. Freud knew that he could help only a few, and even with these it was often uncertain whether they could live a rich and intense life after the completion of the treatment, without lapsing into self-destruction. Freud, as a man, experienced much suffering in his life. His hand-writing shows to what extent he felt oppressed and, at times, threatened by great inner struggles.

What then was Man – in 1900, 1920 and 1933? Man was, above all, his own unresolved past. As a Jew in the old Austria, Freud was conscious of European Jewry and the awakening nations who were anxious to find or even invent an independent past for themselves (as the Czechs did in the Königinhof manuscript, which Masaryk showed to be a forgery). Freud said: 'The experiences of the Ego seem at first to be lost for inheritance, but, when they have been repeated often enough and with sufficient strength in many individuals in successive generations, they transform themselves, so to say, into experiences of the Id, the impressions of which are preserved by heredity. Thus, in the Id, which is capable of being inherited, are harboured residues of the existences of countless Egos.'

A human being is therefore the sum of the unresolved conflicts of his childhood, as well as of the known and hidden conflicts of world history – particularly in the early period of humanity.

In those years, when the National Socialist movement was gaining possession of more and more hearts and minds, Freud, the Viennese Jew, groped his way back to Moses. Moses was the man whom he saw as the inventor of the Jewish God, of the Law and the great divine burden which weighs upon the Jewish people and, marking it off from all other peoples, ordained its terrible fate.

Freud kept back his study of Moses when he was in Vienna: he did not wish to publish it in hard-pressed Austria and to endanger professionally his colleagues, the Jewish psychoanalysts. He feared intervention from the Vatican on the grounds of 'offence to religion'. *Moses and Monotheism* first appeared in London in 1939, the year the Second World War began. Freud said of his work, which was intended to explain the Jewish religion as a gigantic historical Oedipus complex: 'It can be called an attack on religion only insofar as any scientific investigation of religious belief presupposes disbelief. Neither in my private life nor in my writings have I ever made a secret of my being an out-and-out unbeliever. Anyone considering the book from this point of view will have to admit that it is only Jewry and not Christianity which has reason to feel offended by its conclusions. For only a few individual remarks, which say nothing that has not been said before, allude to Christianity. At most one can quote the old adage: "Caught together, hanged together".'

'Needless to say, I do not like offending my own people either. I have spent my whole life standing up for what I have considered to be the scientific truth, even when it was uncomfortable and unpleasant for my fellow-men ... Well, we Jews have been reproached for growing cowardly in the course of centuries. (Once upon a time we were a valiant nation.) In this transformation I had no share. So I must risk it.'

In the 'few individual remarks' on Christianity in *Moses and Monotheism* we read: 'We must not forget that all the peoples who now excel in the practice of anti-Semitism became Christians only in relatively recent times. One might say that they are all "badly christened"; under a thin veneer of Christianity they have remained what their ancestors were – barbarically polytheistic. They have not yet overcome their grudge against the new religion which was forced on them, and they have projected it on the source from which Christianity came to them. The fact that the Gospels tell a story which is enacted among Jews, and in truth treats only of Jews, has facilitated such a projection. Their hatred for Judaism is at bottom hatred of Christians ...' (Hans Ornstein, in commenting on this passage, has observed that 'hatred of Christians' should really read 'hatred of Christianity'.) Freud continues: 'And it is not surprising that in the German National Socialist revolution this close connection of the two monotheistic religions finds such clear expression in the hostile treatment of both.'

The close connection of the two monotheistic religions, Judaism and Christianity, was overlooked or even denied by most Christians in Hitler's Reich. The 'Aryan' Christ was regarded as the 'first anti-Semite'. Heinrich Heine before Freud – and also National Socialists like Alfred Rosenberg and many others – realized that Christianity was only a 'thin veneer'. It was not very difficult to rub it off, as they very soon found out.

Since the Second World War the Christian community has gradually begun to grapple with the problem that Freud, the great Jewish doctor, was chiefly concerned about, namely, that religions are powerless in the contemporary world. They cannot restrain that wounded animal, Man: they provide no protection against murder or suicide, against war or civil strife.

'If only men can be made good and happy, with or without religion, the good God will give his benevolent approval to such work . . . It pains me very much that the theologians are so pitifully backward, and fail. I have been working on this now for more than eighteen years . . . The theologians have too often been distracted by unprofitable quarrelling over principles and have not been able to pay much attention to the spiritual welfare of the laity or of themselves.' Oskar Pfister (1873–1956), the Zurich pastor, teacher and depth psychologist, wrote these words in a letter to Freud on 10 September 1926. He corresponded regularly with Freud from 1909 until Freud's death. In Freud's views on religion Pfister saw 'basically the eighteenth-century ideas of the Enlightenment' and thought that the essential difference between him and Freud lay in the fact 'that you grew up in a world of pathological religious forms and mistook them for real religion, whilst I, fortunately, was able to turn to a free type of religion. This seems to you to deprive Christianity of its content, but I see in it the central message and substance of the Gospel.' (It may be recalled that Zwingli, the founder of the Zurich Protestant Church, acknowledged the influence of Erasmus of Rotterdam, and thought that a Christian should be a man of peace, a person who imparted peace.)

After Freud's death Pfister wrote on 12 December 1939 to the widow of his great adversary in London about his impressions of Freud's family life: 'I, who grew up without a father and suffered all my life from a too one-sidedly indulgent upbringing, was dazzled by the beauty of this family life which breathed freedom and joy because, for all his superhuman stature and his profound seriousness, he, as head of the family, displayed love and sparkling humour. In your house it was like being in a sunny spring garden: one heard the joyful singing of larks and blackbirds; saw bright flowerbeds and was conscious of the rich blessing of summer. That much of this blessing was due to you, and that you, with your gentle and kind nature, were always providing your husband with new strength for life's hard struggle, was at once clear to the guest. The more men seemed to him a rabble (he used this expression in one of his letters), the more that "ferocious pair of gods, Ananke and Logos" (again his own expression) forced him into their cruel service, the more he needed you; and, without you, even this giant could not have achieved all that was presented to "worthless humanity" in his life's work.'

'The Jew is made for joy,' Freud wrote to his fiancée on 23 July 1882. Joy in Eros, above all in Eros between man and woman within the bosom of the family, has made the Jewish family a centre of resistance to suffering and persecution right up to the 'final solution'. Jewish fathers, mothers and grandparents embraced and fondled their children as together, naked, they waited to enter the gas chamber.

In his letter to Freud's widow Pastor Pfister continued: 'In recent years I have often thought of a moving passage in a letter he sent me on 6 March 1910. I think I ought to repeat it to you. It said: "I cannot reconcile myself to life without work. Imagination and work for me go together. I take pleasure in nothing else." ' Pfister quoted at some length from this letter which Freud wrote to him in 1910, and in which he expressed anxiety lest he should succumb to illness: 'One cannot rid oneself of the fear of this possibility. So while I accept my fate as an honourable man should, I have a secret request that there should be no infirmity, no crippling of my powers through physical ailments. At least let us die with harness on our back, to use Macbeth's words.'

Pfister added: 'At any rate, the wish for mental clarity, for death in the royal harness of a thinker has been fulfilled.' He ended his letter of condolence to Freud's widow with the words: 'I am working on several projects which, with my limited ability, continue your husband's kind of work. If this wretched time prefers to make music for the Devil of lies to dance to rather than to hear the symphonies of truth, I believe with your husband that *la vérité est en marche.*'

This letter was dated 12 December 1939. The belief that truth would prevail was the belief of the French Revolution and, before it, of the political humanism of the eighteenth-century Enlightenment. Pfister, who had earlier criticized Freud's eighteenth-century philosophic attitude, now – at a time when the great Nazi campaign of murder had already begun in Poland – paid tribute to it.

It was a time in which millions of Christians succumbed to an anxiety neurosis – and not only in German lands. And Christianity was not able to restrain the monstrous fears in the depth of the human heart. (Freud said that men were predominantly afraid of punishment, women of being deprived of love.)

In his compendious work *Das Christentum und die Angst* (Christianity and Fear) Oskar Pfister showed how in the course of history Christianity had very often not banished fears, but had rather intensified them. He used the example of old-fashioned Lutheran Protestant orthodoxy to show how this had created an anxiety obsession and formed a pathological, anxiety-obsessed community which demanded vast human sacrifices of 'crypto-Calvinists' within the German Lutheran church, as well as of witches and papists outside. Pfister could equally well have found his example in many aspects of contemporary life. Anxiety-obsessed Christians were unable to defend themselves, and they could not, or would not, save the scapegoat from slaughter, the Jew from being crushed between the Cross and the swastika.

I I

Crushed Between Cross
and Swastika

'Brothers in Christ! Arise, and arm yourselves with courage and strength against the enemy of our faith. The time has come to suppress the race of Christ's murderers before they become masters over you and your descendants. For the Jewish gang is beginning proudly to raise its head . . . Down with them before they crucify our priests, defile our sanctuaries and destroy our temples. We still have power over them . . . therefore let us now execute on them the judgment they have passed on themselves . . .'

This comes from a proclamation in Catholic Würzburg dated 1819, in this year of widespread disappointment at the failure of the ruling princes to keep the promises they had made during the wars of liberation. Jewish pogroms spread from Würzburg all over Germany.

The court chaplain Adolf Stöcker, who was a member of the Reichstag in Berlin for nearly thirty years, had this to say when the Reichstag was discussing a ritual murder trial in Xanten in 1892: 'No one with any knowledge of history will deny that Christians, and particulary children, have for hundreds of years died at the hands of Jews through fanaticism or superstition.'

In Innsbruck, on 9 December 1954, Bishop Paul Rusch, one of the most unprejudiced and progressive bishops in Central Europe, gave the following reply to Dr Albert Massiczek, the Viennese historian and state librarian, who had asked him in a letter to forbid the ritual murder festival plays in Rinn in the Tirol: 'With some difficulty and with the help of Father von Wilten, I succeeded a few weeks ago in persuading these people not to perform this play for another five years. Before that I had absolutely no knowledge that the play was being performed. As for the purely historical aspect of the ritual murders, historians differ in their opinions about them. Many are certainly not disposed to accept your opinion. We have therefore to take into account here that there are other well-founded views. In any case, in looking at the whole question, we must accept that it was the Jews who crucified Our Lord Jesus Christ. Because they were unjustly persecuted under the Nazis, they cannot now suddenly pretend that they have never perpetrated an injustice in history. No nation, not even Austria, can make this claim. Finally, I would observe that there was no question of an anti-Jewish demonstration in Rinn:

it was simply a play, which, in its popular form, seems to give pleasure. In similar plays the peasants also are often made fun of, or have their legs pulled, without anyone taking offence.'

In Cologne in 1961 one of two persons who had been involved in the desecration of local synagogues during the previous Christmas made this reply to the court when asked what he had against the Jews: 'They are not Germans, and they crucified Christ.'

'They are not Germans . . .' Every crisis in Germany from 1819 to 1930 produced a national mood of anti-Semitism which expressed itself in this charge that the Jews 'are not Germans', and in the demand for special regulations, the withdrawal of full civic rights and expulsion – ultimately, liquidation.

' . . . and they crucified Christ.' German Protestant anti-Judaism led directly to Julius Streicher and the 'evangelical Christians' who participated, actively and passively, in Hitler's 'final solution' of the Jewish problem. German Catholic anti-Judaism led through the nineteenth and twentieth centuries to those Catholic theologians who showed enthusiasm for Hitler and to those prominent Catholics such as Arthur Seyss-Inquart, Reich minister without portfolio, later the Reich commissioner in occupied Holland, who played an energetic role in the 'final solution'.

Christians who distort the truth and historical facts have tried to keep the Cross and the swastika as far apart from each other as possible, and to represent them as opposites. Certainly the Cross and the swastika stood for opposites in the minds and consciences of certain individuals whose warnings were not welcome in the church – men like Father Friedrich Muckermann, S.J. 'Theodor Haecker and Reinhold Schneider, whose still unpublished dissertations *Et tu Petrus* . . . took up Hochhuth's theme long before *The Representative* appeared. But in the eyes of the world, and in the cold facts of German history, the Cross and the swastika came ever closer together, until the swastika proclaimed the message of victory from the towers of German cathedrals, swastika flags appeared round altars and Catholic and Protestant theologians, pastors, churchmen and statesmen welcomed the alliance with Hitler. In this sense it is historically consistent that Adolf Eichmann and many other henchmen and officials of the National Socialist liquidation machine should have found the active support of members of Catholic orders, who had been familiar with their functions in the Third Reich, when they fled from Europe to South America and the Arab states. In this sense too it is historically consistent that at the Second Vatican Council no fundamental declaration on the Jews was produced, which might have led to real amends for Christian guilt towards that people. Such a manifesto could have cast doubt on and effectively wiped out a thousand year old tradition. So far no legal action – on the part of any of the Council fathers – has been announced against the authors and distributors of the anti-Jewish pamphlets, brochures and books which were sent to them.

'The literature of the first half of the nineteenth century in Germany frequently described the Jew as the crucifier of Christ and as a man accursed. He was diabolical, sinister and closely associated with horror and death. The Jew was uncivilized and subhuman. The Jewish victims themselves accepted many of these ideas and saw themselves more in the distorting mirror of the world in which they lived rather than as they were. To a large extent their conduct was conditioned by the hostility they encountered. But even those who resisted the accusations were never able to free themselves entirely from the proscription imposed by the limited imagination of their persecutors' (Eleonore Sterling).

The Jewish periodical *Orient* stated in 1843 that the Jews hid their pain behind a smile and even idolized those who injured them. 'A Berlin Jew is in ecstasy if you tell him that there is nothing Jewish about his physical appearance.' In the same year Heinrich Oppenheim wrote in the *Mannheimer Abendzeitung* that 'with the German fatherland the Messiah has come for the German Jews'. Rabbi Samuel Hodheim advised the Prussian minister of culture that 'the German consciousness of the German Jews, particularly those in Prussia, rejects the assumption that they are still a separate Jewish race'.

'For some Jews the desire to be submerged in the community was so strong that they began to adopt the anti-Semitic insults of their adversaries and to direct them against themselves. They clung to the false hope that in this way they would be more readily accepted by society, and fancied that self-denigration would protect them from the attacks of their enemies. Judaism was 'rotten', they said. The Jew was deeply imbued with 'spite, thirst for revenge, anger, cunning and deceit'. According to Joel Jacoby all Jews were full of "passion and irreconcilable hatred against Christians and Christianity".' The convert Friedrich Julius Stahl, the arch-representative of political and Protestant conservatism in Prussia during the nineteenth century, wrote that there was admittedly a certain type of aristocrat Jew, but 'in general the Jews lack honour, self-reliance, manly insistence on their rights and a noble way of life, in a word the sense of honour which forms the natural basis of the Germanic race'.

Prussia and Berlin, old Austria and Vienna were centres of a national German Jewry which only wanted to be German. They were also the homes of those Jewish anti-Semites whose attacks on Judaism formed a welcome arsenal for Christian and National Socialist anti-Semites.

There were highly gifted and sensitive spirits among those whose Jewish self-hatred found literary expression. The poet, Rudolf Borchardt, one of the greatest artists in words in the German language (among other things he translated Dante's *Divine Comedy* into an archaic German of his own invention) wanted to be nothing but a Prussian and a German. In his Italian exile he only narrowly missed liquidation at the hands of Nazi henchmen. Even the mortal danger of those years did not open his eyes. He ignored Judaism, the Jewish destiny and suffering. He saw only the German Reich – a land of great spiritual attainments, whose image he carried in his heart.

On 4 October 1903 a young Jew, Otto Weininger, shot himself in Vienna. His book *Geschlecht und Charakter* (Sex and Character) had appeared a few months before his suicide. The twenty-two year old Weininger saw that humanity fell into two categories: the masculine, which was positive and vital; and the feminine, which was negative and without life. No medieval theologian under the influence of Manichaean and Augustinian thought could be more radical in his anti-feminine and anti-Jewish thinking than this young Viennese Jew. Under the influence of Houston Stewart Chamberlain (who lived twenty years in Vienna) Weininger developed his ideas about the complete inferiority of the Jew. On 21 July 1902 he received his doctorate, and he had himself baptized on the same day.

In the task of 'freeing the world of Judaism', Otto Weininger led the way. He rejected Judaism as an evil, feminine and weak form of non-existence. He declared himself to be an Aryan and demanded to be accepted as an Aryan by Aryans. The Aryan was noble: the Jew was characterless, mean, lacking in nobility and worthless. Of all the Germanic races he thought the English were most like the Jews.

Jesus, the founder of Christianity, was the great conqueror of Judaism and historically the only Jew who had overcome Judaism in himself. The time was perhaps ripe for a new Messiah who, coming from Jewry, would overcome the Judaism in himself and in the world. Weininger saw himself as this Messiah and leader of humanity, as the liberator of civilization from the guilt of woman and the sin of Judaism. The present age was for him one of superficiality and injustice, of anarchism and Communism, and of the most stupid of all interpretations of history, historic materialism.

Weininger saw a new and youthful Christianity emerging from great struggles which, as in the early Christian period, were concerned with the necessary choice between Judaism and Christianity, between business and culture, man and woman, matter and spirit, denial and worship.

A few months after the publication of *Sex and Character* the young 'Führer' rented a room in the house in which Beethoven died in Vienna, and shot himself. He left no words behind.

One of his most brilliant pupils and supporters, Arthur Trebitsch, attributed Weininger's suicide to the fact that he had not succeeded in convincing other people of his miraculous transformation into a noble Aryan. If only a single Aryan had received him in his home as an equal, he might not have committed suicide.

Arthur Trebitsch saw in Weininger's experience a reflection of his own struggle to cast off his Jewish ties and to become a pure Aryan. Trebitsch was born in 1879 – ten years before Hitler – and was the son of a silk merchant in Vienna. He was the brother of Siegfried Trebitsch, who made a name in the German theatre as the translator of Bernard Shaw. Because his family had lived in Vienna for several generations, he felt that he was not a Jew, never had been one and never would be.

Arthur Trebitsch saw the Jewish and Christian religions equally as useless ruins, as the vehicles of a slave's morality. He thought humanity must look for a new, heroic faith. The real danger came, not from the Jewish religion, but from the Jewish race, which was infecting the body of Europe with its poisons. Only a few individuals, like Weininger and himself, had been able after the efforts of generations to ennoble themselves as Aryans in spite of their impure origin. Against the millions of other Jews, and particularly against the dirty human stream of Eastern Jews which was pouring into the West, the only method the Aryan master race could use was one of iron hardness. Here we see a highly gifted Viennese Jew from the Jewish aristocracy anticipating the ideas which Hitler, with the help of his Eichmanns, was later to transform into bloody reality.

Trebitsch thought that if Europe wanted to recover it must expel all its Jews with the exception of those few families who were ready to let their sons endure hard, compulsory physical work in labour battalions in the cause of a re-educative process lasting generations. *Arbeit macht frei* (Work makes us free) was the inscription that could be read above the gates of Hitler's concentration camps.

Trebitsch stressed that Judaism and Teutonism could not co-exist: they were absolute opposites. Either the one or the other must succumb. Trebitsch predicted the *Götterdämmerung* and downfall of noble Germany if it did not succeed in liberating itself from all those (sub-)humans who were infected with the Jewish disease.

In 1919 Arthur Trebitsch published the ideas he had worked out in the First World War in a book entitled *Geist und Judentum* (Spirit and Judaism). His thesis was that Germany had lost the world war as a result of Jewish activities. Jewish revolutionaries were responsible for the fall of the Hohenzollerns and the Hapsburgs. Just as – and here the Catholic and National Socialist anti-Semitic distorters of history followed Trebitsch and his predecessors – the Jews had once brought about the fall of the Persian, Egyptian, Greek and Roman empires, so they now threatened the German Reich, the last strong bulwark of the Aryan world. Britain was the champion of Israel; and under the British mask the Jews were seeking to build up their domination of the world. The decline of the West could not be halted, unless it awoke from its sleep, recognized its implacable mortal enemy and developed a form of antidote against the foreign poison.

Since antidotes were often obtained from poisons, it was advisable, as an antidote against Israel, to employ individuals, like himself, Arthur Trebitsch, who had overcome the Judaism in their own hearts. (This is, amongst other things, a very remarkable inversion of St Paul's experience.) Half-and three-quarter-Jews could help greatly in liberating their beloved German fatherland from Judaism.

Trebitsch referred to the *Protocols of the Elders of Zion* to prove the Jewish aim of world domination. Zion and Rome, the Roman Catholic church and international Jewry had joined together and formed an alliance to defeat the Nordic and Aryan Protestants. ('We build the German cathedral against Judah, Hapsburg and Rome,' were the words sung by the supporters of Schönerer and German nationalists in Austria, who left the Catholic church in hundreds of thousands to demonstrate their wish to become completely German and Protestant.) As the most deadly weapon forged by the Elders of Zion, Bolshevism would be called to their aid in order to strike the German Reich a mortal blow. The church and Zion would then share the spoils. Rome would receive Catholic Austria and Southern Germany: Zion would receive the North. But Rome would not be able to enjoy its spoils for long: all Europe would eventually fall to the Jews and Bolshevism.

It would then be useless to place any hopes on America, Trebitsch declared, for America was already in the hands of Jewish international finance. If Europe should ever sink to America's low level then everything that was noble, superior and Aryan would disappear, and the whole of life would degenerate into senseless automatism.

Arthur Trebitsch offered his services to the National Socialist movement in its early days. In the first years of Austrian National Socialism, he was looked on for a short time as 'Führer'. At his meetings believers, including many women and young people, crowded round him and with tears in their eyes listened zealously to his gospel. Later they went over to Hitler, but they never forgot what Trebitsch had revealed to them about the international Jewish menace and the decision which the Germans would have to face.

Trebitsch died in 1927. Apart from his numerically few German-Jewish supporters and the Aryan faithful, there were in Vienna and in the successor states of old Austria, especially in Prague, a body of Jews who, for other motives, looked forward confidently to the coming of the Third Reich. They were originally National Liberal Jews, heirs to 1848, who were opposed to the Hapsburgs and Rome and looked on Bismarck's state as their own – one which was destined to inherit German Austria. Right up to 1945 some Austrian-Jewish Social Democrats exiled in Britain (such as Ellenbogen) – who were by no means anti-Semitic – retained their conviction that Austria should remain united with Germany.

In his study *Der jüdische Selbsthass* (Jewish Self-Hatred) Theodor Lessing wrote in 1930: 'The world we enter here is a heartrending one.' He described this self-hatred in the lives and works of six Jews: Paul Rée (the strange friend of Nietzsche and of Lou Andreas-Salomé), Arthur Trebitsch, Otto Weininger, Maximilian Harden (the champion of German nationalism in late Bismarckian times), Max Steiner and Walter Calé (both of whom committed suicide when young).

Theodor Lessing, a follower of Maximilian Harden, had himself started off as a German super-nationalist and Jewish anti-Semite. At one time, indeed, Thomas Mann publicly charged him with anti-Semitism. Lessing's study was in fact a piece of self-analysis – an attempt to liberate himself from his self-hatred and to penetrate to the Jewish origins hidden in the depths of his being.

He argued that the Jews were an Asiatic people who could play a unique role in Europe as mediators between both continents. They possessed a sense of responsibility towards their fellow-men and an awareness of suffering, matured by thousands of years of persecution; and they could confront a pitiless destination without fear. As the oldest nobility in the world they could have greatly enriched humanity had they been allowed a normal history. But, after having held back their psychological and intellectual energies for hundreds of years in the ghetto, the Jews were all too suddenly liberated from this way of life in the nineteenth century. They then burst upon the world with all their dreams and sufferings, with all their long pent-up energies. In a few decades this highly gifted people had diffused and exhausted itself in Europe. The result was that the brilliant light of Jewish culture and achievement in the European nineteenth century had now burnt itself out. But only a small *élite* of contemporary Jews had accepted the implications of this collapse and found their way back to the harsh land of Asia – to Palestine.

Jewish hopes now rested not on Europe but on Palestine. While the peoples of Europe destroyed each other in wars, the Jews were beginning to cultivate the hallowed land with their blood and sweat – a land which was once the cradle of human history and now again carried the seed of a spiritual rebirth.

The year was 1929, the year which saw a world economic crisis, the year which gave the Nazi movement its decisive impetus. Theodor Lessing saw Arabs massacring Jews in Palestine with the benevolent acquiescence of the British military authorities, and he saw pogroms in Poland and Rumania. How were the Jews to be helped? Theodor Lessing demanded that every single Jew in Europe should clearly seek and find his own way to salvation: by deliberately re-establishing roots in the new Jewish nation and in Jewish destiny. He argued that the Jews were not only the descendants of beggars and poor devils, but also of Judas Maccabaeus and of Queen Esther. The Jew was a link in a long and honourable chain which went back to Saul, David and Moses.

Theodor Lessing, in his early period an ex-Jew, an anti-Semite and a German nationalist, became in the fullness of his life a man who experienced the miracle of rebirth, of finding roots in the deeper recesses of his personality and his Judaism. And about 1930 his was one of the few lonely but significant voices which gave warning of the coming catastrophe. The National Socialists were aware of his importance. When he fled to Czechoslovakia, they had him murdered by their henchmen in 1933.

The year 1933 was to be the year of destiny for German, Jew and European. Let us look again at the background to this event, confining ourselves to Germany in the nineteenth and twentieth centuries. In 1820 there were 270,000 German Jews; in 1925 there were 564,379 – less than one per cent of the German population.

In the nineteenth century increasing industrialization and urbanization made life for large sections of the population increasingly difficult. The nineteenth century was a particular hot-bed for collective discontent. This concentrated itself chiefly in the fast-growing cities. The Jews moved into the cities. The harassed lower-middle-class German was overtaxed by the rapid social changes and took refuge in a retrogressive nationalism, which had nothing in common with the broad, liberal, good-humoured humanity of those aristocrats and patricians who, in Weimar and in the Berlin of the Humboldt brothers, lived easily and without restraint alongside Jews, Frenchmen, Poles, Russians and people of other nationalities.

After the failure of the 1848 revolution the Jewish citizens did not take the reactionary turn of German liberalism. The Jews turned to 'difficult' and not easily comprehensible ideologies which demanded considerable mental effort – such as democracy in general and Socialism in particular. The majority of the lower middle class sought an 'easy' ideology in which everything was apprehended without difficulty: the good leader, the father of the country, the emperor, the wicked enemies which surrounded Germany. The Jew was particularly suitable as an anti-symbol. When the National Socialists gave free rein to German hate impulses they were only meeting a demand which had been building up since 1871. The masses did not ask for anti-Semitism; they merely wanted to hate. Hitler understood this. He compared the masses to a woman yearning to give herself to a strong man. If there were no Jews, he said, one would have to invent them.

There was no need for that. Not only were they very much there, but they had also already been 'introduced' to the public. In *Hänsel and Gretel*, a picture book by Wilhelm Busch (who was anti-Semitic and anti-Christian), a sorcerer is shown standing beside the witch to help in the murder of the child. The sorcerer has Jewish features. Here, in this very widely read book, we already begin to see the diabolical Jew of the *Stürmer* caricatures of 1933.

Adolf Leschnitzer has pointed out that the persecution of the Jews in the thirteenth and fourteenth centuries was replaced by the persecution of witches. In the nineteenth and twentieth centuries this process was reversed. The heaven of the Christian churches became incredible for many sections of the community. But hell was here on earth and immediate: in the narrow, airless rooms and hovels of the cities as they sprawled in all directions. And *where there was hell, there must be a devil – the Jew.*

What had been brewing in the German spiritual and political underground for over a century all but a few sensitive individual Jews preferred not to see or acknowledge. Before 1933 the German Jews had no fear of pogroms: 'Such things do not happen in Germany', it was said. They rejoiced over the words of Crown Prince Friedrich Wilhelm, who said in 1881: 'Anti-Semitism is the disgrace of our century.' And they were happy when in 1901 a German Jewish relief association was founded to help Eastern Jews who wanted to emigrate to America. This association organized the emigration from Russia in 1904. It was known that Bleichröder was Bismarck's banker and that at the Congress of Berlin in 1878 Bismarck had intervened energetically on behalf of the Rumanian Jews. Paul Nathan, a self-acknowledged Jew and an energetic representative of German national interests, went to Russia to negotiate with members of the government about an improvement in the position of Jews and their protection in the tsar's empire. Germany appeared as the strongest protector of Jewry in Eastern Europe at that time.

Leo Baeck, the Berlin rabbi, maintained that the events of 1933 found many Jews in Germany inwardly unprepared. In Berlin in 1933 there were 160,500 Jews – 32 per cent of all German Jews. The majority of German Jews were, at least around 1900, reformed Jews: they wanted to be part of Germany and the German world, and looked down on the orthodox Jews and the 'uneducated and dirty' Eastern Jews.

Jews had been living in German lands since the time of the Romans – many centuries before the Slav and East European tribes were Germanized between the Elbe and the Oder. The Jews themselves did not become Germanized. In the period between 1690 and 1812 a handful of rich families in Berlin and Vienna were able to rise in society. Between 1810 and 1830 there was a period of quick assimilation and absorption. In 1848 the Jews took part in the uprising, as a reaction to their treatment by the governments in the period 1815–47.

After 1848 it looked as if there was going to be a long and peaceful process of assimilation between Jews and non-Jews in Germany. But from 1872 this development was threatened when the Jewish masses, as distinct from individuals earlier, began to seek symbiosis. This led to conflicts. Broadening contacts did not create friendship, but tensions and friction, breaches and, finally, open hostility.

'The Jews are everywhere.' This cry of British monks in the twelfth century was taken up by the Germans, who already had considerable difficulties in their contacts with one another and who had a characteristic German inability to appreciate the qualities of others.

A sociological imbalance increased the opportunities for friction. Had there been a balanced ratio between Jewish and Christian peasants, workers, seamen, fishermen, soldiers, diplomats, post officials and police, the relations of wide sections of the German population with Jews would have developed differently. But the German Jews made for the cities and penetrated the urban middle class.

German art and scholarship were, from 1800 until 1860, in the hands of the middle class, helped by Jews in the Berlin salons and the circles around Heine and Auerbach. The Jews were essentially a literary people. At the beginning of the German-Jewish symbiosis stands the friendship between Lessing and Mendelssohn, at the end the friendship between Stefan George and his Jewish pupils.

The Jews brought their religious zeal to the new preoccupation with worldly culture. The German university took over the role of a secularized Yeshiva, a Talmud college. Enthusiastically (and sometimes inconsiderately), German Jews, the interlopers, vied with emancipated German middle class citizens to better their lot after the founding of the Reich in 1871. Both this German bourgeoisie and the German Jews made a disagreeable impression: both were spiritually and politically unprepared for their emancipation. The new, successful German citizen made a disagreeable impression on the outside world. The German Jew made a disagreeable impression at home, particularly with his German rivals who, like him, were ambitious, obsessed with prestige, yet at the same time filled with an inferiority complex. German nationalism in the period from 1870 to 1933 had its exact counterpart in a certain type of Jewish 'arrogance'. Both the German bourgeoisie and German Jewry suffered morally in this race for success and social advancement and found themselves in 1933 facing Hitler breathless and inwardly quite unprepared. At first German and Jewish industrialists expected Hitler to do no more than restore the good old times of Kaiser Wilhelm and, with that, economic prosperity.

Both the German middle class and the German Jews lost their politically conscious élite in the catastrophe of 1848–9. In March 1848 many Jews were killed in Berlin. German malcontents emigrating to America after 1848 included many Jews, from whom many famous American Jews are descended, for example, Herbert and Irving Lehman, Brandeis, Bernard Baruch and Abraham Jacobi.

The Jews in Germany had no Disraeli. The German Jew, Lassalle, was killed in a duel over a baron's young daughter. German Christianity found no Gladstone in politics; indeed German politicians looked down on him with great contempt.

In 1872 the new Reich, led by Prussia, brought the full civic emancipation of the Jews. They at once set about climbing the social ladder. They were remarkably successful in their professional lives as businessmen, lawyers, doctors, academics, writers and bankers. But in their private lives during this period of 1872–1933 they were often unhappy figures – something which non-Jewish friends and enemies perceived, but which they themselves did not see. They realized neither their alienation nor their self-alienation. They said: 'We are Germans. Judaism is – or was – just our religion, or the religion of our fathers.' They did not understand that their identification with Germany was at best a matter of a few generations. They were assimilated, but not absorbed. If their appearance was non-Jewish, they were proud: best of all to be blond, blue-eyed and tall. But they did not feel the hatred growing up around them. The German lower middle class and the artisans (the German Commercial Employees' Union was a powerful centre of 'nationalist' pressure groups) began to feel themselves overwhelmed, mortally threatened and crushed by modern industrialization and then by the difficulties of the war and post-war period. Their misery produced a mood of perplexity, helplessness and despair. In addition, they were afraid of being proletarianized; and in the popular imagination the proletariat was falling into the hands of the Devil in the form of the 'Jewish Marxist'.

Adolf Leschnitzer has compared the obsession with witch-hunting in the years between 1575 and 1700 (this proceeded simultaneously with the rise of the natural sciences and a relentless rationalism that was counterbalanced by an irrational background) with the German anti-Semitic movement in the nineteenth and twentieth centuries. In both phases economic, social and emotional motives were mingled.

Most German Jews had no idea of all these preparations for what Karl Kraus called a 'third Walpurgis night'. They lived in an invisible ghetto (as still exists today in some American cities where it 'happens' that only Jews mix with Jews), whose existence they refused to acknowledge. The only ones who saw clearly were small groups of young Zionists, and they were made fun of by 'well-meaning' German Jews who would not dream of exchanging their German homes for huts in the deserts of Palestine. These young Zionists were prepared to abandon a hard-won emancipation in Germany for the sake of a future in the long-forgotten land of their forefathers. A large part of German Jewry up to 1933, and even beyond, dismissed their programme as romantic, foolish and unrealistic – a favourite word of the German bourgeoisie.

A clash was impending between two groups, each confined in a ghetto from which it wanted to break free, yet unable to rise inwardly above its own particular ghetto mentality. On the one hand there were the Jews from the German and (in growing numbers) from the East European ghettoes. On the other hand there were the German middle and lower middle class, artisans and workers. These latter were still living mentally, politically and spiritually in the Middle Ages (as many of them still do, to judge from the debate on capital punishment in the Federal Republic in 1964–5). Prisoners of their own particular ghetto, they held the same ideas about their princes, their God, the Devil and the Jews as their forefathers had done, two hundred years earlier. It is true that among Germans since Lessing's day a small élite (which was not, however, altogether reliable in times of crisis) thought of the Jew in different terms. But it was precisely this élite which had suffered catastrophic defeat in 1848.

For these ghetto Germans the old image of the ghetto Jew persisted long after the ghetto walls had fallen. Was it indeed so long since they had fallen? Goethe's and Börne's descriptions of the Frankfurt ghetto recall 'Ahasuerus, the Eternal Jew' as the popular German book depicted him in 1662. The Jew as Cain, Judas and Ahasuerus (all mythical forms of the Devil) was depicted in 1900 in much the same way as he had been in 1600.

Bismarck and Emperor Wilhelm II viewed the serious social tension in the empire with deep concern. From time to time both were disposed to subdue the Socialist masses, even to have them liquidated. Bismarck sometimes thought of provoking a rebellion so as to be able to intervene militarily. (French Catholic conservatives about 1850 also toyed with the idea of involving the unruly masses in a major war in order to consume their energies.) A turbulent German middle class, small bourgeoisie and artisan class, overwhelmed by industrialization and not rich enough to provide an education for their sons, saw the Jews rising in society and able, in disproportionate numbers, to give their children a higher education. The Jewish percentage of doctors, lawyers and other intellectual professions exceeded in a few decades the percentage of the non-Jewish community. Jews became professors, high school teachers and owners of large stores.

At this point political anti-Semitism in the form of 'the mug's Socialism' (*Sozialismus des dummen Kerls* – the expression is attributed to Kronawetter, the Austrian Social Democrat) provided a mental and political refuge for the lower middle class and the small bourgeoisie. No one dared to attack the real rulers, the big figures in politics, in business and in the church. No one dared to confront them directly and force them to bring about a change. Instead the weakest element in the Wilhelmine empire was attacked – the Jews. The result was that the image of the despised Jew, the ghetto Jew, the miserable, odious and horrible sub-human was held up and maintained in spite of the presence of real, successful Jews in elevated positions.

The real trouble about a minority in the age of nationalism was that it existed, that it was there and was not absorbed in the higher, 'sacred' entity of the fatherland. (As late as 29 March 1945 a Nazi Gauleiter saw the 'sacred fatherland' menaced by the evil, invading 'Jews' of the American Ninth Army and the British troops.)

Unfortunately the extraordinary empire of 1871 displayed little ability to tolerate minorities (unlike the large Eastern empires and the Hapsburg monarchy). Catholics, Poles, Alsatians and Jews seemed predestined for discrimination. In the ensuing *Kulturkampf* the Catholics were outlawed as a minority hostile to the empire, maintaining international (that is to say, anti-national) contacts abroad. Spiteful expressions such as 'Jesuit', 'monk', 'inquisitor' originated in this period of struggle, and were taken up again in the anti-church propaganda of the Third Reich. Unfortunately many Catholics did not see here the bond that linked them to the Jews.

Between 1874 and 1879 the Jew became the official Enemy Number One. This was the period of the worst European economic crisis in the nineteenth century (it will be remembered that National Socialism owed its rise to the world economic crisis of 1929). This period of depression was comparable with that of 1919–24 and of 1929–33. 'The Jews are our misfortune.' Anti-Semitism seemed to be the magic key to understanding the world and all its crises, defeats and catastrophes throughout history. Anti-Semitic propaganda of the late nineteenth century in Germany took the same line as Hitler in *Mein Kampf*: the masses should be presented with only *one* enemy. Liberalism, Socialism, an alien Christianity, Russian Bolshevism, Anglo-Saxon capitalism: these were all only the embodiment of a *single enemy*, the Jew!

In the Middle Ages there was a tendency to see every misfortune, war, famine, pest, earthquake, harvest failure and economic crisis in terms of *guilt* rather than of *causes*. People did not ask what were the causes of this or that catastrophe, but who was to blame for it. And the answer was the Jew, the sorcerer. This mysterious idea of guilt still dominates the mentality and political thought of many Germans today: a neurotic anti-Bolshevism with its devil associations has taken the place of anti-Semitism (with its own devil associations of 'Jewish capitalism' and 'Jewish Bolshevism').

In the stormy period of the Reformation and Counter-Reformation, when the persecution of Jews gave way to the persecution of witches, Jewish rites (or what one imagined them from legends to be) were transferred to the witches and became the 'witch's sabbath', and the mark of the Devil on the body of the witch (a symbol of circumcision). Now, in the nineteenth and twentieth centuries, the Jew was burdened with the emotions and images which had been associated with the witch.

The educated and erudite German-Jewish bourgeoisie did not recognize this process of regression, this return to the insurmountable superstitious fears of the lower classes. German Jews in 1933 still saw the Germany of Goethe, Schiller and Mendelssohn. They overrated the power of German education and the influence of the German classics and of German idealism. These German Jews never heard the warning voice of Henri Brémond proclaiming that German book learning produced monomaniacs and monologists, but no sense of social obligation or ability to communicate with others.

It was not the case that National Socialist terrorization made the Germans abandon their old convictions and their culture. The terror merely revealed that very many Germans had for long had no deeply-rooted moral convictions and cultural standards. The same applies today to Christians at all levels of society. If it were politically expedient, they would cast off their old clothes overnight. The majority of German Jews saw and heard nothing. They failed to understand that the Nazi torture chambers did not come out of the blue, but had been erected behind the façade of a 'culture' which eloquently championed the classics. The German Jews believed in the Germany of poets and thinkers. (I remember some nationalist, conservative German Jews speaking to me once with admiration about neo-classic buildings of the Third Reich.)

The story is told of an elderly judge in East Prussia who sought to reassure a young lawyer who was worried about the new wave of anti-Semitism in the 1930s. He said: 'Dr A., we saw all that fifty years ago. It will pass over.'

Why did 'all that' not 'pass over' again?

Karl Friedrich Borée, who recounted this story in his memoirs *Semiten und Antisemiten, Begegnungen und Erfahrungen* (Semites and Anti-Semites: Encounters and Experiences) which appeared in 1960, was a volunteer in the First World War and came from a National Protestant family (his family subscribed to the *Hammer*, the first leading anti-Semitic publication). Borée observed the social scene in Germany, before and after 1914, at first hand; and in his encounters with Jews and anti-Semites he noticed that Jewish children were beaten in school on the grounds that 'they were only Jews'. There were anti-Semitic professors at Leipzig University, such as Rudolf Sohm, the great authority on ecclesiastical law, who said in a lecture: 'In the primeval forests of Germany there were no Jews.'

We may interpolate here that, long before the advent of Nazi anti-Semitic university teachers, German professors showed themselves to be anti-Semites: jurists of the romantic German school of law who, basing themselves on Savigny, dangerously weakened the German citizens' regard for law by limiting their conception of it to 'historical law'; historians like Treitschke; professors of criminal law like Franz Eduard von Liszt; and political economists like Werner Sombart.

In the nineteenth century, in the field of academic anti-Semitism (which flourished particularly in Vienna), the Berlin political economist Eugen Dühring achieved notoriety by his publication *The Jewish Problem as a Question of Racial Character and its Threat to the Existence and Culture of Nations*. Professor Dühring asked: 'Why does the German spirit at present feel so little at home with itself?' And he gave the answer: 'Because not only in the religious, but equally in the intellectual field it has lost its identity and sold itself to Judaism.'

Dühring called the Jews parasites who settled wherever there was corruption and decay. He regarded literature, the press, all political parties, art, science and law, and above all the Christian religion, as Judaized. With the peculiar logic of his madness (Aristotle, Dante and psychologists have detected a remarkable correlation between logic, madness and the Devil) Dühring declared everything which he disliked to be either Jewish or Judaized. That included both Lessing and Nietzsche – and finally even nationalism and anti-Semitism itself.

Let us return now to Karl Friedrich Borée, who describes his life in German-speaking countries before and after 1914. In the German students' union he inevitably encountered deeply-rooted anti-Semitism (though he would not have done so in 1810, 1830 and 1848). In the German army the Jews struck him as unhappy figures: though wearing the same uniforms, they remained isolated. It was only as a result of the revolution of 1918 that the Jewish citizens achieved social equality, although it had existed on paper for seventy years. In the Weimar Republic Jews forced their way into public life, into city administrations and social affairs. These were matters that did not interest non-Jews. According to Borée, the Jews had a passionate belief in the duty and ability of Man to improve the world. In a thousand years of oppression they had kept alive and developed their sense of justice: inevitably they took the side of the oppressed.

Borée observed the wretched behaviour of the liberal bourgeoisie. It did not participate in the all-party protest meeting after the murder of Rathenau (nor did the Christians – *as* Christians). Throughout the eastern part of Germany the Jews were prominently represented in the social élite of the cities and proved themselves there to be 'in general the most reliable supporters and guardians of German civilization'. These nationalist German Jews were inspired by a naïve belief that Germany would protect them.

But Karl Friedrich Borée also saw a profound melancholy in the faces of educated German Jews. Their dilemma, as they saw it, was this: 'If we adapt ourselves, they will look on it as unscrupulous opportunism; but if we stand aloof, we shall be regarded as aliens, to use no worse expression.' Borée saw *one* source of German anti-Semitism in an unwillingness to accept other people as they were. The weak character with little gift for individuality worked off his inferiority complex by appearing as part of the crowd or majority and letting the weaker element feel his strength. Borée thought that both the depressed German middle class and the upper stratum had lost their self-confidence.

Foreign Jews admired Hitler's successes in Berlin in 1933. One represented a Prague bank, another a Dutch; and both were amazed that Borée had not yet joined the successful victorious movement.

The poet Rudolf G. Binding, a frequent visitor in Jewish homes in Frankfurt, was implored to protest against the anti-Jewish campaign in 1933. His reply was: 'What concern of mine are the Jews? Let them help themselves!' Most Christians thought and acted in the same way. German poets, intellectuals, professors and theologians were weak and morally undeveloped and consequently often characterless. Because their own individuality was undeveloped, they remained immature. Integrated neither in society nor in the time in which they lived, they were incapable of showing resistance.

Hitler managed to win the support of much of the anti-Semitic middle class and drive out the very elements from whose critical intelligence and passionate love of freedom a rebellion was most to be feared. These individual and lonely figures, like Friedrich Wilhelm Foerster, had already left Germany or, like Kunz von Kauffungen, were now forced to flee.

Borée tells of an old Jewish woman in Berlin who refused to emigrate to the USA, though she knew the fate which awaited her in Germany. But she did not want to leave her native soil. Her forebears had for hundreds of years been held in high esteem in Mecklenburg.

Borée's conclusion in 1960 was: 'If the Germans have a collective guilt for the crime of liquidating the Jews, it lies in the fact that the people who set the tone in society in those days tolerated contempt for the Jews.' We might add that this was also the main fault of the churches: they certainly tolerated contempt for the Jews and sometimes tolerated much more.

No bishop and no important theologian emerged in this incubation period of modern German anti-Semitism – that is to say from 1872 – to strike an authoritative, warning note. This role was reserved to the 'anti-Christ', Friedrich Nietzsche. Nietzsche regarded Christianity as the product of Jewish antagonism. But at the same time he saw: 'The hymn in honour of charity which Paul composed is not Christian, but a Jewish flickering of the eternal Semitic flame.' The Jews, like the Greeks, were men of passion and of the will to live and love.

Nietzsche said: 'The Jews have spirit.' They have it because they have suffered and remembered their suffering for a thousand years. Spirit is not without the experience of suffering.

Nietzsche parted company from Richard Wagner on the Jewish question. Nietzsche championed the Jews and a future human race strong in intellect and love. Richard Wagner opted for the people, for immediate success and for anti-Semitism. Nietzsche was the first to recognize the plebeian and revolutionary character of modern German anti-Semitism. (It was historically consistent that Hitler should be attending a performance of *Rheingold* in Bayreuth when Dollfuss, the Austrian Federal Chancellor, was bleeding to death in Vienna, murdered by the Nazis.) Nietzsche parted from his anti-Semitic publisher and from his sister when she married the anti-Semitic leader Förster.

Nietzsche saw that the new German anti-Semitism was a new slaves' revolt of the under-privileged against the wealth, power and intellect of the Jews. Adventurers and factory owners, ambitious men and unsuccessful journalists, pious men and atheists, and hysterical women of both sexes joined hands. Nietzsche was convinced that the 'struggle against the Jews has always been a mark of inferior, envious and cowardly natures. Whoever takes part in it must have something of the plebeian mentality about him.'

But where in this modern Germany was there a class or a group which was not infected by a plebeian mentality?

In one of his Turin farewell notes Nietzsche, now on the verge of insanity, remarked: 'I should like to see all anti-Semites shot.'

The German-Jewish cultural symbiosis of the nineteenth and twentieth centuries made possible the German achievements in science and literature. Men like Borée and ex-President Theodor Heuss (the latter in conversation with me) have seen a close connection between the intellectual stagnation in modern Germany today and the loss of the Jewish community. Borée said: 'It will come to be seen as a great national loss that we have destroyed so much capacity and initiative.'

Friedrich Nietzsche admired the first great symbiosis in Europe – the achievement of the Spanish Jews in the Middle Ages. 'In the darkest periods of the Middle Ages, when the Asiatic hordes had already spread out over Europe, it was Jewish thinkers, scholars and doctors who upheld the banner of enlightenment and intellectual independence in conditions of the greatest personal duress and defended Europe against Asia.' And again, 'If Christianity has done everything to orientalize the West, Judaism has substantially helped it to westernize itself again and again; which to a certain extent means making Europe's historical role a continuation of the Greek role.'

Nietzsche saw the Jews being absorbed in the various nations and countries of his time and wanted to see the process succeed. He thought that, as a result of this inoculation with European-born Jews, the nations of Europe would progress. But to ensure this development in Germany he demanded a ban on the further immigration of non-Europeanized Eastern Jews to Germany. 'Germany has enough Jews,' he said, and for that reason 'the doors to the East must remain closed.' This closing of the doors was precisely in the interests of the German Jews.

Nietzsche warned both the Germans and the German Jews with the mythical call of his Zarathustra, 'It is time, indeed high time.'

From early days Jews were fascinated by Nietzsche. In the eighties of the last century Nietzsche discussed with the Viennese Jew, Dr Paneth, the possibility of a popular Jewish renaissance – in Palestine. Nietzsche thought Palestine should be a model for the new organization of the world and for life this side of the grave. There would be properly planned settlements; efficient land utilization and higher educational opportunities. In Palestine the Jews would set up a model colony as a pattern for the future of humanity.

Nietzsche saw very great opportunities and very great dangers emerging in centuries to come – for the European, for Man and for the Jew. He foresaw that 'one of the spectacles to which we will be invited in the next century will be the fate of the European Jews'. Europe was threatened with the loss of part of its European people; and Nietzsche asked: 'What would be left of the European mind if we took away the Jews?'

Nietzsche said of the Jews: 'In Europe ... they have had eighteen centuries of experience, such as no other people here can show, with the result that, if not the community, all the more so the individuals within it have been able to profit from this terrible period of trial. Every Jew has in the history of his father and grandfather a store of examples of cool presence of mind and tenacity in formidable situations, of subtle stratagems, and of the ability to exploit misfortune and chance. Their courage in the guise of miserable subjection, their heroism in *spernere et se sperni* exceed the virtues of all the saints. The world sought to make them contemptible by treating them with contempt for two thousand years and by barring their way to all honours and all that is honourable, and for this they were cast all the more deeply into the shabbier trades. And, in truth, they have not become cleaner in the process. But contemptible? They themselves have never ceased to believe that they have been called to higher things and thus the virtues of all sufferers have never ceased to adorn them.'

Nietzsche's warnings, imprecations and praise of the Jewish destiny in Europe now sound like an obituary.

The anti-Semitic publisher from whom Nietzsche parted came from Saxony. Saxony, and in particular Leipzig with its publishing trade, was the centre of modern anti-Semitism in the publishing world (Leipzig was the home of the Hammer publishing house; of Wilhelm Marr, who coined the phrase 'anti-Semitism' in 1879; and of the 'father' of German anti-Semitism, Theodor Fritsch). A second centre was Vienna.

At the beginning of the nineteenth century imperial Vienna, surrounded by its ramparts and bastions which had held against the Turks and which were still to resist Napoleon, was a small city with magnificent Baroque buildings, among them the Hofburg and the palaces of Schönbrunn and Belvedere. On the eve of the 1914 war these two places were to become symbols of the two opposing elements in the house of Hapsburg. Schönbrunn stood for the old Emperor Franz Joseph, who looked on the fate of his peoples with profound concern and feared a revolt from below and the collapse of his empire. Belvedere, once the palace of Prince Eugene to whom the Austrians owed their rise to the status of a great power in South-eastern Europe, was the seat of the heir to the throne, the Archduke Franz Ferdinand, who had relations with the Christian Socialists and whose spokesman and adviser was Dr Friedrich Funder and his *Reichspost*.

Vienna, the imperial city in the early nineteenth century, was not anti-Semitic. The salon of Fanny von Arnstein received the brilliant figures of the Congress of Vienna. The small, sad man of the people, Franz Schubert, wrote his *German Mass* for his Christian friends and his Hebrew spiritual music for his Jewish friend, the choirmaster Salomon Sulzer. In imperial Vienna at the middle of the century, and then again in the last third of the nineteenth century, there was no anti-Semitism, either in the house of Hapsburg, or in the homes of the great nobility, who occasionally married rich Jewesses. The Villa Wertheimstein, in which Austrian poets like Ferdinand von Saar and later the young Hofmannsthal found a spiritual home, may be regarded as a symbol of that patrician and Jewish patronage of poetry, education and culture which gave the stamp to this Vienna of the 'gay Apocalypse'. Hermann Broch, in his great Hofmannsthal essay, coined the phrase of Vienna's 'gay Apocalypse' in the 1880s.

The names of Arthur Schnitzler, Stefan Zweig, Richard Beer-Hofmann, Peter Altenberg, Felix Salten and Hugo von Hofmannsthal still remind us today of that literary Vienna in which Jewish professors, doctors, lawyers, financiers, press and theatre figures played an important part between 1880 and 1914 and again, though to a much lesser extent, in the period between the two world wars. It was the Vienna of the composer Mahler, of the poet Franz Werfel and of the society of artists and literary figures centred round the woman who became the wife of both men, Alma Mahler-Werfel, who died at a great age in America in 1962.

In fine society the Viennese did not talk about Jews. But at lower social levels they talked all the more. The middle bourgeoisie looked with foreboding at the Jewish lawyers, doctors, and tradesmen; and the lower middle class was learning increasingly to fear Jewish competition. This was intensified when, terrified by the pogroms and persecutions in the East, Jews streamed from Russia, Poland, Rumania and Hungary, to Vienna – to the protection of the house of Hapsburg which from the thirteenth century onwards had earned for itself both praise and heavy criticism for its policy of protecting the Jews. The middle class and the lower bourgeoisie were at first brought together by anti-Semitic clergy and then by anti-Semitic politicians. But here there developed a rivalry between the two forms of anti-Semitism: one was Christian Social, Catholic, Austrian and pro-Hapsburg; the other was German nationalist, anti-Catholic and anti-Hapsburg.

Adolf Hitler, who with the eyes of an impoverished member of a middle-class family looked up in admiration at the wonderful buildings of Vienna, but looked also with hate (like the unsuccessful journalists in the Paris of Drumont) at 'Jew-infested' Vienna, was nurtured on both Christian Social and German nationalist anti-Semitism in Vienna.

The powerful protagonist of the Catholic church's anti-Semitism was the polemical and highly gifted Father Sebastian Brunner (1814–93), the editor of the *Kirchenzeitung* (Church Newspaper). He was the great spiritual leader of anti-Semitism in Austria-Hungary and was highly regarded in Rome and in Paris, where he was known as the 'father of Austrian anti-Semitism'. Viennese journalists in priests' robes and Austrian clerics played an important part in church anti-Semitism as speakers at meetings, as authors of tracts and pamphlets and as preachers from the end of the nineteenth century right up to 1933. But in about 1880 there appeared a keen rival: Georg von Schönerer and the German nationalists. The 'Linz programme' of 1883 was expressly anti-Semitic (Adolf Hitler chose Linz as his artistic capital in the

Ostmark – the Nazi name for Austria after the Anschluss.) To reach the small man a busy industry of trinkets with anti-Semitic slogans came into being (a model for the later Munich and Nuremberg Nazi trash).

The 'first anti-Semitic reading room' was established in a Vienna coffee house. Here all the domestic and foreign anti-Semitic papers were put out to read. Lovers of anti-Semitic student songs, of walking-sticks and pipes decorated with Schönerer's portrait could immerse themselves not only in German nationalist, but also in Catholic anti-Semitic papers and periodicals. (This is important: there have never ceased – even occasionally to this day – to be cross-connections and offers of alliance between individual Catholic, Christian Social and German nationalist groups and circles. The link has been anti-Semitism.)

They came together then – and quickly parted. There was something sectarian about the German nationalist groups in Austria, a constant tendency to split up. There were people associated with the anti-Semitic weekly *Sonntagsruhe* (Sunday Rest), others with the Christian Social Association of 1887 and others with the Anti-Liberal League of 1888 (a collection of various anti-Semitic groups). Schönerer's periodical *Unverfälschte Deutsche Worte* (literally, Undistorted German Words), founded in 1883, lasted until 1903. Latterly it carried the sub-title: 'A Monthly Journal of German Popular Education and Improvement, Pan-German Politics, Economics, Art and Literature'. All these themes were later to be mastered by Adolf Hitler – or so he himself believed.

The anti-Semitic middle and lower middle classes gathered together in the *Deutscher Schulverein* (German School Association), in the *Turnerbund* (Gymnastics Club) and in the guilds. In 1889, the year of Hitler's birth, the student associations of Austria formed a single body in Linz, which was openly anti-Semitic. On 20 April 1897 (Hitler's eighth birthday), Dr Karl Lueger, the leader of the Christian Social Party, who had been elected for the fifth time mayor of Vienna, received for the first time the imperial confirmation of his appointment. The first big Christian Social party conference in Vienna (on 23 April 1896) was held under the banner of anti-Semitism.

In 1935 there appeared in Dresden and Vienna a pictorial volume published by Austrian Catholic National Socialists honouring Lueger, Sebastian Brunner, and the 'courageous soldier of God, Pastor Dr Josef Deckert of Vienna'. The latter had demanded an aliens' law for the Jews in 1897 and had said: 'The Jews must be rendered harmless for the Christian peoples. They must come under an aliens' law. The emancipation of the Jews must go.'

'The Jews must be rendered harmless': only a question of method distinguished Catholic from Protestant Christian anti-Semitism.

An election poster of the Christian Social party in 1920 informed 'German Christians' that the diabolical Jewish dragon of liberalism, democracy, Socialism and Bolshevism was strangling the Austrian eagle. An essay by

Pastor Gaston Ritter on *Jewry and the Shadows of the Anti-Christ* issued a warning against 'Jewry and the Satanic teachings of its protocols' – a reference to the *Protocols of the Elders of Zion*. In 1935 it was triumphantly stated that 'a Catholic bishop – the prince bishop of Seckau, Dr Pawlikowski, has by his imprimatur given this book the blessing of the church'.

Austrian Catholicism in the first Austrian Republic (1918–33) showed itself, in the person of leading representatives and influential circles and groups, to be strongly anti-liberal, anti-democratic, anti-Socialist and anti-Semitic. Its rejection, or at least profound distrust, of democracy and its open hostility towards liberalism (which was identified with educated and cultivated Jewry) formed a bond with German Catholicism and contributed to the weakness of both in the struggle against Nazism.

The Catholic church in Germany and Austria was unable to find any common language of humanity or politics with people of other beliefs – no platform on which its members might have come together in a joint resistance to National Socialism. When we consider how deeply Austrian Catholicism was infected with anti-democratic, illiberal, anti-humanist and anti-Semitic elements, it may seem surprising that it was in fact a number of Austrian Catholics who were the first in Europe fearlessly to take up the struggle against Hitler when Hitler was finding support – or at least polite acceptance – in the Vatican and in Rome, in London, Paris, Belgrade, Warsaw and Budapest.

The struggle of these Austrian Catholics against Hitler and against his confederates in their own country during the years 1933 to 1938 has not yet received adequate appraisal abroad. When in March 1939 Austria collapsed, the only state which was prepared to speak up for her was Socialist Mexico.

But here we are concerned, not with these, but with the Austrian Catholics who were infected by National Socialism.

A young Catholic historian from Vienna, Erika Weinzierl-Fischer, has courageously tried to provide documentary evidence of the way Austrian Catholics slid into National Socialism. (The 'forgetfulness' of Christians, who today do not wish to remember what they then said, did or did not do, shows how strong the temptation still is amongst clergy, theologians and laity to sweep things under the carpet.)

'In Catholic Austria anti-Semitism has for centuries been a matter of faith.' In the eighteenth century the writings of the professor of theology August Rohling showed symptoms of an anti-Semitism aimed at the physical destruction of Jewry. In the last decade of the nineteenth century anti-Semites in the nobility joined hands in Austria with the clergy. It was against them and the Christian Social lower classes that an association to strengthen resistance against anti-Semitism was founded in Vienna in 1891. Baron Arthur Gundacher von Suttner (the husband and colleague of Bertha von Suttner, the great champion of the world peace movement, at whose suggestion Alfred Nobel instituted the Nobel Peace Prize) and Count

Hoyos took a leading part in founding the association. In March 1938 National Socialist henchmen made a later Count Hoyos clean the streets.

The anti-Semitism of the Christian Social party found support in Vienna from the two theologians Sebastian Brunner and his successor Albert Wiesinger, editors of the *Kirchenzeitung*. The historian Richard Charmatz has called Father Wiesinger 'an altruistic fanatic of hate'. The Christian Social party organ *Reichspost* adopted the strongly anti-Semitic tone of the Vienna *Kirchenzeitung*, but had to modify this somewhat after 1895 on the instructions of Cardinal Secretary Rampolla as a result of complaints made against it in Rome by Catholic conservatives.

Karl Freiherr von Vogelsang, theoretician of the Christian Social movement, identified the Jews with capitalism: 'As long as we fail to remove the Jew from our own hearts, we shall continue to feel his foot on our necks.' Disciples of Vogelsang continued until 1938, and still continue even today, to identify 'the Jew, Mammon' with 'the diabolical spirit of Jewish capitalism within us.' 'Nothing but Jews . . .'. In Vienna Jews were everywhere, said Dr Karl Lueger in a famous anti-Semitic speech in the Reichsrat in 1890. He attacked the Jews for their 'unbelievably fanatical hatred and their insatiable love of revenge', and asked: 'What are wolves, lions, panthers, leopards, tigers and men in comparison with these beasts of prey in human form?' That is a language reminiscent of St John Chrysostom, Abraham a Sancta Clara and the sermons of many more recent pastors.

Father Scheicher complained in his biography of Sebastian Brunner in 1888 that the country showed no gratitude to those who wanted to defend 'our Aryan race against corruption and oppression at the hands of an alien nomadic people'. Anti-Semitic preachers and journalists in Vienna devised the jargon which Hitler was later to speak and write.

The Christian Social party programme after 1918 included a promise to fight against 'the excessive power of disruptive Jewish influences'. Commenting on this in 1927 in the periodical *Schönere Zukunft*, the Christian Social chancellor Mgr Dr Ignaz-Seipel wrote: 'The fact that the leaders and propagandists of Russian Bolshevism, of their Communistic allies in Germany and Austria and of the very radical and anti-clerical Austrian Socialists are mostly Jews, is surely explanation enough for the anti-Semitic flavour of public opinion.'

The *Schönere Zukunft* was a leading anti-democratic cultural periodical, which was also widely read in Catholic circles outside Austria. Seipel had hoped to play a leading political role in the empire. After 1918 he flirted for a while with democracy, then gave his support to a Fascist para-military organization, the *Heimwehr*, which was to become a deadly threat to his own Christian Social party.

'We have lost our emperor overnight.' Austrian bishops were of one mind with those many monarch-loving clergy who later pressed in Rome for the beatification of the 'martyr emperor' Charles, and who looked upon the

'Jewish' republic with fear and distrust. Official pronouncements by Austrian bishops against liberalism, Socialism and Bolshevism (they formed an inseparable trinity, first in the historical imagination of these bishops and then of the National Socialists) and their sceptical views on the 'so-called democratic constitution' were scarcely conducive (any more than in France during the nineteenth century) to Catholic acceptance of the new age.

A champion of anti-democratic Catholicism in the world of journalism was the eloquent Swabian, Dr Joseph Eberle. From 1913 to 1918 he was on the editorial staff of the *Reichspost*. He then founded the periodical *Die Monarchie*, which he renamed *Das Neue Reich* after the collapse of Austria. His favourite theme was: 'Democracy leads to bankruptcy'. He criticized the new Austrian constitution of 1 October 1920 with the devastating remark that 'The unrestricted right to vote contradicts the principles of Christian social teaching', and added: 'We expect salvation principally from the restoration of a strong ruling authority.'

Joseph Eberle called for an 'independent Christian dictator'; for the 'great saviour', for 'strong authority'. When the Fascist wave began to break over Europe, a section of the Catholic clergy in Italy, Germany, Spain, Portugal, Hungary, Slovakia, Croatia and Poland co-operated with governments which combined Fascist with older authoritarian elements.

Mgr Seipel, who died in the year Hitler seized power, caused a stir in 1929 by his criticism of democracy in a speech to students of Munich and Tübingen universities. At the end of 1932, in an interview in the *Berliner Börsenzeitung*, he declared that the contemporary form of democracy was quite alien to the German people. In some vital questions conscientious personal leadership was necessary, and 'better parliaments than we have at the moment' were no substitute for this. 'The nation itself,' he said, 'is at bottom tired of the glorification of an inflated parliamentary régime, and wants to see this development.'

There was, in fact, no question of 'glorifying' the parliamentary régime either in Austria or the dying Weimar Republic. The clever Mgr Seipel was, like some other churchmen, the victim here of a politico-religious form of language which proved very useful in preparing the way for National Socialism. It talked of 'people', 'race', 'leader', 'destiny', 'providence' – and also of the Jewish question being 'the final question'.

That was the principal theme of Joseph Eberle, who in 1925 built up the *Schönere Zukunft* as his mouthpiece when the *Neues Reich* proved insufficiently polemical.

On 18 April 1926 Eberle, Austria's Veuillot and Drumont, defined his attitude on the question of Catholics and Jews. He argued in favour of Catholic anti-Semitism and attacked what he called 'shallow humanism' and 'dangerous tolerance'. As models for the Austrian and German Catholic intelligentsia he pointed to Veuillot, Görres, Windthorst and 'the heroes of the Counter-Reformation and the romantic movement'. Eberle claimed: 'Resistance to Judaism is not un-Christian, but represents a return to the traditions of the church which have merely become dormant as a result of the Renaissance and the Reformation.'

Here Joseph Eberle was historically correct. He quoted the Catholic Richard von Kralik (who was campaigning against the more liberal Munich Catholicism): 'Culture is . . . necessarily anti-Semitic. Judaism as a principle is opposed to culture: it is the very opposite of culture.' Richard von Kralik was a very talented man, a prolific essayist, who collected a vast amount of material on the cultural history of Vienna and also wrote a large number of plays. Kralik had given his support in 1919 to a proposal for a national anthem for the Austrian Republic. This included the words: 'God preserve and protect our country from the Jews.' (Earlier it had been: 'God preserve Franz, the emperor . . .'.)

Eberle demanded early in his career that in all branches of economic and cultural life the Jews should be limited to the percentage they represented of the population. The Jews should also be placed under a special law. He argued that the interests of society required 'the confiscation of many large Jewish properties beyond a certain size, limited entry into many professions, and for other professions, as well as for certain institutions, the complete exclusion of Jews'.

The most outspoken writer and speaker was the Catholic social reformer, Anton Orel. His writings between 1921 and 1934 were aggressive and in tone like the *Stürmer* of the Nazi Julius Streicher. Orel combined strictures on Judah and the Mammon of Jewish and liberal capitalism with a condemnation of 'our miserable Jewish republic'. For Eberle too parliamentary democracy smelled 'too strongly of Polish ghettoes'. At Christmas 1927 Eberle evolved the campaign slogan which the Nazis after 1933 were to put into action much more brutally: 'Christians, buy at Christian shops.'

Orel thought that the God of the Jews was the Devil. This 'theological', politico-religious propaganda fell on fertile ground among the Christian Social population, in which anti-Semitism was becoming increasingly apparent, particularly after 1933. The university professors Oswald Menghin and Emmerich Czermak, at one time minister of education (in November 1933 he became the acting leader of the Christian Social party) may be regarded as the leading political spokesman of this anti-Semitic Catholicism.

In his *Ordnung in der Judenfrage* (Order in the Jewish Question) Czermak quoted indiscriminately Bishop Gföllner's pastoral letter, Goebbels, Rosenberg and Johannes von Leers (who later worked for Nasser's propaganda machine). Opposed to Czermak was the Jesuit Bela Bangha, who wrote *Katholizismus und Judentum* (Catholicism and Judaism). There was some internal Catholic resistance to 'exaggerated anti-Semitism' as well as efforts to differentiate a 'Christian' and church anti-Judaism from Nazi anti-Semitism. The *Neues Reich* (from which Eberle had just parted), the philosopher Dietrich von Hildebrandt, as well as the democrats in the Christian Social camp were also opposed to this anti-Semitism.

But more important – and of greater consequence for the future – was this. It was precisely the most prominent spiritual leaders and church leaders of Austrian Catholicism who, in their struggle against National Socialism, supported a 'Christian anti-Semitism' which in effect gave aid to the Nazis' more pernicious brand of anti-Semitism. In this context three men should be named: Father Wilhelm Schmidt SVD (Redemptorist), Father Georg Bichlmair SJ and the bishop of Linz, Gföllner.

In his letters Sigmund Freud saw in Father Wilhelm Schmidt, his declared opponent, an extremely influential man, both in the Vatican and among the leading Christian Social members of the Austrian government in Vienna. A biography of this grey eminence of political and spiritual Catholicism in Austria would provide interesting reading. Schmidt came from a poor artisan's family in what is now North Rhine-Westphalia. He worked himself up with perseverance and industry to become the head (with Koppers) of a Catholic school of ethnology, which depicted the peoples of earliest times in search of a 'Supreme Being' and taught a theory of 'primitive monotheism' which was propagated with missionary zeal throughout the Catholic world. A huge scientific and political apparatus was built up to persuade the learned Catholic world to accept this theory.

Wilhelm Georg Mühlmann, the Heidelberg ethnologist, said of this: 'Schmidt's picture is fantasy, not reality.' Schmidt had sketched an 'ideal, idyllic and romantic picture of "primitive peoples", which in no way related to the hard reality of the struggle for existence of barely civilized groups of humanity' (that is to say peoples in their natural state). 'We hear sentimental disquisitions on "love in the primeval forest" and on the "passionate love of flowers" of the primitive peoples, and learn at the same time that they regarded sexual relations as sinful.'

Mühlmann declared that Father Schmidt lacked any understanding of socio-religious factors. 'Development' for Schmidt, the anti-democrat, was merely the principle of deterioration. 'Development' always involved merely decline and degeneration. 'The application of Christian theological conceptions to quite different untheological facts is bound to produce distortions.'

The case of Wilhelm Schmidt is a good example of the way certain sciences arise from specific spiritual and political backgrounds. Schmidt had close contacts all his life with the Hapsburg dynasty, and fought its political cause. He emigrated to Freiburg in Switzerland before the arrival of the National Socialists, and after 1945 thoroughly settled accounts with anti-Christian Nazism – theologically, intellectually and politically.

Father Schmidt must never have realized how his own anti-Jewish, anti-democratic and mystical thinking, in all good faith, assisted the 'anti-Christ'. In 1934, that fateful year for Austria, he made a racial and anti-Semitic speech at a meeting of the leaders of Catholic Action of Vienna which finally caused an outcry in the Catholic world. In this speech he produced a variant of the anti-democratic theme which he had formulated at a Catholic conference in Vienna before the election of 1920. This was that the conquest of Vienna by the Turks in 1683 'would not have been as disastrous and disgraceful . . . as Vienna continuing to tolerate this alien Jewish domination.'

Turkey, we may observe, was the only country which erected a memorial to Benedict xv, the pope whose efforts to achieve peace in the First World War failed, not least because of the bitter resistance of nationalistic Italian, German and French Catholics. (In the sixteenth century the Jews came to Hungary with and under the protection of the Turks.)

On 18 March 1936 Father Georg Bichlmair SJ gave a lecture in Vienna which caused a stir: it was entitled 'The Jew and the Christian'. He said the Jewish people were depraved – collectively depraved – because of their apostasy. Bichlmair was against Jewish converts being admitted to senior positions, on account of their 'evil inherited characteristics', and he was of the opinion that the stipulations about Aryans in individual unions and associations could not, as a matter of Christian ethics, be rejected.

Bichlmair's extremely ambivalent speech – he himself was aware of this ambivalence – left the door open for either a mild or a severe form of anti-Semitism. Father Bichlmair was the nominal leader of the *Paulus-Werk*, which served the cause of Christian-Jewish understanding. He was also a co-founder of the 'K' movement (named after a social worker of that time, Countess Manuela Kielmansegg), which was devoted to the welfare of Jewish-born Christians. Later in the Third Reich a handful of brave Catholic men and women set up a relief organization for persecuted Jewish-born Christians under the personal protection of Cardinal Innitzer.

From 1933 onwards Nazi propaganda and publications loved to quote the pastoral letter of Bishop Gföllner of Linz. In this, dated 21 January 1933, the breaking of the harmful influence of Judaism was demanded not only as a right but 'as a matter of strict conscience for every convinced Christian'.

Dr Johannes Maria Gföllner had studied at the German School in Rome. He became bishop of Linz in 1915 and died in 1941. Gföllner was a legitimist, and was regarded as one of the biggest opponents of the Nazis in Austria. He was the political reporter at the Austrian bishops' conference, and in 1938 he was the only bishop who did not publish in his diocesan gazette the pledge of loyalty and the appeal of the Austrian bishops to vote for Hitler (after the Anschluss had been effected).

The pastoral letter of 21 January 1933 which, appearing as it did in Linz (Hitler's favourite town in Austria), was clearly in competition with National Socialism and its anti-Semitism, declared: 'Without doubt many Jews who are strangers to God exercise a very harmful influence in almost all fields of modern cultural life.' They were trying to 'poison the Christian national soul'. It went on to say: 'Degenerate Judaism in league with international freemasonry is also largely the pillar of Mammonist capitalism and largely the founder and apostle of Socialism and Communism, the herald and pacemaker of Bolshevism. To break down the harmful influence of Judaism is not only a right, but also a matter of strict conscience for every convinced Christian; and it is much to be desired that Aryans and Christians should appreciate the dangers and harm caused by the Jewish spirit, should combat them more effectively and not, openly or covertly, imitate and encourage them.'

Bishop Gföllner mentioned the – obviously very effective – ghettoes, which were just then being re-established in Germany: 'Our modern society does not need to expel the Jews from the country, but should, through its laws and administration, provide a strong barrier against all the intellectual rubbish and moral slime which, coming largely from Jewry, threatens to flood the world. At the same time we must agree, without any qualification, that there are also noble characters among the Jews. If National Socialism wants to incorporate only this spiritual and ethical form of anti-Semitism into its programme, there is nothing to stop it . . .'

'Nothing to stop it . . .' National Socialism was never 'stopped' in its anti-Semitism, anti-humanism, anti-liberalism, anti-democracy and anti-Socialism by the leaders of German Catholicism, who believed in 1933 that their hour had come too. But in Austria the bishops were horrified by the brutal events in Germany in this year 1933. In December the entire Austrian episcopate released a pastoral letter drafted by Bishop Gföllner which condemned 'the Nazi racial folly which would – indeed must – lead to racial hatred and international conflicts'. It also condemned the sterilization law and 'radical racial anti-Semitism'.

But *Schönere Zukunft*, which was the authoritative organ for the liveliest minds among educated Catholics, declared its solidarity with the Nazi burning of books on 8 May 1933. The murder of the Viennese philosopher, Moritz Schlick, in 1936 by one of his former pupils was taken as an opportunity to underline the unhealthy intellectual influence of Judaism. It did not occur to the inveterate anti-Semites of *Schönere Zukunft* that Moritz Schlick was not a Jew and that he derived his first name from his ancestor, Ernst Moritz Arndt. But, of course, he 'must' have been a Jew, because he disseminated a 'godless' and profoundly 'disruptive' positivist philosophy.

Catholic professors, theologians and publicists worked hard between 1931 and 1938 to reconcile church and National Socialism in Austria and to prepare the way for the Anschluss (though on that point they were not all in agreement). For the church leaders a statement of the Nuncio Sibilia in 1932 was significant. This declared: 'The important thing in deciding our attitude to National Socialism is whether or not it is hostile to the church. Two questions, in particular, have to be examined. First, the marriage question. Secondly, religious education in schools. If National Socialism is seen to be hostile to the church on these two questions, Catholics cannot give their votes to National Socialists in the elections. If National Socialism gives guarantees that it is not hostile to the church, then we should not fight it.'

In this ruling we see in a nutshell the whole tragedy of German and Austrian church Catholicism from 1933 onwards. The bishops and the Vatican tried to get from Hitler the assurance, that is to say, the promise of certain special rights to safeguard church interests. And in return for these they were ready to renounce human rights for all other people – including, by implication, Catholics.

In 1933 the Sudeten German university professor Dr Theodor Innitzer became archbishop of Vienna and cardinal. Innitzer, who was born in a very poor lower-middle-class family in Weipert-Neugeschrei, was an *anima candida*, essentially non-political and sincerely anxious to do the right thing. From his earliest days he was filled with a childlike faith in Germany. Although after 1945 Innitzer was much criticized by French and Swiss Catholics, and even in the Vatican, for his 'lapse' in March 1938 after Hitler's troops marched in, he had been in fact the first priest in the early autumn of 1938 who dared, in a sermon in St Stephen's Cathedral, to call for resistance to National Socialist terror.

The pastoral letter of Bishop Gföllner of Linz in January 1933 had, in addition to its reference to the strict duty of all Catholics to adopt a 'moral form of anti-Semitism', declared that it was impossible 'to be at the same time a good Catholic and a true National Socialist'. This pastoral letter quickly went through eight editions, was translated into foreign languages and produced a two-fold reaction among the Nazis. On Maundy Thursday 1933 National Socialists stuck a poster on the door of the Catholic press club building in Linz, which depicted Christ as a criminal hanging from a swastika. Beneath was the inscription: 'Once he was delivered up by Jewish gangs and crucified by Aryan Romans. Now, as Hitler's redeemer commandeth, we hang Christ on the swastika. Heil Hitler! Judah-Christ, die like a dog!'

This poster and this inscription might have served as a dire warning to European Catholics to remember the brother of Jesus in every persecuted individual and especially in every persecuted Jew.

But, for Catholic National Socialists, another interpretation of Gföllner's pastoral letter was both possible and typical. We can see it in a work produced by Austrian National Socialists of Catholic and German nationalist background. This was a fully illustrated popular book, which appeared in Dresden and Vienna in 1935, entitled *Antisemitismus der Welt in Wort und Bild* (Anti-Semitism throughout the World in Words and Pictures) with the subtitle 'The World Conflict and the Jewish Question'. The writer Dr Robert Körber and the professor Dr Theodor Pugel, a teacher of history, were the editors and principal authors. A civil servant, Professor Dr Benno Imendörffer, and a lawyer, Dr Erich Führer, were given as contributors. They thus formed a representative cross-section of the anti-Semitic professional world in Austria.

The work of these Austrians was dedicated to the Franconian leader, Julius Streicher. He, with his *Stürmer*, was systematically going about his ambitious task of bringing anti-Semitism to every German state school and every family within reach.

The history teacher Pugel informed his readers that the Jews were 'a kind of mulatto, compounded of off-white and black', far closer to the Negroes than to Aryans. 'The Jew is essentially a man of this world, and therefore a materialist.' (Here the old Manichaean 'Christian' disparagement of 'evil matter' asserts itself.) 'His true deity is the Golden Calf.' (That was an old theme for Catholic pulpit orators of the eighteenth century.) 'Moses was the first Jewish world revolutionary' – a favourite topic of conversation between Adolf Hitler and his close friend Dietrich Eckart in Munich in 1922–3. St Augustine had been an anti-Semite. Or Mordecai Pugel remarked that 'the founder of the international Jews' party called Social Democracy bore the same name'. That was also the conviction of many members of the Christian Social party in Vienna right up to Mgr Seipel's time, who believed that Judaism and Socialism were inseparable. Catacomb pictures showed the Aryan Christ – 'Christ, "the Galilean", the most outspoken anti-Semite of all time.'

'When the Jews of Palestine were driven out into all the provinces of the Roman empire, the seeds were sown of the future Jewish world revolution, the idea of which has not been completely banished even in the twentieth century.' (From Munich to Rome, from Ireland to Spain, Catholics saw Hitler as the saviour against the Jewish-Bolshevist world revolution).

Even as early as AD 131 the 'Jewish world revolutionaries' were at work, according to Pugel, instancing the activities of Akiba ben Joseph under Emperor Trajan, when 'the daemonic forces of the whole of world Jewry were working on the gigantic task of establishing the Jewish world empire.' 'Gigantic' is the only word that fits the world revolutionary activities of those diabolical supermen, the Jews. They could be outmatched only by the 'gigantic' edifice of the Third Reich and the searchlights of the Wehrmacht at the Nuremberg party rallies.

Now for Professor Pugel on the subject of 'early Christian anti-Semitism in the East'. The Aryan Christ and his apostles, he claimed, looked on anti-Semitism as the fundamental basis of the Gospel. 'With his merciless campaign against the Pharisees and Sadducees the "Galilean" Christ proclaimed to the world his anti-Semitic attitude . . . Christ, the non-Jew, the "Galilean" accomplished, by overthrowing the Mosaic law, the most significant act in human history. Christianity became the universal anti-Semitic bulwark against Judaization in the Roman empire.'

Here we may observe that if this was madness, there was method in it, and it was in line with an old tradition. Pugel followed the theological expropriation (to use Karl Marx's phrase for 'dispossession') of the Old Testament by the church fathers to its logical conclusion. If the Holy Scriptures did not belong to the Jews, as the church fathers claimed, why should Christ belong to them?

St Paul was chosen by Christ to be the 'spiritual bridge to the Aryan world'. 'In St Paul the anti-Semitic spirit of Christ prevailed.' Paul was no racial Jew. 'In Paul's case Aryan blood was in terrible conflict with the Mosaic law, which had probably been inculcated in him by converted ancestors.' Many theologians and priests have seen in St Paul the heroic fighter against the Jews.

A picture in the book showed the statue of St Peter in Rome. St Peter also was a 'Galilean' and a non-Jew (this formed a bridge to the alliance with the papacy). 'Christianity preserved the Mediterranean peoples from diabolical religious chaos under Jewish leadership.' In early Christian Rome, 'the great early Christian anti-Semite Justin' and 'the anti-Semitic Pope Callistus I' were prominent.

The book claimed that 'the famous church fathers, St Jerome . . . then Origen . . . and St Ambrose . . . were also anti-Semites.' And to Origen was attributed the statement that the Jews taught that Christians slaughtered boys and devoured them, and indulged in irregular sexual relations. 'The profiles of many South Tiroleans show undeniable Jewish strains,' according to the old Viennese nationalist Pugel. This evil miscegenation had probably taken place in Carolingian times. Charlemagne himself had been possibly of Jewish origin. 'His physiognomy is that of an aged Jew.' He kept a harem like an oriental despot (Author's note: the young Adolf Hitler in Vienna was subject to sexual envy in regard to the Jews) – and 'was filled with diabolical hatred of everything that was German'. He had Jewish monks as his advisers and the Jew, Ephraim, acted as his finance minister. (The theologians responsible for Pinay's *Conspiracy against the Church* in 1963 treated Charlemagne in just the same way.)

'The Grand Inquisitor of Spain was the baptized Jew Torquemada, to whose bloodthirstiness hundreds of thousands of Aryan Christians fell victim.' At this point in the argument the paths between Pugel and Pinay divide, only to meet again: 'Pope Gregory VII must be regarded as the most assiduous anti-Semite of the Middle Ages.' Innocent III, also, 'was an emphatic anti-Semite'. The good Christian had to be a racial anti-Semite 'if he wants to be regarded as a true disciple of Christ in the sense of the Gospel'. Here Pugel and Pinay are speaking the same language. A picture of Innocent III taken from a mosaic was captioned 'The mighty pope and fearless anti-Semite' who finally forced the Jews into the ghetto in 1215.

On the subject of ritual murders, pictures showed the place Judenstein near Rinn 'where the murder took place' of Andreas Oxner (Anderl von Rinn). The Bull of Pope Benedict XIV of 22 February 1755, honouring the 'blessed Andrew', was suitably acclaimed.

At the beginning of the modern period came 'the most powerful and most fearless anti-Semite in priest's robes', John Capestrano (1386–1456). The Christian, Catholic and National Socialist hagiographers, striving in this book to represent to the Christians of 1935 the thousand-year-old struggle of the saints and heroes against the diabolical Jew, devote much attention to him in words and pictures.

Capestrano had Jews hanged in Breslau and Schweidnitz. He was canonized under Pope Alexander VIII in 1690. 'Here is the proof that radical anti-Semitism was not opposed to true Christianity.'

Here indeed was an eye-opener for a hesitant Christian people! If a saint could kill Jews, why should one not approve similar actions today or tomorrow?

The persecution of the German nation after the appearance of Luther was principally the work of the Jews. 'The notorious Jew, Pope Alexander VI' and the Jewish nuncio in Germany, Aleander, were chiefly responsible for the split in the German nation. Pictures of that great man, Martin Luther, but pictures too of Savonarola, 'the heroic fighter for a pure and genuine Christianity' – an interesting example of Protestant and Catholic reconciliation under the banner of a joint struggle against Judaism.

But the great man Luther came in for some criticism: 'If Luther had been an anti-Semite from the beginning, there would no longer be a Jewish problem in many states of Europe in the twentieth century.'

The Thirty Years' War from 1618 to 1648 was 'the diabolical result of a Jewish world policy designed to destroy the German people'. The Enlightenment (throughout the nineteenth century and to some extent still the butt of Catholic writers and educationalists) was part of Jewry's attempts to achieve world domination. 'That hateful flower of the Enlightenment, freemasonry, founded in London on 24 June 1717, is deeply enmeshed in international Judaism.'

Worried Catholics of the nineteenth and twentieth centuries, imprisoned in their own ghetto, had an inner need to see their mortal enemies presented in a simple form: Jewish freemasonry was one of the most obvious. Adolf Hitler met this need for simplification.

'The French Revolution, which was the product of the racially infected sewer of humanity in southern France, was on the side of Judaism.' The Jacobins were led by Judaism. 'Since all the humanitarian fuss during the Enlightenment, Hebraic domination has spread like wildfire.'

'Humanitarian fuss': even to this day we still encounter this inhuman language in Catholic and other pronouncements, for instance, on the question of capital punishment.

Austrian anti-Semites tried early – about 1880 – to establish contacts with anti-Semites in France, Germany, and other countries. In Pugel's picture primer appropriate space was given to descriptions of anti-Semitism in Africa, amongst the Arabs and in America (picture of Henry Ford and speech of Congressman Luis McFadden on 29 May 1933: 'The Jews are conquering America', as well as England and France. Pictures showed the propagandist work of 'The Britons' in England. Their stickers 'Bolshevism is Judaism' and 'Can a Jew be an Englishman?' had their models in the Viennese anti-Semitic propaganda industry sixty years before. France was said to have had a great and wonderful anti-Semitic history. There was a tribute to Drumont. Today, we were told, French anti-Semitism was taking a political form and 'the national and elemental forces of the French people' were awakening. 'Anti-Semitism is daily on the increase in France too: the papers *Le Jour* and *Libre Parole* are clear proofs of it.'

Great horizons were opening up for the member of the German and Austrian Catholic lower middle class who had felt his isolation and encirclement in the modern world and in the past. He would not be alone if he became a National Socialist: for he would find himself in a thousand-year-old company of saints and great men of all periods, in the midst of a winning world movement of anti-Semitism. The anti-Semite Internationale would overcome the diabolical Internationale of the reds, the liberals and the freemasons.

The description of French anti-Semitism ended with the pious wish: 'God grant that the die will be cast for the salvation of Aryan humanity, and that in France also new life will blossom out of the ruins of a foundering liberal, democratic, Marxist world.'

'God grant . . .' On a National Socialist election poster in 1933 the papal nuncio in Bavaria, Vasallo di Torregrossa, greeted the Führer with these words: 'For a long time I did not understand you. But I long tried to do so. Today I understand you.' The election poster added: 'And every German Catholic today understands Adolf Hitler and will vote "Yes" on 12 November.'

Pugel defended the pogroms and excesses of Russian and Polish Christians against the Jews by referring to the revelations on the subject of Jewish murder (ritual murders and poisonings) made by the professor of theology August Rohling and the periodical *Civiltà Cattolica* in Rome. Pugel declared: 'According to *Civiltà Cattolica*, a periodical published by the Jesuits and of unimpeachable authority, the use of Christians' blood in food and drinks, at the circumcision, marriage and death of an orthodox Jew, on the great day of atonement or at the Feast of the Passover – in the mazzoth and in wine – and at the Feast of Purim, were regarded as a means of salvation for the Jewish soul.

'It must be stated categorically . . . that it is a *scientific* fact, affirmed by the Catholic church, that Jewish circles, and perhaps also secret sects, subscribed to blood mysteries in all ages.' From this it was shown that Bolshevism was one vast, gigantic blood orgy which found a model in the ritual murders of Christians. 'Terrible are the bloody deeds in Russian history which were devised, ordered or carried out by Jews.' 'The shots fired at the Austrian heir to the throne, Archduke Franz Ferdinand, at Sarajevo on 28 June 1914 by representatives of Jewish freemasonry were also gun salutes to the new champions of Jewish world domination, who had for long regarded Russia as their first prey.'

Judaism was Bolshevism and Bolshevism was Judaism in practice. 'The tsarina was an anti-Semite. The White Guard judge who investigated the tragedy of the tsar in Ekaterinburg, Sokolov by name, found carved on the window post of the tsar's room, next to the tsarina's beloved swastika sign, the date of arrival in Ekaterinburg (the present Sverdlovsk) – 17 April 1918.'

Pugel, the history teacher, had identified Judaism with Bolshevism. But with the inevitable absence of logic of the anti-Semite – for whom the laws of logic and contradiction seem suspended in his state of political mysticism and alchemy when brought face to face with the overwhelming phenomenon of the diabolical Jewish superman or sub-human – he noticed that there was also Bolshevist anti-Semitism. He commented: 'Yet, even under the bloody Communist tyranny, hostility to the Jews is one of the strongest features of Bolshevist Russia.' Since 1930 there had been an anti-Semite opposition within the Russian Communist party.

After Russia, the Viennese civil servant Benno Imendörffer dealt in a detailed and well-informed way with anti-Semitism in the old Austro-Hungarian empire. Anti-Semitism in modern Austria was described by Dr Erich Führer, who was to have an important career in Austria in 1938 after the Anschluss. Führer dealt in detail with Bishop Gföllner's pastoral letter of 21 January 1933, which 'called for a struggle against Judaism', and he quoted a comment on it from *Die Schönere Zukunft*: 'Austria is certainly the most Judaized of all the German lands, and so it was only right that an Austrian bishop should refer openly to this unfortunate state of affairs.'

It is perhaps of interest that the Christian National Socialist anti-Semites of Austria suggested in this book a kind of 'Austrian solution' of the Jewish question: 'No serious-minded anti-Semite . . . wants a return of the ghetto or the yellow badge.' Another Austrian solution was needed, for the benefit of both German and Jewish peoples – and that was a special status for the Jews. This corresponded exactly with the proposals made by Catholic theologians and leading Christian Social politicians in Vienna between 1920 and 1933.

Robert Körber described anti-Semitism in the German Reich up to 1931. He observed with pain that Eisenmenger's book *Das entdeckte Judentum* (Judaism Discovered) was confiscated by the imperial court in Vienna. Fortunately, it has been possible to get two copies to Berlin under the protection of King Frederick 1, who had the book printed at his own expense, after lengthy and fruitless interventions with the Austrian emperor on Eisenmenger's behalf:

Picture of a Talmud school, with the observation: 'Here we see the anti-Christ and anti-German in the flesh'. In the nineteenth century Judaism broke upon the defenceless German people: 'Revolutionary sub-humans and

Asiatic literary figures constituted the "leadership" which the Germans believed in 1812, ran after in 1848 and blindly obeyed in 1918 ... The revolution of 1848 can be described as the real beginning of present-day Jewish domination. What happened between 1812 and 1848 was only the prelude to the great German tragedy after 1848 – the peaceful conquest of Germany by a Jewish people alien to Europe.'

Walther Rathenau was quoted (*Impressionen*, 1902): 'Strange vision! In the midst of German life a separate, alien human tribe ... an Asian horde on the sands of Brandenburg! Thus they live in a semi-voluntary ghetto, not a vital limb of the nation but a foreign organism in its body ...' This confession, in which Jewish experience of suffering, Jewish self-criticism and Jewish self-hate were painfully compounded, was used here as king's evidence against Judaism.

There was a large picture of Richard Wagner, chief witness in the cause of anti-Semitism. Then followed: 'The father of anti-Judaism, the faithful guardian of the German people, Theodor Fritsch.' Like one crying in the wilderness. [The writer apparently did not notice that with these words he was himself using an expression connected with Jewish prophets in the Old Testament] he stood, the unyielding and never-tiring hero, who sacrificed property and freedom and devoted everything to this holy war against Asia in Europe.' This holy war began in 1939 and for many is not ended even today.

Then there was a quotation from Paul de Lagarde (1827–91): 'We Europeans, we Christians, are not what we should be when there are still Jews amongst us.' Lagarde demanded, in exemplary fashion, that the Jews be expelled from Europe.

The book then returned to the present age: 'Whoever travels with open eyes through German lands or asks German girls ... will find that it is precisely they who are pursued by the Jews and treated as sexual booty.' In fact, of course, Jews often prove attractive to such girls – just as educated clerics in medieval courts had more success with the noble ladies than their ignorant knights. Sexual envy acted as a driving force both in the case of Adolf Hitler and in the propaganda of the *Stürmer*.

'When we consider what vast power Jewish businessmen (store owners, lawyers, film and theatre agents, providers of services and many others) exercise over the army of working German women, and when we realize how they regard Aryan women only as girls like their own, then we are bound to recognize their satanic danger.' A German actress had 'first to give her body to the Asiatics before she could bring her art to the German people'.

Here, in fact, an especially sensitive aspect of German-Jewish relations was broached. Distorted and exaggerated it may be, but a certain sexual tyranny did make itself felt, which the Jew shared in some fields, such as cinema, theatre and publicity, with his 'Aryan' colleagues: an unscrupulous tendency to exploit the economic dependence and the professional prospects of women seeking work and employment. The Jews concerned came mainly from the East and were therefore rootless, *déracinés*. Some of them early saw the possibilities of exploiting sex commercially in magazines and the like. The old German Jewry in Prussia tended to be puritan, and its members lived out their passions and sufferings within the narrow circle of their own closely supervised families. The fact that some of these attacks on the sexual tyranny of Jewish managers were partly justified contributed substantially to the political ensnarement of some Christian circles.

The founding of the Weimar Republic ('the Jewish revolution of 1918') was described as the 'greatest victory of Judaism on German soil'. 'And on the ruins of the German spiritual cathedral the satanic edifice of Jewish cultural Bolshevism was established.' The heading 'cultural Bolshevism' included practically everything that was connected, or was thought to be connected, with modern art, poetry and literature – from Picasso to Thomas Mann.

With the evil slogan 'The Jewish Revolution of 1918', National Socialism killed several birds with one stone; the Social Democrats, whose support for the Weimar Republic was half-hearted; the radical left, which fought openly against the Republic; and the Centre party, which had only partially and hesitantly committed itself to it. So, finally, it was able to win over the right wing which, though split into little groups and oddments, was nevertheless united on the one issue of hatred towards the Weimar Republic.

Writing about anti-Semitism in the German Reich after 1932, Robert Körber remarked: 'The church's anti-Semitism is almost as old as the church of Christ itself.' Pope Innocent III, the nineteenth-century Bishop Konrad Martin of Paderborn and the bishop of Linz, Johannes Maria Gföllner, were paraded for the benefit of Christian and National Socialist anti-Semites. In addition, there were references to Anton Orel, Emmerich Czermak (the acting chairman of the Austrian Christian Social party), Oswald Menghin and Joseph Eberle: 'Resistance to Judaism means a resumption of church traditions which have become dormant.' This awakening of the sleeping church in the souls of men was to prove disastrous. The call 'Rome, awake!' came to be identified with the call 'Germany, awake!' Both Rome and Germany were to be roused from their slumber by the anti-Semitic movement.

The doctrine of 'equal rights for every human being' must 'be rejected with moral indignation as an unnatural attempt to overthrow the order willed by God. It must be rejected by every truth-loving and responsible civilized man who is still able to see and hear Man as he really is and speaks ... "The strength of a people and their fatherland lies in the blood and in the home." These prophetic words were spoken by no less a person than the cardinal prince bishop of Vienna, Dr Theodor Innitzer, at the Catholic Action festival meeting in the diocese of Seckau on 26 March 1933. As for the application of these prophetic words, we read: 'If, from a Christian point of view, the death penalty is justified for criminals, then we can justify before Our Lord the sterilization of persons with criminal characteristics, which does not involve any loss of life.' 'Is an army of idiots, lunatics and congenital criminals to be permanently accommodated in hygienic institutions at the expense of healthy people, while the latter often have to live in cellars?' 'Is then the idea of a planned selection, improvement and increase of those favoured by the lord of Creation and the careful reduction, neutralization and *elimination* [my italics] of those who suffer from hereditary weakness through the *unkindness* of fate or the fault of their parents, "inhuman", "un-Christian" or "barbaric"?' Körber's answer was: 'No: it was rather true Christianity in action'!

This is an example of test case politics. The question was: How far could one go in practice without encountering strong resistance from the church and Christians? Between 1933 and 1939 National Socialism tested the reaction of the churches and public opinion in Germany, abroad and all over the world by stages: first to the disfranchisement, then to the expropriation, expulsion and collection in concentration camps of Jews, Socialists and other opponents. Later it indulged in preliminary testing-out of the 'final solution' of the Jewish question – by introducing compulsory sterilization and then liquidation of 'people unfit to live'. Here National Socialism encountered a decisive rejection by the church. It did not, however, encounter any opposition to its 'efforts to solve the Jewish question' or to its destruction and 'neutralization' of liberals, democrats, Socialists and Communists.

Anti-Semitism throughout the World now returned to the individual Jew, claiming that we were standing at the 'deathbed of the German soul'. The most widely read books in the German world were the trashy works of Jewish writers. 'Do not most of our women dance to the tunes of the sensual desert people?' it asked. The Jewish-Asiatic libertine seduced the German woman into becoming his whore. It gave the Jew 'an ecstatic feeling of revenge' to subjugate 'women of the blond and noble German race' by means of sexual intercourse. Here Jewish self-incriminatory evidence of a dubious kind was cited – Anselma Heine about the poet Jakobowski in 1912.

As for the solution of the Jewish question, the slogan was: 'The domination of all our cultural institutions by the Jews can no longer continue.' This slogan was taken from a speech in Vienna in 1933 by the grey eminence of the Christian Social party, Father Wilhelm Schmidt – a case of the churchman going along with National Socialism to the point where theories become practice.

'Down the ages war was always for the Jews merely good business, while for the Aryans it meant a terrible loss of blood . . .' 'No honest man can any longer deny that Judaism wants to destroy us. To help ensure that this does not happen is the task and duty of every German, Christian and Aryan today.'

These sentences stood in bold print like commandments in this bible of anti-Semitism. What was dangerous was the confidence of the assertion that the Jews wanted to destroy Christians and Germans. How was this intention to be frustrated? The author left the question open – or rather he answered without words: by the destruction of the Jews.

'Since the Jewish people brought the Saviour to the Cross, it has no longer been the chosen but the *accursed* [my italics] people . . .'

Caption to a picture: 'The courageous soldier of God, Fahter Josef Deckert of Vienna.' This was the man who as early as 1897 had called for an aliens' law for the Jews. Father Deckert had demanded: 'The Jews must be *rendered harmless* to the Christian peoples: they must come under an aliens' law. The emancipation of the Jews must go.'

Leading Catholics like Father Wilhelm Schmidt and Oswald Menghin were again quoted. 'The Jew remains a Jew even after baptism.' Any sort of pastoral care for baptized Jews would be very difficult. This led to the demand: 'In its own interest the church must co-operate with the Nordic idea . . .' What about the pogrom? 'It is not the Christians who persecute the Jews, but the Jews the Christians.' 'If anyone is responsible for pogroms, then it is partly the intellectuals among the people concerned, because they fail to support the people in its struggle against Judaism. It is also partly the responsibility of the Jews themselves, whose predatory habits cause conflict and whose intellectual and financial brow-beating of the upper stratum of the nation (the professional classes, press, business, consumers, banking, etc.) deprives the people of leadership and consequently leads to violence.'

Picture of a poster proclaiming: 'Between 1910 and 1925, thirteen Jews entered Germany daily from Eastern Europe.' Underneath the picture was the comment: 'Thanks to the chaotic racial ideas of liberal democracy Germany has become a colonial land for Eastern Jews in the twentieth century.'

The book concluded: 'Whoever still has respect for historical facts and does not reject the spiritual authority of our great poets and thinkers must accept anti-Semitism as a sacred duty in the defence of our people, our culture and our fatherland.'

The authors of this Christian-Catholic and National Socialist primer of anti-Semitism strictly condemned individual acts of violence against the Jews. They confidently left the solution of the Jewish problem in the hands of the Führer and his loyal paladins – such as the Franconian leader Julius Streicher, to whom this work was dedicated.

The last picture showed the hero Siegfried as a god of Light, wielding his sword Notung against Satan and the powers of Darkness (Richard Wagner's *Siegfried* – Act I).

Österreich unter Judas Stern (Austria under Judah's Star, Vienna, 1912) was the title of a book by Dietrich Eckart. This poet and journalist sat at his favourite table in the 'Brennessel' wine-parlour in Schwabing, the Munich artists' quarter, holding forth to friends and all others who believed in the future. Berlin and Weimar were no good, a new party had to be formed with a leader who was a man of the people. He should preferably be a bachelor – to attract the women.

Dietrich Eckart took part with his close friend Adolf Hitler in the march to the Munich Feldherrnhalle on 8–9 November 1923. This was Hitler's first attempt at a putsch. Eckart was taken into custody and died shortly after his release. On 1 March 1924 the Hoheneichen Verlag in Munich published his unfinished manuscript *Der Bolschewismus von Moses bis Lenin* (Bolshevism from Moses to Lenin), subtitled 'Dialogue between Adolf Hitler and Myself, as a testimony to the Christian attitude of the national movement'. The publishers included in it a postscript, which said: 'We express the hope that after the high treason trial at present impending against him, Adolf Hitler will be good enough to complete this almost finished work.'

Adolf Hitler did, after his fashion, complete his talks with Dietrich Eckart – by writing *Mein Kampf* during the period of his detention. Eckart's 'Dialogue between Adolf Hitler and Myself' is more intimate and less reserved than *Mein Kampf* (which certainly is not lacking in threats of violence) and conveys a clever picture of the seething, explosive intellectual world of these frustrated coffee-house litérateurs, journalists, agents and hacks of political adventurers in Munich.

The Paris of Edouard Drumont and the Vienna of Jörg Lanz von Lieben-fels with its 'First Anti-Semitic Reading Room' in the Landstrasse, join hands with the Munich of this period, which has the distinction of having kept Hitler in Germany. Under the patronage of conservative Christian Catholic circles, Hitler was able to form his political plans before the November putsch and maintain himself after his release from prison. The Bavarian People's party, which split away from the Centre party in the Weimar Republic, stabbed both the Centre party and democracy in the back. Among other things it helped Hindenburg, the candidate of the anti-democratic national front, to become president in preference to the Centre party candidate, Marx.

Today we can no longer know for certain to what extent Eckart put his own views into the mouth of his friend Hitler. But the fundamental intellectual and political tenets they held in common are obvious. Moreover, Hitler was described with an intimacy of authentic detail which has been confirmed by other and later observers of his 'table talk'. These early conversations, as far as the Jews were concerned, already contained a foretaste of the final solution.

'Adolf Hitler indicated the hidden, secret force which ordered everything in a certain way. "It's there. It's been there since the beginning of history. You know what it's called – the Jew!" '

'Taking the Old Testament, he quickly went through the pages, and said, "There, look at it, the recipe for the way the Jews have always concocted their hellish brew. We anti-Semites are fools. We hit on everything except what is most important." And he read with a harsh voice, emphasizing each word: "And I will set the Egyptians against the Egyptians and they shall fight, everyone against his brother, and everyone against his neighbour, city against city, and kingdom against kingdom . . ." '

The Old Testament was quoted to show the Bolshevist background, the thousand-year-old Jewish world revolution. Then, to demonstrate the incapacity of the Jew to fit into human society Henry Ford, Walther Rathenau and Heine were quoted – or rather interpreted.

England was Judaized. Since Cromwell's time it had been totally Judaized. 'I once saw that leading freemason Edward VII in person: it was the classical picture of a Stock Exchange Jew. And he had a lot of Jews round him. Since then the centre seems to have been moved to America.' According to Sombart, Jews made Columbus' first voyage possible: that was one of Dietrich Eckart's contributions to the conversation.

There was a discussion about Theodor Herzl, Zionism and the new Jewish state. There were references to Luther, to the Aryan Jesus Christ, to the church and its campaign against ritual murder. The conversation ebbed and flowed. It roamed excitedly and impulsively over the depths and heights of world history. Everywhere the diabolical Jew was at work, seducing and corrupting the nations. Dietrich Eckart mentioned Jesus Christ's struggle against the Jews. 'Although he said "Love your enemies",' Hitler replied. ' "Peace certainly, with a proper enemy, an open one, even a brutal one, whom one can still love. One can at least respect him, and that is what Christ meant. But that we should take to our hearts sheer beasts, men whom no love in the world could deter from poisoning our souls and bodies, it never occurred to Christ to accept that. He didn't do it himself. On the contrary he hit as hard as he could . . ." '

I might add here that in many conversations with Catholic clergy and laity after 1945 on the subject of the Christian attitude to Communists, I have heard the same arguments concerning Christ advanced as those expressed by Hitler in 1922 with regard to the Jews.

In their talk Hitler and Eckart quoted Luther and St Thomas Aquinas – against the Jews. Then Hitler made an attack on Jewish popes and Jewish church dignitaries. And here he added: 'Was that Catholicism which they represented? No, it was Judaism. Let us take only one example: the selling of indulgences. That was the Jewish spirit, its very essence. *We both are Catholics* [my italics]; but may we not say that?'

Hitler and Dietrich Eckart, in their intimate conversations, were as little inhibited as the authors of the essays in Pinay's *Conspiracy against the Church* which was handed to all the Vatican Council fathers in 1962.

Hitler continued: 'Do they really mean to tell us that the church was never at fault? It is just *because* we are Catholics that we say it. It has nothing to do with Catholicism. We know that would remain untouched even if half the hierarchy consisted of Jews.' (Hitler in 1922 was far more 'optimistic' and moderate than Pinay in 1962!) 'In general one can say that the popes of Germanic origin were a purer embodiment of Catholicism than the Italians or the Spaniards. The German Hildebrand, as Gregory VII, upheld it with greater consistency than any other. So long as he was at the helm, there was no pernicious equality for the Jews.'

Dietrich Eckart spoke up: ' "And what is the position *now*?" I interrupted him. "One Catholic priest after another is being tortured to death in Russia last gasp. Satan and Judas have their monuments [Catholic anti-Communist propaganda has the same images to depict the 'synagogue of Satan' which is Bolshevism.] Rome is unable to give the child its proper name. Sometimes there's a small move and then it's finished. Catholicism wants to speak up, but its tongue is paralysed by Judaism. You know, of course, what Trebitsch said: Once Germany is Bolshevist the Jews will deal with Rome. As a Jew, he should know." ' (Here Hitler was referring to the Viennese anti-Semitic Jew, Arthur Trebitsch, who regarded himself as the leader of an Aryan world.)

'Hitler then changed his ground and said: "Rome will pull itself together, but only after we have done the same. Only the solidity of the German can open the eyes of the world. A second Hildebrand will appear, an even greater one who will separate the chaff from the grain. And one day it will be said that the division of the church is a thing of the *past*." '

A second Hildebrand: a pope who, together with the Führer of the German Reich, would deliver the world from Bolshevism. Up to 1945 Catholics thought of Pope Pius XII in this role beside the Führer; and when the Führer disappeared, they ascribed it to the pope alone.

The conversation then assumed a strongly anti-Protestant tone. Ex-Jewish theologians and church dignitaries were cited to show how the Evangelical church and its theology had been Judaized.

Hitler declared: 'There is no hope for our Protestants. Honest people but simple fellows, the Protestant Schopenhauer calls them. The Bible is not a cookery book.' The positive and negative aspects of Luther were discussed in detail, and Hitler acknowledged Luther as both a friend and an enemy to the Jews. Dietrich Eckart feared the Jews 'would represent even Luther as a Jew'. Hitler nodded earnestly and replied: 'I know. *The most terrible tragedy.* [Emphasis in original.] A guilt of such terrible consequence that today our whole culture is threatened with ruin from it – and done in all innocence! One of the greatest Germans, the innocent cause of the German collapse! Luther, the mighty opponent of the Jews, unconsciously becomes their fateful herald. Incredible, I tell you, incredible! And just a wretched ten to twenty years too late! When everything had been settled. Earlier he was body and soul for the betrayer. Then the Hebrew were still cousins and brothers of

Our Lord, and we Christians only relations by marriage and outsiders . . .
Erzberger when he was alive could not have acted more insanely.'

Matthias Erzberger, here likened by Hitler to Luther, was a well-known
Centre party politician who was murdered by right-wing extremists as a
betrayer of Germany. But Hitler claimed to be greatly impressed by 'Luther,
the man of the people, the son of humble folk'. In this sense, he was prepared
to concede that Luther had, to a certain extent, prepared the way for his own
work. 'All the same, Luther was a great man, a giant. With one blow he
heralded the new dawn! He saw the Jew as we are only now beginning to see
him today. But unfortunately too late, and not where he did the most harm –
within Christianity itself. Ah, if he had seen the Jew at work there, seen him
in his youth! Then he would not have attacked Catholicism, but the Jew
behind it. Instead of totally rejecting the church, he would have thrown his
whole passionate weight against the *real* culprits. Instead of glorifying the
Old Testament, he would have branded it as the armoury of the anti-Christ.
And the Jew, the Jew would have stood there in his terrible nakedness, as a
perpetual warning. The Jew would have had to leave the church, society, the
halls of princes, the castles of knights, and the houses of citizens. For Luther
had the strength and the courage and the invincible will. There would never
have been a split in the church nor the war which, in accordance with the
wishes of the Jews, caused Aryan blood to flow in rivers for thirty years.'

The conversation turned directly to Bolshevism, to the 'blood-stained
Jewish dictatorship in Russia'. Dietrich Eckart suspected that Rome wanted
to come to a diplomatic agreement with it. Hitler wished to hear from Rome
a language towards Jewish Bolshevism like that spoken by 'Gregory VII, the
church fathers St Chrysostom and St Thomas Aquinas, and all genuine
Christians of outstanding calibre'. (Pinay's *Conspiracy against the Church* of 1962
adopted exactly the same tone.) The conversation then turned on the historical débâcle of Protestantism: from the standpoint of two Catholics in
Catholic Munich in 1922.

Protestantism, Hitler and Eckart agreed, was early undermined and
wrecked by Jews. Dietrich Eckart then drew attention to the sad fate of the
Jesuits: 'The knightly Loyola attacked the spirit which he thought was
Lutheranism. But in a trice the Polish Jew Polanco pulled the wool over his
eyes and the Jews had the reins in their hands. The moral theology of the
Jesuits looks damnably like the moral teaching of the Talmud. The majority
of Jesuits fought Protestantism and freemasonry in good faith, and the
majority of Protestants and freemasons fought Jesuitism.' The wire-pullers,
the Jews, laughed at both.

Later in the conversation, in which Hitler also came to talk about 'the
wonder of modern Jewry: Moses Mendelssohn' and the Judaized Berlin of
his time, Dietrich Eckart again drew attention to Luther and his demands
that synagogues and Jewish schools should be burnt down. To this Adolf
Hitler replied: 'The burning would have helped us damned little. The

point is that, even if there never had been a synagogue, a Jewish school, the Old Testament and the Talmud, the Jewish spirit would still have been there and been doing its work. It has been there since the beginning, and no Jew, not a single one, has failed to embody it. This comes out very clearly in the case of the so-called enlightened Jews.'

Here a thought suggested itself which, however, Hitler did not actually express: if every Jew embodies the evil, diabolical Jewish spirit, then it is not sufficient to burn synagogues, as in 1928: every Jew would have to be exterminated.

Almost automatically the conversation returned to the subject of Jewish Bolshevism. Hitler's thought processes concerning this were compulsive: in his speeches and his intimate table talk in the Führer headquarters during the war he always came back to the same themes. In his view Jewish Bolshevism had transformed Russia into a desert, as the Elders of Zion had demanded, and it was now trying to destroy Germany through Communism. Hitler declared that the Communist party in Germany was being maintained by Jews.

With the following remarks by Hitler the unfinished manuscript of Dietrich Eckart broke off: 'It is,' he said, 'as you once wrote. We can only understand the Jew when we know what he is finally aiming at. It is something beyond world domination, the *destruction* of the world. He thinks he must bring the whole of humanity under his subjection, to be able to create for it a paradise on earth, as he conceives it. [This is an indirect recognition of the Messianic hope and effort of the Jews to lead the whole of humanity into God's kingdom – on this earth.] Only he can do this, he believes, and it will certainly turn out like that. But we see from the methods he uses that he has secretly some other aim. While he pretends to help humanity, he drives it to desperation, madness and destruction. If he is not stopped, he will destroy it. That is what he wants and aims at – although he has a vague idea that in the process he will destroy himself. He cannot avoid it: he has to do it. [In this passage Adolf Hitler draws a self-portrait of his own dark urges, his despair and his will for self-destruction which he expressed by leading the German people to death.] This feeling that his own existence depends entirely on that of his victim seems to me to be the main reason for his hate. It is a question of having to destroy someone with all means at one's disposal, but of suspecting at the same time that that will inevitably lead to one's own destruction. If you like, it is the tragedy of Lucifer.'

Catholic and other Christian apologists of the attitude of the churches under National Socialism have tended to obscure the very concrete social, political and theological reasons that caused the churches to slip down into the service of Hitler. They in particular have preferred to make mystical references to Hitler's 'satanic', 'demoniac' and 'Lucifer-like' character. The *writer* Adolf Hitler – for this is what he called himself – here stands self-revealed in this conversation with probably his most intimate friend Dietrich

Eckart in Munich 1922–3. He has described his own subconscious state, with all its hatred, despair, will to destroy and urge towards self-destruction. Into his fixation with the mortal enemy he has projected everything which resided in his own ego. Hitler's 'Jew' is a reflex of his 'death wish', of his undeveloped, immature and frustrated underground.

In the early hours of 29 April Adolf Hitler, as Führer and Chancellor, wrote his personal and political testament in the bunker of the Berlin Reichskanzlei. He was, as Alan Bullock has said, 'still recognizably the old Hitler. From first to last there is not a word of regret, nor a suggestion of remorse. The fault is that of others, above all that of the Jews, for even now the old hatred is unappeased.'

Adolf Hitler in his political testament said of the Second World War: 'I did not want this war. It was desired and instigated solely by those international statesmen who were either of Jewish descent or worked for Jewish interests.

'Centuries will pass, but out of the ruins of our towns and monuments, hatred will always revive against the people ultimately responsible, whom we have to thank for everything: international Jewry and its helpers! . . . I have also made it plain that, if the nations of Europe are again to be regarded as mere bundles of shares to be bought and sold by those international conspirators in money and finance, then that race, Jewry, which is the real cause of this murderous struggle, will be saddled with the responsibility . . .'

The political testament ended with the words: 'Above all, I charge the leaders of the nation and those under them scrupulously to observe the laws of race and mercilessly to oppose the universal poisoner of all peoples, international Jewry.'

On Sunday, 29 April 1945 at four o'clock in the morning, the testament was signed and witnessed by Goebbels, Bormann, Burgdorf and Krebs. In his private testament Adolf Hitler gave, among other things, the following instructions: 'My pictures, in the collection which I bought over the years, were never assembled for private purposes, but only for the establishment of a gallery in my home town of Linz on the Danube. It is my heartfelt wish that this bequest should be duly executed.'

Adolf Hitler saw himself primarily as an artist, and left no doubt about this conviction of his in his talks with Henderson and in his table talk and sketches and plans during the war. It was circumstances that had unfortunately compelled him to concern himself temporarily with hateful politics. Adolf Hitler was an artist of a peculiar sort: he wanted to shape the world in accordance with his hopes and fears. After an outburst of anger on Hitler's part, Guderian (who on 9 January 1945 had tried to draw Hitler's attention to the serious situation) noted: 'He had a certain picture of the world, and every fact had to be fitted into this fantasy. The world had to be as he imagined it: but in reality it was a picture of another world.'

Millions of Christians and non-Christians, ordinary middle-class citizens and distinguished princes of the church, have only been able to conceive the world in terms of their preconceived ideas and their desires and fears. In this sense they have a fundamental rapport with Adolf Hitler's conception of the world. Hitler's words and ideas still make themselves felt in the minds of many Germans in their image of the world – something that perceptive Catholic observers like Franz Greiner and Vincent Berning have noticed – and exercise a strong influence outside Europe.

In the bunker of the Reichskanzlei Adolf Hitler remembered his early days in Vienna, thanked his secretaries with a *Küss die Hand*, abused the philistine Himmler, who wanted to be his successor, and the Prussian generals and officers. The later Adolf Hitler was in his thought processes still the Hitler of Vienna 1909–13. *Hitler did not undergo any development*; he adhered to the end to the ideas in which he had been caught up as a boy.

Adolf Hitler, the complete provincial, came of a comfortable middle-class background (though he sought to conceal the fact in *Mein Kampf*). Was he a quarter Jewish? William Patrick Hitler, his nephew, drew his attention in 1930 to his possibly Jewish origin. Hitler, his legal adviser Hans Frank, and anti-Nazi papers all took up this question at the time, and it has never yet been clarified (see Note). Adolf Hitler unconsciously hated his father and his relations and, after the Anschluss with Austria, had his father's home district, Döllersheim and its surroundings, transformed into a military manœuvre area. The birthplace of his father and the site of his grandmother's grave were shot to pieces by the Wehrmacht and flattened. 'It rather looks as if the destruction of Döllersheim took place on the direct orders of the Führer – out of a mad hatred for his father, who perhaps had a Jewish father.'

The young Adolf Hitler, who may once have shovelled snow in Vienna and who indiscriminately devoured tracts and all kinds of 'literature', would have been an ideal patient for Sigmund Freud. The Hitler family, like many thousand other German and Austrian families, had a Jewish doctor by the name of Bloch. 'Adolf Hitler used to send him postcards from Vienna with views painted by himself. Dr Bloch paid twenty kronen for each one, which Adolf warmly acknowledged. In the year 1938, when Hitler became master of Austria, the Gestapo brutally deprived the old doctor of his letters and cards, and, despite many requests and reminders that he had been Hitler's family doctor, Bloch was forced as a Jew to leave his Austrian homeland. He died in America' (Franz Jetzinger). Hitler as a young man seems at one time often to have cultivated 'friendly' contacts with Jews. A Hungarian Jew, Neumann, who lived in the same hostel with him and dealt in second-hand clothes, sent him an overcoat which came down over his knees.

'But Vienna was, and remained, for me a hard school, even if it taught me the most profound lessons of my life,' Hitler wrote in *Mein Kampf*. Vienna, in Adolf Hitler's memory, signified utter frustration – ever since his failure in the entrance examination for the Academy of Fine Arts in September 1907. Vienna meant for him an asylum for homeless people (September 1908 to the end of 1909) and a men's hostel (1910 to 1913). (In 1913 he went to Munich to avoid conscription.) Vienna, the opulent city of pleasure, was for him a mine of hate, a serpents' pit of envy. Here Adolf Hitler indulged his hate and found targets for it among the Social Democrats, the priests, the capitalists, the Hapsburgs and the Jews.

'Today it is hard, if not impossible, for me to say when the word "Jew" first began to raise any particular thought in my mind. I do not remember even having heard the word at home in my father's life-time.' Hitler later thought it was due to the 'more or less cosmopolitan views' which his father retained in spite of his strong patriotism. We should not make too much of this silence; but it is very remarkable and has not been adequately taken into account. Are we to accept that, at a time when 'the Jew' was assuming so much importance in Christian, Catholic and nationalist middle class and lower-middle-class families in the old Austria (thanks to sermons and nationalist and Christian Socialist anti-Semitic propaganda) the word 'Jew' was never heard in this middle-class pan-German Austrian household? Was Hitler's father concealing the Jew or was Hitler concealing the Jew from himself and his father?

We have it on his own authority that Hitler was not an anti-Semite when he came to Vienna as a young man. He read the liberal papers and said he was repelled by the vulgar tone of the anti-Semitic press. He regarded anti-Semitism as 'a form of cultural backwardness', which is what the Viennese Social Democrats also called it. But in the course of two years – from the autumn of 1910 to the summer of 1912 he gradually became an anti-Semite and claimed that this change in his views was the most painful transformation he had ever experienced in his life.

These years saw his professional frustration, his decline from the status of being a sheltered, middle-class son to a member of the proletariat, a 'suburban hypochondriac', a refugee and an inmate of a men's hostel. The susceptible and in his way sensitive, very ambitious young man, who looked up in admiration at the splendid buildings of Vienna, suffered a profound shock, social, political – and also personal. Was it true, as those who knew him at that time asserted later, that the charming blonde and blue-eyed Viennese girls of Schnitzler's pages were 'snatched' away from him by 'Jewish boys'? The strong sexual emphasis in his anti-Semitism betrays a very personal flavour: the Jew is shameless and lewd and 'took' Christian girls.

'Was there any shady undertaking, any form of foulness, especially in the cultural sphere, in which at least one Jew could not be found participating?' 'The part which Jews played in prostitution and more especially in the white slave traffic could be studied better here in Vienna than in any other West European city, with the possible exception of the ports of Southern France.' 'The black-haired Jewish youth lies in wait for hours on end – with satanic joy in his face – for the unsuspecting girl whom he plans to seduce, adulterating her blood and taking her from her own people . . .' For hours, day and night, the young unemployed Hitler walked through the streets of Vienna and saw Jewish youths standing at corners and waiting for girls to come out into the still light and warm spring evening after the shops had closed. From now onwards this vision pursued Hitler by day and night. He himself spoke of the 'nightmare visions of the seduction of hundreds of thousands of girls by repulsive, bandy-legged Jewish bastards'.

Jewish youths 'took' Christian girls. And Jews, as leaders of the Jewish-controlled Social Democracy, 'took' the German people. A powerful form of sexual envy always asserted itself in Hitler's personality: Germany was to be a 'bride'; he would 'take' the masses waiting like a woman to be taken by a man. And from the Jew he would save them all – Germany, women and the masses. One evening in 1938 Hitler said in the presence of Hans Frank (who in the early 'thirties had defended him in court cases against the accusation of being of Jewish origin), 'In the Gospels the Jews called out to Pilate when he refused to crucify Jesus: "His blood be upon us and our children's children!" Perhaps I have to fulfil this curse.'

The passage quoted here (St Matthew 27, 15) played no part in the disputes between Christians and Jews during the first centuries of Christianity. But from the fourth and fifth centuries until today it has had an important place in anti-Semitic Christian preaching. Hitler and the Gospels; Hitler and the churches; Hitler and God – in what, then, did Adolf Hitler believe?

Adolf Hitler did not believe in a new paganism, in the *Myth of the Twentieth Century* of his party colleague, Rosenberg, or in any Germanic, pagan or Christian 'humbug'. Hitler did not believe in a personal God, in Jesus Christ, the Gospels or in the immortality of individual souls.

Adolf Hitler believed in himself, and he found this belief confirmed by his success and daily in his speeches, when the masses gave themselves to him like a woman and he united with his 'bride' in ecstasy, in cold calculation and even in passion. Adolf Hitler was his own evangelist. He felt himself to be a saviour when he heard the cries of 'Heil Hitler' drowning the church bells and scattering the old evil spirits.

'I go the way that Providence has directed me, with the assurance of a sleepwalker.' This 'Providence', which he sometimes also called 'God Almighty', denoted a radiant power he felt within himself as heir to Shamanist magicians, to plebeian and politico-religious popular leaders from the common people, who from the twelfth to the eighteenth centuries had conjured up salvation from the depths of their own personalities. Hitler had many features in common with the visionary leaders of the Reformation period. His own relative, the poet Robert Hamerling, who died the year Hitler was born, foresaw in his Anabaptist epic the fate of his great nephew. The Prussian Friedrich von Reck-Malleczewen, who died in a concentration camp, had Hitler directly in mind in *his* Anabaptist novel of 1933.

'How conscious we must feel at this moment of the miracle that has brought us together! You once heard the voice of a man, and it struck your hearts. It awakened you, and you followed this voice. You followed this voice for years without ever having seen its owner. You only heard a voice and followed.' As his own voice in the wilderness, as his own John the Baptist and St John the Evangelist, Hitler spoke thus to the political leaders of his party in 1936: 'When we meet here, we are all filled with the miracle of this gathering. Not everyone can see me, nor can I see each of you. But I feel your presence and you mine. It is our belief in our people that has made us little men great, that has made us poor men rich, us hesitant and fearful men brave and courageous. It has made us who were confused see and has led us to each other.

'And so one day you come to this city from your small villages, your market towns, your cities, your mines, your factories and your ploughs. You come from the humble background of your daily round and your struggle for Germany and our people so that you may have the feeling that we are now one, we are with him and he is with us and we are now Germany . . . It is a wonderful experience for me to be able to be your Führer.'

'We are with him and he is with us' . . . Communion between the Führer and his bride, Germany. Communion between the lonely, the fatherless, the godless and the leaderless and their Führer. The communion of millions of women: one had to see it to believe it: the way they gave themselves to their Führer with light in their eyes.

There is a pious picture of the boy Adolf seen kneeling before the gateway of a monastery with rays of light falling from the coat of arms on to his outstretched hands. The model for this was St Francis receiving the stigmata of the Lord. But the legend behind the picture was not quite correct. The small Adolf did not learn about the swastika from an abbot's coat of arms in the monastery of Lambach. Probably he first learnt about it in the *Ostara* pamphlets of the Cistercian monk Georg Lanz von Liebenfels, who came from the Heiligenkreuz monastery near Vienna. It was he who, in the first decade of our century, hoisted the swastika flag on Danube castles and in his writings preached the doctrine of the eternal struggle fought by a diabolical race of sub-humans against the Aryan men of Light.

But the picture connecting Hitler with St Francis draws attention to one thing. The young Adolf went to school for two years in the monastery at Lambach. Here he received singing lessons in the monastery's choir school and declared that he wanted to become an abbot. Later he recalled: 'There I had a wonderful opportunity to drink in again and again the solemn splendour of the very magnificent church festivals. It was only natural that the office of abbot should seem to me to be an ideal infinitely worth striving for.'

The coat of arms of Abbot Theoderich Hagen at the gateway of the monastery at Lambach had a certain similarity with the swastika. But for us today it is far more important to establish the fact that *Adolf Hitler was a Catholic*. He still regarded himself as a Catholic in the early Munich days; he never left the church; he received the highest recognition from the highest princes of the church – including a personal letter from Pope Pius XII on his fiftieth birthday; and he was never expelled from the church.

The Catholic Adolf Hitler very soon became a Catholic atheist. He could have said of himself, as did Charles Maurras: *je suis athée, mais je suis catholique* – I am an atheist, but I am a Catholic. The supporters of Charles Maurras (whose *Action Française* was, as we have already mentioned, condemned by the church after the First World War but restored to favour by Pope Pius XII in 1939) insofar as they claimed to be Catholic atheists, had no personal faith. They did not believe in the Jew Jesus, but they did believe in the authority, discipline and rule of a strong church. To the end of his life Adolf Hitler showed his extraordinary respect for the Catholic church's capacity for political rule. He knew that it would survive him. He tried to create a grand council of the National Socialist movement, after the model of the College of Cardinals, which would among other things appoint his successors in the Thousand Year Reich.

Hitler was profoundly indebted to the church for his own ability to lead the masses and to manipulate the propaganda weapons of joy and terror. For hundreds of years the church had deeply impressed the masses with its preachings about hell and the Devil. Hitler had heard in the Viennese Prater pleasure gardens the delighted, terrified shrieks of the public on the ghost railway there. He said: 'Cruelty impresses. People need a healthy fear. They want to be afraid of something. They want someone to make them afraid, to subject themselves to someone in fear. Have you not noticed that after a fight in a meeting-hall it is always the men who were beaten up who are the first to apply to join the party? Why do you babble about cruelty and become indignant about suffering? The masses want it. They want something to horrify them.'

Hitler conquered the German masses with his propaganda weapons of joy and terror. And he was convinced that he could win the war with the same methods. In his table talk at the Führer headquarters he declared that 'this war is an exact replica of the period of our political struggle. What happened then at home in the struggle between parties is now taking place externally in a struggle between nations.' That was Adolf Hitler's greatest political mistake.

Hitler's admiration for the organization of the historic Catholic church and its traditional ability to subdue and tame the stupid and helpless masses did not extend to the Protestant church. He had no high opinion of Protestant clergy: 'They are insignificant little people, submissive as dogs, and they sweat with embarrassment when you talk to them. They have neither a religion which they can take seriously nor a great position to defend, like Rome.'

Hitler did not allow anyone, not even Bormann, Himmler or Goebbels, to pick a quarrel during the war with the church leaders, or to single out for

attention a Bishop Galen or Cardinal Faulhaber or even the pope himself.
Later, after the war, it was his intention to liquidate this whole group, dis-
possess it and enforce the unconditional obedience of the rest of the clergy.
Adolf Hitler, the Catholic, knew very well how concerned this clergy was
about its position and the pay it received from the state. The Christian
question would be solved after the war. But first it was the Jews' turn: they
had to be destroyed first.

Adolf Hitler realized – though only on the surface, knowing in his subconscious mind that it would never have been possible for him – that he
could have first built up his party financially with the help of German Jews
and then have gained possession of a whole world with the help of European
and perhaps American Jewish and non-Jewish circles. He, the great enemy
of Bolshevism, enjoyed great admiration, particularly in England (and not
only from the Britons who had married into the family of Richard Wagner)
and in America. The anti-Semitic National Socialist press proudly reported
in May 1934 the speech of the president of the American Chamber of
Commerce in Berlin, E.B.Peirce, who said, 'We could no longer today speak
of a sound economy if Germany had not saved Europe from the danger of
Bolshevism.'

Hitler's power to establish order was recognized in the Vatican, in anti-
Bolshevist America, in Spain, Ireland and in almost every country of Europe.
Why did Hitler have to pick a quarrel with the Jews? Hundreds of thousands
of Jews could not understand this even after he had seized power. Why did he
have to have his war? And why inextricably connect the war with the
liquidation of the Jews? In his Reichstag speech on 30 January 1939 he
himself prophesied: 'Should international Jewish finance succeed, within and
outside Europe, in involving the nations in another world war, it will not
result in the Bolshevization of the world and with it the victory of Judaism
but, instead, in the destruction of the Jewish race in Europe . . .'

Against the background of this Reichstag speech, made in the year in which
he was to start his world war, let us call back to mind the young Hitler in
Vienna in 1910–12 and in his talks with Dietrich Eckart in Munich in 1922–3.
Why did Hitler need the Jews? To destroy himself? To obliterate himself and
his deeply concealed and hated ego in their destruction (after destroying the
locality in which his paternal ancestors had been born)?

Like many political Catholics whose religion has been transformed into a
political faith, and like many other Catholics, at least since the Middle Ages,
the Catholic atheist Adolf Hitler did not believe in God – but he did believe
in the Devil. Devout Catholics cannot, of course, consciously admit to themselves that they have less faith in God (a good, just, almighty, powerful God
in this wicked world) than in the Devil.

The cancer of European Christianity, Manichaeism, has ever since the
Middle Ages always begun to spread at times when popular religious and
political movements produce feelings of fear and despair. Hitler's brown – the

brown of his brown-shirted columns – was the brown of the confederate shoe in the peasants' wars of the sixteenth and seventeenth centuries. As for the Devil, there was so much to expunge from one's own heart and to combat in the wicked world. Behind the internal war in one's own heart and the external war in the outside world was the Devil, the Enemy Number One who had many helpers in this world – hunger, leprosy, pestilence and war. These things were all brought to a country by the Devil's accomplices, the sorcerer and the Jew.

Adolf Hitler, a very gifted human being, had much to expunge from his own heart: a brutal and uncontrolled sexuality (which among other things drove to death his much loved niece Geli Raubal: she was found shot in Hitler's Munich flat on 18 September 1931); difficult and hate-ridden relations with his father and mother; and severe disappointments in Vienna which prevented his becoming an architect of a new world. Adolf Hitler saw in the outside world strong and evil opponents whom he regarded as mortal enemies: the upper classes, the intellectuals, the Social Democrats (Hitler had never read or studied Karl Marx). The abundant anti-Semitic literature in Vienna, and later in Munich, made it possible for him to identify and put his hands on the Devil and on the Devil's agents, the Jews. The Devil was behind Jewish liberalism, Jewish democracy, Jewish Socialism, Jewish Bolshevism and Jewish intellectual Bolshevism. In all this church leaders, theologians and preachers, both Catholic and Protestant, agreed with Hitler. But Hitler went further than them in saying that the Jews were also behind Christianity, in both its churches. Germany, he thought, should be purified of the Jews, and that meant also of Christians.

How is it that – at bottom even today – the Christian churches were not able to see the monstrous challenge that Adolf Hitler signified for them? A Prussian, Colonel Kühlenthal, in the Reich war ministry in Berlin recognized it as early as May 1930 (according to the report of the British military attaché, Colonel J.H.Marshall-Cornwall, to his government): 'The National Socialist movement is a real danger and a much greater threat to the present constitution than Communism. The problem of the "brown shirts" lies in the fact that their principles and theories are completely destructive.' Colonel Kühlenthal drew the attention of his British colleague to the susceptibility of a number of young officers to the National Socialist movement and observed: 'Another menacing feature of this movement is the powerful mastery which its leader, Adolf Hitler, can command. He is an extraordinarily good speaker and has a marvellous ability to hypnotize his listeners and to win supporters. Although his programme is entirely negative, he is able by his gifts of persuasion to win over quite reasonable people to his views. That is the main danger of the movement.'

'Quite reasonable people': how was it that Adolf Hitler was put into power by conservative men and groups, and was able right up to his death to enjoy the support of responsible leaders of both major Christian churches?

The Weimar Republic (1918–33) was the child of Germany's collapse in the First World War: an unloved child, unwanted by its parents. Ebert, the leader of the German Social Democrats, said he hated the revolution like sin. His party really wanted to maintain the monarchy. 'The completely incompetent Noske', as Kurt Tucholsky described the first minister of the interior in the Republic, at once concluded a pact with the generals, in order to be able to suppress left-wing Socialist and Communist uprisings. The general staff, which at first backed the Republic, subsequently turned against it. Its chief, Seeckt, thought himself of becoming a 'leader' (see the letter to Wiedtfeld of 4 November 1923). In Eschenburg's words, the Weimar constitution was a sort of 'substitute monarchy'. When the 'substitute Kaiser', Hindenburg, who was a declared opponent of the Republic and democracy, became president of the Reich, the Republic's fate was sealed in advance.

In 1918–19 Germany got an improvised democracy, as did the successor states of the Hapsburg monarchy, Rumania and the Balkan countries. The main responsibility devolved on the two political parties which had, in the days of the empire, been dominant in the opposition: the Social Democratic party and the Centre party of the Catholics, which, however, also got some support from non-Catholic voters. Neither party was able, however, to breach the ghetto in which German Catholics had immured themselves since the founding of the Reich in 1871.

The Social Democrats were led by party politicians who were often philistine, doctrinaire, bureaucratic and centralist; and the Social Democrat masses were insulated from the outside world by barriers of fear erected above all against wicked left-wing Socialists and Communists. Before the Nazis took over in the Reich, Social Democrats worked principally in local government and in the *Länder* (provincial) governments. In national government they always showed a tendency to panic. In 1920 and again in 1930 they left the government, in 1930 overthrowing their own chancellor, Hermann Müller, and with him the last majority government. In this way it made the path free for the 'authoritarian experiments of Brüning, Papen and Schleicher', as Karl Dietrich Bracher has put it. Although the strongest party, the Social Democrats always chose the unhappy role of opposition and, their eyes fixed on the arch-enemy and source of all their anxieties, the Communists, shirked real responsibility. Important Social Democrats like Julius Leber (who was to be hanged after 20 July 1944) pondered ruefully on their missed opportunities after Hitler came to power.

The whole of the left (with the exception of a few intellectuals and outsiders like Bloch, who recognized early the irrational basis of the National Socialist movement and the existing, emotional vacuum in which the doctrinaire politicians of the left forgot the German people) failed to notice what was developing with Hitler and his movement. In using the false slogan of 'Fascism', they lumped National Socialists together with German nationalist reactionaries, whom they knew all about – or so they thought.

Though they despised Hitler, it was the Communists the Social Democrats really feared. For them Communism was a profoundly irrational fixation. Communism was a devil that, like Hitler's Jew, dwelt in their own hearts. Deep down they feared the revenge of the great 'red brother', their founder Karl Marx, ignored but feared from early days, to whom they now made even rarer acknowledgement in official speeches. The panic fear of leading Social Democrats against Communism undeniably betrayed much more than a mere concern not to lose votes. Sober conservative Prussian observers saw things much more clearly. They knew that Communism in the thirties had no chance of achieving power in Germany.

'The year 1932 was an unbroken line of misfortune. It should be smashed to pieces. Outside in the streets Christmas spreads its peace. I sit alone at home and ponder over so many things. The past has been difficult and the future is dark and gloomy. All hopes and prospects have completely disappeared. The whole house looks dead. I am overcome by the most terrible feeling of loneliness – a sort of dull despair comes over me.'

That is what Joseph Goebbels wrote in his diary on 23 December 1932. Shortly afterwards he advanced, limping slightly, but radiant, to enjoy the fruits of power with Hitler.

Hitler spoke of his 'seizure of power' and, at the same time, of his legal assumption of power. Neither term is correct. Hindenburg appointed Hitler chancellor on 30 January 1933. The conservative Papen-Meissner group, 'the grave-diggers of democracy', appeared with that to have achieved their aim. They thought they could use Hitler and then dispose of him. Walther Hofer declared: 'In the last analysis Hitler was not carried to power on the back of an irresistible political movement: he was legally put into power by the above-mentioned wire-pullers round Hindenburg. Hugenberg and Papen, the conservative monarchists, hoped they could use the rabble-rouser Hitler for their own purposes. They thought they had "made sure" of him. It did not worry these men of conservative-monarchist sympathies and the millions who thought like that at all that Hitler's avowed intention was to abolish the democratic republic.' (Nor did this seen undesirable to the German bishops.)

The meteoric rise of the NSDAP in elections between 1929 and 1932 was due to the world economic crisis which had its origins in Wall Street in 1929. The millions of German unemployed streamed into the NSDAP and the Communist KPD. These two parties often formed opportunist alliances both in the streets and in the Reichstag, against the weak coalition governments. Most of the governmental crises in the Weimar Republic were the result of internal crises among the coalition partners. In 1928–9 industry, the army and Hindenburg himself began to look with favour on the idea of an authoritarian government which would use strong arm tactics against the parties, the Marxists and the provincial parliaments. After the failure of the last majority government in 1930, the Reich chancellors could govern only with the help of emergency decrees supported by Hindenburg. When this 'substitute Kaiser' withdrew his support from Reich Chancellor Brüning, the days of the democracy 'which no one wanted' were over.

National Socialism owed its election successes to the petty bourgeois, small peasant and Protestant areas of North-east and Northern Germany. In the summer of 1932 it achieved its greatest victory at elections. Then there was a set-back, and in the late autumn the movement was threatened by an internal split. It looked as if Reich Chancellor Brüning was being successful in bringing about a great German recovery. Constitutionally Hitler had never received more than one-third of the electorate's votes. In the summer of 1932 there were signs that the great turning point on the road to Germany's recovery was at hand. Leading National Socialists recognized that very clearly and were desperate. The party treasury was empty; there were whisperings of a putsch against Hitler.

Even in the elections of 5 March 1933, in which Hitler was able to use every available weapon of terror, fifty-six per cent of the electorate voted against the NSDAP. 'In thousands of electoral communities and districts, the impeded and persecuted opposition parties were able to poll many more votes than the NSDAP. If one looks at the statistics, one finds many towns and parishes, particularly in Westphalia, the Rhineland and Bavaria, where the NSDAP was not able to get even ten per cent, sometimes hardly five per cent, of the votes, while the Centre party had a stable two-thirds or three-quarters majority and, in some cases, even up to eighty-five per cent. There was also 'red' Berlin and Hamburg and certain industrial towns and communities in Thuringia, Saxony and Hesse, where a clear decision against the National Socialist seizure of power and against the NSDAP's exclusive claim to represent the nation was borne out by the great majority of Socialist votes' (Bracher).

The National Socialists, like the whole of the right, based its campaign against the 'Jewish Weimar Republic' on the legend of a 'stab in the back', on the betrayal of Germany and her undefeated and invincible army by Judas, 'the arrant knave Judas' (Abraham a Sancta Clara). Germany, the *German republic*, had, in fact, been itself betrayed. The stab in the back came from the clique around Hindenburg, backed by landowners who feared for their estates in East Prussia, but the betrayal had been perpetrated in fact by the leaders of the Social Democrats and Centre, who in an involuntary act of self-betrayal refused to lead the masses of their loyal supporters into battle. In their fear of the devil Communism, the bureaucrats of the Social Democratic party had suppressed or driven out all the independent, dynamic and belligerent elements in the party and the trade unions. The trade union leaders allowed themselves to be thrust aside by Hitler with humiliating alacrity.

There was no stratum of society, no group or party in the Weimar state which did not share responsibility for its destruction. A certain form of postwar nationalism and anti-democracy could often be detected in even the best individuals. In 1918 Thomas Mann was opposed to democracy; and the great man of Weimar foreign policy, Stresemann, produced a programme in 1925 and 1927 which in many respects anticipated the aims of Hitler's foreign policy. After the old Western frontiers of the Reich had been recovered, demands were to be made in the East: the Polish corridor, Danzig, the smashing of Poland, the Anschluss with Austria and the 'protection' of twelve million 'oppressed' *Volksdeutsche*. And in 1935 Heinrich Brüning, the last important chancellor of the Weimar Republic, now living abroad, criticized Hitler for his 'accommodating' attitude towards the Poles.

According to J.C.Fest, 'the face of the Third Reich was the face of the entire people'. K.D.Bracher has said: 'The history of National Socialism is substantially the history of how it was underestimated.' Schools, technical colleges and universities; the law (whose judges had earned much praise for discrediting the Weimar Republic in their political judgments); elementary school-teachers who voluntarily took up subsidiary roles in the Nazi movement; and broad strata of the lower middle class, the middle class, the small peasants and the agricultural workers – all these made up the material which fell into Hitler's hands.

Power was conveyed to him, secured for him, and assigned to him by people at the top. Hugenberg and his German nationalists, industrialists (somewhat tardily) and, not least, army officers helped Hitler achieve power.

On the night that brought Hitler victory, a celebratory torchlight procession in the beautiful old Catholic town of Würzburg was led by an enthusiastic young army lieutenant, by name Count Stauffenberg. It was the same Count Stauffenberg who was later to prove the great driving force in the resistance movement of the men of 20 July 1944. In this movement an élite of the Prussian Protestant nobility and officer corps were involved: the Catholic German nobility stood aside.

It is now time to throw some light on the responsibility which Catholics in Germany and in Rome share for the liquidation of Europe's Jews. German Catholicism and the Vatican come together in the fateful figure of Eugenio Pacelli.

'We feel in conscience obliged to accept the German republic, and I believe it will depend on the loyalty of the Catholic community in Germany whether or not the German republic survives.'

That is what Dr Spiecker, as spokesman of the loyal republicans, said at the conference of the Centre party in Kassel in November 1925. As Heinrich Lutz has observed: 'It took place after the Reich presidential election which, as is known, had decided against the Centre party leader, Marx, and for Hindenburg. At the Kassel meeting, against the background of the defeat which the right-wing groups had imposed on the centre groups, the party discussed openly for the first time its attitude towards the republic.'

On the eve of Hitler's assumption of power German Catholicism presented to the eyes of the world an imposing force with its multiplicity of organizations and associations. In Europe only German and Austrian Social Democracy could compare with it for organizational cohesion. There were many friendly ties between German and Austrian Catholics, between Vienna and Cologne, between Vienna and Munich, between Salzburg and the academic world of the Rhineland. The Salzburg Catholic University weeks, which were intended to lay the foundations for the reconstruction of Salzburg University as a Catholic university for all Germans, were held under the slogan 'Christianity, Antiquity and the Germanic world'. Austrian and German educationalists saw in Catholicism a reminder of the Holy Roman Empire. At the jointly organized university weeks in Salzburg no one talked about the republic or democracy; but there was much talk of the 'Holy Empire'.

But, although they had much in common, there were also important differences between German and Austrian Catholics – and not only in their mentality. German Catholicism, which was concentrated in the rural areas and small and medium-sized towns of Westphalia, the Rhineland, South-West Germany and Bavaria, was by no means as strongly influenced by anti-Semitism as Austrian Catholicism. In Germany the Jew was not automatically made the symbol and the scapegoat for everything that caused grief and confusion. In place of the Jew there arose a different kind of anti-symbol and anathema to which one could transfer one's own uncertainty and fear of the present and future: the republic, democracy.

The majority of German Catholics were really a-political and non-political – without any political education or influence. Politics were left to the political leaders of their own party, the Centre, and the ultimate leadership was left to the very reverend bishops. 'They' – the masses – were loyal to the Kaiser, and with all other Germans they had loyally accepted all the burdens, suffering and sacrifices on all the battlefields to which the Kaiser sent his people up to the final defeat. A programme of peace and reconciliation, for which the Centre Party politician Erzberger had been almost the only advocate in 1917 (and for which he was murdered in 1921), was scarcely known to the majority of Catholics. 'In the minds of many Catholics the old ideas of victory and conquest again prevailed over the peace and reconciliation programme of 1917, insofar as this programme had ever entered the consciousness of the propaganda-fed masses.'

The Catholic historian Heinrich Lutz has broached the question: 'How did the political conscience and moral sense of Catholics cope with the inheritance of an unsuccessful war?'

It must be said that this political conscience was not, in the case of the majority, trained and educated to be a strong enough moral sense to rid itself of the illusions and follies of propaganda. Theodor Haecker, one of the best Catholic minds in Germany, used in his introduction to a translation of Newman the following sentences, and the Munich *Hochland*, the most progressive and cultivated German Catholic periodical, took over the passage in 1921 under the heading: 'The blasphemy of Versailles': 'It is indeed an oppressive sign that the British, as slaves of an un-Christian idea, have allowed their political honour since the blasphemy of Versailles to be tarnished and to fall into disrepute by associating with the refuse of France's hysterical and psychopathic apostates of the faith and advocates of the past, her power-hungry, imbecile white nigger marshals and dishonourable bandit generals.'

The *Allgemeine Rundschau*, an influential Catholic weekly, made an appeal in its New Year number of 1920 to foreign Catholics. It called for an 'awakening on the part of international Catholicism' and a protest by it against the 'crime' of Versailles. 'Just as once the Christians were thrown to the lions in the Circus Maximus of pagan Rome, so we are, it seems to us, thrown as fodder to the finance hyenas of masonic and Jewish international plutocracy.' That is the language of Hitler – and in 1920! These German Catholics entirely overlooked the fact that they had just marched through the whole of Europe as part of 'the greatest army in world history' and had approved all the demands of a 'victorious peace' – the permanent occupation of Belgium, the 'acquisition' of the 'Eastern lands' and of Brest-Litovsk.

Monarchists among the senior clergy – such as the Regensburg Cathedral provost and Würzburg Professor Franz Xaver Kiefl – strongly opposed the republic. Archbishop Faulhaber, in his Lent pastoral letter of 1920, indulged in polemics against the Reich constitution (political polemics – implying that the others are always responsible – have since 1945 again become a feature of Lent pastoral letters. An odd form of contemplation and atonement: suppression instead of confession!). It was based on the words of the Gospel: 'Every plant which my heavenly Father hath not planted, shall be rooted up.' Faulhaber acted as 'the spokesman of a radical view' which cast doubt on the Weimar state 'from the point of view of the moral unacceptability of the revolution'.

The sixty-second General Assembly of German Catholics in Munich, which took place from 27 to 31 August 1922 and was the first major Assembly since the war, already played with Hitler's fire. Pacelli spoke at the opening. The archbishop of Salzburg transmitted brotherly greetings from Austria. A representative of the Catholics in the Saar – they were mobilized in support of Hitler in 1935 – said: 'We Catholics from the Saar have faith that God will frustrate the lie of the imposed peace.' The representative of the Danzig Catholics – the Second World War began with the struggle for Danzig – said: 'We want to remain in spiritual contact with you until the hour of reunion strikes again. Something so unnatural as the dismemberment of the German East cannot be permanent.' The speaker for the Germans in Bohemia said: 'We have come in order to make closer the community of faith and race [a foreshadowing here of Hitler's 'community of race'] . . . May Germany's self-laceration cease. Then the day of the German people will come – for us, too, who groan under a foreign yoke.'

The president of the Catholics' Conference, Konrad Adenauer, spoke against 'the imposed peace of Versailles' and appealed to French Catholics jointly with the Germans 'to find a way which will help our two countries'. Cardinal Faulhaber spoke about 'the church's power for peace' and made strong attacks on France and the League of Nations . . . 'The League of Nations in its present form is a noose to throttle the economy of a people. It is not a pillar of world peace, but fuel for new world wars, a gambling hell of big capitalism.' Cardinal Faulhaber openly attacked the constitution of the Weimar Republic and its spokesmen in the Centre party: 'The revolution was perjury and high treason: it will go down in history as a tainted inheritance, branded with the mark of Cain.' On this point there was a controversy between Adenauer and Faulhaber at the Catholics' Conference: Konrad Adenauer defended the Weimar constitution.

The good and well-meaning Adolf Hitler unfortunately had some bad advisers. That, at any rate, was what Faulhaber said about him in a speech in the Löwenbräu-Keller in Munich on 15 February 1924. The massive attacks on the republic at the first pan-German Catholics' Conference after the war later appalled Catholics. The workers' leader, Joseph Joos, spoke of 'predictions which sound like a prophetic intimation of Hitler's putsch in the following year.

'Sometimes it seems as if some of the leaders of the Bavarian people have no clear idea of what can happen when one plays with fire . . .'

Bavaria's leading political Catholics played with fire from 1918 onwards. They prepared their assumption of power before Hitler's Munich putsch, and after it they protected Hitler, an Austrian subject, who would have been expelled from Germany if the judicial authorities had been in democratic hands. Bavaria openly rebelled against the Reich government in Berlin when, under Stresemann's influence, the latter abandoned passive resistance to the French occupation troops on 24 September 1923. Bavaria proclaimed a state of emergency and appointed Dr von Kahr as state commissioner. Eschenburg has written: 'Bavaria was then the eldorado of nationalist, racial and monarchist organizations which were generally supported by the state commissioner, von Kahr. In spite of their different aims these associations were united in their anti-democratic and anti-Marxist attitude and their hatred of "red" Berlin. They not only dreamed of a march on Berlin: they actually prepared for one.'

In 1925 the Centre party was already threatening to break up. Disastrously weakened by the secession of the Bavarian Catholics, who created for themselves in the Bavarian People's party a strong right-wing movement with monarchist leanings, it was no longer able to effect a real reconciliation between the republicans and the monarchists and other enemies of the

Republic. Count Westarp declared openly on behalf of his Centre party people: 'For us all, politics means support for the privileged state of the old Prussian caste system which we never want to give up.'

The advocates of a Christian democracy, who had their supporters in the Rhineland, in the South-west and scattered throughout the North German towns – Marx, Wirth, Spiecker, Adenauer, Krone – could not really succeed against the champions of the monarchist, authoritarian and anti-republican wing. The crisis of the Centre party which had been festering for so many years was eventually solved by a compromise. To prevent a split in the party, they decided no longer to elect a layman as chairman but a priest, Mgr Kaas, who then proceeded to bring in clergymen to other leading positions. In 1933 Kaas led the Centre to self-destruction.

Joseph Wirth, in the passionate discussions in the Centre party in 1925 about the political role of the Republic, appealed to his right-wing nationalist party colleagues: 'See for yourself to what extent nationalist ideas have already partly confused our Catholic youth.'

Like the confusion of the masses within the church, the political confusion of Catholic youth came from above, from the best minds of educated German Catholicism. In the Catholic youth movement, whose spiritual leader was Romano Guardini, there were a number of individuals and groups centred on the *Quickborn* and round the periodical *Die Schildgenossen* who sought contacts with democracy and industrial society; but the majority was romanticist, hostile to the Republic, anti-urban and anti-democratic. They looked for 'leadership' and a 'Führer'. Romano Guardini called for 'a sense of responsibility and creative leadership' for 'authority within an hierarchic order', for political 'authority' and said in 1925 that the attempt to substitute 'leadership' for office was only a preliminary form of solution. 'Order, and with it authority, if they are to be valid, cannot be tied up with the specific qualities of the person exercising them, but must have an independent existence. They always stem in some way from God's grace.'

In 1922 voices could be heard in *Quickborn* which directly heralded 1933: 'We do not believe in national salvation through a parliamentary system inherited from the liberal West, even when it dresses itself in the fine cloak of an outwardly pure democracy.'

In 1928 *Die Schildgenossen* took on as a writer Carl Schmitt, the very interesting German legal thinker, who later became the leading lawyer of the Third Reich and a most persuasive 'wrecker of confidence in the rule of law and parliamentary and democratic ways among young Catholics'. The authority of the church and its hierarchy, which had been over-emphasized in the nineteenth century, fused in the minds of these young Catholics with the dream of a strong state authority, a Germany which would impose order in Europe. Catholic democrats and people like the men connected with the *Rhein-Mainische Volkszeitung* (Walter Dirks, Ernst Michel, Heinrich Scharp), the *Westdeutsche Arbeiterzeitung*, and the Catholic peace movement (Nikolaus

303

Ehlen) – all these gave vain warnings against the path to the abyss which German Catholicism was treading.

In autumn 1933 this truly remarkable thought appeared in *Die Schildge-nossen*: 'When in 1870 the doctrine of papal infallibility was formulated, the church at the highest level anticipated that historical decision which is to be taken today at the political level: for authority and against discussion; for the pope and against the authority of the council; for the leader and against Parliament.'

Here the great political decision was proclaimed. The anti-democratic spiritual leaders of German Catholicism and the anti-democratic 'German Pope' Pius XII, an opponent of discussion and parliamentary government, led German Catholicism into the Third Reich. The attitude – or lack of attitude – of both towards the vital question of the Jews in Europe is only intelligible when seen as part of their overall theological, ecclesiastical and political thinking. Why should the church concern itself with the fate of liberals, democrats, pacifists, Jews, Socialists and Bolshevists? They argued: 'We are here to save the church and the rights of the church which we, the clergy, lead and represent. Catholic political parties are a nuisance and often disobedient. Let us throw them away.' Thus it was that in 1923 the Christian Democratic party of Italy (PPI) was cast aside, then the German Centre party in 1933; and in 1953 attempts were made to discard Alcide de Gasperi, the outstanding leader of the Italian Christian Democrats, in order to make possible an alliance with the neo-Fascists and monarchists.

As early as 1939 Theodor Haecker predicted that the Germans would forget the way in which they had slithered to ruin. But to 'forget' means to suppress. The historian is like the psychotherapist in his attempt to stir the memory, to recover what is suppressed and to suggest self-analysis. This is because he knows (with Santayana): 'Those who cannot remember the past are condemned to repeat it.'

In 1920 a 'Catholic League for National Policy' was founded. In 1924 a branch of it brought out the publication *Der Rütlischwur* (later *Der Völkische Katholik*) in Munich. These extremist right-wing Catholics campaigned against Marxists, Jews and freemasons. The curate Josef Roth, who later became a senior official in Hitler's church ministry, made anti-Semitic speeches in these circles. Here also Abbot Albanus Schachleitner made his appearance. He had earlier been abbot of the Emmaus monastery in Prague. (Since the days of Jan Hus, when Emmaus was the centre of Czech reformed Catholicism, German and Czech nationalism had clashed there, and in both cases religion acted as the driving force.) Abbot Schachleitner was the only Catholic prelate who maintained friendly personal contacts with Hitler right up to his death.

These Catholic National Socialists represented no more than an insignificant and peripheral aspect of German Catholicism. The German bishops as a whole supported the Centre party and the Bavarian People's party and from 1930 onwards gave warnings against National Socialism in their sermons and pastoral letters. Not a single one of them can be regarded as National Socialist. How was it then that they all – without exception – stumbled into the Third Reich?

In 1930 these German bishops, who had little of the unprejudiced and intellectually courageous Catholicism seen a century earlier, in Bishop Sailer, Franz von Baader and Möhler and later in Ignaz von Döllinger, were the spiritual offspring of that authoritarian clerical rule which had triumphed at the First Vatican Council. Only one of them had also studied lay subjects: Konrad von Preysing, bishop of Eichstätt and subsequently of Berlin. He was originally a student of law and only later became a priest. He alone had a proper insight into the totalitarian aspirations of the Nazi régime. Most of the bishops were men in their sixties with narrow political horizons, conditioned by their experiences of imperial Germany before 1914.

To these senior clergy National Socialism appeared as the enemy of liberalism, democracy (which they distrusted) and Bolshevism. All German bishops recognized the 'patriotic motives' behind National Socialism. Their own constant emphasis on patriotism unintentionally helped National Socialism to command greater respect in the eyes of the Catholic masses – although the intention had been otherwise. It had been meant to take the wind out of the sails of the hotheads; but in fact it merely increased their ardour. Take one example of the nationalist oratory of these bishops. At the great Catholic youth demonstration in Berlin at the end of March 1932 (a decisive year for Germany) Bishop Bares of Hildesheim said: 'We are patriots to our very bones, German through and through, prepared for *veery* [my italics] sacrifice for nation and fatherland.'

In the political programmes of the 'People's Union for Catholic Germany', use was made in 1931 of nationalist slogans and a demagogy that came very close to National Socialism. The culprit was the wicked West!

There was a broad anti-Western and anti-democratic front in German Catholicism, derived from Görres and Adam Müller. It was opposed to the wicked French Revolution, to the Enlightenment and to liberalism. Liberalism was always identified with atheism (despite cautious attempts by Catholic historians and jurists to correct this impression). The election of Mgr Ludwig Kaas as leader of the Centre party finally emasculated the party politically. From being a party of Catholics (and other Christians), which had fought – under August Windthorst – for human and civic rights, it became an instrument designed by the clergy to defend their canonical rights.

Chancellor Heinrich Brüning, who had been a reserve officer in the First World War and felt deep obligations to his military master Hindenburg, himself established early contacts with Hitler and was ready to take him into his government (1930–1). Another Centre party man, who stood even further to the right, Franz von Papen, acted as Hitler's stirrup-holder when he was helped into power.

L

In *Die Katholiken und die Diktatur* (Catholics and Dictatorship) at the end of 1932 Walter Dirks warned Germans, in the light of the unhappy Italian example of the Vatican's alliance with Fascism, about the path they were treading towards the abyss.

Hitler seized power. The nuncio in Berlin, Cesare Orsenigo, expressed his great pleasure at the event. The Vatican saw in Hitler a bulwark against Bolshevism. Cardinal Faulhaber reported to the Bavarian bishops on his visit to Rome: Pope Pius xi, he said, had publicly praised Hitler, at the council of cardinals on 13 March 1933, for his commendable attitude towards Communism. International press opinion emanating from Rome confirmed that the Vatican was well disposed towards Hitler.

In his negotiations with the Centre party leaders Kaas, Stegerwald (the leader of the Catholic trade unions who had earlier demanded an alliance with the nationalists against the Social Democrats) and Hackelsberger, Hitler promised (20–22 March 1933) everything they wanted – or better still, what they wanted to hear. The political and church leaders of German Catholicism from then onwards developed an unfortunate tendency to read into Hitler's words everything that they wished to hear in their fond imagination. They became victims of their own wishful thinking.

Mgr Kaas announced the Centre party's agreement to Hitler's enabling law on 23 March 1933. The bishops lifted their ban and pledged Catholics to co-operate positively with Hitler's régime. From now on, terrorist acts against sectarians, Socialists and Communists were 'overlooked', especially among young people and workers.

On 30 March 1933 Mgr Föhr, the leader of the Centre party in Baden, enthusiastically welcomed the work of the Führer. Archbishop Gröber of Freiburg became a so-called 'contributing member' of the SS (in January 1938 he was expelled: he did not want to resign). On 3 April 1933 the Catholic organization *Kreuz und Adler* (Cross and Eagle) was founded for the purpose of close co-operation with the National Socialist movement. At their first meeting in Berlin on 15 June Papen said that National Socialism represented a victory over liberalism and that the Third Reich was a Christian counter-revolution to 1789. Joseph Goebbels put it this way: 'With 1933 the year 1789 has been expunged from history.'

The popes of the nineteenth century had fought against the French Revolution, against liberalism and against democracy. And on precisely this basis – that of extinguishing 1789 – the spiritual leaders of German Catholicism accepted the Hitler régime in 1933 and in the years that followed.

In Rome Pacelli was in constant contact with Mgr Kaas who, without consulting the other Centre party leaders, moved to Rome on 7 April 1933 and remained there till his death. From Rome he called on German Catholics to co-operate with the new régime. The Bavarian minister at the Vatican, Baron Ritter, reported to Munich that Pacelli and other leading cardinals favoured co-operation with Hitler. The German bishops were told that the

Vatican respected National Socialism particularly because of its campaigns against Bolshevism and against immorality! The complete immorality of the régime, which had already ten years' experience of murdering its colleagues and pioneers (secret tribunal murders and, later, the murders of the SA) was 'overlooked'. Papen and Goering made a good impression in the Vatican during their state visit. These gentlemen were so different from such poor devils as the Catholic reform theologians who from 1832 to 1957 humbly prostrated themselves before the popes and begged for toleration.

On 26 April 1933 Hitler had a conversation with Bishop Berning and Mgr Steinmann. The subject was the common fight against liberalism, Socialism, and Bolshevism, discussed in the friendliest terms. In the course of the conversation Hitler said that he was only doing to the Jews what the church had done to them over the past fifteen hundred years. The prelates did not contradict him. Hitler acknowledged himself to be a Catholic and said that trouble was brewing with Poland. Germany would need obedient soldiers – so there was a case for retaining religious schools! In other words, the German bishops knew in 1933 that Hitler was preparing his war and that it would be their duty and responsibility to provide obedient human material.

The Concordat of 20 July 1933 crowned Pacelli's work. He had been working for this since 1920. It was his triumph. Mgr Kaas had been on friendly terms with Pacelli since 1925.

In Pacelli's negotiations in Berlin before 1933 the question of the rank of the military bishop, the *episcopus castrensis*, had always cropped up. In Italy he was an archbishop, and the Germans wanted the same. Another important issue was that of the church schools.

The Vatican threw over the Centre party as, ten years earlier, the *Popolari* of Don Sturzo had thrown over the Italian Christian Socialists. In Germany, Nazi terror against the church and Catholics effectively helped the Concordat negotiations in Rome. Pius xi had great fear of Communism and gave his support to the Concordat. He saw in Germany and Italy the heart of the Christian and Catholic world.

The self-dissolution of the Centre party was the price paid for the Concordat. Papen, Pacelli, Kaas and Gröber were in charge of the final negotiations. Hitler grasped in full the great opportunities abroad which the Concordat offered him. He spoke about them at a cabinet meeting on 14 July: there was now, he said, a possibility of intensifying the campaign against international Judaism and against Austria (where the anti-Nazi wing of Austrian Catholicism had managed to assert itself in the government and had National Socialism declared hostile to the church). German Catholicism obediently supported the Nazi state. Catholic organizations were dissolved. On 4 July Mussolini told the German ambassador, Ulrich von Hassell, that the conclusion of the Concordat represented a great moral victory for Hitler and would win for him the support of Catholic opinion throughout the world.

There was a solemn signing of the Concordat by Pacelli and Papen on 20 July 1933. Eleven years later to the day the noblest elements of the German Protestant aristocracy and officer corps rose against Hitler.

Article 16 of the Concordat laid down that newly-appointed bishops must take an oath of loyalty to the Nazi régime. Article 27 included provisions for pastoral care in the armed forces. Article 30 provided for prayers for the government and German people to be spoken after every high mass.

The *Volkischer Beobachter* rightly celebrated the Concordat on 23 July 1933 as a solemn recognition of National Socialism by the church and as a great moral strengthening of the reputation of the Third Reich. On 10 September Cardinal Bertram of Breslau asked Pacelli whether the Vatican would say a word on behalf of the Jewish converts – even at this early stage the Vatican was being asked to play the petitioner to Hitler . . . On this very day (10 September 1933) the Concordat was ratified. With it the back of all Catholic resistance to Hitler was broken. From then up to 1945 the German diocesan authorities treated priests and laymen who supported the resistance, or were put in concentration camps for other reasons, as social lepers.

Guenter Lewy has rightly observed that in a certain sense both sides – Hitler and the Vatican – played with false cards in 1933. The Vatican thought the Concordat would last long after Hitler. It was right: on 26 March 1957 the government of the German Federal Republic recognized the validity of the Concordat. Archbishop Gröber in the *Handbuch der religiösen Gegenwartsfragen* (Handbook of Contemporary Religious Questions), which was published with official church approval in Freiburg in 1937 and which gave the authoritative view of the German churches on all political and religious questions of the Nazi period, declared the Concordat to be 'a proof that two powers, totalitarian in character, can reach an agreement, if their spheres are clearly differentiated . . .'

The Fulda bishops' conference (30 May to 1 June 1933) announced in a long pastoral letter that, for Catholics, there was a deep continuity in their love for the fatherland (this was an attempt to whitewash nationalism) and in their belief in authority, even vis-à-vis the temporal state. The pastoral letter argued the case for *Lebensraum* for the German nation (Hitler's talks with Berning and Steinmann were already bearing fruit) and for 'breaking the chains [of Versailles]'. Thanks were expressed to the government that unbelief, immorality and Bolshevism were no longer a threat to the German soul. (How often had Catholic publications spoken of this three-fold threat as a specifically Jewish threat to the 'German soul'!)

As far as immorality was concerned, a Catholic theology deeply tinged with Manichaeism concentrated on 'immodest' films and writings and on sex, ignoring the murderous immorality of social and political structures and systems of government.

After 1945 Bishop Neuhäusler edited this pastoral letter and, by making twenty-one cuts, falsified its meaning.

The French Catholic historian, Count Robert d'Harcourt, a scion of one of the oldest families in France (an ancestor had fought at the Battle of Hastings in 1066) and a good friend to the Germans, remarked in 1939 that in this pastoral letter the German bishops had attempted to reconcile what was incapable of reconciliation. They tried to flatter the executioner and to comfort the victims by their unreserved recognition of the new state, whose real nature they failed to recognize. The bishops had no criticism to make of the one-party system. 'They spoke of moral renewal at a time when the Brown Terror was perpetrating murder and persecution.' In addition, a long tradition associating throne and altar had distorted their vision of reality.

German Catholicism under the leadership of the church marched confidently into the Third Reich. Bishop Bornewasser told Catholic young people in the cathedral of Trier: 'With our heads high and with firm steps we have entered the new Reich and are ready to serve it body and soul.' The Berlin Catholics' Conference on 25 June 1933 was held in the presence of the papal nuncio. Hitler had been invited but he did not appear – he avoided the personal overtures of the leaders of German Catholicism. The leader of Catholic Action, Erich Klausener, who was to be murdered on 30 June 1934, said the awakening of the German nation imposed important tasks on German Catholics.

On 11 July 1933 Bishop Berning of Osnabrück was appointed by Goering to the Prussian State Council (Goering, who organized the first concentration camps, had a motto: 'I thank my Creator that I do not know what objectivity is'). There were endless pledges of loyalty to Hitler from the bishops in spite of the continuing terror against Catholics. Cardinal Faulhaber sent a personal letter to Hitler on 24 July 1933 which said: 'What the old parliaments and parties failed to do in sixty years you achieved in six months by your statesmanlike foresight in the Concordat.' The letter ended: 'God preserve the Reich Chancellor for our people.'

There were enthusiastic telegrams and demonstrations for Hitler at the festival of the Sacred Robe in Trier. The Berlin Vicar-General, Steinmann, greeted the masses with 'Heil Hitler!' and spoke in glowing terms to the Catholic youths marching in front of him. The *Völkischer Beobachter* produced a picture of this which was published in New York in the periodical *Aurora und Christliche Woche* with a critical comment. Mgr Steinmann replied in an open letter. German Catholics, he said, saw Hitler's government as a God-given authority, a bulwark against Bolshevism. It had destroyed Bolshevism, liquidated the atheist-Marxist movement and freed the German people from the plague of dirty literature. (Was it not extraordinarily naïve to imagine that, as a result of energetic action during a few months in 1933, world movements and other great phenomena could be liquidated and destroyed?)

The declaration of the *Neudeutsche Jugend* (New German Youth) in September 1933 reflected the beliefs of these leaders of German Catholicism:

'We Germans of today affirm the total claims of our state and of our religion. Our profound desire is to harmonize and fuse together these two total claims.'

Cross and swastika were coming ever closer. Between the two, Man was to be crushed: the Jew and many others.

Catholic theologians rightly discovered many affinities between Nazi ideology and Catholicism. Michael Schmaus argued that Catholic and liberal thought were irreconcilable, but Catholicism and National Socialism could, and must, march hand in hand. Karl Adam wrote that National Socialism and Catholicism belonged together like nature and grace. Hitler had revealed to us the *homo germanus*.

Schmaus, the author of an ambitious dogmatic philosophy (and after 1945 rector of Munich University), and Karl Adam, the Nestor of contemporary Catholic theological thought, were, together with the highly significant church historian Joseph Lortz, the leading minds of European, and not merely German Catholicism. They were on firm historical ground in connecting National Socialism with the development of absolutism in the Curia and its condemnation of liberalism, Socialism and democracy in the nineteenth century.

In *Stimmen der Zeit*, the main periodical of the German Jesuits, which often showed great courage (Alfred Delp, who established contacts with the men of 20 July 1944, was on the editorial staff), Father Ludwig Koch announced the happy news that the swastika had proved its creative potential. This symbol of nature found its completion and fulfilment in the symbol of grace – the Cross.

Nature and grace: the swastika and the Cross. The church bowed to 'nature' in the form of the Nazi régime and exalted its brave struggle with its own sacraments and blessings right to the bitter end in 1945.

In the meantime Nazi bands stormed the last remaining Catholic institutions, beat up Catholic youths and arrested Catholic officials.

Completely surprised, the leaders of the church in Germany permitted their flock to be attacked. Pope Pius xi was disturbed and dismayed; but he let himself be reassured by Pacelli, who saw matters 'realistically', as Diego von Bergen reported back to Berlin.

The muzzling of the independent Catholic press (there were 400 Catholic daily papers at the beginning of the Third Reich) went quite smoothly: it was preceded by a wide-scale voluntary decision to accept the situation and to be silent. Many church papers now began to do more than Berlin had demanded from them and became virtually propaganda organs of National Socialism. Father Friedrich Muckermann, who had fled to Holland and there produced the resistance periodical *Der Deutsche Weg* (was it read in Rome by Pacelli?), called the Catholic press in the Third Reich an unsavoury medium of mendacity. The press worked smoothly in the service of the war propaganda machine, as, for instance, in preparing the offensive against the plutocratic capitalist West in March 1940. The war against the West was in accordance with natural law and papal teaching (*Haec Loquere et Exhortare*, XXXIV, 1940, 145: Mauritius Volk OSB: 'Plutocracy').

Ideologically there was a conflict with Alfred Rosenberg and his *Myth of the Twentieth Century*. But Rosenberg was never taken seriously by Hitler. Hitler himself was never excommunicated, nor were his books ever placed on the Index. Even much later, in the encyclical *Mit brennender Sorge* (With great perturbation) of 21 March 1937, one could still clearly detect a desire for reconciliation and co-operation with the system.

In *Nationale Erziehung und Religionsunterricht* (National Education and Religious Instruction, Regensburg 1934) the talented priest Anton Stonner SJ, drew parallels between the Christian mission, the cloister and the monastery and the SS and the SA. Stonner was highly praised by church papers and his book received official church approval. For decades, indeed nearly a century, the church had fought for its own schools; now Catholic schoolchildren in Catholic schools were taught in their religious instruction about the close affinity between Cross and swastika.

The bloody excesses and murders committed by the régime on 30 June 1934 did nothing to inhibit the many overtures of the bishops, prelates and theologians towards the régime. The line was consistently adopted that the church had been authoritarian and totalitarian from the beginning, and that in consequence it was in perfect harmony with the new age. Cardinal Bertram declared at the diocesan synod of the Breslau archbishopric in 1935 that the church had always recognized the importance of race, blood, and soil. Both Cardinal Faulhaber (in 1936) and the Würzburg Vicar-General, Miltenberger (in 1937) expressed themselves similarly in favour of blood and race. The articles on 'race', 'enlightenment', 'individualism', and 'honour' in Archbishop Gröber's *Handbook of Contemporary Religious Questions* were geared to the new National Socialist catechism: the Führer had liberated Germany and brought her back to the old Germanic virtues of honour, loyalty and courage. The Catholic fallen of the 1914–18 war were now frequently evoked, and the readiness of German Catholics to die on the battlefield proclaimed (as, for instance, in Faulhaber's Advent sermon in Munich in November 1936).

The world began to tremble in anticipation of a war brought about by Hitler. The important theologian, Otto Schilling, had been justifying the claim to greater *Lebensraum* and colonies since 1934. The article dealing with peace among nations in Gröber's handbook expressed the opinion that war was justified in certain circumstances.

The National Socialists themselves were not enamoured of these attempts to integrate German Catholicism with the Nazi régime. They disliked the way Catholics had adopted their own language with such phrases as 'Jesus is our Leader'. In Vienna Dietrich von Hildebrand, who had emigrated from Munich, criticized the overtures of the German Catholics and their attempts to outdo the National Socialists in chauvinism.

As late as February 1938 Bishop Ehrenfried of Würzburg expressed the hope that the totalitarianism of the state and the totalitarianism of the church could co-exist without conflict.

No German bishop spoke up against the abolition of all human and political rights by the régime. Nothing was said about the putsch of 30 June 1934, to which leading Catholics also fell victim, for example, Erich Klausener, Adalbert Probst, the courageous journalist Fritz Gerlich, and Fritz Beck. In Switzerland the German Catholic Waldemar Gurian wrote a pamphlet about the disgraceful silence of the church on the subject of these murders. (It was a silence that corresponded to the silence of the American church about Hiroshima and to the silence of the church and Catholicism about present preparations for Christendom's suicide. We shall return to it later.) Gurian said this silence destroyed the last moral authority in Germany and would lead to loss of confidence in the church. In Vienna Dietrich von Hildebrand said the same: 'The last mask has fallen.'

The church was silent about the concentration camps which had been established in 1933. Only the provost of Berlin Cathedral, Bernhard Lichtenberg (to whom, among others, Hochhuth's *The Representative* was dedicated) wrote to Goering on the subject. All the church tried to do was to get permission from Hitler for confession and mass to be held in the concentration camps.

In June 1936 Bishop Berning, who was a member of the Prussian state council, visited some concentration camps in his diocese of Osnabrück. He called on the inmates of Aschendorfer Moor camp to be obedient and loyal to the state and nation and praised the work of the staff and guards of the camp. And he ended with three Sieg Heils to the Führer. This also happened in the Papenburg concentration camp on 1 July 1936. The Catholic *Kölnische Volkszeitung* carried a report on it.

Friedrich Muckermann had been appealing to the church throughout the world since 1934 to protest against this barbarism and murder, but the international church and the international conscience of Catholicism did not react. After 1945 the many church appeals on behalf of the 'church of silence', the 'church in distress', in the 'trap of Bolshevist Satan' were remarkable attempts to conceal its own silence over the tortures and murders in Catholic dictatorships and authoritarian states of Europe, Africa, Asia and South America. Above all, they were attempts to conceal these things from its own consciousness.

In correspondence with each other the German bishops showed that they were profoundly pessimistic and anxious about the attitude of German Catholics. They believed that these would not remain loyal to the church if there were a breach with the régime. Only a small minority would stand by the church. That was a correct analysis. But the German bishops overlooked then – and to a certain extent still do today – that they had done nothing to educate the German Catholics politically and to train them in the religious sense to be mature people capable of resistance, instead of obedient children. The bishops also overlooked the fact that they themselves were steeped in a political image of the world which, in many respects, corresponded with the National Socialist image.

Foreign observers had different ideas about German Catholics. The British Catholic writer William Teeling, for instance, after spending two years in Germany and Austria, remarked in 1937 that they were confused by the lack of leadership and guidance from their bishops. Pope and episcopate had shown a lack of leadership and courage. This view was also expressed by Cardinal Tisserant in a letter to Archbishop Suhard on 11 June 1940.

On 13 March 1938, the very day the Anschluss with Austria was effected, Friedrich Muckermann declared in his periodical *Der Deutsche Weg* that the bishops had failed: they had not defended human freedom and were therefore incapable of defending the freedom of the church. The same conviction ran like a thread through the reflections of Father Alfred Delp in the prison at Berlin-Plötzensee, where in 1944-5 he waited in chains for his execution. In his periodical *Stimmen der Zeit* only one lonely voice of conscience was heard: Max Pribilla SJ in his article on 'Character' in 1935.

An important cause of the German bishops' slipping into the clutches of National Socialism was their patriotism. The church supported Hitler's foreign policy from beginning to end. Election appeals by German bishops called for participation in the plebiscite on the secession of Germany from the League of Nations. The Saar plebiscite in 1935 produced a marked similarity in the propaganda of the Catholic church and the National Socialists. *Le Matin* had said as early as 1922 that, for the German bishop of Speyer, love of Germany was a hundred times more important than love of God. (That was not quite correct, and in any case, French Catholicism, with its extreme chauvinism, which did not hesitate to identify the cause of France with that of God, was by no means entitled to make such a statement.)

In 1935 the bishops of Trier and Speyer, Bornewasser and Sebastian, adopted a very nationalist attitude towards France. Pacelli sent from Rome, in quick succession, two pro-Fascist and pro-National Socialist papal delegates as apostolic visitors to the Saar: Testa and Panico. *Der Deutsche Katholik in der Saar* which appeared from 1 October 1934, with its illustrated supplement 'The battle cry against the Anti-Christ', showed atrocity pictures from Bolshevist Russia, and beside them Hitler as the saviour from the Bolshevist peril.

When, after a rapturous church propaganda campaign, the Saar was incorporated into Germany, and shortly afterwards church organizations were suppressed, the bishop of Speyer turned to Rome for help. The office of the state secretary said it had expected nothing else. But shortly before, it had given free rein to Catholic National Socialist propaganda.

In November 1935 Adolf Hitler declared that Germany was the bulwark

L* 313

of the West against Bolshevism. The German bishops took up these words of Hitler with enthusiasm. The Fulda pastoral letter acclaimed Hitler's foreign policy (19 August 1936). On 9 September 1936 Hitler 'preached' against Bolshevism at the Nuremberg party rally; while Pius XI spoke against Bolshevism to Spanish refugees in the Vatican. The sermon of the new bishop of Passau, Landesdorfer, at his inauguration, struck the same note. On 4 November 1936 Cardinal Faulhaber had a long and friendly talk with Hitler over lunch on the Obersalzberg. Hitler boasted he was the only protection against Bolshevism. He assured the cardinal that National Socialism and the church would fight together against Bolshevism, or go down to defeat.

Faulhaber was deeply impressed. He heard what he wanted to hear; and Hitler knew what the cardinal wanted to hear. Faulhaber reported back to the bishops about this talk, declaring that the Führer knew more about diplomacy and social etiquette than a born monarch. The baker's son, Faulhaber, was the first Catholic bishop in the First World War to receive the Iron Cross for his spiritual work, as senior military chaplain with the Bavarian troops, and he had shown himself from the very first to be the mortal enemy of the Weimar Republic.

As a result of Faulhaber's report, the German bishops published a joint pastoral letter against Bolshevism. This appeared on 24 December 1936 and was read from the pulpits on 3 January 1937. The bishops said the hour of destiny had struck: Bolshevism was preparing to advance against Europe. In this way the German bishops identified themselves completely with Hitler's pre-war propaganda. In 1936 Stalin was preoccupied with opposition at home and many other difficulties. The bishops took the same opportunity to warn their flocks against discontent and criticism of the National Socialist régime. Faulhaber himself was critical of Catholic refugees who spoke and wrote disagreeable things about Hitler, like Waldemar Gurian in his *Deutsche Briefe* in Lucerne and Father Muckermann in *Der Deutsche Weg* in Holland.

All church bells in Germany and Austria rang on the evening before the day of the 'Greater German Reich' on 10 April. The only German bishop not to vote in the 'plebiscite' in the Ostmark was Sproll of Rottenburg. He was hounded from his diocese. In the declaration of the Austrian bishops, which was published in the Vienna diocesan gazette on 22 March 1938 and had previously appeared on all advertising pillars and street posters, it was stated that the 'thousand-year-old desire of our people for union in a great German Reich' had found its fulfilment. This was a plain lie taken over directly from Nazi propaganda. The bishops said they 'gladly recognized that the National Socialist movement has done, and continues to do, excellent work in the sphere of national and economic construction and in the social field for the German people, particularly the poorest sections . . . On the day of the plebiscite it will be for us bishops an obvious national duty to opt as Germans for the German Reich. We also expect all Christian believers to appreciate what they owe to their people.'

From several thousand Austrian Catholics the bishops could no longer expect such appreciation, for these had already been seized, thrown into prison, and transported to Dachau along with legitimists, Socialists, Jews and Communists. Many other Austrians were forced to commit suicide.

On 1 October 1938 the Germans marched into Czechoslovakia: the Sudetenland was occupied. Faulhaber sent a telegram of thanks to the Führer in the name of the German episcopate: the Führer had ensured peace. Thanksgiving services were held in all German churches on the following Sunday. In the Berlin diocese a message was read from the pulpits saying that God had listened to Christendom's prayer for peace. There was a *Te Deum* for the peaceful incorporation of the people of the Sudetenland into the Reich. The German ambassador at the Vatican, Diego von Bergen, reported to Berlin on 22 March 1939 that the pope had rejected French attempts to persuade him to protest against the annexation of Bohemia and Moravia. He did not wish to intervene in historical processes in which, from the political point of view, the church was not interested.

Pacelli, the new Pope Pius XII, sent the first news of his election on 3 March 1939 to Hitler. He violated protocol by himself signing the German version of the letter, expressing warm hopes of friendly relations.

There were church bells, swastika flags on church towers and thanksgiving services for Hitler's birthday in 1939. That the new wind blowing from the Vatican was favourable to Hitler was well understood: Pius XI had been much more reserved. Votive masses took place in all churches in honour of the Archangel Michael, imploring God's blessing on the Führer. (In popular belief the Archangel had led the army of the Holy Roman Empire in the Middle Ages.) Sermons and diocesan papers celebrated Hitler on this day as the 'extender' o the Reich: this was an old title of the Roman emperor.

The church stood behind Hitler when he went to war. As Guenter Lewy has written: 'The church had no eyes for Hitler's blood purge of 1934 and the barbarities of the concentration camps. She was in no position, politically or intellectually, to oppose him now, when he plunged the world into a war that was to cause unimaginable misery and the death of millions of human beings.'

Of about thirty-two million German Catholics – fifteen and a half million of whom were men – only seven openly refused military service. Six of these were Austrians.

The German bishops, at the time of the Second World War, were prisoners of an image of the world which had been formed before the First World War in imperial Germany, and to a large extent, they continued to be so even after 1945.

It was precisely those princes of the church Galen and Faulhaber, celebrated after 1945 as 'heroes' of the resistance against Hitler, who stood most profoundly under this spell of historical continuity. Galen, a feudal reactionary, thought on the same political lines in 1917, 1933 and 1945. In 1932 Faulhaber dared to take an initial step towards a theology of peace: he became the patron of the 'German Catholics' League of Peace'. Gröber also spoke up for a theology of peace in 1931, but in 1935 he was again supporting the old war theology. For Galen, German soldiers in 1944 were still martyrs who had fought against 'atheist Bolshevism' and 'the anti-Christ'.

In German pastoral letters during the Second World War the love of Christ was perverted into a war mentality. Here is only one example, taken from the pastoral letter of the eight Bavarian bishops of 25 February 1941, after Poland had been drowned in blood and Russia was about to be attacked: 'The time in which we live will be decisive for far into the distant future . . . We therefore address to you, dear members of the dioceses, in a spirit of fatherly love and care, a word of exhortation to encourage you to devote all your strength to the service of the fatherland and your dear country by conscientiously carrying out your duty and taking a serious view of your calling. We Germans form a great living community of destiny: we are also a community in our faith in Christ and in our love of Christ. And if the commandment of love is always the greatest of all commandments, this is especially so in times of danger and suffering . . . We saw with pride and joy in the first years of the [First] World War what great things unity brings about. But we were also to see at the end of the World War how lack of unity again destroys all those great things. [This is an acknowledgment of the legend of the 'stab in the back'.] To be united is now therefore the great commandment in this grave hour. We must be united in the love and service of the fatherland: we must create a unique community ready to work and make sacrifices to protect our country.'

This myth of unity is again being peddled about in contemporary Germany. The German atom bomb theology and its atrocity propaganda against the diabolical arch-enemy of 'international Communism', are a direct continuation of the tradition of 1939–45.

In 1937 the Fulda bishops' conference began to honour the military chaplains of the First World War. After 1937 many books appeared dealing with priests as war heroes. In July 1939 the bishops were instructed, as a matter of the utmost secrecy, to prepare a cadre of military chaplains. At the Fulda bishops' conference, 22–24 August 1939, the bishops already knew that war was imminent.

On 17 September 1939 the German bishops issued a joint statement. In this Catholic soldiers were specially called on to show obedience to the Führer. All church bells rang for Hitler's first great victory – the conquest of Warsaw – on the orders of Cardinal Bertram of Breslau. On the feast of the patron saint of Poland, St Hedwig, the German army bishop Rarkowski rejoiced over the defeat of Poland: 'One would not be a man or a Christian, one would lack the profound German spirit, if one had not been moved when the Führer raised his voice in solemn entreaty to warn those who want to stir up a world conflagration and provoke the nations into a cruel war.'

Among the many Poles executed in this bloody autumn of 1939 were 214 priests, including the whole cathedral chapter of Pelphin. At the end of 1939 there were about a thousand Polish clergy in prison and concentration camps. On 21 September Cardinal Hlond protested to the pope about German acts of cruelty. Both Radio Vatican and the *Osservatore Romano* reported his protest. But there was no reaction from the German bishops. The diocesan gazettes celebrated Germany's 'holy war', particularly in Berlin and Breslau. (How does it look in Berlin and Breslau today?) Germany was fighting a holy struggle for her vital rights, among them 'the right of the German people to Lebensraum'.

After the victory over France the church bells rang for a whole week. Swastika flags flew for ten days on the churches. Cross and swastika came ever closer together, crushing the nations and then the Jews.

Rise up against England, the old bastion of capitalism! (This was the call in the Freiburg diocesan gazette *St Konradsblatt*.) Onwards with God's help to victory! The war against Russia and against Bolshevism was welcomed enthusiastically. Bishops made statements supporting the struggle against the Slav 'subhumans'. Archbishop Jäger of Paderborn (who became a cardinal in 1965) said in his Lent pastoral letter of 11 February 1942 that, as a result of their hostility to God and their hatred of Christ, the Russians had degenerated almost to the state of animals. Even in January 1945 Archbishop Jäger was exhorting German Catholics to play their part in the mighty struggle against Germany's two great enemies – 'liberalism and individualism on the one hand, and collectivism on the other'. (In contemporary pastoral letters this theme always recurs. But today the enemies are Eastern and Western materialism.)

In April 1945 Count Galen, 'the lion of Münster', refused to receive British and American journalists because they were representatives of the enemy. In his first statement after the occupation, at Easter 1945, he said his heart bled at the sight of passing enemy troops. He was thinking in terms of the 'German God', the *deus teutonicus*. For that God the German imperial bishops had marched to the East in the twelfth century. In 1945 the German God, who had no eyes for the sufferings of others, was contained.

German military chaplains witnessed the killing and persecution of Russian prisoners of war in the East. As Guenter Lewy has said: 'The Catholic episcopate must therefore bear some share of the responsibility for the immeasurable suffering which Hitler's armies inflicted upon Europe.' The American Catholic historian, Gordon C. Zahn, who was not a refugee as German Catholic papers have suggested, has shown how the church became an 'agency of the Third Reich'. He remarks that the German episcopate learned nothing from the Second World War. We would like to qualify this view: it has rather learned too little, because it cannot make up its mind to rid itself of old theological and political conceptions of the world. The American historian notes in this connection that there was not a single protest by the church in the USA against the two atomic bombs dropped on Japan.

The most macabre actor in the drama of German war-time Catholicism was the army bishop Franz Josef Rarkowski. He was a creature of the Roman prelate Benigni, who in the time of Pius x had covered the whole of Europe with a traditionalist 'Gestapo' of the Curia. In the First World War a German officer who belonged to a religious order accidentally discovered a file concerning this movement in occupied Belgium. Throughout Catholic Europe Benigni's organization, centred on the *Sodalitium Pianum*, the Pius Society in Rome, had branches which supplied it with material about 'suspect' theologians, priests, members of orders and laymen, who either as 'modernists' condemned the authoritarian line of the Curia or were at least guilty of 'theological deviations'.

Contemporary Catholic theologians and sociologists have often observed that Catholicism has not yet recovered from the deep scars left by this witchhunt that claimed as its victims outstanding Catholic theologians, professors and academics.

From the political point of view it is important to observe that the theological authoritarianism which divides the world into two great military camps, one of God and the other of the Devil, with its Augustinian and profoundly pessimistic anthropology, *forms the broad basis of ecclesiastical absolutism and papal dictatorship*. It takes into account neither the rights of bishops nor those of other men. Pius xii was until his death the patron of this authoritarianism to which, after 1945, the 'new theology' of the Jesuits, Dominicans and Carmelites fell victim. The worker-priests' movement was another victim.

On 20 February 1938 – the day on which Hitler was brow-beating Austria's chancellor Schuschnigg in Berchtesgaden – the nuncio Orsenigo ordained Franz Josef Rarkowski *episcopus castrensis* (army bishop) in Berlin in the presence of Preysing and Galen. This army bishop accompanied Hitler's campaigns with orders and circulars addressed to German Catholic soldiers, couched in a language no longer readable today, advocating a 'European crusade' against 'Bolshevist subhumans' and so on.

These military chaplains mentioned morality, but – in a typically traditionalist way – they meant the private sexual morals of the soldiers. There was no word about the immorality of war, of murdering, plundering and oppressing foreign nations. But behind this was an illustrious Augustinian tradition ('What seekest thou?' 'God and the salvation of my soul.' 'Nothing else?' 'Nothing else!')

On 8 December 1939 Pope Pius xii addressed a pastoral letter to the military chaplains of all nations. (There were about 560 Catholic chaplains in the German armies; Hermann Goering's Luftwaffe had no use for any.) The pope declared that the present war should be seen and accepted as a manifestation of divine providence and as the will of God, who always transformed evil into good. The chaplains were called on to fight for the church under the flag of their respective countries.

Here the tragedy of Pope Pius XII is already apparent. This fundamentally lonely man was a prisoner of tradition and of ecclesiastical traditionalism. Until the end of his life he believed in the traditional Catholic theological view of the 'just war' – in spite of Hitler and nuclear weapons. He believed in the historical role of Concordats – even with murderers and dictators. He believed in the traditional theology about the Jews, in precisely the sense in which the important church historian of the Papal University in Rome, Father Georg Hertling SJ, described it in his essay on the Jews written for *Civiltà Cattolica* in 1962. The sufferings of the Jews were, to some extent, to be seen as the proof of God's grace. At the instigation of State Secretary Cicognani this essay was withdrawn in Rome, but it later appeared in the highly regarded German Jesuit publication, *Stimmen der Zeit* (No. 171).

The Vatican sacrificed Catholic Poland to the dictator Hitler after the pope had made attempts in Berlin, before Hitler's invasion, to get his assurance that the interests of the church in Poland would be safeguarded. As a result of German complaints, Radio Vatican stopped its broadcasts in Polish in January 1940. The Vatican repeatedly gave the German ambassador, Bergen, to understand that it did not condemn the German military actions against Poland, Holland and Belgium. After the war the former Polish foreign minister, Beck, declared: 'One of the main sources of responsibility for the tragedy of my country was the Vatican. I realized too late that we were pursuing a foreign policy in the interests of the Catholic church.'

The surrender of Poland by the Vatican had important consequences, not only for the Polish intelligentsia and the upper strata of the Polish nation, who were liquidated, but also for the whole of European Jewry: Poland was to become the deathbed of Europe's Jews. Pius XII could not foresee that; but he deliberately sacrificed Catholic Poland to the dictator Hitler. He was under the spell of that unfortunate scholastic teaching which accepts the lesser evil to avoid the greater one. What represented the greater evil was made clear after the crushing of Poland, when the pope spoke at a reception of the college of cardinals on 25 December 1939: 'Let us end this war between brothers and unite our forces against the common enemy of atheism.'

In 1938, on the occasion of the Eucharistic Congress in Budapest in Fascist Hungary – not far from occupied Austria, where at the time, Catholics loyal to Rome were being persecuted to death – Pacelli had similarly drawn attention to the coming crusade against Bolshevism. Until the end of the war Pius XII hoped to reconcile Hitler and the Western powers and to unite them in a common alliance against Russia.

The Vatican greatly feared a German defeat in Russia. The church – that is to say, the Curia and the German episcopate – was anxious not to weaken Hitler, but to strengthen him internally. Michael Serafian, the Jesuit Martin, put it in 1964 this way: 'It cannot be denied that Pius' XII's closest advisers for some time regarded Hitler's armoured divisions as the right hand of God, with whose help the prophecy of Fatima concerning the conversion of Russia would be fulfilled.'

It was a sad spectacle. The German episcopate and its organs of publicity constantly made overtures to Hitler during the Second World War and assured him of their complete and unreserved support. Hitler and the National Socialists for their part made considerable efforts to free themselves from these unwanted allies in the Catholic church.

At the height of Hitler's military victories in 1941 there occurred the first conflict with the church. The church was not prepared in Germany to co-operate with Hitler's euthanasia policy. It protested and was successful. Thus did the power of public opinion show itself in the middle of the war, at the climax of Hitler's military victories. There was a close connection between the killing of the mentally infirm and the liquidation of the Jews. The 'elimination of useless lives' was a *ballon d'essai* which, above all, was meant to test the technical possibilities of mass extermination. But here clergy of both churches, generals, senior officials and even Gauleiters raised their voices in protest.

By August 1941 this chorus had become a hurricane. Hitler then postponed his euthanasia programme 'for the duration of the war'. As Guenter Lewy observes: 'Had German public opinion shown a similar response against other crimes of the Nazi régime committed on an even greater scale, such as the extermination of the Jews in Europe, the results might well have been similarly telling.' Why did it not happen in the case of the Jews?

'As far as the Jews are concerned, they have crucified God and so have made themselves guilty. And for this reason God has cursed them for all time. Their sufferings down the centuries ever since are only a divine revenge for this crime and for their refusal to be converted to Christianity.' Michael Serafian quoted this traditional doctrine as representing the present con-victions of conservative circles in the Curia. In private discussions with Catholics it is still possible today to hear the view expressed that Hitler in his treatment of the Jews was the instrument of divine providence.

Of German nineteenth-century Catholics, Bishop Martin of Paderborn (1812–79) and Bishop Keppler of Rottenburg (1852–1926) were particularly well known for their anti-Semitic views, which were often quoted by the National Socialists. The Centre party press began an anti-Semitic campaign against Jews and liberals in the summer of 1875. Erzberger, the man of the so-called left wing of the Centre party, was critical of the 'strongly Judaized' Social Democratic trade unions. Gustav Gundlach SJ, in the article on anti-Semitism in the official *Lexicon for Theology and Church* (2nd edition, 1930), argued that political anti-Semitism should be tolerated so long as it employed morally permissible methods. Bishop Michael Buchberger used the same argument in 1931 in *Gibt es noch eine Rettung?* (Is Salvation Possible?, Regensburg, 1931). Vicar-General Dr Mayer of Mainz was of the opinion that Hitler in *Mein Kampf* had correctly described the evil influence of the Jews in the press, the theatre and in literature, but he was opposed to racial discrimination. Without ever being prosecuted or censured, Josef Roth announced that Jews were an inferior race, that action against them was justified and did not violate the principle of Christian love. Wilhelm Maria Senn, a member of a Catholic order, even described German Catholicism in 1931 as 'Judaized'. He considered the Hitler movement, in spite of certain excesses, 'the last big chance to shake off the Jewish yoke'.

Of great importance was, of course, that popular form of anti-Semitism still encountered today in certain 'pious customs' specially protected by the church. In Deggendorf in Bavaria there is each year a week-long church festival in remembrance of a massacre which took place on 30 September 1337. On that day the people of Deggendorf killed all the Jews in the locality as a form of thanks for the miraculous saving of a small child from ritual murder. Part of the festivities consisted of a morality play presented by a Benedictine monk. This morality play would still be performed today but for Dr Franz Rödel, the founder of a Catholic-Jewish institute in Jetzendorf to enlighten Catholics. Rödel presented a petition to the Bavarian bishops' conference in 1960, requesting that the festivities be abolished. He received no answer. Only when the periodical *Der Spiegel* took up the case did the church authorities begin to do anything about it. But the overall festival of the *Deggendorfer Gnad* still continues.

Only a few Catholic priests and laymen resisted the anti-Semitic wave in the Catholic world at the time of the Weimar Republic. Such exceptions were Franz Rödel and the journalist Franz Steffen, who in 1925 prophesied in Berlin that the National Socialists would fall on the Catholics – after the Jews.

In the Weimar Republic not a word from the bishops was heard in protest against Nazi anti-Semitism. The roots of the church's failure to protest against or resist the later Nazi policy of liquidation lay precisely here: in the still ambivalent attitude of the church towards the Jews. We can trace this attitude from the early days of Christendom to Hitler's assumption of power and beyond.

Hitler knew very well the anti-Jewish attitude of the church stretching over fifteen centuries and referred to it in his conversation with Bishop Berning and Mgr Steinmann on 26 April 1933. We do not know the precise answer the two church leaders gave Hitler, but after this meeting German bishops began to proclaim the importance they attached to matters of race and racial purity.

Many attempts have been made since 1945 to depict a resistance movement of the church against Hitler; in fact, the only resistance lay in the defence of the clergy's rights in their narrowest sense. In addition to carefully edited sermons by Galen and Faulhaber (with some tactful omissions), the 'heroic defence' of the Jews in Cardinal Faulhaber's famous Advent sermons of 1933 always plays a conspicuous role.

In these sermons the Munich cardinal defended the Old Testament (no cardinal would ever have dared attack it); but in the same breath he said that he did not intend to defend his Jewish contemporaries: one must make a distinction between Jews before and after the death of Christ. When in 1934 foreigners were wicked and hostile enough to suppose that he was defending the Jews, Cardinal Faulhaber expressly rejected this malicious supposition. He said he had never intended to defend the Jews. In 1943, when the extermination of the Hungarian Jews was at its height, the papal nuncio in Budapest made a similar statement. He declared that the protest of the Vatican against the crude form the deportations took was not the result of a 'false feeling of pity'. These are examples of that attitude towards 'humanitarian fuss' which used to crop up in National Socialist and Catholic publications – and still does today.

The Jews were robbed of their sacred past and thereby exposed to a murderous future. A canon of Regensburg Cathedral instructed Catholic teachers in the Bavarian *Klerusblatt* in 1939 to show their schoolchildren how the holy books of the Old Testament were in direct conflict with the Jewish mentality. The great miracle of the Bible was that it showed how true religion was able to prevail over the voice of Semitism.

Christianity was not Jewish; but Marxism was Jewish. 'Bolshevism is an Asiatic despotism in the service of a group of terrorists led by Jews': that is what the article on Marxism said in Gröber's *Handbook of Contemporary Religious Questions*. Here it was also proclaimed that the Führer had correctly described Europe's struggle against this Asiatic barbarism.

Whoever among the thousands of Catholic officers on the Eastern front saw how the 'Jewish Bolsheviks' were handled as prisoners could, with a clear conscience, refer to the guidance provided for all educated Catholics in this handbook.

The Jews were responsible for the Weimar Republic, for Marxism and for the 1918 revolution. This was the claim made in an article in 1935 in *Klerusblatt* entitled 'Marxism over Germany seventeen years ago'. Ever since 1914 the question had arisen of the Jews' betrayal of the German people. These 'subhumans' brought about the revolution of 1918. The Jews did more harm than good to the German people, according to Gustav Lehmacher SJ in an essay called 'Racial Values' in *Stimmen der Zeit* in 1933. And the Benedictine Bogler, in *Der Glaube von gestern und heute* (Faith Yesterday and

Today, Cologne, 1939), proclaimed that the Jews killed Jesus and that their boundless hatred still put them today in the front rank of all destroyers of the church. The book was published with official church approval.

Waldemar Gurian, a democratic Catholic refugee, recognized in his *Deutsche Briefe* on 27 September 1935 that the Nuremberg racial laws constituted a step towards the complete physical extermination of the Jews. On the other hand, a civil servant named Münsterer declared in the *Klerusblatt* in 1936 that these laws were an indispensable safeguard for the maintenance of the German people. Bishop Hudal in Rome welcomed the Nuremberg laws as being in the old tradition of the church's struggle against the Jews.

It is well known that State Secretary Dr Globke, who was for many years Dr Adenauer's close associate, won special recognition for his work on the Nuremberg laws. He was understandably exonerated by Catholic bishops after 1945.

Viewed against the background of the 'final solution', the church's zealous co-operation in looking for proof of Aryan blood is seen to be highly dubious. Without the co-operation of many thousands of priests' offices, it would not have been possible to produce the proof.

Baptized Jews received only limited help. The silence of the church on the persecution of the Jews prompted one priest to say in 1934 that it was the duty of the church to oppose the rising wave of hatred. The Jewish question would provide a good opportunity for a genuine 'Catholic Action' ('The Catholic Church and the Jewish Question' – an anonymous contribution in *Eine Heilige Kirche*, 1934).

The bishops were silent on the subject of the *Kristallnacht*, on the burning of the synagogues and on the tormenting of many Jews. They were silent about the 'final solution'. They were silent because they did not want to endanger the Führer's great final struggle against Bolshevism.

From the end of 1941 onwards soldiers brought news of murders of Jews to Germany from the East. In 1942 the murder of three hundred thousand Jews in Poland was reported. In August of the same year the Protestant SS leader, Kurt Gerstein, tried to inform the nuncio in Berlin about the gas chambers in Lublin. But Orsenigo refused to listen to him. Gerstein then reported this information to Dr Winter, the legal adviser to Bishop Preysing, and to others. He also asked that his report should be forwarded to the Holy See. At the same time other reports from Catholic officers in Poland and Russia about the beginning of the 'final solution' reached the German bishops. One of these German officers, Alfons Hildenbrand, took special leave from his unit near Minsk in order to report to Cardinal Faulhaber. The Bavarian Catholic politician Joseph Müller, who became very well known in German politics after the war, persisted for a long time in informing Faulhaber and the German episcopate about the atrocities in Poland.

The German bishops were silent or phrased their protests in very general terms when it was a matter of killing 'innocent' people. But the Jew was guilty – the theologians had proved that a thousand times. Of course, the bishops never spoke of Jews or non-Aryans. For that reason, being under the spell of this inner fixation, they do not talk today about genocide, but rather of war. This great silence lay like a cloak of ice over the German people, nearly half of whom were Catholics in 1939 – 43.1 per cent. Even in the SS nearly a quarter – 22.7 per cent on 31 December 1938 – belonged to the Catholic church.

The church had declared itself opposed to duelling and cremation; but the annihilation machine ran on undisturbed. There was not a single excommunication. Only one German churchman protested: Provost Bernhard Lichtenberg of Berlin Cathedral. He was arrested on 23 October 1941 and died in a concentration camp. The Cross of Christ, the Cross of the Jew Jesus was, with the complicity of both churches, imposed on the Jews.

The passivity of the German bishops was in contrast to the behaviour of the French, Belgian and Dutch bishops. In 1942 the Dutch bishops protested against the first deportations of Dutch Jews. In 1943 they forbade Dutch Catholic police – even at the risk of losing their jobs – from taking part in the hunting down of Jews. Similar attitudes were known to have been shown in Belgium and France. On 15 March 1941 Archbishop Gröber of Freiburg referred to the curse which the Jews had brought on themselves. The Jews' saying, 'His blood be on us and on our children' was, he said, still being fulfilled today. A monstrous 'justification', showing to what extent the German bishops were still prisoners of their own anti-Semitic teachings.

It was only in Berlin that Jews were concealed in any numbers, and then chiefly by workers, male and female, who had no connection with the church, as the Protestant Dean Grüber testified.

'It has been said that the church protects the Hebrews and has changed its discipline. That is not true. The church maintains its laws and discipline. The church has said nothing and done nothing to defend the Hebrews, the Jews and Judaism.' The bishop of Cremona made this solemn declaration on 6 January 1939 in his Epiphany sermon – the day the Italians celebrate Christmas.

This terrible statement is part of a tradition, fifteen hundred years old. The bishop of Cremona was not a prophet; but he rightly saw that the Roman Catholic church would not speak up in the years to come – not even when Jews in Rome were snatched from the gates of the Vatican by Fascist soldiers and sent to their deaths.

'I know Herr Hitler. He is a fool and a nobody, but a fanatical nobody – an intolerable talker! . . . Tell your Jews that they don't need to be afraid of him.' That was what Benito Mussolini said in a conversation with Nahum Goldmann in 1934. It was a remarkably incorrect assessment. Italy is a country which has hardly been affected by anti-Semitism. With their sound common sense, derived from hundreds of years of experience, the Italians could not imagine what Hitler would actually do. Yet even in Italy it was possible to find henchmen for the final solution. The way for their participation had been prepared by Fascist ideologists associated with Nicolo Giani and the periodical *Dottrina Fascista*. The editors were Vito Mussolini, Fernando Mezzasoma and Nicolo Giani, professor of history and Fascist ideology at Pavia University.

Perché siamo antisemiti (Why we are anti-Semites): under this title there appeared in 1939 a number of the *Quaderni della Scuola di mistica fascista Sandro Italico Mussolini*. The author was Giani. What was significant about this publication was its aggressive anti-liberal and anti-democratic attitude and the constant references to anti-Semitic essays by theologians, particularly in *La Civiltà Cattolica*. Close connections have survived to this day between Roman conservative circles in the Curia and Roman Jesuits on the one hand and Fascists on the other – former Fascists and neo-Fascists. In 1952–3 this unholy alliance almost succeeded in defeating the Christian Democrat ruling party and its leading statesman, Alcide de Gasperi, in breaking up the party, and in putting a Fascist-conservative-Catholic combination in its place. This alliance cast a heavy shadow over the Second Vatican Council and probably barred the way to the great opening of the door to the Jews and other non-Christians. Cardinals of the Curia, supported by their Fascist friends combined to fight with all their strength against *sinistrismo*, against a deviation from the inexorable 'pure teaching' of the church and against any concession to the left-wing socialism. In 1945, after the Jewish massacre, they remained of the same opinion as Nicolo Giani before the massacre.

Giani said in 1939 that two hostile worlds were then engaged in a life and death struggle – Fascism on the one side and democracy under the leadership of Roosevelt and the Jews on the other. Judaism was the common factor in *demoliberalsocialcommunismo* – a portmanteau word covering Communists, liberals, democrats, freemasons and Socialists. Behind all these stood the Jews.

Being Roman meant being at the same time a Catholic and a Fascist. Leading articles in the *Osservatore Romano* proclaimed the Romans to be the basis of Christianity and a bulwark against the left. Giani found his confirmation in Father Agostino Gemelli, the highly regarded rector of the Catholic univerisity in Milan, who defended National Socialism and Fascism against its enemies. He called the Hebrews the physical negation of Rome, the church and the state. Giani quoted Cato, Cicero, Tacitus, Juvenal and the Roman emperors and referred to the strictness and severity of the church fathers towards the Jews. And he then recalled an outstandingly important event: on 21 March 1928 the Holy Office had condemned the society *Amici d'Israeli* (the Friends of Israel). Dutch theologians had started it with the idea of creating a small centre within the Roman Catholic church where Jews and Christians could meet. The Holy Office put paid to it. Such a 'spirit of reconciliation' was contrary to the teaching of the church and its traditions. The decision was confirmed by the pope on 22 March 1928 and recorded in the *Acta Apostolicae Sedis*.

The silence of Pope Pius XII on the subject of the Jews, right up to his death, must have had its deepest objective basis here. The subjective bases arising from his personality we shall look at later. This pope wished to maintain the whole tradition of the church intact, and the anti-Judaism which had existed from the fourth right up to the twentieth century was part of that tradition. For fear that the whole structure of the church would collapse, he would not touch a single stone in the edifice.

Like so many theologians, Giani considered the French Revolution the root of all evil. He referred to the *Protocols of the Elders of Zion* and argued that, even if in their present form they were forgeries, their content and spirit were authentic Judaism. The Jesuits had recognized that as early as 1892.

Giani mentioned an anti-Semitic statement of the Duce on 4 June 1919, and he issued an appeal: 'It is now, in 1939, up to us. Let us do our duty in the struggle against Judaism, as the martyrs of the church, the Crusaders and the Templars did theirs. God has reserved to us the honour of the struggle, the privilege of sacrifice and pride in being able to fight for an ideal of salvation and power.'

Giani, the Fascist of 1939, produced Faulhaber's sermons on the Jews, which had appeared in Italian in Brescia in 1934, as evidence of his Catholic anti-Semitism. He also referred to the great anti-Semitic tradition of *Civiltà Cattolica*, the leading Roman Jesuit periodical, which was so close to the Vatican.

The encyclical *Mit brennender Sorge*, which concerned itself in March 1937 with National Socialism and which was published far too late, was phrased in a very conciliatory tone – something which was later conveniently over-looked. Reconciliation with the right was an honourable thing: reconciliation with the left was blasphemy. This encyclical did not mention anti-Semitism with so much as a single word, although that constituted the pivot of National Socialist philosophy and practice. Anti-Semitism was not mentioned in the eight condemned theses of Nazi ideology or in the statement of the Roman congregation of seminaries and universities (*La Croix*, 17 September 1938). The words of Pope Pius XI, addressed to Belgian pilgrims on 7 September 1938 (they were often quoted after 1945), 'We Christians are all spiritual Semites,' were not reported at the time in any Italian paper – not even in *Osservatore Romano*.

The Holy See had little objection to the anti-Jewish legislation introduced by the Catholic Vichy state. Its ambassador, Léon Bérard, had sounded the Vatican on its opinion. Twice in the year 1942 Roosevelt approached the pope through his personal representative at the Holy See, Myron C. Taylor, to remind him of the persecution of the Jews. In a conversation with Ciano in Rome in October 1942 Himmler praised the 'discretion' shown by the Vatican in the Jewish question. Himmler was very fulsome in his praise of the pope. Ciano recalled this in his diaries.

On 11 June 1940 Cardinal Tisserant wrote in great concern from the Curia to the archbishop of Paris, Cardinal Suhard. This letter was later found by the Germans in the archbishop's palace in Paris. It said: 'Our superiors do not wish to understand the real nature of the conflict, and they obstinately cling to the idea that this is a war like others in the past. But Fascist and Hitlerite ideology has transformed the conscience of young people, and those under thirty-five are ready to perform any kind of misdeed in a cause which their leader orders.' Tisserant feared that the German policy of annihilation which had been tried out in Poland would also be applied in France. 'I have constantly begged the Holy Father since the beginning of December to issue an encyclical on the duty of every individual to listen to the call of conscience, for there lies the essence of Christianity . . .'

We may observe here that it was precisely the role of the individual's conscience which was carefully suppressed by Roman traditionalism. They wanted obedient servants, not partners. Pius xii never left any doubt about that: he did not want colleagues, but executive organs or 'instruments'.

Tisserant wrote: 'I fear that history will be justified in charging the Holy See with having pursued a policy of selfish convenience and little more. That is extremely sad, especially for those of us who have lived under Pius xi. And everyone relies on the fact that, after Rome has been declared an open city, no one in the Curia will have to suffer. That is disgraceful . . . My life here is one of complete uselessness. I am held back here, although I have asked the Holy Father to send me to France.'

'That is disgraceful.' The disgrace was manifest in Rome itself in 1943–4. The Jews were removed from Rome. The German ambassador, von Weizsäcker, in his report to Berlin, praised the pope's silence, although the latter must have feared that this silence would be held against Catholicism in the Western world. Weizsäcker reported on 28 October 1943: 'The pope has refused to make any demonstrative statement against the deportation of the Jews from Rome.' The pope did not wish to injure relations with the German government. The *Osservatore Romano* reported on 25–6 October the pope's charity and his fatherly care for all men without distinction of nationality, religion or race. Weizsäcker remarked in this connection: 'There is all the less reason to object to this statement since the text, a translation of which is provided, will only be understood by very few to have special reference to the Jewish question.'

How right Weizsäcker was! Edoardo Senatro, Berlin correspondent of *Osservatore Romano*, asked Pius xii why he did not protest against the liquidation of the Jews. The pope replied: 'Dear friend, do not forget that millions of Catholics are serving in the German armies. Am I to involve them in a conflict of conscience?' That, indeed, would have been the duty of the pope in this case.

On 15 August 1945 Pius xii praised in his letter to the Bavarian bishops those millions of Catholics who fought against the demoniac forces which had governed Germany. But only a little while before the church had strongly condemned all resistance to Hitler. The German bishops had condemned any uprising against him. Even Count Galen, 'the lion of Münster', had consistently opposed any form of resistance movement to Hitler in his famous sermons against the Gestapo in July and August 1941.

The church did not mobilize the power of public opinion in Germany against Hitler, but only in its own cause. In 1941 the Catholics forced the cancellation of the crucifix decree, involving the removal of crosses from schools in Bavaria. While many thousands of opponents of the régime were being beaten, tortured and murdered in concentration camps, the church still spoke of its support for the wonderful moral rebirth which Hitler's régime had brought to Germany.

In those years the church did not condemn any dictatorial régime of the right, but it did condemn left-wing régimes. The armed rebellion against the republic of Mexico in 1927 was praised by Pius XI in an encyclical of 28 March 1937. And the later Pope Pius XII blessed Franco's uprising.

The German Catholic Hans Kühner-Wolfskehl wrote the following report concerning Pius XII: 'During the Nazi terror in Rome in 1943–4 I belonged to a resistance group whose business was to hide the victims of persecution, Jewish or otherwise. Apart from private premises, it was necessary to guarantee the extra-territorial status of church premises. The air attaché Baron Herbert von Veltheim, who has since died, deserves the credit for creating the necessary conditions for this . . . I remember the day when they began to arrest the Jews . . . Justice certainly demands that we remember the material help – even if it was in vain – given by the pope to the (later converted) chief rabbi on behalf of the Roman Jews, as well as the help of the many monasteries and institutions which unreservedly took up the cause of the persecuted. To be effective an appeal by the pope should have been registered at latest on the day the first groups of Jewish Roman citizens were carried off to their miserable death. From our direct knowledge of the situation, our opinion at the time was that the death convoys would never have left Rome if the pope had made an energetic personal intervention, and the arrests would immediately have stopped. When he wished, as in the case of both bombings of Rome, Pius XII was capable of appearing with surprising speed on the scene. But in the case of the deportation of Jewish citizens, we in the resistance waited in vain for a single cardinal to appear. It may be said clearly today – and here Hochhuth's judgment is correct – that the threat of an interdict and a repeal of the unhappy Concordat uniting the papacy with Hitlerite Germany, which was continually being violated by Hitler's Reich, could have had a very considerable impact.'

On 25 October 1943 the German Jesuit Alfred Delp spoke at a conference of the Bavarian diocesan authorites. He attempted to appeal to the conscience of the Bavarian clergy. He said the silence of the church concerning the monstrous fate of the Jews in Poland would prejudice the acceptance of the church in Germany after the fall of the National Socialist régime. Alfred Delp concerned himself, right up to his death on the scaffold in Berlin-Plötzensee, with the question: Are Christians – and he was thinking naturally of Catholics – able and willing to champion the cause of *Man* and not merely the interests of their clergy's church?

Guenter Lewy closes his weighty book *The Catholic Church and Nazi Germany* (1964) with the hope that if mankind were ever again to be faced with moral challenges of the enormity presented by Hitler's régime, it might have better moral guidance than that provided by the Catholic church.

On 2 November 1954 Pope Pius XII made a speech in which he declared that all the affairs of men, in politics, social affairs and economics, concerned the church and were subject to its authority. Here the pope was making gigantic claims, similar to those made by Innocent III and later by Paul VI, who saw in the pope the *rector mundi*, the leader and judge of all the world.

This spiritual imperialism, which sees the kingdom of God and the kingdom of Christ in the Roman Catholic Church – and specifically in Rome – is part of a thousand-year-old tradition which basically begs the question of the Jews. When Christians today consider the Jewish problem they find themselves at the crossroads. They must either challenge the tradition of the church or continue on the path the popes have consistently trod up to Pius XII.

Cardinal Tardini has spoken about Pius XII's anxious character. Tardini was one of his closest subordinates and assistants. The anxieties of Pacelli as a human being had deep foundations. Some were thousands of years old, others were related to his spiritual life – his failure to develop.

Like all neurotically anxious men, Pacelli never underwent an inner development. Men of this kind break off the 'dialogue with the enemy' early in their hearts – often in first youth – and remain fixed in their fears all their lives. Here in psychological terms a comparison is possible with Adolf Hitler, who was otherwise so different. On the eve of his death Hitler proclaimed in his testament the same beliefs about Judaism, Bolshevism and liberalism that he had expressed in conversation with Dietrich Eckart in Munich in 1922. Pope Pius XII, on the eve of his death, proclaimed the same beliefs and the same political and religious convictions that he had disclosed in Munich in an interview with Jules Sauerwein which appeared on the front page of *Le Matin* on 25 September 1921.

The man who breaks off 'the dialogue with the enemy' too early, that is to say the debate in his heart between 'higher' and 'lower', 'left' and 'right', between the various layers of feeling and consciousness in himself, remains all his life a prisoner of his unacknowledged doubts and uncertainties. He does not see the 'devil' in his own heart. Robert Kaiser has said: 'Pius remains a prisoner of the church's past.' *He remained a prisoner because he was a prisoner of his own unresolved personal past.* The man who does not undergo development in his own heart, who does not transform himself from year to year and from decade to decade, will never be creative; he remains philistine, spiritually frustrated and without confidence in a positive future – whether it is the future of the church, the future of dogma, the future of theology or the future of Communism.

Pacelli's condemnations of 'diabolical Communism', Pierre Teilhard de Chardin, evolution and biblical research, when it was seriously undertaken and did not merely consist of adjustments, were a mark of his spiritual inflexibility. They were also a mark of a rigid Augustinian philosophy: the kingdom of God and the kingdom of the Devil face each other like great blocks, without any mutual contact.

'The Council, like all great events in the church, represents a battle between the *Civitas Dei* and the *Civitas Diaboli*' was the way the *Osservatore della Domenica* wrote of the opening of the Second Vatican Council. That was exactly how Pius XII would have spoken. This Augustinian fixation forms the theological basis for the alliance with Fascism, still extant today in leading circles of the Curia. Pius XII and the powerful Jesuit general, Vladimir Ledochowski – a crude man of force, a Polish aristocrat who ruled his young Jesuits as if they were his serfs, a man of profoundly Manichaean and dualistic stamp – accepted the Rome-Berlin axis as a bulwark against Communism, just as, centuries before, popes allied themselves with temporal powers like the Turkish sultan, the anti-clerical king of France, and the Protestant German emperor in Bismarck's time.

When the Jesuit Pierre Charles in Belgium and Father Friedrich Muckermann began their lonely campaign against the murderous Rome-Berlin axis, they were silenced by Ledochowski: they were told not to undermine the work of God, who was using Mussolini and Hitler to bring about a new order.

Pius XII was a man of order. But order is the great idol and mark of all those men who, in their own hearts, have broken off the process of development and condemned inner argument and conflict to silence. At this psychological level traditionalist theologians, cardinals of the Curia and Catholic atheists still meet even today. Hitler was a Catholic atheist who also wanted to create order. Charles Maurras, whose ideas poisoned generations of daring French minds, was also a Catholic atheist. On 10 July 1939 Pius XII rescinded the church's judgment on the *Action Française*. Mario Tedeschi, the handsome young editor of the Fascist paper *Il Borghese* and a rabid anti-Bolshevik, freely admitted in a conversation with Robert Kaiser that he himself had no religion but that he thought the Roman Catholic church the best bulwark against Communism and Socialism. During the Second Vatican Council Tedeschi was in close contact with Cardinal Ottaviani.

He who is creatively gifted is made young through difficult inner struggles in which there is ceaseless spiritual questioning. In this sense Eugenio Pacelli was young when, as peace envoy of Pope Benedict XIV in imperial Germany, he experienced great disappointments. Kaiser Wilhelm II was very polite to him, but completely negative on the issue at stake. The unfortunate experience which marked Pacelli and determined his outlook to the end of his life was his clash with some Communists in Munich during the brief episode of the government of soviets. In his interview with Sauerwein for *Le Matin*, Pacelli recalled the spring days of 1919 and produced a picture which showed, in a monstrously one-sided way, the Bolsheviks as the Devil and the right-wing extremist Munich and Bavaria of General Ludendorff as God's country, as the only bulwark in Germany against red ruin.

It was in this Munich, in which Hitler experienced the decisive events of 1922–3, that Pacelli's political, spiritual and philosophic outlook was finally formed. Pacelli honoured in Bavaria the men of order who supported Hitler and protected him in his imprisonment and later helped him to come to power. Pacelli praised the men who suppressed the Russian-led Bolsheviks in Munich. One of these Bolsheviks even threatened him with a pistol, Pacelli told his interviewer.

Dr Galeazzi-Lisi, Pope Pius XII's physician, reported that the pope often recounted his dreams to him in the morning. 'The Holy Father had a dream which recurred with oppressive frequency. He saw himself pursued by monsters who forced their way into his office. Perhaps that was an unconscious memory of the Communist pressure to which he was exposed while nuncio in Munich.'

Galeazzi-Lisi added that he had tried to dissipate the pope's nightmares by means of psychoanalysis. But that may be doubted: the pope's physician, who had the reputation of not being altogether reliable, was surely exaggerating here. Pope Pius XII would never have submitted himself to analysis, or would quickly have broken it off if it had begun. He resisted the dialogue in his own heart, and consequently he also resisted an open dialogue in the church. This inhibited pope, who could only tolerate executive organs and instruments but no colleagues, sought refuge in the public eye. He wanted to be the great father-figure, the leader of obedient and childlike masses. The pope who could not lean back in his chair and who could not eat a morsel in company, shunned discussion and open theological argument. It was fear that made him oppose the 'young' theologians of 1943 and 1950. Carefully he rehearsed his public role and flooded the world with a stream of proclamations, which hardly anyone read because they seldom contained anything concrete.

On 20 February 1965 *La Civiltà Cattolica* published a study of Pius XII and Hitler by Angelo Martini SJ. This unintentionally revealed the helplessness of this great prisoner of his inner self. Martini described how, immediately after his election as pope, Pius XII wanted to reassure and pacify the Führer and the Reich government. In the last days of Pius XI they had been annoyed by the hardening attitude of the Vatican. In particular they had been upset by a speech of the archbishop of Chicago, Cardinal Mundelein, who, at a private assembly of priests of his diocese on 18 May 1937, had asked how it was possible that a nation of sixty-six million intelligent people could subject themselves to an Austrian paperhanger (and an inferior one at that), and to a few comrades like Goebbels and Goering, who decided every move of the German people.

Perhaps Berlin had heard something about Pius xi's intention of taking more energetic steps against them – he had intimated as much to the British chargé d'affaires shortly before his death. This pope, according to Cardinal Tisserant in a letter to Suhard in 1940, clearly recognized the difference between the Cross and the swastika. He referred to it in his speech of 3 May 1938 in Castelgandolfo, when he called the swastika a 'cross hostile to the Cross of Christ'.

In his essay Martini frankly describes the efforts of the newly-elected pope to come to an arrangement with Hitler. 'The death of Pope Pius xi on 10 February 1939 seemed to provide an opportunity to halt the conflict for a moment and to make an attempt to improve the relationship . . . A gesture of relaxation at the beginning of the pontificate thus lay in the nature of things.'

It might be observed that the expression 'the nature of things' is just as conveniently misused here as the formula 'natural right' when invoked to justify everything conceivable – from slavery to atomic weapons. In 1939 the nature of things was this: Hitler had for some time been revealing himself to the world as a murderer and persecutor of men. The German bishops knew from Hitler himself and from instructions they had received that he was preparing for war; and they prepared themselves for this war by increasing the provision of chaplains and by intensifying their theological war propaganda. That was the true 'nature of things' in 1939 when Pius xii, immediately after his election, discussed the possibilities of 'a resumption of fruitful contacts' with the German government. His partners in the discussion were the German cardinals, Bertram of Breslau, Schulte of Cologne, Faulhaber of Munich and Innitzer of Vienna. (Like almost all the other world powers, the Vatican had not protested against the Anschluss.)

The German cardinals were enthusiastic. 'Bertram was of the opinion that they would have to deal with the fairly widely held view that the clergy and the church at home and abroad were hostile to the régime and its achievements. This view was constantly heard in the form that, after the victory over Bolshevism and Judaism, the Catholic church would be left as the only enemy of the present régime. Faulhaber, for his part, had some reservations about the expression "the cross hostile to the Cross of Christ", because the swastika had not been chosen with the express purpose of opposing Christianity, and it was now a symbol of sovereignty, which any state was free to choose for itself. Likewise, he thought an expression in the encyclical *Mit brennender Sorge* was too inexact – as if the new government had intended to persecute the church from the very beginning and as a matter of principle.' Faulhaber wanted to adhere to Hitler's statement of March 1933.

Faulhaber also favoured an ostrich-like policy: 'We sometimes wonder whether the senior party authorities have any real desire for peace. They behave so belligerently that it looks as if they prefer to have reasons for quarrelling – especially when it is a question of acting against the church. But I think we bishops should behave as if we saw nothing. [Here, with a vengeance is the silent church! After 1945 anti-Communist propaganda in the West liked to project the image of 'the silent church in the East': an unconscious counter-image to the silent church of the West.] Therefore we should be most humbly grateful to your Holiness if an attempt to procure peace were made.'

The Führer conveyed his 'warmest congratulations' on the election of the pope through his ambassador, von Bergen, who was received in person by the pope. The pope then discussed with the German cardinals his letter to the Führer. At the suggestion of Faulhaber it was written, contrary to protocol, in German. And, at the suggestion of Cardinal Innitzer of Vienna, the second person singular (the usual form of address from the pope to one of his flock) was replaced by the more respectful second person plural. It was also agreed to use the form 'much honoured' instead of 'much esteemed' (*molto onorando* instead of *molto rispettabile* in the Italian text). Likewise, they avoided the form of address 'Dear Son', 'which was not deserved, and which, in addition, was hardly acceptable to the recipient'.

In this letter the pope assured Hitler: 'At the beginning of our pontificate we wish to assure you that we remain devoted in our hearts to the German people entrusted to your care and, in a spirit of fatherly love for the same, we beseech from Almighty God that true good which draws nourishment from religion.' Pius xii recalled the many years he had served as nuncio in Germany. 'We cherish the hope that our ardent wish, closely bound up as it is with the welfare of the German people and the sure growth of order of every kind, may with God's help find fulfilment. In the meantime we shall pray for the protection of Heaven and the blessing of Almighty God for you and all members of your nation.' Rome, 6 March 1939.

But in March 1939 Hitler was already on the brink of war. Here in this letter Pope Pius xii expressed trust in a man who had shattered the trust of the whole world and who had ignored all treaties with other governments – first with Austria and then with Czechoslovakia. Soon it would be the turn of Poland.

On 30 September 1941 Pius xii wrote a letter to the bishop of Berlin, Preysing, congratulating him for championing 'the cause of God and the holy church' and assuring him that in this endeavour he would always enjoy the support of the pope. 'It should not be thought that the efforts of bishops to uphold against their own government the rights of religion, the church and the individual, those without protection and those who have suffered violations by the state – whether children of the church or outsiders – might harm your fatherland in the eyes of the world. That kind of courageous championing of what is right and humane does not expose your fatherland, but rather earns respect in the world both for it and for yourself, and will ultimately prove to its best advantage.'

This letter was unearthed after the Second World War. How different things might have been if the pope and the bishops in Germany had adhered to this principle!

In this letter the pope spoke – for the first and only time – approvingly of the fact 'that Catholics, and especially Berlin Catholics, have shown the so-called non-Aryans much love in their oppression'. 'In this connection we extend a special word of fatherly recognition and deep sympathy to Father Lichtenberg in his imprisonment.' (Rolf Hochhuth's play *The Representative* is dedicated jointly to Lichtenberg and to the Polish priest Maximilian Kolbe, who voluntarily gave his life for a fellow inmate of Auschwitz.)

The representative of Jesus Christ, Pope Pius xii, unsealed his lips on 2 June 1945. In what Angelo Martini has called a 'moving address' to the cardinals he passed a devastating judgment on National Socialism, though he did once more defend his Concordat with Hitler. He said: 'One must recognize that the Concordat in subsequent years brought various advantages, or at least prevented greater misfortune.' So here again the disastrous doctrine of greater and lesser evil was pressed into service. The pope referred to the encyclical *Mit brennender Sorge* and stated: 'In any case, no one could accuse the church of having been slow to recognize the true character of the National Socialist movement and to reveal the dangers to which it exposed Christian culture.'

This claim has a hollow ring when one remembers how church bells pealed uninterruptedly as human beings were being liquidated in gas chambers.

The pope then recalled the sufferings of Catholic priests and laymen in Dachau. 'Nor can we pass over in silence the priests who belong to the occupied countries, Holland, Belgium, France – with the bishop of Clermont among the French priests – Luxemburg, Slovenia and Italy. Many of these priests and laymen have borne unspeakable suffering for their faith and calling.'

Not a word about the killing of millions of Jews. But it would be unfair to make Pope Pius xii the scapegoat for fifteen hundred years of an erring Christian tradition. Pius xii merely did not wish to alter by one iota this tradition that made an eternal scapegoat of the Jew. If Pope John xxiii had not, by his own initiative, changed the Good Friday liturgy and so made possible a total revision of the Jewish question at the church's centre, this old tradition would probably still dominate Catholic thought even today.

Pope Pius xii acted in precisely the same way as his predecessors. In his church state he protected 'his' Jews, as far as possible. To pardon the Jews historically; indeed to recognize them and defend them as cross-bearers, as the brothers of the crucified Christ, as the most prominent, most numerous and most tormented of all the millions who have crosses to bear today – all that lay beyond the mental and theological range of Pope Pius XII. Until his death it was right and proper for the church to care only for its own flock. All the rest constituted the enemy: the liberal, the Protestant, the heretic, the Jew. They could be tolerated in non-Catholic states, but their human rights and their right to live were no concern of the Catholics. The perturbation expressed in *Mit brennender Sorge*, the encyclical on National Socialism, and in all other encyclicals related only to the members of the Catholic church and their spiritual salvation.

John XXIII dared to leap across these centuries. Under his protection an old German servant of the church, Augustin Bea, who had declined a cardinal's hat from Pope Pius XII, ventured to open the church's door for a meeting between Christians and God's people of the old covenant.

We do not know what thoughts were present in the death agony of the lonely man in the chair of St Peter, Pope Pius XII, tormented by thousand-year-old Augustinian anxieties and fears emanating from his own arrested development. We know only that Father Bea was for a long time the father confessor of Pope Pius XII. Do we see in Cardinal Bea's later work an expression of the deep concern of this pope who wished to do the best for the church entrusted to his care, yet was powerless in the face of terror?

12

Collaborators in the Final Solution

The active support which the Austrian Catholic Adolf Hitler received for his 'final solution' of the Jewish problem exceeded even his wildest hopes and expectations. Hitler had unwitting and sometime unwilling allies in the popular anti-Semitism of Russians, Ukrainians, Latvians, Poles, Rumanians and Hungarians – Eastern peoples whom he and his racialists held in such contempt – and also in the more refined theological anti-Semitism of French and English Catholic writers, whose attitude to the beginning of Jewish immigration into Palestine was one of scorn and malice. Other collaborators were German industrialists, field marshals, British officers in Palestine, senior Swiss officials, American government circles and all the diplomats who failed to suggest any positive action to save the Jews of Europe. They had nothing to propose either at the thirty-two nation conference which Roosevelt convened in Evian in 1938–9 or at the refugee conference in Bermuda in 1943.

Adolf Hitler waited until 1941. And when he saw that no one wanted the Jews and no major power was prepared to pay ransom, he struck.

Reports about the beginnings of his work of destruction were dismissed as 'atrocity propaganda' in Britain and the United States, often with the help of Jews themselves. The Americans had always been reluctant to believe the stories told by German refugees. State Department officials suppressed news about anti-Jewish atrocities so as not to draw public attention to the fact that Jewish refugees were not getting any official help in the USA.

Josué Jéhouda, who tried to mobilize the conscience of the Jews and the world with his *Revue juive de Genève*, published between 1932 and 1939, called this period the years of decision for the Jews. In silent admiration the world watched the audacity and brutality with which the National Socialists were setting about the solution of their problems. National Socialist anti-Semites realized with surprise that the international community was not going to put up any serious resistance to the extermination of the Jews. Emancipated Jews did not dare to fight openly themselves against this militant anti-Semitism. All they were prepared to do was to offer anonymous assistance in individual cases. This enabled the National Socialists calmly to round up the Jews all over Europe like cattle, without arousing any international reaction.

Let us first take a look at Poland, where the largest number of Jews was murdered. Anti-Semitism among Polish nationalists and Catholics had prepared the country for its role at the centre of the National Socialist death machine.

Anti-Semitism is part of the Poles' hatred of all so-called minorities in Greater Poland, although these 'minorities' often constituted majorities in the districts in which Byelorussians, Ukrainians and Jews were settled. The anti-Semitism of the Polish Catholics dates back to the thirteenth century. Neither before 1939 nor after 1945, when anti-Semitism immediately revived in Poland, did the country's ecclesiastical leaders immunize or even warn their loyal supporters, the Polish peasants, against anti-Semitism.

In 1932 the Sejm (the Polish parliament) passed anti-Jewish laws excluding the Jews from official posts and barring them from various occupations. People who had suffered in the Polish concentration camp of Bereza Kartuska between 1934 and 1939 and were later sent to German camps, said the Polish camps were even worse.

When on 12 December 1941 General Anders conferred with Stalin, he said that no Jews would be accepted in the new Polish army. Stalin agreed that Jews made poor soldiers. Anti-Jewish pamphlets distributed among the Polish underground army said the Germans had solved the Jewish problem for the Poles. There would be no room for Jews in post-war Poland. The Polish legionaries regarded all Jews as Bolsheviks.

In his autobiography *Life without a Star* Charles Goldstein gave a personal account of the four months he spent in a cellar after the abortive Warsaw rising, together with six other Jews and a Polish priest. He spoke of the deep hatred of Jews, especially among Polish resistance fighters: 'Scum! Goddam swine, these Jews! We don't need any Jews! They ought to be killed, the lot of them!' In fact these resistance men did shoot Jews.

In 1946 bloody pogroms were staged in Kielce in Poland and in Kunmadaras in Hungary. At the last plenary meeting of the Communist party before the 'Polish October' a great debate was held on whether Poland should get rid of her Jews. Should there be a return to the anti-Semitic policy of the *Endecja*, the extremist anti-Jewish party of the pre-war years? On 25 April 1957 Gomulka issued a kind of pastoral letter, deploring anti-Semitism in the party and Polish nation. On 8 July 1956 *Pro Prostu* published 'Fragments of a Diary' written by a Jewish Communist, a woman, who had returned to Poland in 1954 after studying in Paris and was aghast at the anti-Semitism in her country. On 6 January 1957 reports of anti-Semitic excesses in Poland appeared in *Pro Prostu* along with some readers' letters. One said that the entire Polish nation would heartily welcome the expulsion of the Jews. Another stated even more explicitly: 'We shall settle their fate as Hitler did. God himself sent Hitler against the Jews.' And a third read: 'The Jews must be strung up or drowned like dogs.'

In 1957 a Polish Communist and liberal élite spoke out against this brutal anti-Semitism. But it remained deeply rooted among the lower clergy and the Catholic peasantry. François Fejtö, a Hungarian Jew living in Paris, who made a study of anti-Semitism in Communist Eastern Europe, commented: 'It seems that the Catholic church, which enjoys great authority in Poland, is somewhat reluctant to support Gomulka's policy in this matter.' In the years of violence there were some individual Poles in the country who helped persecuted Jewish refugees of their own free will. But these Jews would have found more support from the peasants if the Polish bishops had at least issued a pastoral letter in their defence.

Four Hungarian prime ministers – Gömbös, Teleki, Brádossy and Kállay – have declared that Hungary was Europe's guide on the road to anti-Semitism. From 1932 onwards hostility against the Jews – and also against the Germans in Hungary – was manifested quite publicly under the Gömbös régime. In 1938 there existed nine Magyar National Socialist parties. Adolf Eichmann worked closely with the Hungarian government.

Jews had come to Hungary together with the Turks in fairly large numbers – mostly Jews of Balkan-Spanish-Moorish descent. And when Galicia became part of Austria under Maria Theresa, the influx of Jews into Hungary increased. In 1875 Viktor Istóczy, the pioneer of Hungarian anti-Semitism, entered the scene. Descended from an aristocratic family, he became a judge and, in 1872, a member of Parliament. In 1878 Istóczy moved in the House of Deputies that the government should compel Turkey to give up Palestine so that the Jews could be settled there. The motion caused immense amusement. Later Istóczy founded an anti-Semitic periodical.

Racial hatred was stirred up over an alleged ritual murder in Tiszaeszlar in 1881 (this was the subject of a film by G.W.Pabst in 1946) and led to anti-Semitic riots in Pressburg, Oedenburg, Budapest and Zalaegerszeg. When Admiral Horthy, after crushing Béla Kun's Communist dictatorship, rode into Budapest on his white horse, the 'white terror' began against the Jews in Hungary. Jews and trade union leaders were murdered with impunity.

Horthy was a Calvinist. Catholic anti-Semitism in Hungary was guided and fanned by some brilliant intellectuals including Father Béla Bangha SJ, a leading exponent of the 'Christian stream' of anti-Semitism in the 1920s and author of an essay 'Catholicism and Jewry', which was published in Hungarian and German. He also edited a periodical *Magyar Kultura* and two daily newspapers which were among the chief mouthpieces of Hungarian anti-Semitism. Bishop Ottokar Proháska, a pioneer of a Catholic reform movement, opposed the assimilation of the Jews, arguing that Israel was cursed by God. Israel, he declared, ought to become a nation-state once more and later embrace Christianity. Proháska propounded this interesting thesis in an essay entitled 'The Jewish question in Hungary', which appeared in 1921 in the Hamburg journal, *Hammerschläge*.

Hungary's anti-Semites early established contacts with German circles.

Julius Gömbös and his racialist friends Ulain, Mecsér and Eckardt were in touch with Hitler from 1923 onwards. Soon plans were being devised for the bloody extermination of Hungary's Jews.

Father Béla Bangha originally wrote his essay 'Catholicism and Jewry' for his Catholic friends in Austria, and it was published in a collective volume under the title *Klärung der Judenfrage* (Clarification of the Jewish Question) in Vienna in 1934. He wrote: 'All the volcanic eruptions of Jewish persecution throughout the centuries show a desire for a final reckoning after many provocations endured in silence. Unfortunately the Jews have always refused to face this fact, and thus they have again proved themselves to be the real authors of anti-Semitism.' The distinguished theologian was here merely stating what 'Christian people' had long known: the Jew is to blame – even for anti-Semitism.

Parliamentary debates on anti-Jewish legislation, which were to go on for years, began in 1938. Cardinal Justinian *(nomen est omen!)* Serédi, archbishop of Budapest and primate of Hungary, raised no objection in May 1938 in the Upper House to the bill, except as regards baptized Jews, and here he only called for some modifications. The publication of the encyclical *Mit brennender Sorge*, already mentioned in the last chapter, is said to have been considerably delayed, owing to Serédi's intervention in Rome.

On 1 July 1941 Josef Közi-Horváth, a representative in Parliament of the Christian Association, read out a declaration on behalf of his parliamentary colleagues who were Catholic priests. This said: 'For many years the Catholic clergy and leading protagonists of a Christian policy have been campaigning in favour of restraining the excessive spiritual and material influence of the Jews and against permitting mixed marriages and the introduction of more permissive marriage laws . . . The Catholic priests and the majority of Christian politicians have never for an instant abandoned the struggle, though subjected to the full fury of press and propaganda media controlled by the Jewish-masonic-liberal front.'

Liberalism, democracy, Jewry, freemasonry, Socialism and Communism were all lumped together and assailed by the Catholics in Hungary, just as in Germany and Austria. Josef Kösi-Horváth said: 'We are guided exclusively by our Christian convictions and love of our race.'

The anti-Semitic measures brought in by the Kállay government opened the way to the 'final solution'. On 20 April 1942 – Hitler's birthday – Miklós Kállay declared: 'There is no other solution but to expel the eight hundred thousand Jews from Hungary.' On 10 April 1941 Horthy told the army: 'The God of the Magyars and the nation's thoughts are with you now. Forward to the thousand-year-old southern frontier of Hungary!' Hungary had become one of Hitler's satellites.

On 18 October 1942 Prime Minister Kállay spoke out in praise of Hungary: 'It is a fact that we Magyars were the initiators and pioneers of the idea that now prevails in Europe. We were the first to fight for it and you will see it will prevail throughout the world ... We are the pioneers of Christian thought ... Magyar truth has been made Europe's truth by our allies ...'

In Hungary followers of the Arrow Cross movement demonstratively posed as Catholics, arranged for masses to be read in support of their political aims and murdered thousands of Jews. The Arrow Cross atrocities under the Szalasi régime led directly to collaboration in Eichmann's 'final solution' of the Jewish question.

Even Hitler and Himmler were surprised, almost disconcerted, at being outdone by members of the Rumanian government in eager search of a 'final solution'. At the Berlin Congress in 1878 German Jews made strong representations to Bismarck on behalf of Rumanian Jews, who were languishing under the harshest oppression anywhere in Europe with the exception of Russia. The pogroms of the 1880s were the direct forerunners of the massacres of 1941 and 1942 in Iasi, and other Rumanian towns and villages. Collaboration with the German henchmen went with exemplary smoothness. Only once, on 1 June 1943, did Eberhard von Thadden of the foreign affairs ministry in Berlin, with his colleagues Franz Rademacher and secretary of state, Martin Luther – enthusiastic advocates of Jewish extermination – find cause to fear that some Jewish children might escape from Rumania across the sea to Palestine. The children did not escape.

In Croatia the prime effort was directed at exterminating the Orthodox Serbs – numbering between six hundred thousand and seven hundred thousand, including children. Catholic priests helped actively, and Rome gave silent consent. Croatia, like Poland, Hungary and Rumania, were predominantly agrarian countries whose partly illiterate population (they had the highest illiteracy rate in Europe), misled by its preachers and priests, sought a scapegoat for the many incomprehensible, confusing, oppressive and menacing features of incipient industrialization and dictatorial government. They found an easy scapegoat in the Jew. If they could not get at their masters, these poor peasants could at least take it out on their masters' slaves, the Jews.

The social and mental make-up of the highly educated, manicured, aggressive anti-Semites of Western Europe was entirely different. France had an 'aristocratic' anti-Semitic tradition, the leading exponents of which had included members of the nobility and clergy since the days of Drumont. The French commissioner-general for Jewish affairs in Laval's Vichy government bore the proud name of Darquier de Pellepoix. One of the champions of Vichy's official anti-Semitic policy, Xavier Vallat, at his trial after the war, quoted St Thomas Aquinas and referred to his own strictly ecclesiastical anti-Semitic education. In Catholic education the Jews were either ignored or branded as deicides in liturgical and theological writings. The standard work *La Chrétienté médiévale* by Augustin Fliche (Paris, 1929), which deals with the period between 395 and 1254, does not even mention the word 'Jew'. Drumont's tradition was very much alive among French Catholics of this type.

On 5 February 1938 Jacques Maritain delivered a lecture in Paris on the Christian world's callous indifference to the tragedy of the Jews. But his appeal to the Roman Catholics of Poland was in vain. Behind this indifference lay an acquiescence and approval that people were seeking to conceal from their own conscience. And it was this indifference that enabled Hitler to turn Europe into a graveyard of Jews.

One example, the book *Synthèse de l'antisémitisme*, published in Brussels in 1941, must suffice to illustrate Western Europe's spiritual, theological and political collaboration with Hitler in the Jewish question. Its author, Edmond Picard, was a lawyer. His expert witnesses – de Bonald, Toussenel, Proudhon, Stöcker, Schönerer and Drumont – were not, he said, poisoners, as had been alleged, but healers. Christianity, he claimed, had flourished only on Aryan soil. If the Turks, the Semites [*sic*] had conquered Vienna in 1683, the Aryans would have been exterminated. Don John of Austria in the naval battle of Lepanto and King Sobieski in the battle of Vienna had finally stopped the Semitic hordes and given the Christians security in Europe. An understanding of the Turkish and Jewish questions provided the magic key to all doors and offered guidance through the labyrinths of world history. The Koran, not the Old Testament – which was so deeply imbued with Aryan sentiment – was the continuation of the old, barbaric bible of the Hebrews. Picard described the Rothschilds as the incarnation of the Jewish race, personifying money, gold and avarice. Wherever the Semite had gained ascendancy over the Aryan, the civilization of the Aryan had decayed. The Semites were incapable of progress and fit only to engage in sterile agitation. Contact between Semite and Aryan must be avoided; any intermingling was dangerous. And Jewish overlordship was pernicious.

Picard also declared that Jesus may have been Jewish by nationality, but not by race. Portraits of Christ rightly show the Aryan Jesus of Galilee: a young man with a fair beard, brown hair, gentle blue eyes, a big nose and oval face.

Picard urged his contemporaries of 1941 to ask themselves seriously: have all the wars against the Persians, the Phoenicians and the Turks – all these world wars against the Semites – been in vain? All over Europe the Aryan hearts answered: No! And rose up in a European anti-Semitic rebellion. Picard looked around for remedies to liberate the Christian West from the Jews. Baptism offered no genuine solution. Once a Jew, always a Jew. There was only one way out: the Jews must not hold office anywhere and must be completely separated from Aryan society. Public opinion in Europe had already understood this, but the bourgeoisie still hesitated.

'The Jews must be completely separated.' Soon the trains would be ready to effect this separation.

In conclusion Picard repeated emphatically: Jesus and St Paul were in no way Jews, but Aryans. It was St Paul, the genius of the Aryan race, who had divided Christianity from Judaism.

The Englishman has a hidden soul. Ernest Barker has compared the life of the English (and for that matter of any nation) to an iceberg: the much larger, invisible part below the surface preserves the coherence and continuity of this strange structure. The English do not talk about what lies below the surface. 'English anti-Semitism has nearly always been an underground movement, protected by the pretence that it does not exist' (Malcolm Hay). There are only indirect references and insinuations – so as not to fall foul of the law – which, however, both conceal and at the same time expose this anti-Semitism. This can be easily seen in three particular instances: in British Catholic literature and theology; in the anti-Semitism of British military officers in Palestine: and (in what may be its most innocuous form) – in the publications and activities of British political groups which were the English equivalent of the Nazis.

English and Catholic theologians and writers in the nineteenth and twentieth centuries have quite openly talked about the spiritual and religious infertility of the Jews. Clerics have echoed in chorus that the Jews have no religion and no spirituality. These poor souls have apparently never realized that they themselves live entirely by Jewish religion and spirituality: by the two Testaments and Jewish liturgy. The liturgical movement initiated at the monastery of Solesmes was given a strongly anti-Jewish tinge by Dom Guéranger, many of those writings have been translated into English. Hilaire Belloc borrowed ideas and even his manner of expressing them from Drumont. Oratorians, such as W.B.Morris, and Dominicans, such as Bede Jarrett, excelled in 'spiritual' anti-Semitism. But it always had political as well as ecclesiastical implications.

Jewry and Bolshevism were declared identical by Hilaire Belloc in *The Jews* in 1922. Like many other anti-Semites, he opened his attack with the ritual formula: 'Many of my best friends are Jews.' Ribbentrop said the same thing at the Nuremberg trials. Belloc invented a new name for anti-Semitism: 'defence organization'. Catholics, he declared, have been on the defensive for centuries. They have had to defend the honour of their offended God, their insulted sacraments, their affronted sweet Lord Jesus and the Mother of God against Protestants, Jews and freemasons. And defence has been their form of attack on the Jews.

342

The political implications of Catholic anti-Semitism in English literature and theology were patent in the sneers and mockery which Catholic priests, monks and writers poured on the Zionist settlement of Palestine. The plan was bound to fail, they asserted, because the Jews were utterly incapable of creative state-building.

The Palestine enterprise was doomed to failure: this was the conviction of British officers and senior officials in the military government during the fateful inter-war years and even after that. In the pogroms of 1929, the British military government protected the persecutors, the Arabs, and not the Jews. That year was the turning point which made possible Hitler's rise to power.

'The conduct of the British authorities in Palestine convinced the Arabs that Jews could be killed with impunity.' Malcolm Hay, who wrote this sentence, is a gallant Scottish Catholic who went to war in France in 1914 with the First Gordon Highlanders. Describing the attitude of senior members of the military government, he said the Nazis of Berlin had their prototypes in Palestine. Hitler's *Mein Kampf* was available in both English and Arabic versions, as were the *Protocols of the Elders of Zion*. On the other hand, the British censor prohibited the sale of the Brown Book on the Hitler terror.

On 21 July 1938 *The Times* published a letter from Josiah Wedgwood which said that, for two years, murder and destruction of Jewish property in Palestine had gone unpunished under British rule. The administration was continuing to be strictly impartial between the murderers and murdered. Wedgwood said he knew of no comparable black page of incompetence and hypocrisy in British history.

'The Jews are the scum of humanity.' So said the great Bossuet, the most outstanding pulpit preacher of French Catholicism and author of a short history of the world which has been used for centuries in Catholic seminaries, monastic schools and other closed establishments. A similar term to scum was used in the Belsen trial in 1948 by a British officer, defending the SS leader Kramer. He pleaded for leniency because, he said, it was 'the dregs of the ghettoes of Central Europe' that came together in the concentration camps.

A good introduction to the mentality of these British officers is a book by Wing Commander Leonard Young published in London in 1956 by the Britons Publishing Society. Its title, *Deadlier than the H-Bomb*, signified that the Jews are more dangerous than the atom bomb. Leonard Young had been a professional soldier since 1919. His book started with England's early history – 2000 BC. It seems possible (he said) that even King Solomon thought out a scheme for a peaceful conquest of the whole world by Sion through economic infiltration. The Jews came to England in 1066 in the wake of William the Conqueror. They were probably the authors of the Domesday Book, the first record of lands in England, and used for the purposes of taxation.

The Jews had always advocated nihilism, Socialism and Communism. For some time they were even in favour of Pan-Germanism. This was claimed by French propagandists during the Dreyfus era because Germany was the base of Jewish financiers and because Pan-Germanism was a means of weakening the Nordic races and sowing the seeds of Communism. Calvin was most likely a Cohen by birth, and Cromwell was financed by the Jews in Amsterdam.

Leonard Young used as his authorities such untrustworthy English historians as Nesta Webster, whose books were also favourite sources for Pinay's *Conspiracy against the Church*, and were quoted by centralist anti-Semitic theologians at the Second Vatican Council.

In 1956 – so Young said – the Church of England and the British government were dominated by Jews and freemasons. (Hitler and his propagandists alleged this to the end.) The Jews were behind the Moors in Spain, the freemasons and all enemies of Christendom. The Jews spread internationalism and Socialism. The Jews were the destroyers of the monarchy and aristocracy and were preparing for Jewish world control and the reign of anti-Christ. Here Young invoked Mgr George E. Dillon (Edinburgh, 1884); Lt-Col Greagh Scott (*Hidden Government*); and A.K. Chesterton.

'Since the cynically insincere opportunist Disraeli injected his liberal and radical Jewish poison into the Tory party, it has become less and less Tory and more and more Socialist and internationalist in effect, until it is now for all practical purposes as completely under the control of the Sanhedrin as is the Socialist party.'

The horde of German and Russian-speaking Jews who poured into Britain managed to find a large number of Gentile dupes to work for them. Socialism (Young wrote) was the work of international Jewish financiers. The members of the Fabian Society, in common with the Communists and Zionists, were agents of the Sanhedrin, out to destroy the resistance of the British people to the Satanic plot of Jewish world dominion.

We might add that this is exactly the line taken by American anti-Semites and anti-Communists trying to 'unmask' President Kennedy (after Roosevelt) as an agent of Jewish Bolshevism.

Young wrote that, after the First World War, Jewish poison used in the service of the Germans and the Soviets [*sic*] had a devastating effect in the USA. During the Weimar Republic these 'American' (i.e. Jewish) financiers of Wall Street and their allies perpetrated a colossal fraud at the expense of the American people. Huge sums were sent to Germany and Russia, both of which were to be rebuilt by American Jews, while Britain was weakened by a terroristic finance policy. The League of Nations, according to Young, was nothing but a Jewish conspiracy to prepare Jewish world rule.

This RAF officer gave Hitler a tremendous panegyric in 1956. Germany (he said) was the first country in history openly to oppose the Jewish plot against the rest of mankind. He called *Mein Kampf* a magnificent work, in which Hitler propounded his two great themes: the exposure of Jewish Marxism and his admiration and longing for friendship with Britain. At

Dunkirk Hitler saved the British army – a fact about which details might be found in the book *The Nameless War* by the late Captain A.M.Ramsay, a former Conservative MP and friend of Neville Chamberlain.

According to Young it was the Jews who organized the revolution in Spain in 1936. He had no wish to talk about the German concentration camps, about which (he said) many lies had been spread. Hitler had done a great deal of good in Germany. (Many people in the German Federal Republic have been answering questions about Hitler in exactly the same vein during the last ten years.) There were, of course, some traitors who worked for Hitler's destruction, just as Napoleon had men like Talleyrand and Fouché around him.

It might here be remarked that the German nationalist underground – and today even more open nationalists – can find in such 'authorities' as Young in Britain and David Hoggan in the USA plenty of material on which to build a new 'stab-in-the-back' legend.

Let Young continue. According to him 'Hitler was in effect, if not in intention, the tool of the Sanhedrin' in the destruction of the German nation. There can be no doubt about this. For propagandist reasons, the Jews spread grossly exaggerated stories about their persecution by the National Socialists. It was the Sanhedrin which was responsible for the great slaughter of the Second World War and for Hitler's murder of the Jews. Both were instigated by this supreme authority of the Elders of Zion. Young, with the remarkable madness which inspired both him and his like in Germany, France, Spain and America, declared: 'The Sanhedrin is completely callous and would not hesitate to allow a number of Jews to be slaughtered for propaganda purposes if considered worth it.'

The last war between Britain and Germany, Young wrote, was entirely unnecessary. 'Neville Chamberlain was the last British Prime Minister this country had and he was also an honest man.' Rudolf Hess sacrificed himself in an heroic attempt to bring the unnecessary war to an end. If Winston Churchill had had any sense of responsibility, he would have allowed Hitler to get on with destroying Communism and the Jewish menace while he (Churchill) concentrated on building up the strength of Britain and the empire. (Young, who served many years as a training officer in India, was a British imperialist and, if he had had his way, the British would still be ruling in India.)

Young also claimed that President Roosevelt had plotted the destruction of the British empire and the support of Communism. Even after Roosevelt all American governments were in the service of Bernard Baruch, acting in the interests of the Jews and Communists. The subservient American government deliberately handed China over to the Communists and stopped General McArthur and van Fleet from turning the Communists out of Korea. The United Nations, like the League of Nations, were a Jewish creation and a step on the road to Jewish world domination. The same applied to NATO,

EEC and SEATO(!). Young noted that the pale blue and white colours of UNO were also those of Israel. And nearly all the key positions in UNO were held by Jews or their fellow-travellers. UNO seemed to function properly only when Jewish interests were at stake.

One must admit there is method in this madness. And if there is such a thing as a theatre in hell, Adolf Hitler must be watching the show put on by Wing Commander Young and his friends with great satisfaction from his box.

Young also drew a picture of post-war Britain: The hordes of Jews, Negroes, Indians, Pakistanis, Cypriots and other non-Nordic aliens flooding into Britain had been deliberately introduced by the Sanhedrin to 'pollute our race' and to provide alien, degenerate, urban mobs which could be used for revolutionary purposes under the prevailing 'democratic' i.e. Jewish or Communist system. For ten years, according to Young, all British governments had cravenly submitted to these Jewish moves to destroy Britain.

Like conservative Catholic authors in Germany and France during the nineteenth and early twentieth centuries, Young regarded urbanization and industrialization as the Jews' choice instruments in the pursuit of world control. They needed the mobs of big cities for the world revolution.

Wing Commander Young, filled with eschatological fear, proclaimed that the end of the world was imminent, that the second advent of Christ would occur before the end of this century. Little time was left to fight and to hold high the flag against Satan, anti-Christ and the Jew. 'World government is what Satan and his instruments, the Jews, are working for. It would be a police world.' We must decide now whether we stand for Christ or anti-Christ, for our queen and country or for Jewry, for freedom of the individual or abject slavery.

We must fight for decentralization, against urbanization, for a return to common law and agriculture, and for conservative, Christian principles. In this return and in the struggle against the Jews and Satan lay the only remedy.

Leonard Young cited St Thomas Aquinas and Luther, British anti-Semitic authors such as Richard St Barbé Baker, A.K.Chesterton, C.H.Douglas, Sir Albert Howard, Arnold Leese, J.C.Thomson, Prof.L.A.Waddell, Nesta Webster and C.H.Welch. And he drew on works published by the Covenant Publishing Company, the Britons Publishing Society, K.R.P. Publications and the magazines *Candour, Free Britain, The Farmer, The Social Crediter* and *Voice*.

On 25 January 1939 all diplomatic and consular representatives abroad were sent a memorandum by the foreign ministry in Berlin, headed 'The Jewish Question as a Foreign Policy Factor in 1938'. This stated that all the countries into which migrants were beginning to flood – North America, Latin America, France, Holland, Scandinavia and Greece – were already registering a distinct rise in anti-Semitism. 'The press and official news media in North America currently report anti-Jewish demonstrations by the people,' said the memorandum. 'It is probably symptomatic of the internal political trend in US politics that the well known anti-Jewish radio priest, Father Coughlin, now has an audience of more than twenty million.'

One of the National Socialists' favourite quotations was from a speech Benjamin Franklin made in 1789 in the American Congress. Franklin's speech, quoted to draw attention to the venerable age of American anti-Semitism, referred to the Jews as a danger greater even to the USA than the Roman Catholics. The Jews were vampires, living off other nations. 'I warn you, gentlemen: unless you exclude the Jews for all time, your children's children will curse you in your graves!' As Asiatics, threatening America, Jews ought to be constitutionally barred from living in the USA.

This is the kind of puritanic race hatred which is today propagated by members of the reformed church in South Africa among others.

In 1881 the English historian Edward Freeman, one of nineteenth-century England's leading protagonists of race hatred, visited the USA. It would be a great country (he wrote) if only every Irishman were to kill a Negro and were then hanged for it himself. Freeman's American friends in Massachusetts made their child pray: 'Good night, father: I hope you sleep well and everyone sleeps well – except the Jews.'

Malcolm Hay observes that there is a gentleman's agreement in the United States: No one talks about his own anti-Semitism. There is the anti-Semitism of the common man – particularly aggressive and dangerous in unsuccessful, frustrated people. (Nietzsche noted the rise of this plebeian anti-Semitism around 1880 among the 'under-privileged' in Germany.) Then there is the anti-Semitism of the successful. They despise the 'Hebes', the Jews, yet join other anti-Semites in saying: 'Some of my best friends are Jews.' Hay writes that religious toleration is legal in the United States, but in practice it is a well-mannered fraud. Bigotry and prejudice are not dead, but often concealed. They can be stirred as easily as the waters of a pond. The anti-Semite does not understand that this portrait which he places over the face of every Jew is actually the image of his own darker Self, a picture of the Judas in his soul who betrays the Christ within him again and again. All these passages from Hay's book (first published in 1950 under the title *The Foot of Pride* and then in 1960 in the USA as *Europe and the Jews*) apply as much to yesterday's Spaniards and Germans as they do to present-day Americans. 'We are as infected as they were, because we are no better Christians than they were; we are only more comfortable with our consciences, and less in need, at the moment, of a scapegoat for our sins.'

'At the moment': after 1945 vast numbers of Americans have been very much in need of scapegoats to understand and bear the reverses of American policy in Asia and Europe and the frustrations of their personal lives. They have needed the Communists, Jews, Negroes, Puerto Ricans, Fidel Castro, the Chinese and all the other hideous coloured people and non-conformists who do not want to adopt Babbitt's American way of life.

'Recently I actually got a letter from a professor of literature in the state of Ohio, who says that by my hostility to the entirely unprovocative régime in Germany I incited the world to war against them, and that I am responsible for the three hundred billion dollars America has already had to spend on the war. The least I could do, the professor says, is to urge a quick reconciliation and peace. A fool, you'll say. But the world is full of fools, and these are really sinister words to read.'

Thomas Mann wrote these lines from Pacific Palisades, California, to his American friend, Agnes E. Meyer, on 3 June 1944. And on 1 December 1946 he wrote to this same influential American lady: 'But if Fascism does come, I can point out that I once had lunch with you and Senator Taft. That may save me from the concentration camp.'

Thomas Mann kept an alert eye on events in Europe, and, even back in 1940 or so, he was afraid that America might turn Fascist and that he might have to look around for another haven, perhaps Peking. In January 1943 he realized that Fascism still had a great future. (And ten years later, Vatican circles nearly succeeded in toppling de Gasperi and in installing a Fascist-monarchist-right wing government.) Thomas Mann feared that Roosevelt might agree to a Catholic-Fascist peace in Europe.

Psychologically American mass society is as susceptible to volcanic eruptions of hatred, despair and aggressiveness as Europe with its German, French, Polish, Rumanian and Russian background. In 1950 sociologists and psychoanalysts, including T. W. Adorno, Else Frenkel-Brunswick, Daniel J. Levinson and R. Nevil Sanford, published in New York studies of the American unconscious mind which offer a revealing insight into the sinister panorama of the human mentality first discovered by Sigmund Freud in Vienna in about 1910.

'Observers have noted that the amount of outspoken anti-Semitism in pre-Hitler Germany was less than in this country [the USA] at the present time,' – it is stated in the foreword to *The Authoritarian Personality*, published in New York in 1950.

German Catholics were members of an in-group, often a community of frustrated people anxiously shutting itself off against outsiders. In imperial Germany they were not admitted to high offices of state and positions of leadership; and 'under-privileged' even in the scientific and educated world of modern times, they were taught to fight shy of liberalism, democracy, Socialism and Jewry. Authoritarian upbringing at home, at school, in seminaries and the church turned them into nervous, ego-alien characters similar to those authoritarian-minded characters who in America form the bulk of that section of the masses most susceptible to Fascism, anti-democratic movements, racial fear and hatred.

Both groups, the German Catholic and authoritarian-minded Americans, are often pseudo-conservatives. They acknowledge and pay lip-service to the values of their society and its glorious nationalist or democratic past, yet at the same time are consumed by an unadmitted desire to rebel against the hierarchy that rules them. German Catholics – including many clerics – consciously or unconsciously hate and despise their church hierarchy. Authoritarian types in America hate the leaders of democracy but very rarely have the courage to say so openly. Yet a target has to be found for this hatred, and it is invariably the Jew, the Negro, the foreigner, the Socialist or the radical.

These studies of American society show that broad strata of the middle-class – a type corresponding to the German petit-bourgeois *Bürger* – think in ready-made clichés. And most Americans belong intellectually to this type. They are incapable of seeing individuals, of treating a Jew or Negro as a separate identity. For them there is only the abstract conception of 'the Jew', 'the Negro', 'the enemy'.

The long lists of anti-Jewish clichés registered in the United States contained more or less all the ideas of the Christian Social supporters of pre-1933 Austria and of their co-religionists and party associates in Germany. The great fear of Jewish economic predominance, the connection between militarist and nationalist views and anti-Jewish sentiments – these were present on both sides of the Atlantic. Mistaken upbringing, and the failure to produce a mature, emotionally vigorous personality had pernicious social and political repercussions. Children brought up in an authoritarian atmosphere, who have much to repress in their own selves, are especially susceptible to anti-Semitism and similar prejudices. Such young people *must* become aggressive towards suspect and feared out-groups such as Jews, Negroes, the poor, trade unionists and 'radicals', because they dare not hold their parents and teachers responsible.

These types – superstitious, inflexible, emotionally cold, loth to think for themselves – feel themselves constantly menaced, as much from within as from without. And, unable to grasp the enemy within (their immature egos), they seek to 'defend' themselves against external enemies. This is why the anti-Semitic radio priest Father Coughlin (like his well-known contemporary South American successor) evolved a 'defence mechanism' designed to protect non-Jews from Jewish attacks.

The loudly professed 'love' of parent-authority, that is to say, of authority imposed by political, ecclesiastical and educational bodies, is not a genuine emotion. Deep down in the unconscious mind there is a resentment and hostility against these authorities which stands in direct contrast to their stereotyped and orthodox glorification. The German authoritarian family has rightly been described as the breeding ground of Fascist and pseudo-conservative rebellion – an assertion contested only by people who are still prisoners of the authoritarian milieu of their own childhood. This German family had its replica in the authoritarian American parents who, anxious to maintain their social status, developed a hard, aggressive morality: 'good' in America was what helped a man's social status, and 'good' in Germany was what was useful to the party and the nation, but above all to the Führer. 'Bad' was anything that differed, deviated or was socially inferior. The weak and the sick were bad; so were the humble, the lowly and the coloured people.

The stereotyped relationship between children and parents had its equivalent in the stereotyped relations between the 'children' – who throughout their lives remain at the pre-puberty stage – and 'others'. Excessive conformity, manifested in the child's unquestioning acceptance of the ideals of parents and leaders of society, has an oppressive effect on personality: it builds up hatred and a will to destroy. Everything that has to be repressed as being 'ugly', 'unsuitable', 'dirty' and sexually disreputable is said to be the fault of 'the others'. To puritanical Americans just as to German seminarists and the sons of Protestant clergymen, the Jew is the lascivious success-seeker, the over-sexed, super-potent male – a negative ideal and a caricature of their own dreams and passions.

The transference of repressed hostility against one's own father to external 'fathers' and 'super-fathers' encourages anti-Semitism. It is no coincidence that Judaism is considered the religion of the father and Christianity that of the son. The most pathetically biased image of the Jew is the one of an old man with a beard, a father come down in the world and humiliated. During the Second World War Wehrmacht propaganda pictures showed young German soldiers cutting the beards off old Jews, thereby rendering them impotent. In tsarist Russia – the home of the pogroms – Dostoyevsky in his *Brothers Karamasov* drew a powerful portrait of a disgraced father who in the end is killed by his sons – though not directly murdered.

The weak, miserable, repulsed father is the Father-God who cannot be openly attacked. Only a few Americans have dared to assail the Father-God as the parent of a terroristic society and mortal enemy of democracy as openly as Thornton Wilder in his Frankfurt Peace Prize speech and Eugene O'Neill in his play *Strange Interlude*.

The struggle against the Christian God, of the Jewish God and the Father-God in the United States is by no means an open one. Society's puritanical superstructure, with its draconic laws and sanctions against 'blasphemy', is still too strong for that. The religious basis of American anti-Semitism is obscured for another reason too: simply that many people no longer realize how deeply their clichés are rooted in religion. And yet it is aggressive American anti-Semitism that most closely reflects the struggle between the Redeemer and Satan. The Jew is the Devil, and the Devil is a Jew. The Jewish financier and moneylender of anti-Semitic propaganda is modelled on the Biblical archetype of the money-lenders whom Jesus chased from the temple. The wicked Jewish intellectual and sophist is the final replica of the Pharisee, denounced in Christian sermons and religious lessons at school.

The underlying anti-Semitism of the United States, in a society of poorly educated masses, fundamentally exposes the catastrophe of an education policy which does not deserve the name – and of systems of education that have proved unfit to promote individualism and develop the human personality. A proper policy was not embarked upon until President John F. Kennedy took office.

In their neurotic search for the quickest possible means of adapting the young to standard values and non-values, to achievements and failures of an extrovert mass society, these methods of education have produced intellectually and emotionally feeble human beings who are unsure of themselves, deeply nervous and repressed. They cannot work off all their aggression by simply reading of atrocities in comics, or by adulating sex-stars, gangsters and other criminals.

As long as democratic values determine the standards of conformity, these pseudo-conservatives continue to behave like 'democrats'. It is no accident that tests in the large penitentiary of San Quentin have shown its inmates to be politically ultra-conservative. These criminals are not revolutionaries: they are simply working off their discontent in pseudo-rebellions against the formal laws of capitalist society, just as schoolchildren resolve their frustrations with the aid of their comics, teenagers with their sex parties and 'adults' with their crime novels and horror films.

In a society of this sort anti-Semitism fulfils a concrete function and satisfies, above all, psychological needs. How many fears and frustrations there are which need a concrete object to seize on! 'Jews are everywhere', and everywhere they are the enemies of the peace-loving American people. Together with that wicked man Roosevelt, they hounded the United States into an entirely unnecessary war with Hitler Germany. A twenty-six-year-old woman declared: 'I am not particularly sorry because of what the Germans did to the Jews. I feel the Jews would do the same type of thing to me.'

Young Americans who, when questioned, openly supported the National Socialist extermination policy, were fond of starting with the stereotyped phrase: Some of my best friends are Jews. The Jews themselves, they said, were to blame for the way Hitler treated them. Officers, students and women all said the same. 'If I had been in Germany I would have done the same thing as the Nazis,' said a twenty-seven-year-old student who had served in the war. Another young man, studying to become a dentist, declared: 'I think that what Hitler did to the Jews was right. When I had difficulties with a chap with whom I was negotiating I often wished Hitler would come here. I think the time will come when we will have to kill the bastards.'

In the psychodrama of Man a kind of court trial is held, with the prosecutor also acting as judge. The prosecutor represents the unfulfilled instincts, compulsions and passions. Conscience plays the judge. But the two roles – prosecutor and judge – are merged into one within the individual who is the prisoner of his own fixed ideas, prejudices and clichés. Therefore the Jews do not stand a chance of being allowed to speak in this travesty of a trial. They are always condemned, because the judge sees them through the eyes of the prosecutor.

Court practice in National Socialist Germany followed this psychodrama pattern to the letter. The Jews never had a chance of defending their case. 'Makes no difference: the Jew will be burned.' This is the motto of Lessing's drama *Nathan the Wise*, which raised the curtain on Germany's psychodrama of the nineteenth and twentieth centuries. At its other end we see bureaucrats, professors, theologians, industrialists and field-marshals. All of them are armchair-murderers, middle-class beings both intellectually and spiritually. Towards the end of the psychodrama men like Martin Luther and Adolf Eichmann make their appearance – two German Christians with a Protestant upbringing.

This is not the Martin Luther of the sixteenth century (though he too in his later years lashed out against the Jews), but his twentieth-century namesake, a secretary of state in the German foreign ministry, who in 1941 declared: 'I am still without any proposals from Belgrade. Generalities do not help solve the question. Please telephone Ambassador von Rintelen. Make it a special call.' The question was the liquidation of eight thousand Serbian Jews. A senior official was sent from Berlin to organize the extermination. The official, Franz Rademacher, reported on 25 October 1941: 'The male Jews will be shot by the end of this week. This settles the problem mentioned in the embassy's report.'

'Shooting the Jews is simpler than shooting gypsies. One must admit that the Jews go to their death with great composure. They stand very calmly, while the gypsies howl, scream and constantly move when they are at the place of execution . . . At the beginning my soldiers were not impressed. But on the second day it became obvious that one or the other did not have the nerve to carry out shootings over a lengthy period. My personal impression is that one has no moral qualms during the shooting. But they come days later when one reflects on it quietly in the evenings.' Thus wrote Lieutenant Walter, commanding the Ninth Infantry Regiment 433, on 1 November 1941. Moral qualms over the Jews had been obliterated over the past thousand years.

On 3 January 1946 Colonel John Harlan Amen of the American prosecution team at the Nuremberg trials put this question to Ohlendorf, the third in command in the Reich security office: 'When you say "liquidate", do you mean "kill"? – Ohlendorf: 'Yes, I mean kill.'

On 20 November 1941 von Manstein, Army High Command 11, had this communication circulated down to regimental and even battalion level: 'The Jews are the middlemen between the enemy at the rear and the remaining fighting units of the Red Army and the Red Command. The Jews hold all key posts in the political administration, commerce and trade more strongly than elsewhere in Europe and continue to form the nucleus of unrest and possible rebellion. The Jewish-Bolshevik system must be rooted out, once and for all. Never again must it encroach on our European Lebensraum. Soldiers must understand the necessity of *harsh expiation* [the italics for this theological expression are mine] to be exacted from the Jews, the spiritual fathers of the Bolshevik terror.'

In an order of the day dated 10 October 1941 concerning the Eastern territories Field-Marshal von Reichenau, Army High Command 6, said: 'The supreme aim of the campaign against the Jewish-Bolshevik system is the complete destruction of its power and the eradication of Asiatic influence on European civilization.' (Author's note: Note the use in an army order of those corrupt theological and idealistic slogans which had been propagated for decades in sermons and philosophical lectures.) 'In the East, our soldiers are not only fighting in accordance with the precepts of the art of war. As representatives of the unbending ideology of our nation, they are also exacting revenge for all the bestialities committed against the German and related peoples. The fear of German countermeasures must be stronger than the threats from roaming Bolshevik remnants.' In the late autumn of 1941 Hitler had proclaimed that the Red Army was no more than a force of such 'remnants'. Von Reichenau's order of the day ended with these words: 'Quite apart from any political considerations for the future, our soldiers have two tasks to fulfil: (1) the *complete destruction of the Bolshevik heresy*, the Soviet state and its armed forces; (2) the merciless extermination of alien malice and cruelty and thereby the protection of the life of the German soldiers in Russia. Thus alone shall we do justice to our historic task of liberating the German nation for ever from the Asiatic-Jewish peril.'

The German soldier was thus elevated to the position of a crusader wielding fire and sword, pledged to fulfilling the tasks the Inquisition had set itself since the extermination of the Albigenses.

Alfred Metzner gave this *affidavit* on the shooting of Jews: 'This action was the job of special SS units, who carried out the executions inspired by idealism — and without liquor.'

Idealism was also the watchword of Adolf Eichmann at his trial in Jerusalem. And the theologians contributing to Pinay's *Conspiracy against the Church* invoked it as well.

In Nuremberg, at the hearing on 7 January 1946, A. Thoma, counsel for the defence of A. Rosenberg, asked Erich von dem Bach-Zelewski, a general of the Waffen-SS, about Himmler's command for the extermination of thirty million Slavs. Bach-Zelewski replied: 'I think this followed logically from our ideology . . . If you preach for years and years that the Slavs are an inferior race and that the Jews are not even human, then you are bound to get such an explosion in the end.'

Bach-Zelewski's statement about preaching might also apply to the Christian hate campaign against the Jews which persisted not only through years, but unbroken centuries up to the 'final solution'. From early childhood millions of Christians had it hammered into their heads that the Jews were murderers of Christ and deserved to be exterminated. On the eve of the 'final solution' in 1939 Fritsch's *Handbook on the Jewish Question* in a revised edition (45th printing) listed a long series of devastating court verdicts which denied the devilish Jews the very right to live. This was done for the benefit of good National Socialists, Catholics and Protestants and all schoolchildren in Germany and throughout the world. 'Judaism is a single fighting organization, acting as needed under political, religious, economic or humanitarian guise. Its goal is Zion, that is to say, domination by the Jew. We are witnessing the dramatic final struggle for control of the world: is the Aryan born of Light or the Jew from the underworld to shape life on this earth according to his precept? Jewry has been waging this struggle for the past two thousand, five hundred years – and, in accordance with its nature, it works underground.'

Fritsch's *Handbook* was anti-Christian as well as anti-Jewish, seeing in Christianity the fruit of Jewish seed and in Christian churches the pathfinders of Jewish world supremacy. But, being intended for readers with a Christian upbringing, it made a point of quoting ecclesiastical opinions on the Jews. Catholic clergymen were cited as crown witnesses on ritual murder, Luther quoted *in extenso* advocating the burning of synagogues and destruction of Jewish homes. This Martin Luther (the reformer, not his namesake in the German foreign ministry of 1939) claimed that the Jews never ceased killing Christians. 'For myself I would only like to add that, if God were to give me no other Messiah than the one the Jews want and hope for, I would much rather be a swine than a man.'

But 'God' did give the Germans that other Messiah: Adolf Hitler. The 'Heil Hitler' greeting stirred the fervent faith of millions whose Christianity had dried up in their veins and now sprang forth in substitute belief in Hitler as the German Messiah.

But to return to Luther, a thousand years of rejection of the Jewish Messianic faith did indeed turn many Christians into 'swine'. The vision of the distant hereafter vanished and life on earth – divorced from its Messianic duty to work for the future kingdom of God on earth – became a 'materialistic swamp' in which a handful of overlords, especially in Catholic Spain, France, Italy and Latin America, drove themselves to death in orgies of luxury and pleasure while abandoning the masses to the mercies of the accursed earth.

Martin Luther described the Jews as children of the Devil and dastardly murderers. And the *Handbook on the Jewish Question* proudly claimed that some of the most distinguished Catholic ecclesiastics agreed with that view. It instanced the fate of the 'Society of the Friends of Israel', formed in 1928 in Rome by Dutch Catholics. In the same year the Holy Office disbanded the society. The reason given was that 'words and deeds have begun to intrude into the Society of the Friends of Israel which deviate from the concepts of the church, the spirit of the holy fathers and the sacred liturgy.' And it is true that the words and deeds that prevailed between 1939 and 1945 were more in keeping with the tenets of St Ambrose and St John Chrysostom.

'In future no one shall be allowed to write or publish books or other works which in any way favour such heretic tendencies.' This prohibition is of great significance: it means that on the eve of Hitler's rise to power, the supreme authority of the Roman Catholic church forbade any theological and journalistic campaigning against anti-Semitism. The *Handbook* cited a comment of 19 May 1928 which appeared in *Civiltà Cattolica* in connection with this prohibition under the heading 'The Jewish danger and the Friends of Israel'.

It said: 'The Jewish danger threatens the whole world by its corrupting influence or despicable intermingling with Christian nations, especially with Roman Catholics and Latin peoples where a traditional, blind liberalism has strongly favoured the Jews and at the same time damaged Catholicism and the ecclesiastical orders in particular. The danger is growing day by day . . .' The tremendous power the Jews had in financial and government circles could only be explained by 'secret Jewish influence', and (*Civiltà Cattolica* added) 'the so-called League of Nations also favours secret Jewish interference.'

The *Handbook of the Jewish Question* in 1939 rightly said about this semi-official Roman commentary on the dissolution of the Friends of Israel: 'One could scarcely have expected greater insight from these circles. Is it not a splendid justification of the attitude of National Socialist Germany?' Indeed, it was a splendid justification.

In May 1944 Adolf Eichmann's death trains were rolling through Hungary, day and night. The world knew that Hitler's Reich had entered its final battle and that its downfall had begun. The Vatican made a protest, after a 'deluge of protests from neutral countries' had swept over the Horthy régime. The papal nuncio in Budapest, on conveying the message, took the opportunity to state that the Vatican's protest was by no means due to 'false feelings of pity' for the Jews. No, there can be no room for 'false pity' for the people who murdered Christ.

'In 1932 Germany had only two choices: either to perish in the Jewish-Marxist morass of political parties, the racial chaos of sub-humans and the degrading enslavement by Jewish financiers, or to arise from the disgrace of Jewish dominance, racial pollution and economic misery through the defeat of Jewry and the rebirth of a nation of pure German blood.' This is quoted from E.V. von Rudolf's *Der Judenspiegel* (The Mirror of the Jews), published in 1938 by the SA for the encouragement of its members. How many pastoral letters, essays in church magazines and publications by German theologians welcomes this 'rising' and 'rebirth' of the German people and saw their continuation in Hitler's war!

In the 'final struggle' against devilish Jewish Bolshevism concentration on these themes of rising and rebirth ensured that the extermination of the Jews was kept conveniently out of sight.

Giving evidence on oath about mass shootings of Jews and others, Ernst Rode, chief of staff of the SS command, said, 'These methods, rejected by the majority of SS and police officers and, I think, by most Army officers, were naturally often discussed in my presence during conferences at the Supreme Command of the Armed Forces and the Army High Command. On those occasions I always pointed out that it would have been within the powers of the commanders-in-chief of the army groups to oppose such actions. I am firmly convinced that a determined and united protest by all the field-marshals would have brought about a change in the assignments and methods. In my view it would be stupid, even cowardly, to suggest that if these men had been removed they would have been succeeded by even harsher commanding officers.'

According to this statement, if the Vatican and European cardinals and bishops had issued a resolute appeal to stop this mass murder it could have aroused, co-ordinated and activated resistance right up to the top ranks of the SS.

Brutal SS authorities including Himmler himself yielded when their attempts to apply the 'final solution' met with real opposition, as for instance in France and Denmark, where the National Socialist authorities were clearly impressed by the resistance of the Danish people. A similar situation arose in Bulgaria where the metropolitan of Sofia, Stephan, sheltered the chief rabbi. His public condemnation of the persecution of the Jews was more explicit than anything the Vatican ever said.

In Germany, where the Christian community as a whole no longer had an informed collective conscience, individual men and women displayed a high sense of moral responsibility yet remained untouched by the Nazi murder machine.

Kurt Schmit, Reich minister of economics from 30 June 1933 till the beginning of 1935, left the cabinet because of deep disagreement with Hitler's and the government's policies. 'I told Hitler, Goering, Gürtner, Schacht, von Papen and Blomberg why I disagreed ... Even then [in 1934] I realized that this policy would lead to war and to a dreadful disaster. I also regarded the action of 30 June 1934 as murder by the régime, and I said so to US Ambassador Dodd in the autumn of 1935.' The government's policy was becoming increasingly obvious to the members of the cabinet. 'But when I put this to Blomberg, who was then defence minister, he said he was a soldier and these events were decreed by fate.'

Baron von Eltz, minister of posts and communications, submitted his resignation in a letter to Hitler of 30 January 1937, in which he also refused to accept the Golden Party Badge. The reason he gave was that as a devout Christian he felt compelled to take this step on account of the increasing official party attacks on Christians and people trying to remain true to their religious beliefs.

Senior officers protested at the crimes that were being committed. Nothing happened to them. On 4 July 1944 – shortly before the attempt on Hitler's life on 20 July – a legation secretary, Reinhard Henschel, submitted his resignation to the foreign ministry. It was accepted on forfeit of his pension rights. In a statement explaining his action, Henschel later said: 'In my opinion many of those whose position involved them in a conflict of conscience or compelled them to authorize evil ought to have made, and could have made at least an attempt to get out of their untenable situation. All officials were in a position to recognize the point at which their work made them accomplices in crime.' With some material sacrifice and skill such officials could have saved themselves and their families.

A lively, charming Viennese sergeant named Anton Schmidt was, in civilian life, the co-owner of a clothing store. In his thirties, he was tall and slim, had brown hair and looked a little like Hitler with his black moustache. A sportsman who loved wine, women and song, Sergeant Schmidt was not a meek character or a regular church-goer. Sent to Vilna, he worked unceasingly to save Lithuanian Jews, for whom, when he was discovered, he sacrificed his own life. Anton Schmidt, friend of the Jewish poet Hermann Adler, had early taken an interest in Zionism. The priest who regularly visited him in his prison cell confirmed: 'This is a man with very positive ideas.' Schmidt looked upon God as a symbol of the higher senses. But he also believed that 'repentance is something for little children'.

The man who professed this latter view was Adolf Eichmann, and it is held today by millions of ordinary citizens and Christians. The leading political mouthpiece of Catholic conservatives in the Federal German Republic, the *Rheinische Merkur*, said rightly in 1961: 'In the Federal Republic one would expect Eichmann to be acquitted.' In the same distinguished paper, which claims to influence opinion among the German élite, a high Protestant dignitary, Erwin Wilken, spoke out decisively in 1963 against trials of Nazi criminals and against 'too magnanimous' confessions of guilt. The conviction of a limited number of criminals, he wrote, would cause all others to feel that they had now really been 'absolved from any reproach of complicity in a higher sense'.

Well, the overwhelming majority of ordinary citizens today do feel absolved from any reproach of complicity, in whatever sense of the word one cares to name. As Hannah Arendt has rightly said: 'There are few people who are capable of truly realizing that they have done wrong – let alone of feeling regret or shame.' Neither church nor school nor university has done anything towards developing a mature and articulate conscience.

Adolf Eichmann is a normal, typical case. Millions like him are today working in factories making weapons and equipment for nuclear war. Ordinary citizens and good Christians can go to communion in the morning, attend mass, then take breakfast in the officers' mess and drop gas bombs before noon (as in Italy's war against Abyssinia) or even on Good Friday (the day of Mussolini's treacherous attack on Albania). Then they have a good lunch, and in the afternoon press a button to release a stick of atom bombs. And in the evening they listen to *The Merry Widow*. (In the summer of 1944 inmates of Auschwitz concentration camp were marched to the gas chambers to the sound of music from *The Merry Widow*.)

At his trial in Jerusalem Eichmann said fifteen times: 'Not guilty in the terms of the indictment', and he also said: 'I am not guilty of shedding blood.' Eichmann did not deny what he had done, but he acknowledged no personal responsibility for doing it. His evidence conformed to the 'sound sense of the people', which secular and ecclesiastical authorities in Central Europe have cultivated in the last two centuries.

Nearly all the important henchmen of the 'final solution' came, like Eichmann, from good middle-class families. There was hardly one head of department at the *Reichssicherheitshauptamt* who did not sport a doctor's title on his office door: Dr Kaltenbrunner, Dr Höttl, Dr Wisliceny, Dr Grell, Dr Pütz, Dr Mengele, Dr Mildner, Prof. Dr Hirt. In the concentration camps university professors and physicians carried out unspeakably cruel experiments on living human material with the same calm as Eichmann. Some of them, as for example Dr Lucas, may have been gentle in manner and well thought of – even by the camp inmates themselves. But there was truth in the statement that another of the accused, Stefan Baretzki, flung in Dr Lucas's face at the Auschwitz trial in Frankfurt in February-March 1965: 'Within half an hour he sent five thousand people to the gas chamber, and now he tries to pose as a saviour.'

'Many SS leaders were Catholics or Protestants. Kaltenbrunner, Müller, the Gestapo chief Hoess, the commandant of Auschwitz – all came from Catholic families' (Bernd Nellessen). Himmler's godfather was a bishop of Bamberg. In his youth the Protestant Adolf Eichmann belonged to a Bible class run by the YMCA. A Franciscan monk, fully aware of Eichmann's identity, helped him to escape to Argentina. Many German, Slovak and Ukrainian auxiliaries collaborated with the SS in the Eastern territories, and numerous Croat Catholics, who had killed more than half a million Orthodox Serbs, fled via Rome to South America and to Arab countries. Sano Mach, minister of the interior in the Catholic government of Slovakia, recommended successfully that even baptized Jews should be taken off to die.

'I was an idealist,' said Eichmann on 12 July 1961, 'and I was in this Jewish business out of idealism as long as there was something constructive in it, but not once its purpose became destructive. I never did negative things for reasons of idealism, but rather in a spirit of pessimism.'

For Eichmann, the man who had fallen a bit below his social class, the die was cast at the Wannsee conference in January 1942. Heydrich had invited senior officials there to discuss how the 'final solution' was to be put into practice, for (as Hannah Arendt has said) 'this programme depended on the active co-operation of all ministries and the entire apparatus of officials'.

To Heydrich's great surprise and satisfaction none of the senior civil servants present raised any objection. Heydrich had expected great difficulties, for this was a matter of making technical preparations for the murder of eleven million Jews. The civil servants and other senior officials dealt briskly with the whole business, just like the planners of military exercises today who reckon out the killed in terms of twenty, forty or sixty million.

Years later, on 26 June 1961, Eichmann expressed the deep satisfaction he had felt back in January 1942: 'At that moment I sensed a kind of contentment such as Pilate must have experienced, because I felt completely free of any guilt. Here at this Wannsee conference the most proment people of the Reich were stating their views. The *"popes" were giving orders* [my italics]. Mine was to obey, and that is what I remembered in all the years to come.'

At that conference Heydrich outlined the programme for the final solution: the first stage would be the deportation of the European Jews to the East. Heydrich reckoned this would involve eleven million people. To start with, these Jews would be turned into forced labourers. The heavy work would kill the weak, and the survivors would then have to be put to death. The plan was approved unanimously. There were no objections. In 1961 Eichmann commented: 'Then we went on to discuss the various possible ways of killing them.'

On 13 December 1961 Eichmann addressed the court in Jerusalem for the last time. Since the destruction of the temple by the Romans, this was the first trial at which Jews were judging a man who had committed a crime against their own people. In his final plea Eichmann said: 'Mass murder must be blamed on the political leaders alone . . . I emphasize again that my guilt lies in my obedience . . . It is quite wrong to say that I was a fanatical persecutor of the Jews . . . I am not guilty of shedding blood . . . No one ever came to me to object to the way I was doing my job. Not even the witness Prior Grüber alleged that . . . [Grüber had come to the trial only in order to put forward mitigating circumstances on some counts.] The guiding principle in my life, which I was taught when I was a boy, has been to strive to realize ethical values . . Official language is the only language I know.'

Adolf Eichmann – the unimaginative, ordinary citizen and (until he left the Protestant church in 1937) the stereotyped ordinary Christian – never really understood the crime he was committing. Similarly, millions of normal citizens and ordinary Christians (before the last two world wars and a possible third one) did not and do not understand what modern war – genocide – means.

Eichmann's Germany, the Germany of so many Eichmanns, had lost its conscience. The 'other Germany', the Germany of the 'internal emigrés' and of the plotters of 20 July, was deeply divided. Goerdeler, the political brain behind the plotters, considered a just peace to include the incorporation of the Sudetenland, Austria and possibly South Tyrol in the German Reich. His solution of the Jewish question closely resembled Eichmann's early projects and the National Socialist solution in its early stages.

Adolf Hitler, the Austrian Catholic, was able to carry out his schemes without hindrance, indeed with the co-operation (at first only passive) of the whole world. Hitler's plans were there for all to see in *Mein Kampf*. They were restated in many speeches and then turned into grim reality by brown-shirted murderers.

Let us record a few landmarks on this road of terror. 1 April 1933: boycott of Jewish shops. 30 June–2 July 1934: murder of political and ideological adversaries in the Roehm putsch, with SS and Gestapo going into action. 25 July 1934: Nazi putsch in Austria; Federal Chancellor Dollfuss assassinated. 1935: Hitler works out his euthanasia scheme, which formed the basis for his 'final solution'. 15 September 1935: proclamation of the anti-Semitic Nuremberg Laws, drafted by Hans Globke, in later years adviser to Federal Chancellor Adenauer. After 1945 Globke was 'exonerated' by Catholic ecclesiastical authorities in Germany. One provision of the Nuremberg Laws – the special passport stamps required by Jews – made it easy to apprehend German Jews anywhere in Europe. 9 November 1938: the *Kristallnacht* when, all over the Reich, synagogues were set on fire, mass arrests made of Jews and their property seized. 1 September 1939: Germany invades Poland. 30 April 1940: the first Polish ghetto set up in Lodz. 31 July 1941: Goering orders Heydrich to deport all European Jews. 23 September 1941: experimental killings in gas chambers in Auschwitz. 28 September 1941: Jewish pogrom in Kiev: thirty-four thousand massacred. 20 October 1941: first deportations from Germany ordered. End of 1941: permanent gas chambers set up at Chelmo near Posen. 20 Janary 1942: conference at Wannsee: discussion of the 'final solution' of the Jewish question. 16 March 1942: death camp of Belzec set up. 11 June 1943: Himmler orders liquidation of inmates of Polish ghettoes.

On President Roosevelt's initiative, a conference of thirty-two countries was called at the lovely Swiss resort of Evian in the summer of 1938 to discuss refugee problems. There were long discussions on where to send the European Jews. Not only Germany, but also the Polish and Rumanian governments, had repeatedly made it publicly known that they wanted to get rid of their Jews. The representatives of the thirty-two countries could not find any place for them, not even for the children. In 1938 an American writer (W. Ziff) asked: 'What is to be done with these people, with the millions who are clawing like frantic beasts at the dark walls of the suffocating chambers where they are imprisoned? The Christian world has practically abandoned them, and sits by with hardly an observable twinge of conscience in the midst of this terrible catastrophe. The Western Jews, still potent and powerful, rotate in their smug self-satisfied orbits, and confine themselves to genteel charity.'

That was in the year 1938 when – for all who wanted to see – the Jews of Europe could be seen locked up like cattle awaiting the slaughter, while the Christian world just looked on. As for the Western Jews – we shall come back to them later.

'The Jewish blood spilt by the National Socialists is on the hands of all of us,' said Jean-Paul Sartre, a decided non-Christian. 'The conference was a striking failure and proved disastrous to the German Jews,' wrote Hannah Arendt. Not until two years later, in the autumn of 1941, did the Hitler government prohibit Jewish emigration. Hitler waited till 1941, and when he saw that no one was willing to stand by the Jews, he struck.

More than a million children could have been saved. But between 1941 and 1943 the British government refused to issue any entry visas to Palestine and other territories. In those years the British and the United States governments discussed what steps could or should be taken to save the Jews. The American Secretary of State, Cordell Hull, declared that they were seeking places of rescue for the Jews in Madagascar, Cyrenaica, Palestine, French North Africa, and even in the Dominican Republic and Ecuador.

The 'Christian world' was thoroughly sick of the Jews, sick of them to the depths of its Christian soul, though not daring to admit it. So, both actively and passively, it helped to exterminate them. As in the sixteenth and seventeenth centuries, the principal country in Europe to give shelter to the Jews was Islamic Turkey. Istanbul and Ankara became the headquarters of the clandestine stream of European emigrants on their way to Palestine.

In the spring of 1943 the Bermuda Refugee Conference was held. The twentieth century has evolved the macabre technique of discussing the life and death of millions at luxury hotels in health resorts. It would have been more realistic to move the seat of the conference geographically a little nearer to the scenes of murder. The Bermuda Conference refused to deal with the Jews in isolation as a separate issue. The World Jewish Congress asked the delegates to enter into negotiations with the Axis powers in order to obtain the release of the Jews from concentration and labour camps, or at least to enable food parcels to be sent to these camps. The United States declined to relax American immigration laws. Great Britain would not permit Jewish children to enter Palestine. 'The only result of the Bermuda Conference was to strengthen Hitler's conviction that the world did not really care very much what happened to the Jews, and to fortify his resolution to exterminate them' (Malcolm Hay).

Hundreds of thousands of children could have been saved at the cost of a few million dollars. This was later confirmed by Secretary of State Cordell

Hull. But during the war American government officials prevented news of Hitler's exercise in extermination from becoming known in the United States.

And so Hitler really enlisted the whole world as collaborators in his 'final solution' of the Jewish problem, though (to be just) they were often unwitting and unwilling. But basically all – French Jews, Protestant Christians in the United States and Scottish Catholics like Malcolm Hay – are agreed: Germany's responsibility for these crimes was only secondary. The prime responsibility lay with ten centuries of Christian tradition.

But we must also examine the difficult question of the extent to which the Jews shared responsibility for this unparalleled catastrophe. It was the first time that the Jews had experienced the downfall of their whole world – as an overture to the downfall of the Christian world, which was preparing its own suicide after having hounded the kinsfolk of the Jew Jesus to their deaths for fifteen hundred years. In earlier persecutions Jews had always been sure that the people of Israel would live, even if individual Jews died. But this time it was a case of genocide: the entire Jewish race was being exterminated.

How far then did the Jews collaborate in the 'final solution'? The National Socialists regarded collaboration with Jewish leaders as a vital element in policy. Without it the extermination might have proved technically impossible; it would certainly have been more difficult and protracted. At his trial in Jerusalem, Adolf Eichmann repeatedly mentioned 'good collaboration' with Jewish leaders. Eichmann and the Nazi Gauleiter Wilhelm Kube, commissioner-general for Byelorussia, made a distinction between the 'bestial hordes' i.e. East European Jews, and German Jews from 'our own cultured sphere'. Gauleiter Kube was a kind of National Socialist heretic. According to a file entry by a high SS official dated 1 October 1942, Kube was against the suppression of Jewish artistic achievements, such as the music of Mendelssohn and Offenbach; one could not simply pretend that Mendelssohn and other Jews had not contributed anything to the treasury of music.

There was no mention at the Eichmann trial, either in the indictment or the verdict, of any distinction between East and West or Central European Jews. Yet this distinction was important: German and German-educated Jewish victims from Central Europe still had something in common with the German managers of the 'final solution'. Both looked down on the 'Asiatic hordes' from the East. German Jews whom Golo Mann met in a French internment camp in the Pyrenees praised the orderliness in Dachau in comparison with the situation in their French camp.

On 3 October 1932 President Hindenburg sent the following letter to Dr Löwenstein: 'Many thanks to the Reich League of Jewish Ex-Servicemen for the good wishes, the beautiful flowers and the memorial volume you sent me for my eighty-fifth birthday. In respectful memory of the Jewish comrades who gave their lives for the fatherland I accept the book, which I am placing in my war library. Comradely greetings.'

The Reich League of Jewish Ex-Servicemen published this book in 1932 under the title *The Jewish Dead of the German Army, Navy and Colonial Troops 1914–18: A Memorial Volume*. In 1914 there were five hundred and fifty thousand Jews of German nationality; of these, one hundred thousand fought in the war and twelve thousand died. When the book was ceremonially presented, Lieutenant Ott expressed a vote of thanks on behalf of the minister of defence and said: 'We shall hold this book about our Jewish comrades who died in the World War in high honour . . . in memory of these loyal and true sons of our German nation.'

The ceremony took place in Berlin on 17 November 1932. Six years later the *Verband nationaldeutscher Juden* (Association of German Jews), which had been founded in 1921, was disbanded. After Hitler's advent to power the association had planned to become 'Adolf Hitler's most loyal opposition'.

Not only German Jews in the Reich, but also German-speaking and German-educated Jews in the post-war Danube states believed with un-shakeable tenacity in the greatness and humanity of the 'nation of poets and philosophers'. To them Germany was the nation of Schiller and Goethe, a country with a highly disciplined and efficient economy and an incomparably brave army. This Jewish faith in Germany had to be literally rooted out, burnt and gassed to death. It was ineradicable as long as its bearers were alive.

This deep-rooted, irrational faith in Germany among Central European and German Jews resembled the exiled Spanish Jews' belief in Spain which lasted into the early twentieth century. The Jews credited even Hitler with the 'noble reason' of a nation that had produced the philosopher Kant, whom Eichmann earnestly cited in his defence at the Jerusalem trial. They thought: 'Surely, he won't be that mad.' These German-educated Jews simply could not believe that the Führer and Reich Chancellor would irrationally destroy his highly gifted Jews who were so eager to be of service.

The faith of these German Jews in Germany cannot simply be equated with that politico-religious belief which certain National Socialist Jews displayed in Prague, Berlin and Vienna. These Jews secularized the ancient Messianic faith and pinned their hopes on Hitler, as Fascist Jews did on the Duce – or as Socialist Jews do on Socialism or Communism.

The driving force within these Jewish National Socialists was often a Jewish self-hatred of the kind we have already encountered in Trebitsch and similar Jewish forerunners of National Socialism. Joseph Gabel, a French Jew who has written some excellent studies on forms of alienation has said:

'The true anti-Semite, who is simply anti-Semitic and nothing else, is un-doubtedly the anti-Semitic Jew, of whom there are more than one thinks.' Gabel, who made this observation in a study of Kafka, commented: 'Far be it from us to include the author of *Metamorphosis* in this category. But it is certain that his Jewishness took a highly problematical form. His bio-graphers have reported some astounding remarks which he is said to have made. And few anti-Semites have written crueller things about Israel than Kafka in his story *Jackals and Arabs*.

To find tragedy we must search the peaks and not the valleys: Kafka's struggle to defeat alienation leads from the battle with his Jewish God-Father and his own father to the complex aspects of 'problematic Jewishness'. If we except orthodox East European Jews and the numerically insignificant pockets of orthodox Jews in other parts of Europe, we find that the over-whelming majority of Central and West European Jews had become doubtful of their own Jewishness, especially in the years before Hitler's rise to power.

National Socialist propaganda, with its sewer mentality, uncovered the festering sores and weak spots of democratic France and Britain. It also sensed the deep crisis in European and German Jewry and published a mass of evidence of Jewish self-recrimination, ranging from the most sublime spiritual self-criticism in the face of the living God – in the Bible – to the self-accusatory utterances of morbid minds.

The spirit of the West European Jews was broken and their defences shattered. Feeling doomed and forsaken by their God, they were unable to stand and fight an enemy whose power was reaching gigantic proportions. In the hope of escaping the hangmen, anti-Semitic Jews began to commit suicide by rushing into their arms. Often the persecuted imitated the persecutors and took over even their brutal terminology and slogans.

On the eve of 1933 and of 1939 many European Jews were no longer conscious of being Jewish. One was a Jew by reason of atavism, habit, con-formism, indolence, but chiefly because of spiritual idleness (Josué Jéhouda). Moreover, liberal Jewish theologians, endeavouring in all innocence to keep up with the times, had undermined the faith of their ancestors.

On 7 November 1909 Rabbi Léonard Lévy preached in the temple of the *Union israélite libérale* in Paris. In the course of his sermon he referred to the tomb of St Carlo Borromeo (Pope John XXIII's favourite saint) in Milan Cathedral. There lay the bones of the great archbishop (the rabbi said), the mitre crowning the skull and the skeleton's hands bedecked with jewels. He went on: 'I should like to compare traditionalist Jewry with this precious relic. Certainly it is laden with jewels and priceless ornaments, with experience, wisdom and great historic deeds. But it looks like a dead man.'

For many Jews this ghostly relic had by 1933 lost all live-giving power and inspiration. Josué Jéhouda, a lone fighter for religious Judaism, who lived in Geneva through the bitter years of struggle from 1933 to 1945, said in 1958: 'Today many Jews are Jews only by the grace of Hitler.' For it was Hitler who forced them to recognize their Jewishness.

The abandonment of the Jewish heritage in the years before the 'final solution' took any one of the four following forms: there was firstly what one might call pink assimilation – submersion in a liberal and nationalist German, French or English Jewry; secondly the red assimilation within Marxism, Socialism, radicalism and Communism; thirdly, a blue assimilation – with atheistic, secularized nationalists seeking to establish a state of Israel on the Western pattern; and, finally, a black assimilation – spiritual regression into an orthodox sixteenth-century ghetto mentality.

Josué Jéhouda's analysis of Jewish reaction to the provocations of European anti-Semites between 1914 and 1932 led him to this conclusion: 'The grand offensives of European anti-Semitism in press, literature, politics and church were met by an utterly feeble, half-hearted response.' Racial anti-Semitism was directed against a Jewry that had lost its moral roots and disintegrated into numerous hostile and segregated clans, without hope for the future, spiritually amorphous and confused and plagued by fear and scepticism. These Jews, completely rent asunder, submitted to the terrible blows of anti-Semitism in fatalistic resignation. By the time the Second World War came, racial anti-Semitism had already made such devastating inroads into the Jewish and non-Jewish conscience that public opinion, focused on the war, remained silent when in 1942 details became known of the monstrous campaign to hunt down and destroy the Jews.

Robert Neumann, whose books had been burnt by the Nazis, spent the war years in England. He describes in his book *The Excuses of Conscience* how he was visited there by a leading Jewish Social Democrat from Poland, who told him everything that was going on. 'And I refused to make use of the horrifying details I had been told.' He found them impossible to believe.

Throughout the war Robert Neumann worked with a British organization devoted to the study of German affairs. When the Russians handed over some captured diaries and letters from German soldiers the first reaction, even among those who came from Germany, was that they could not be genuine. Later Neumann was to discover that the Nazis were aware of this inability of others to believe what they could do – and took advantage of it.

Salcia Landmann has published a collection of Jewish jokes which contains examples reflecting the contorted attitude of German Jews in the early days of the Third Reich. She comments: 'Before the Hitler era, the Jews of Germany were mostly enthusiastic German nationalists and militarists.' Among her 'jokes' is one about two German Jews who had escaped from a Nazi concentration camp near the Dutch frontier and managed to get to Holland, where they were enthusiastically received. 'Escorted by Dutch troops further into the country, one Jew turned to the other and whispered sadly: "And this is what the Dutch call marching! What would *our* SA think?" '

The Jewish European joke – first a symptom of enlightenment and slackening belief and then of complete loss of faith – mirrored not only the decay and self-betrayal of West European Jewry, but also the profound doubts and uncertainties besetting East European Jews. Caught as they were between a superstitious belief in Chassidim mystic rabbis with their harsh, inflexible orthodoxy and the temptation of being liberated by the West from the God of Sinai, they were beginning to crack spiritually.

Many East Jewish jokes revolve round the unspoken question that worries especially true believers: What can God do? What can the God of Job do to the faithful? It sounds harmless enough when put this way: 'Jankel, I worry already all day. What d'you think: Can God create a stone which is so heavy He can't lift it?'

In 1949 an Austrian Jew tried to free himself from his despair in the God of Israel by writing a huge book entitled *Bibel und Zeitgeist* (The Bible and the Spirit of our Age). Using the pseudonym Robert Jaromir, the author first reflected on his experience in the police prison of occupied Vienna in July 1938. Jews, Catholics, Socialists and others had all been thrown in there after the Anschluss. Jaromir's Jewish mind was desperately absorbed with the Jewish tragedy – constantly seeking a way out by renouncing the God of Sinai. One Jewish 'joke' touches upon this tremendous preoccupation of all ex-Jews: 'You are a rich man. Would you not make a small contribution towards my pilgrimage to the Holy Land?' – 'Gladly; but on one condition.' The rich man takes the Bible from his bookshelf and gives it to the visitor. 'When you get there, be so kind as to put this back on Mount Sinai.'

In many countries children are fond of war games. They play Red Indians, cops and robbers, or, as in England, recall Guy Fawkes' plot to blow up the Houses of Parliament. Children's games revive memories of old disasters, but very rarely do they enact a future catastrophe.

Here is a child's letter of thanks to the Nazi magazine *Der Stürmer*, written from the youth hostel Gross-Möllen on 16 April 1936: 'Every Saturday our warden does a puppet play about the Jews. We have a puppet that looks just like a real Jew. It has a nose like the Devil. Today we saw a play in which the Devil persuaded the Jew to shoot a brave National Socialist. [To this day devotional pictures in places of pilgrimage, e.g. at Mariazell and elsewhere, show how Jews, prompted by the Devil, attack and murder priests and God-fearing Christians.] This play really made us understand how the Jew sets about his evil business.'

This was written by a child in 1936. Millions of children learn at school in their lessons on religion how the Jews killed Christ. It stands to reason that people who can murder Christ *must* also murder human beings.

Dr Aharon Peretz, a gynaecologist, wrote about the ghetto in Kovno on 4 May 1961: 'I think the greatest tragedy of the Jewish people is the tragedy of its children. In the ghetto the children played and laughed, but their play showed the tragedy of the Jewish nation. They played funerals. They dug a grave, put a child in it and called him Hitler. They played near the gates of the ghetto. Some of the children were Germans, others were Jews. The German children insulted and hit the Jewish ones.'

Children no older than three or four fully grasped the seriousness of the situation. Yet 'children' of fifty or sixty – Christian children, officers, bishops and professors – were incapable of doing the same! And what of the Jewish 'children' – the leaders of the Jewish communities in Hitler-dominated countries?

The Nazi régime deported and sent to their death Jews from 33,914 places in Germany, Austria, Estonia, Latvia, Lithuania, Holland, Luxembourg, Norway, Poland, Czechoslovakia, Rumania and the Soviet Union. There are no details available about other countries such as Greece, though it is known that Salonika's entire Sephardic community, descendants of Jews exiled from Spain in 1492, was deported to Auschwitz.

Jewish central authorities and Jewish police units which the Nazis had set up in occupied territories were instrumental in the 'final solution'. Indeed, without them, the mass deportations would have been technically impossible. Jewish authorities were organized by the Nazis side by side with the quisling governments in occupied countries. 'Where the National Socialists failed to install puppet governments, they also failed to mobilize Jewish collaboration. But whereas quisling governments were usually staffed by ex-opposition members, the Jewish councils were as a rule composed of the recognized Jewish leaders of the country. The Nazis gave these men enormous authority – power over life and death – until they themselves were deported, usually "only" to Terezin or Bergen-Belsen, if they were of Central or West European origin, but to Auschwitz if they were East European Jews.

'This participation of Jewish leaders in the destruction of their own people is, beyond doubt, the darkest chapter in the whole tragic story. As far as collaboration was concerned, there was no difference between largely assimilated Jewish communities of Central and Western Europe and the Yiddish-speaking masses from the East. In Austria as in Warsaw, in Berlin as in Budapest, the Nazis were able to rely on Jewish officials to compile lists of people and property, extract money from the victims for their own deportation and destruction, keep an eye on vacant houses, and supply policemen to round up and help bring the Jews to the trains. They helped up to the bitter end, to the handing over of Jewish communal property so that it could be properly confiscated' (Hannah Arendt).

Some of these Jewish leaders saw themselves as sea captains who 'had managed to bring their sinking ships safely into port by throwing much of their precious cargo overboard'. They were saviours of the Jewish nation who 'rescued a thousand by sacrificing a hundred, and ten thousand at the cost of a thousand'. Hannah Arendt comments: 'Reality looked quite different. In Hungary, for example, Dr Kastner bought the salvation of exactly 1,684 people by sacrificing about 476,000.'

This Jewish catastrophe can only be understood against the background of wholesale terror and the 'total moral collapse which the Nazis caused in all sections, especially in the upper strata, of society throughout Europe'.

It was particularly the most intelligent and deeply sensitive Jews who felt utterly forsaken – by God, by the Christians and all non-Jewish human beings.

We know from many reports from Hitler's and Stalin's concentration camps how the fight for a crust or a sip of water could turn human beings into murderers or even cannibals who tore the livers from the bodies of their dead comrades. Excessive pain and perpetual terror undermine and destroy a man's moral resistance. The Jews in *Prison Europe* and in *Ghetto Europe* knew they were forsaken by all. Individual acts of charity – like that of Cardinal Innitzer, who sheltered Jews in his palace, in Roman monasteries and elsewhere – do not mitigate the cruel fact that not one Christian church in Germany, Poland, Hungary or Rumania intervened on behalf of the persecuted Jews.

'The utter failure of ecclesiastical leaders, committees and administrators is obvious. Generally speaking, they sent the non-Aryan pastors into the desert and were glad to be rid of them' (Martin Niemoeller). Apart from Holland and some areas of France, the Protestant and Catholic churches were not even capable of defending baptized Jews and their own Jewish-Christian clergy, let alone the Jews themselves. In 1933 the Protestant church in Germany drew up its own Aryan clause; in 1939 the Protestant ecclesiastical authorities demanded proof of Aryan origin even from students of theology. On 17 December 1941 Protestant church leaders published a statement on the position of Protestant Jews within the church. 'The National Socialist leadership of Germany has given irrefutable documentary proof that this world war was instigated by the Jews . . . As members of the German national community, the undersigned Protestant provincial churches and church leaders stand in the front line of this historic struggle, which has made necessary such measures as the official police recognition of Jews as the *born enemies of the Reich and the world*. Even Martin Luther, from bitter experience, advocated stringent measures against the Jews and demanded their expulsion from Germany. From the Crucifixion to this day the Jews have fought against Christendom or exploited and misrepresented it for their own ends. Baptism changes nothing in the racial separateness, national status or biological character of the Jew. The task of any German Evangelical church is to cultivate and promote the religious life of Germans. Christians who are

Jewish by race have no place and no rights in this church. The undersigned German Protestant churches and church leaders have therefore severed all links with Jewish Christians. We are determined not to tolerate any Jewish influence on German religious life.'

Anyone who feels inclined to pass judgment on the collaboration of Jewish leaders and authorities in the 'final solution' would do well to reflect also on this infamous ecclesiastical document. Logically it would have obliged the German Protestant churches to join in the destruction of the synagogues, the expulsion of the Jews and the burning of both Testaments. Among the things the churches forgot in issuing this shameful statement was the fact that orthodox Protestant theology of the nineteenth century owed much to Jewish-Christians such as Neander, and that the neo-conservative political movement of German Protestantism drew its inspiration from such men as Stahl.

The Protestant failure had its parallels in the Catholic church. Cardinal Michael Faulhaber, the Roman Catholic dignitary most highly respected in Germany and abroad, sent numerous letters to German National Socialist authorities and foreign papers in 1934, emphatically protesting at the monstrous imputation that he had delivered a sermon *against* racial hatred and anti-Semitism.

In August of that year the *Sozialdemokrat*, the paper of the German Social Democrats in Prague, had published a sermon by the Cardinal which he had in fact never delivered. Faulhaber protested against the publication of what he called 'a disgraceful inflammatory article based on a Marxist forgery'. He demanded that the government should stop the sale of the newspaper and that the 'public be told the truth about this barefaced lie without delay'. When – to use the terminology of Faulhaber's official gazette – the 'alleged pro-Jewish sermon was seized upon' by the hard-pressed Jewish World Conference in Geneva at the end of 1934, Faulhaber wrote to the conference, protesting resolutely against the use of his name by a conference which was calling for a trade boycott of Germany.

In 1936 Faulhaber, in a sermon he did deliver, hailed Pope Pius XI as the best, and at the beginning, the only friend of the National Socialist Reich. He declared: 'The most spiteful falsehood about the Holy Father, Pope Pius XI, was presented to the German people by a German newspaper on the first day of this year: he was alleged to be half Jewish, and his mother was said to have been a Dutch Jewess. I can see the congregation starting in horror. This lie is eminently calculated to expose the pope to mockery in Germany.'

In making this pronouncement, Cardinal Faulhaber – the most prominent and representative church leader in Germany – not only overlooked the fact that Jesus was a Jew, but also that, if he was condemning the Jews to banishment, it was the Christians he was exposing to mockery, since National Socialist pamphlets had rumoured it abroad (in Munich too) that in the course of its history the church had had more than a little to do with the Jewish God and the Jew Jesus. In this context we should recall once more the statement of the papal nuncio in Budapest at the height of the 'final solution' in 1944, in which he emphasized that the Vatican's protest at the continuing extermination of the Jews had not been prompted by 'false feelings of pity'.

The collaboration of the Jewish leaders and authorities in Europe with the Nazis must therefore be regarded as a parallel to the failure of their counterparts in the two principal Christian churches. But it should nevertheless not be forgotten that, whereas the great majority of the church leaders remained unmolested in their palaces and official residences, the leaders of the Jews were daily facing death. To escape their constant despair and sense of futility, they took refuge in work, in collaborating in the counting, sifting, organizing and assembling of Jewish 'human material'.

Even today something similar is going on among vast numbers of people who are working themselves to death, committing secret suicide by degrees in their efforts to escape from the emptiness of their souls and the futility of their lives. Distraction in work was the motto which these Jewish leaders and authorities also adopted in the face of the daily threat of death.

Freud, the grand old man from Vienna who had managed to escape to England before the gates of the concentration camp of Europe slammed shut, had thought a great deal about Man's death wish in the years before the 'final solution'. The Freudian concept of the death wish contains a specifically Jewish element: despair – the hidden despair of a race so many of whose members had been done to death in Europe in the past thousand years. The zeal with which Jewish authorities served the Nazis had therefore a second cause: their despairing doubts about God and the human race.

In the autumn of 1938, after I myself had spent some time in prison, I met one of my former Jewish teachers in the Ringstrasse in Vienna. He was a man of great knowledge who had been barred from an academic career at Vienna University because he was a Jew. He told me that Germany's hour had now struck, and the Germans, fulfilling their historic mission in the world, were doing away with the Jews. He himself was now working in the first 'model' Jewish offices which Eichmann had set up in Vienna. He and his young wife ended up in the gas chamber. He was a deeply despairing man, a 'guilty' man, an accomplice, yet I hold his memory in honour. For a discerning Christian the question: 'Cain, where is Abel thy brother?' has been replaced by the much bigger question: *'Christian, where is Israel thy brother?'*

In Spain and in many other Christian kingdoms, the Jewish community of a town, province or country were time and again held responsible for the crimes of individual Jews. This liability chiefly took the form of payments, special contributions of huge amounts of money and valuables which Christian kings and princes exacted from 'their' Jews through the Jewish leaders. The provision of countless millions in money and property was part of the ancient tradition that in the 'final solution' became the provision of millions of lives. It was the last ransom that the Jewish leaders and authorities were called on to pay to their Christian masters.

Jewish observers, historians, sociologists and psychoanalysts who have studied the attitude of the Jews between 1933 and 1944 have established that these Jews had a 'tremendous capacity for self-delusion'. Jews went to their death refusing to believe in the death they themselves had helped to prepare. Today millions of people, Christians and non-Christians alike, have this same capacity for self-delusion as they help to prepare their own 'final solution' – the suicide of mankind by atomic war.

Deep down Adolf Hitler had a suicide fixation. And among the SA and SS leaders there were quite a few uprooted and despairing men who were also working unconsciously towards their own suicide.

In the summer of 1944 a female leader in the SS went around Bavaria exhorting the peasants to hold out and stand firm. She told them that a good German need not fear defeat. Should it come, the Führer in his kindness had prepared a gentle death by gas for the German people. Friedrich von Reck-Malleczewen reported this in his posthumous *Tagebuch eines Verzweifelten* (Diary of a Man in Despair). The same writer provided in a novel about the Anabaptists a visionary description of Hitler's downfall.

In 1961 a doctor, Hans Lehndorff, reported in his *Ostpreussisches Tagebuch* (East Prussian Diary) how in a refugee camp in Koenigsberg he had tried in January 1945 to persuade a woman to escape. She replied: 'Our Führer won't let the Russians get us; he'd rather gas us first.' Lehndorff added: 'I glanced around unobtrusively, but no one seemed to find anything odd in her remark.'

13

Christian Suicide or Christian Jewish Rebirth

There are no memorials over Babij Yar.
Only an abrupt bank like a crude epitaph rears.
I stand terror-stricken,
Today I'm as ancient in years
as the Jewish people themselves are.
It seems to me at this moment —
I am an Israelite.
Now I'm wandering over ancient Egypt in captivity.
And now on the cross I perish, crucified,
and to this day the marks of the nails are on me.
I am Dreyfus now,
  inside my mind.
My informer and judge
  the Philistines.
I am behind bars . . .
It seems to me —
  I'm a boy in Bialystok.
Blood flows over the floor, red-running.
Outrages are committed by bullies of vodka shops,
stinking of drink and raw onions.
I lie helpless, by jackboots kicked about.
I plead to the pogromites in vain,
'Beat the Yids! Save Russia!' they shout:
My mother by shopkeeper is beaten and flayed . . .

I am Anna Frank
  It seems to me
as frail as a twig
  in April weather
And I love.
  And for empty phrases have no need . . .

Over Babij Yar only rustling wild grasses move.
The trees watch sternly
  like judges arrayed.

How silence itself cries aloud –
  my hat I remove,
and feel
  I am gradually going grey.
And I myself
  am like an endless soundless cry
over these thousands and thousands of buried ones.
Each one
    of these murdered old men am I.
I
  am each of their murdered sons.
Nothing will ever forget this within me.
Let the 'International' thunder its might
When will be buried for eternity
the earth's last anti-Semite.
No Jewish blood my veins runs through,
but I am hated with an encrusted passion,
by all anti-Semites, as if I were a Jew,
and because of that
    I'm a genuine Russian!

YEVGENY YEVTUSHENKO

No memorial or monument stands in the gorge of Babij Yar, in which 75,000 Jews, with a few kindred Ukrainians and gypsies, were led to their deaths by the Ukrainian police and shot by Germans.

'When in February 1963 an audience of nine thousand gathered in the Lenin sports palace in Moscow to hear poetry readings, it was almost exclusively poems against anti-Semites which were read. Some poems contained a direct attack on them, others descriptions of the annihilation of Jews in Nazi concentration camps. Anne Frank was the heroine of many poems' (Boris Lewyczkyi).

Young Russians were here setting themselves up against the party bureaucracy, against the still mighty shadow of Stalin, the destroyer of Communist hope, who in the last years of his life had reverted to Jewish persecution. Russian youth identified itself in Yevtushenko's poem with the Jew as the cross-bearer of humanity.

The Italian film director Pasolini, an atheistic Communist, wanted Yevtushenko to play Jesus in his film *The Gospel according to St Matthew*. Yevtushenko agreed, but was not granted an exit permit by the Soviet Union.

After 1945 all the crises of the Cold War, all civil wars and internal tensions were accompanied by new waves of anti-Semitism. In both East and West the Devil retained his thousand-year-old identity in Christian minds with the Jew.

In the Soviet Union, Poland, Hungary, both Germanies, Austria, Switzerland, France, England, in the whole of America and in the Arab states the symptom of anti-Semitism has risen to show the state of health of a sick society. In South Africa (according to a report by Hilda Bernstein) a drunken policeman repeatedly shouted 'I am Eichmann' as he beat up a white political prisoner.

Let us begin our quick survey of the post-1945 situation with Eastern Europe.

In the Soviet Union anti-Semitism is a part of the unconquered past and the unconquered present. The anti-Semitism of the tsarist era was followed by the anti-Semitism of the Stalin era and then of our own time. Pasternak portrayed in *Doctor Zhivago* anti-Semitic excesses near the front in the First World War. Ilya Ehrenburg portrayed in the third part of his autobiography *People, Years, Lives* the most difficult period of his life: at the end of 1948 the Jewish Anti-Fascist Committee was dissolved. All the leading members – with the exception of Ehrenburg – were arrested and murdered. The Jewish paper *Emes* was closed down and the Yiddish poets and novelists Pfeffer, Kuitko, Bergelsen and others taken prisoner. In January 1949 newspapers informed their readers of the discovery of an 'anti-patriotic' group of Jewish theatre critics. Shortly after that the fight began against 'rootless cosmopolitans', the Jewish intellectuals. In 1952 persons arrested in the 'Crimean affair' were shot. The political secret police accused an élite of Jewish intellectuals of attempting to occupy the Crimean peninsula and to sever it from the Soviet Union at the behest of Zionists and American imperialists. Shortly before his death Stalin tried, by inventing a 'conspiracy of doctors', to create new victims for his persecution mania.

Prominent Jewish intellectuals had devoted themselves with religious zeal to the cause of the revolution, which for them was inextricably bound up, above all in Russia, with the world revolution of Man. Leading Bolshevists – Trotsky, Zinovyev, Kamenev, Litvinov, Kaganovich – were Jews and were regarded as Jews in the eyes of the general public. Lenin said angrily to Gorky, who was pleading the legitimacy of the Zionist movement: 'Are there not enough states and armies in the world?' In order to check the Zionist movement in the provinces of the Soviet Union, it was decided to found a Palestine inside the Soviet Union, the autonomous Jewish province of Birobidjan, which was to become a 'centre of Jewish national culture for the entire working Jewish population of the USSR'. On 7 May 1934 this came into being. But it was unable to develop, in an unhealthy climate, with no economic support and repeated acts of sabotage by anti-Jewish Communists. In 1959 it had 162,000 inhabitants, of whom only 14,200 were Jews.

The crisis began with the transition from the heroic phase of revolutionary Communism to the bureaucratic Communism of Stalin. In a masterly manner Trotsky portrayed in his memoirs this seizure of power by the red bourgeois and bureaucrats – who also attacked Yevtushenko. The Jews seized by the revolutionary spirit had a different conception of Communism from that of the bureaucrats and myrmidons of a Stalinist neo-nationalism. Jews soon became suspect. Stalin's intellectual inferiority complex, his fear of superior critical minds confronting him in the very central committee itself in the shape of Jews, was shared by the non-Jewish bureaucrats. What they all wanted was not movement, spiritual and political unrest, but the simple fulfilment of plans imposed from above.

The Jews in Russia tended to become more Russian than the other nationalities inside the Soviet Union, such as Poles and Ukrainians. They were hated by the non-Russian peoples in the Soviet Union as Russians and representatives of the Communist ruling class. The Stalinist bureaucrats and their successors saw here a good chance of diverting dissatisfaction with themselves on to the Jewish scapegoat, especially since the old orthodox and national anti-Semitism was still alive, hidden only skin-deep.

The article on the Jews in the 1932 edition of the *Great Soviet Encyclopaedia* under the heading 'Hebrews' was spread over sixty columns. In 1952 (under the heading 'Jews') it was brutally cut to eight columns. The Jews were usurers and capitalists in the Middle Ages; Zionism was a reactionary, nationalist and bourgeois movement.

In 1957, after the 'Polish October', there appeared in the Polish Yiddish journal *Folks-Sztyme* (Voice of the People) on 24 and 26 February a far-reaching criticism of this denunciatory article from the pen of the Polish Jewish Communist Michael Mirsky, which found wide response in Poland and Russia.

The Soviet press in 1957–9 was rich in anti-Semitic articles connected with the 'Israel complex of the Soviet Union' (François Fejtö). This corresponded to the earlier Tito complex and propaganda against 'the reactionary essence of the Jewish religion'. A malicious press compared the Jews with fleas and dirty insects. Moses was a hypocrite, a deceiver, a false magician dressed as a prophet. In 1959 a systematic 'process of enlightenment' was carried out against Judaism and was particularly virulent in the Ukraine. Ukrainian murderers of Jews had carried on their hideous trade ever since the sixteenth century, right up to the period of Hitler's Ukrainian SS and police auxiliaries. In 1959 there appeared in Kiev a brochure *On the Judaic Religion* by T.K.Kitschko in the Ukrainian language, and a year later *What is the Talmud?* by M.S.Belesinski in the Russian language. 'Both pamphlets were in no way inferior to the *Stürmer*' (Lewyczkyi).

On 29 September 1959 the *Pravda* of Kiev accused Moses of having preached against stealing, yet at the same time he advised the Jews to take all golden and silver vessels and pieces of jewellery with them on their exodus from Egypt. It was this very Bible passage that the old church fathers had seized on in order to justify their own takeover of ancient heathen beliefs and practices in the interests of their church.

In the Soviet population census of 1959, 2,200,000 persons described themselves as Jews. This is about one-third of the number of Jews in 1941. Only

20.8 per cent gave Yiddish as their mother-tongue, the rest mostly Russian. In 1952, fourteen Jews were studying at the school for rabbis at the great Moscow synagogue. The Jews in the Soviet Union possessed only sixty to seventy synagogues. Yet despite these conditions, an official campaign against Israel and the Jews was able to rekindle old, deeply rooted Russian resentments. Close observers of political movements in Russia and prominent emigrés have observed that, if one day these men were to come to power there, the pogroms of the tsarist era would be renewed.

A hint of it can be seen by what happened in Malakhovka, a small town in the neighbourhood of Moscow, on 4 October 1959, the first day of the Jewish new year. The town had three thousand Jewish inhabitants. On that day the synagogue was set on fire and wild riots broke out.

Hundreds of anti-Semitic placards had beforehand been stuck on the walls. They said: 'Down with the Jews – save Russia,' and were signed by the Central Committee for the Liberation of the Russian People.

The text of one proclamation ran: 'We Russians saved the Jews from the Germans, who showed themselves by their treatment to be more intelligent than we are . . . The Jews are a stain on our nation.' – The old cry is raised: beat the Jew and save Russia.

On 9 June 1957 one of the best known Jewish Communist writers in America, Howard Fast, took leave of the party in a letter to Boris Polevoi. In it he summarized the motives which, in both East and West, had moved Jewish people, and above all intellectuals, to join the Communist movement and in many cases to remain true to it to the end.

Fast wrote that two strong forces impelled him to become a Communist. One was the idea of brotherhood and justice as taught by Jewry, by Isaiah and the prophets and then by Jesus Christ. The second force was the idea of a living democracy as lived and taught by Jefferson and Lincoln and then, in most recent history, by the activities of the working class. Now he was witnessing the persecution of Jews in the Soviet Union, following the extermination of six millions by the National Socialists. Fast went on to say that Ehrenburg, who alone was spared, was obviously regarded as an 'honorary Aryan' in the Soviet Union.

In 1956 the curtain was pulled aside on the extermination of the literary and artistic Jewish élite in the Soviet Union, which had taken place during the years 1948–53. Parallel phenomena were to be found in Czechoslovakia in the Slansky trial of 1952, and previously in the arrest of Zionist leaders in Czechoslovakia and Rumania in 1949 and in anti-Semitic propaganda in Hungary under the régime of Rákosi, himself a Jew.

The true cause of the Slansky trial in Prague was the struggle for power between the state apparatus and that of the party. The state won: the party secretariat, the economic and foreign ministries were purged of Jews. The trial was conducted in an openly anti-Semitic manner with all the usual old slogans. On 20 November 1952 Radio Prague raged against the 'Talmudic spirit of Slansky'.

The Polish Communists, pressing for reform in the 'Polish October', can be given the credit of having brought the causes of the anti-Semitism which flared up again in the Socialist countries after 1945 out into the open. It became evident here that a long and undisturbed economic, political and spiritual reconstruction would have been necessary to de-contaminate the minds of the people. Exposed after Hitler to further terrorization by Communist bureaucrats and policemen, the people regarded Jews as scapegoats for all outrages of the reign of terror before 1956. The central organ of the Polish workers' party, *Trybuna Ludu*, acknowledged on 25 April 1957 that twelve years of work against inveterate anti-Semitism had borne very little fruit. As a rule it had led only to vague and empty proclamations.

An awakening Polish, Hungarian, Russian intelligentsia of young people, struggling for internal freedom, have opened battle in the last few years against the mighty forces of political reaction, against the unholy alliance with anti-Semitism and a narrow-minded bourgeoisie, against the archaic spiritual attitudes of all the many who on the subjects of war, capital punishment, Jews and enemies still think and act like their forebears of the sixteenth to nineteenth centuries.

Jewish Communists are once more playing a definite part in the self-critical reform movements within East European Communism. They are thus resuming their true function in world politics – to be agitators, disruptive elements – but in a positive sense as chemical agents and catalysts. Many Jewish Communists were passionate supporters of Nagy in the Hungarian rising of 1956: Georg Lukács, Julius Háy, Tibor Déry, Tibor Tardos, Zoltán Zelk, Josef Gali, Miklós Gunes.

In an essay entitled *Anti-Semitism in East Germany* Robert Neumann observed in 1965: 'The circumstances with regard to anti-Semitism are completely different in the two German political systems which today go under the name of German Democratic Republic and Federal Republic of Germany. The fear of the West in East Germany is increased – if I saw correctly – by the fact that their partners – Russians, Poles, Czechs, Hungarians – have an attitude of rejection and mistrust towards the West Germans. While West Germany, for the present, is still on the sunny side of the Cold War, the East German people live in dreadful isolation: they are the real losers of the war, it is they who are atoning, paying for the whole nation: they, as regards rejection by the world around them, are the heirs of murdered Jewry . . . Far more important, these East Germans are alarmed to see that in West Germany, the hunting of Communists is becoming more and more clearly to resemble the former hunting of Jews.'

In the Federal Republic of Germany, a political product of the victorious

N*

Western powers (Karl Jaspers), the rich potential of anti-Semitic ideas and images was able from the very start to find an outlet in 'new' old conceptions of 'Jewish' Communism, Socialism, Bolshevism and 'Eastern hordes.' Hostility towards the Democratic Republic also made it possible to parade before the world the contrast between 'good' (meaning West) Germans and 'bad' (meaning East) Germans, who are the myrmidons of – Jewish – Bolshevism and the 'hangmen' of Ulbricht's state, the régime of Soviet occupation.

After 1945 churches, trades unions, professors and theologians, men of letters, politicians and non-politicians had a common interest in camouflaging, or at least minimizing, their role in the National Socialist régime. Manufacturers and industrialists who delivered equipment for gas chambers seldom possessed – in the years before they entered into business with Nasser – the courage of a Konstantin von Neurath, who at the Nuremberg trials in 1946 stuck to what he had said in 1933: 'Germany must be purged of Jews.' Von Neurath added in 1946: 'That is exactly my opinion today, but with different methods.'

Since the important thing was to win American money, American politicians and soldiers for the common cause of the struggle against 'Jewish' Communism and Bolshevism, machinery was built up which skilfully enrolled the surviving Jews themselves in the deception. Through collections, payments of money to Israel, through 'reparation funds' and friendly declarations to representatives of Jewish organizations, the West German state got itself a reputation as the very epitome of democracy. 'Useful idiots' (by this, right-wing politicians in the Federal Republic meant intellectuals who had allegedly fallen under Stalin's sway, as they themselves had once fallen under Hitler's) – individuals of independent mind, who cared deeply about a true reconciliation with Israel, were roped in to help in a very remarkable ritual of deception. An annual 'Brotherhood Week' proved very effective in concealing the lack of brotherly feelings during the rest of the year towards those fellow men who thought differently. Ladies in both camps who find pleasure in attending rallies and social functions and appearing on TV began to practise philo-Semitism in a way that made it look like a special form of the old anti-Semitism.

This masked ball was stage-managed by ruthless men who no longer found it necessary to conceal their nationalistic outlook and could openly pursue their own interests in Bonn and Munich, having been assured that their anti-Semitic aggression would not stand in their way. The only difference now was that they were obliged, for reasons of tact, to refer to 'world Communism' instead of 'international Jewry', 'agents of the Kremlin' instead of 'Wall Street Jews', and 'Bolshevik synagogue of Satan' in place of 'Jewish satanism'.

Splendidly masked murderers, and their accomplices, moved quietly and inexorably into high positions, into the police, into the judiciary and into ministries in Bonn. This quiet seizure of power would presumably have gone on uninterrupted if two very unexpected things had not occurred, which caused considerable repercussions.

The desecration of synagogues, the daubing of Jewish gravestones and other individual acts could easily be explained away as part of the international wave of anti-Semitism which broke out in 1960, provoked by the fear of war and by internal crises in many states. The two events which whipped off the masks overnight were the arrest of Eichmann in Argentina, and the production of Rolf Hochhuth's play *The Representative*.

The political transactions necessitated by the Eichmann trial released a chain reaction of revelations. Now at last a serious effort was made to bring the murderers of the 'final solution' and their accomplices to trial. Hochhuth's play *The Representative* focused attention on the share of responsibility borne by the Christian churches for everything which had happened between 1918 and 1945, in and around Germany, and in Europe as a whole.

It was revealed then that in Western Europe, in Germany and in Austria, the minds of men were still as full of subconscious anxieties and anti-Semitic complexes today as they had been twenty or thirty years ago. They were no more truly cured than the Eastern peoples of Europe.

Through its close connection with the Vichy régime, the old anti-democratic, ecclesiastical and right-wing religious and political anti-Semitism in France had been so compromised that it withdrew after the liberation into the recesses of the unconscious, into the political underground, and into North Africa and Algeria. The writer Louis-Ferdinand Céline, who in his novels had advocated an aggressive anti-Semitism, fled with the remnants of the Vichy government first into Germany, and then into Denmark. De Gaulle demanded from the new nuncio in Paris, Roncalli, a cleansing process among the French episcopacy; Roncalli was skilful enough to reconcile the re-established republic and the church. In Belgium the leaders of the militant Catholic-Fascist movement, once grouped around the Rexist movement of Léon Degrelle and closely connected with the National Socialist régime, either fled to Spain and South America, or were arrested in Belgium. Belgium, France and the Netherlands had anyway plenty to occupy them after 1944–5, and had little room left in their political souls for anti-Semitic excesses.

The Netherlands had lost a great colonial empire, and their country had been a theatre of war. The Netherlands were in any case of all countries the least affected by the disease of anti-Semitism, and they share today with Denmark the glory of having unanimously resisted the National Socialist persecution of Jews.

In France the war continued, first in Indo-China, then in North Africa. The two Frances entered into a deadly enmity in this struggle which brought the country to the brink of disaster.

In Great Britain, what there had been of anti-Semitic feeling began slowly to reassemble around active and retired military officers who, in India and Palestine and other places overseas, had coupled an imperialist outlook dating from the 1890s with a racial attitude of more recent date. However, the austerity programme and the enormous problems of reconstruction and mental adjustment to the problems of the atomic age did not leave over all that much strength to devote to the hobby of anti-Semitism.

When, in the summer of 1964, it was no longer possible to overlook the signs of increasing anti-Semitism in Canada – acts of terror, attacks on rabbis in Toronto, swastikas painted on synagogues in Winnipeg – the matter was investigated, and it was found that this anti-Semitism had been imported from the United States. The head office of the anti-Semites in Toronto had been supplied with printed matter and pamphlets from the USA, and the American anti-Semite Rockwell had instigated the first acts of violence. An independent Canadian anti-Semitic movement was discovered within the Social Credit Party.

We have seen how in Spain in the fifteenth and sixteenth centuries and in Germany in the nineteenth and early twentieth centuries, the Jews played an important part in the struggle for evolution as a nation, only to be evicted at the end as disturbers of the peace. The fusion of races, classes, religions and ethnic groups from other continents into an American society has been, and still is, a lengthy and difficult process. It is vulnerable to all internal and external crises – China, Japan, the struggle for the Far East, the struggle with Stalinist Communism in Europe, the veiled recession, automation. Basically there is no problem of human society on the eve of the atomic age which does not have its effect on the fusion of Jews, Catholics, negroes, Eastern Europeans, Puerto Ricans, Chinese, the people from the deep South and from the lower stratum of society, into an American nation.

The fear of negroes among the 'poor whites' in the Southern states, the inferiority complexes which the white middle classes of other states show towards Jews on an intellectual and cultural level – all this created a mental reservoir out of which movements around first McCarthy and then around Senator Goldwater could make political capital. The investigations made around 1950 into the connections between faith in authority, pseudo-conservatism and anti-Semitism showed how susceptible the 'authoritarian personality' in the USA is to extreme right-wing and anti-Semitic movements.

The racial problem and the problem of education are the two greatest internal questions in the United States. Upon their solution will depend whether the United States is to become a neurotic mass-herd, convulsed by concealed internal unrest, and therefore a source of infection to the rest of mankind, or whether it will succeed in its protracted and difficult task of building a free, open society. The Jewish problem is connected with the racial problem; both are vital questions of the first order for the America of today and tomorrow. This explains the lively interest taken by American bishops in a declaration on the Jewish question at the Second Vatican Council. It also explains the enthusiasm with which Cardinal Bea and the Swiss theologian Köng were taken up as champions of a liberal Catholicism, giving first place to human rights – and the opposition to them as well.

A role similar to that played by the radio-priest Father Coughlin in the USA, with his anti-Semitic sermons during the fateful years before 1940, is played today by the Catholic priest Dr Julio Meinvielle in Argentina. He works in conjunction with the extreme right-wing organization *Tacuara*, the students of which are often the sons of prominent Argentinian personalities. The Argentinian police force is strongly permeated by anti-Semitic elements. Meinvielle has declared, on the subject of attacks on Jewish institutions and persons, that these attacks were either provoked by the Jews themselves or were plain lies. Meinvielle has published books and brochures attacking liberalism, democracy, Communism and the Jews.

The arrest of Adolf Eichmann in Argentina turned the attention of the world to a country in which many Germans have been long established and many National Socialist emigrants found a promised land after 1945. In his last words before his execution, Adolf Eichmann wished three countries well in the future: Germany, Austria and Argentina.

In the last few years anti-Semitic activities in Argentina and Uruguay have met with increasing opposition. Representatives of the church, as well as of the government, have spoken out against Dr Meinvielle. The whole vocabulary of this Argentinian priest can be found in the Austrian and German anti-Semitic propaganda of the first half of this century. Meinvielle sees in the Jews the key to world history – like Hitler and his friends in Vienna around 1912, and in Munich around 1922. *El Judio en al misterio de la historia* is the title of one of his books: the Jew is the secret of world history, he is at the centre of all conspiracies against mankind. *Los Judios son hijos del diablo*: the Jews are sons of the Devil. Here Meinvielle concurs with the authors in *Conspiracy against the Church*, that collection of essays which can be regarded as a model for a widespread Catholic anti-Semitism which, under the cover of formal declarations of friendship and 'appreciations' of Jewry, still colours the thinking of the broad masses, as well as influential personalities, to this day.

A basic theme of this book, to which some of the highest officials in the Curia have given their blessing, is that the anti-Christ has 'loyal accomplices among the highest dignitaries of the church'. The church is to become a satellite of the anti-Christ and of the 'synagogue of Satan'. One of the most influential Catholic conservative journalists in Germany today, Anton Böhm, formerly of the *Schönere Zukunft* in Vienna and today chief editor of the *Rheinischer Merkur*, deals with Communism in his book *Die Epoche des Teufels* (The Epoch of the Devil, 1955) as the 'synagogue of Satan'. Pope Pius IX and even Leo XIII spoke of freemasonry as the 'synagogue of Satan'.

'The unanimous teaching of the great church fathers, that *unanimis consensus Patrum* which the church views as the source of all faith, damned the unbelieving Jews and pronounced the fight against them good and necessary.' The authors of *Conspiracy against the Church* cite – correctly – St Ambrose, St Jerome, St Augustine, St John Chrysostom, St Athanasius, St Bernard.

'The Church has been fighting energetically for nineteen centuries against the Jews, as we shall prove by means of authentic documents.' The 'Jewish masonic and Communist conspirators' were planning a 'surprise coup' at the Second Vatican Council; they intended to 'ensure that anti-Semitism or any other move against the Jews should be condemned'. 'We intend to show that Christ Himself, the Gospels, and the Catholic church are among the sources of anti-Semitism.' By condemning anti-Semitism the church would condemn itself, since it would put numerous church councils, popes and saints in the dock.

'There can be no doubt that the Jews are the inventors of Communism.' Stalin belonged to the Jewish race [*sic*]; Khrushchev was a Jew whose real name was Pearlmutter; Khrushchev's wife Nina was also Jewish; 'Marshal Tito, whose true Jewish name is Josef Walter Weiss, comes from Poland.' *La Civiltà Cattolica* was brought in as a witness, together with German, French, Hungarian and Rumanian anti-Semitic literature. There was no other alternative: 'Either Jewish and Communist domination – or extermination.'

A pioneering force behind Jewish Communism was freemasonry, which had been created by Jews. To prove it, Pope Leo xii was quoted, as well as the primate of Chile, Cardinal José Maria Caro, Archbishop Léon Meurin SJ, Drumont and many other French Catholic anti-Semites. 'All the defenders of Dreyfus were freemasons, and Jews into the bargain.' Freemasons had committed important murders: Louis xvi and many other historical personalities. (In Germany Mathilde Ludendorff had specialized in this subject: according to her, almost all significant personalities of free German intellectual life, including Schiller and Mozart, were murdered by masons.)

The long struggle of the church against the Jewish religion and its rites was not due, as has been erroneously maintained, to the religious intolerance of Catholicism, but to the monstrous villainy of the Jewish religion itself. God had repeatedly cursed the Jews. The Inquisition had rightly persecuted them. The Jewish blood-baths throughout history and the mass exterminations by the Nazis were fulfilments of the judgment of God. (In Vienna, a Capuchin priest preached in this vein in the Kapuzinerkirche, next to the tomb of the Hapsburg emperors, in 1955.)

These blood-baths among Jews should be seen as a punishment ordained by God Himself. 'They – the Jews – shout themselves hoarse with their assertion that the Catholic church condemns anti-Semitism.' That was not true: the church had, for example, condemned the Friends of Israel in 1928.

This condemnation by Pius XI was described in detail. Among the items condemned was the assertion that the Jewish people was not responsible for Christ's death: this contradicted what the church had been representing for almost twenty centuries.

The chief witness against the Jews was the Gospel according to St John.

At the end of the fifteenth century Christendom had been on the point of winning the final victory over all its enemies and over the Jews as the synagogue of Satan. (In the minds of all Catholic centralists, as of National Socialists, the eschatological idea of 'final victory' plays a vital role in their strategic thinking.) But then the Jews exercised a diabolical cunning; they appealed to Christian charity and awoke the sympathy of the princes of the church. There was already at that time a fifth column of Jews representing the Devil inside the church – in the clergy itself! This fifth column was made up of the descendants of Jews who had been converted to Christianity in previous centuries, but had preserved their Jewish faith in secret synagogues. They smuggled, and were still smuggling, crypto-Jewish Christians into the seminaries and into leading positions inside the church. That was 'the octopus which is strangling Christendom'. – 'In the Middle Ages the popes and the church councils succeeded in destroying the Jewish revolutionary movements': Cathars, Albigenses, Hussites, Illuminati. 'Thanks to the Inquisition, the Holy Church was able to overthrow the Jews and postpone for several centuries the catastrophe which now threatens mankind.'

This fifth column was represented today by the 'progressive priests'. Catholic priests were trying to inveigle Catholic students in Spain, Portugal, Paraguay, Guatamala and other countries into Communism. (We might add that this reproach is directed against a small circle of Catholic reformers, who are no longer satisfied with the four centuries old Manichaean and feudalistic domination of the masses in Latin America, and who are pressing vigorously for social, economic and political reform.)

'These traitors must quickly be called to account in Rome.' They were wolves in sheeps' clothing, raging against the Inquisition and 'those patriots who are defending their peoples against Communism, Jewry and freemasonry'.

The authors of this work, calling for purges and trials reminiscent of the worst excesses in Stalinist Russia during the period 1934 to 1938, are particularly fond of summoning St Paul and St Augustine to their aid.

The Jews were the progenitors of the Gnostics. For conservative Catholic sociologists and historians, Gnosticism remains to this day the mother of all spiritual world revolutions from Hegel to Marx. 'The underground movements of modern Jewry are to a large extent a replica of the teachings of the great Gnostic revolution . . . With the conversion of Constantine the victory of the church over heathenism, Gnosticism and Jewry was complete.' If we are logical, we should be able to deduce from this statement that final victory had been achieved. But far from it: the Jews were still alive. And so they continued to assail the church. The Jew [sic] Arius founded the Arian heresy, which denied the divinity of Jesus Christ. The Jews acted as allies of Julian the Apostate. St John Chrysostom and St Ambrose condemned the Jews. 'Today clergymen and laymen of that type are needed to save Christendom and the whole of mankind from the threat of Communism, masonry and the synagogue of Satan, which is behind the whole conspiracy.'

Over and over again, on almost every page of this book, the council fathers are entreated to follow these illustrious examples. St Augustine, St Jerome and other church fathers condemned the Jews: this inflammatory theme is repeated with monotonous regularity.

The measures adopted against the Jews by weak Visigoth kings under pressure from a fanatical clergy at a time of permanent civil war are here set up as models for the present and the future. It is rightly stated: 'There can be no doubt that St Isidore of Seville and the metropolitans and bishops of the Fourth Council of Toledo, had they lived in our wretched present age, would immediately have been accused of racialism or anti-Semitism or of being Nazi criminals, not only by Jews but also by clergymen who pass themselves off as Christians, though they are in fact in the service of the Jews.'

After a lengthy description of the model persecutions of the Jews by the Visigoths, it is maintained that the subsequent reconciliation between Christians and Jews was the prelude to the collapse of the Visigoth empire owing to Jewish corruption. Today, twelve hundred years later, we are experiencing the same thing: 'They – the Jews – want to overthrow the governments of the USA, England and other Western countries, and hence they sow the seeds of depravity and immorality there.' (Similar assertions about the seduction of the Germans are to be found in pastoral letters by German bishops, who were continually thanking Hitler for having restored morality to the country.) In this collection of essays the arguments about 'Jewish imperialism' and the 'Jewish struggle for world dominion' bear a remarkable resemblance to the remarks to be found in German newspapers and Goebbels' propaganda right up to the end of the Third Reich.

One great truth must be understood by a Christian: 'The more fanatical he is [fanaticism is looked upon here as a virtue!], a Christian must also be fanatical in his opposition to the Jews, since they are the chief enemies of Christendom and of the human race.'

Many Germanic soldiers in the Roman legions took part in the destruction of the temple of Jerusalem. [What a prospect for Nasser and his German collaborators today!] Unfortunately, however, they brought Jewish women back to the Rhine and Main as their wives. Thus it is clear 'that the Nazis made the gravest mistake when they thought they could ascertain all secret ramifications of Jewry by a genealogical investigation of only three generations.'

The worthy and strict Catholic co-initiator of the Nuremberg racial laws, Hans Globke, who invented the idea of supplementary names in the passports of German Jews, now knows – for these Italian, French and Spanish theologians have told him – that he was not thorough enough in his demands for proof of Aryan descent.

Charlemagne fell victim to Jewish cunning. Under him, and above all under his son Louis the Pious, whose court was totally under Jewish influence, the Jews almost succeeded in bringing the Holy Roman Empire under Jewish control. All honour to Vienna, for St Bernard, the archbishop of Vienna, and Agobard of Lyons took up the struggle against this danger. (The none-too-learned authors here confused the Austrian capital with Vienne in Burgundy.) The case of the pro-Jewish Empress Judith showed 'how commonly philo-Semitism and the protection of Jews, can lead to anti-Christian activity and domination of Christians by Jews'.

'One of the most significant successes of the Jews in Judaizing the Holy Roman Empire was the conversion of one of the Christian philo-Semitic bishops to Jewry, a man who had enjoyed great trust at the court of the emperor and was one of his chief advisers.' This was the confessor of Louis the Pious, Bishop Bodo. Here he is portrayed as the precursor of Cardinal Bea, who is not mentioned by name, but is always represented as a dreadful example in several historical instances. Pinay observed: 'We do not know exactly whether this Bodo [i.e., Bodo-Bea] was secretly a Jewish bishop who carried out his theatrical conversion for propaganda purposes . . . or whether he was in fact a bishop who was induced by his dangerous philo-Semitism to lapse, turn apostate and embrace Judaism.'

The pamphlets which were distributed at the Second Vatican Council against Cardinal Bea and 'progressive' cardinals and theologians likewise left the question open: are these men crypto-Jews who insinuate themselves into the church in order to destroy it from inside, or are they only criminally stupid philo-Semites who have 'lapsed'? But Pinay issued a warning to all politicians and others, that they should learn their lesson from these 'ablest rogues in the world' who made themselves at home at the court of Louis the Pious.

What is to be done? Tchernyschevsky and then Lenin asked this question of three generations of an awakening Russian youth. Pinay and his colleagues have an answer of their own: the church and the world should make use of *anti-Semitic propaganda on a wide scale* among all political parties and all religious confessions, including above all the Arabs and Islam. The anti-Semitic activities of the church in the ninth century should be copied and we should print 'short but clear brochures for the working masses and books for the educated classes, which for the most part must be distributed free to individual households and to individual people, so that everyone may be enlightened about the danger of Jewish imperialism and its revolutionary activities.'

Officers, politicians, academicians, students, radio and television staff, the youth of all levels, the clergy of all churches, must be worked on. The churches and the wealthy must finance this propaganda, otherwise death or the concentration camp of Communism await them.

The men around Ottaviani, Siri and the reactionaries within the Roman Curia who are bound up with Fascism have managed successfully to present this bogey to Pope Paul VI. The left-wing ideas and philo-Semitism of the unfortunate Pope John XXIII are opening the gates of Italy to Communism. Italian big capitalists will, they warn, let the Vatican slide, if it does not go their way.

According to Pinay, Jews infiltrated into the clergy at an early stage, particularly its highest ranks. A Jewish cardinal became Pope Anacletus. St Bernard of Clairvaux wrote to Emperor Lothaire: 'It is a disgrace to Christ that a Jew sits on the throne of St Peter.' (We recall the remark of Cardinal Faulhaber about Pius XI.) The Jews were also secretly behind the Albigenses and employed the same tactics as are used by Bolshevists today: the destruction of the church from inside by Jews.

In the Russian Orthodox church, too, a Jewish fifth column had been for a long time successfully at work. It prepared the way for Bolshevism: it was 'a band of Jewish criminals, which has terrorized the Russian people to the present day'. That is the great danger: a pact between the church and the Devil, between the church and Communism. 'The American nation, which has already been weakened by the treachery of many of its rulers [from McCarthy to Goldwater the American political plot theory has appealed to many Catholics, since they have been conditioned to this cliché by their church over one hundred and fifty years] would be completely disheartened if it noticed that the church was throwing its sheep to the wolves and making a pact with the Devil.' This was the Jewish plan for the next Ecumenical Council.

But the dragon of hell would not conquer. 'At the Council a new Anastasius, St Ambrose, St John Chrysostom or St Bernard will appear and at the critical moment bring to nought the dark plans of Jewish Communism and its fifth column in the clergy, even if they believe that the Council is under their control and break out into shouts of joy.' These villains intended to proclaim peaceful co-existence with the anti-Christ, with the 'Jewish gang in the Kremlin'.

Many Russian, Rumanian and other emigrants from Eastern Europe, an unholy alliance of reactionaries, were helping in this work.

Pinay was almost right in the end. The men he favoured had a partial victory at the Council, but it was won, not with the fiery eloquence and candour of an Anastasius, St Ambrose or St John Chrysostom, but with practised hypocrisy, lies, terrorization, forgery, and procrastination – particularly terrorization.

The Jews were disseminating the cult of Satan throughout the world. All worshippers of Satan were Jews. Monsignor Meurin, the archbishop of Port Louis, referred to the arch-fraud Leo Taxil.

The Inquisition had fought heroically against this permanent Jewish conspiracy in the church. Today it was the Holy Office, which did in fact try from time to time at the Council to impose its will on the pope and the Council. 'In our time, on the other hand, these heretical accomplices – cardinals, bishops and clergymen of all ranks – while boasting of their orthodoxy, are contributing in various ways to the progress of the masonic and Communist revolutions. They betray the church and their country without being dismissed for their criminal activities . . . At the time of the Inquisition they would no doubt have been locked up, thrown out of the clergy and in some cases reduced to lay status in order to be executed.'

Pinay and his colleagues in the Curia and in the Holy Office did not only wish for a return to the purges of the era of Pius x, Pius xi and above all of Pius xii, in which distinguished Catholic priests and scholars were continuously terrorized, denounced and excommunicated. They were demanding a great clear-out, comparable in every way to the great purge under Stalin in 1936. Laconically Pinay stated that there were cardinals and bishops today who were secret Communists. 'If there were today a court of justice with methods of investigation as effective as those of the Inquisition at the time of which we are speaking, then it would certainly be recognized that there are many Jews among those cardinals, archbishops, abbots, canons and monks who so vigorously and eagerly – if also so hypocritically – press the cause of freemasonry and Communism, or defend Jews with far more fanaticism and success than they have ever shown in the cause of the holy church.' We might add that these monstrous accusations were brought at the beginning of the Second Vatican Council, but not a single father demanded a judicial inquiry.

Pinay urged that these progressive bishops and clergymen should be charged before the ecclesiastical courts with heresy (as at the Lateran Council of 1179). 'Today Christendom, if it wishes to save itself, must adopt the same measures for its defence which saved it at that time.'

The rules of the monastic orders should be changed so that they could be thrown into the battle against Communism, masonry and Jewry. Once again Pinay recalled the great Pope Innocent iii and the famous Fourth Lateran Council. Both had given their blessing to what the Jews call race hatred and anti-Semitism. Of especial significance then had been the marking of Jews by special clothing and signs in order to hinder their escape. Pinay goes on to say that, if Innocent iii and his assistants had been alive today, they would be accused of being Nazis and condemned for race hatred and anti-Semitism. 'For that reason the proposals planned in secret meetings between the synagogue and Communism are so dangerous, seeking as they do that the next Vatican Council should condemn race hatred and anti-Semitism.' The church would be made to contradict itself; the faithful would be confused; and the churches would stand empty.

Pinay, and the members of the Curia connected with him, demanded a grand alliance against the Jews, freemasons and Communists: an alliance of Christians – Catholics, Protestants and members of the Orthodox church. (French emigrants and their disciples around Metternich and then around Tsar Alexander I had once made similar demands.) One thing only was at stake: the need to destroy the synagogue. 'The synagogue was for close on two thousand years less a temple for the veneration of God than the head-quarters of the most dangerous and most powerful band of criminals of all time.'

Hitler and Himmler and their spokesmen could not have expressed themselves more clearly. Pinay even corrected the Nazis: 'In the race hatred of the Nazis one must differentiate carefully between the purely defensive and the aggressive or imperialistic aspects. Pinay expressed allegiance to the first: *'The Nazis only did what the holy Catholic church had commanded on various occasions during the last fourteen centuries, as measures to guard Christendom against the attempts of Jewish infiltrators to conquer and overthrow it.'*

Popes, church fathers and saints fought against and condemned the Jews. St Ambrose and St Thomas Aquinas thought it right to hold the Jews in perpetual servitude. The bull *Hebreorum Genus* of 26 February 1569, expelling the Jews from the Vatican State, was cited, together with the broadsides of St Gregory of Nyssa against the Jews. 'Not even Hitler used so few words to pronounce so many accusations as did the bishop of Nyssa sixteen hundred years ago.' The invectives of St John Capestrano against the 'Jewish beast' in the fifteenth century were put forward as models for the present. This saint deserved 'to be regarded by the patriotic organizations at present struggling against Jewry as their patron saint.'

The great hope lay in the anti-Jewish, anti-Communist movements in the USA, in Latin America, in the Islamic world and in Europe. Pinay pleaded for an alliance of peoples and religions in a 'feeling of true brotherhood' against the Jews and Communists.

One particular chapter of this book, which must be taken as a politico-religious declaration of intent by those centralist circles prepared to use all means to achieve the 'final solution' of the Jewish question, was devoted to the 'Jewish-masonic infiltration of the Jesuit orders'. Cardinal Bea, a Jesuit, was the main target of the attacks which Ottaviani, Siri, Carli and the Curia centralists directed against any liberalization of the church.

Pinay declared that in some parts of the order of St Ignatius there was a noticeable process of Judaization in progress. Jesuits were carrying out tenacious subversive activities against the few Catholic governments still left in the world. The good aggressive Jesuits who were fighting against Jewry, freemasonry and Communism were under attack from within the order itself. The Society of Jesus could, however, still be saved from disaster.

What, however, is the true position with regard to the Jesuits? Ignatius de Loyola had heroically overcome his personal aversion to the Jews. He brought Jews to Rome from Spain and accepted them into the Society of Jesus. The fervour of Jews inspired by a Messianic faith contributed much to the initial spread of the Society of Jesus. Thirty-five years after the death of Ignatius, Italians and members of the Curia overcame the Spanish leadership of the Society and introduced the 'Aryan paragraphs'. National Socialist anti-Semitic propaganda – as previously Fritsch's classic *Handbook of the Jewish Question* – seized on this anti-Jewish exclusivity of the Society of Jesus and continuously quoted the malicious excesses of the Jesuit periodical *Civiltà Cattolica* against the 'Jewish people who murdered Christ'.

In the nineteenth and twentieth centuries, in particular, Jesuits were quite often to be found at both extremes of the Catholic church, among the most progressive as well as the most reactionary. The German demagogue Father Leppich in our day speaks a language reminiscent of the Third Reich. Johovah's Witnesses – together with the Jews the most persecuted martyrs of the Third Reich – he refers to as troublesome people 'who, like bedbugs, are always with us' – and the best way to deal with bedbugs is to exterminate them). The Roman and Italian Jesuits tend to think like Father Leppich. On the other hand German, French, American, Spanish and Irish Jesuits belong to that small group of explorers who are trying to guide the church out of the straits of its traditional beliefs.

In 1946 the Society of Jesus abolished its 'Aryan paragraphs'. Father Bea, the confessor of Pope Pius xii, became, after the death of this unhappy pope, the tireless advocate of a Christian encounter with the 'first people of God'. On Good Friday, 27 March 1959, Pope John xxiii performed a truly revolutionary act: by striking the *perfidia judaica* and the *perfidis* from the Good Friday intercession service he broke the back of anti-Semitism in the church.

John xxiii summoned the Second Vatican Council. It was meant to take a step forward in the history of the church. But those members of the Curia who saw themselves at this Council as heirs and attorneys of the Inquisition, succeeded in imposing their will more than once after the death of Pope John xxiii. Cardinal Bea soon aroused the anger of the Holy Office with his plans in connection with the Jews which struck at the very heart of theological anti-Semitism. When the Holy Office came to know of them, it immediately began to stir up the Arab states. Their diplomats made representations to the Holy See, and Bea had to withdraw before his scheme could be presented in June 1962 to the steering commission. 'I wouldn't have believed all this if I hadn't seen it,' an American bishop told Robert Kaiser.

The Irish Jesuit Martin, a former lecturer at the papal Bible Institute in

Rome, has written (under the name of Michael Serafian) in his book *The Pilgrim*, dedicated to Pope Paul vi, about the present opinion of the leading men of the Curia concerning the Jews. This takes the line that the Jews crucified Christ and were therefore guilty men. For that reason God had cursed them for all time. Their sufferings through the succeeding centuries were only a divine reprisal for this crime and for their refusal to be converted to Christianity. In support of this thesis the important church historian of the Universita Pontificia Gregoriana in Rome, the Jesuit Hertling, wrote an article for *Civiltà Cattolica* which, on the suggestion of Secretary of State Cicognani, was withdrawn before publication. It subsequently appeared in the journal *Stimmen der Zeit*. In this article the author came to the 'regretful conclusion that one must regard the sufferings of the Jews to some extent as a proof of God's mercy'.

The Jews and the Council in the Light of the Holy Scriptures and of Tradition is the title of a brochure which was distributed at the Council. Behind the author's pseudonym of Bernardus stand concealed the figures of Ottaviani and Ruffini and (as probable direct author) Bishop Luigi Maria Carli. Here it was written that the Holy Scriptures had established unequivocally that the Jews were the deliberate murderers of Christ. The church fathers, St Thomas Aquinas and the popes all confirmed that the Jews were members of a world-wide conspiracy intent on destroying the church. Thus the faithful must be on their guard against the Jews and must take care not to offend against a basic dogma of the church.

In 1960 Cardinal Bea had prepared, on instructions from Pope John xxiii, a draft for an official declaration by the Council on the Jews. This laid down that neither the Jews of Christ's lifetime, nor the Jews of today were guilty of Christ's death. The Jewish nation was to be absolved of blame for the collective murder of Christ. The crime was to be ascribed to mankind as a whole. It was unjust to reproach the Jews for murdering Christ, as Christians did, and to make them atone for it up to the present day. The concept of a divine curse, pursuing Jews throughout the centuries, could not be proved by means of the Bible.

'Against Bea's draft, a hundred doubts and objections of a biblical, theological, pastoral and political nature were mobilized, with the invited aid of Arab nationalists. Finally all that remained of his draft was: "The Jews *of our time* should not be reproached with what happened during the Passion of our Lord" ... Even this unrecognizably watered down draft, was to be further cut down on the dubious written command of three cardinals of the Curia, until it said nothing at all' (Hans Wirtz).

This 'improved' declaration on the Jews was presented at the penultimate meeting of the third session of the Council in 1964 under the innocuous title *On non-Christians*. It was provisionally adopted by 1657 votes to 99. Of those in favour, 242 expressed reservations.

'It is not enough just to wash away the imaginary bloodstains of the murder of Christ with our tears; we must also keep in sight our close relationship with the children of Abraham and live in accordance with it.' So said Pope Paul vi early in his pontificate. He was distressed by the accusation which had hung over Pope Pius xii since Hochhuth's drama *The Representative*. Paul vi consulted the archivists of the state secretariat about Hochhuth, and was told that it would be better for the moment not to publish a white paper on the attitude of Pius xii to the Jewish problem.

Meanwhile the German episcopate had assumed the task of exonerating Pius xii, and had decided to bear a part of the costs for the investigation of this gigantic problem themselves. They were right to do so, for these bishops were responsible for the conduct of the church in Germany, both in the recent past and at present.

'*The reconciliation with Jewry will not take place.*' Under this title a German-born Jew, Fritz Sonnenberg, wrote a commentary on the journey of Pope Paul vi to the Holy Land and on the prospects for the Jews at the ecumenical meeting of the Council in March 1964.

In November 1963 the leaders of the Curia apparently managed to make Pope Paul vi their prisoner (since 1870 the popes had been the prisoners of their so-called centralist partisans and of the senior curial bureaucrats). In March 1965 these men went over to open attack. In the widely-read weekly paper of the Italian clergy *La Palestra del Clero* the bishop of Segni, Luigi Maria Carli, who was also secretary of the council commission of bishops, wrote that the Jews of today were also 'accursed and rejected by God'. He continued: 'I consider it proper to assert that the whole Jewish people at the time of Jesus was answerable for the crime of the murder of Christ, even if only the leaders, followed by a part of their supporters, actually carried out the crime.' Bishop Carli's answer to the question of Jewish responsibility today was as follows: 'In this very precise sense even the Judaism of the times after Our Lord objectively share the responsibility for the murder of Christ to the extent that this Judaism represents a voluntary extension of the Jewry of that time.' On these grounds the Jews could, according to Bishop Carli, be considered 'accursed and rejected by God'.

A careful study of the history of Christendom in Europe can lead one to the conclusion that the species which God cursed and rejected, the people guilty of the murder of Christ and of men, are the Christians themselves. As early as the second century, to the horror of Julian the Apostate, they began to fight with all means – forgery, persecution, killing – against other Christians. Heretics were deprived of their reputations and not infrequently of their lives. From the fourth century onwards, this permanent cold and hot civil war in and around the Christian churches began to spread out externally as well – against non-Christians, 'heathens' and others. Fifteen centuries of

Jewish persecution was accompanied by fifteen centuries of pathological self-hatred, self-torment and persecution of fellow Christians.

The Jesuit Martin (Michael Serafian) who dedicated his book to Pope Paul VI as 'proof of the author's devotion to the Church of Christ and to the great cause to which your Holiness has pledged his life', openly states there what the world, outside the doors of a church pathologically wrapped up in itself, already knows:

'No one who is aware of the basic facts of modern Europe can deny that the stakes and furnaces, the poisonous smoke and stench in the extermination camps of National Socialist Germany are, if not exactly the logical result, nevertheless at least a drastic consequence of the attitude adopted by the average Christian towards the Jews. Here Christendom stands close to the abyss of self-destruction.'

Christendom today stands close to the abyss of self-destruction through nuclear weapons. This suicide follows in historical terms logically from the practice, stretching over fifteen hundred years, of killing the blood relations of the Jew Jesus, the son of the Jewess Miriam, Mary. It is being prepared at deeply concealed levels of the subconscious. This subconscious is aware that Christendom has failed in its attempts to liquidate the Jews and to conquer the world. The greatest bankruptcy in the history of the world has been revealed in two world wars, for which the whole of Christendom shares the responsibility, and in the extermination of six million Jews. The word 'bankruptcy' is here used in a completely literal sense. Bankruptcy meant originally that the tables and benches of financiers who could not meet their obligations were publicly smashed as a sign of their failure. *World history has smashed the illustrious thousand-year-old tradition of Christianity*, and with it the images of God and of men, through which for centuries right down to the present day, millions, perhaps even thousands of millions of people had sought and are still seeking their life's meaning.

This situation is deadly serious. In order to conceal it from themselves human beings take refuge in further killings, in a new war which is revealing itself as the suicide of Christendom. In December 1963 the official paper of the Vatican, *L'Osservatore Romano*, proudly published statistics to show that there are 974,489,630 Christians in the world, of whom 584,869,340 are Catholics, 256,457,440 Protestants and 133,153,850 Orthodox.

Without going further into the strict census character of these statistics, we can nevertheless say that there are therefore close on *one thousand million Christians who have literally nothing to say about the preparation of their 'final solution': their self-destruction through nuclear weapons*. The valiant efforts of individuals and small Christian groups, such as the Quakers, have failed to achieve any change of outlook in Christendom as a whole.

Let me quote but a single instance to show the connection between this silence and the silence which met the 'final solution' of the Jewish question. A German bishop, who had supported Hitler and his wars, declared a few years ago in a sermon, that the sins of mankind – he was looking towards the East – had already become so great again that God would certainly punish them with a third world war. This was the bishop of Passau, Simon Konrad Landersdorfer, speaking in 1959.

This sense of fatalism and defeatism springs from the pessimistic Augustinian conceptions with which both the major churches are impregnated. It is the flight into a hereafter, into an eventless eternity, abandoning this earth to the mercies of murderers and suicides. Here are three examples which I myself experienced a few years ago within a few days of each other.

At a convention of Protestant students in Vienna I spoke about a Christian's responsibility for the future. In the ensuing discussion, a Protestant theologian put forward the view that there was no need for us to be concerned about the future, since the future was in God's hands. And he referred to the Revelation of St John and the impending Day of Judgment. This theologian, and many of his like-minded Protestant and Catholic fellow theologians, overlook the fact that St John's revelation was addressed to a small band of persecuted Christians exposed to the mercies of some brutal Roman emperors. This small band had no direct responsibility for the murderous activities of their murderers. *Today millions of Christians share the responsibility for preparing the suicide both of the churches and of mankind.*

The second example: French Catholic friends told me of their attempts to induce a German cardinal (now dead) to intercede on behalf of starving Algerian children in French concentration camps. The cardinal declined: it was perhaps better that these children should die, since, if they were to grow up, they would in all probability become Mohammedans and not Christians.

The third example was reported to me by Rolf Hochhuth – who in the same conversation said that his play should have been written by a Catholic. He received a visit in Basle from an important German Jesuit who had written a lofty review of Hochhuth's play. Now in private conversation this truly important theologian declared: 'Herr Hochhuth, you would be right if the humanists were right. For God, however, it is a matter of complete indifference whether He receives these Jewish sacrifices in the form of small children, fourteen-year-old girls or adults.'

Behind this declaration lie the legitimate theological traditions of a thousand years – and also the greatest temptation to which Christians can succumb: to love God at the expense of human beings. In this case, however, the word 'God' is a cipher for the imaginings and fears and dreams of the Ego confronted with a confusingly different world. In this same tradition stand those famous justifications of the use of atomic weapons which were voiced by Father Gundlach and Father Hirschmann, but they at least were critically received by a handful of German Catholics, though not condemned by the ecclesiastical authorities. Hirschmann spoke of 'Franciscan courage' in connection with the use of the atom bomb, while Gundlach said that the honour of God could in certain circumstances demand that mankind

393

should perish in a nuclear war against Communism in defence of its highest beliefs. Such statements are, however, equally an expression of the death wish, buried deep in the subconscious mind. In earlier times this impulse was often openly expressed. Saints and many less than saints longed daily, hourly to be taken from this sinful earth and redeemed. Nowadays this dissolution impulse is more indirectly stated.

The great Leibniz once accused Calvinism of being a theology of death and the glorification of the Devil. All Christian theologians of today and tomorrow should be examined in the same light. To what extent are they inherently theologians of death, of killing and of suicide, unfitted to cope with life in a world where millions of people think differently from themselves?

For centuries Christians have been feeling offended, wronged and spiritually wounded by the advent of the new era. Many German Catholics sighed with relief when in 1950 Romano Guardini showed them, in a successful book, that the new era was coming to an end. Orthodox Protestants have, since the time of Luther's last years, felt threatened by heretics, fanatics and mortal enemies of pure doctrine. All attempts to suppress the nonconformist movements, perpetually arising anew from the orphaned spiritual Unconscious failed. From the womb of a specifically Protestant piety, Bible science emerged to analyse the word of God, and its researches into every word of the Bible have succeeded in raising doubt in the minds of literal minded Protestants.

For the past four hundred years the Catholic church has been fighting desperate defensive actions against a hostile world. Wishing to be seen as the bulwark of Christian orderliness and peace in Europe, the Catholic church first surrendered its role of peacemaker by refusing to accept the treaty of Westphalia, which ended the Thirty Years War – the first great European civil war. This treaty could be regarded as a great work for peace, since it did after all ensure the European balance of power until the French Revolution. The papal objection to this peace was eventually ignored by both the Catholic and the Protestant nations.

Throughout the nineteenth century the Curia fought for the preservation of its papal state. It sought help from the emperor in Vienna, from the Russian tsars, from Napoleon III, from Bismarck. Having made an enemy of the new Italy, it shut itself up with its prisoner, the pope, in a dungeon of its own choice. That made it possible for the Italian government successfully to sabotage the efforts of the solitary Pope Benedict XI (1914–22) to intervene in international politics and to take part in preparation of peace treaties from 1918 onwards. In the Second World War the lonely and tragic Pope Pius XII wanted to be the great peacemaker. He had thoughts of a new Vienna Congress – perhaps in Rome? – and wanted to bring the Axis powers and the Western powers together against the Soviet Union. He failed. His radio speeches and New Year addresses from 1945 onwards in the cause of democracy sounded strange in the mouth of a man who sat at the head of a ruling system that to this day has never practised, or learnt, the meaning of democracy.

Walled in and excluded from any meaningful contributions to the solution of the world's great problems, the major churches turned in on themselves. *The church became an end in itself*, in which every serious attempt to open it up was denounced as an insult to the holy mother church. The old allegory of the church as a woman, in contrast to the female symbol of the synagogue – we have dealt with its historical genesis – is here understood quite materialistically. Not wanting to admit that one feels insulted as a human being or as a representative of the church one speaks of an insult to God, to Mother Church, to the Holy Father.

Sigmund Freud has spoken of the three great matters in which human vanity and self-conceit feels outraged (he discovered them in the course of his researches). The first is connected with the name of Copernicus. Man experiences to his grief that the earth – his earth – is not the centre of the solar system, of the universe. The second outrage is connected with the name of Darwin. Man – the king of creation, the first beloved child of God, the son of God on earth – is revealed as the laborious late-product of a difficult evolution, connecting him through millions and thousands of millions of years with the other creatures on this earth. Man is a grandson of the worm and the brother of apes.

The third outrage of Man Freud saw revealed in the work which he himself began – in psychoanalysis. Man discovered to his horror that he is a patricide, an Oedipus, a suicide caught up in a web of impulses which not only give birth to his highest ideals and his most sacred values, but also nourishes them, and, under certain circumstances, destroys them again.

Copernicus, Darwin, Freud, modern natural science and biblical science: these fundamentally upset the balance of a species that saw itself as lords of creation and owners of God – by the word of the Scriptures and God's strong citadel in the church. These outraged victims of a specifically European egoistic self-conceit – equally evident in people who have or profess no church faith, yet under the skin are also hemmed in by Christian complexes and doubts – are now joined by insulted Christians who are only now beginning to feel the full force of their outrage.

Let us now place beside Copernicus, Darwin and Freud three causes of a specifically Christian sense of outrage.

First, the Jew Jesus. What is one to make of the Jew Jesus and of Christ in the face of non-Christian theistic and atheistic world religions which are in some cases much older than Christianity? – *Asien missioniert im Abendland* (Asia Seeks Converts in the West) is the title of a collection of essays published by a Protestant firm in Stuttgart. It deals mainly with Islamic and Buddhist missions in Europe today.

Second, in fifteen centuries of Christian deicide – every murder of a man is deicide, every denunciation is a betrayal of the godhead, which is thus denied the power and the right to reveal itself through the unique personality of the person denounced – Christendom has shown itself to be the people guilty of God's murder. The Jew became the cross-bearer, successor and representative of the Jew Jesus, and was hounded to his death. The most illustrious and oldest traditions of the church are thereby thrown into doubt, and must be replaced in a positive way. St Paul and St Augustine must be challenged, that is to say, examined anew. How, however, can Christendom, which for centuries has considered itself mortally wronged, bear so appalling an insult? It could do so only if it were to accept this insult as a command and dispensation of God – demonstrated by the power of world history to show up errors and set them right.

Third, throughout their history, which has become through them a tale of suffering for Christians, Jews and non-Christians alike, the churches have continuously made grave mistakes. Their theological questionings have served not infrequently to conceal the real great questions. Their solutions have very often been solutions in appearance only, such as their treatment of heretics from the second right through to the twentieth centuries. These false solutions have thus only led to a worsening of the explosive situation. There has never been a world religion or a human society which has stored up so much explosive material inside itself as the 'Christian society'. The successive explosions concerning Albigenses, Hussites, witches and Jews have revealed a Christianity consumed in self-loathing. Not daring to acknowledge its own complexes, it was forced to create from century to century new enemies and scapegoats for itself in order to divert attention from the deep intellectual, spiritual and mental disturbances in its own heart.

Imprisoned in this vicious circle, it had to drag new witches, devil worshippers, Jews, Socialists, Communists before the gates of its church to be branded. *Thus the church turned itself into a permanent stake* on which 'heretics', people who deviated to the right or to the left, were burned. Even the burning of books can be seen as a sort of burning of men outlawed from society and from the church.

Within the deeply sick community of Man dwell deeply sick churches, and they form the centres of pathological processes constantly leading to new explosions.

The venerable Protestant theologian Paul Schütz concerned himself in 1960 in his large-scale work *Parusia – Hoffnung und Prophetie* (Parusia – Hope and Prophesy) with the tendency of the church to shut itself off from a society which is equally closed. Such a church can see nothing but self-defence at all costs, even at the cost of a nuclear war. It has become an end in itself, hiding from the truth and paying enormous prices in human life and in spiritual life to maintain its self-concealment. 'Theology is Man's most dangerous adventure.' In the Thirty Years War the two Christian Gods – the Gods of two closed church societies – lost the battle against each other. (This statement of the Protestant theologian Paul Schütz in 1960 was anticipated in

1915 by the excommunicated Catholic theologian Alfred Loisy, whose lectures on the battle of the various national Gods in the First World War has been dealt with in an earlier chapter.)

Paul Schütz concludes: 'Christendom has failed to bring hope to the world.' A church which expends all its strength in shutting itself off and in defending its hidden self can give the world no life, no hope, but only death.

There has been as yet no major scientific investigation by Catholics themselves into the pathological element inside their church, but there is in existence a remarkable demonstration of it. That is the *Index Romanus*, the *index librorum prohibitorum*, the catalogue of books and publications which Catholics are forbidden to read under pain of committing a mortal sin. The Catholic Hans Kühner-Wolfskehl, member during the Second World War of a resistance group which had voluntarily taken on the task of saving persecuted Jews, produced in 1963 a concise study of this product of a pathological situation which had persisted for four hundred years, kept alive by a continued supply of new fuel to burn.

A high percentage of the work of the creative human spirit in Europe – in philosophy, literature and theology – can still be found in this unique catalogue of condemnation and destruction: from Johannes Scotus Erigena in the ninth century, via Maimonides to Albertus Magnus, to Dante (until 1921 right through to modern times). 'It is a matter of deep shame to see Montaigne's masterpiece, the *Essays*, Kant's *Critique of Pure Reason*, Pascal's *Pensées* and the *Provinciales*, Spinoza's *Tractatus* and Lessing's mighty thoughts *On the Education of the Human Race* still on the Index and to see their readers accused of a serious sin.'

'The long dramatic history of the Index began in 1557. It was compiled at the command of Paul IV Carafa, a glacial, unChristian despot filled with an almost pathological hatred, who of all popes embodied the Inquisition in its harshest form.' The German theologian Albert Sleumer, whose shortened edition of the Index went through eleven editions up to 1957, resolutely defended the Index, with the argument that temporal states also ban and burn books. That can certainly be maintained without contradiction in a country such as Catholic Germany, where not long before, the burning of books had been a prelude to the burning of men.

The *Index Romanus* has lived largely on a system of denunciation. It has borne witness also to that dangerous tendency to keep men in a childlike state, to which the leaders of the church often fell victim in the nineteenth and twentieth centuries. It was in this sense that *L'Osservatore Romano* spoke, when a book by the Louvainian theologian Camille Muller was placed on the Index in 1954, because he had dealt critically with the scientific side of Pius XII's encyclical, *Humani Generis*. Learned Catholics, said *L'Osservatore Romano*, should note that they had in future 'to demonstrate a more childlike devotion towards the teaching of the church'.

Alongside some of the greatest works of Italian, German and English literature, the Index impounded with particular partiality French works, from Fénelon through Voltaire to Sartre. (No doubt French denunciations in Rome helped.) Emile Zola was four times placed on the Index, the first time immediately after his public protest, *J'accuse*, during the Dreyfus scandal. There is some significance in this. The inflammatory hate-filled anti-Semitic books, essays and tracts, which in the nineteenth and twentieth centuries paved the way in print for the involvement of Christians in the 'final solution', are not to be found on the Index. Pinay's *Conspiracy against the Church* in 1963 could hardly be placed on the Index, unless the men of the Holy Office had been prepared to put themselves on it, or unless the request which Archbishop Roberts SJ put to the Second Vatican Council had been accepted – that there should be a holy inquiry by the Council into the most Holy Office.

A new self-appreciation – that is what theologians and others are trying to wrest from the church today. It is realized, at least in small circles, that this new self-appreciation will call for new and more open relationships with the world and the worldly realities of love, sex, other world religions, 'atheistic humanism' and hence also of Judaism and Israel. Very much has been achieved by individuals such as the courageous Gertrud Luckner and Karl Thieme in Catholic Germany and by small groups of Catholic and Protestant theologians in Germany, France and America. The aim has been to prepare a first meeting between the Christians and the Jews – between the new and the old people of God, as it is often expressed. For domestic political reasons (since the racial struggle threatens the whole existence of the USA) American bishops and cardinals have in recent years become particular advocates of Christian-Jewish rapprochement.

However, these efforts by individuals and small groups can succeed only if Christianity replaces its exclusivity and self-concealment with self-analysis. It would lead back through a chain of centuries-old, deeply-rooted errors, failures and misjudgments, first to the Jew Jesus, then to Israel, and then to 'the heart of all things' – to Meister Eckhart's conception of a *weiselose Gottheit*, a divinity which cannot become the property of any exclusive society or pressure group or be neatly defined by a self-protective theology; a divinity which insists upon the commandment: Thou shalt not make any graven image.

Self-analysis is a journey through hell, the hell of one's own subconscious depths. Would it be possible to find, within a Christianity very largely composed of wounded, outraged and sick souls and minds, personalities strong enough to take on this arduous task?

Three theologians were prepared to do it. They did not know each other, even by name, and all three spent their years of imprisonment wrestling with the vast problems of preserving the effective essence of Christianity after the death of the Christian 'religion'. These three theologians were the Protestant Dietrich Bonhoeffer, the German Jesuit Alfred Delp and the Austrian Austin canon Karl Roman Scholz. Delp was executed in Berlin, Bonhoeffer in Flossenburg and Scholz in Vienna in 1945, after four years spent in various prisons in Germany. Scholz was a poet, history teacher and active fighter for the Austrian resistance, but the group he founded was betrayed into the hands of Hitler's henchmen in May 1940.

The poverty of church life today has been demonstrated, as regards the Protestant half of Christianity – though it can be taken to apply to Catholicism as well – by a Protestant theologian in the USA, Peter L.Berger (a former Austrian Jew) in his book *The Noise of Solemn Assemblies : Christian Commitment and the Religious Establishment in America*. Berger reveals that in the USA a hundred million dollars might be spent in a single month on building new churches. These often pretentious American churches are class institutions of a social and political religion – *the American way of life*. Sorrow, death and pain have no place here. In this religion God is an opium, religion a psychological tranquillizer. And God is also an ideological weapon in the world conflict, in the struggle against 'un-American' activities and against Communism.

In the age of nuclear war this marriage of church and state clings as unthinkingly to its militant religiosity as ever Prussia did in 1812 and 1914, or the Russian and Austro-Hungarian empires in their time.

Religion for these churches consists largely of a specific social, political and psychological task: the increasingly perfect assimilation of the individual into a society dominated by economic considerations. Religious, mental and spiritual restlessness is looked at askance. Belief in authority, nationalism and religious conformity makes for an intense unity in these churches, which, as closed communities, regard self-assertion and self-perpetuation as their only aim.

These churches are cut off from the dynamic forces of society. One can see from their monumental appearance that in America the religious protest of the Jew Jesus and the religious protest of the awakening human being must almost inevitably take an anti-religious, anti-church and anti-Christian form. In the introduction to the German edition of this American book (entitled, significantly, *Kirche ohne Auftrag* – Church without a Task) Bolewski draws attention to some of Berger's conclusions, which in his opinion give a valid general picture of the position of the church in the last two centuries: religion as an organization and guardian of dogma has been the province of the church; religion, in the sense of religious fervour and living faith, has been largely kept alive by the anti-religious.

Bolewski remarks with regard to the German situation: 'During the last hundred years there has been on the one hand a movement towards ever greater uniformity within the church, and on the other a silent withdrawal from the church of all those groups which the church, in this monolithic condition, was unable to satisfy.'

During the period of the two world wars and the liquidation of the Jews, these unsatisfied groups saw with horror that the inward-looking church was too busy with its own affairs to take any notice of the *passio hominis*, the crucifixion of mankind in the persons of Jews and other victims of persecution. In a discussion of Hochhuth's *The Representative* the suffragan bishop of Limburg, Walter Kampe, remarked that the assumptions and habits of the church have never included the idea of coming directly to the help of non-Catholics.

Under the protection of a closed church – this closed character was the great Catholic achievement of the nineteenth century – 'this beautiful country of Germany can feel secure from the threat of Christ's message.' Carl Amery, the son of the distinguished Catholic scholar and church historian Anton Mayer-Pfannholz, makes this point in his study *Die Kapitulation oder Deutscher Katholizismus* (Capitulation or German Catholicism).

Bishop Bernard Hanssler, who as chairman of the central committee of German Catholics has acquired a reputation as a spokesman of German church life, underlines Amery's irony with his remark that Jesus 'forbade the taking up of an essentially critical attitude'. Here we have a statement which is as much against the true spirit of Christ as it is anti-Jewish and ecclesiastically orthodox. Hanssler reviles the nineteenth century, the critical century, in the style of Goebbels. As in any form of closed society, there are close internal and external links between Nazi, Fascist and clerical ways of self-assertion. The distinguished Catholic church historian, Joseph Lortz, was right to see a continuous movement of resistance to criticism and self-criticism running from the popes of the nineteenth century, from Gregory XVI and Pius IX, right up to the Catholic Adolf Hitler.

This self-isolation of the church from the world, from truth and from history, has recently provoked concern even in orthodox ecclesiastical quarters. The failure of theology and the church to master the concrete problems of humanity has led to a crisis in Catholic education. Many posts cannot be filled by church-going Christians. A German specialist in ecclesiastical education, Karl Erlinghagen AJ, has warned the leaders of the church of the great vacuum which their policies have produced: 'Since the beginning of the modern era the church has been frightened by threatening historical developments into a dangerous withdrawal from the world; and only gradually is it now venturing on the slow process of return . . . The church is still suffering as a result of historical shocks . . . The shock administered by the Enlightenment has still not been overcome. The fear of the world which resulted from it, and which restricted the creative intellectual life, above all of German Catholics, in the nineteenth century, is still perceptible . . This fear takes two forms, though these ultimately have the same origin: the world is seen either as a temptation or as a threat. Since these two forms have the same source – the Christian's existential uncertainty in his own belief – they react to some extent on one another.'

Erlinghagen speaks of a sort of 'society-phobia' in German Catholicism, a withdrawal from the society of other groups: 'Withdrawal into the society of like-minded people, into part voluntary, part involuntary occupation of a stronghold, is quite understandable. Nevertheless, the withdrawal has frequently borne the marks of escapism.

'Present-day theology scarcely concerns itself with the problems of the world, of history, of artistic creation and technical production, of the distinctively religious area of life, of power, politics, jobs, the family, education, nature, life, and the whole complex of activities in which the human spirit expresses itself. These things are not taught, because they have not received theological treatment. But it is precisely these things which are the constituents of the life of educated people; and with such people the present-day preachers of the word of God achieve no true contact.

'The basic religious aim of getting to heaven at all costs can imply a dangerous narrowing of outlook and a diminution of Christianity's mastery of the problems of existence. The minister whose injunction is simply an individualistic "Save your soul" is misleading the flock which has been entrusted to him.'

We may comment that here – as in other areas – the Augustinian principle must be abandoned and replaced by a return to the Old Testament roots of Christ's own piety and to even older roots – to the original faith in which Man felt himself to be both God's creature and his responsible partner.

Erlinghagen goes on: 'The theology of worldly realities, which has remained stunted till the present, has dealt with the world in its own characteristic way. In dogma an authoritative treatment of the world is completely lacking – at least in the dogmatic equipment which the present-day theologian is given for his life and work. The world only really finds a place in moral theology, though it ought also to be found in other departments. And in moral theology the world, and everything which makes it worthwhile to people in our time, is treated not in a positive sense, as having a value of its own, but simply *sub ratione peccati*. One can merely infer from it that the world concerns the Christian only insofar as it represents the risk of sin. The approach is negative – the less men have to do with the world, the better. Could not Nietzsche's cry, "Remain faithful to the earth" be interpreted as the cry of protest of a misunderstood and mistreated world, and be echoed in its truest sense by the Christian? . . . The contempt for the world of which we speak goes far beyond contempt for the material and the basely sensual: it extends to the purest realms of the spirit.'

In illustration of this last remark, we may instance not only the Roman Index, but in general the lordly, arrogant and dismissive attitude of ecclesiastical authorities to the achievements and personalities of creative artists, scholars and scientists, to men who, as heralds of the future, are trying to lead humanity and the church itself away from the impasse of their own deathwish.

To see the world *sub ratione peccati*, to reduce morality to the question of private sexual morality – this has fateful consequences both for the role of the church and for mankind. We may anticipate our conclusion by saying that *the disregard of the fate of the Jews between 1918 and 1945 can only be understood as part of a general disregard for Man and the world.*

Once again, in Germany and elsewhere, ecclesiastical campaigns are now being mounted against sex and the alleged increase in sexual immorality. They are based on Augustinian and Manichaean assumptions. Latent Manichaeism is the cancer of Christianity; and anti-Semitism is its natural outgrowth. Unlike individual people, great institutions, such as churches and religions, can be sick for thousands of years with spiritual cancers, and still not die.

Basing their theology on Augustinian and Manichaean principles, blinkered by celibacy and by an enclosed education in seminaries, Catholic boarding-schools and theological colleges, the modern clergy has developed an obsession with the crudely sexual. This can be seen not only in standard works of moral theology since Alfonso de' Liguori, but also in the whole thought and action of broad sections of the priesthood.

Sin is above all sexual immorality, and the whole of morality revolves around sex. The unholy alliance between the German bishops and Hitler was founded on approval for his battle against immorality (pornographic literature and so on). Then, as now, the leaders of the church overlooked the fact that there is a more important morality than that of the individual: the morality and immorality of a whole society. The immorality of economic exploitation, of a war economy and of political relationships within society – all this is overlooked. Why? Simply because consideration of these matters would involve an obligation to try to change them, and the thought of this frightens the princes of the church back into confining their attentions to the moral problems of teenagers, sexually frustrated housewives and elderly men on holiday. They ignore the fact that the sex crisis is only a secondary phenomenon. A post-Christian society, still largely shaped by 'Christian' obligations and attitudes, has been left in a moral vacuum, as far as creative self-realization and responsibility in life are concerned, by a theology and a church which are not seriously involved in these 'worldly' questions.

Let us return to Erlinghagen's argument: 'The problems posed by these areas of life are felt by theologians to be marginal to their true concerns, if not actually intrusive; and their individual dealings with them nearly always remain amateurish. The preaching of the word of God in sermons, speeches, private instruction and conversation often demands from priests, little versed in worldly affairs, judgments which they are not capable of making. They usually pass them without even realizing that it would have been much better to abstain.' We might add at this point that most of the political attitudes taken up by twentieth-century bishops – even long after Hitler – could be put in this category of an amateurish meddling with vast unknown quantities.

'The hasty judgments of the church on technology, advertising, mass communications, politics, the acquisitive society, property and professional ambition not only blur the Christian message, but often alienate the audience which they are trying to direct, being, as they mostly are, mere prejudices . . . Anyone who examines the attitude of the average theologian during the last two hundred years *to anything new, such as democracy*, modern art and literature, technology and even teaching methods, will be forced to acknowledge the truth of what has been said above.' Thus spoke the German Jesuit, Professor Karl Erlinghagen in 1965.

The intellectual, spiritual and political mentality of broad sections of European Catholicism is essentially the same today as in those fateful decades when the Austrian Catholic Adolf Hitler was preparing the final solution of the Jewish question, and at the same time (unknowingly), the final destruction of the German people. This Christianity has as little to say about the prospect of a third world war as about the final solution of the Jewish question.

A self-critical symposium *Deutscher Katholizismus nach 1945* (German Catholicism since 1945, published 1964), to which seven Catholic theologians, historians, sociologists and philosophers contributed, reaches the conclusion that post-war German Catholic society is a post-Fascist society, in which all the elements of Fascism and Nazism are still at work. The vocabulary of the barbarian is still the vocabulary of the current German language.

German society and German Catholics are still imbued with the poison of Nazism (Franz Greiner). This post-Fascist Catholic society is successfully suppressing the history of its collaboration with the Third Reich. Any attempt to recall Catholic resistance thinkers and writers is strictly taboo, and their memory is suppressed or distorted. No one wants to know of Father Friedrich Muckermann and the German Catholic emigrants who, from Switzerland and Holland, tried to carry the outlook of the resistance back into Germany. The only honour for Father Delp, the brave and open-minded Jesuit who, from his prison, clearly saw and described the church's share of guilt in the suppression of the individual and the downward slide to dictatorship, has been to have a military barracks named after him by the former German defence minister, Franz-Josef Strauss!

In barracks and church the old friend-foe ideology is still nourished. Nothing can be heard from Reinhold Schneider, whom Edzard Schaper called the conscience of Germany, and who has passionately denounced the church for its part in preparing for an atomic war. His letters on this subject and his poem cycle *Tu es Petrus*, which long before Hochhuth took up the theme of papal failure, have not been published. Instead, we can read the conventional Christian tracts from which he has inwardly dissociated himself.

The bishop of the Austrian diocese to which the peasant Franz Jägerstätter belonged – the Catholic who was executed for refusing to take an oath of loyalty to Hitler – forebade the publication of the story of his martyrdom, on the ground that those who had fought in the war were the greater heroes.

The suppression of the memory of this one brave man among millions of collaborators was so completely successful in Austria (where the Catholic mentality is very similar to that of the Bavarian Catholics) that the Viennese Cardinal Franz König had never even heard of Jägerstätter until I showed him the American Gordon C. Zahn's book *In Solitary Witness*.

Back now to the present day and the essays in *German Catholicism since 1945*. The cure of souls is treated as a religious 'amenity'; the church has become a spare-time activity. The most eager churchgoers are those who feel frustrated in a technological society. Modern industrial and technical civilization and the modern universities have developed without the help of the Catholics. The apparent revival of the church after 1945 has long since been shown to have been a sterile one. Heinz Robert Schlette affirms that for a high percentage of Germans Catholicism is only a formal 'religion': a kind of religious self-gratification rather than a genuine faith. Faith would require a responsible moulding of the personal life and of society, an unreserved confidence in Yahweh, the *Dieu d'avant*, the coming God (Schlette). Our own comment here would be that German Catholics have thoroughly cleansed themselves from this Jewish God, from the Jew Jesus and from Jewish piety and experience of the divine; and that in doing so they have cut themselves off from their own roots.

'Let us face the fact, which many already know and have already formulated, that Christianity is conceived of by Christians and non-Christians as an ethic, as an institutional guarantee for our political life and public safety, as a cultural value. Christians stand helpless and uncomprehending in face of the basic statements and challenges of the New Testament. One has only to think of basic words like congregation, eschatology, communion, witness, glad tidings, epiphany. In place of the demands made from the faithful by the New Testament, we have the doctrine of individual salvation through organized religion, eudaemonism and mythological hopes, expressing themselves in the outward forms of Christian piety and mysticism.'

In such a mass church, prone to collective neurosis (the devilish and subversive Jews have now been replaced by Socialists and Communists), the true faith is assailed, while the religious forms go largely uncriticized. For belief demands vigilance and resistance, whereas religion offers a perfect and painless integration into the existing social system.

'Anyone who believes and wants to believe, finds that the struggle to interpret the messages of the Bible, and particularly to give a radical existential content to the Gospel message, brings him up against the most arduous tests, existential obscurities and almost insoluble enigmas.' In contrast to this, every day brings proof 'that Catholicism as a religion is not seriously touched by these and other difficulties; it does not take any cognizance of these problems, maintaining its stand on the apparently firm ground of the creed into which it has grown, or fallen.'

'The question might be asked, in the light of this division between faith and religion, whether there is not some justification for the old accusation that Catholicism has an interest in keeping the people in a state of stupidity and theological ignorance.'

The Catholic popular press in the Weimar Republic and the Third Reich comes to mind in this connection. This nurtured all the collective anxieties and delusions from the stab-in-the-back legend to anti-Semitism, which were connected with the 'national' withdrawal from contact with a very complex reality. The same situation exists today, but the new mode of expression has shifted the line of attack from the capitalistic and Jewish West to the Marxist and Jewish East.

'The Catholic popular press is almost exclusively concerned with the interests of a Catholicism which sees and expresses itself as a religion. This is true not only of its political and social, but also of its religious and spiritual utterances. If one considers the vast circulation of these papers, and the uncritical approach of the average Catholic reader, one realizes what a danger they constitute.'

We would add here that this Catholic press, with all its taboos and its refusal to come radically to grips with the burning questions of Christianity and human life, is still as dangerous today as it was in the period of incubation of Nazism and in the years from 1933–45.

Schlette's conclusion is clear: 'The task which faces Catholicism is quite simply this: Catholicism as a religion must publicly identify itself as such and clearly distinguish itself from Catholicism as a faith, if this faith is to be preserved for the present and for the future. We may adopt here a formulation of Amery's, though our understanding of the problem perhaps needs even stronger terms: "*Sentire cum Ecclesia may demand from us a break with existing Catholicism.*" '

Sentire cum Ecclesia – to feel, to think, to share responsibility with the church: Franz-Martin Schmölz, the Dominican church historian and sociologist, states in this volume of essays that for the Catholic nineteenth century the church was 'an earthly kingdom of ecclesiastical power, a sort of papal state'. He goes on: 'In 1894 the Catholic official dictionary accepted a somewhat elaborated translation of Palmieri's well-known definition of the church (*ecclesia est regnum Christi in terris auctoritate apostolica regendum*): The church is the visible kingdom of Christ on earth, which unites under Him, its invisible head, all the faithful in the unity of doctrine and the communion of the sacraments.' In the nineteenth century the church was in practical and theological terms identified with the hierarchy, true religion with the church, the term Christian with the term ecclesiastical. 'The greater a person's allegiance to the church, the more Christian he is . . . The application of the principle *extra ecclesiam nulla salus* to this conception of the church was bound to lead to intolerance, and thereby to the total isolation of the church from the outside world. Why should we bother about the world, the state, society and politics?' Why should we bother about the imprisonment of wicked liberals and Socialists in concentration camps, and the extermination of the Jews?

The Dominican Schmölz, at present a lecturer in Catholic theology at Salzburg University, remarks in this connection: 'The fact that, for a whole century, the idea of democracy was presented to the church only through the distorting mirror of liberalism, and that the church itself rejected democracy as a result of an unaccountable adherence to the medieval conception of *Imperium-Sacerdotium*, is one of those tragic occurrences only too frequent in history'. Our comment on this would be that the political, social, theological and psychological reasons for this adherence are perfectly obvious and only 'unaccountable' to those who dare not venture on a serious self-inquiry.

But what is the church's conception of itself today? Basically it has not altered since the times of Innocent XIII and Gregory XVI. The Jesuit Walter Kerber formulates it in this volume as follows: 'The task of the church as such relates exclusively to the next world, that is to say, it carries on Christ's work of salvation, which is an absolute gift from above. More earthly tasks may be the duty of Christians, but not of the church as such.'

Here we come to the heart of the matter, the very essence of this book: the churches and Christianity have so often fallen under the spell of this conception that the church has of itself become blind to history, to reality, to God, to mankind, to the world. The gaze of Christians has been deflected upwards, away from Man and his sufferings, from the *passio hominis*, from the sufferings of the Son of God in His brothers and sisters on earth, because the church has been engaged in the defence of eternal rights and truths which must not be shaken.

The withdrawal of the church from history has created that specifically Christian and ecclesiastical irresponsibility – towards the world, the Jew, the other person, even the Christian himself, considered as a human being – which was the ultimate cause of past catastrophes and may be the cause of a final catastrophe in the future.

'Eternal church, eternal truths, eternal rights': this very eternity is a static eternity originating in Platonic and Greek philosophy, which has no place in the range of experience of the Old or the New Testaments. For His chosen people in the Old Testament God was a God who revealed Himself in history; Christianity as a branch on the tree of God's chosen people is the historical religion *par excellence*. No other religion on this earth (and we do not know of any other religions of possible other creatures on other planets) is to such an extent a historical religion and a religion of history.

The church's creed invokes historical fact – as no other religious or philosophical creed has done – the fact that Jesus, the son of Mary, was crucified under Pontius Pilate. Everything, literally everything in the church and in Christianity, starts from completely concrete historical situations and facts.

The Roman Catholic church always used historical arguments in its battle with emperors, kings and heresies, and the claims of bishops and patriarchs in East and West to be descendants of St Peter and St Paul have frequently been supported by falsifications and dangerous manipulations of history.

No dogma, no papal declaration, can be considered apart from its historical context, however much it may thunder 'from above', proclaiming 'eternal truths' – like Michelangelo's Jupiter-Christ in the Sistine Chapel, or like the Jupiter-Moses, Pope Julian II, who rode armed into the battle. Every dogma, every papal message, every ecclesiastical law was formulated at a specific historical moment – and often bears to this day the chains, scars and marks of the arduous struggles which called it into existence.

'We become all we fight': these words, written by the English Catholic poet Roy Campbell during the London blitz, contain the same meaning as my own saying: 'Who turns the spit remains stuck fast to it' – the meaning being that all positions, propositions, doctrines, all theological explanations and formulations of the church are ultimately connected with the particular oppositions and antagonisms out of which they emerged.

Every word of the liturgy, of the mass, of the sacraments, is a word rooted in history: born at a particular moment in history, in the Jews' struggle with their God and with their enemies, and within their own breasts. The liturgy of the Roman Catholic church is the product of a historical process. It began with the taking over of elements from Jewish, Oriental and Greek cults and institutions in the service of the new Lord. As the Revelation of St John took the symbols and colours of the cult of the emperors into the service of the new king, Christ; as the golden city of papal Rome took over the golden palace of Nero, so too the whole development of the liturgy has been bound up with historical situations. From the brutal battles with the Arians; from the aspirations and interventions of the lords of the Visigothic church and of the Frankish and Carolingian kings; from the struggle of the papacy in the Middle Ages to take over all the sacred signs of dominion, all the rites and linguistic forms of the hostile imperial party which was now condemned to a new secularity; through the struggles of the early modern period to the liturgies of new saints and the festivals of Mary in the eighteenth to twentieth centuries; right up to the Festival of Christ the King in 1925 (with its momentous anti-Jewish interpolation – three years before the banning of the Friends of Israel in 1928); the whole liturgy of the church has grown up through a historical process, and it reflects as many deformities and perversions as the history of the church as a whole.

The church's retreat from history, and hence from responsibility for mankind, can best be seen in its self-complaisant handling of the liturgy. While outside the church doors Jewish women and children were being dragged away to death, thousands of priests and monks inside were calmly intoning – as they still do – the psalms of the Jewish people, without seeing that they were applying to themselves the cry of distress of the Jew.

The heavenly liturgy, the service of the Heavenly King brought down to this earth – this has been the interpretation of the mass by liturgists in the Carolingian period, in Germany and France in the twelfth century, in the Baroque period and in the liturgical movements of the nineteenth and twentieth centuries. Is it only a coincidence that leaders of the liturgical movement, like Dom Prosper Guéranger in France (whose books have also had wide currency in English-speaking countries), and of the German movement centring around Maria Laach, have been explicitly anti-Semitic in their attitudes? In their enthusiasm for a synthesis of classical Christian and German elements, they perhaps deliberately (at least at the subconscious level) disregarded the fact that by far the greater part of the material of the liturgy was Jewish, recounting the sufferings of God's people Israel and the experiences of Jewish Man with God's first love.

By denuding the liturgy of its historical content, the church made it possible to disregard completely the sufferings of the Jews, Christians and non-Christians who were being murdered – literally as individuals, and in a broader sense as a people – outside the very doors of the churches. Direct references to the Jews, as in the Good Friday prayer, had a specifically anti-Jewish purpose. Millions of masses were read in the 'Christian West', millions of psalms and prayers were offered up by monks, nuns and priests, without its being noticed that, outside, the blood relations of the Lord were being murdered.

In the same way a completely non-historical *Confiteor* is said in the mass – a confession of sin which has no relation to the present ('God is the God of the present' preached Meister Eckhart in the true spirit of Jewish piety). This *Confiteor* has no relation to the *passio hominis* of today, to the history of suffering of Jewish, Christian and non-Christian fellow beings. It is a timeless. devitalized, ritualized *Confiteor* which in no way engages the depths of the person. Since Adrian VI acknowledged his guilt in 1522, the Roman Catholic church has never risked a concrete confession of sins which takes full account of history. The ritual used daily by millions of clergy and laymen provides the easiest way of suppressing guilt and avoiding responsibility and self-analysis. *This purely formal confession of guilt absolves from the actual acknowledgement of guilt which leads to a living sense of responsibility and to action.*

As an impressive instance of suppression of responsibility we may relate the experience of one of the most prominent and progressive Catholic theologians of our time, the Dominican Yves M.J.Congar. At the beginning of the 1950s he became a victim of the purge directed, during the last years of Pius XII, particularly against the French Dominicans, Jesuits, Carmelites and worker-priests. Leading theologians like Lubac and Congar lost their positions as professors and were transferred to other places. Congar had the good fortune to be able to retreat into an exceptional place: to Jerusalem.

Jerusalem, April to September 1954: let a simple Christian layman picture to himself one of the most clear-sighted of theologians standing daily before the temple, in the very place where Jesus, the son of Mary, taught and suffered. It was just ten years after the liberation of France from the terror of the Nazis and the Vichy leaders. On what does a French theologian of this stature meditate as he stands before the temple? Dreyfus perhaps, or the leading Catholic collaborators of the Vichy régime, justifying their support for it by reference to St Thomas Aquinas and to the doctrine and practice of the church? What strikes this great theologian in Jerusalem? (I use the adjective 'great' sincerely: one must look at a tragedy in its highest and not its lowest manifestations, and that is precisely why I have chosen Congar as an example.)

Congar wrote a book *Le Mystère du Temple*, in which he considered God's plan for Man's salvation. God builds His temple – the new temple of Jerusalem, the church – out of living stones, out of the faithful. The first part of the book deals with the presence of God in Old Testament history. His presence for the prophets and in Jewish piety and Jewish thought. The second part is entitled *The Temple or the Presence of God in the Messianic Period*. It discusses Jesus and the temple; Christ and the church, the holy temple; St Paul and the body of the Christian as a spiritual temple. The church is the concrete spiritual and bodily temple; the apocalypse is the eschatological temple. The final chapter deals with 'the providential economy of God's presence in the world' (*L'économie providentielle de la présence de Dieu dans le monde*).

The presence of God in the world, in the temple, in the church, in the history of salvation: in this ritualized, sacramentalized history the real person, the historical person does not figure at all! And that is why history of this sort has become, in the actual story of living Man, a history of disaster and damnation.

Congar embraces world history in a single sentence, just as in medieval churches world history is depicted in a few symbolic figures: Adam, Cain and Abel, Christ, the Last Judgment. '*Cette histoire va d'un Paradis à un Ciel, par un entre-deux de peine.*' This history extends from the Garden of Eden to Heaven, through an intermediate period of suffering. Such a history of salvation slurs over the whole true history of mankind, and completely disregards the liquidation of the Jews. For *Ecclesia ab Abel* – the church is already present in Abel. Jesus is the new temple, which is quite different from the old temple. John the Baptist represents the destruction of the old temple and the construction of a new spiritual temple. The history of Israel is entirely worldly, profane – only from above and outside does God occasionally intervene in it. But since Jesus, history has become radically different. Jesus is embodied in the church and ever-present within it. In his beautiful book, Congar speaks often of God's presence in the world, and this is how he sees it. God has become Man – in the corpus of the church.

St Thomas is used to support the view of the church as successor to the temple and the synagogue. It took over from these two in their own life-time. Yet no – in the strictest sense there are no longer any Jews; they no longer have a meaningful place in the history of salvation!

Congar, however, still thinks it useful to have a passing debate with the Protestant view of the church as expressed by Calvin. Calvin makes no distinction between the sacraments of the synagogue and those of the church. The church is for him a continuation of the synagogue. The Catholic con-ception is totally different: the church as represented by the new temple of Jesus is something completely new. *As the new temple, it is the destroyer of the old.* It never seems to have occurred to this great theologian that it might be the refusal of Calvinism to deny its Jewish roots that has kept the Calvinist countries free from the bloody persecutions of the Jews which have characterized the Catholic countries.

Congar comments in a foot-note on the strange fact that Jesus so seldom (author's note: in fact, never) speaks of the church, but always of the kingdom of God. But he does not come on the reason, which is that Jesus thought of Himself as a Jew, not as a Christian – and never as a church Christian.

Congar concludes, basing himself on St John and St Paul, that with the coming of Jesus we have moved on from the very human history of the Old Testament, in which God merely intervened, to a truly heavenly order of existence. What was once only hoped for in terms of an eschatological Messianism has now been given us by Jesus Christ and is experienced in the church through the grace of the Holy Ghost. *World history, the epoch of an 'histoire très humaine', is over; all hope, all eschatological hope has been fulfilled in the church. It is the living God and Christ present amongst us.*

To sum up: this lofty view of world history as the history of salvation eliminates all real events, dismissing them as of no significance. This includes the whole story, past and present, of the Jews and (by extension) of Christians and the whole of humanity. All that is unimportant. The only truth, the only reality is the eternal presence of Christ, of God in the church. This presence can be experienced each time mass is said and in all the sacraments of the church.

Untouched by the murder of a million Jewish children, priests and their 'blessed people' read, on Holy Innocents' Day, the account of Herod's killing of the new-born. Christmas, with the birth of Jesus from Mary's womb, Easter with the story of the Passion (and Easter week has since the Middle Ages often been the Passion week of the Jews): the whole holy story, as it is re-enacted and recalled as a divine presence in the liturgy, overlooks the Jews, overlooks the *histoire très humaine* of the church.

And this brings us to the second dreadful consequence of this dissolution of world history in the history of salvation: the holy Mother Church – who is also the living Christ – this unspoiled virgin has only a sacred history. In the strict theological sense there is no other history of the church. Naturally there are minor incidents and oddities on the edge of the great central stream which flows from God – *Ecclesia ab Abel* – and which flows back to God through Christ. But of these little incidents, which can always be put down to the climate of the times, the good Catholic does not speak. The task of writing an *histoire sincère* of the church (Charles Seignobos wrote an *Histoire sincère de la Nation Française*) is left to heretics and enemies of the church.

'Rome has no need to defend itself' (Paul vi). Since the only essential history is the history of salvation, the gift of the eternal truths through the eternal Christ in the church, all else – this *entre-deux de peine* – can be left out of account. Church history, as it has been written until very recent times, makes no mention of the Jews in the Middle Ages. The 'monstrous inhumanity' as Martin Buber calls it, of these recurrent 'periods of heightened emotion' (Hans Kühner), in which heretics, Jews, witches and others are persecuted and killed, is thus excused or made to look innocuous – or in most cases completely disregarded.

This disregard is beginning to strike alert Christians, even Catholics. German moral theologians pointed out in a petition to the Second Vatican Council that the church had never officially dissociated itself from the evil events of the past. And the brave archbishop's coadjutor of Strasbourg, A. Elchinger, said in full council: 'Now is the time to admit the historical truth and to make a public confession – even if that truth is bitter.'

The truth about mankind is always bitter. The descent into the hidden depths of the individual soul is a journey through hell. And the self-analysis to which Christianity must subject itself is as perilous as the psychoanalysis of a single person. But only such analysis can make Christianity fruitful again for the future. Openness to the future involves open publication and positive renunciation of the events of the past.

Like deeply neurotic invididuals, the church and Christendom have hitherto concealed their past – and never more resolutely than in times of crisis. It was this neurotic condition of Christianity in the nineteenth and twentieth centuries, as in the third and fourth centuries, in the twelfth and thirteenth centuries, in the late Middle Ages and the sixteenth century, which sparked off civil wars and world wars, conflicts within the church and between the church and the world.

'Dogma is a compulsive striving to overcome doubt. Just as visions are used to banish doubt, so dogma is used to banish heresy.' This interpretation of dogma by the early psychoanalytical thinker Th. Reik – *Dogma und Zwangsidee* (Dogma and Compulsion, *Imago* xiii, Vienna, 1927) and earlier still *Der Eigene und der fremde Gott* (The Personal and the Alien God, Vienna, 1923) – perhaps goes too far, but pinpoints an essential component in the formation of all dogma. Its severity corresponds to the vigorous efforts which the 'true believer' has to make in order to banish the doubt in his own breast and to fix it on the heretic. The stronger his doubt in his own loudly-proclaimed truth (which he does not experience personally and existentially as the truth), the more violently must the enemy outside be combated. The fight against disbelief, that forbidden 'belief' which the individual feels inside him, projects disbelief on to the enemy. And on to the enemy is likewise projected all that is passionately desired in the dark inferno of the Unconscious – the pleasures of sex and enjoyment of worldly goods. Once theologians looked on as the torturers applied their selected instruments to the naked bodies of witches, projecting on to them their own sexual obsessions. Sex-ridden priests projected their scarcely concealed concupiscence on to their victims, the 'bewitched' women. Their own worldliness was projected on to the 'materialistic' Jew, their own immature sexual desires on to the 'lascivious' Jew.

Fanatical and murderous Christian anti-Semitism is a product of the fourth century. During this century, theologians of the main body of the church won a truly bloody battle against Arianism. Arianism had preserved the lore of the early centuries after Christ concerning the man Jesus. But in the battle for a 'personal God' – which was often only a psychological cover name for personal desires, anxieties and power lusts – the Jew Jesus, the son of Miriam, was pushed further and further away into a higher unhistorical world. All the church's better theologians agree that this struggle for Christ's deification went much too far: Jesus Christ was elevated so high above men that ever since humanity has not had its due in the church and in Christianity.

In comparison with Manichaeism, the monophysite doctrine has been a hidden – and sometimes an open – disease of Christianity. Since the fourth century Christian inhumanity has frequently been due to the fact that the God of the Christians – God as their banner, sword or leader into battle – had become so remote. Jesus the man, the friend of prostitutes, publicans and children, the lover of simple people, but also the accomplished theological debater – this whole man Jesus was elevated to a timeless heaven in which he was enthroned and unapproachable.

This dangerous process of deification had three momentous consequences for Christianity and for those 'outsiders' who had the misfortune to come up against these God-fixated Christians during the next fifteen hundred years. The first was the development of a special cult of Mary; secondly, the development of a brutal intolerance towards 'heretics' – that is, those who held other beliefs; and thirdly, the cutting off of Christianity from its roots, from its foundations in the Old Testament and in the piety of the people of Israel.

Let us consider this first development, the special cult of Mary. Important Catholic theologians like Otto Karrer, Karl Rahner and Michael Schmaus have recognized that in the struggle against Arianism in the fourth century 'direct devotion to Christ was replaced by an excessive stress on the divinity of Christ, so that His character as brother and human example was obscured

. . . Many people then proceeded to fill the place formerly occupied by the humanity of Christ, our brother and intercessor, with the merciful figure of Mary, transferring to her all the characteristics of Christ mentioned in the Bible.'

A mediator was needed between them and the remote and awesome Christ-God. This role was filled by the mother of Christ, who remained human and cared for the wretched sinner. Medieval Germany made no distinction in language or thought between God, God the Father and Christ.

'God' is both the Christ-God who has absorbed the Father into His awesome divinity, and God the Father who has absorbed the Son. St Bernard of Clairvaux, whose fanatical warfare against heretics, unbelievers, Islam, Abelard and intellectuals we have already briefly encountered, determined the character of this devotion to Mary for the next five centuries. In a famous sermon he said, for instance, of the text 'For our God is a consuming fire' (Hebrews, 12, 29): 'How should the sinner not fear to be destroyed if he approach God, even as wax melts near the flame?' Therefore we have need of a mediator – Mary.

Mary has a softening effect on her harsh Son, on the anger of this awesome God: she is exalted to the position of 'mediator of all mercies', of 'co-redeemer'. Without Mary, God (Christ) can achieve nothing; her will is law to Him, the Son. The believer flees to Mary, dedicates to her his whole life and his family. Popes have pledged the whole of the human race to the heart of Mary. Mary is the universal remedy against liberalism, questioning intellectuality and doubt, against the spirit of the moderns and Bolshevism.

The harsh popes of the nineteenth century and the Piuses of the twentieth century were extreme devotees of Mary. It was in the time of Pius XII that the dogma of the *assumptio Mariae* was proclaimed – a doctrine which would have been a theological impossibility for St Thomas Aquinas. Pius XII ordered Catholic households to dedicate themselves annually to the Mother of God, meaning that all requests were to be made to Mary. This intense monophysite exaltation of Mary – there exists also a healthy worship of Mary which is not merely the reflection of a lack of humanity in a harsh, masculine church of judges and administrators – fulfils important functions in a clerical church standing outside history. Before Mary all questions are silenced, nothing is discussed. Instead, the children of the church, confused by the wicked world, run to her embrace like obedient children.

This cult of Mary has reached proportions far exceeding those of church orthodoxy, as a result of constant propaganda in church newspapers, pamphlets, sermons and pastoral exhortations. It has also met with all too little opposition from the church and the church's responsible leaders, since they themselves have been driven by their own doubts to the refuge of the bosom of Mary, mediator of all mercies. The cult of Mary has in any case been the most effective means of keeping the masses in a state of infantilism. And this cult, in which Mary was worshipped as the universal remedy against all evil, as the opposite pole to the Devil and the Jew (fanatical worship of Mary and aggressive anti-Semitism often went hand in hand, as in the history of the Franciscan order), has proved to be the best means of postponing the long-overdue self-analysis of the individual believer and the church as a whole.

This Mother of God fulfils really frightening functions in a church which conceals from itself its origin, its past and its future. A troubled German Catholic layman, Kerstiens, has pointed out in this connection how, in specifically Catholic countries, Christianity has been swallowed up by the more primitive and archaic religion of the *magna mater*. The prelate Dr Straubinger wrote from Argentina just before his death a disturbing letter about the devilish way in which the religion of Christ had been supplanted by an extravagant cult of the Madonna in South America. Here God had surrendered all power to Mary, and for most people Christ survived only in the host.

We see Christianity vanishing here without trace in the primeval forest of an ancient mother-religion, as old churches and temples are overgrown by the jungle or buried in the desert sand.

It was the popes of the nineteenth and twentieth centuries who in particular promoted the cult of Mary as a practical and effective spiritual attitude. In this the popes were leaders yielding to the pressure of the masses, who then themselves in their turn were able to lean on the spiritually and mentally retarded leaders of the church. An official ecclesiastical document, a petition to Pius XII signed by more than fifty South American bishops supporting the proclamation of the dogma of the *assumptio Mariae* at the beginning of 1950, refers to the miraculous removal from Ephesus to Loreto of the house where Mary lived and died.

'In their encyclicals concerning the proper worship of the Mother of God, particularly in their recommendation of the use of the rosary, the popes Leo XIII, Pius XI and Pius XII were obviously influenced by Mary's appearances in Lourdes and Fatima' (Kerstiens).

Important theologians of the present day have investigated the authenticity of the Lourdes and Fatima appearances. Whatever the truth may be, the historian can state as a fact that in the nineteenth century the French Catholic church, burdened with neuroses and anxiety, turned to the Mother of God at Lourdes as a political remedy against the evil of the times, against the liberal and Jewish spirit of the age, and against the republic. And it was the same in Portugal; an anxiety-ridden people fled to Mary of Fatima: she would save the country, free it from the revolution and save Russia from Bolshevism.

Such was the solution to the problems of world history envisaged by the masses, kept in a state of infantilism primarily by their own priests and pastors: Mary would save Russia and the human race; she would placate her Son's anger if her sympathy could be gained; otherwise the end would come;

the Last Judgment and the dreadful extermination of the sinful human race.

So here, too, we have *flight from history* – to Mary, who was seen as a panacea, a wonderful image of grace able to triumph over Satan, the Bolshevik the evil spirit of the age, the Jew.

The Jew – the man Jesus – no longer exists in this religion of Mary. The victory of the monophysite conception of Christ in the great dispute in the fourth century opened the way for this gradual development of the cult of Mary.

The second momentous result of this distorting total deification of the man Jesus was the development, in the struggle against Arianism, of a brutal intolerance of heretics and of unorthodox beliefs and opinions, and in particular within the church itself.

This deification of the man Jesus made impossible psychic demands on the 'barbarians' of the fourth century. It would have been much healthier for most people if they had turned at that time to Arian Christianity, or had not been torn violently away from it, as were the Ostrogoths and Visigoths. A more human conception of Christ would not have made such colossal demands on the spiritual resources of the individual, the theologians and the church. Arian people remained tolerant. But as soon as they became Roman Catholics they succumbed to an aggressive intolerance. In the face of heathens, 'unbelievers' and the remaining Arians the exclusivity of a Christ-God could only be defended at great psychic cost, especially when this God was the subject of deep and unavowed doubts within His advocates themselves.

The deification of the Jew Jesus of Nazareth demanded too much of the spiritual and mental resources of Christianity. In the raging struggles of theologians in the fourth, twelfth and sixteenth centuries – Lutheran theologians raged as violently against the neo-Arian Socinian-Unitarians as against the Jews – the dangerous phenomenon arose of people transferring their own doubts about the divinity of Jesus on to those enemies who would not acknowledge belief in this God. This was bound to have particularly disastrous results, since there was never a victory to point to. Illness and death – declared by St Paul to have been conquered in Christ – plague, violence, hunger, wretchedness and spiritual affliction continued to exist, within the church as in the rest of the world, just as clearly as in the times before Christ's ascension.

The spiritual resources of most Christians, even today, would cope much more easily with a conception of Christ that was nearer to the more human Arian conception. To profess, in the midst of millions of unbelievers, belief in a Christ-God who lived as a human being on earth – and to profess it not only with one's lips but in one's whole way of life – this calls for a mental and spiritual maturity so far attained by only very few.

Hölderlin's complaint in *Hyperion* that the Germans had become even more barbaric as a result of religion still applies to all the barbarian peoples from the fourth to the twentieth centuries. Their exclusive Christ-God became for them a dreadful weapon of self-assertion directed both outwards and inwards, into their own breasts, where all doubts were 'mortified' – the word 'mortification', a keyword of a certain brand of Christian asceticism, is revealing in a most sinister way.

This Christ-God led inwards on to the battle-fields of the soul, and outwards on to the actual battle-fields of the Crusades. The Mohammedan Arabs were taken completely by surprise by the First Crusade. In Arab and other Islamic countries people had lived for centuries in peaceful co-existence. As early as the thirteenth century, Crusades overseas gave way to Crusades within Europe, which were considered by leading theologians and canon-lawyers of the church as worthier causes – campaigns against heretics, Albigenses, Waldenses, Wends, Hussites, Protestants, liberals and Socialists.

The maturity necessary for belief in a Man-God, Christ, can only be gained by those who have prepared themselves in body and mind, who have not abandoned the dialogue with their doubts in their own hearts – a dialogue in which, as Reinhold Schneider has stated, belief nourishes doubt and doubt nourishes belief. It can only be acquired by those who are ready and able to subject themselves to self-analysis, for whom life itself is a constant process of self-analysis, an endless journey through the hell of their own depths – *descensus ad infernos*. Only at this depth, the depths inhabited by the Eumenides below the temples of the Acropolis (the superstructure of the consciousness) – only by this journey through hell can rebirth and the releasing of creative forces be won.

This is at the root of the sterility of so-called Christian art in the eighteenth to twentieth centuries and of the well-known hostility of many clerics towards art or any creative activity. Spiritual and intellectual sterilization is the fate of anyone who recoils from the descent into his own depths, or who does not daily experience both despair and the confident will to resist.

The great missionary Charles de Foucauld (previously a life-loving soldier) who lived among and was eventually killed by nomads in North Africa during the First World War, came to the conclusion that for these people and for the North African 'barbarians' Mohammedanism was the most appropriate religion. Christianity was not suitable for their state of consciousness or for their level of intellectual development. (His spiritual descendants, the Community of the Little Brothers of Charles de Foucauld, have renounced the task of conversion.)

If this discovery of Foucauld's had been made by the aggressive church leaders of the fourth century, they would not have had to 'mortify' so cruelly their own doubts about their Christ-God by persecuting Arians, Jews and heathens.

History shows that the peoples of North Africa and Spain were mostly converted overnight to Mohammedanism – without any compulsion – since the devotional style of this religion, which also includes elements of Jewish and Christian origin, bore a closer relation to their general intellectual and spiritual disposition than did the compulsory belief in a Christ-God far removed from the history of mankind.

A small body of ecclesiastical theologians and Christian laymen today have worked out certain practical measures – now already under way – to root out this thousand-year-old intolerance of Islam and other world religions such as Buddhism (in the Catholic Middle Ages Buddha was worshipped under slightly different guise as a saint of the church, in accordance with the legend of Barlaam and Josaphat). But such measures can become historically effective only when Christianity has put down roots again in the piety and spirituality of Israel, in the soil of the Old Testament, in the piety of the Jew Jesus.

Our present-day Christianity is like the huge trees on the slopes of the Alps which are ripped up in storms because they are rooted among rocks and not in deep soil. 'Upon this rock I will build my church.' These words of Christ, often invoked in self-justification by Petrine mysticism and the papal church, were frequently disastrously misinterpreted in history. Jesus never intended to uproot His disciples, to tear them from the parent soil of Israel. Simone Weil, the great Jewess who is so close to Christianity, has recognized that the masses in the industrial age need to put down roots. *Only through self-analysis can Christianity re-establish its roots in the ancient soil of its Jewish fatherland.* This self-analysis leads back to the Jew Jesus, and to the rich streams of Jewish piety and spirituality; and these streams can only be tapped by a recognition and condemnation of Christianity's murder of their Christ over the centuries in His blood-relations, the Jews.

This painful process, which can only offer a solution to the future by the positive dissolution of the past, may be briefly illustrated by two Christian examples, one Protestant, one Catholic.

'The church needs the Jews; the Jews need the church; those who belong to each other need each other . . . God entered into an eternal covenant with Israel. This was not annulled by the Crucifixion but – as the prophets promised – extended to include the heathens. The new covenant grew out of the old. At bottom there is only one unrevoked covenant, by which God has united Israel and the other races, both to Himself and to each other. The fact that Jews and Christians have a different apprehension of God and the world is not a violation of the covenant. God has chosen both for salvation, and makes history with both.'

This was written by the Protestant theologian Dietrich Goldschmidt and Hans-Joachim Kraus in the foreword to their account of the transactions of the Tenth Evangelical Church Congress in Berlin (20–2 July 1961) which considered relations between Christians and Jews.

The Protestant opponents of these public discussions attacked their conclusions as a betrayal of church history. Exactly the same arguments were
used at the Curia in Rome by cardinals, bishops and theologians who wanted
to preserve the long-standing anti-Jewish tradition of the church. What is
here called a betrayal we can see in a more positive light as the melting of a
petrified mass.

The gallant Protestant delegates in Berlin in 1961 dared to make the following conclusions: where Jesus is no more than a memory, a phenomenon
of the past, people need atomic weapons to survive. The exodus from history
will be followed by an exodus – by means of suicide and murder – from the
earth into a worse hereafter. Even today, theologians and churchmen who
have written terrible things about the Jews do not show any remorse.
(Remorse would of course require rigorous self-analysis.) The Calvinist
Dutch Reformed church has shown greater sympathy with Israel than the
Lutheran, Catholic and Orthodox churches. St Paul was already fighting
against the church's dangerous tendency to usurp Israel's place when he
struggled with this temptation within his own breast. The church, as younger
sister of the Chosen People, must readjust its views. Israel remains the
Chosen People. We Christians have by our own conduct made the name of
Jesus stink in Jewish nostrils – such were the words of an Anglican bishop.
Christian books on religion let Jewish history end with the year AD 70. The
subsequent liquidation of the Jews has been staged by the Christians on
their own.

These German Protestant theologians also dared in 1961 to proclaim what
remained unspoken in 1945: that a direct line leads from Luther to Julius
Streicher and *Der Stürmer*, and to the murder of Jews perpetrated in the
world it represented. The Lateran Council of 1215 prepared the way for this
development. The conservative, Protestant-controlled state policy of
Germany towards the Jews in the nineteenth and twentieth centuries provides
surprising parallels with the Jewish policy of Soviet Russia.

Christian theologians still rage today against the Jews, totally unaffected
by all that has happened. The elements of insecurity, fear and arrogance in
German nationalism strengthen German anti-Semitism. The German anti-
Communism of today is the heir of German anti-Semitism. The inadequate
response of Protestant theology to the Jewish catastrophe has continued from
1932 right up to the present.

The Protestant church remained silent on the 'final solution'. At Easter
1943 Christian laymen in Bavaria approached their bishop to protest against
the church's silence. 'But the church remained silent.' Only Bishop Wurm
dared to approach the Nazi government in 1943 about the extermination of
the Jews.

The indecision of the church continued after 1945. In 1948 a warning was
issued to Protestant pastors: 'Guard against any form of anti-Semitism.'
Christmas 1959/60 saw a new wave of anti-Semitism. In 1960 there was a

joint Catholic-Protestant educationalists' conference in Bergneustadt which produced six recommendations for the writing of religious books and the teaching of religion.

The Berlin theologian Helmut Gollwitzer said of the overwhelming majority of Protestant Christians: 'On this question of the Jews, there is in our congregations as yet simply no recognition of the fact that, after living with the Jews for fifteen hundred years in Germany and in the other countries of Europe, we Christians have reached the point where we cannot look a Jew straight in the face. And this is due precisely to the failure of our Christian witness towards them, the total witness of word and action which would have made them welcome guests, and which would, in the words of St Paul (Romans 11), have provoked them to jealousy of the splendours of the Gospel. This did not happen; the history of Jewry in Germany as in the other countries of Europe is a history of dreadful suffering inflicted on the Jews by the Christians.'

The most important conclusions reached at the Berlin congress in 1961 were that the church is the younger sister of Judaism; that throughout history, and right up to the present day, the Jews have been bearers of the Cross to an incomparably greater extent than the victorious church: and that most theologians and leaders of the church have still to embark on the necessary readjustment of their views. In this connection a significant question was posed: why have the Jews always been attacked as the murderers of Christ, and never thought of as the race which gave us Christ?

Let us now place a Catholic example beside this Protestant invitation to self-analysis by the church and by Christianity.

On 8 March 1965 the Catholic rector and theologian Heinrich Spaemann broadcast a talk on Jews, Christians and the New Testament in the Südwestfunk radio in Baden-Baden. In it he said:

In our thinking and our attitude towards Israel we have been guilty of three sins. Firstly, we have doubted God's loyalty to the people whom He singled out from among all the others to be His chosen people, to whom He revealed Himself and to whom He entrusted the task of transmitting the revelation to the rest of humanity ... Jesus knew He had been sent as a partner of the old Sinai covenant. Israel was to be the source of salvation. Salvation comes from the Jews ... For who are the firstlings of the Redemption? Mary, the apostles, the disciples, the eye-witnesses of the Resurrection, the first Pentecostal gathering, the apostle of the peoples – St Paul – and all of them are Jews ... We have only noticed the thief on the left of the Cross, not the one on the right. Both were Jews. The whole of the eleventh chapter of St Paul's Epistle to the Romans is directed against the idea that the Jews were the *former* Chosen People.

The second sin in our attitude to Israel is the identification of this people with the Crucifixion of Jesus ... We have preserved in our memories the misdeeds of this race and effaced its virtues. We have nailed this people to its guilt, as if the Crucifixion did not imply just as much its redemption as our own . . . and as if it were permissible even for a single instant for one who has himself been redeemed by Jesus's Crucifixion to go on nailing another to his guilt. Whoever does that is continuing to crucify Jesus Himself.

Our third sin is presumption. We have behaved as if we ourselves had no share in the Crucifixion of Jesus, as if similar things had not happened in our own lifetime – and in our own country and among our own people. And in what a dreadful form did it happen, among us and through us . . . As Jesus identified Himself with the innocent children of Bethlehem (and the church acknowledges that in celebrating their memory), how can we doubt for one moment that He was identified with the millions who lost their lives in Auschwitz?

Israel and Jewry had survived constant persecution throughout the centuries. 'Then came the darkest hour, the time of unspeakable torture and mass-murder in the gas-chambers under Hitler. Jewry suffered a passion as painful as the Passion and Crucifixion of Jesus. And out of this night of suffering and death arose the resurrection of Israel as a nation.

'God allowed this people to survive the fluctuations of fortune and the appalling catastrophes of world history in order to lead it to its final salvation. What an event – and how much should it stir Christianity in preparing for the Day of Judgment! Stir it, above all, to awareness of its bonds with the first-born people of God – its elder brother in God's inheritance.

'Herod was reincarnated in Hitler. Among those Hitler murdered were more than a million children. This happened some twenty years ago. Herod's child massacre took place two thousand years ago. On that occasion perhaps twenty children were killed. We should be grossly irresponsible – especially we in Germany – if we continued to remember the Jewish children of Bethlehem in our liturgy, our sermons and catechisms, while keeping silent before our altars and obliterating from our memories the extermination, for similar reasons, of the millions in Auschwitz and elsewhere. If we were not to remember these victims, it would make it appallingly clear how liturgy can become an end in itself, a harmless ritual drained of any appeal to the conscience, a mere glorification of its own existence.

'May I say once more: How can one celebrate the festival of the Holy Innocents of Bethlehem, enriching it with an attractive folk-lore, while remaining quite unmoved by the appalling fact that twenty years ago more than a million innocent children were murdered by a Herod produced by our nation and speaking our language? Not to mention the other millions who were killed in the most dreadful way, simply because they belonged to the race of Israel. This is beyond all comprehension. It shows what *can* happen to our church services, not what *must* happen. Instead of being an occasion for an encounter with truth – the truth which faces us today – they can become mere routine in which everything is pre-arranged – an imposition by means of which one discharges one's responsibility. When God becomes an imposition one is really dispensing with Him.

'The greatest obstacle in the way of Christians overcoming their strange indifference towards the fate of Jews in particular – and they bear responsibility for Auschwitz, possibly Christianity's greatest defeat by not having prevented such things – is the idea, still deeply rooted in many minds today, that the Jews are the people who crucified Jesus.'

Rector Spaemann refuted this charge of Jewish guilt. Pope Paul VI revived it again in a sermon on Monte Mario on Passion Sunday, 1965, which provoked two leading Jewish personalities in Italy to write a telegram of protest to Cardinal Secretary of State Cicognani. Spaemann observed:

From the theological point of view, Jesus was crucified in every part of the world . . . Israel was and is the people of humanity. It has never been able to think without God, and thus has never been separate from the rest of humanity . . . It was standing for all sinners when once the proud and mighty among it crucified Jesus. And can we any longer overlook the fact that it was Israel, once more standing for the whole of humanity in its irrevocable closeness to Jesus, that has borne in unspeakable sufferings (which the other races of the world were spared) the consequences of that sinfulness which led us all, Jews and Gentiles, to crucify Jesus?

No other race on earth has shared with Jesus this suffering unto death to the same extent as the Jews. And Christians inflicted this suffering, thereby in their own fashion piercing the heart of their God. Fifty years ago Léon Bloy said of anti-Semitism in Christians: 'The most dreadful blow which the Lord received in the course of His still-continuing Passion is the blow struck by Christians at the face of His Jewish mother.' What would Léon Bloy have said only thirty years later?

It appears to us, as we said before, as if this crucifixion of the Jews, which has continued for almost two thousand years, reached its final culmination in the appalling horrors which were perpetrated by the German people during the Third Reich; as if, therefore, even in the furnaces of Auschwitz and all the other dreadful places, Heaven had repeated the words of the hour of Golgotha: *Consummatum est* – it is finished. For out of this very night of darkness and death, as it seems to us, came the beginnings of the resurrection of Israel which was foretold in Ezekiel Chapter 37.

The Catholic theologian Spaemann declared that the duty of Christians was now 'to recognize and love this people as our elder brother in God's inheritance. Only recognition of the brother can lead to recognition of God, for him and for us.' The Christian will only become a whole human being 'when the confession of guilt owed by Ecclesia to Synagogue has been publicly proclaimed: a confession such as Paul VI addressed to our Christian brothers who are separated from us – only here we are dealing with quite different abysses of guilt.'

We might comment here that these abysses of guilt could only be acknowledged by a Christian – and then later on by a church – who has, by means of self-analysis, classified the history of his life and of the church, going right back to the Jew Jesus and to the early church's reactions to the delay in the Second Coming of the Messiah.

Spaemann asked further: 'What is it that divides us? . . . And how can we cross this divide? It is a question we have not considered for centuries. Should we not follow St Paul's example and bidding to the Jews, and become Jews ourselves in order to speak with them as brother to brother? But who takes this idea seriously? Who is making a serious attempt to know and love this people?'

According to Spaemann, the Jews possess a 'dynamic power of action' lacking in Christians. They are always putting it into practice 'always eager to give concrete form to the duties of the covenant'. Zealous observance of the faith was and is more common in Israel than in Christianity. 'God's special grace to the Jews both urged and enabled them to act. They received this grace manifestly when the Word was made flesh in one of their race. In Christ's Gospel the emphasis on action and realization is unmistakeable!'

Action and realization: here today and tomorrow. We may complete Spaemann's thought by saying that Christians who worship the exalted monophysite Christ-God escape responsibility here and now by referring it 'upwards'. To continue with Spaemann: 'If we have a tendency to see things the wrong way round, and if this brings about, in large areas of Christianity, a glaring disparity between doctrine and life, between the spirit and the real world, this is because we have allowed ourselves to be too much influenced by Greek and Platonic ways of thought, *instead of letting our own roots feed us*. [My italics.] And this came about because we were only a church of Gentiles, estranged from Israel.

'What are the implications of a church of Gentiles without a church of Jews? Firstly, that there was, taking into consideration the whole of Christianity, above all a lack of the charismatic urge to action, which was a feature of the Jews. Secondly, that a conception of the church asserted itself which was far too static, abstract and unhistorical; and that Christianity still largely lacks the vital awareness, which Israel could have contributed, of being one family with the people of Abraham, with God's first Chosen People. Israel would have brought this awareness as a heritage. And thirdly, that we know all about political alliances and their scope, but pathetically little in our hearts about God's covenant.' Here we might interpolate: NATO and other military alliances have replaced the alliance between God's people and God. In this sense the Protestant theologian Gollwitzer could justifiably say at the Berlin Congress in 1961: 'Where Jesus is only a memory, a figure of the past, one must needs use the weapons of this world to survive; Christianity must be defended with atomic weapons and people kept within the church by political pressure. And with all this nothing will be achieved.'

Spaemann went on: 'But the words "covenant with God", which are so absolutely essential for Israel, are very remote for many Christians, who therefore cannot sufficiently appreciate the priceless consequences to be gained from an existence within and based upon this covenant.

'The fourth point follows on from here – a lack of belief in the Promised Land, and a lack of courage for the exodus into the desert, for the journey into the kingdom of God with the dynamic, non-complacent existence that it implies.

'Fifthly it implies a lack of that Messianic impatience peculiar to the Jews, which the last words of Jesus in the Bible – "Surely, I come quickly" – were designed to raise and keep alive in us.'

'Surely, I come quickly.' *But the longed-for Christ did not come quickly. Generations of Christians waited for His return and constantly found themselves being told by Jews that Christ's failure to come was proof that the Jew Jesus was not the true Messiah.* In his study *Über den Hass* (On Hatred) Manès Sperber remarked: 'Behind all the theological disputes and countless heresies [during the first centuries of the Christian era] was the great question of the Second Coming. For without this Second Coming there was a danger that the Messianic claim of Christianity could become the fraud of which the Jews never tired of accusing the Christians. F.Lovsky quotes a text from the fourth century on the Second Coming, without which it is impossible to believe in the First, since the latter has not fulfilled all prophecies. For this reason the Jews refuse to believe: since the prophecies concerning the glorious coming have not yet been realized. They do not believe that it was the Messiah who came at that time.'

F.Lovsky said of this fourth-century text: 'The further the hopes of the church receded, the more powerful anti-Semitism became within the bosom of Christianity. In the fourth century, in which the theological anti-Semitic theses triumphed, the City of God gradually repressed the hope of an eschatological kingdom in Christian thought and faith. We may certainly ask whether it was not Christ's delay in coming that was the cause of certain reproaches being made against the Jews.'

To this Manès Sperber replied: 'The facts speak for themselves. There can be no doubt about cause and effect. The baptized were subjected to the same terrors and catastrophes as before the Redemption; the earth was not transformed into the Kingdom of God; death prevailed as before; neither sickness nor chaos disappeared; neither the slavery or misery of the poor, nor the pride of the mighty were broken. For all these reasons the eschatological hope had to be abandoned and replaced by excuses which instilled fear in the hearts of the doubters. Henceforth they would say that it was "obstinacy" that made the Jews refuse to believe in the birth and divinity of their brother, Jesus of Nazareth. They would say that it was the crime of this people, who threw away their spiritual and worldly heritage and thus prevented the Second Coming. [The same sort of argument was used by the churches in the Middle Ages and later, much more vehemently, by Martin Luther.] And they would proclaim that a curse burdened this race which had "murdered" Christ.

'Until the fourth century, however, the Jews often lived well and prosperously and even enjoyed great riches throughout the Roman Empire. But now it had to be shown that they were responsible for the failure of the

Messiah to return. From then on they were set apart, subjected to ignominious laws and systematically humiliated in order to demonstrate their exclusion from salvation to the whole Christian world . . . That insane propaganda of hate, whose consequences we still see today, particularly where God has been deposed, then joined forces with that extraordinary invention which was to plunge the souls of the faithful into a permanent state of fear – that is to say, with the threat of hell, which in its pious trappings now began to terrorize mankind . . . It was proclaimed that the Devil was to be found everywhere: and he was most to be feared in those matters in which he made use of his most faithful servants – the apostates and the Jews.

'It was precisely the magnificent cathedrals, those royal graves of an extinguished hope, those fortresses of the *ecclesia triumphans*, which proclaimed the final defeat of eschatological Christianity. The Christianity of the churches no longer looked to the future, to a Second Coming, but sought to justify itself by its past record, by the sufferings of the saints who had everywhere displaced the old local divinities. The cult of the Madonna and Child answered the needs of souls longing for the goddesses of fertility and love. Illiteracy protected the people from any doubts which might have been aroused by reading the Bible. Those who appealed to Holy Writ were condemned as heretics and cast aside.'

That applied to the Middle Ages and indeed was the case up to the nineteenth century. Church bans on the Bible being read in the language of the people were very frequent in the late Middle Ages and recurred right into the nineteenth century. But no ban could overcome the doubt, the sorrow and the hatred deep down in the human personality and in the collective consciousness of the church.

Once more we find ourselves in the fourth century, in that unhappy key period of Christendom. Who was responsible for the failure of the Messiah to return, for the obvious corruption of the church, for the withdrawal of intellectuals – and not only in the circle of Julian the Apostate – and for the defection of the ordinary people from Christianity?

Naturally, the Jew was to blame. It was he who declared 'cynically' and 'subversively', as it has been said all the way from the fourth to the twentieth centuries, that the Jew Jesus was not the Messiah. The Jews were waiting, hoping and suffering in expectation of the true Messiah, who would establish the kingdom of God on earth, a kingdom of joy and freedom, of peace and justice – here on this earth, and for all mankind.

The Jew was to blame. In the minds of anxious, despairing Christians there arose this unspoken conviction (which even today is deeply repressed and passed over in silence) that *the Jew Jesus was to blame*. The Jew Jesus had to be repressed. In His place was set a king of heaven who had nothing in common with the happy and confident young Jew from Galilee who made His way through the regions of the Holy Land abundant with flowers, vines and fish, proclaiming the Gospel of the impending kingdom of God.

From the fourth to the twentieth centuries the Christians' murderous hatred of the Jews was, at bottom, directed against the Jew Jesus, of whom Christians despaired, whom they hated and blamed – with the Devil and the Jews – for the heavy burden of history. The Jew Jesus was killed off in thousands of images: Christ, the emperor and king of Heaven, assumed imperial, papal, royal and Jupiter-like features. Such was still the case in Michelangelo's time. The Jew Jesus was to blame. We can now understand the trembling indignation with which Cardinal Faulhaber defended himself against the charge of having taken up the cause of the Jews and defended Pope Pius XI against the monstrous charge of being half-Jewish in origin.

A psychoanalytical investigation of Christian theologians and laymen, of princes of the church and their flocks, might often provide an insight into this abyss in the depths of the soul where there is hatred for the Jew Jesus.

In 1952 the psychoanalysis of a thirty-year-old Catholic woman revealed that deep down this woman prayed to Wotan. It was uniquely symbolic of how a German Catholic could lapse into the Nazi faith, believing that salvation could come from Hitler. This woman composed in the process of analysis the following poem:

> When that other pale and gentle God from Nazareth
> has ceased to suffer and rattle in His throat
> and, dying, is laid in the grave,
> then, indeed, O Mighty One, your time will come!
> With raging breath, Lord of the winds, you will go forth
> and drive the clouds and waves furiously before you.
> The ripening world, seared by the deathly spirit of Golgotha,
> will burst forth again ever more fruitfully at your touch.
> How the fields will swell in your morning radiance
> and the roaring sea echo your voice,
> in which the last cry is stifled on the Cross!
> My soul shouts with joy for you.
> Freed from Heaven's dominion, I can hate again
> and take up my sword with heady courage.
> Already the steel whistles through the air
> and with awesome horror I breathe the scent
> of warm blood!

'Freed from Heaven's dominion, I can hate again.' From the heyday of the Middle Ages, at least, very many Christians could only believe in the Devil. *In this Devil the Jew Christ was absorbed.*

'Take up my sword with heady courage.' Christ, the sword of the German and Western Middle Ages, the leader, *Truchtin* or *Trochtin* and lord of hosts led His men to the Crusades and killed the Jews and the Jew Jesus.

It would be simple to demonstrate in a very striking way this 'Christian' hatred of the Jew Jesus. If, say, in Easter Week, in hundreds of cathedrals and churches in town and country, a large picture were put up overnight above the altar, showing a thirty-year-old Jew as Jesus racked with pain, there would be a cry of horror and indignation. And this would be because it had laid bare the profound concealment and repression which attaches to the Jew Jesus and his whole Jewish tribe. For many clerics and laymen, princes of the church and pastors, such a picture of a young Jew – say, a photograph taken shortly before the victim was gassed in 1944 – would appear to be a terrible blasphemy.

But it is only by a self-analysis of the Christian man and his church, which takes us into and through the hell of Christian hatred of the Jew, that one will find the key to the past and its roots, and from there to the future.

If this understanding is achieved, first in the hearts of individuals and then in the knowledge, conscience, and consciousness of the church and Christendom, then very great energies will be released – energies and radiations from Israel's potential, from its piety and experience of God and the world.

By rooting itself in its true soil, Christianity would achieve the great acceptance of the world – the acceptance of 'earthly' love. Only Eros can dissolve the neuroses and pathological self-isolation of Christianity in relation to the Jew Jesus, to Man's history and to itself.

This great acceptance of the world, of love and of sexual love between man and woman, is bound up with the acceptance of God in history. In history the God who is to come demands obedience – in thought, action, and suffering: in the daily assumption of political and social responsibility towards one's fellow-men. A Christendom which ran away from history denounced the future and abandoned it to enthusiasts, Communists, 'Utopians' and 'fools'. Attempts to inject Messianic and eschatological elements into a historically feeble and inflexible body were denounced – and still often are today – as Utopian.

A Christendom which ran away from the world was able for centuries to disregard the Jew and the outsider, the enslavement of peoples and the terrorizing of the bodies and souls of so many Christians. Indeed, it was able to justify all that by gazing upwards towards the 'eternal values' and a God who was constantly insulted by immodest and impermissible questions.

A Christendom enriched by Israel and Jewish piety would recognize that the so-called eternal values are only true and genuine when they are made incarnate, when they become flesh in history and when they are realized in the society of Man. Otherwise, they are a pseudo-ideology, a camouflage-ideology, a mask for ends which are, in fact, aggressively pursued on this earth: highly material interests for which religious orders have furiously fought against other orders, bishops against bishops, abbots against abbots, and popes against emperors, kings and spiritual and worldly princes.

The Jew has received the call to submit all religions to the judgment of criticism and self-criticism and to show them up as new attempts to construct the Tower of Babel. The prophets employed this destructive criticism when dealing with the temple, the priests of the temple and their kings. The prophetic heritage lives on today, in its secular form in men like Marx and Freud, and in its religious form in the brilliant minds of Judaism and Christianity.

The Jew is said to be materialistic. But the Creation, the whole world and all matter is of God. The great acceptance of matter – Pierre Teilhard de Chardin's *Messe sur le Monde* – can only take root in Christian and post-Christian men and women, if they seek a religious soil for it in the acceptance of the world, in the books, songs and living experience of Jews steeped in God and the world.

The Jew is said to be lascivious and worldly. But the much-deplored emphasis on sex, the sex-wave of a society possessed by the devil of sex, can only be banished in a positive sense by a spirituality, a piety and an experience of the body which introduces to the present age the joyous knowledge of the Song of Songs. A pious and profound consideration of Chagall's pictures of love, which are inspired by a Jewish and Chassidim concept of love, could bring salvation to Christians and relieve them of their complexes. For they have allowed their eyes, hearts and souls to be corrupted by sexless pictures of the 'sweet lord Jesus', by homosexual pictures of angels and lascivious pictures of Mary Magdalene.

The Jew is said to stand for world revolution and to prepare the world for liberalism, Socialism and Communism. But both Jew and Christian are called on – and indeed are under an obligation – actively and passively to promote the 'world revolution' of the kingdom of God in a Messianic spirit of expectation.

The Jew is said to be a pacifist. The production of vast quantities of war materials appears to Christians and post-Christians to play a necessary role in safeguarding physical and spiritual values in the present state of transition. In his active (and sometimes leading) participation in international organizations the Jew is constantly reminding his fellow-men that God intends this earth to be a place of justice and peace. Every struggle, every effort made on behalf of justice and peace is a service to God and to Man. 'The good God is to be found in small things.' True piety is attested, renewed and reborn every day in the service of one's fellow-men. After what has happened – and if the same or worse is not to continue to happen – Christians need, in addition to a sense of private sin, a feeling of responsibility which takes cognizance of Man's violations, persecutions and killings in this world: and not merely the violation of a young girl who achieves canonization like Maria Goretti.

Church fathers, monastic reformers, humanists and apostles of enlightenment have all raised the cry: *ad fontes*, back to the sources and origins. But they have understood and practised this in very different ways. Today and tomorrow, the call *ad fontes* would mean, for a Christendom which felt a complete sense of responsibility towards humanity, an opening up of sources which have often been poisoned at an early stage, and then become silted up and stagnant. Honest hope, the *docta spes* of a spiritual and religious rebirth, could be achieved by a self-analysis of Christianity.

Today aggrieved Christians and aggrieved Jews confront each other. Both have often very little idea of how to cope with the monstrous challenge to which they have been subjected: a challenge to liberate themselves in a positive sense, to release their own basic potential.

It is fashionable to speak today of friendly relations amongst the religions of the world. Islam and Buddhism have now come into the Christians' field of vision. Interblending and mutual infusions could enrich, fertilize and open up all the world religions in their process of development. But no religion requires an interblending and an infusion – of Jewish piety and spirituality – as much as Christianity: an infusion of the experience of a thousand years of suffering, of the great Crucifixion – not self-crucifixion and killing. The 'worldly' Jew can perform for Christians a spiritual task of the greatest importance, if both understand the vital importance of the monstrous challenge to which they are subjected: a call to open up the ultimate sources and potentials revealing, unlocking and deciphering their own history with all its virtues and errors.

Exhausted by the terrible blood-letting, very many Jews in the West take refuge in the shells they have built for themselves in industrial society. The Israelis have other preoccupations than that of returning *ad fontes*, to the sources. All their strength is needed in the struggle to survive in the face of the Arab states. It must fall to the Jewish Diaspora to take up the work of intellectual and spiritual rebirth. As in Christendom, a number of religious thinkers and divines are engaged in this task.

But at the moment a large proportion of so-called world Jewry refuses to see the danger which threatens not only the Jew, but all minorities, special groups, non-conformists, outsiders and heretics who do not accept the opinion of the majority, exactly as in the incubation period of National Socialism. A courageous Viennese Jew with Socialist views, Fritz Flesch, has for years been conducting, together with his wife, a lonely struggle in Detroit against the ostrich-like policy of leading South African Jews and their collaborators in America and elsewhere, against a persistent effort to ignore the racial policy of the South African government. Another Viennese Jew, Karl Kraus, conducted, single-handed, a thirty years' war against a Viennese press busy provoking the events which led up to the First World War.

Since many Jews today adopt the same sort of attitudes as were adopted in the past fifty years – attitudes which in Europe led to the rise of Hitler – they should ponder these words: 'However much malicious people may warn against Jewish solidarity, the fact remains that it does not exist and must not be allowed to arise!' Hitler proved the correctness of this terrible judgment, which comes from Walther Rathenau, one of the greatest and most significant Jewish minds of our century.

The concept of solidarity is just as misunderstood by Jewish charitable organizations, which have mobilized large sums of money, as it is by the church's charity workers: as if solidarity should, or must, be concerned exclusively or mainly, with charitable work! A solidarity which does not take into account the whole political, social, and mental situation of both persecuted and persecutors is nothing but a particular form of collaboration with the persecutors. Charitable work which is only concerned with material aspects, and disregards the general issues concerning all involved, is at least as suspect as the conception of the Red Cross as a means of supporting war, whereas Henri Dunant founded it as an active weapon *against* war.

Solidarity which takes the form of material help exclusively for one's own 'ghetto' group overlooks the fact that in a sick civilization the Jew – and the Christian – can only be helped if the sicknesses of society are treated by education and sheer hard work. The vast funds at present being devoted to suicidal armaments should be harnessed to this cause.

Let us for a moment consider once again that specifically Jewish failure to grasp the international threat of the period 1914–39. It will help us to get into perspective the extent of today's failure. Josué Jéhouda pointed out that in the period 1914–32 European Jews reacted weakly and quite helplessly to the protracted offensives against them in the press, literature, and politics. The assimilated and converted Jews indeed reacted by themselves adopting the lies of anti-Semitism. Racial anti-Semitism attacked a Jewry which was morally dislocated and divided into many warring clans: a resigned Jewry without hope for the future, spiritually amorphous and victim to scepticism and anxiety. This Western Jewry met the attacks of anti-Semitism in a mood of fatalistic resignation.

Neither in Europe nor in America was emancipated Jewry capable of developing a doctrine, a teaching, a philosophy or idea to counter the lies and attacks of racial anti-Semitism everywhere. Only small isolated groups took up the fight. But the great Jewish organizations sabotaged these efforts: they were only interested in philanthropic aid for individual victims of anti-Semitism.

Like the churches, these Jewish organizations laboured under a double delusion, a mortal form of self-deception. Civil war, which is spreading today on an international scale through all societies and generations, and even among individuals, cannot be overcome by charitable work. Nuclear war, total war, cannot be prevented by the Red Cross, nor by agreements on 'clean atomic weapons' from showing its true face. It is genocide, the murder and suicide of entire peoples, and it follows logically from the genocide and murder of six million Jews.

Anti-Semitism is the most obvious manifestation of a sick civilization which prepares its own catastrophes by not knowing how to cope with its own inner complexes and growth problems. And one of the reasons in this case is because the wisdom of great Jewish doctors and teachers like Jesus of Nazareth, Maimonides, Spinoza and Freud is either disregarded or perverted.

The great question for Judaism and Christianity now and in the future is primarily this: will those isolated individuals, the great doctors of the soul and the spirit and the teachers produced by European Jewry in the nineteenth and twentieth centuries, be able to exert an influence over the broad masses of human society that slumber and stagnate in a cosmopolitan civilization divorced from history or settle down in archaic spiritual states, uninterested in the problems of truth and reality?

In terms of spirituality and mental and psychological alertness there are wide and dangerous gaps between the leaders of Jewish intellectual life and the majority of Jews, as there are also in Christendom, where men like Dietrich Bonhoeffer, Alfred Delp and Reinhold Schneider seem to be as far removed from the mentality of the church-going masses as Neanderthal Man was from the Greek of the fifth century B C.

The intellectual isolation of Martin Buber in modern Israel has its counterpart in the isolation of great Jewish and Christian spiritual minds throughout the nineteenth and twentieth centuries.

Simon Dubnow, a great historian and man of learning, was shot dead by a Latvian militiaman when the National Socialists liquidated the Riga ghetto in the night 7–8 December 1941.

'God is so near to me.' These were the words Simon Dubnow wrote in his diary in 1910, as he recalled his Chassidim grandfather, Rabbi Bentsion. Dubnow experienced the Russian pogroms organized by the régime of Tsar Nicholas II in 1903–5. In 1915, as a result of Dubnow's writings, Maxim Gorki, Leonid Andreyev, Fedor Sologub and others founded a league to combat anti-Semitism. On 9 June 1917 Simon Dubnow spoke at a great Jewish meeting in St Petersburg. Russia, he said, was standing between revolution and counter-revolution. Could the oldest civilized people in the world, which had had its own great social revolutionaries in the prophets two thousand years ago (who dared to say to their kings what was now being said to the deposed tsar), accept without protest the present anarchy – this childhood illness of culturally backward nations? It was true, Dubnow said, that some of the demagogues came from Jewish circles. They worked under cover of Russian pseudonyms because they were ashamed of their Jewish origins (Trotsky, Zinoviev and others). But it would be better to say that their Jewish names were pseudonyms, for they were not rooted in the Jewish people.

Opposing the Bolsheviks, Dubnow declared himself for the democratic revolution and for pacifism as the thousand-year-old heritage of Judaism. On 23 April 1922 he left Russia.

Simon Dubnow believed that Jews were, above all, a spiritual nation.

Every generation of Jews carried within it the remnants and ruins of vanished worlds through which the Jewish people had passed. The Jews lived as a cultural and spiritual nation in the midst of political nations.

Dubnow founded the *Folkspartay*, which stood for Jewish autonomy as a synthesis between the opposites of assimilation and isolation, for the purpose of preserving the Jews in Russia and elsewhere in the world. He believed that, as a spiritual nation, Jewry could not be destroyed. Dubnow thought that Jewish history was the inner history of Man, basic history, the history of the intellectual and religious struggle, advances and retreats of mankind. If mankind progressed, the whole history of mankind would in this sense become basic history.

'What is a Jew to do in Haman's times?' In view of the future, this was the question which faced all Jews. It was ignored by many. But Dubnow put the question to himself and his friends in 1939 in a letter to the publisher of *Oyfn Sheydveg* (At the Cross-roads), and he answered it in this way:

The year 1937, he said, recalled the two thousandth anniversary of the abduction of the first Jewish prisoners from Jerusalem to Rome (63 BC). The two years of the Hitler régime (1938–9) led many men to think that that represented the beginning of the end of European Jewry: the main centre of Jewry would be transferred to America or Asia. The Jews were going through one of the worst crises of their history. Dubnow recalled the period of the Crusades, the plague of 1348 and the expulsion from Spain. He recalled the Polish-Ukrainian Jewish catastrophe in 1648–9 and the Russian and Ukrainian pogroms of 1881–2, 1903–4, and 1919–20. 'The anti-Jewish measures in Central Europe today combine all the sufferings of the past with the most modern system of cruelty, vandalism and torture, as can be created only by the inquisitorial fantasy of a Hitler, a Goering or a Streicher. Today we truly live in Haman's times. Hitler's system of extermination is only another version of Haman's plans to kill, destroy and overcome all Jews.' The only difference was that in those days Haman's onslaught evoked the organized resistance of the Jews. Now that was lacking.

Simon Dubnow appealed to world Jewry, at what was truly the eleventh hour, to create an international organization to fight this band of murderers. Bodies must be set up to find homes for the refugees and those who had been expelled. In his entreaty Dubnow said: 'All the active forces of Jewry must unite in this terrible battle to cleanse Europe of this evil and save Europe's Jewry from destruction.'

Dubnow called for an economic and moral boycott and blockade of the Axis powers. (We know who the principal blockade breakers were: the Christian churches.)

He begged the opposing groups and movements within Jewry to stand together in this period of the utmost gravity. And he reminded his readers of the French Revolution: 'We stand or fall with the advance or retreat of all humanity, and not with just some of its degenerate elements.'

431

Dubnow thought that the call 'back to the ghetto' was an illusion. Progressive Jews would never return to the medieval ghetto and its Judaism.
'The call "Back to God and our traditional orthodoxy" will have as much
success as similar appeals by the Christian churches to their members. The
religious masses will remain loyal to their faith, but the progressives will not
be driven back to the synagogue or the church.'

A century before, the founder of the neo-orthodox movement, Samson
Raphael Hirsch, had declared that it was not the task of the Torah to adapt
itself to life, but life to adapt itself to the Torah. Recent generations had,
however, shown (Dubnow declared) that the essence of Jewry could be
preserved only by conforming to modern life. There were now religious Jews
and national Jews, or a combination of the two. Each group should be
allowed to go its own way. No single group was entitled to monopolize the
whole of Jewry. Competition of the spirit must be retained.

Simon Dubnow, the great Jewish historian and religious thinker, was himself the product of those two great spiritual forces whose struggles and rivalries
and alliances brought about a renewal of Jewish piety and intellect in the
nineteenth and twentieth centuries. They are still at work, in America and in
Europe, everywhere in fact where Jews venture to strive for more than
passive conformity, absorption or withdrawal into a ghetto. These spiritual
forces are the memory of a specifically Eastern Jewish intellectual and
religious awakening, and a specifically West European intelligence, based
essentially on the ideas of the great German philosophers of Kant's time and
of the period of German idealism.

Dubnow, the pupil of a West European scientific enlightenment, stood at
the centre of the great Eastern Jewish renaissance, to which such differing
personalities as Ahad Ha-Am (Asher Ginzberg) and Chaim Nachman Bialik
belong.

In Germany at the beginning of the nineteenth century there was a small
but important group of Berlin Jews, headed by Leopold Zunz and Heinrich
Graetz, which called itself the *Wissenschaft des Judentums* and was based on the
ideas of Hegel. Heinrich Heine belonged to this group in his student days.
Most of its believers became converted to Christianity, which helps to
explain why Rabbi Samson Raphael Hirsch's neo-orthodox reaction against
Jewish worldliness and self-liquidation was so violent.

An important manifestation of German idealism combined with Jewish
rationalism emerged in the work of the German Jewish philosopher Hermann
Cohen. It was sparked off by Treitschke's attack on the Jews in 1879. Cohen,
professor of philosophy at Marburg (1842–1918) praised Luther and German
Protestantism, seeing them as closely related to his own form of enlightened
Jewish monotheism. He returned to Judaism by identifying Jewish monotheism and Messianism – full of German Jewish emotionalism – with an
idealistic form of Socialism.

Cohen claimed that the future would see the victory of ideas, the perfection of Man and Nature. Zionism he rejected completely: he was concerned with the whole of mankind. In his book *Religion der Vernunft, aus den Quellen des Judentums* (The Religion of Reason Based on Judaism), which appeared in 1918, the year of his death, he declared that religion was concerned with men, not with God. God was a correlate of Man, helping him to transcend his animal nature. Hermann Cohen believed – in the spirit of Kant and the prophets' descendants – in a future family of nations.

The essence of Messianism is a belief in the ultimate victory of good over evil. Full of German idealism and Jewish piety, Hermann Cohen attacked the myth of original sin. Each of us, he said, is responsible for his own sins, and we learn to understand ourselves through an examination of our own sins (a contact here with psychoanalysis). To the prophets the Jewish people constituted a signpost on the road to the united nations of mankind.

Cohen's Socialism stemmed from the same German and Jewish sources. The God of the prophets is the God of the poor people. In God's eyes all men are poor. God is a twofold Creator: He created mankind and He created the spirit of human brotherhood. Man has been given the task of discovering Man as a fellow being. The sanctity of Man lies in the sanctity of the Self. This has no limits, and is never static; it lives in struggle and growth. Immortality and resurrection signify the correlation between God and Man, which is endless. What is at stake is the attainment of a Messianic future for the whole of mankind, not the miraculous appearance of a personal Messiah. It is a question of justice, integrity and the destruction of idols, such as those set up by Christians.

Cohen saw the Crucifixion as a symbol of the suffering of the Jewish people in the cause of unity, of the Messianic future of all mankind. He died in the very year in which all the horrors of the near future were beginning to form around the legend of a stab in the back in a Germany that could not accept Cohen's vision – inspired by Kant, Hegel and German idealists from Lessing to Schleiermacher – of peace, happiness and freedom for a single family of Man.

Martin Buber, while acknowledging Cohen as a great doctrinist, considered that he had failed. Cohen, he wrote, had erected the last home for the God of the philosophers. It was against the God of the philosophers that Blaise Pascal turned at the time of his conversion, opting instead for the God of Abraham, Isaac and Jacob. Yet Pascal was bound by all the cords of his intellect to the philosophic enlightenment which he condemned. The leading philosophers of the Jewish religious renaissance in Germany, Leo Baeck, Franz Rosenzweig and Martin Buber, are all of them unthinkable without the background of their constant inner battles with German philosophy and with Christianity as experienced by them in German lands.

At the turn of the century Adolf von Harnack, the spiritual leader of a liberal Protestant theology, delivered to students of all faculties at Berlin University his famous series of lectures on the nature of Christianity. Harnack, who was well in favour with Kaiser Wilhelm II (for whom he prepared the war manifesto in 1914), was in a position to repulse the attacks of the orthodox, and in his lectures he disputed all Jewish claims to separate identity and creative power in modern times. It was against Harnack that Leo Baeck published in 1905 his *Wesen des Judentums* (The Nature of Jewry), a comprehensive defence of the Jewish 'mother religion' against the Jewish 'daughter religions', namely, Christianity, Mohammedanism and Socialism. They had all, he said, borrowed the missionary idea from the Jews, who had discovered and long practised it.

Baeck was quite ready to acknowledge the rights and historical significance of these Jewish daughter religions, but he did not feel that they were under an obligation to kill their mother.

Leo Baeck, who as a rabbi in Berlin suffered with his people in Terezin, then proceeded to make a detailed criticism of Christianity which is of great significance not only in relation to the Christian-Jewish debate of our day, but also to a self-critical analysis of Christianity during the past two thousand years. Leo Baeck's strength emerges more powerfully in this criticism than in his exposition of a Jewish theology of his own.

Baeck saw Christianity as a 'romantic' religion, from the time of St Paul to Friedrich Schlegel, the convert from an idealistic Protestantism to an idealistic Catholicism. The romantic seeks his goal in a dreamland, in a Hereafter, and despises the world, history and the grim realities of every-day life. A romantic religion that consoles its believers with the prospect of a Hereafter beyond history restricts Man to his own worries and to thoughts of his own individual salvation. He is completely passive, child-like, obedient and free of individual responsibility. It is a conception that demands the presence of an exclusive church to guard its lambs from the dangerous world outside.

Baeck then proceeded to a detailed criticism of St Augustine and St Paul. (And it is true that, if Christianity ever ventures on a self-analysis, it will have – like him – to concern itself primarily with those two.) He quoted St Augustine's well-known saying that he would not accept the Gospels without the church's authority. And his criticism of St Paul centred round the charge that by adopting ancient religious rites he really created a romantic myth: through sacramental rites the human being is transported out of the world from above and transformed.

According to Baeck, Christianity had turned its back on time, on history and the Creation. It was therefore unable to take seriously Man's ethical duty to change the world. In complete contrast, the Jewish religion imposed on Man the duty to fulfil God's word here on earth, and actively – with complete responsibility towards all creatures – to fight for justice, freedom and peace.

Leo Baeck's dispute with Christianity was continued and transformed in a very conciliatory spirit by his friends Franz Rosenzweig and Martin Buber. Rosenzweig in his *Stern der Erlösung* (Star of Redemption, 1921) saw Christianity and Judaism as close relatives in a community of love. The Jewish emergence from old beliefs was a direct invitation to Christians to allow themselves to be fertilized, enriched and inspired by Jews.

Martin Buber, the great solitary mind of Israel, born in Vienna, intellectually shaped by German education and the German way of life, yet rooted in Jewry through his Chassidim grandfather, brings us right into the middle of our present-day debate – a debate which is only just beginning between Jews and Christians both striving to build anew on the best of their past in the fluid conditions of modern thought.

An interesting light is thrown on the problems of both by such a problematic non-believing Jew as William S. Schlamm, also by birth a product of the old Austro-Hungarian empire. As a motto for his book *Wer ist Jude? – Ein Selbstgespräch* (Who is a Jew? A Monologue, 1964) Schlamm chose a passage from Martin Buber. 'Today the question is repeatedly asked: how is Jewish life possible after Auschwitz? I should like to put the question more correctly: how, in a time that has known Auschwitz, is a life with God possible? The mystery has become too cruel, the concealment too deep . . .'

Martin Buber asks, 'Can one still call on him?' – and points to Job. 'But what God tells him does not answer the charge, is not even relevant to it. The true answer that Job receives is God's appearance, and only that. Distance changes to proximity. His eye sees Him, so that he will know Him again. But nothing is explained, nothing solved. Wrong does not become right, nor cruelty compassion. Nothing has happened, except that once again Man hears God's word. The mystery remains an enigma, but it has become Man's own. And we? How is it with us?'

And we? How is it with us? Schlamm voices a complaint that will today be understood by Jews and Christians struggling to form roots at a deeper spiritual and historical level. What would have happened to the world, he asks, if Christianity had remained true to Jesus the Jew? Pontius Pilate's successors have provided the popes over two thousand years, while the successors of Jesus's Jewish apostles rank as the successors of Judas Iscariot. The churches are afraid of a confrontation with the Jews.

'Christianity proclaims the mystery of Jesus Christ within the Trinity, a mystery of world redemption and resurrection enacted on the Cross. Judaism proclaims the identity of the one and only God with His Creation and His Chosen People; the single responsibility of a human being for his future redemption; and the significance solely of life on earth in justice. Basically these are the positions of each of the two religions, and the comparison reveals – perhaps somewhat surprisingly – that the modern world is essentially more Judaistic in outlook than Christian.'

Schlamm develops this surprising statement as follows: 'Can it be seriously doubted that contemporary Man finds it easier to believe in a single impersonal God than in the Trinity? In Man's essential goodness rather than in original sin? In the unity of faith and knowledge rather than in the division of body and soul? In Man's responsibility for his own actions rather than in the grace of God? If Jewishness did not happen to be regarded as a defect, can it be seriously doubted that modern Man would not willingly find his way back to the early Judaistic form of Christianity?'

This, according to Schlamm, is the grotesque position today: 'The more Christians tend to become involuntary Jews, the less Jews wish to remain Jews. The development in opposite directions has a single cause: both Christians and Jews are moving further and further away from their original religious positions.'

And what does the future hold in store? 'The essential religious experience of the Western world was, is and will continue to be the dispute between the Jews and Jesus Christ. Now, after twenty centuries of hair-raising diversions, the world has finally got back again to this original dispute.

'The Jews, to whom Jesus was sent, were the first Christians. And perhaps they will be the last.

'The divine mission – first and last duty of a church – will either be a crusade against the unbelieving world, or it will be in vain . . . If the church, which was founded by Jews, wants finally to reach the Jews, it must at last become Christian.'

But if the church is to become Christian through the Jews, what is to happen to the Jews themselves?

Schlamm declares: 'There are problems which are insoluble; and Jewry is one of them.' The Jewish problem is 'the reaction of one human being to another'. Having lived through twenty centuries defending himself from myths, the Jew *must* have become an intelligent being. The pluralistic society of today needs Jewish sensibility (and consciousness of suffering) more urgently than ever before. The foundation of the state of Israel has given Jews for the first time in their history the chance of making free decisions: 'Subject only to his own conscience, a Jew can now decide whether or not to be a member of the Jewish people and their state; whether to believe in the Jewish God or the Christian God or in no God at all; whether to be a Jew or not. Each of these decisions has now become possible, permissible and honourable.'

'From the extraordinary suffering of the Jews there has grown an extra-ordinary freedom, from the last crisis of the illness a good chance of recovery. And so the history of the Jews has had its significance: those who were last in the brutal collective throng have now become the first who are free to make their own decisions. May the Jews desire their new freedom!'

436

And may mankind as a whole desire its new freedom to achieve through constant self-analysis liberation from those terrible psychological impulses which seek to find scapegoats in others, to invent devils and mortal foes, to wage wars and civil wars because it fears to explore its own inner depths. It is a great challenge to all religions, including Christianity.

That Jewish piety and spirituality are able to hold their own today in the concert of world religions can be seen in the anthology *Die Antwort der Religionen* (The Answers of the World Religions), which was published in Munich in 1964. Gerhard Szczesny, an acknowledged humanist, put thirty-one questions to prominent Jews, Catholics and Protestants (two distinct Christian religions, though many today try to deny or ignore the fact), Mohammedans, Hindus and Buddhists. In contrast to the philosophically forced, brilliantly intellectual and sometimes tortuous replies of the Christian representatives, the Jewish answers are distinguished by their brevity, precision and directness. The Christians (the Catholic theologians Karl Rahner and Johannes Baptist Metz and the Protestant theologian Ernst Wolf) do not reply at all to some of the questions, such as those concerning atomic weapons and the treatment of Communists. This silence is more revealing than many of the voluminous replies to questions concerning miracles, for example.

Basic to all the Jewish answers is the principle that in Judaism all religious activity involves one's fellow beings. 'A fellow being may be my enemy, but he does not for that reason cease to be my fellow being. "If thou meet thine enemy's ox or his ass going astray, thou shalt surely bring it back to him again" (Exodus 23, 4). The Hebrew word for ethical duty is *zedaka*, which means justice and piousness in one. The man practising it is called *zaddik*, the pious man, because he has shown justice to a fellow being' (Rabbi Kurt Wilhelm).

The greatest gifts that the people of Israel had received from God in their sufferings were the Law, the land of Israel and the world to come. 'No image obscures the Jew's spiritual conception of immortality. That is God's own secret. As the Talmud says: No eye has seen the coming world: only God knows it.

'No Jew has ever declared this world to be a vale of tears, thus playing off life in the next world against life in this. The questions of personal immortality, of pre-existence and the continuing existence of the soul are bound up with the eternal existence of the Jewish people itself. As explained in a Midrash commentary, all the souls which will ever enter into a Jewish body were present on Sinai and entered there into the eternal covenant between God and Israel. We Jews were with our Father on Sinai; we do not need the Son to give us access to our Father.

'We live for ever: with this song on their lips Jews entered the gas chambers.'

Here is an excerpt from a diary: 'Early today two Jewesses went out into the village: a mother and her daughter. As luck would have it, some Germans from Rudki came into Bodzentyn to fetch potatoes and met these two Jewesses. When they saw the Germans they ran away, but the Germans overtook and grabbed them. They wanted to shoot them at once in the village, but the mayor would not allow it. So they went to the edge of the woods and shot them there. The Jewish police went along immediately afterwards to fetch them for burial. When the cart arrived, it was full of blood. Who . . .'

With that word the diary of David Rubinowicz breaks off. In careful childish handwriting the twelve-year-old David had recorded events between March 1940 and June 1942 in five school exercise books. His father sold milk in the village of Krajino. In the spring of 1942 the SS rounded up all the Jews in the neighbourhood and sent them to the little town of Bodzentyn. where they were put in cattle trucks and carted off to their deaths. In the plundered Rubinowicz home a neighbour discovered David's exercise books and hid them in a barn. During a clear-out some years later they were thrown on the rubbish heap, where a woman found them.

Everything that constitutes Europe's Christian world has been influenced and shaped through two thousand years by the Psalms. Neither the works of Goethe nor of Bert Brecht would have been possible without the Psalms, which are the living memory of the bliss and the suffering, the guilt and the repentance, the death agony and the delight in love of Israel, God's chosen people and first love. The immeasurable, inconceivable Jewish catastrophe of the twentieth century has found its expression – as far as that is humanly possible – not in a theology or philosophy or an epic work, but in a body of Jewish songs and poems which might be regarded in its unresolved, uncompleted inherent wholeness as a *New Psalter*.

It is a psalter of voices (not infrequently of men, women and children facing imminent death) from Russia, Poland, Germany, France, England and America reaching out to us who remain. Many of their creations in the face of death vanished in smoke and ashes, like the bodies of the creators:

> Each day behind the barrack sheds
> I see smoke rising to the sky.
> Jewish people, bend your heads:
> No one here will pass it by . . .

That is the beginning of a poem *Kamin* (Fireside) by a thirteen-year-old Viennese girl, Ruth Klüger. It was written in 1944 in Auschwitz. Beside the lament of a child stand the laments of venerable men like Zalman Schneour, Louis Golding, Robert Nathan, Chaim Nachman Bialik, Israel Zangwill and of women such as Hannah Senesh. This very talented young woman (1921–44) left Hungary to become an early settler in Israel. During the war she made a parachute landing in Hungary in the service of an underground organization formed to help the prisoners in the death camps. She was captured and killed in a concentration camp. Hannah Senesh, who freely chose death, wrote of her own decision in a poem *The Blessed Match* (originally written in Yiddish). She herself is the match lighting the flame of resistance in the surviving Jewish youth of Europe:

> Blessed the match that was burned
> And ignited flames!
> Blessed the flame that blazes up
> In the secret places of the heart.
> Blessed the heart that throbbed its last beat in honour;
> Blessed the match that was burned and ignited flames.

Jewish women like Gertrud Kolmar, Gertrud Kantorowicz, Ilse Weber and Ilse Blumenthal-Weiss sang of their own death and the death of the people of Israel in their last poems. 'I cannot hate' was the theme of *Prayer* by Ilse Blumenthal-Weiss (see page 2), whose husband was gassed in Auschwitz and whose son was murdered in Mauthausen. She herself, a German Jewish woman who had once corresponded with Rainer Maria Rilke, had been in two concentration camps.

Genuine piety can include anger and despair – the cry of Job as uttered in our days by Jizchak Katzenelson, who wrote his *Song of the Last Jew* and buried the manuscript in three bottles in a French concentration camp before being deported to Auschwitz. (Extracts from his poem are on page 13.) The opinion of the Catholic theologian J.B. Metz that a human being might interpret a true personal religious experience as atheism should be borne in mind when reading this great song of despair with its deep religious undertones.

Somewhat akin in theme to this incomparable ode by Jizchak Katzenelson is *Genesis* by Jules Alan Wein. The seven days of the Creation are treated as stages in the destruction of the Jews:

> In the beginning there were transports . . .
> A most scientific transport
> Yet a child cries, 'Hold me, Mama! . . .
> I have fear'
> And it was evening and it was morning
> The first day.
> And the second day was sorting
>
> The old men sorted from the young men
> The young men sorted from their wives
> The children sorted from their mothers.

A careful sorting
A most scientific sorting . . .

On the fifth day there was gas.
Visgadal v'yiskadash . . .
And weeping . . .
For the old bewildered men,
For the young men with thin arms,
For the matrons shrieking for their children.
A careful gassing
A most scientific gassing.

The sixth day: the rising in the Warsaw ghetto. The seventh day: the destruction of the Warsaw ghetto. Triumph in death:

And it was evening, the seventh day
And death was but the birthcry of the morrow.

Songs of comfort and despair, elegies on the death of a wife, of fathers, mothers and children. Odes on the martyrs of Troyes in the thirteenth century and the suffering and extermination of the Jews on the Rhine in the twelfth and thirteenth centuries have a permanent place in Jewish liturgy. In the psalter of tomorrow's men there will be songs recalling the 'final solution'. And in this psalter of a new piety and spirituality among the single family of Man the poems of Nelly Sachs, a Jewess from Berlin, and Paul Celan from the borderlands of old Austria will have a special place.

In *Eli*, which Nelly Sachs has herself described as a mystery play of Israel's suffering, the basic theme is spoken by Dajan. Rightly understood, it explains Christian and post-Christian hatred of the Jews:

But they do not know the beginning,
the eternal beginning –
and that is why they hate us . . .

The beginning: God's covenant with his first love, the people of Israel. A dead child addresses its killers:

Hands,
What did you do
When you were the hands of little children?
Did you hold a mouth organ, or the mane
Of a rocking-horse, or in darkness clutch your mother's skirt?
Did you point to a word in your reading book –
Was it God perhaps, or Man?

You throttling hands,
Was your mother dead

440

Or your wife or child?
That now you held only death in your hands,
In your throttling hands?

Sublime 'revenge': that a Jewish woman, whose husband-to-be and many of whose relations were murdered, should sing in German of the 'Hands of Death's Gardeners'.

Paul Celan's *Todesfuge* (Death Fugue, 1945) is the great requiem of a young Jew whose mother was murdered. With large, wide-open eyes he looks on the golden-haired Margarete, on Germany, and on the ashen-haired Sulamith, Israel:

He cries play death sweeter death is a master from Germany
he cries fiddle lower then you'll rise in the air as smoke
then you'll have a grave in the clouds you won't lie cramped there
Black milk of the dawn we drink you nights
we drink you noon death is a master from Germany
we drink you evenings and mornings we drink and drink
death is a master from Germany his eye is blue
he strikes you with leaden balls his aim is true
a man lives in the house your golden hair Margarete
he sicks his hounds on us he gives us the gift of a grave in the air
he plays with the snakes death is a master from Germany

your golden hair Margarete
your ashen hair Sulamith

Two short verses recalling the great German-Jewish symbiosis that lasted a hundred years before, in 1933–45, it was turned to smoke and ashes.

Death is a master from Germany: *Death is a master in all places where life is not mastered.* And where today, in our vast industrial society, is life being mastered?

Do we not see all around us millions of frustrated people, men and women, young and old, their life's expectation disappointed and unfulfilled? Deeply estranged, they know nothing of that full and crowded life that will enable them at the end to die with a blessing on their lips.

In this world of people who cannot master their life, death is master – that death which in Germany showed its prowess in the slaughter of millions of Jews. It was a Germany in which despair prevailed, the despair of broad masses who had failed to come to terms with East and West, with the burden of freedom and the difficulties of democracy. They could reconcile themselves neither with the past, nor the present, nor the future. Christians were unreconciled with the new age, with liberalism, Socialism and the Jews.

Unmastered life longs for death and unfolds mighty forces of destruction. Unmastered life looks eagerly for scapegoats on which it can off-load its burden and vent its fear and hatred – a hatred which deep down is self-hatred, a lack of faith that deep down is lack of faith in the chosen God.

It is the cliché of 'the people who killed Christ' that is seized on by all Christian and post-Christian societies to denigrate the enemy who is blamed for the collapse and non-mastery of their own lives, whether they be coloured people, Japanese, Communists or Jews.

In places where it does not appear expedient at the moment to cite the Jew, it is now usually the Communist who takes his place. Thus it is in Catholic Germany, as the following example shows. In Königstein in the Taunus, annual congresses are held in which leading Catholic theologians and laymen deal with the position of the church in East Europe. In recent years an attempt has been made to evolve certain speech formulations which would dispel the reproach that spiritual preparations for a third world war are going on. Thus one speaks of atheism rather than of Communism. In his final speech at the 1964 congress on the subject of transcending love, the well-known popular priest Werenfried van Straaten declared that in the Communist states the persecution of God (by which he meant the harassing of the church) had increased rather than diminished. The 'atheistic régime' did not grant God the right to speak. This Premonstratensian priest seems to have been completely unaware that God has often also not been granted the right to speak under 'Christian' régimes, as a thousand years of history up to the present has shown. He also failed to realize that God is not obliged to express Himself in our language and according to our formulations. After so many desecrations of His name and of human dignity in the cause of religion, He might well choose to make use of another language than that of our theologians!

Werenfried van Straaten ended with the words: 'The church is in mortal danger' – from betrayers without and within. His conclusion accords remarkably with the theme of *Conspiracy against the Church*, which ascribes all blame to the Jews inside and around the church. 'And you can pray for the conversion of the traitors, for strength for the afflicted, light for the straying, sagacity for the Vatican diplomats, protection for the witnesses who wrote to me and a flaming sword for the Archangel Michael that he may with God's help thrust Satan back into hell.'

For very many Christians that is the last word in their Gospel: love transcending becomes a prayer for a flaming sword for the Archangel Michael. The Crusaders called on him, and before them the warriors of the Holy Roman Empire, to lead them and fight with them in all their battles with rebels against God and the empire.

But who shall wield the archangel's sword on earth today? That is a matter of burning political discussion. Is it to be lodged in the distant Pentagon or (closer still) with the mortal enemy from the East – perhaps in an atom-bomb-proof shelter, not too far away from Hitler's last bunker in the Reichskanzlei?

The very last word that these Christians at the congress in Königstein addressed to history, to hundreds of millions of fellow beings they do not understand, is – as it has been before – hell.

Hell is the others. The key to a Christianity struggling with the greatest crisis in its history turns out to be a well-known quotation from Sartre's *Huit clos*. The appallingly perilous situation in world politics today is here shown in a new light: at the very moment when mankind must gird itself to a physical, mental and spiritual leap forward if it is to master the great effort of living together in one huge community of hundreds of millions of fellow beings, Christianity is expending its strength in despairing attempts to maintain its false identity. It starts back in fear from dissolving its past, lest the whole structure of the church collapse.

In the Protestant church questioning theologians encounter bitter opposition from traditionalists intent on defending their Bible, their Jesus and their Luther against what they regard as destructive intellectual criticism. In Catholic circles few dare to say, as the Catholic professor Renée Marcic did at Salzburg University in a lecture entitled 'Is Anti-Semitism a Crime?', that the Pauline concept has come to grief. Marcic declared: 'What according to that [i.e., the Pauline tradition] was theologically impossible, nevertheless happened in practice: the Jewish synagogue lived on as a social and religious centre in the Diaspora even after the nation was dispersed.'

What a Christian religion unreconciled with itself and all others has regarded as theologically impossible over a period of fifteen centuries has been: a peaceful co-existence in political and practical terms and a religious and spiritual collaboration with heretics, Jews, Mohammedans, Turks, Protestants, Papists, Calvinists . . .

The problem of anti-Semitism (and all its offspring such as racialism, anti-Communism, clericalism and anti-clericalism) can be successfully solved only on this condition: that outraged Christians become reconciled with themselves, that an exclusive Christian religion seeks and finds reconciliation with men of other religions and beliefs.

This reconciliation can be achieved only through a process of self-analysis that leads us back to Jesus the man and Jesus the Jew.

Christendom will find the humanity it so urgently needs only by facing Jesus the man and planting its roots in the piety and spirituality of His people, who were and are God's first love. The bond between them must become insoluble.

But it will be achieved only through a tremendous inner struggle. The great and increasingly perilous battle for the future will take place inside the human heart.

Mankind is standing at the cross-roads. Will a few significant groups and individuals succeed in putting into men's hearts that strength that will enable them to overcome all their many disappointments, cherished illusions and implacably guarded imaginings of false heavens and hells? Will hate, frustration, death wishes and subconscious suicidal tendencies be mastered and the way opened to recovery and new life?

Anti-Semites in the nineteenth and twentieth centuries regarded the Jews as the key problem of world history. They were right, but in a different way than they thought. In the Jews, in whom they saw the driving force of human history over the past four thousand years, lurks not the Devil, but *the hidden God, who unmasks the living lie in every human being. The God of burning fire, whose fire consumes all the idols, all the religions and all the systems of Man.*

In the conflagrations of two world wars, in the fires of Hitler's concentration camps the God of Sinai stood behind the 'destructive', 'devilish', 'anti-Christian' Jews. He, a terrible God, sacrificed His firstborn sons, His Jews, to open up to all humanity ways of breaking through ancient petrifications, prejudices, mistaken ideas and deeds.

This God is the coming God: a God of the present and of the future, in which He will submerge the brutal past.

Notes and Bibliography

Translator's note: In the original German text the author has supplied detailed references to his sources in all the books mentioned in the bibliography. While leaving the bibliography intact, I have quoted detailed references only in the case of books of English or American origin or easily available in English translation. My reason for doing this is that readers with a sufficient knowledge of German to follow up all the quoted sources will also be more likely to read this book in the original German than in my translation.

CHAPTER I: GOD'S FIRST LOVE

Arendt, H.: Eichmann in Jerusalem, Munich 1964

Eckert, W.P., and Ehrlich, E.L.: Judenhass – Schuld der Christen? Versuch eines Gesprächs, Essen 1964

Hay, Malcolm: Europe and the Jews – The Pressure of Christendom on the People of Israel for 1,900 Years, Boston 1960

Jéhouda, Josué: L'antisémitisme, miroir du monde, Geneva 1958

Loewenstein, R.: Psychanalyse de l'antisémitisme, Paris 1952

Long, E.J.: 2,000 Years – A History of Anti-Semitism, New York 1953

Ornstein, H.: Der antijüdische Komplex, Zurich 1949

Poliakov, Léon: Histoire de l'antisémitisme, 2 vols, Paris 1955

Schlösser, M. (Editor): An den Wind geschrieben, Darmstadt 1960

Schoenbach, P.: Reaktionen auf die antisemitische Welle im Winter 1959/60, Frankfurt 1961

Thieme, Karl: Judenfeindschaft, Darstellung und Analysen, Frankfurt 1963

Page

2 *Gebet* by Ilse Blumenthal-Weiss: German text in Schlösser (Ed.).

CHAPTER 2: EXODUS INTO HISTORY

Ausubel, Nathan and Marynn (Editors): A Treasury of Jewish Poetry, New York 1957

Benemozegh, E.: Israël et l'humanité, Paris 1914

Bevan, E.R., and Singer, C. (Editors): The Legacy of Israel, Oxford 1953

Brod, Max: Johannes Reuchlin und sein Kampf, Stuttgart 1965

Fleg, E. (Editor): Anthologie juive des origines à nos jours, Paris 1951

Geis, R.R.: Vom unbekannten Judentum, Freiburg 1961

Goldschmidt, H.L.: Die Botschaft des Judentums, Frankfurt 1960

Jaromir, R.: Bibel und Zeitgeist, Eine religionssoziologische Untersuchung, Affoltern 1949

Kahler, E.von: Die Verantwortung des Geistes, Frankfurt 1952

Klesse, M.: Vom Alten zum Neuen Israel, Ein Beitrag zur Genesis der Judenfrage und des Antisemitismus, Frankfurt 1965

Levine, E. (Editor): The Jewish Heritage, London 1955

Loretz, O.: Quohelet und der alte Orient, Freiburg 1964

Roth, B.Cecil: Die Kunst der Juden, Frankfurt 1963

Schlösser, M. (Editor): An den Wind geschrieben, Darmstadt 1960

Szczesny, G. (Editor): Die Antwort der Religionen, Munich 1964

Page

5 *Wir ziehn* by Karl Wolfskehl translated from the German by Carol North Valhope and Ernst Morwitz (*A Treasury of Jewish Poetry*, ed. Ausubel).

7 Priests and prophets: F.L.Moriarty, The Prophets – Bearers of the Word, in *The Bridge* II, 1956.

8 The Sabbath, God's greatest gift to Israel, anchored in the Creation: K.Wilhelm in Szczesny (Ed.). In interviews with prominent representatives of world religions, the two Christian theologians had nothing to say on the subject of happiness – in contrast to the Jewish reply.

9 The Jews as the people of a book: A.Cohen and A.J.Polack in *The Jewish Heritage* (Ed. Levine).

10 Collective guilt: A.Cohen in *The Jewish Heritage* (Ed. Levine).

10 Zangwill's poem: see Ausubel (Ed.). Consciousness and experience of pain: do., 121ff, 132ff, 150ff, 161ff.

10 The educational role of Psalms and Psalter: G.A.Smith and W.B.Selbie in *The Legacy of Israel* (Ed. Bevan and Singer).

12 A French Jewish philosopher: Leon Werth in Fleg (Ed.).

12 The Book of Job: B.Ulanov, Job and His Comforters, in *The Bridge* II, 1956.

13 *Botschaft an die sieben Himmel* by Jizchak Katzenelson: German text in Schlösser (Ed.).

14 The book Quohelet: B.Hessler, Kohelet – the Veiled God, in *The Bridge* I, 1955.

14 Jewish striving for justice, sense of responsibility, Messianic belief: Levine (Ed.); A.J.Polack, D.Daiches-Raphael and Leon Roth in The Legacy of Israel (Ed. Bevan and Singer).

14 The remark of the theologian Paul Tillich: '*Die Wahrheit kann nicht gedacht, sie muss getan werden*' (Truth is not a matter of thought, but of action) corresponds to ancient Jewish thinking.

CHAPTER 3: JEWS, GREEKS AND ROMANS

Baum, G.: Die Juden und das Evangelium, Einsiedeln 1963
Deschner, K. (Editor): Jesusbilder in theologischer Sicht, Munich 1966
Goldschmidt, H.L.: Die Botschaft des Judentums, Frankfurt 1960
Heer, F.: Europa, Mutter der Revolutionen, 1965 (to be published in English as Europe, Mother of Revolutions)
Isaac, Jules: Genèse de l'antisémitisme, Paris 1956
Klesse, M.: Vom Alten zum Neuen Israel, Frankfurt 1965
Lewy, Guenter: The Catholic Church and Nazi Germany, London and New York 1964
Parkes, James: The Conflict of the Church and the Synagogue – A Study in the Origins of Anti-Semitism, New York 1961 (First ed. 1934)
Parkes, James: The Jew and his Neighbour – A Study of the Causes of Anti-Semitism, London 1930
Poliakov, Léon: Histoire de l'antisémitisme, Paris 1955
Roth, B.Cecil: Die Kunst der Juden, Frankfurt 1962
Stauffer, E.: Jerusalem und Rom im Zeitalter Jesu Christi, Berne 1957
Stauffer, E.: Jesus – Gestalt und Geschichte, Berne 1957
Thieme, Karl: Judenfeindschaft, Darstellung und Analysen, Frankfurt 1963
Winter, P.: On the Trial of Jesus, Berlin 1961

Page
15 Greeks and Jews in Alexandria: Parkes (Conflict), 14ff.
16 *Pia fraus:* On this problem, which has persisted through the centuries, see later chapters 4–6. Religious authors after 1945 have not been averse to falsifying Nazi documents. On the many falsifications at the First Vatican Council, see the exchange of letters between Lord Acton and Dr Döllinger.
19 Pontius Pilate: among others, H.Duesburg, The Trial of the Messiah, in *The Bridge* I, 1955.

CHAPTER 4: JESUS AND THE JEWS

Balthasar, Hans Urs v.: Herrlichkeit – eine theologische Aesthetik, Einsiedeln 1962
Baum, G.: Die Juden und das Evangelium, Einsiedeln 1963

Brandon, S.G.F.: The Fall of Jerusalem and the Christian Church, London 1951

Böhlig, H.: Die Geisteskultur von Tarsus im augusteischen Zeitalter, Heidelberg 1913

Bultmann, R.: Geschichte und Eschatologie, Tübingen 1958

Congar, Yves M.J.: Le mystère du Temple, Paris 1959

Deschner, K. (Editor): Jesusbilder in theologischer Sicht, Munich 1966

Dibelius, M.: Paulus und die Mystik, Munich 1941

Dix, Gregory: Jew and Greek – A Study in the Primitive Church, New York 1953

Ebner, Ferdinand: Gesammelte Schriften, Munich 1963

Eckert, W.P., and Ehrlich, E.L.: Judenhass – Schuld der Christen?, Essen 1964

Eichrodt, W.: Theologie des Alten Testaments, Stuttgart 1957

Finkel, A.: The Pharisees and the Teacher of Nazareth, Leiden 1964

Freed, Edwin D.: Old Testament Quotations in the Gospel of John, Leiden 1965

Goppelt, L.: Christentum und Judentum im ersten und zweiten Jahrhundert, Gütersloh 1954

Graesser, E.: Das Problem der Parusieverzögerung in den synoptischen Evangelien und in der Apostelgeschichte, Berlin 1957

Isaac, Jules: Genèse de l'antisémitisme, Paris 1956

Isaac, Jules: Jésus et Israël, Paris 1948

Jaromir, R.: Bibel und Zeitgeist, Affoltern 1949

Jéhouda, Josué: L'antisémitisme, miroir du monde, Geneva 1958

Jocz, J.: The Jewish People and Jesus Christ, London 1949

Kahler, E.von: Die Verantwortung des Geistes, Frankfurt 1952

Kaplan, M.: The Purpose and Meaning of Jewish Existence, Philadelphia 1964

Klesse, M.: Vom Alten zum Neuen Israel, Frankfurt 1965

Köhler, L.: Theologie des Alten Testaments, Tübingen 1953

Küng, Hans: Freiheit in der Welt, Einsiedeln 1964

Loretz, O.: Die Wahrheit der Bibel, Freiburg 1964

Mansor, Menahem: The Dead Sea Scrolls, Leiden 1964

Maybaum, Ignaz: The Face of God after Auschwitz, Amsterdam 1965

Paillard, Jean: Vier Evangelisten – vier Welten, Frankfurt 1960

Parkes, James: The Conflict of the Church and the Synagogue, New York 1961

Pauly (Editor): Die Pharisäer und das Neue Testament, Frankfurt 1961

Schlösser, M. (Editor): An den Wind geschrieben, Darmstadt 1960

Schneider, Karl: Das Frühchristentum als antisemitische Bewegung, Bremen 1940

Schoeps, H.J.: Aus frühchristlicher Zeit, Tübingen 1950

Schoeps, H.J.: Theologie und Geschichte des Judenchristentums, Tübingen 1949

Schoeps, H.J.: Paulus – Die Theologie des Apostels Paulus im Lichte der jüdischen Religionsgeschichte, Tübingen 1959

Stauffer, E.: Jesus – Gestalt und Geschichte, Berne 1957

Stauffer, E.: Die Botschaft Jesu damals und heute, Berne 1959

Stauffer, E.: Jerusalem und Rom im Zeitalter Jesu Christi, Berne 1957

Thieme, Karl: Judenfeindschaft, Darstellung und Analysen, Frankfurt 1963

Werner, Martin: Glaube und Aberglaube, Stuttgart 1957

Werner, Martin: Der protestantische Weg des Glaubens, Berne 1955

Windisch, H.: Paulus und das Judentum, Stuttgart 1935

Page

22 *Gang durch die Via Dolorosa* by Georg Mannheimer: German text in Schlösser (Ed.).

23 Gospel according to St John a theological, not a historical document: Freed. See also Pierre Benoit in *Cross Currents* 1965, 339ff.

23 Anti-Semitism in the Gospels: among others Parkes, 27ff, 38ff; R.Kugelmann, Hebrew, Israelite, Jew in the New Testament, *The Bridge* I. 1955.

23 The Gospels and Christ as a historical figure: The motion of the Theological Commission at the Second Vatican Council was very cautiously expressed: 'The Gospels provide a true and honest report of the life of Jesus.' Pope Paul VI proposed the insertion of the words, '. . . the historical truth of the life of Jesus'. This seemed to the majority of the commission to go too far. Cardinal Bea proposed the adoption of an amendment proposed by a bishop, which stated, 'The Gospels proclaim the truth necessary for salvation.' The final outcome is contained in the official records.

23 Hans Küng, with church approval, ventures on the phrase: 'Peter, *the brothers of the Lord* [my italics] and the other apostles took their wives with them when preaching the gospel.'

24 Qumran writings: among others, Mansor.

24 The Pharisees: For modern Jewish attitudes towards them: Kaplan, 67f. For older assessments: Finkel. Wolfgang Beilner was the first Catholic (1959) to point out Christ's friendship with the Pharisees.

24 Anti-Judaism in St John: Parkes, 27ff. 'St John's mode of expression is understandable only against the background of anti-Judaism at the close of the first century' (C.Thoma in Eckert-Ehrlich).

24 Pauline and Johannine theology: see P.Benoit in A Contrast, *Cross Currents XVI*, 1965 (also in *New Testament Studies* IX, 1962–3).

24 At the death of Paul, Christianity was still a Jewish sect: Parkes, 77ff.

25 Schoeps draws attention in the foreword to his St Paul biography to the internal censorship to which – for the most part subconsciously – denominational researchers are prone. The reader 'must bear in mind that the historian striving to reach understanding of the apostles through

the particular problems of Jewish religious history is bound to speak of misunderstandings in matters in which Christian theologians detect divine guidance . . .'

Schoeps also points out St Paul's lack of interest in the man Jesus, whom he never saw. Among others, he quotes Albert Schweitzer: 'If we had only St Paul to guide us, we should not know that Jesus spoke in parables, that He spoke the Sermon on the Mount and taught His people the Lord's Prayer.' St Paul attributes his experience on the road to Damascus to a higher authority than the words and teachings of the mortal Jesus (cf. Galatians 1, 12–13). This claim lies certainly behind II Corinthians 5, 16, which might be translated hypothetically: even if we had known Christ after the flesh, we no longer know Him thus. St Paul preaches belief in Jesus and not the belief *of* Jesus. His portrait of the Kyrios Jesus is not based on Christ's life on earth: his is a pre-existent, supernatural Jesus. Schoeps comments: 'Only from this point does it become really clear that St Paul fundamentally changed Christ's teaching. In his missionary desire he was obliged to judge the world in a way different from the way it appeared in Christ's thinking.'

25 In later Jewish Christian writings. St Paul is portrayed under the pseudonym of Simon as a sort of anti-Christ, proclaiming the fall of Moses. He is regarded as a pseudo-apostle.

25 Schoeps: 'It can be said that St Paul's position in early Christendom was a very controversial and questionable one.' His Jewish Christian contemporaries would have been incredulous if told that St Paul's preaching would prevail, and 'they themselves fall by the wayside and only a few generations later even be denounced as heretics. At that time St Paul and Pauline theology represented only one direction among several – and then by no means the most important. In fact it did not really find acceptance in the church until after AD 70.'

26 The basically non-Jewish element in St Paul is his belief in the Son of God, originating from heathen, mythological conceptions filtered through the Hellenistic syncretism of his time. St Paul's Christ 'has become a supernatural figure, approaching in essence those gnostic dwellers in heaven who descend to earth. He even managed during the Israelites' journey through the desert to turn Himself into a rock (1 Corinthians 10, 4). *This celestial Christ seems to have absorbed entirely the historical Jesus.* As pre-existing Son of God and agent of the Creation, He is almost a mythical figure, whose contact with the world and earthly things is only very weak. The myth of a celestial being descending to earth, clearly apparent here, points to pagan origins and can only very implausibly be reconciled with Jewish-Hellenistic speculations' (Schoeps).

26 Schoeps: 'The Jewish Christians saw in Jesus only a remarkable prophet like Moses and worked from the hypothesis of a double parousia – one

in humilitate, manifested in Christ's earthly existence, and one *in gloria*, when He will come again as the Messiah and Son of Man ... They bear witness to the fact that the original Kerygma was open to another interpretation than that of St Paul.'

26 Catholics are still somewhat reluctant to accept Hans Küng's suggestion (in *Theologie und Kirche*) that 'what is needed today is an exegesis ... that does not argue away the multifarious humanity and frailty of the Biblical witnesses'. Theology requires a passionate love of truth which is not to be repressed by hypocrisy and fear of reprisals. Küng emphasizes the fragmentary character of all our formulations of faith. 'Truth can often be uncomfortable, unpleasant, unwanted, inopportune – even *piis auribus offensivae*.'

26 Catholic researchers will be able to deal freely with St Paul only when they are prepared to take seriously Karl Rahner's remarks: 'In the Bible there is a development of dogma as well as of theology ... St Paul's teaching – for example, the sacrificial nature of the Crucifixion, Christ as the second Adam, original sin, many points of eschatology etc., a large part of Johannine theology *etc.* – are *theological developments of a few quite simple statements* made by Jesus concerning the mystery of His person and the experience of His Resurrection.' [The italics, including the 'etc.', are mine.]

26 The Jew Saul in his Jewish and Hellenistic surroundings: see among others, Dix, and also J.Edgar Burns in *The Bridge* I, 317ff.

26 The 'Aryan, anti-Semitic' St Paul around 1933: see chapters 11 and 12.

26 The Pauline church of Christ is the new and genuine Israel: Congar, in the true Catholic tradition, maintains that Jesus – the new temple – is quite different from the old temple: the Gospel of St John signifies the destruction of the old temple and the re-erection of a spiritual temple which is the church.

26 The greatest act of robbery in history: Schoeps quotes with approval Nietzsche (*Morgenröte*, Aph.84): 'What can one expect from the after-effects of a religion that, in the centuries since its foundation, has enacted that incredible philological farce of trying to filch the Old Testament from the Jews, on the grounds that it contains nothing but Christian teaching and belongs to the Christians as the true people of Israel, whereas the Jews had adapted themselves to it?'

The classic Catholic version (*Dictionnaire de Théologie Catholique*, Paris 1932), states under 'Liturgie' [the italics are mine]: 'Le théologien ... sait que l'Eglise a succédé à la Synagogue, *qu'elle est l'héritière de tous ses livres*, que le peuple Juif, rejeté *par son infidélité, a été remplacé* par le peuple chrétien, qui est devenu le peuple de Dieu.' That is why (as it is explained here in great detail) the church prays in its liturgy *plebs tuas populus tuus, familia tua* – to indicate 'the substitution of the Jewish *race* by the Christian *race*'. The French liturgical movement has been ever since Solesmes (Gueranger) particularly anti-Semitic in tone. See chapter 11.

26 On the *perfidia* of the Jews see J.Oesterreicher in *Theological Studies* 8, 1947, and K.Sullivan in *The Bridge* II, 1956.

27 St Paul's inability to see his adversaries other than through a distorting mirror: Schoeps describes as St Paul's basic mistake, his failure to understand the Law as the saving principle of the old covenant. In a way obviously customary among Diaspora Jews, St Paul curtailed and divided the Law. 'He reduced the Torah, which for the Jews meant both law and teaching, to an ethical and ritual law; and on the other hand he separated the Law from its overall context of God's covenant with Israel, and isolated it.' This was the cause of his mistaken exaggeration of the antithesis between Christ and the Law.

'The whole literature of Jewish Hellenism reveals either a rationalization or a spiritualization of the Torah laws, both of them straining away from the realm of Jewish belief ... And so Pauline theology sets out from its author's fatal error of tearing covenant and Law apart and introducing Christ in their place as the fulfilment of the Law' (Schoeps).

27 St Paul's question whether the Law as a whole was capable of fulfilment is completely meaningless to Jews, and it also shows 'that the essentially Jewish beliefs – in JJWH's gift of grace and Man's freedom, even in regard to his evil impulses – were unknown to him.' Schoeps goes on to deplore the fact that the Christian church allowed 'a converted Jew of the Hellenistic Diaspora, estranged from the beliefs of his fathers', to provide it with a completely distorted picture of the Jewish Law. 'And it is even more surprising that over two thousand years, Christian theology has attributed St Paul's lack of impact on the Jews to Jewish obstinacy, and has hardly ever asked itself whether the reason might not be that the apostle was, as far as the Jews were concerned, talking beside the point, since he had misinterpreted everything from the start.'

27 Jules Isaac points out that the Jewish religion was neither decadent nor ossified in the lifetime of Jesus. In Israel the Jewish religion was in full flower, and Jesus preached in the temple and in the synagogue. He wanted to live within the Law, not to destroy it, and the Jewish masses received Him enthusiastically. As Isaac says, if one wants to assert that the Jewish people rejected Christ or the Messiah, one would have to demonstrate that Christ revealed Himself to the Jewish people, the masses, as the Messiah. But that never happened.

28 The Messianic idea: St Paul 'made a myth of the Messiah' (Schoeps), in contrast to Jewish doctrine, which says that the Messiah is not seen as a redeemer or a person with supernatural powers, but simply as the agent of God. 'The Messianic age is in Jewish eyes more important than the person of the Messianic king' (Schoeps).

28 'Jewish eschatology always was, and still is, directed entirely to the

future.' With St Paul it was the other way round, as his interpretation of the Resurrection shows. The situation constantly recurring well into the twentieth century was based on this theological principle: *Christians live with their backs to the future*, and fight (and suppress) any advance in world history – because *their future lies in the past*.

28 'St Paul's eschatology was not directed towards a distant future but, like all true eschatology, based immediately on tomorrow' (Schoeps). Cf. 1 Thessalonians 1, 10; Philippians 4, 5; Romans 8, 9. It is irrelevant to compare Christ's eschatology with St Paul's. 'St Paul's hopes really were fixed on the immediate future, and he was disappointed when they failed to materialize. This is the parousia delay, which lasts to this day [and which present-day theologians like Roger Troisfontaines SJ have ceased to expect at all]. Like all the Qumran people, St Paul found the delay hard to bear, but took it as a call to intensify the certainty of faith even further, since the Last Judgment was at hand and would certainly come as Habakkuk (2, 3) predicted ... It cannot be disputed that the true course of history has put New Testament eschatology in the wrong' (Schoeps).

28 To this gigantic problem belong the remarks of the Catholic physicist Gernot Eder in the Catholic periodical *Wort und Wahrheit* (November 1964): 'The canonization of specific New Testament writings has preserved the purity of doctrine, hemmed in the Holy Ghost, and forced the subsequent evangelists into bloody legends and sects.'

28 Austria's greatest religious thinker in the first half of the twentieth century, the existentialist Ferdinand Ebner, spent a lifetime grappling with the early distortions of Christianity in the church. 'One day,' he wrote, 'the huge edifice of the church will have to collapse in order to set free the Glad Tidings.' In 1919 Ebner asked the vital question whether the church was not producing only neurotic Christians.

28 Looking back to Auschwitz and Hiroshima, to the Christians' centuries-old disassociation from history, Rabbi Ignaz Maybaum (an Austrian by birth) writes in *The Face of God after Auschwitz*: 'There is no holy history as distinct from the history of Man. The medieval dream is ended.'

29 St Paul condemns women to silence in the church: Catholic theology regards the edict as genuine, and uses it to protest against the ordaining of women in the Evangelical church (the most significant breach of Pauline doctrine yet in a major Christian church). Protestant research has shown St Paul's edict to be a later interpolation. The Catholic theologian Schelke is of the opinion that St Paul allowed women to speak in the community (1 Corinthians 11, 5), but he still considers the ban on speech in the church (1 Corinthians 14, 34ff) genuine. Ferdinand Ebner, remembering St Paul and St Augustine, points out quite rightly that anti-feminism and anti-Semitism are, to a far greater

extent than might be realized, the consequence of a celibate 'idealism'. Ebner refers to celibacy as 'a perversion of the intellectual and spiritual life'.

30 St Augustine, the killer of hope: Balthasar, in his chapter on Charles Péguy, points out that Péguy, the great Catholic philosopher of hope and solidarity, breaks down the constraint of centuries: ... 'the theology of St Augustine and the West, in which the concept of predestination logically excluded a final solidarity. According to St Augustine, a man can hope only for himself, but not for his neighbour.'

30 Yves M.Congar (*Concilium* I, 1965) admits: 'It looks as if our definition of religion primarily as a cult and a moral obligation (a definition taken from the classicists of the seventeenth century) has sacrificed something of the feeling that Christianity means hope, an all-embracing hope, even for the so-called material world.'

31 The cosmocrat Christ: In direct contrast to this cosmocratic ideology certain Catholic theologians are today turning their attention back again to the historical Jesus. '*His life ended in bankruptcy*,' writes Herbert Haag SJ in *Am Morgen der Zeit*.

CHAPTER 5: CHRISTIANITY ON THE WAY TO THE IMPERIAL CHURCH

Ausubel, Nathan and Marynn (Editors): A Treasury of Jewish Poetry, New York 1957

Balthasar, Hans Urs v.: Herrlichkeit – eine theologische Aesthetik, Einsiedeln 1962

Balthasar, Hans Urs v.: Origines, 1950

Baum, G.: Die Juden und das Evangelium, Einsiedeln 1963

Bérard, P.: Saint-Augustin et les Juifs, Besançon 1913

Berkhof, H.: Kirche und Kaiser, Zollikon-Zurich 1946

Blumenkranz, B.: Die Judenpredigt Augustins, Basle 1946

Brod, Max: Johannes Reuchlin und sein Kampf, Stuttgart 1965

Deane, Herbert A.: The Political and Social Ideas of St Augustine, 1963

Dempf, A.: Geistesgeschichte der alt-christlichen Kultur, Stuttgart 1964

Deschner, K. (Editor): Jesusbilder in theologischer Sicht, Munich 1966

Harnack, A.von: Lehrbuch der Dogmengeschichte, 1931

Hasler, V.E.: Gesetz und Evangelium in der alten Kirche bis Origines, Zurich 1958

Hay, Malcolm: Europe and the Jews, Boston 1960

Hedenquist, Göte (Editor): The Church and the Jewish People, Edinburgh 1954

Heer, F.: Die dritte Kraft, 1959

Heer, F.: Europa, Mutter der Revolutionen, 1965 (English: Europe, Mother of Revolutions, London 1970)

Heer, F.: The Intellectual History of Europe, London and Cleveland 1966

Hernegger, R.: Macht ohne Auftrag – Die Entstehung der Staats- und Volkskirche, Olten 1963

Isaac, Jules: Genèse de l'antisémitisme, Paris 1956

Ivanka, E.von: Plato Christianus – Übernahme und Umgestaltung des Platonismus durch die Väter, Einsiedeln 1965

Jaromir, R.: Bibel und Zeitgeist, Affoltern 1949

Jéhouda, Josué: L'antisémitisme, miroir du monde, Geneva 1958

Kamen, H.: The Spanish Inquisition, London 1966

Klesse, M.: Vom Alten zum Neuen Israel, Frankfurt 1965

Levine, E. (Editor): The Jewish Heritage, London 1955

Levy, J.: Auf der Suche nach dem Menschen, Salzburg 1960

Loretz, O.: Die Wahrheit der Bibel, Freiburg 1964

Lubac, Henri de: Der geistige Sinn der Schrift, Einsiedeln 1952

Lucas, L.: Zur Geschichte der Juden im vierten Jahrhundert, Berlin 1910

Marmorstein, A.: Judaism and Christianity in the Middle of the Third Century (in Studies in Jewish Theology, London 1950)

Parkes, James: The Conflict of the Church and the Synagogue, New York 1961

Poliakov, Léon: Histoire de l'antisémitisme, Paris 1955

Schoeps, H.J.: Israel und Christenheit, Munich 1961

Simon, M.: La polémique antijuive de St Jean Chrysostome, Brussels 1936

Simon, M.: Verus Israël, Étude sur les relations entre Chrétiens et Juifs dans l'Empire Romain, Paris 1949

Spanneut, M.: Le stoicisme des pères de l'Eglise, Paris 1957

Thieme, Karl: Judenfeindschaft, Darstellung und Analysen, Frankfurt 1963

Ullmann, W.: Medieval Papalism, the Political Theories of the Medieval Canonists, London 1949

Vogt, J.: Der Niedergang Roms – Metamorphose der antiken Kultur, Zurich 1965

Widengren, G.: Mani und der Manichäismus, Stuttgart 1961

Williams, A.Lukyn: Adversus Judaeos, a Bird's-Eye View of Christian Apologiae until the Renaissance, Cambridge 1935

Zaehner, R.C.: The Dawn and Twilight of Zoroastrianism, London 1961

Page

32 Two churches in exile: Parkes, 77ff.

32 Creation of an official Jewish attitude to Christianity: among others, Parkes, 106ff.

33 The tragic history of the Jewish Christians after separation: Parkes, 92ff.

33 Jesus in the Talmud: Parkes, 109f.

33 The church never ceased to fear the rival influence of Jewry: Parkes, 120f, and chapters 5, 6, 7, 8 and 13 of this book.

34 The development of dogma in the fourth century, which set the direction (as in the 'Jewish problem') for the next fifteen hundred years: The

problems arising from that have still not been fully solved by the Roman Catholic church. K.Rahner (in *Schriften zur Theologie* IV) says that the real problem has been deliberately passed over. In all questions of dogma the pressure of the superstitious masses played an important role. Rahner pleads with modern theologians to work against this 'popular' form of piety, which dominated church councils and controversies on dogma in the fourth and nineteenth centuries. Hans Küng calls for a historical approach, which considers church dogma itself as a historical phenomenon.

34 Texts of Christian anti-Jewish polemics in Williams. 'They did not understand the mind of the Jews' (417f).

37 St John Chrysostom and the Jews: Malcolm Hay remarks of his sermons: 'Such logic would justify the German race murderers. St John Chrysostom could have preached a powerful sermon beside the mass grave at Dubno.'

38 Sexual lust was obscene: cf. Ebner: 'Anyone who tries to explain Christianity in ascetic terms is guilty of misunderstanding it.'

39 The Song of Songs: For the Jewish interpretation see Ausubel (Ed.), XLIIIff. Christian interpretations: bibliography in Balthasar. The great Spanish religious poet Luis de Leon (who was of Jewish extraction) was accused of translating the Song as a worldly love-song (Kamen, 84).

40 Catholic monastic interpretation of the Song holds firm to the old tradition. The Carmelite R.O.Lucien-Marie de Saint-Joseph, reviewing a new French translation in 1953, observes: 'La rencontre dans ce volume d'un traducteur juif et d'un préfacier chrétien s'inspire d'un esprit d'amitié aux sources communes de leur foi respective.' But he holds firm to the purely spiritual character of the Song, with God-Christ as the bridegroom and the church, Mary, the soul as the lovely bride.

40 The Jewish-born Catholic Jacques Lévy, who died in Auschwitz, contrasts Renan's interpretation of the Song as an erotic love-song with St Paul, who sees the love between man and woman as a mystic union.

40 St Augustine's historical significance: among others Deane, Heer (Intellectual History).

42 St Thomas Aquinas was the first who dared to respond properly to St Augustine's invitation to his readers (*De Trinitate* I) to criticize his theology.

42 St Augustine's views on concupiscence and on Jews are closely related to his views on the Mother of Christ. The Virgin Mary is free of all concupiscence. Early Christians understand the birth of Christ quite naturally: through conception. Clement of Alexandria (*Stromateis* VII) wrote in the second century that most Christians were in favour of a natural birth, and only 'some say' that Mary was found to be a virgin after the birth. In line with the rapidly developing monasticism of Christianity, Athanasius, St John Chrysostom, St Ambrose and St

Augustine (all of them extremely anti-Jewish) began to talk of the untouched hymen and genital passages. The great Jesuit theologian F.Suarez later expended several pages on the question of the afterbirth at the birth of Jesus.

42 Hereditary service in the Roman Empire and St Augustine's ideas on original sin: The erection of the Roman church as a citadel of orthodox faith should be seen in relation to the development of the *Imperium Romanum* as a fortress under Diocletian. Cf. Tertullian's militarization of Christianity. The connection of the individual to the collective salvation of the church can be compared with the connection of the *coloni* to the land under Constantine. Slaves and *coloni*: the descent of large sections of the peasant population to a position of bondage under Theodosius is related to the process of building up the church.

43 Cardinals and bishops assume to this day the titles (Eminence, Excellency) and wear the clothes of Constantinian and Byzantine imperial court officials.

43 St Augustine and the Donatists: among others, Deane.

43 *Servi adscripticii:* Ullmann.

43 Bishops and theologians seated on their exalted thrones: see, for example, the *auto-da-fé* picture (c. 1500) in the Madrid National Gallery (Fig. 8 in *The Legacy of Israel*, Oxford 1953).

44 St Augustine and the Jews: According to Guido Kisch, St Augustine formulated the momentous phrase *Judaeus servus est Christiani* (the Jew is slave to the Christian) some years after Emperor Honorius had excluded Jews from military service. A high percentage of theological definitions represents the belated execution of political decisions – from the fourth up to the twentieth centuries.

45 St Augustine and the fall of Rome: among others, Deane.

45 The process of eliminating Judaism from the church is closely related to its Hellenization. In the second and third centuries the church fathers were characterized by an optimistic, rationalistic and monastic stoicism. Around A D 250 the great wave of Neo-Platonism carried all before it. Clement of Alexandria marks the transition from stoicism to Neo-Platonism in Christian thought.

46 Athanasius: Parkes, 186f.

48 Cyril of Alexandria: 'Ritual murder, the poisoning of wells, the profanation of the Host, all these are natural growths from the picture created by a Chrysostom or a Cyril' (Parkes, 376).

48 St Epiphanius: Parkes, 168ff.

48 The Councils of the fourth century: Parkes, 174f.

48 Constantius: Parkes, 180.

48 Emperor Theodosius' Code: Parkes, 199ff.

48 Justinian's legislation against the Jews: Parkes, 245ff, 255.

49 Theodoric and the Ostrogoths tolerant towards Jews: Parkes, 206ff.

49 Jewish reactions to persecution in the later Roman Empire: Parkes, 121ff, 145ff.

49 Talmudic Judaism and Jewish orthodoxy: see Isidore Epstein, *The Rabbinic Tradition*, in Levine (Ed.).

CHAPTER 6: THE CHRISTIAN AND JEWISH MIDDLE AGES

Ausubel, Nathan and Marynn (Editors): A Treasury of Jewish Poetry, New York 1957

Bevan, E.R., and Singer, C. (Editors): The Legacy of Israel, Oxford 1953

Blumenkranz, B.: Juifs et chrétiens dans le monde oriental (430–1096), Paris 1960

Bressolles, Mgr.: Saint Agobard, évêque de Lyon, Paris 1949

Brod, Max: Johannes Reuchlin und sein Kampf, Stuttgart 1965

Browe, P.: Die Judenmission im Mittelalter und die Päpste, Rome 1942

Dubnow, Simon: Die Geschichte des jüdischen Volkes in Europa, Berlin 1926. (Abridged English translation by B.Mowskowitch, London 1936: A History of the Jewish People)

Eckert, W.P., and Ehrlich, E.L.: Judenhass – Schuld der Christen?, Essen 1964

Falco, G.: Geist des Mittelalters, Zurich 1958

Fleg, E. (Editor): Anthologie juive des origines à nos jours, Paris 1951

Günther, Hans F.K.: Rassenkunde des jüdischen Volkes, Munich 1930

Hay, Malcolm: Europe and the Jews, Boston 1960

Hoffmann, D.: Der Schulchan Aruch und die Rabbiner über das Verhältnis der Juden zu Andersgläubigen, Berlin 1885

Holtzmann, R.: Geschichte der sächsischen Kaiserzeit (900–1024), Munich 1941

Isaac, Jules: Genèse de l'antisémitisme, Paris 1956

Kaplan, M.M.: The Purpose and Meaning of Jewish Existence, Philadelphia 1964

Leschnitzer, A.: The Magic Background of Modern Anti-Semitism, New York 1956

Levine, E. (Editor): The Jewish Heritage, London 1955

Liebermann, A.: Zur jüdischen Moral, Berlin 1920

Long, E.J.: 2,000 Years – A History of Anti-Semitism, New York 1953

Maurer, W.: Kirche und Synagoge, Stuttgart 1953

Newman, L.J.: Jewish Influence on Christian Reform Movements, New York 1925

Parkes, James: The Conflict of the Church and the Synagogue, New York 1961

Poliakov, Léon: Du Christ aux juifs de cour, Paris 1955

Roth, B.Cecil: Die Kunst der Juden, Frankfurt 1962

Runciman, S.: A History of the Crusades, London 1951 (paperback ed., 1965)

Seiferth, W.: Synagoge und Kirche im Mittelalter, Munich 1964

Thieme, Karl: Judenfeindschaft, Darstellung und Analysen, Frankfurt 1963

Trachtenberg, J.: The Devil and the Jews, New Haven 1943

Waas, A.: Geschichte der Kreuzzüge, Freiburg 1956

Williams, A. Lukyn: Adversus Judaeos, Cambridge 1935

Page

54 R. Travers Herford in *The Legacy of Israel* (Ed. Bevan and Singer).

55 Visigothic Spain: among others, Dubnow, Parkes, 345ff. Anti-Jewish Spanish writers and texts from fifth to fifteenth centuries: Williams, 206.

58 French anti-Semitism in the nineteenth century: see chapter 9.

58 Jews at the court of Charlemagne and Louis the Pious: among others, Dubnow.

58 The religious and political climate of the Carolingian court: Williams writes (348): 'The early part of the ninth century was a remarkable period in the history of France, for thoughts came to the surface then, and ideals were seen, which afterwards were long lost sight of, not to say buried, and were revived and put into practice only after nearly a thousand years had passed away.'

59 Agobard, archbishop of Lyon: among others, Williams, 348ff.

60 Amulo of Lyon: texts in Williams, 348ff.

62 Alterations to Good Friday liturgy: among others, John M. Oesterreicher, *Pro perfidis Judaeis*, in *Theological Studies*, 1947. Isaac rightly remarks that some Catholic studies have obscured the historical situation.

64 In his excellent study on the position of the Jews in Catholic liturgy, John Hennig (in Eckert-Ehrlich) remarks that Christian veneration of Old Testament saints in religious art and literature reached its climax at a time when Jewish persecution was particularly rife in Christian Europe.

64 The killing of Jews in the Crusades condoned by Catholic writers of the eighteenth to twentieth centuries: texts in Hay, 47ff.

65 Anti-Jewish echoes in Chaucer's Canterbury Tales: see R. J. Schoeck, *Chaucer's Prioress, Mercy and Tender Heart* in *The Bridge* II, 239ff.

67 St Bernard of Clairvaux: among others, Hay, 40ff, 56.

68 Petrus Venerabilis and Sir Evelyn Parker: Hay, 47f.

68 Summary of Catholic writers and historians in the nineteenth and twentieth centuries: Hay, 62ff.

68 Abelard, the great exception in his attitude to Jews: Hay, 67f.

70 Accusations of ritual murder in modern times: Hay, 310ff. Ritual murder: among others, Hay, 111ff; Parkes, 367f. Accusations of ritual murder in the antique world, China etc.: Long, 105ff.

71 Albigenses opposed to doctrine of transubstantiation: In the middle of

the twelfth century a dying man refused communion from the priest Ekbert von Schönau, saying with a scornful smile: 'If the Lord's body were as large as the Hermelstein [a rock near Coblenz], it would have been eaten up entirely in the time since people first began to eat it.'

71 Ritual murder legends in England: Hay, 122f.

71 Anderl of Rinn and the bull *Beatus Andreas*: among others, Hay, 129f. In 1955 the peasants were still defending their Anderl: 'How can the pope in Rome know what happened here four hundred years ago?'

72 Sermons and acts of violence against 'the people who killed Christ' in the Middle Ages: Hay, 33ff.

72 The Lateran Council of 1215 and the Jews: among others, Hay, 86ff, Dubnow.

72 Innocent III's two letters: Hay, 76f.

73 Jewish marks after 1215: Hay, 86ff.

74 Gregory IX warns the bishops: Hay, 96f.

74 Judah Halevi: among others, Dubnow and M. Simon in *The Jewish Heritage* (Ed. Levine).

75 Triple culture Spain and the Jews: among others, Dubnow, Charles and Dorothea Singer in *The Legacy of Israel* (Ed. Bevan and Singer), 184ff.

76 Maimonides: Singer in *The Legacy of Israel*, 192ff, 251ff, 257ff, 267ff; Simon in *The Jewish Heritage* (Ed. Levine), 119ff; Kaplan, 36ff.

77 Public debates between Jews and Christians in the twelfth and thirteenth centuries: Bevan and Singer (Ed.), 294ff, Dubnow.

77 Immanuel di Roma: Ausubel (Ed.), LIff, 176f; Fleg.

78 Ecclesia and Synagogue in Bamberg Cathedral: In 1965 Jewish tombstones were desecrated in Bamberg and anti-Jewish pamphlets distributed throughout the town.

82 Jewish liturgies of mourning in the Middle Ages: Dubnow, Ausubel (Ed.), LIff, 177ff (Meir von Rothenburg).

82 Les Martyrs de Troyes, 1288: Texts in Fleg (Ed.), 281ff.

84 England and the Jews in the Middle Ages: Dubnow; Long, 54f; R. J. Schoeck in *The Bridge* II, 239ff; B. Ulanov in *The Bridge* I, 266ff.

90 Francesco Traini's altar-piece depicting the victory of St Thomas Aquinas over Averroes: Fig. 44 in *The Legacy of Israel* (Ed. Bevan and Singer).

91 Belief in witches, witch hunts and Jewish persecution: Leschnitzer, 97ff, 103ff, 145ff.

CHAPTER 7: SPAIN: HEAVEN AND HELL OF THE JEWS

Bevan, E.R., and Singer, C. (Editors): The Legacy of Israel, Oxford 1953

Dubnow, Simon: Die Geschichte des jüdischen Volkes in Europe, Berlin 1926 (English, abridged: A History of the Jewish People, London 1936)

Gebhardt, C. (Editor): Die Schriften des Uriel da Costa, Amsterdam 1922
Heer, F.: Aufgang Europas, 1949
Heer, F.: Die Dritte Kraft, 1959
Heer, F.: Erasmus von Rotterdam, Frankfurt 1962
Heer, F.: Europa, Mutter der Revolutionen, 1965 (English translation: Europe, Mother of Revolutions)
Heer, F.: Heiliges Römisches Reich, 1967 (English: The Holy Roman Empire, 1968)
Heer, F.: The Intellectual History of Europe, London and Cleveland 1966
Jaromir, R.: Bibel und Zeitgeist, Affoltern 1949
Kamen, H.: The Spanish Inquisition, London 1965
Levine, E. (Editor): The Jewish Heritage, London 1955
Long, E.J.: 2,000 Years – A History of Anti-Semitism, New York 1953
Pinay, M.: Verschwörung gegen die Kirche, Madrid 1963
Poliakov, Léon: Du Christ aux juifs de cour, Paris 1955
Rahner, H.: Ignatius von Loyola als Mensch und Theologe, Freiburg 1964
Rahner, H.: Ignatius von Loyola – Briefwechsel mit Frauen, Freiburg 1956
Randa, Alex. von: Das Weltreich, Wagnis und Auftrag Europas im sechzehnten und siebzehnten Jahrhundert, Freiburg 1962
Schneider, Reinhold: Winter in Wien, Vienna 1958
Schurhammer, G.: Franz Xaver, Freiburg 1955
Thieme, Karl: Judenfeindschaft, Darstellung und Analysen, Frankfurt 1963

Page
94 Spanish anti-Semitism in the twentieth century: Kamen, 229f.
94 For a more detailed account of Pinay's *Conspiracy against the Church* see chapter 13.
96 Ramon Lull: see Heer (Intellectual History).
97 Luis de Leon: see Heer (Intellectual History).
99 Georges Bernanos and his experiences in Majorca: P. Anderson in *Continuum* II, 1964, 194ff.
102 Marranos: among others Dubnow, Kamen, 15, 31.
105 Columbus and the Jews: Heer (Intellectual History); Long, 73f.
107 Leo Baeck: see chapter 13.
107 *Conversos*: Kamen, 14ff, 29ff, 63f, 71, 82, 122ff.
108 The Jesuits and the Inquisition: Kamen, 88f, 128f, 156, 252f, 274, 281, 304.
108 Hernando de Talavera: Heer (Intellectual History).
108 Francisco Ximenes de Cisneros: Heer (Intellectual History).
109 Illuminists: Kamen, 71ff, 76, 82.
109 Fray Melchor: Heer (Intellectual History).
109 Revolutionary Puritanism in England and Scotland: Heer (Intellectual History). On the eve of the French Revolution . . .: ditto.

110 Erasmus and Spain: Kamen, 67ff, 88f, 93ff; Heer (Intellectual History).

110 Dr Vergara: Kamen, 67, 69, 72ff, 124; Heer (Intellectual History).

111 The Cazalla family: Kamen, 72f, 77, 79ff; Heer (Intellectual History).

111 The Valdes Index: Kamen, 88ff, 26off, 268ff; Heer (Intellectual History).

111 Pope Paul IV: Kamen, 124, 159, 233; Heer (Intellectual History).

112 Loyola admits a woman to the Society: She was the daughter of Emperor Charles V, the Infanta Juana, and she was admitted under the name of Mateo Sanchez (related in Rahner's *Ignatius von Loyola – Briefwechsel mit Frauen*).

112 Jesuits and Jews at the time of Loyola: among others, Kamen, 128ff, 252ff.

113 Archbishop Siliceo: among others, Kamen, 64, 82, 122ff, 128f, 156f.

113 Number of people burnt at the stake: Kamen, 26ff, 177ff.

113 The 'business-like' Inquisition: Kamen claims (p. 50) that the Inquisition represented the interests of the vast majority of the Spanish people against a small but significant minority.

113 Philip II, the 'bureaucratic king': Kamen, 137ff.

114 Lucero's monster trial: Kamen, 55ff, Dubnow.

116 Archbishop Siliceo's plot allegations: Kamen, 122ff, Dubnow.

117 Portuguese Inquisition: Kamen, 144, 170f, 215ff.

120 Spinoza and the Jews: See Leon Roth in *The Legacy of Israel* (Ed. Bevan and Singer) and D. Daiches-Raphael in *The Jewish Heritage* (Ed. Levine).

120 *Limpieza de sangre*: among others, Kamen, 125ff, 130ff, 144ff, 162ff.

121 The Last Words of Don Henriquez: Translated from the Yiddish by Joseph Leftwich (in *A Treasury of Jewish Poetry*, Ed. Ausubel).

CHAPTER 8: EASTWARDS

Balthasar, Hans Urs v.: Herrlichkeit – eine theologische Aesthetik, Einsiedeln 1962

Benz, E.: Die Ostkirche im Lichte der protestantischen Geschichtsschreibung, Freiburg 1952

Brod, Max: Johannes Reuchlin und sein Kampf, Stuttgart 1965

Byrnes, R.F.: Anti-Semitism in Modern France, New Brunswick 1950

Dubnow, Simon: Die Geschichte des jüdischen Volkes in Europa, Berlin 1926 (English, abridged: A History of the Jewish People, London 1936)

Erikson, Erik H.: Young Man Luther – A Study in Psycho-analysis and History, London 1959

Feder, E.: Paul Nathan – Politiker und Philanthrop, Stuttgart 1963

Goldschmidt, D. and Kraus, H.J. (Editors): Der ungekündigte Bund, Stuttgart 1962

Grau, W.: Antisemitismus im späten Mittelalter, Berlin 1939

Harnack, A.von: Lehrbuch der Dogmengeschichte, 1931

Hay, Malcolm: Europe and the Jews, Boston 1960

Heer, F.: The Intellectual History of Europe, London and Cleveland 1966

Hutten, K., and Kortzfleisch, S.v. (Editors): Asien missioniert im Abendland, Stuttgart 1962

Jaromir, R.: Bibel und Zeitgeist, Affoltern 1949

Klesse, M.: Vom Alten zum Neuen Israel, Frankfurt 1965

Leschnitzer, A.: The Magic Background of Modern Anti-Semitism, New York 1956

Lewy, Guenter: The Catholic Church and Nazi Germany, London and New York 1964

Long, E.J.: 2,000 Years – A History of Anti-Semitism, New York 1953

Musurillo, H. (Editor): The Acts of the Pagan Martyrs, 1954

Pfister, O.: Das Christentum und die Angst, Zurich 1944

Poliakov, Léon: Du Christ aux juifs de cour, Paris 1955

Ullmann, W.: The Growth of Papal Government in the Middle Ages, London 1955

Werner, M.: Der protestantische Weg des Glaubens, Berne 1955

Winter, E.: Russland und das Papsttum, Berlin 1960

Page

127 Christian converts to Buddhism: E.Benz deals with this in the *Eranos-Jahrbuch 1958* (Zurich 1959), where he speaks of one Italian and two German monks as Buddhist missionaries. In Hutten and Kortzfleisch (Editors) there are questions addressed by a German Buddhist to the Christian West.

128 Reuchlin: among others, Dubnow and Heer (Intellectual History).

128 Martin Luther: Balthasar, who of all Catholic theologians penetrates most deeply into Luther's spirituality, traces the many connections between him and Catholic spiritual and philosophical traditions in European history. In his criticism of Luther from a Protestant point of view, that remarkable theologian of a reformed church, M.Werner, reveals convincingly how Luther distorted the Bible in the cause of his existential situation.

129 Luther and the Jews: among others, Hay, 166ff.

129 For more on Adorno's researches into authoritarian personality, see chapter 13.

130 For more on Hitler's conversations with Dietrich Eckart, see chapter 11.

131 'His words could adorn the gates of the police headquarters and concentration camps of our time' (Erikson): At the tenth Protestant church congress in 1961 in Berlin a Protestant working group for the first time connected Luther with Julius Streicher and Nazi policy towards the Jews. A fuller account of this congress (recorded in *Der ungekündigte Bund*, ed. Goldschmidt and Kraus) is contained in chapter 13. Hay

(p. 169) remarks that the first National Socialist pogrom in November 1938 (the *Kristallnacht*) took place on Luther's birthday. Hay also quotes Dean Inge (p. 166): 'The worst evil genius of Germany is not Hitler, or Bismarck, or Frederick the Great, but Martin Luther.'

135 Popular anti-Semitism in Poland after 1945: see chapter 13.

140 Russian anti-Semitism under Stalin and in 1965: see chapter 13.

141 The Black Hundreds: Long, 124ff, who also deals with Russian anti-Semitism in the nineteenth century on 117ff.

141 The Protocols of the Elders of Zion: among others, Long, 177f, and Pierre Charles SJ in *The Bridge* I, 1955. See also chapters 11 and 12.

141 Pious forgeries concerning the acts of the martyrs: on the literary aspects of pious forgery the great Bollandist Hippolyte Delehaye has done some vital pioneer work (*Les passions des martyrs et les genres littéraires*, 1921). See also Musurillo (Ed.). Ullmann deals extensively with the Donation of Constantine, which falsely maintains that Emperor Constantine bequeathed Rome and certain other territories to the pope. Forgeries in connection with the First Vatican Council are richly documented in the correspondence between Lord Acton and Dr Döllinger.

141 Forgeries in connection with the Second Vatican Council, in the reproduction of the encyclical *Pacem in terris*, etc.: The American Jesuit Conway has pointed out forty serious mistakes in the official Italian translation of the original Latin text, as well as omissions of whole sentences, interpolations of other sentences, rearrangements of whole paragraphs. For a time after 1945 it was customary among German church historians dealing with the German church in Hitler's time to doctor their sources according to need (Lewy provides several examples). For Catholic forgeries in the Dreyfus affair, see chapter 9.

142 French plot theory: Heer (Intellectual History).

143 Tsarist approval of anti-Semitism and pogroms after 1881: Byrnes, 88ff.

CHAPTER 9: THE FRENCH VERSUS JEWRY

Arendt, H.: Eichmann in Jerusalem, Munich 1964
Arnoulin, G.: Edmond Drumont et les Jésuites, Paris 1902
Barrès, Maurice: Scènes et doctrines du nationalisme, Paris 1902
Bernanos, G.: La grande peur des bien-pensants, Edmond Drumont, Paris 1931
Boisnadré, A.: Napoléon antisémite, Paris 1938
Byrnes, R.F.: Anti-Semitism in Modern France, New Brunswick 1950
Coudenhove-Kalergi, R.: Eine Idee erobert Europa, Vienna 1958
Czempiel, E.O.: Das deutsche Dreyfus-Geheimnis, Munich 1966
De Gasperi, M.R.C.: De Gasperi uomo solo, Milan 1964
Donos, Charles de: Morès – sa vie, sa mort, Paris 1899

Duployé, P.: La religion de Péguy, Paris 1965

Fleg, E. (Editor): Anthologie juive, Paris 1951

Frank, Walter: Nationalismus und Demokratie im Frankreich der dritten Republik, Hamburg 1933

Guérin, J.: Les trafiquants de l'antisémitisme, Paris 1905

Hay, Malcolm: Europe and the Jews, Boston 1960

Heer, F.: Europa, Mutter der Revolutionen, 1965 (English translation: Europe, Mother of Revolutions)

Jéhouda, Josué: L'antisémitisme, miroir du monde, Geneva 1958

Labroul, H.: Voltaire antijuif, Paris 1942

Lazare, Bernard: L'antisémitisme, Paris 1934

Lesca, Charles: Quand Israël se venge, Paris 1941 (11th ed.)

Loisy, A.: La guerre et la religion, Paris 1915

Loisy, A.: Mémoires pour servir à l'histoire religieuse de notre temps, Paris 1930–1

Pinson, Koppel (Editor): Essays on Anti-Semitism, New York 1964

Poliakov, Léon: Du Christ aux juifs de cour, Paris 1955

Schlamm, W.: Wer ist Jude?, Stuttgart 1964

Thalheimer, S.: Macht und Gerechtigkeit – ein Beitrag zur Geschichte des Falles Dreyfus, Munich 1958

Thieme, Karl: Judenfeindschaft, Darstellung und Analysen, Frankfurt 1963

Weber, Eugene: Action Française, Stanford (Calif.) 1962

Page

146 Jews had affected Russia with syphilis: Hay, 191.

146 Bernanos praises *La France Juive*: La grande peur, 185.

146 A long anti-Jewish tradition in France: Hay, 171ff.

146 Bossuet: Hay, 173ff. Pascal, Voltaire, Rousseau, etc.: Hay, 171ff.

147 Isaac Berr: Fleg (Ed.), 318f.

147 The French Revolution and the Jews: Fleg (Ed.), 315ff.

147 Karl Marx and the Jews: see chapter 10.

148 The Dreyfus affair as the severest crisis of modern democratic society: Byrnes in the introduction to his first volume.

149 The Third Republic in France as the child of defeat: see Byrnes, I, 23ff.

149 Hippolyte Taine: Byrnes, 48ff.

149 Action Française rehabilitated by Pope Pius xii: see chapter 11.

150 Maurras in *Chemin de Paradis*: Hay, 19.

150 French Catholic anti-Semites were attentively watching: Byrnes, I, 78ff.

150 Polish anti-Semitism: R. Mahler in *Essays on Antisemitism* (Ed. Pinson), 145ff. See also chapter 13.

150 The tsar gave approximately twelve million roubles: Byrnes, 89.

151 Number of Jews in France: Byrnes, I, 92ff.

151 Jewish attitude towards anti-Semitism: Byrnes, I, 97ff.

151 Zadoc Kahn: Byrnes, I, 101. Thalheimer says that he recommended Esterhazy to Baron E. de Rothschild!

152 Gobineau: among others, Byrnes, I, 112ff.

152 Pope Pius IX blessed Henri Gougenot des Mousseaux (one of Hitler's sources!): Byrnes, I, 113.

152 Left-wing anti-Semitism before 1880/5: Byrnes, I, 114ff.

153 Right-wing, Catholic and conservative anti-Semitism in France: Byrnes, I, 125ff.

153 French Catholics and freemasonry: Byrnes, I, 126ff.

154 Edmond Drumont and *La France Juive*: among others, Heer (Europe, Mother of Revolutions) and Byrnes, I, 137ff, 140ff.

155 French clerics in favour of Drumont: Byrnes, I, 179ff.

156 *La Civiltà Cattolica* supported French anti-Semites in the Dreyfus trial: Hay, 201f.

157 First congress of the Christian Democrats in Lyon: Byrnes, I, 209ff.

157 Morès: Byrnes, I, 225ff, 237ff, 242ff; also Barrès.

159 French provincial clergy: Byrnes, I, 201ff, 298ff; Hay, 176ff. Military officers: Byrnes, I, 263f.

160 Unemployed journalists, etc.: Byrnes, I, 269f, 290. Anti-Semitic caricaturists: Byrnes, I, 291ff.

161 The Jews are either Germans or agents of the Germans: Hay, 211ff. Bonsirven: Hay, 226.

161 Anti-Semitic books written by priests: Byrnes, I, 298ff. Anti-American clergy: Byrnes, I, 301ff.

162 Leo Taxil: among others, Byrnes, I, 304ff, 313ff, 315, 317.

165 *Civiltà Cattolica* and the Dreyfus trial: this periodical, which remained strongly Fascist in tone until only a few years ago, declared at that time: 'In the mouth of a Catholic the word tolerance is a mortal sin.'

166 Esterhazy to David Christie Murray: in Thalheimer, who has provided source material for all written here on the Dreyfus trial.

168 Charles Péguy: Thalheimer, Heer (Europe, Mother of Revolutions), Duployé. Yves M.J.Congar wrote in *Dokumente* of October 1965: 'Péguy found his way into the community of saints even without the sacraments.' Congar, a Dominican, realized that Péguy could not reconcile himself with the actual church and with Catholicism in France: 'He was conscious of the tendency of all powerful organizations to become tyrannical with that sort of *respected authority which Jesus, Joan of Arc and Dreyfus condemned*. Bergson had fallen victim to its censure, and now it was threatening him.'

169 Leading circles in the Curia were on the side of Dreyfus's enemies: Hay, 201.

170 Drumont's challenge to Pope Leo XIII: Byrnes, I, 334; Hay, 208.

170 Rampolla's joy at Dreyfus's conviction: Hay, 207. Rampolla was the

great protector in Rome of the Austrian anti-Semites of the Christian Social party before, and at the time of, Lueger.

170 'Friends of Israel', *Action Française* and the Vatican: see chapters 11 and 13.

CHAPTER 10: THE GREAT DREAM

Arendt, H.: Rahel Varnhagen, Munich 1959

Bloch, E.: Das Prinzip Hoffnung, Frankfurt 1963

Borée, K.F.: Semiten und Antisemiten – Begegnungen und Erfahrungen, Frankfurt 1960

Borries, A.von (Editor): Selbstzeugnisse des deutschen Judentums 1870–1945, Frankfurt 1962

Cohen, Arthur A.: The Natural and the Supernatural Jew, New York 1962

De Sinoja, J.E.: Das Antisemitentum in der Musik, Zurich-Vienna 1933

Deutscher, I.: Trotzki, Stuttgart 1962

Dubnow, Simon: Nationalism and History, Essays on Old and New Judaism, New York 1961

Eckert, W.P. and Ehrlich, E.L.: Judenhass – Schuld der Christen?, Essen 1964

Ferenczi, S.: Versuch einer Genitaltheorie, Vienna 1924

Fleg, E. (Editor): Anthologie juive, Paris 1951

Freud, S.: Briefe 1873–1939, Frankfurt 1960

Freud, S. (with Oskar Pfister): Briefe 1909–39, Frankfurt 1965

Freud, S.: Briefe an Wilhelm Fliess, Frankfurt 1950

Freud, S.: Das Unbewusste – Schriften zur Psychoanalyse, Frankfurt 1960

Fürst, J. Henriette Herz, Berlin 1950

Goldschmidt, H.L.: Die Botschaft des Judentums, 1960

Goldschmidt, H.L.: Das Vermächtnis des deutschen Judentums, Frankfurt 1957

Heer, F.: Europa, Mutter der Revolutionen, 1965 (English translation: Europe, Mother of Revolutions)

Heer, F.: The Intellectual History of Europe, London and Cleveland 1966

Hofstätter, Peter R.: Einführung in die Tiefenpsychologie, Vienna 1948

Jacob, H.E.: Felix Mendelssohn und seine Zeit, Frankfurt 1959

Jaspers, Karl: Kleine Schule philosophischen Denkens, Munich 1965

Jetzinger, F.: Hitlers Jugend, Vienna 1956

Kahler, E.v.: Die Verantwortung des Geistes, Frankfurt 1952

Kemper, Werner: Der Traum und seine Be-Deutung, Hamburg 1955

Klesse, M.: Vom Alten zum Neuen Israel, Frankfurt 1965

Küng, Hans: Kirche und Freiheit, Einsiedeln 1964

Leschnitzer, A.: The Magic Background of Modern Anti-Semitism, New York 1956

Liptzin, S.: Germany's Step-children, New York 1961

Loewenstein, R.: Psychanalyse de l'antisémitisme, Paris 1952
Maas, Hermann (Editor): Den Unvergessenen Opfern des Wahns 1933 bis 1945, Heildelberg 1952
Marcuse, L.: Obszön, Munich 1963 (on Schlegel's *Lucinde*)
Müller-Claudius, M.: Deutsche und jüdische Tragik, Frankfurt 1955
Nobécourt, J.: 'Le Vicaire' et l'Histoire, Paris 1964
Nuttin, J.: Psychoanalyse und Persönlichkeit, Freiburg 1956
Ornstein, Hans: Der antijüdische Komplex, Zurich 1949
Popitz, H.: Der entfremdete Mensch, Basle 1953
Pulzer, P.G.J.: The Rise of Political Anti-Semitism in Germany and Austria, New York 1964
Rathenau, Walter: Schriften und Reden (edited H.W.Richter), Frankfurt 1964
Reichmann, Eva G.: Hostages of Civilization, London 1950
Richter, W.: Bismarck, Frankfurt 1962
Rosenberg, Alfred: Der Mythus des XX. Jahrhunderts, Munich 1935
Rühle, J.: Literatur und Revolution, Frankfurt 1963
Schlamm, William S.: Wer ist Jude? – Ein Selbstgespräch, Stuttgart 1964
Schoeps, H.J.: Israel und Christenheit, Frankfurt 1961 (re-issue)
Schoeps, H.J. (Editor): Jüdische Geisteswelt – Zeugnisse aus zwei Jahrtausenden, Darmstadt 1953
Spiel, Hilde: Fanny von Arnstein oder Die Emanzipation, Frankfurt 1962
Stadelmann, R.: Soziale und politische Geschichte der Revolution 1848, Munich 1948
Sterling, Eleonore: Er ist wie du – Aus der Frühgeschichte des Antisemitismus in Deutschland (1815–50), Munich 1956
Stransky, E.: Staatsführung und Psychopathie, Vienna 1952
Thieme, Karl: Judenfeindschaft, Darstellung und Analysen, Frankfurt 1963
Trotzky, Leon: My Life, London 1930
Weltsch, R. (Editor): Deutsches Judentum–Aufstieg und Krise, Stuttgart 1963
Wittgenstein, Ludwig: Schriften, Frankfurt 1960
Wulf, J.: Das Dritte Reich und seine Diener, Berlin 1956
Zilboorg, G.: Freud and Religion, London 1959
Die Juden und die Kultur (anthology), Stuttgart 1961

Page

172 The ghetto broke open: 'The opening of the ghetto gates had revolutionary implications for European Jews, since they had in the space of a single generation to achieve an intellectual development which had occupied the West for three thousand years' (Schoeps, *Jüdische Geisteswelt*).

173 The literary salons of Jewish ladies: among others, Liptzin, 9ff, 12ff.

173 The first mention of Jews in Berlin: in 1510, thirty-eight of them were tortured and burnt (Max Brod, *Johannes Reuchlin*).

174 Goldschmidt's population statistics in *Das Vermächtnis*.

175 Moses Mendelssohn: among others Liptzin, 9f, 23, 146; Dubnow, 6, 92, 133, 314ff; Cohen, 19ff, 59, 75.

176 Christian Wilhelm Dohm: among others, Cohen, 22f.

177 Leo Baeck and Moses Mendelssohn: Leo Baeck, Types of Jewish Understanding from Moses Mendelssohn to Franz Rosenzweig, translated by H.C.Stevens, *Judaism*, vol. IX, notes 1 and 2.

179 Rahel Varnhagen: Among others, Liptzin, 12ff.

180 Prince de Ligne and the Jews: Among others, Liptzin, 12; Fleg (Ed.), 366f.

180 Fichte and the Jews: Among others, Reichmann.

180 Friedrich von Gentz: The great Austrian poet, Franz Grillparzer, has painted an excellent portrait of this questionable character in his political essays. Grillparzer maintains that Gentz had an unfortunate influence on Metternich, who was much given to the pleasures of life as he grew old and was anyway (in Grillparzer's opinion) no great statesman.

182 Heinrich Heine: among others, Dubnow, 12, 94, 316f; Cohen, 18, 42, 56, 198.

182 'Show some respect, Jew!' (*Mach Mores, Jud!*): Kiptzin, 29.

182 Ludwig Börne: Liptzin, 9, 27ff, 48, 55, 63, 69, 82, 88f, 91, and others.

183 Karl Beck: Liptzin, 45ff, 55, 63.

183 Joel Jacoby and David Friedrich Koreff: Liptzin, 48ff, 57ff.

184 Heine: Liptzin, 12, 63ff, 91, 96, 103, 137, 237, and others.

186 Heine's poem 'Peace' translated by Emma Lazarus (Hartsdale House, New York 1947).

188 Rene König on Marx in the anthology *Die Juden und die Kultur*.

190 Börne's statement 'Some reproach me for being a Jew': Max Wehrli in the anthology *Die Juden und die Kultur*.

193 Moses Hess: Heer (both books); Kiptzin, 93ff, 101ff, 260; Cohen, 54ff.

195 Ferdinand Lassalle: Heer (Europe); Reichmann; Dubnow, 94, 317.

197 Split into orthodox and liberal Jews in the nineteenth century: Fleg, 358ff; 375ff; Dubnow, 314ff; Cohen, 29ff; and others.

198 The quotations from Trotsky's autobiography are taken from the edition published in London in 1930 by Thornton Butterworth, Ltd.

199 Trotsky before the commission in Mexico: Deutscher.

199 Trotsky's last words in his autobiography, proclaiming his belief in world revolution, contain elements of Proudhon, Rosa Luxemburg and Teilhard de Chardin, who was completely unknown to him.

200 Trotsky's death: Deutscher.

201 Trotsky's lament on the death of his favourite son: Deutscher.

201 Trotsky and Lenin: frequent references in Trotsky's autobiography and in Deutscher.

203 Trotsky's will: Deutscher.

207 Gustav Landauer: Liptzin, 229ff, 270, and others.
207 Pacelli's shocking experience in Munich: Nobécourt; report of his doctor, Galeazzi-Lisi.
208 Walther Rathenau: Liptzin, 139ff, 181. In *Selbstzeugnisse des deutschen Judentums* (ed. Borries) E.Feder relates a conversation in which Paul Nathan deplored Rathenau's decision to join the Weimar government: 'He should not have done that. He will not die a natural death.' A biography of Rathenau by H.Kessler (published in London by Gerald Howe in 1929) contains a chapter on the *Breviarium Mysticum*. An English translation of *Von kommenden Dingen* (In Days to Come) was published by Allen and Unwin in 1921.
208 'Jesus in a tail-coat' (*Jesus im Frack*): Richter.
208 A favourite of the National Socialists: see chapters 11 and 12.
210 Jews as Prussian patriots: the writings of the Prussian Jew H.J.Schoeps provide an interesting illustration, together with the contributions of Ernst Simon, Ernst Feder and David S.Landes in the anthology *Deutsches Judentum – Aufstieg und Krisse* (ed. Weltsch).
210 Moritz Itzig: Liptzin, 17ff.
216 A high officer of the SS and one of Hitler's governors: SS-Obersturm-bannführer Rauch in a memo dated 2 October 1942 concerning Gauleiter Wilhelm Kube, governor of Ruthenia. (Related in Wulf.)
218 Richard Wagner and Mendelssohn: Among others, Reichmann and Heer (Europe).
219 Berthold Auerbach: Liptzin, 88ff.
220 Auerbach's suggestion for a German university in America: Liptzin, 100.
221 Hitler's Jewish family doctor: Dr Bloch (Jetzinger).
222 Haseloff: in the anthology *Die Juden und die Kultur*.
223 René König on Gundolf: in the anthology *Die Juden und die Kultur*.
224 Hermann Cohen: Cohen, 73ff, and chapter 13 of this book.
226 Happiness belongs only to childhood': Freud's letter to Wilhelm Fliess.
227 With Lueger in the caves of St Canzian: letter to Fliess. Lueger: see chapter 11.
227 Congratulations on his eightieth birthday: letter to Arnold Zweig, 31 May 1936.
227 Freud's family life: letters to Oskar Pfister.
228 Tsar Nicholas: letter to Fliess.
228 Freud on Emperor Franz Josef: letter to Fliess.
228 Exchange of letters between Freud and Einstein: in *Einstein on Peace*, edited by Otto Nathan and Heinz Norden (London 1963), from which translated excerpts are taken.
234 Freud as Jacob struggling with the angel: letter to Fliess.
234 Freud on psychoanalysis and Judaism: Jaspers's rejection of Freud (and Marx) stems from an anti-Semitic attitude of which Jaspers himself was probably unconscious, and which his distinguished pupil

Hannah Arendt would probably deny. Anti-Semitism assumes a far more open form in Freud's former pupil and subsequent opponent, C. G. Jung, who early welcomed National Socialism and openly sympathized with it. Anti-Semitism in Switzerland: see chapter 13.

235 The 'enthroned idol, Meynert': letter to Fliess.

236 The gods had three functions to fulfil: Freud, *The Future of an Illusion*. (Translator's note: The quotations from Freud used here have been taken, where available, from the edition of Freud's works published in London by the Hogarth Press. These include: *Moses and Monotheism, The Ego and the Id* and *The Future of an Illusion* (all by Freud); *Letters of Sigmund Freud*, selected and edited by Ernest L. Freud; and the three-volume biography *Sigmund Freud – Life and Works* by Ernest Jones.)

237 The strength of religious illusions: from Freud's *The Future of an Illusion*. His correspondence with Pfister touches on this book.

238 'Immortality, retribution . . .': letter to Fliess.

238 'Our god Logos': *The Future of an Illusion*.

242 Freud's obituary tribute to Ferenczi appeared in the *Internationale Zeitschrift für Psychoanalyse* 19, 1933.

243 'The experiences of the Ego . . .': from *The Ego and the Id*.

243 Freud on Moses: letter dated 31 October 1938 to Charles Singer on his *Moses and Monotheism*.

243 The 'Aryan' Christ as the 'first anti-Semite': see chapters 11 and 12.

CHAPTER 11: CRUSHED BETWEEN CROSS AND SWASTIKA

Amery, C.: Die Kapitulation – oder deutscher Katholizismus heute, Hamburg 1963

Arendt, H.: Eichmann in Jerusalem, Munich 1964

Bahr, H.: Der Antisemitismus – ein internationales Interview, Berlin 1894

Berdyaev, H.: Christianity and Anti-Semitism, Kent 1952

Berneri, C.: Le juif antisémite, Paris 1935

Bogler, Theodor: Der Glaube von gestern und heute, Cologne 1939

Borée, K.F.: Semiten und Antisemiten – Begegnungen und Erfahrungen, Frankfurt 1960

Bracher, K.D.: Die Auflösung der Weimer Republik, Villingen 1960

Bracher, K.D.: Deutschland zwischen Demokratie und Diktatur, Berne 1964

Buchow, W.: 50 Jahre antisemitische Bewegung, Munich 1937

Bullock, Alan: Hitler, A Study in Tyranny, London 1952

Byrnes, R.F.: Anti-Semitism in Modern France, New Brunswick 1960

Cohn, Norman: The Pursuit of the Millennium, London 1957

Coudenhove-Kalergi, R.N.: Eine Idee erobert Europa, Vienna 1958

Coudenhove-Kalergi, R.N.: Judenhass von heute, Vienna 1935

Daim, W.: Der Mann, der Hitler die Ideen gab, Munich 1958

De Gasperi, R.M.C.: De Gasperi, uomo solo, Milan 1964
Delp, A.: Zwishen Gott und Welt, Frankfurt 1957
Deschner, K. (Editor): Jesusbilder in theologischer Sicht, Munich 1966
Diebow, H.: 265 Bilddokumente, der ewige Jude, Munich 1937
Eckart, Dietrich: Der Bolschewismus von Moses bis Lenin – Zwiegespräch
  zwischen Adolf Hitler und mir, Munich 1924
Eckert, W.P., and Ehrlich, E.L.: Judenhass – Schuld der Christen?, Essen
  1964
Erlinghagen, K.: Katholisches Bildungsdefizit, Freiburg 1965
Eschenburg, T.: Die improvisierte Demokratie, Munich 1963
Falconi, Carlo: Il silenzio di Pio XII, Milan 1965
Förster, F.W.: Erlebte Weltgeschichte 1869–1953, Nuremberg 1953
Förster, F.W.: Die jüdische Frage, Freiburg 1959
Frank, Hans: Im Angesicht des Galgens, Munich-Gräfelfing 1953
Fried, Jakob: Nationalsozialismus und katholische Kirche in Österreich,
  Vienna 1947
Galeazzi-Lisi, R.: Dans l'ombre et la lumière de Pie XII, Paris 1960
Gamm, H.J.: Führung und Verführung – Pädagogik des Nationalsozialismus,
  Munich 1964
Giani, N.: Perché siamo antisemiti, Milan 1939
Gibson, B.H. (Editor): The Ciano Diaries, 1939–43, New York 1946
Gilbert, G.M.: Nürnberger Tagebuch, 1962
Giovannetti, A.: Der Vatikan und der Krieg, Cologne 1961
Goldschmidt, D., and Kraus, H.J. (Editors): Der ungekündigte Bund,
  Stuttgart 1962
Gollwitzer, H. etc. (Editors): Du hast mich heimgesucht bei Nacht –
  Abschiedsbriefe und Aufzeichnungen des Widerstandes, Munich (undated)
Grossmann, Kurt R.: Ossietzky, Munich 1963
Haecker, T.: Satire und Polemik, Munich 1961
Haeuser, P.: Jud und Christ, Regensburg 1923
Harand, Irene: Sein Kampf – Antwort an Hitler, Vienna 1935
Harand, Irene: So oder so? Die Wahrheit über den Antisemitismus, Vienna
  1933
Hay, Malcolm: Europe and the Jews, Boston 1960
Heydecker-Leeb: Der Nürnberger Prozess, Cologne 1958
Janaczek, F.: Zeittafeln zur Fackel, Munich 1965 (on Karl Kraus)
Jaromir, R.: Bibel und Zeitgeist, Affoltern 1949
Jéhouda, Josué: L'antisémitisme, miroir du monde, Geneva 1958
Jetzinger, F.: Hitlers Jugend, Vienna 1956
Kaiser, R.: Inside the Council, London 1963
Kaplan, Mordecai M.: The Purpose and Meaning of Jewish Existence,
  Philadelphia 1964
Kirchmann, S.: St Ambrosius und die deutschen Bischöfe, Lucerne 1934
Klesse, M.: Vom Alten zum Neuen Israel, Frankfurt 1965

Körber, R. (Editor): Antisemitismus der Welt in Wort und Bild, Dresden 1935 (simultaneously in Vienna as: Israel und die Völker)

Kuehnelt-Leddihn, E.v.: Freiheit oder Gleichheit?, Salzburg 1953

Landmann, Salcia: Der jüdische Witz, Olten 1960

Leers, J.von: Juden sehen Dich an, 1933 (4th edition)

Leschnitzer, A.: The Magic Background of Modern Anti-Semitism, New York 1956

Lewy, Guenter: The Catholic Church and Nazi Germany, London and New York 1964

Lilge, F.: The Abuse of Learning – The Failure of the German University, New York 1948

Liptzin, S.: Germany's Step-children, New York 1961

Loewenstein, R.: Psychanalyse de l'antisémitisme, Paris 1952

Lonsbach, R.M.: Friedrich Nietzsche und die Juden, Stockholm 1939

Lutz, H.: Demokratie im Zwielicht, Munich 1963

Maier, Hans (Editor): Katholizismus nach 1945, Munich 1964

Mann, Golo: Der Antisemitismus, Munich 1960

Marburg, F.: Der Antisemitismus in der Deutschen Republik, Vienna 1931

Massing, P.W.: Rchearsal for Destruction – A Study of Political Anti-Semitism in Imperial Germany, New York 1949

Maybaum, Ignaz: The Face of God after Auschwitz, Amsterdam 1965

Mitscherlich, A., and Mielke, F. (Editors): Medizin ohne Menschlichkeit, Frankfurt 1960 (on the Nazi doctors' trials in Nuremberg)

Mosse, W.E. (Editor): Entscheidungsjahr 1932 – Zur Judenfrage in der Endphase der Weimarer Republik, Tübingen 1965

Mühlmann, W.G.: Homo Creator, Wiesbaden 1962 (on Pater Schmidt)

Müller, H.: Kirche und Nationalsozialismus, Dokumente 1930–35, Munich 1963

Neumann, R.: Ausflüchte unseres Gewissens, Hanover 1960

Nobécourt, J.: 'Le Vicaire' et l'Histoire, Paris 1964

Poliakov, L., and Wulf, J.: Das Dritte Reich und seine Diener, Berlin 1956

Pross, H.: Vor und nach Hitler, Olten (undated)

Pulzer, P.G.J.: The Rise of Political Anti-Semitism in Germany and Austria, New York 1964

Raddatz, F.J. (Editor): Summa iniuria oder – Durfte der Papst schweigen?, Hamburg 1963

Rauschning, H.: Gespräche mit Hitler, 1940 (re-issued 1964)

Reichmann, Eva G.: Hostages of Civilizations, London 1950

Reimann, V.: Innitzer, Kardinal zwischen Hitler und Rom, Vienna 1967

Rost, H.: Gedanken und Wahrheiten zur Judenfrage, Trier 1907

Roth, Josef: Katholizismus und Judenfrage, Munich 1923

Royce, H., Zimmermann, E., Jacobsen, H.: 20. Juli 1944, Bonn 1960

Rudolf, E.V.v.: Georg Ritter von Schönerer, Munich 1936

Schlund, E.: Katholizismus und Vaterland, Munich 1923

Schmidt, G.: Selektion in der Heilanstalt, Stuttgart 1965 (on murderous activities of Nazi doctors)

Senn, W.M.: Katholizismus und Nationalsozialismus, Münster 1931

Staff, Ilse (Editor): Justiz im Dritten Reich, Frankfurt 1964

Steffen, F.: Antisemitische und deutschvölkische Bewegung im Lichte des Katholizismus, Berlin 1925

Steinhausen, H.: Die Judenfrage – eine Christenfrage, Lucerne 1939

Sterling, Eleonore: Er ist wie du, Munich 1956

Stonner, A.: Nationale Erziehung und Religionsunterricht, Regensburg 1934

Sulzbach, W.: Die zwei Wurzeln und Formeln des Judenhasses, Stuttgart 1959

Thieme, Karl: Judenfeindschaft, Darstellung und Analysen, Frankfurt 1963

Tucholsky, K.: Morgen wieder?, Frankfurt 1963

Valentin, H.: Antisemitenspiegel, Vienna 1937

Webster, Richard A.: The Cross and the Fasces – Christian Democracy and Fascism in Italy, Stanford 1960

Weisenborn, G. (Editor): Der lautlose Aufstand, Hamburg 1953 (on 20 July 1944)

Weltsch, R. (Editor): Deutsches Judentum – Aufstieg und Krise, Stuttgart 1963

Wengraf, E.: St Georg von Zwettl, Vienna 1887 (on Schönerer)

Wild, A.: Nationalsozialismus und Religion, Augsburg 1930

Zahn, Gordon C.: German Catholics and Hitler's Wars, New York 1962

Zahn, Gordon C.: A Solitary Witness; Franz Jägerstätter, New York 1964

Zeller, E.: Geist der Freiheit – der 20. Juli 1944, Munich (undated)

Zolli, E.: Antisemitismo, Rome 1945

Page

246 The correspondence between Rusch and Massiczek is published in Eckert-Ehrlich (Ed.). It might be compared with the statements that Cardinal Frings of Cologne made to Rabbi Max Nussbaum (*Der Spiegel*, 30 January 1967).

247 German Protestant anti-Judaism led directly to Julius Streicher: German Protestant recognition of this fact is contained in *Der ungekündigte Bund* (ed. Goldschmidt and Kraus), recording the findings of a Protestant congress in Berlin in 1961. The congress is dealt with in chapter 13.

247 Seyss-Inquart: His brother was for a time a Catholic padre during the First World War (Reimann).

247 The swastika in German churches: plenty of material in Zahn (German Catholics) and Lewy.

249 Otto Weininger: Liptzin, 152, 165, 184ff, 192f, 213.

249 The English were most like the Jews: This idea of Weininger's became a Nazi propaganda slogan. It was also held by French Catholic anti-Semites in the nineteenth century (cf. Byrnes) and in Russia by Tsar

Nicholas II, who said: 'An Englishman is a Jew' (Barbara Tuchmann, *August 1914*).

249 Arthur Trebitsch: Liptzin, 189ff.

251 Jewish self-hatred: Jaromir's *Bibel und Zeitgeist*, written by an Austrian Jew (R. Unger), is itself the product of a tragic Jewish self-hatred. See also Liptzin, 152ff, 165ff, 184ff; Kaplan, 288; Loewenstein and Jéhouda.

252 Theodor Lessing: Liptzin, 152ff, 218.

252 Arabs massacring Jews with the acquiescence of the British authorities: Hay, 288ff.

253 Hitler compares the masses to a woman: *Mein Kampf*, 44.

254 Anti-Semitism in Wilhelm Busch: Leschnitzer, 223.

254 Conceptions of heaven and hell in the nineteenth and twentieth centuries: I am preparing a monograph on this vast subject, so here simply a short note: When the French Jesuit Roger Troisfontaines in 1958 asked many French Catholics how they visualized the Hereafter, he found that their ideas on heaven constituted a *'chef d'oeuvre d'ennui'*.

254 The events of 1933 found many Jews inwardly unprepared: Leschnitzer, 150ff, and others.

254 The position of the Jews after 1848: Leschnitzer, 65ff; Reichmann.

254 The position of the Jews after 1871: Leschnitzer, 77ff; Reichmann.

254 The German Jews made for the cities: Reichmann, Pulzer, and others.

255 Famous American Jews descended from 1848 malcontents: Leschnitzer, 65.

257 A Nazi Gauleiter: Florian, addressing the people of Düsseldorf. His proclamation (reproduced in facsimile in the *Rheinische Post* of 27 February 1965) begins: 'The enemy fighting so pitilessly under Jewish leadership against us is lying in its speeches and writings as it has always lied.' Tucholsky relates that during the First World War an illustrator in the Tenth German Army was instructed always to make Wilson look strongly Jewish.

258 Between 1874 and 1879 the Jew became the official Enemy Number One: Leschnitzer, 138f.

258 Jewish rites and marks transferred to witches: Leschnitzer, 146ff.

258 It was not the case that National Socialist terrorization made the Germans abandon . . . : Leschnitzer, 154.

259 Eugen Dühring: Liptzin, 114; Reichmann. The German title of his publication: *Die Judenfrage als Frage des Rassencharakters und seine Schädlichkeiten für Existenz und Kultur der Völker*.

263 Imperial Vienna: In the bulletin for members of the Society of Friends of the Leo Baeck Institute (no. 10, Tel Aviv 1960) occurs the following sentence: 'Nowadays one tends easily to forget the fact that it was in the territories of the old Austrian monarchy that the new Jewry was born.'

264 Catholic and national anti-Semitism in Vienna: among others, Byrnes, I, 83ff, 90ff.

264 Anti-Semitic priests as publishers and journalists in Vienna: Hay, 311ff; Byrnes, I, 83ff, 85f, 90ff.

264 Adolf Hitler as artist: among others, Bullock, 35ff, 386ff.

265 Georg von Schönerer: Schönerer was depicted on postcards as St George killing the Jewish dragon, just as Hitler was later to be shown. An essay by O. Karbach, *The Founder of Political Anti-Semitism, Georg von Schönerer*, appeared in *Jewish Social Studies*, VII, No. 1 (New York 1945).

265 In 1935 there appeared in Dresden and Vienna . . .: Listed in bibliography under Körber, R. (Editor).

266 Erika Weinzierl-Fischer: 'Österreichs Katholiken und der National-sozialismus' in *Wort und Wahrheit*, XVIII, June–July 1963.

268 Austrian aristocrats against anti-Semitism: Richard Coudenhove-Kalergi writes in *Eine Idee erobert Europa* about his father, Heinrich Graf Coudenhove-Kalergi, who took part in the struggle against anti-Semitism in the Austro-Hungarian empire.

270 Father Wilhelm Schmidt: see Freud's letter dated 30 September 1934.

271 Turkey received Jews persecuted by Hitler: Hay, 301ff.

271 Bishop Gföllner's pastoral letter: printed in Fried, Reimann and in *Wort und Wahrheit* (Weinzierl-Fischer).

273 Cardinal Theodor Innitzer: The biography by Viktor Reimann was published in 1967. In my present sketch I base myself on my personal acquaintance with this much misjudged, humanly outstanding personality.

274 Conversations between Hitler and Eckart: see bibliography under Eckart, Dietrich.

274 From Munich to Rome: From numerous conversations since 1945 with Spanish, American and Irish Catholics I have learnt that many still regard Hitler as the great warrior against Bolshevism.

276 Martin Luther: At the Nuremberg trials Julius Streicher evoked the name of Luther, a fact that the world press in 1946 failed to note. Streicher said: 'I must bear my cross: the Jews are crucifying me now.'

276 The Enlightenment (*Aufklärung*): Present-day opposition to it in the Catholic press and in Catholic schools is closely connected with the ghetto mentality, through which German Catholics since 1870 have tried to create a 'special society' to protect their members from the wicked world outside.

276 Humanitarian fuss: A typical specimen of this inhuman language was provided recently by a university professor from Hamburg who, describing himself as 'Christian to the depths of his being', went on to speak of 'inhuman monsters, who must be crushed like vermin'.

277 The papal nuncio in Bavaria on an election poster: cf. Lewy, 25ff.

283 Dietrich Eckart: among others, Bullock, 74, 76f.

284 Theodor Herzl was regarded with a certain sympathy in Nazi circles, among them Eichmann (Arendt).

288 Hitler's testament: Bullock, 794ff.

288 Hitler saw himself primarily as an artist: among others, Bullock, 386ff. According to Fest, Hitler had a sketch made depicting the huge projected congress hall as a ruin.

288 Guderian: 'He had a certain picture of the world': Bullock, 767. On Guderian himself: Bullock, 588, 591, 764ff, 770ff.

289 Greiner and Berning both in *Katholizismus nach 1945* (ed. Maier). See also Bracher (Deutschland) and Pross. As good judges of their German people Hess, Rosenberg and other Nazi leaders foresaw a revival of their ideas and of Nazism in Germany after twenty years. Gilbert quotes Goering on the subject of permanent German nationalism.

289 Hitler in the Reichskanzlei bunker: Bullock, 777ff. Albert Speer spoke about Hitler's Austrian charm in the issue of *Der Spiegel* for 7 November 1966.

289 The German publisher of this book (Bechtle Verlag, Munich) supplies the following note concerning Hitler's parentage: In the first volume of his Hitler biography (Bechtle Verlag 1968) *Adolf Hitler – sein Weg bis 1924* Werner Maser clears up questions of Hitler's descent, particularly with regard to the obscure figure of his maternal grandfather. Maser's researches have considerably altered the existing picture. Among other things, he has shown that there is no foundation in fact for the allegation that Hitler's grandmother, Maria-Anna Schicklgruber, had an affair with the Jew Frankenberger from Graz, which resulted in the birth of Alois Schicklgruber. The publisher draws attention in this connection to Bullock, to William L. Shirer's *The Rise and Fall of the Third Reich*, two other books by Werner Maser (*Die Frühgeschichte der NSDAP*, Frankfurt 1965, and *Hitlers Mein Kampf*, Munich 1966) and *Adolf Hitler – Versuch einer Deutung* by Hans Bernd Gisevius (Munich 1963).

289 Hitler and the Jew Neumann: Bullock, 30, 32.

289 Hitler in Vienna 1907–13: Bullock, 25ff; Jetzinger and others.

290 'Today it is hard, if not impossible . . .': *Mein Kampf*, 54f.

290 The strong sexual emphasis in his anti-Semitism: Gamm.

290 'Was there any shady undertaking . . .' and following quotations: *Mein Kampf*.

291 'In the Gospels the Jews called out to Pilate . . .': related by Hans Frank in his *Im Angesicht des Galgens*.

291 Hitler did not believe in a new paganism: Fest. Gilbert says that none of the men accused at Nuremberg had read Rosenberg's book. Hitler once said in conversation with Bishop Berning: 'That is why I turned against Ludendorff, and that is why I reject Rosenberg's book' (document 48 in Müller).

291 Hitler believed in himself: among others, Bullock, 672ff.

291 Hitler as heir to Shamanist magicians: I have been saying this for many years; now the same view is expressed by Cohn (*Pursuit of the Millennium*).

291 Maybaum is right to emphasize (p. 22 of his book) the medieval character of the Catholic mentality in Germany, Austria and Poland around 1933: it was by its very nature very susceptible to Hitler's religio-political sermons.

292 Communion between the lonely: Goering once said: 'I do not live, but Hitler lives in me'; and again: 'I have no conscience. My conscience is Adolf Hitler and, just as for Catholics the pope is infallible, so Hitler is for me.' Cf. Fest.

293 Hitler's respect for the church's capacity for political rule: see *Mein Kampf*, 481f.

293 Hitler had no high opinion of the Protestant clergy: cf. Bullock, 389. Hitler's view is remarkably akin to Heine's.

294 Hitler's awareness of the clergy's concern about its pay: Rauschning, Lewy.

294 The speech of the president of the American Chamber of Commerce: Körber (ed.).

294 Hitler's power to establish order was recognized in the Vatican: Zahn (German Catholics), 211ff; Lewy.

295 Hitler and Geli Raubal: Bullock, 19f, 130, 145, 392f.

295 Hitler had never read Marx: Jetzinger. His hatred of Social Democrats: Bullock, 34, 39, 73, 279f; of Communism: Bullock, 36f, 114, 125, 193ff, 333; of parliamentary democracy: Bullock, 37, 53, 139f, 157f.

295 Colonel Kühlenthal and the report of Colonel Marshall-Cornwall: see Grossmann's *Ossietzky*.

301 Though Haecker, in his raging polemics after 1918, could vie in tone with the Nazi press, he could be equally violent against (for example) 'wartime Christians', Cardinal Mercier and the 'busy Archbishop Faulhaber'. As Haecker rightly said: these German 'state Christians' would have put a steel helmet on Christ's head and sent him into the dugouts.

301 The Sixty-Second General Assembly of German Catholics: Lutz, Lewy.

302 Faulhaber on Hitler: Lewy (cf. Zahn, German Catholics, 101ff).

304 The anti-democratic spiritual leaders of German Catholicism: The German prelate Karl Forster remarked in 1964: 'In the field of active negotiation the Catholic church has not yet found the right attitude towards democratic national and social forms.' This appears in *Deutscher Katholizismus nach 1945* (ed. Maier), where, on the other hand, Walter Kerber SJ writes: 'The church's task is strictly other-worldly, that is to say, it is concerned with the work of salvation which Christ began and which is an absolute gift from above.' But Kerber does make the following admission: 'Christians will have to take their responsibilities towards the world considerably more seriously than they have in past centuries.'

304 Attempts were made to discard Alcide de Gasperi: *De Gasperi, uomo solo,*

written by de Gasperi's daughter and secretary, Maria Romana Catti de Gasperi, is both a richly documented book and at the same time a shattering revelation – not least of the betrayal of the freedom of Italian Catholics by church leaders up to the highest level.

304 Roth, Schachleitner: Lewy.

305 The German bishops in 1930 and during the Third Reich: Zahn (German Catholics), 6off; Lewy.

305 Konrad von Preysing: Lewy, 12f.

305 All bishops recognized the 'patriotic motives': Lewy, 14f.

305 Bares of Hildesheim: Lewy, 16.

305 Ludwig Kaas: Lewy, 18ff; Bullock, 256, 268

305 Heinrich Brüning: among others, Lewy, 21f.

305 Franz von Papen: among others, Bullock, 206ff, 242ff, 428ff.

306 Walter Dirks's warning: cf. Lewy, 23f.

306 Faulhaber reports pope's praise of Hitler: Lewy, 31.

306 Hitler's promises to the Centre party leaders: Lewy, 33ff.

306 The bishops lifted their ban: Lewy, 36ff.

307 Pacelli and Kaas: Lewy, 47f.

307 Hitler's conversation with Berning and Steinmann: Lewy, 50ff.

307 The Concordat of 20 July 1933: Lewy, 57ff.

307 The Vatican threw over the Centre party: Lewy, 69f, 74f, 86. Lewy remarks: 'In a sense it is accurate to say that both sides in 1933 played with false cards.'

308 The Fulda bishops' conference: Lewy, 94ff.

309 Robert d'Harcourt: *The German Catholics*, trans. R. J. Dingle, London 1939, 84.

309 Bornewasser: Lewy, 100f.

309 Faulhaber to Hitler, 24 July 1933: Lewy, 104.

310 Steinmann: Lewy, 105.

310 Lortz, Schmaus, Adam: Lewy, 107f.

310 Pope Pius XI reassured by Pacelli: Lewy, 113ff.

311 The war against the West was in accordance with natural law: Lewy, 145. In the great debate on war and atomic weapons which took place at the Second Vatican Council in October 1965 the German bishops remained absolutely silent.

311 Bertram, Faulhaber, Gröber: Lewy, 162ff.

311 Dietrich von Hildebrand criticized . . .: in *Der christliche Ständestaat*, Vienna 1936. I know from my own experience that Christian Social supporters either rejected this journal or did not read it at all.

312 No German bishop spoke up . . .: Lewy, 168ff.

312 Waldemar Gurian: even after 1945 this important German Catholic writer continued to be ignored. His pamphlet: *St Ambrosius und die deutschen Bischöfe* by Stefan Kirchmann (pseudonym).

312 Bishop Berning visited some concentration camps: Lewy, 171ff.

313 The bishops steeped in a political image . . .: cf. Zahn (German Catholics), 60ff, 83ff, 101ff, 143ff. Zahn maintains that the German episcopate learned nothing from the Second World War. Cf. with this the remarks which the eighty-year-old Cardinal Frings made in January 1967 to an American rabbi and the following press controversy in German and Jewish papers.

313 William Teeling: Lewy, 174.

313 Tisserant to Suhard: Tisserant watched with alarm from the Vatican how orthodox Serbs were destroyed by Catholic Croats, with the help of the Franciscans: Falconi, 386ff, 487ff.

313 The church supported Hitler's foreign policy: Lewy, 176ff.

313 The Saar plebiscite: Lewy, 182ff.

314 The joint Nazi-Catholic campaign against Bolshevism: Lewy, 205f. Tucholsky quotes the following words of Geheimrat Krüger: 'Bolshevism is everything one cannot agree with.'

314 Hitler and Faulhaber: Lewy, 207f. Zahn (German Catholics) deals with Faulhaber on 101ff, 109f.

314 The German bishops' joint pastoral letter: Lewy, 208.

315 The bishops' attitude to the annexation of Austria: Lewy, 211ff.

315 The invasion of Czechoslovakia: Lewy, 218ff.

315 Pacelli sent the first news of his election as pope to Hitler: Giovannetti.

315 The church stood behind Hitler when he went to war: Lewy, 221ff.

315 German and Austrian Catholics refused military service: Lewy, 234; Zahn, 54f. Zahn has devoted a book to one of these – Franz Jägerstätter. The bishop of Linz prevented the publicizing of Jägerstätter's martyrdom after 1945 on the grounds that those who took part in the war were the greater heroes: see Zahn in *Werkhefte* XVI, August-September 1962, p. 8f. In 1965 W.H.Auden recalled Jägerstätter in his poem on Josef Weinheber.

315 German bishops as prisoners of an image of the world formed before the First World War: Zahn (German Catholics), 60ff, 88ff, 102ff, 124f, 126ff, 217f.

316 Galen: Zahn (German Catholics), 88ff.

316 Gröber's war theology: Zahn (German Catholics), 126ff, 130f, 139f. Gröber against the resistance fighters of 20 July 1944: Zahn (German Catholics), 133.

316 The love of Christ perverted into a war mentality: examples in Zahn (German Catholics), 73, 78f, 80f, 82ff.

316 Bishops instructed to prepare secretly a cadre of military chaplains: Lewy, 226.

316 The church and the conquest of Poland: Lewy, 227ff. Copious excerpts from Polish archives in Falconi. Present-day disputes can only be understood against the background of this attitude of the German church towards Poland. Cf. for example *Tygodnik Katolikow* (October 1965) with

Cardinal Döpfner, etc., and the celebrations of the Polish episcopate in Wroclav (Breslau) on 31 August 1965 in connection with the twentieth anniversary of the re-establishment of church life in the Western and Northern territories of Poland. In their pastoral letter of 15 August, the Polish bishops recalled the anti-German Emperor Otto III.

317 Rise up against England: Lewy, 229f.

317 Archbishop Jäger: Lewy, 232.

317 Galen in April 1945: Lewy, 231; Zahn (German Catholics), 91ff, 94f.

317 The church as 'agency of the Third Reich': Zahn (German Catholics), 202.

318 Rarkowski: Zahn, 143ff; Lewy, 236ff.

318 With Benigni and his organization, I deal more fully in my *Intellectual History* and also in my forthcoming book on the faith of Adolf Hitler.

318 Theological authoritarianism: cf. Kaiser: 'Pius XII was a traditionalist, an autocrat, a man whose ecclesiology was founded on the old Augustinian dualism' (p. 88ff). And again: 'He took for granted the fission of the world into two blocs: it had been that way in Augustine's time, it was like that in the time of Innocent III. It was like that at the Reformation, and again in 1870. It would always be like that.' Kaiser says that the Second Vatican Council was confronted with two completely opposed systems of theology: the centralist one, 'a theology of pessimism and fear', which regarded the incarnation as a unique historical factor (after the Ascension it became the church's task to maintain a pure and unblemished faith); and on the other side a progressive theology, 'a theology of optimism and hope', which maintained that the process of incarnation was still in progress. Many references to centralism, papal absolutism and Augustinian theology in the nineteenth century are contained in the correspondence between Lord Acton and Döllinger. Kaiser maintains that even John XXIII was to become a prisoner of the curialists.

319 The Vatican sacrificed Catholic Poland to Hitler: Lewy, 246f; Falconi; Nobécourt.

319 The pope's silence in face of the bestialities in Poland was foreshadowed by the silence of Pope Pius XI and Pacelli with regard to Mussolini's war in Abyssinia, when 'thousands of Abyssinians were being cooked in gas' and 'the pope's quietest whisper' would 'immediately have drowned the whistling of the bombs' (Bernanos in his Brazilian journal).

319 Pius XII hoped to reconcile Hitler and the Western powers and to unite them in a common alliance against Russia: When the Jesuit Pierre Charles in Belgium and Friedrich Muckermann in Germany wrote against the Rome-Berlin axis, they were silenced by the pope and the head of their order with the instruction that they should not interfere with the work of God, who was setting up a new order through Mussolini and Hitler. See Kaiser, 24f. M.R.C. de Gasperi relates that a few days

before war broke out in 1939 the Prince of Hesse gave Pius XII a Madonna as a present from Hitler. The pope's private secretary, Robert Leiber SJ, a very worthy and well-informed man, has confirmed in *Summa iniuria* (Ed. Raddatz) that for Pius XII Bolshevism was the principal enemy both of the world and the church. He could see no solution other than the military defeat of the Soviet Union. Nikolaus Koch, writing in *Evangelisch-Katholisches Forum* 4, 1964, comments: 'Taking that into consideration, one can understand the pope's failure. This is realistic political thinking in the manner of ordinary diplomats. But in terms of realistic politics the pope is powerless and knows he is powerless . . .'

320 The Vatican greatly feared a German defeat in Russia: Lewy, 249, 250; Falconi.

320 The German episcopate made overtures to Hitler: Lewy, 251ff, 257.

320 Bishops Martin and Keppler: Lewy, 269f.

321 The Deggendorf festival and Rödel: Lewy, 273.

322 Faulhaber's Advent sermons: Lewy, 276.

323 There is a certain historical irony in the fact that it was Hudal who later became one of Hochhuth's chief informants regarding the régime of Pius XII. Hudal has also confirmed to me in several letters his agreement with my views on the problem of the Catholic church and the Jews. Hudal's role as intermediary between the Austrian church and the Nazis is dealt with by Reimann in his Innitzer biography. According to the Russian journalist Besymenski, writing about the hunt for Martin Bormann, it was Hudal who procured Eichmann a passport under the name of Ricardo Clemente for his escape to South America.

323 Church help in obtaining proof of Aryan blood: Lewy, 281ff.

323 Baptized Jews received only limited help: Lewy, 283. An exception in this connection was the Viennese Cardinal Innitzer (cf. Reimann).

323 Gerstein: Lewy, 288, among others.

323 Dr Alfons Hildenbrand's report to Faulhaber: Lewy in a conversation with Dr Gertrud Luckner, the great pioneer of Christian and Jewish reconciliation and helper of the Jews in the Nazi period.

324 The bishops never spoke of Jews or non-Aryans: Lewy, 292. The great exception was Cardinal Innitzer (Reimann).

324 Nearly a quarter of the members of the SS were Catholics: Internal SS report in NA Washington, T-580, roll 42, file 245; Lewy, 292.

324 The bishop of Cremona's Epiphany sermon: in *Regime Fascista* XVII: 'L'omelia del Vescovo nella festività dell Epifania, 7.1.1939.' See also Giani (*Perché siamo antisemiti*, 1939).

324 'I know Herr Hitler. He is a fool . . .': Jakob Dränger in his Goldmann biography, 1956.

326 Vichy anti-Jewish legislation: Lewy, 297; and Nobécourt, who recalls that Xavier Vallat, the minister in charge of Jewish affairs in the Pétain

government, based his ideas on the anti-Jewish doctrine of the church from St Paul to St Thomas Aquinas and his own Thomist upbringing.

326 Roosevelt approached the pope: VS Diplomatic Papers 1942, III, 772.

327 Tisserant to Suhard: Lewy, 307; Nobécourt, Falconi.

327 Pius XII did not want colleagues, but 'instruments': Kaiser, 38f, 88ff; Nobécourt. Pius XII wanted only church subjects for his policy of church absolutism, and he pledged them to war – even nuclear war. Cf. N.Koch in *Evangelisch-Katholisches Forum* 4, 1964: 'Helpless bishops, helpless priests and helpless laymen were all that remained, the shuttlecocks and victims of a totalitarian world . . . It revealed the weakness not only of the pope, but of the whole church.'

327 Edoardo Senatro asked Pius XII . . .: revealed in a public discussion in Berlin on 11 March 1963. See *Summa iniuria* (ed. Raddatz); also Lewy, 304.

327 On 15 August 1945 Pius XII praised in his letter . . .: Lewy, 309f.

328 Galen against any form of resistance: Lewy, 316f. Cf. Zahn (German Catholics), 94ff.

328 The church and the German resistance movement: Lewy, 310ff.

328 The Catholics forced the cancellation of the crucifix decree: Lewy, 313.

328 Pacelli blessed Franco's uprising: Lewy, 312.

328 Hans Kühner-Wolfskehl's report: *Summa iniuria* (ed. Raddatz).

328 Alfred Delp: Lewy, 307f. Delp's concern with Christian championship of the cause of mankind can be seen in his book *Zwischen Gott und Welt*.

329 Pacelli-Pius XII: See also my *Europe, Mother of Revolutions*; Kaiser, 88ff, 245; Nobécourt; and Falconi. In the *Evangelisch-Katholisches Forum* of October 1964, N.Koch wrote: 'That was the pope's final trouble: he did what the Curia before him had been used to doing.' The German Catholic Koch, after careful argument, comes to the conclusion: 'People who, like Hochhuth, demand such things are challenging fifteen centuries of church history. They must be prepared to put this history in question . . . The question of church complicity in the German crime of murdering the Jews becomes an instance of a resort by the church to temporal power. Criticism that takes the implications of a pope's actual historical behaviour seriously becomes not only a criticism of the pope, but of the church itself. And criticism of the church must of necessity become ecumenical criticism, since practically all historical attitudes of the Catholic *Imperium Romanum* fall victim to it.'

329 Pacelli's interview with Sauerwein: Nobécourt.

330 Pius XII's habit of thinking in terms of inimical blocks: Kaiser, 24f, 88ff, 132.

330 Charles Maurras, the Catholic atheist: 'This is their revenge for the Dreyfus affair,' Maurras said in January 1945 when charged in Lyons with being a collaborator. The Vienna edition of the *Völkischer Beobachter*

of 30 January 1945 reported this under the heading 'Old hatred never dies'.

330 Tedeschi and Kaiser: Zahn (German Catholics), 93.

330 Pacelli in imperial Germany and his clash with Communists in Munich: Nobécourt.

331 Falconi's careful researches reveal that between 1939 and 1945 Pius xii was constantly bombarded with news and petitions concerning the killing of Jews and Orthodox Serbs (by Catholic Croats) and suffered a severe guilt complex which he was always trying to work off.

331 He wanted to be the great father-figure: Kaiser, 38f.

335 Augustin Bea declined a cardinal's hat: Kaiser, 36.

335 The growing flood of literature about Pius xii can be divided into four main categories, though individual works may come into more than one of these. They are (1) devotional works; (2) hagiography; (3) apologiae; (4) historical works. In the last group a distinction might be made between (a) works which paint a portrait of the pope in a historical context and (b) works of historical criticism.

Devotional works: These owe their origin to the need of the faithful to honour the pope as Christ's representative, as the beacon of Christianity, the teacher of mankind, the leader who brought the church safely through a night of barbarity.

Hagiography: These are aimed directly or indirectly at the canonization of Pope Pius xii (proposed by Pope Paul vi at the conclusion of the Second Vatican Council).

Apologiae: These are severely critical of Hochhuth's *The Representative*, Saul Friedländer's *Pius XII and the Third Reich* and all voices raised against the attitude of the 'German pope' towards the Jews and the Orthodox Serbs during the war and after, as well as his approval of a 'just' defensive war with nuclear weapons.

Historical works: Up to the present (1967) the majority fall into the first sub-division: they are portraits in a historical setting. The time for a truly historical biography does not yet seem to have come. The work of editing the historical sources which are relevant to his time is still going on. The life and work of Pius xii is, for instance, bound up inextricably with the lives and works of the Popes Pius ix to xi, in the light of whose unity and union Pius xii must be considered.

I gave here a few notes on individual works which have a certain significance.

Devotion, hagiography and apologetics are combined in the works by P.Bargellini, Paul Dahm, Nazareno Padellari, Elisabeth von Schmidt-Pauli, Alexis Curvers, Renée Casin and many others. To take two examples: Alexis Curvers's *Pie XII, Le Pape outragé* (Paris 1964) presents Pius xii as the victim of a conspiracy involving all the evil spirits of our age and in particular the church reformers, whom the pope condemned, who banded together to blacken the reputation of this unique and saintly representative of Christ. In historical documents, such as Cardinal Tisserant's letter to Suhard concerning the historic guilt of the Curia, Curvers (himself a Belgian) sees nothing but the understandable reluctance of a French prelate to remain in Rome during the war. Critical studies of Pius XII (such as that of P.Marlé SJ) are considered as intimately connected with the reassessment after the pope's death of heretics whom he had condemned. Teilhard de Chardin, for example – three times condemned by the church – is now spreading himself in church magazines and elbowing his way right up to the doors of the Holy Office. Impertinent young Jesuits are poking fun at the veneration of the Virgin Mary which lay so close to the pope's heart. In these confused times, in which Satan is making his influence felt inside the church, it is high time (according to Curvers) that the guiding light of Pius XII should be held up to a foolish and malicious world that has been led astray by new-fangled modernists.

In her *Mensonges et silences sur Pie XII* (Monte Carlo 1965), Renée Casin, Lauréate de l'Académie Française, voices the great need of millions of women to venerate in Pius XII the true leader, father and guide to mankind (the psychological connection with the devotional feminine Führer-worship in Germany is clear to see). Renée Casin originally called her book *Mensonges et silences du Vicaire*, thus emphasizing the contrast to Hochhuth's *The Representative*. She writes of 'the great opportunity presented to us (Catholics) to raise our eyes to a chief who not only represents from a theological point of view the tangible presence of the Holy Ghost, but also from a human point of view a magnetic pole of purity, courage, genius and saintliness.' Loyalty to Christ is possible only through loyalty to the pope. It is interesting to note that Renée Casin specifically draws attention to French vituperation during the First World War against Benedict XV, whom Clemenceau called the *pape boche* and Léon Bloy Pilate XV, while the famous Dominican Sertillanges exhorted Frenchmen from the pulpit of the Madeleine to defy him. She draws a line from Benedict XV to Pius XII – without, however, recognizing the true inner relationship as Buonaiuti (for instance) has defined it.

Renée Casin joins battle particularly with Hochhuth and Saul Friedländer and summons Jewish witnesses to testify to the pope's charitable work on behalf of the Jews. It is interesting to observe, both in this and in German devotional apologetics, that the very authors who demand most from the pope in terms of world leadership are content with examples of his actual achievements as a sort of charity manager.

Other works on similar lines to Curvers and Renée Casin are: Paul Rassinier, *L'opération de Vicaire – le role de Pie XII devant l'histoire* (Paris 1965); Josef-Matthias Goergen, *Pius XII, Katholische Kirche und Hochhuths*

Stellvertreter (Buxheim 1964); and Walter Adolph, *Verfälschte Geschichte –
Antwortan Rolf Hochhuth* (Berlin 1963).

The religio-political background to a certain type of German devotion
to Pius XII can be clearly seen in: Joh. Maria Hoecht, *Fatima und
Pius XII. Maria, Schützerin des Abendlandes. Der Kampf um Russland und die
Abwendung des dritten Weltkrieges* (Wiesbaden 1957).

The book by José Antonio Almeida, *Das Menschheitsproblem des
Atomkrieges – Pius XII und die Atomwaffen*, published with church approval
in Essen in 1961, is dedicated to 'the land and people of Germany, which
I admire and love'. As Father Eberhard Welty points out in his foreword, the author (himself a theologian) makes clear that Pius XII 'in
certain circumstances recognizes the moral correctness, indeed the moral
duty to repel an enemy with nuclear weapons when the physical or
spiritual existence of a nation is threatened and the successful outcome
of such defensive action can be hoped for.' As highest authority for a
potential 'German' war aimed at correcting the results of the Second
World War Pius XII is indispensable to German Catholics. Almeida's
very tactful study returns again and again to St Augustine and classical
Catholic war theology and justifiably quotes 'the teaching of Pius XII
regarding nuclear warfare' in its support.

The presumptive enemy, Soviet Russia, is spoken of in terms that
Pius XII would have approved: 'Under a system that recognizes the
rights of neither God nor Man, and will stop at nothing to achieve its
aim, everything that is sacred to free men and to Christians will be
destroyed.' (One single meeting with a dozen young Soviet Russians
would have convinced Pius XII – who received so many young German
soldiers in audience – and Almeida that young Russians are no less
humane and unspoilt than young Germans can be.)

In this connection it is worth recalling the war correspondence
between President Roosevelt and Pope Pius XII, which was published in
a highly official edition edited by Myron C. Taylor and with forewords
by Harry S. Truman and Pius XII. In this Roosevelt is seen, in his letter
of 3 September 1941, trying vainly to make his war alliance with Russia
comprehensible to the pope. Roosevelt knew how distasteful this alliance
was to Catholics in America and Europe, but he believed that Russia's
survival would be much less dangerous to religion and the church and
mankind in general, than a survival of German dictatorship would have
been. And how right Roosevelt was! How would Europe, the church and
mankind have looked twenty years after a victory by Hitler? But Pius
XII did not share Roosevelt's opinion. Polite as he was, he did not even
mention Russia in his reply of 20 September 1941. It is almost eerie to
see these two distinguished correspondents speaking and writing to each
other with many respectful epithets and references to Christianity, but
at complete cross purposes. Though Pius XII was obviously against

Roosevelt's demand for unconditional surrender, he said simply that it was no concern of the pope what form a peace treaty with the Hitler régime took. Roosevelt as spokesman and champion of an armed American democracy of a puritanical, Calvinistic stamp comes through more convincingly than the pope. This is no accident: Roosevelt was mobilizing millions of men for the fight with Hitler. What was Pius XII mobilizing? Reading this correspondence again, one finds even more significance in Ernesto Buonaiuti's remark that in it Roosevelt emerges as a prophet and true spokesman for Christianity, while Pius speaks evasively like a politician. The two had exchanged their roles.

The frontispiece of Cardinal Domenico Tardini's *Pio XII*, issued by the Vatican in 1960, shows the pope, dressed completely in white, standing with arms outstretched and eyes raised to heaven against the red background of an empty stage. Was he an actor? He once called himself the showman of God. Other colour pictures in the book show Pius XII in cinematic poses, or rather in those 'living pictures' which were fashionable in the eighties of the last century: praying on 9 May 1947; kissing the feet of a crucifix on 1 December 1956; distributing caramels to orphan children on 30 September 1958; praying again, on his *prie-dieu*, on 21 January 1957. Pius XII was the last baroque-style pope, but not the last representative of that magic world that honours the celestial hierarchy in earthly-celestial images. Not only these pictures, but many speeches and sayings of Pope Pius XII tell us as much.

Cardinal Tardini's laudation for Pius XII was preceded by a laudation by the subsequent Pope John XXIII in Venice on 11 October 1958, shortly after the death of Pius XII. Roncalli (John XXIII) said: 'In the time of Jesus the miracles spoke. With Pius XII this voice gained in power and penetration until it became the voice of world-wide agreement.' Roncalli had watched on television as the body was conveyed from Castelgandolfo to St Peter's and he asked himself whether this ceremony could not be compared with the triumphal procession of an ancient Roman emperor. 'With our blessed father Pius XII we are present at the opening of new heavens (*una apertura evidente di nuovi cieli*), at the improvement of contacts between the civil order and the religious and political order . . . The whole world gathered round the dying pope as Christ's disciples on the Mount of Olives to accompany him with eyes and hearts on his ascension to heaven.'

Here Roncalli was speaking the language of the *Osservatore Romano*, in accordance with the image that Pius XII had projected of himself and the image of his appearance on earth projected in the *Osservatore* liturgical reports on audiences, etc.

Tardini's laudation was delivered on 20 October 1959 in the presence of Pope John XXIII and a distinguished audience. It is a masterpiece in which every word deserves serious consideration. Tardini served Pope

Pius XII for many years, and in his speech he recalled that famous saying of Pius XII: I do not want colleagues but executives (*Io non voglio callaboratori, ma essecutori*), which he spoke to Tardini on 5 November 1944. Tardini here used to some extent the language of Pius himself, a sort of papal liturgy, but discreetly mixed with it were the words of an acute observer of humanity. Tardini praised Pius XII as a great devotee of truth, as a great pacifier of peoples, as a great judge of sinful humanity and as a bearer of Christ's crown of thorns.

In contrast to the *papificatio Christi*, which the great German Catholic Franz von Baader deplored, one might speak of the *christificatio* of the pope, who, like Christ, drained the cup of sorrow to the dregs. Tardini praised Pius XII in a single breath as a humanist and as a connoisseur of literary style (*apprezava le belle frasi letterarie, come un umanista del Rinascimento*) and said that his laughter was as happy as a child's.

Tardini stressed in particular two aspects of the pope's character: firstly, his solitariness, which set him inwardly apart from other men; and secondly, his gentleness, which bordered on timidity (*Pio XII era, per naturale temperamento, mite e piuttosto timido*). This sensitive man did not ever like to say no: his natural tendency was to avoid rather than to accept strife.

Tardini ended his laudation with a description of the ritual gesture with which Pius XII always ended his public audiences. First he would lift his head and raise his eyes to heaven: a gesture of supplication. Then he would spread out his arms, as if to take the whole of mankind in a fatherly embrace: a gesture of consecration. Maintaining this attitude, he appeared like a man crucified: a gesture of sacrifice. He stood before us, the true representative of Christ, in a realistic liturgical interpretation of the Crucifixion.

From the Constantinian Christ-Emperor, the Christ in the liturgy of the imperial church, a direct path, spanning fifteen centuries, led to Pius XII's acted spectacle of the crucified Christ.

Every gesture, every word addressed to a world in which Christ was a Roman (cf. the pope's speeches in *Pius XII: Roma nella parola di Pio XII, Roma onde Cristo è Romano, a cura di O.Galassi Paluzzi*, Rome 1943) depicted Pius XII as Christ on earth (in the tradition of Innocent III). It was a liturgical conception which caused controversy within the Curia itself, and after the pope's death it broke out explosively. But in fact this Christ-pope liturgy was completely in line with the fixed forms of an archaic religiosity in which every object, man or angel has its known place in the hierarchy. In this fixed pattern everything has been ordained by God, and the hierarchy of the church on earth reflects the hierarchical order in Heaven. Pius XII said as much in the encyclical *Mediator Dei* of 30 November 1947, a proclamation which brought from Aldo Capitini (*Discuto la religione di Pio XII*, Parenti 1957) the remark that 'institutionalized authoritarianism (the church) here joins hands with mythology'.

Aldo Capitini questions this fixed religiosity of Pius xii from the standpoint of his own, more open, religion. Capitini's book *Religione aperta* (Parma 1955) had been placed on the Index. The decree appeared in 1956 on the anniversary of the very day on which the Concordat between the Vatican and the Fascist régime had been signed. Capitini recalls the pope's encyclical *Summi Pontificatus* of 20 October 1939, celebrating this reconciliation with the Fascist state as 'the peace of Christ that has been granted again to Italy'. But Capitini reminds his readers what grave injuries to human dignity and conscience had been brought about by this Concordat.

Capitini maintains that Pius xii's fixed form of religion, based on clear divisions between friends and foes, made any form of spiritual, intellectual or political co-operation with others impossible. He criticizes the illogicality of this usually so logical pope towards the United Nations. Pius xii proclaimed his wish to strengthen this organization, but at the same time made any practical collaboration with others impossible by refusing to recognize their spiritual validity.

Capitini then goes on to consider what he sees as the unrealistic social teaching of the pope (and all other popes). In this God is seen not as a creator, but as a copier of nature: there must always be rich and poor, and everything has its place in a pre-established order (or rather lack of order). The creative process is replaced by charitable 'virtues'. This pope had no conception of a dynamic relationship between heaven and earth, in which the kingdom of God, or belief in the kingdom of God, is constantly influencing and changing life on earth. His war theology was in line with his static and hierarchical social order.

Capitini recalls the fourth edition of *Moralità della guerra*, published by *Civiltà Cattolica* in 1944 with the approval of the church. The author, Angelo Brucculeri, a Jesuit and supporter of papal centralism, states in this that not only defensive, but also aggressive, war was morally and theologically permissible.

Pius xii's Christmas message of 1956 does not recognize the right of a conscientious objector to replace armed service with civil duties, but pledges Catholics to armed service, even in a nuclear war.

Capitini declares in connection with this: 'I cannot conclude that Pius xii was right when he said on 3 December 1939: "Is not the church itself divine progress in the world and the mother of the greatest spiritual and moral advance of humanity and the civil life of nations?" ' A single glance back into the history of the past decades and centuries compels one to answer no to this rhetorical question.

Turning to the mythical and supernatural aspects of the pope's religious outlook, Capitini deals with the pope's views on the *Corpus*

Mysticum Christ-church-pope, with his conception of the priesthood (which was particularly tinged with archaic elements of magic), with his attitude towards the modernists and with his mythology. In his encyclical of 30 September 1943, Pius XII describes the Bible as a collection of 'paternal letters from the throne of His Majesty' addressed to mankind and entrusted for eternal safe-keeping to the church.

Capitini sees the pope's cult of angels, and of Rome, as particularly revealing expressions of his archaic religious outlook. His cult of the Virgin Mary and of Christ and his belief in hell are the corner-stones of that remarkable revival of the baroque period which Pius XII brought about.

In an address (5 February 1955) to Italian Catholic lawyers, Pius XII gave a striking demonstration of his belief in hell, retaining all the force of old church tradition. He declared that God could have chosen another form of punishment in the after-life than hell. But hell, eternal hell, was what He wanted. About the facts of eternal and unalterable damnation in hell there could be no dispute. God, the highest lawgiver, had here made use of His omnipotent power and would permit no change. And so the unlimited term of punishment in hell was accepted law (Dunque questa durata senza limiti è diritto vigente).

Pius XII was not prepared to change the old church tradition by a single iota. He was the prisoner, not only of ecclesiastical tradition, but also of that religio-political tradition which, through the refusal of the Curia to recognize the Treaty of Westphalia, had forced the Vatican into growing isolationism and non-participation in the political decisions of the nineteenth and twentieth centuries. This was how Ernesto Buonaiuti saw the historical role of Pius XII in his book *Pio XII*, published in Rome in 1946, and now once again held in high regard.

Together with Giovanni Roncalli, Buonaiuti was a pupil of Monsignore Benigni in Rome. As pope, Roncalli did not forget the pain and suffering of Ernesto Buonaiuti: he himself was in 1946 one of the few survivors of that witch-hunt against modernists to which many fine young priests and theologians in Italy had fallen victim. Buonaiuti was twice condemned by an authoritarian and centralist church which worked so smoothly with the dictatorships of Mussolini and Franco and strove so many years for acceptance by Hitler's régime. At one time Buonaiuti was excommunicated, but at the Second Vatican Council many of his most significant proposals for reform had become common property among the alert members of a younger generation of theologians. Buonaiuti fell victim to the unholy alliance between the church and the Fascist régime for the second time when he was deprived of his teaching post at the secular university of Rome. The Concordat of 1929 had pledged the Fascist régime not to employ ex-priests in the service of the state.

In 1946 Buonaiuti had only the following sources at his disposal: his knowledge of church history and his attentive reading of the speeches and writings of Pope Pius XII and of the *Osservatore Romano*. It is these very limitations that make his book so extraordinarily significant as a human document and a historical essay.

Buonaiuti does not with a single word impugn the human personality of Pius XII, his integrity or his moral virtues.

Buonaiuti considers the first Thirty Years War of 1618–48 in close connection with a second Thirty Years War of 1914–45. In this epoch both Catholicism and the church underwent a huge and momentous deformation. The individual conscience of the post-Tridentine Catholic shrunk to an obsessional fear of hell-fire and forgot the obligation to spread the kingdom of God, with its glad tidings of joy and freedom, on this earth. In the same way the church shrunk to an organization of clerics concerned only with their own privileges, which they sought to ensure first through military and political alliances and later through Concordats.

Buonaiuti deals in a masterly manner with the mania for Concordats which characterized the era of Pius XI and his pupil Pius XII. While a convulsed Europe was falling apart, this curial church was exerting all its efforts in making Concordats with ephemeral governments in Lithuania, etc., and with dictatorships. This self-absorbed church was quite incapable of providing the forces necessary for the spiritual, intellectual and religious recovery of the struggling peoples. Buonaiuti shows strikingly how the destruction of an élite of the Italian clergy in the modernist controversy rendered their successors incapable of providing resistance to the Fascist régime.

As nuncio in Germany during the First World War, Pius XII had believed almost to the last in German victory. In the Second World War he retained his belief in German victory, at least until 1943. Buonaiuti finds impressive examples to illustrate the extent of the church's collaboration with the Fascists. Of particular interest is his description of a visit paid by Cardinal Schuster of Milan to the *Scuola di mistica fascista*: it was from this stronghold of 'Fascist mysticism' that a radical brand of anti-Semitic propaganda, ostensibly based on church teaching, emerged during the Second World War. Of even more significance, as Buonaiuti shows, was Pius XII's fatal subservience to tradition which prevented him from finding the spiritual and intellectual means to deal effectively with the terrible enemy of mankind in Germany and Italy. As one sees from numerous examples in Buonaiuti's book, his addresses hovered literally in the clouds, the baroque-style language descending at times to a bathos which reminds one ominously of the rhetoric of Goebbels. For example, speaking in Rome to the Poles on 30 September 1939, he referred to Polish tears over the terrible situation of their people. Christ recognized the special value of these tears, he said. The tears themselves held their own sweetness. He called Chopin to mind, whose art was distilled from tears. (After the fall of Stalingrad, Goebbels compared the town to a painting which looked crude when seen near to, and only revealed its high qualities at a distance.)

While Europe was drowning in a sea of blood, Pius XII, enthroned on his baroque cloud, spoke on 29 June 1941 (and on throughout the war in the same vein) on the radio of the heroic deeds of the defenders of Christian civilization, inspired by fervent love for their country, noble spirits ready for any sacrifice. (*Valore magnanimo in difensa dei fondamenti della civiltà cristiana e fiducioso sperante per il loro trionfo, fortissimo amore di patria. Atti eroici di virtú. Anime elette pronte e preste ad ogni sacrificio. Dedizioni generose. Largo risveglio di fede e di pietà.*)

As significant as these operatic speeches was the silence that met acts of brutality. Buonaiuti deals with the silences of Pius XII, and more particularly with the silences of the Vatican paper *Osservatore Romano*, which had literally not a word to say about Mussolini's Eastertide invasion of Albania, about Fascist atrocities in Italy and Nazi atrocities in Europe – even in Rome itself.

Buonaiuti pays tribute in his last chapter to the integrity of the pope's personal character. Viewing his political activities as a whole, he comes to the conclusion that his failures, the complete lack of accord between his words and deeds and the facts of reality, must not be blamed on the individual man, but solely on the ideas and values of an official Catholic orthodoxy striving to preserve conventions long proved false by history and Man's experience.

In conclusion Ernesto Buonaiuti poses the question which is as open today as it was in 1946. The second Thirty Years War was the crucial test of the Christian spirit. Can Christendom survive it? And, if so, in what form?

CHAPTER 12: COLLABORATORS IN THE FINAL SOLUTION

Adorno, T.W. (Editor): The Authoritarian Personality, New York 1950
Aldag, Peter: Juden beherrschen England, Berlin 1939
Arendt, H.: Eichmann in Jerusalem, Munich 1964
Brod, Max: Johannes Reuchlin und sein Kampf, Stuttgart 1965
Clarke, E.G.: The British Union and the Jews, London c. 1936
Deschner, K. (Editor): Das Jahrhundert der Barbarei, Munich 1966
Deschner, K. (Editor): Jesusbilder in theologischer Sicht, Munich 1966
Deutschkron, Inge: Denn ihrer war die Hölle – Kinder in Ghettos und Lagern, Cologne 1965
Erlinghagen, K.: Katholisches Bildungsdefizit, Freiburfi 1965
Eschenburg, T.: Die improvisierte Demokratie, Munich 1963
Falconi, Carlo: Il silenzio di Pio XII, Milan 1965

Fejtö, F.: Les juifs et l'antisémitisme dans les pays communistes, Paris 1960

Fleg, E. (Editor): Anthologie juive des origines à nos jours, Paris 1951

Fritsch, T.: Handbuch der Judenfrage, Leipzig 1939 (45th printing)

Gabel, Joseph: Formen der Entfremdung, Frankfurt 1964

Hay, Malcolm: Europe and the Jews, Boston 1960

Hilberg, R.: The Destruction of the European Jews, Chicago 1961

Jaromir, R.: Bibel und Zeitgeist, Affoltern 1949

Jéhouda, Josué: L'antisémitisme, miroir du monde, Geneva 1958

Koestler, Arthur: The Trail of the Dinosaur, London 1955

Körber, R. (Editor): Antisemitismus der Welt in Wort und Bild, Dresden 1935 (published in Vienna as: Israel und die Völker)

Landmann, Salcia: Der jüdische Witz, Olten 1960

Lewy, Guenter: The Catholic Church and Nazi Germany, London and New York 1964

Maier, Hans (Editor): Deutscher Katholizismus nach 1945, Munich 1966

Maybaum, I.: The Face of God after Auschwitz, Amsterdam 1965

Mitscherlich, A. and Mielke, F. (Editors): Medizin ohne Menschlichkeit, Frankfurt 1960

Motzkin, L.: La campagne antisémite en Pologne, Paris 1932

Nellessen, B.: Der Prozess von Jerusalem, Düsseldorf 1965 (on Eichmann)

Neumann, R.: Ausflüchte unseres Gewissens – Dokumente zu Hitlers Endlösung der Judenfrage, Hanover 1960

Nobécourt, J.: 'Le Vicaire' et l'Histoire, Paris 1964

Ostrowski, W.: Anti-Semitism in Byelo-Russia and Its Origin, London 1960

Picard, E.: Synthèse de l'antisémitisme, Brussels 1941

Poliakov, L., and Wulf, J.: Das Dritte Reich und seine Diener, Berlin 1956

Reck-Malleczewen, F.von: Tagebuch eines Verzweifelten, Stuttgart 1947

Rippmann, P.: Unbewältigte schweizerische Vergangenheit, Basle 1965

Rudolf, E.V.von: Das Judenspiegel, Munich 1938

Sharf, A.: The British Press and the Jews under Nazi Rule, Oxford 1965

Weidlein, J. (Editor): Der ungarische Antisemitismus in Dokumenten, Schorndorf 1962

Weltsch, R. (Editor): Deutsches Judentum – Aufstieg und Krise, Stuttgart 1963

Young, Leonard: Deadlier than the H-Bomb, London 1956

Ziff, W.: The Rape of Palestine, 1939

Page
336 The conference in Evian, 1938: Hay, 5f; Ziff. It is also dealt with in Hans Habe's novel *The Mission*.

336 The refugee conference in Bermuda: Hay, 302f.

336 Hitler waited until 1941: Hay, 300f; Jéhouda.

336 Reports dismissed as 'atrocity propaganda': Sharf deals with the curious

attitude of the British press, the one notable exception being the *Manchester Guardian*.

337 The *Kriegstagebuch des Kommandostabes Reichsführer SS*, published by the Europa-Verlag in Vienna in 1965, provides copious examples of the language formula employed by the perpetrators of the 'final solution'. Extermination, for instance, becomes *Befriedung* (pacification). As examples of 'objective' reporting: 'About 800 Jews and Jewesses in the age range 16 to 60 were shot'; 'two horses lost in the bog, about 300 Jews shot'; 'total number shot: 722 Jews, 13 partisans'. The shooting of children was described as *Aktionen nach Kriegsbrauch* (actions in accordance with the practices of war). 'Four men, four women and seven children were given special treatment (*sonderbehandelt*) as suspected terrorists (*bandenverdächtig*).' '*1000 Stück Juden aus Wien eingetroffen*' (A thousand head of Jews arrived from Vienna). And so on. The diary also relates that a Jewish mechanic saved the lives of some SS men.

337 Polish anti-Semitism: Ostrowski, in whose book the Polish concentration camp of Bereza Kartuska in the period 1934–9 is described. Books by survivors include: C. Goldstein, *Leben ohne Stern* (Munich 1965); Stefan Szende, *Der letzte Jude aus Polen* (Zurich 1945); and Koppel Holzman, *Die Höhlen der Hölle* (Graz 1961).

337 At the last plenary meeting of the Communist party . . . : Fejtö.

337 Gomulka's letter and *Pro Prostu*: both Fejtö.

338 Maybaum says that a single word from one Polish bishop could have saved the lives of some Jews.

338 The Polish church under Nazi occupation: Falconi.

338 Hungarian anti-Semitism: Weidlein.

338 Eichmann in Hungary: Arendt.

340 Followers of the Arrow Cross movement arranged for masses to be read: the Ustacha in Croatia did the same.

The great Hungarian historian Julius Szekfü recalls in *Forradalom után* (After the Revolution, Budapest 1947) that Catholics went to the sacraments believing that they were serving their church, 'but at the same time their hearts were full of hatred, envy and revenge, for they considered everybody who did not belong to their party or did not believe in Hitler as an outlaw.'

On 1 August 1946 Cardinal Mindszenty issued a pastoral letter pleading for a general amnesty, since 'in this way a revival of anti-Semitism, which is threatening today in new forms, could be prevented'.

340 Rumanian anti-Semitism at the Berlin Congress of 1878: N. M. Gelber in Weltsch (Ed.).

340 Eberhard von Thadden and Dr Martin Luther: Poliakov-Wulf.

340 The extermination of Orthodox Serbs: among others, Falconi, who states that Cardinal Tisserant was the only person in the Vatican to speak openly against the murders.

340 Darquier de Pellepoix and his assistants: among others, Nobécourt. Arthur Miller's play *Incident in Vichy* deals with the position of the Jews in Vichy France.

341 A form of French liturgical anti-Semitism was spread throughout the world in translations of the anti-Semitic *L'année liturgique* of Dom Prosper Guéranger, the abbot of Solesmes: see Hay, 342.

341 Maritain's lecture was first delivered at the Théâtre des Ambassadeurs in Paris, and repeated in New York on 14 December 1938. It also appeared in London in 1939. In it he described the witch-hunting German background to Jewish persecution. Catholics (he said) should not – as they were widely doing – describe racialism as neo-paganism: that was an insult to the pagans. Maritain recognized the deadly danger of anti-Semitism, particularly to the Christians, and revealed to the world (in 1938!) terrible examples of Nazi brutality. He dealt with anti-Semitism in Russia, Poland and Rumania (where the anti-Semitic head of government was the Rumanian patriarch), and posed the question: What must be done? Were all Jews to be massacred? The church gave no answer to Maritain, who was already at that time advocating a pluralistic society and was regarded in the Vatican with deep suspicion. Maritain, who with his wife Raissa and her sister Vera (both of them Russian Jewesses) was baptized into the Catholic church in 1906, felt himself in debt to Israel. See *Carnet de Notes*, Paris 1965.

342 Anti-Semitism in British Catholic literature and theology: copious examples in Hay, 236ff, 250ff, 264ff.

342 British military officers in Palestine: Hay, 262.

342 Hilaire Belloc borrowed from Drumont: Hay, 214ff, 236ff.

343 Catholic sneers at the Zionist settlement in Palestine: Hay, 256ff.

343 The British military government protected the persecutors: Hay, 288 and (quoting H.V.Morton and others) 290ff.

343 Wing-Commander Leonard Young: RAF officers are to some extent strongly anti-Semitic in outlook.

344 For the works of Nesta Webster and other British anti-Semites, see the bibliography of Young's book.

344 Cf. Young's picture of post-war Britain with the Nazi view: 'England is the refuge and centre of world Jewry. Jewish elements have there succeeded in taking over the most important and decisive positions' (Peter Aldag, 1939).

346 The memorandum of the foreign ministry in Berlin: German title: *Die Judenfrage als Faktor der Aussenpolitik im Jahre 1938*. Father Coughlin: Adorno (Ed.), 240ff.

347 Franklin's speech is reprinted in Fritsch's *Handbuch der Judenfrage*.

347 Puritanic race hatred as in South Africa: cf. the 'Aryanization' of Christ into a white man. 'Although the Catholic Church early recognized Christ as a Jew, it engaged in a progressive Aryanization of Him in strict

accordance with the logic of symbolism' (Roger Bastide in 'Race and Colour', *Congress for Cultural Freedom, Reports*, 9 July 1966).

347 Edward Freeman in the United States: Hay, 213f.

348 In 1950 sociologists and psycho-analysts . . .: See also Adorno, 'Anti-Semitism and Fascist Propaganda' in E.Simmel (Editor), *Anti-Semitism, a Social Disease* (New York 1946); Adorno, 'The Psychological Technique of Martin Luther Thomas's Radio-Speeches' (in the archives of the Institute of Social Research, New York); R.N.Sandford, 'Identification with the Enemy: Case Study of an American Quisling' (in *Journal of Personality*, 1946); O.Fenichel, 'The Psycho-Analysis of Anti-Semitism' (*American Imago*, I, 1940). As Fritsch reveals in his *Handbuch der Judenfrage*, the Nazis kept a watchful eye on anti-Semitism in America: it was their great hope.

348 German Catholics were members of an in-group: see in this connection the chapter 'The Misfit Bourgeois' in Adorno (Ed.).

349 American pseudo-conservatives: Adorno (Ed.), 207f, 357f, 385 and 675ff.

349 Lists of anti-Jewish clichés: Adorno (Ed.), 63ff, 606f.

349 Children brought up in an authoritarian atmosphere: Adorno (Ed.), 337ff, 368ff, 385ff.

349 The loudly professed 'love' of parent-authority: Adorno (Ed.), 257f (Else Frenkel-Brunswik).

350 'The Jew is . . . over-sexed': Adorno (Ed.), 606f.

350 The Jew is the Devil, and the Devil is a Jew: Adorno (Ed.), 728f. Adorno refers to J.Trachtenberg, *The Devil and The Jews* (New Haven 1943).

351 Tests in San Quentin: Adorno (Ed.), 171.

351 In the psychodrama of Man a kind of court trial is held: Adorno (Ed.), 629ff.

352 Court practice in National Socialist Germany: see *Justiz im Dritten Reich*, 1964, edited by Ilse Staff.

352 Dr Martin Luther and Franz Rademacher: Poliakov-Wulf.

352 Von Manstein: Poliakov-Wulf. Also Friedrich Heer in the essay 'Kriege und Kriegsfolgen' in Deschner (Editor, *Das Jahrhundert*).

355 The papal nuncio in Budapest: Arendt.

356 Statement of Dr Kurt Schmitt: Poliakov-Wulf.

357 Resignation of Baron von Eltz and Henschel: Poliakov-Wulf.

357 Anton Schmidt: Poliakov-Wulf; Arendt.

357 Adolf Eichmann is a normal, typical case: Hannah Arendt's book *Eichmann in Jerusalem* has the apt sub-title: *Ein Bericht von der Banalität des Bösen* (A Report on the Banality of Evil).

358 Eichmann said fifteen times: Nellessen – with Arendt the main source of the passages dealing with Eichmann.

358 The Slovak head of government, the prelate Tiso, was anti-Semitic.

360 'What is to be done with these people?': Ziff, 487. See also Hay, 5f.

361 'The Jewish blood spilt by the National Socialists': J.P.Sartre, *Portrait of the Anti-Semite*.

361 More than a million children could have been saved: Hay, 7, 302.

361 Cordell Hull's statement: Hay, 301ff.

361 The Bermuda Conference refused to deal with the Jews in isolation: Hay, 302.

362 American government officials prevented news: Hay, XXIII. In the Swiss Bundesrat the *Vaterländische* (Patriots) got a motion passed forbidding newspapers to print 'atrocity stories' about the mass extermination of the Jews (W.M.Diggelmann in his novel *Die Hinterlassenschaft*, Munich 1965).

362 The church's responsibility: In the first edition of his book *The Conflict of the Church and the Synagogue*, which appeared in 1934, the Anglican historian James Parkes spoke a warning. But, like Maritain, he was ignored.

362 Without the collaboration of Jewish leaders the extermination might have proved technically impossible: Arendt. For an example of the angry contradictions that Hannah Arendt's assertion aroused, see Mary McCarthy in *Partisan Review*, 1964.

362 File entry on Gauleiter Kube: quoted in Poliakov-Wulf.

362 German Jews in a French concentration camp praised the orderliness in Dachau: Golo Mann in *Geschichte und Geschichten* (Frankfurt 1961), which also deals with the nationalist attitudes of German Jews during the Second World War.

363 Hindenburg's letter to Dr Löwenstein: quoted in Poliakov-Wulf.

363 Plans for a German Jewish *Nationalrat*: related by M.H.Sommerfeldt in *Ich war dabei, 1933-9* (Darmstadt 1949).

363 Jewish belief in Germany, even in Hitler: I myself had frequent experience of this during the years 1933-9 in conversation with German Jews in Prague, Berlin and Vienna.

364 Few anti-Semites have written crueller things about Israel than Kafka: Gabel. Kafka's Jewish soul: Brod.

364 Rabbi Léonard Lévy preaching in Paris: Fleg (Ed.).

366 The spiritual problems of the Jew are also evident in the writings of Arthur Koestler. See, for example *The Trail of the Dinosaur* (1955) and *Promise and Fulfilment* (1950). On Koestler's curious 'solution' of the Jewish problem, see Fejtö, 254ff.

366 A child's letter to *Der Stürmer*: quoted in Neumann.

367 Millions of children learn at school: A Catholic teacher, Alice Baum, writing in *Una Sancta*, a periodical devoted to the furtherance of contacts between denominations, in 1963, says that a change of Christian attitudes towards Israel is still very much in its beginning stages in Catholic school books. In *Der neue Mahnruf* 9 (1964) an Israeli writer criticizes West German school books.

367 Dr Aharon Peretz on ghetto children: Nellessen.
367 How bravely Jewish children met their death can be seen from the statements of witnesses in the Auschwitz trial, 27 February 1964. Documentation in Deutschkron.
367 Jews sent to their death from 33,914 places: 'Black Book, Issued on Holocaust' in *The Israel Digest*, VIII, No. 5, 1965.
367 Jewish central authorities: Arendt; Hilberg.
368 'The utter failure of ecclesiastical leaders ...': Niemöller in the *Handbuch des Kirchenkampfes* (1956) in 'Die evangelische Kirche im Dritten Reich'.

CHAPTER 13: CHRISTIAN SUICIDE OR CHRISTIAN-JEWISH REBIRTH

Abrahams, G.: The Jewish Mind, London 1961
Ackerman, N., and Jahoda, M.: Anti-Semitism and Emotional Disorder, New York 1950
Amery C.: Die Kapitulation oder: Deutscher Katholizismus heute, Ham,burg 1963
Ausubel, Nathan: Pictorial History of the Jewish People, New York 1956
Ausubel, N. and M. (Editors): A Treasury of Jewish Poetry, New York 1957
Benamozegh, E.: Israël et l'humanité, Paris 1911
Berger, Peter L.: The Noise of Solemn Assemblies, New York 1961
Bettelheim, B., and Janowitz, M.: Dynamics of Prejudice – a Psychological and Sociological Study of Veterans, New York 1947
Bevan, R., and Singer, C. (Editors): The Legacy of Israel, Oxford 1953
Bloch, J.S.: Israel und die Völker nach jüdischer Lehre, Berlin 1932
Cohen, Arthur A.: The Natural and the Supernatural Jew, New York 1962
Cohen, Elliot E. (Editor): The New Red Anti-Semitism, Boston 1953
Congar, Yves M.J.: Le mystère du temple, Paris 1958
Congar, Yves M.J.: Sainte Eglise – Etudes et approches ecclésiologiques, Paris 1963
Eckert, W.P., and Ehrlich, E.L.: Judenhass–Schuld der Christen?, Essen 1964
Epting, K.: Der geistliche Weg der Simone Weil, Stuttgart 1955
Erlinghagen, K.: Katholisches Bildungsdefizit in Deutschland, Freiburg 1965
Fejtö, F.: Dieu et son juif, Paris 1962
Fejtö, F.: Les juifs et l'antisémitisme dans les pays communistes, Paris 1960
Fleg, E. (Editor): Anthologie juive des origines à nos jours, Paris 1952
Fromm, Erich: The Sane Society, New York 1955
Glatzer, N.M.: Franz Rosenzweig, His Life and Thought, New York 1953
Goldschmidt, D., and Kraus, H.J. (Editors): Der ungekündigte Bund, Stuttgart 1962
Goldschmidt, H.L.: Die Botschaft des Judentums, Frankfurt 1960
Goldschmidt, H.L.: Das Vermächtnis des deutschen Judentums, Frankfurt 1957

Gutfeld, L.: Von der Bibel bis Chagall, Frankfurt 1963

Hammerstein, Franz von: Das Messiasproblem bei Martin Buber, Stuttgart 1958

Heschel, A.J.: The Earth is the Lord: The Inner World of the Jew in East Europe, New York 1950

Heschel, A.J.: The Sabbath: Its Meaning for Moder.. Man, New York 1951

Hutten, K., and Kortzfleisch, S.v. (Editors): Asien r ssioniert im Abendland, Stuttgart 1962

Jéhouda, Josué: L'antisémitisme, miroir du monde, Geneva 1958

Kaiser, Robert: Inside the Council, London 1963

Kaplan, Mordecai M.: The Purpose and Meaning of Jewish Existence, Philadelphia 1964

Kühner, H.: Index Romanus – Auseinandersetzung oder Verbot, Nuremberg 1963

Kühner, H.: Tabus der Kirchengeschichte, Nuremberg 1964

Küng, Hans: Kirche in Freiheit, Einsiedeln 1964

Küng, Hans: Theologe und Kirche, 1964

Leftwich, J. (Editor): The Golden Peacock, a World-wide Treasury of Yiddish Poetry, New York 1961

Levine, E. (Editor): Jewish Heritage, a Symposium, London 1955

Löwenthal, L., and Gutermann, N.: Prophets of Deceit – A Study of the Techniques of the American Agitator, New York 1947

Maier, H. (Editor): Deutscher Katholizismus nach 1945, Munich 1964

Maybaum, Ignaz: The Face of God after Auschwitz, Amsterdam 1965

Ornstein, H.: Der antijüdische Komplex, Zurich 1949

Pallière, Aimée: Le Sanctuaire inconnu, ma conversion au Judaisme, Paris 1926

Pinay, M.: Verschwörung gegen die Kirche, Madrid 1963

Pinson, Koppel S. (Editor): Essays on Anti-Semitism, New York 1946

Pinson, Koppel S. (Editor): Nationalism and History, New York 1958

Poliakov, L., and Wulf, J.: Das Dritte Reich und seine Diener, Berlin 1956

Rahner, K., and Vorgrimler, H.: Kleines Konzilskompendium, Freiburg 1966

Roth, B. Cecil: Die Kunst der Juden, Frankfurt 1962/3

Rubinowicz, David: Das Tagebuch des . . ., Frankfurt 1960

Rudin, Josef (Editor): Neurose und Religion, Olten 1964

Rudy, Zvi: Die Juden in der Sowjetunion, Vienna 1966

Runes, Dagobert D.: The Jews and the Cross, New York 1965

Sartre, J.P.: Betrachtungen zur Judenfrage, Zurich 1948

Schlamm, William S.: Wer ist Jude? Ein Selbstgespräch, Stuttgart 1964

Schlösser, M. (Editor): An den Wind geschrieben, Darmstadt 1960

Schoeps, H.J.: Israel und Christenheit – Jüdisch-christliches Religionsgespräch in neunzehn Jahrhunderten, Frankfurt 1949

Schütz, Paul: Parusia – Hoffnung und Prophetie, Heidelberg 1961

Schwarz, S.M.: Antisemitism v Sovetskom Sojuze, New York 1952
Seeber, David Andreas: Das Zweite Vatikanum-Konzil des Übergangs, Freiburg 1966
Serafian, Michael: Der Pilger
Smith, G.A. (Editor): The Legacy of Israel, Oxford 1953
Spaemann, H.: Die Christen und das Volk der Juden, Munich 1966
Szczesny, G. (Editor): Die Antwort der Religionen auf 31 Fragen, Munich 1965
Tschuppik, Walter, Der Christ und sein Schatten, Leipzig 1923
Weidlein, J.: Der Aufstand in Ungarn und das ungarländische Judentum, Schorndorf 1957
Wiesel, Elie: Die Juden in der UdSSR, Munich 1967

Page
373 'Babij Yar' by Yevtushenko translated by Herbert Marshall (Pergamon Press 1967: copyright by E.P.Dutton and Co. Ltd.)
373 'When in February 1963 ...': B.Lewytzkyj in *Tribüne*, No. 6, 1963.
373 Pasolini wanted Yevtushenko to play Jesus: U. Seelmann-Eggebert in *Dokumente*, No. 1, 1965.
374 Anti-Semitism in the Soviet Union: Fejtö, Rudy.
375 *Pravda* published its first anti-Semitic leading article on 10 September 1965. See the *New York Times* of 11/12 September 1965.
376 Howard Fast's correspondence with Boris Polevoi: *New York Times Magazine*, 9 June 1957.
377 The Polish Communists pressing for reform: Fejtö.
377 Robert Neumann on anti-Semitism in East Germany: *Tribüne*, 1963.
379 The controversy over Hochhuth's *Der Stellvertreter* (The Representative): *Summum jus oder summa injuria*, ed. K.Raddatz, Hamburg 1964; Walter Kampe, Ludwig Marcuse, R.Neumann, Paul Arnsberg in *Tribüne*, 1963; René Marlé in *Dokumente*, No. 1, 1965; *The Commonwealth*, 28 February 1964 (whole issue): *Christianity and Crisis*, 30 March 1964; N.Koch in *Evangelisch-katholisches Forum*, No. 4, 1964.
380 Anti-Semitism in the United States: Kaplan.
380 The racial problem in the United States: Among many others, William Peirce Randel, *Ku-Klux-Klan*, and James Baldwin, *The Fire Next Time*. Baldwin points out that the liberation of the coloured people is a question of the liberation of the white people: the white people must be enticed out of the prison of their guilt.
381 *Conspiracy against the Church* (published in Italian as *Complotto contro la chiesa* and in German as *Verschwörung gegen die Kirche*): see John M. Oesterreicher in Eckert-Ehrlich.
386 The men around Ottaviani have managed successfully ...: Serafian.
386 Terrorization, forgery, etc., at the Second Vatican Council: Kaiser, 60ff, 65ff, 70 ('A Jesuit in Haarlem said publicly that the Holy Office

was "an instrument of spiritual terror" '), 90ff, 176ff. Misleading and false information given by the official press bureau: 67ff.

389 Father Leppich advised a Catholic committee preparing a missionary campaign in Wuppertal to begin by creating a 'religious mass psychosis'. He said, 'You will be amazed what one can do with the stupid masses,' and added, 'Give me three good men and I will terrorize this hall for you. Give me seven men, and I will terrorize a city like Berlin for you.' (See *Werkhefte* 6, 1962.)

389 Arab diplomats made representations: Kaiser, 215.

390 Disputes concerning the official declaration on the Jews: Serafian, Oesterreicher in Eckert-Ehrlich.

392 'No one who is aware of the basic facts . . .' (Serafian). Spaemann has written: 'Auschwitz in the culmination of a tragedy of failure, in which for two thousand years the baptized have failed to recognize fully their guilt. It is an inescapable symbol, on which once again the spirits are dividing.'

392 The valiant efforts of individuals and small Christian groups: for example, the group around Archbishop T. D. Roberts SJ (see *Nuclear Weapons and Christian Conscience*, London 1961).

394 The attitude of the Catholic church to the treaty of Westphalia is dealt with more fully in my book *The Holy Roman Empire*.

395 Since the death of Pius XII there has been a certain reaction against the doctrine of the church as an end in itself. See for example Haag, Küng (*Kirche in Freiheit*) and the contributions by Yves Congar, E. Schillebeeckx and R. P. van Kets in the first issue of the new *Internationale Zeitschrift für Theologie*.

395 Sigmund Freud has spoken of the three great matters: in *Kleinere Schriften zur Neurosenlehre*, IV, Vienna 1918, 553f.

396 *Asien missioniert im Abendland*: see, for instance, the questions of a German Buddhist addressed to the Christian West (235ff) and W. Nigg on hell as the Christian idea of vengeance (244).

396 Deeply sick churches: In *Kirche in Freiheit* Küng maintains that mutual fear between individual members of the Catholic church has led in more recent times to hypocrisy and failure to act. A church absorbed in itself considers only self-defence at any price. It ignores the fact that the church as *ecclesia semper reformanda* and *ecclesia semper reformans* is constantly in a state of change. Seven British Roman Catholics have spoken up against superstition and terrorization in the church in *Objections to Roman Catholicism*, London 1964.

398 A holy inquiry into the most Holy Office: *sancta inquisitio sanctissimae inquisitionis*. Kaiser (67) relates that this threat was made in Archbishop Roberts's words by his successor at Bombay, Cardinal Valerian Gracias, who was vehemently supported by Cardinals Döpfner of Munich, König of Vienna and Liénart of Lille.

398 Bonhoeffer and Delp are today well known throughout the world, whereas Scholz has been known only by his novel *Goneril* and a few poems and letters. Reimann has dealt with him in his biography of Cardinal Innitzer, published in Vienna in 1967.

399 Religion in the sense of religious fervour and living faith: Fromm, quoted approvingly by Bolewski in his foreward to Berger. Berger maintains that religion provides individuals with the means of concealing from themselves the true nature of their being.

400 Walter Kampe: in *Werkhefte*, July 1963.

400 Joseph Lortz in *Katholischer Zugang zum Nationalsozialismus*, 1934, quoted by K.Deschner in *Und abermals krähte der Hahn.*

400 Erlinghagen in *Katholisches Bildungsdefizit in Deutschland*, Freiburg 1965.

402 The modern clergy has developed an obsession with the crudely sexual: But one present-day Catholic moral theologian has declared that the task today is to convert Christianity to sexuality. See H.Waider, *Zum gegenwärtigen Stand der Diskussion über die Lehre von den Ehezwecken* in *Festgabe für Ernst Hippel*, Bonn 1965.

403 Father Delp's criticism of the church: see Lutz in Maier (Ed.) and Delp's own *Im Angesicht des Todes*, Frankfurt 1948.

406 'The task of the church as such relates exclusively to the next world': In this connection it might be remarked that Pope Paul VI sees himself as a Pope Innocent III. His hymn to Rome and return to the patriarchal house of Romanism are in line with this static conception of the church as a hierarchical, other-worldly institution. Paul VI sees himself as *rector mundi*, as pope at the centre of a (pre-Copernican!) world. See P.Heinemann on the first encyclical of Pope Paul VI in *Evangelisch-katholisches Forum*, December 1964.

407 The whole liturgy of the church has grown up through a historical process: The grand master of Catholic research into the history of the Catholic mass, J.A.Jungmann SJ, has shown this in his great life's work, culminating in *Missarum sollemnia*, the fifth edition of which was published in two volumes in Freiburg in 1965.

408 Modern attitudes to the Catholic liturgy: A special issue of *Wort und Wahrheit*, published in 1965 under the title *Liturgiereform und Zukunft der Kirche* prints seventy-four Catholic answers to five questions. The answers reveal a frequent attitude of self-criticism. Several authors disapprove of specifically Jewish and Old Testament references in the liturgy. 'The rigid, unhistorical devotional style easily obscures the topicality of the message, and falsifies it. Prayers are for many un-comprehended and unconsidered formulas. In the opinion of many it will require "much time and patience before *a new liturgy is developed to replace one that has lasted fifteen centuries*" [my italics].'

408 It was Bea who first reminded the church of Pope Adrian's confession

(Kaiser, 40). A true confession is that of Pope John XXIII which I have used as a motto at the beginning of this book.

409 With Congar's relatively strict traditional view of the church in *Le mystère du Temple* one might contrast his collection of ecclesiological studies entitled *Sainte Eglise*, which covers the work of thirty years. The 'meantime' is the time of the church – between the First and Second Comings of Christ. Congar compares this time with the time between Stalingrad and 8 May 1945: from Stalingrad one knew that Hitler (the Devil) had lost his war, but had to wait until 8 May 1945 before victory was acknowledged. In the same way the believer knows that with Christ's 'victory on the Cross' the Devil met his Stalingrad, but victory will be complete only when Christ appears for the second time on day x. This juggling with religious and historical facts shows how little even the best theological minds of today are inclined to treat history seriously. Congar has a profound knowledge of church history. He knows that Catholicism after the Council of Trent was unfortunately often simply anti-Protestantism. He wrestles with the meaning of the Reformation in God's plan of salvation and sees that now for the first time the church recognizes the existence of 'others'. He knows that the authority of the church expressed in a liturgical ceremony is not sufficient to guarantee the reality of the event celebrated. St Thomas Aquinas did not have a very strong sense of history. 'The individual in the middle of the twentieth century thinks historically.' 'Men today are compelled to be completely honest and transparent.' Catholics will have to ask themselves questions concerning their 'separated brothers', the Protestants. 'I for my part am convinced that we must soon acknowledge the shattering conclusion that we cannot evade the questions which were put in the sixteenth century and which were then – except by a few exceptional people – pushed aside or ignored.' Yet this same Congar defends the syllabus of 1864 and the deplorable encyclica *Pascendi* of 1907, which condemned questions, posed by the so-called Modernists, of far more significance to present and future Christianity than the questions of the sixteenth century! Thus we see how even so distinguished a mind as Congar's is confined within the strait-jacket of a system that still demands 'voluntary' submission in matters of knowledge and conscience.

Congar himself ventures the opinion that *our task is to develop and further Jesus Christ*. He himself puts the question: 'Has Catholic theology not been forced back step by step on previously prepared positions under the irresistible pressure of ideas and facts which have gradually wrung from it terrible losses?' And Congar provides the answer: 'We think not.' He believes that 'Catholic theology is progressively developing the means which it possessed from the beginning, while being led at the same time by new facts or a better understanding of already established facts to work out new applications or aspects previously unrealized. *Nova et vetera. Nova ex veteribus.*'

This sounds very good. And of course it can be seen in this way. This leap across fifteen centuries of errors and omissions enables us to ignore the need for self-analysis and self-release which alone would give Christianity and the church control over history. It is in line with the traditional view, which Congar fully shares, of the church as a stopgap during a short period of world history, during which the sole aim is 'that men multiply themselves, atone and work together with God'.

But that of course is the question: *how* to work together with God. From the Council of Trent to this day Catholics have answered this question (which for Lutherans is anyway an inadmissible one) in the following way: The Christian works together with God by obeying the orders which come down from the hierarchy above and by absolving in the church his private sins. In this collaboration there is no room for the 'others' and no place for a positive life's contribution based on love. In contrast to the efforts of Russian and Eastern church thinkers in the nineteenth and twentieth centuries, the church to this day has no theology of the world, of creative human labour or of love (brotherly and sexual love).

411 Rome has no need to defend itself: Kühner (*Tabus*).

411 The need for Christian self-analysis: Congar writes in *Concilium* I (1965): 'The church as an institution has no need to convert itself.' The vast majority of present-day Catholics is probably against the idea of self-analysis. They would say with Robert Leiber SJ, the distinguished secretary of Pope Pius XII: 'I hope that the church has no intention of making a confession of guilt' (a remark that is both very German and very Roman Catholic). The refusal to contemplate self-analysis is typical of all centralists within the church (cf. the harsh rejection of the doctor and priest Marc Oraison by the Holy Office).

412 Monophysite tendencies in the church today: Joseph Rupert Geiselmann expresses the opinion that the average Catholic of our day is monophysite in outlook (*Das katholische Jesusbild* in Deschner, K. (Editor), Munich 1966).

412 Some further points on dogma. Hans Küng (*Theologe und Kirche*) exhorts Catholic theologians to learn to think historically, since church dogma is itself an important historical influence. Discussions at the Second Vatican Council on *schema* 13, dealing with the role of the church in the world today, revealed that the church did not yet possess a real theology of the world (see *Frankfurter Allgemeine Zeitung*, 29 September 1965). The bishop of Innsbruck, Dr Paul Rusch, made an important contribution towards the idea of a self-analysis of the church in his preliminary thoughts about *schema* 13, published in the first supplement to *Pax-Christi-Mitteilungen* (Vienna, July–August 1965).

Rusch points to the dire consequences arising from the separation of the church from the world, and pleads that mankind should once more be given hope. 'We are at a turning point, at which our own times are on trial. To overcome it, we need a man of judgment, initiative and courage.' Rusch calls for freedom of conscience, since conscience is the final subjective standard. At the Council Archbishop Beran of Prague said that the church in Bohemia was still paying for the Catholic abuse of religious freedom in the fifteenth and seventeenth centuries, when the Catholic church ordered the reformer Jan Hus to be burnt at the stake and later compelled Protestants to join the Catholic church. (Reported in the newspaper *Kurier*, Vienna, 21 September 1965). Suffragan Bishop Walter Kampe writes in the foreword to Eckert-Ehrlich (Ed.): 'May Ecclesia become ever increasingly aware of her descent from Synagogue, and the synagogue recognize in the church her younger sister.'

412 Kerstiens: *Nachdenkliches über die Marienfrömmigkeit*, published privately in Münster.

416 Charles de Foucauld: in addition to his own writings and letters, see R. Voillaume: *Au coeur des masses – La vie réligieuse des petits frères du père de Foucauld*, Paris 1950.

416 This spiritually immature, even perverted mentality of many Christians is the source of that hatred which has prompted a Jew of today to ask the question: 'Can't you love without hate?' (Dagobert D. Runes in *The Jews and the Cross*).

417 The transactions of the Tenth Evangelical Church Congress in Berlin: in *Der ungekündigte Bund* (ed. Goldschmidt and Kraus).

419 Heinrich Spaemann's broadcast talk *Juden, Christen und das Neue Testament* has been reprinted in *Hochland* (June 1965) under the title *Die Christen und das Volk der Juden*.

423 *Über den Hass* by Manès Sperber in *Die Achillesferse*, Cologne 1960.

424 St Matthew 27, 25 ('His blood be on us, and on our children') was not identified with the Jewish people until the fourth century: see Goldschmidt and Kraus (Ed.), 269.

425 The psychoanalysis of a thirty-year-old Catholic woman is described by J. Jacobi in Rudin (Editor). This woman painted Wotan with long red hair and wearing a Roman helmet, and prayed to him. It is known that the young Nietzsche and his sister once worshipped at an altar to Wotan. C. G. Jung, also a clergyman's son, had Wotan tendencies in his youth. This Wotan is a symptom of lacking blood vitamins (sex, life) in Christianity.

426 Some few painters in more modern times have depicted Christ with Jewish features. The first was perhaps Matthias Grünewald in the Crucifixion on the Isenheim altar in Kolmar, painted at a time when large sections of the people had lost faith in the idea of a remote

Christ king. This Jewish Christ should be compared with Holbein's picture of the dead Jesus in Basle – a wholly dead human being.

Otto Antonia Graf, the Viennese art historian, has kindly provided me with a list of more modern works in which Christ is depicted with Jewish features. Chief among them are numerous paintings of Christ and the apostles by Emil Nolde, e.g. his life of Christ on nine panels painted in the years 1915–51. Nolde has said: 'I painted them as strong Jewish types, for the men who adopted Christ's revolutionary new teaching were certainly never weaklings.'

Other examples: Lovis Corinth (e.g. *Kreuzabnahme*, 1895; *Kreuzigung*, 1897; *Kreuzigung*, 1906; *Martyrium*, 1907); Ernst Barlach (*Anno Domini MCMXVI post Christum natum*); Schmidt-Rottluff (*Petri Fischzug*); Otto Mueller in his Polish Family as Jewish Holy Family and Gypsy Madonna (two cross-bearing peoples!).

Christ as a Jewish type is plain to see in the early work of Georges Rouault, though it later becomes more abstract. There are also examples in Alexey Jawlensky. Rather more doubtful are James Ensor (his Christ of 1888, in Brussels), Honoré Daumier (*Ecce Homo*), Böcklin (*Kreuzabnahme*, Berlin), Vincent van Gogh (*Mater dolorosa, Pietà*), André Dérain (The Last Supper, 1914), Maurice Denis, Ford Madox Brown and Dante Gabriel Rossetti.

Most striking of all is Marc Chagall in many pictures of Christ and in his self-portrait of 1946, showing himself painting Christ. Chagall paints the Crucifixion as a symbol for the suffering of the Jewish people. Cf. Marie Renate Bach (a Catholic), writing in *Una Sancta* 3, 1966: 'The question might be asked to what extent the events of Good Friday have been repeated in the concentration camps... as culmination of a centuries-old persecution of the – alleged – murderers of Christ.'

426 Psychoanalysis and the church: In the name of ten Latin American bishops the Mexican bishop of Guernavaca, Sergio Mendez Arceo, asserted that the anthropological and psychological bases of the individual should not be ignored, and above all the discoveries of Sigmund Freud should not be left out of account. He added: 'Freud's discoveries are just as significant as those of Darwin and Copernicus.' Bishop Arceo, whose ideas aroused anger in Rome, had members of a monastery in his diocese (with their free consent) psychoanalysed.

426 The Jew has received the call to submit all religions to the judgment of criticism: – and 'to destroy all holy lies' (M. Sperber). Cf. Hermann Cohen's criticisms of the worship of images of God: Kaplan.

427 Christian sin complexes: In *Die chinesische Mauer* the great Viennese writer Karl Kraus has dealt in a masterly way with the Manichaeistic Christian morality of sin, which he describes as dishonest and mortally dangerous. In a review of this re-issued book in *Die Zeit* of 29 January 1965 Richard Schmid observed that in Kraus's opinion the perversity

of Western Man was 'the sickly consequence of a crippled sex life caused by morality and laws against immorality'. It cannot be disputed that 'the sexual envy of the Western Christian male provides the most fruitful breeding-ground for racial tension in Europe and America'.

427 The Jew as pacifist: There is no parallel among present-day Christian publications to the lecture given by the Jewish thinker Günther Anders in Mainz on 24 October 1964. In this forceful, deeply considered plea for peace, an imaginary speech by the victims of three world wars, the 'atheistic', profoundly religious philosopher Anders expresses his conviction that men are responsible for their own destiny, 'since we are living in the final phase, in a time in which we are really able to bring about the end, and since – if we do not take steps to prevent it – this final phase will really become the end of time.' Cf. also Maybaum: Auschwitz and Hiroshima, 38; shalom, 29.

The Jewish fight for world peace is closely connected with the conception of Jewish identity. As Kaplan writes (294): 'For us Jews there can be no higher purpose than that of exemplifying the art of so living individually and collectively as to contribute to the intellectual, moral and spiritual progress of mankind.'

Elias Canetti, an Austrian Jew of Spanish descent who now lives in England, has written: 'Of all the religions of Man, war is the toughest; but even that can be overcome.' And he adds: 'It is not until one is oneself an exile that one realizes to what significant extent the world has always been a world of banished people' (*Neue Rundschau*, 1965).

Walter Tschuppik in his *Der Christ und sein Schatten, oder: Die Geburt des Juden aus dem Geiste der absoluten Moral* (The Christian and his Shadow, or, The Birth of the Jew from the Spirit of Absolute Morality) probes deeply: for example, 'The Jews receive the blows which the betrayed Christian (i.e. the idealist) deals out to the world for not being idealistic or Christian.'

On the subject of Christian self-analysis: Protection from self-analysis is afforded by the definition of the word 'dialogue' given by the editor of the *Osservatore Romano*, Mazzini: 'The purpose of every dialogue is to impart the truth to those who do not possess it.' Mazzini draws attention to Pope Paul vi's call for watchfulness and warns against the danger of polemics among the Catholics themselves. So the necessary inner debate of church and Christianity is to be prohibited before it has even begun!

For recent Anglo-American contributions to the subject of Christian and Jew see *Cross Currents*, XVI, 3, 1966, 354ff.

428 Aggrieved Jews: Runes's *The Jew and the Cross* is a very moving document. 'There is no dialogue necessary between Christians and Jews. All we wish is the pontifical monologue to stop accusing the Jews of deicide' (35). 'The Cross to the Jew is the symbol of pogrom' (67). See 61ff: Pogroms and the Cross. Runes draws lines from St John Chrysostom to

Hitler (65), from Luther to Hitler (25) and from the popes of the fourth century to the popes of the twentieth century (15) – exactly as Pinay did in the opposite sense in his *Conspiracy against the Church*! Runes exhorts Christians to break with their long tradition of murder: 19, 22f, 27.

See also Maybaum: 'The two thousand years of the Christian era were two thousand years of war' (195). Maybaum claims that the fault of the Catholic church in the Nazi period was that it was still a church of the Middle Ages. 'Hitler could trust the Vatican' (25). He maintains that one single word from a bishop in Poland could have saved Jewish lives (26). 'The Golgotha of modern mankind is Auschwitz' (36, and see 77ff). Defining Jewish reproaches against Christendom, Maybaum asserts: 'The Christian needs the Jew at his side' (170ff and 193).

428 A courageous Viennese Jew with Socialist views: Fritz Flesch, 8094 Whitcomb, Detroit 28, Michigan, has kindly placed at my disposal his collection of documents.

429 'However much malicious people may warn against Jewish solidarity': cf. Rathenau's self-portrait of his 'divided existence' in the speech he made on his fiftieth birthday, 29 September 1917. See also S.Dubnow's *Jewish Werther* in *Nationalism and History* (Ed. Pinson), 143ff.

430 The great question for Judaism and Christianity: Nahum Goldmann said in 1962 that the Jews were in danger of disintegrating because (a) there was no longer any religious obligation, and (b) they were no longer physically persecuted. See Kaplan, 287.

430 Simon Dubnow's death: *Vi azoy di nazis hobn dermordet professor S. Dubnow* by Hillel Melamed in *Zukunft*, LI, 1946: quoted in *Nationalism and History* (ed. Pinson), 363.

432 A small but important group of Berlin Jews: Goldschmidt; Arthur A. Cohen, 39ff.

432 Rabbi Samson Raphael Hirsch: A. A. Cohen, 49ff.

432 Hermann Cohen: among others, A. A. Cohen, 73–102, 173ff; Kaplan, 42ff, 61–254 (Epitome of Hermann Cohen's Rational-Religion).

On Kaplan's criticism of Jewish orthodoxy and reformism, see A. A. Cohen, 206ff.

433 The Crucifixion as a symbol of the suffering of the Jewish people: The Catholic Jew Jacques Lévy joyfully accepted death in Auschwitz in the cause of Israel 'out of love for the Jew Jesus as a Jew' (M.G.Morelli in *Jacques Lévy, Auf der Suche nach dem Menschen*, Salzburg 1960).

434 Leo Baeck: among others, A. A. Cohen, 102ff, 173ff. Leo Baeck in the concentration camp of Terezin: Maybaum, 113ff.

434 Baeck saw Christianity as a 'romantic' religion: A. A. Cohen, 110ff. Baeck's criticism of St Augustine and St Paul: A. A. Cohen, 114ff.

435 Franz Rosenzweig: among others, A.A.Cohen, 120–48, 160f, 173ff.

435 Martin Buber: among others, A. A. Cohen, 145f, 149–76, 267f.

435 Pontius Pilate's successors have provided the popes over two thousand years: see also Runes, 34, 40f, 45ff, 49ff, who emphasizes that the Romans (the predecessors of the popes and cardinals) crucified Christ a thousand times in their persecution of the Christians. Robert Raphael Geis (in Eckert-Ehrlich) poses the final question: Will Christianity continue to the end of time to 'permit itself the luxury of a theology, the costs of which have to be borne by others?'

437 *Die Antwort der Religionen*: Other participants, beside those mentioned in the main text, were Muhammad Asad 'by birth an Austrian Jew' for Mohammedism and B.H.Ben Maharaj for Hinduism. Kurt Wilhelm is the chief rabbi of Sweden.

438 The influence of the Psalms on Christian Europe: W.B.Selbie in Bevan and Singer (Ed.), 423ff.

438 *Kamin* by Ruth Klüger: German text in M.Schlösser (Ed.).

438 Poems of Zalman Schneour, Louis Golding, Robert Nathan, Bialik, Israel Zangwill in N. and M.Ausubel (Ed.).

439 *The Blessed Match* by Hannah Senesh: in N. and M.Ausubel (Ed.).

439 Poems of Gertrud Kolmar, Gertrud Kantorowicz, Ilse Weber and Ilse Blumenthal-Weiss in Schlösser (Ed.).

439 *Genesis* by Jules Alan Wein in N. and M.Ausubel (Ed.).

440 Poems by Nelly Sachs (who was awarded the Nobel prize for literature in 1966): *Das Leiden Israels, Eli, In den Wohnungen des Todes, Sternverdunkelung*, published in Frankfurt 1964.

441 *Death Fugue* by Paul Celan: in N. and M.Ausubel (Ed.). Translated from the German by Clement Greenberg.

443 The Christians' last word: Runes poses the cardinal question: 'Can't you love without hate? Is your faith so weak, is your devotion so poor, that you must have the Jewish hate story as part of your theological structure?' (82, 83, 88f). For 'Jewish' any other hate object can be substituted at will.

443 A change of heart? At the proclamation ceremony of five declarations – including that concerning the non-Christian religions – at the Second Vatican Council on 27 October 1965, the Psalm 132 ('Lord, remember David') was sung. This ends with praise of Zion. Thus the connection between the messages of the Old and the New Testaments was demonstrated (*Frankfurter Allgemeine Zeitung*, 28 October 1965.

'When Christians individually succumb to anti-Semitism, it should not in future be possible for them to base their arguments on the church' (Mgr Otto Mauer in *Mitteilungen der Katholischen Akademikerseelsorge*, Vienna, October–December 1965). A Protestant observer at the Second Vatican Council, Pastor Johann Christoph Hampe, observed: 'Non-Catholic Christians must have an interest in seeing that the Catholic church mkes its peace with Israel . . . It would have helped tremendously to clear the atmosphere if the bishops had said that with this declaration the church was turning its back on the Middle Ages, in which the church identified the world with Christianity and thus logically ignored the heathens outside and confined the Jews within its walls to ghettos. The Christian origin of anti-Semitism is obvious enough, but the churches – all of them together – are not yet capable of realizing that' (*Rheinische Post*, 6 November 1965).

Willem Visser't Hooft, general secretary (up to 1966) of the World Council of Churches, described the section of the Council's declaration dealing with the other world religions as 'terribly weak'.

Catholic recognition of the Jewish faith today: Père H.Cazelles in *Cross Currents*, XIV, 1964 ('Our Two Fidelities').

In the decrees of the Second Vatican Council there are occasional assertions, reminiscent in style of Pius XII, which attempt to wipe out centuries-old historical realities with a single sentence. For instance, in the decree concerning missionaries the bold assertion is made: 'In truth throughout history, both sacred and profane, the Gospels have provided mankind with the leaven of freedom and progress, and continue to provide the leaven of brotherly love, unity and peace.' If Pope Gregory XVI had been confronted with this sentence in 1832, he would have had every right to condemn it as the work of heretical reformists, since it contradicts a tradition stemming from St Augustine and the laws of the early Christian emperors that remained intact until 1958 at least.

Schema 13 (which has been described as the great wastepaper basket of the Council) contains one sentence which might be seen as the confession of faith for which so many people persecuted by the church (and above all believing and non-believing Jews) have lived and died: 'We may rightly assume that the future destiny of mankind lies in the hands of those who can impart to future generations the driving forces of life and hope.'

Index

References to the Notes and Bibliography are italicized